Street by Stre

C000143663

SHEFFIELD

BARNSLEY, CHESTERFIELD, DONCASTER, ROTHERHAM

Chapeltown, Conisbrough, Dronfield, Mexborough, Mosborough,
Rawmarsh, Stocksbridge, Thurnscoe, Wath upon Dearne, Wombwell

1st edition May 2001

© Automobile Association Developments
Limited 2004

Ordnance Survey® This product includes map data licensed from Ordnance Survey® with the permission of the Controller of Her Majesty's Stationery Office. © Crown copyright 2004. All rights reserved. Licence Number 399221.

Published by AA Publishing (a trading name of Automobile Association Developments Limited, whose registered office is Millstream, Maidenhead Road, Windsor, Berkshire SL4 5GD. Registered number 1878835).

The Post Office is a registered trademark of Post Office Ltd. in the UK and other countries.

Mapping produced by the Cartography Department of The Automobile Association. (A02098)

A CIP Catalogue record for this book is available from the British Library.

Printed by G. Canale & C. S.P.A., Torino, Italy

The contents of this atlas are believed to be correct at the time of the latest revision. However, the publishers cannot be held responsible for loss occasioned to any person acting or refraining from action as a result of any material in this atlas, nor for any errors, omissions or changes in such material. This does not affect your statutory rights. The publishers would welcome information to correct any errors or omissions and to keep this atlas up to date. Please write to Publishing, The Automobile Association, Fanum House (FH17), Basing View, Basingstoke, Hampshire, RG21 4EA.

Ref: MD072

Key to map pages ii-iii

Key to map symbols iv-1

Enlarged scale pages 2-11

Street by Street 12-191

Index – towns & villages 192-193

Index – streets 194-237

Index – featured places 238-244

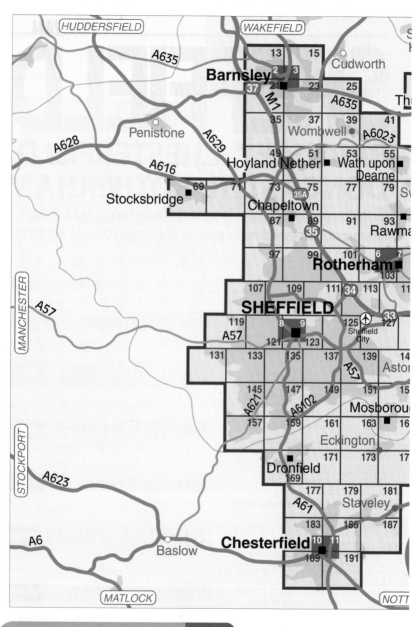

HUDDERSFIELD WAKEFIELD

A635

Barnsley 13 15 Cudworth

2 3
37 21 23 25
M1 A635 Th

35 37 39 41
Penistone Wombwell A6023
A628 A629

A616 49 51 53 55
Hoyland Nether Wath upon
Dearne

69 71 73 75 77 79 Sw
Stocksbridge 35A
Chapeltown

87 89 91 93
35 Rawma

97 99 101 6 7
Rotherham 103

107 109 111 34 113 11

SHEFFIELD

119 8 9 125 127
A57 Sheffield 33
City
121 123

MANCHESTER A57

131 133 135 137 139 14
Aston
A57

145 147 149 151 15
A621 A6102 Mosborou

157 159 161 163 16

STOCKPORT Eckington

A623 171 173 17
Dronfield
169

A6 177 179 181
A61 Staveley

183 185 187

Chesterfield 10 11
Baslow 189 191

MATLOCK NOTT

Enlarged scale pages 1:10,000 6.3 inches to 1 mile

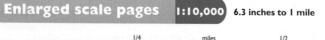

0 1/4 miles 1/2

0 1/4 1/2 kilometres 3/4 1

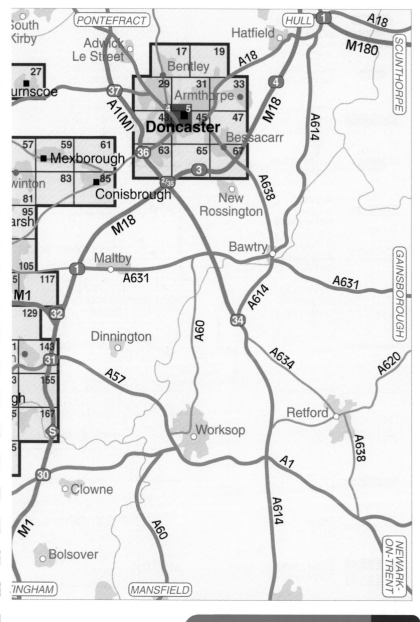

4.2 inches to 1 mile   **Scale of main map pages** 1:15,000

iv

Junction 9	Motorway & junction	**P+🚌**	Park & Ride
Services	Motorway service area	🚌	Bus/coach station
	Primary road single/dual carriageway		Railway & main railway station
Services	Primary road service area		Railway & minor railway station
	A road single/dual carriageway	⊖	Underground station
	B road single/dual carriageway	⊖	Light railway & station
	Other road single/dual carriageway	+++++++++	Preserved private railway
	Restricted road	*LC*	Level crossing
	Private road	•—•—•—	Tramway
←　　←	One way street	----------	Ferry route
	Pedestrian street	·················	Airport runway
=========	Track/ footpath	—··—··—··—	Boundaries-borough/ district
	Road under construction	⌄⌄⌄⌄⌄⌄⌄	Mounds
]==={	Road tunnel	**93**	Page continuation 1:15,000
P	Parking	**7**	Page continuation to enlarged scale 1:10,000

∿	River/canal lake, pier		♿	Toilet with disabled facilities
⤳	Aqueduct lock, weir		⛽	Petrol station
465 ▲ Winter Hill	Peak (with height in metres)		PH	Public house
	Beach		PO	Post Office
	Coniferous woodland		📖	Public library
	Broadleaved woodland		i	Tourist Information Centre
	Mixed woodland		♜	Castle
	Park		🏛	Historic house/ building
	Cemetery		Wakehurst Place NT	National Trust property
	Built-up area		M	Museum/ art gallery
	Featured building		†	Church/chapel
⊓⊓⊓⊓	City wall		♛	Country park
A&E	Accident & Emergency hospital		🎭	Theatre/ performing arts
🚻	Toilet		🎥	Cinema

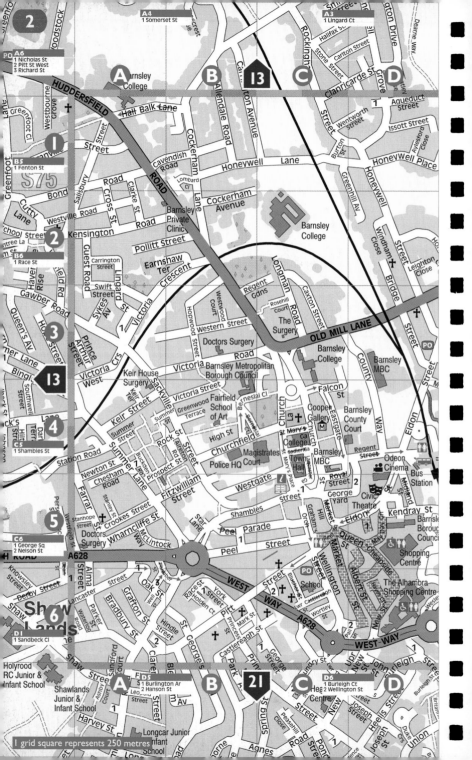

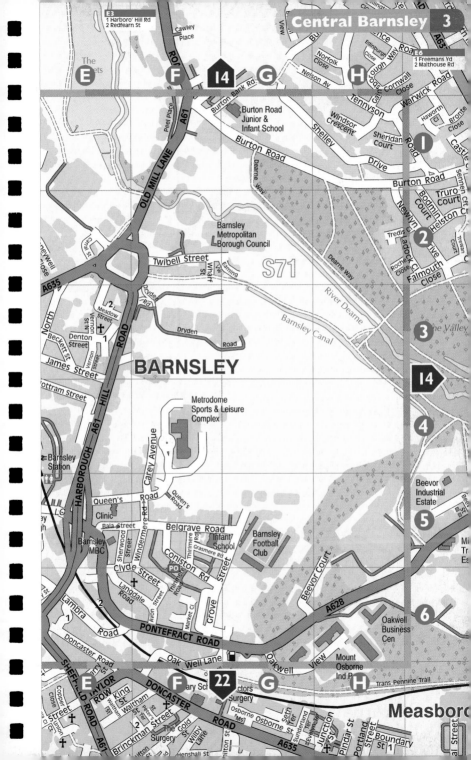

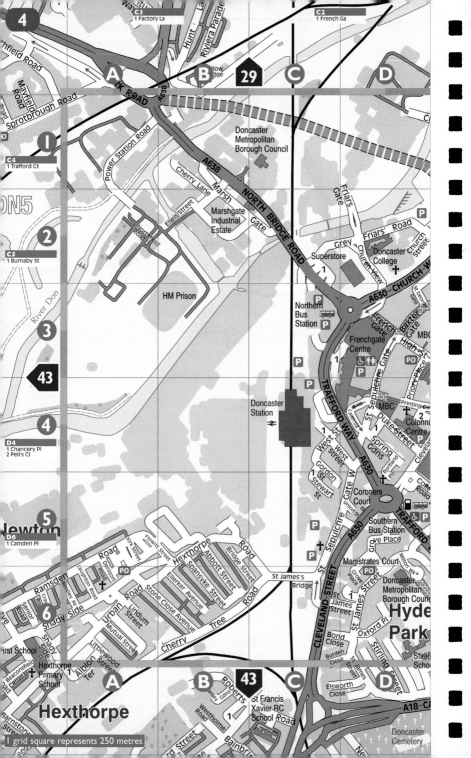

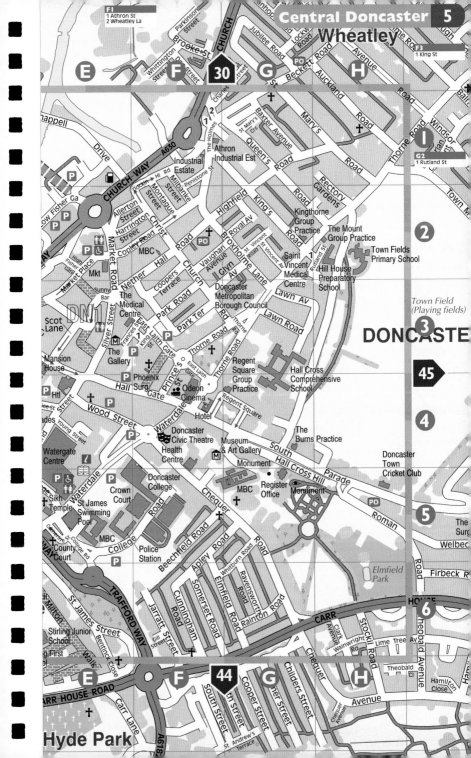

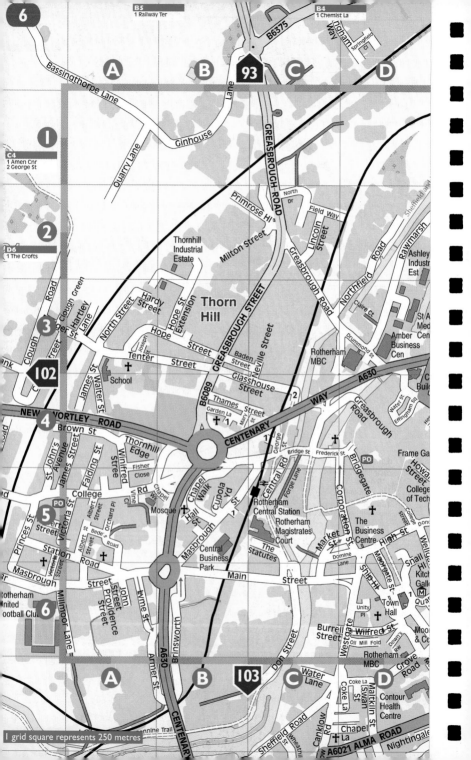

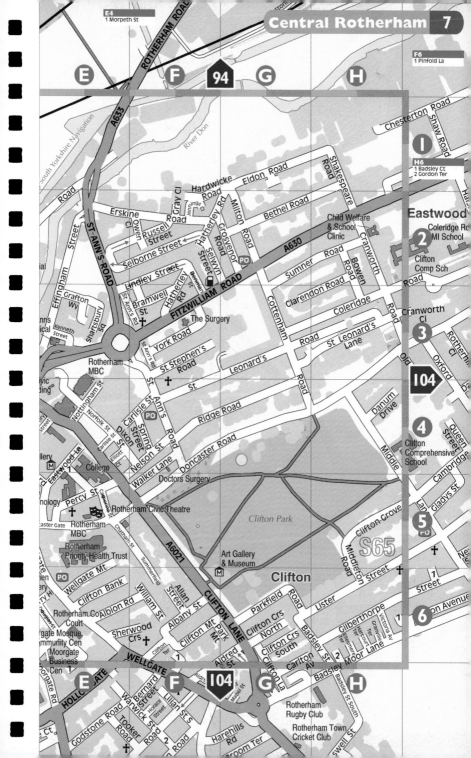

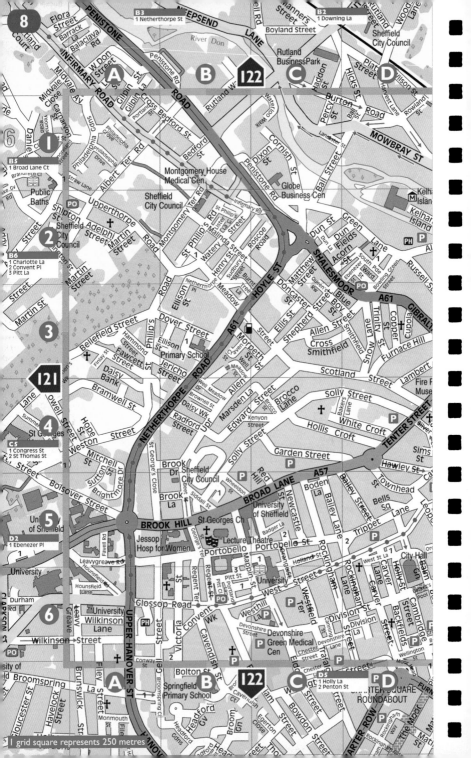

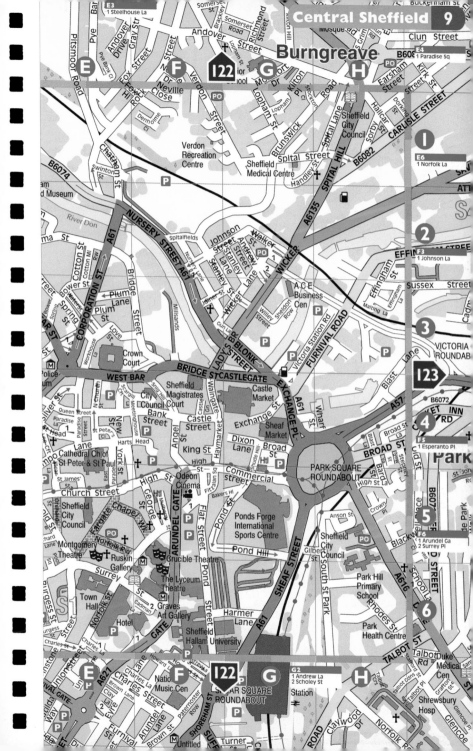

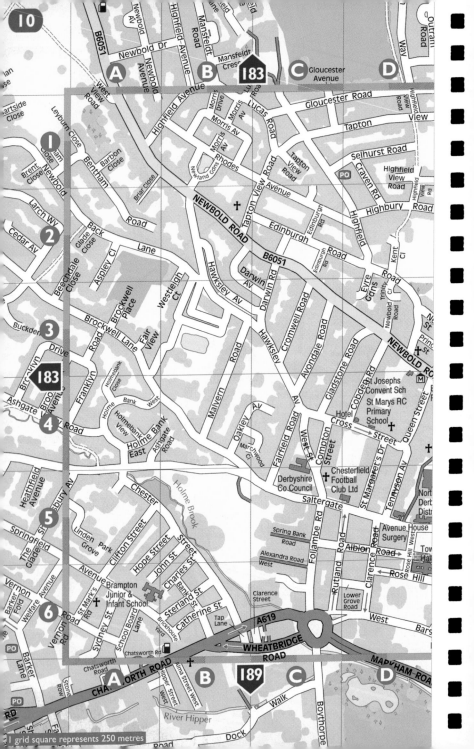

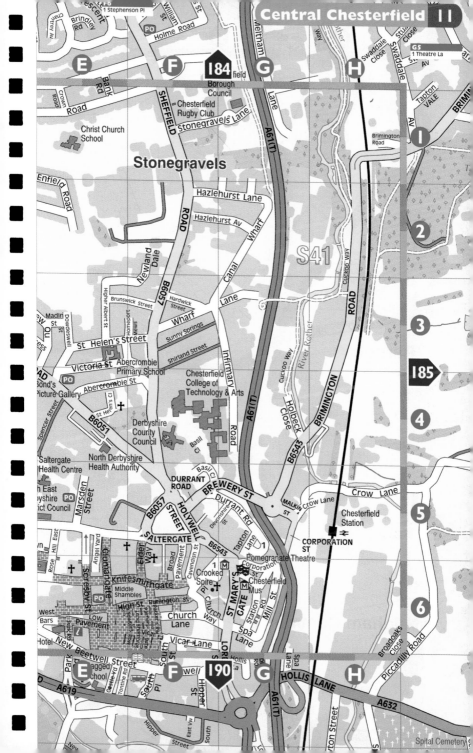

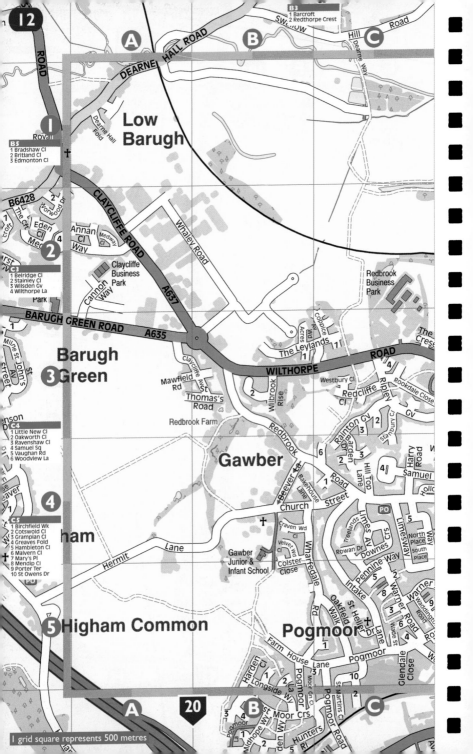

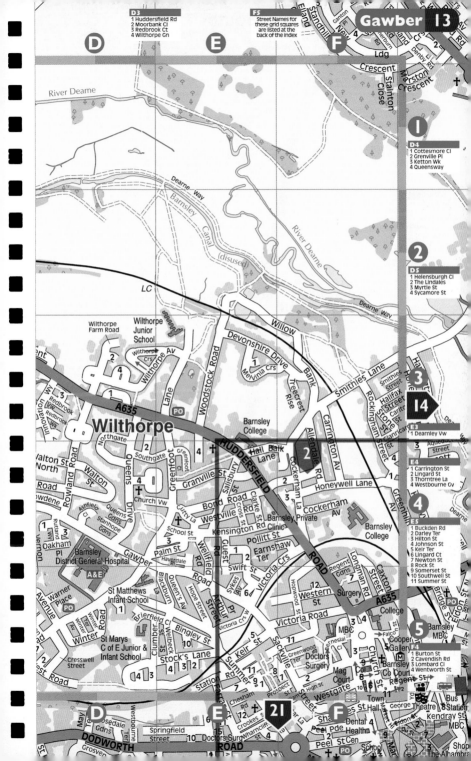

D3
1 Huddersfield Rd
2 Moorbank Cl
3 Redbrook Ct
4 Wilthorpe Gn

F5
Street Names for
these grid squares
are listed at the
back of the index

River Dearne

Dearne Way

Barnsley Canal

River Dearne

Dearne Way

(disused)

LC

D4
1 Cottesmore Cl
2 Grenville Pl
3 Ketton Wk
4 Queensway

D5
1 Helensburgh Cl
2 The Lindales
3 Myrtle St
4 Sycamore St

Wilthorpe Farm Road

Wilthorpe Junior School

Wilthorpe Crs

Wilthorpe Av

Devonshire Drive

Willow

Treecrest Rise

Smithies Lane

Smithies Street

Halifax Street

Rockingham Stone Street

Carlto

Woodstock Road

Wilthorpe Lane

Melvinia Crs

Bank

Carrington Av

Allendale Rd

Greenhill

Dearne

E3
1 Dearnley Vw

E4
1 Carrington St
2 Lingard St
3 Thorntree La
4 Westbourne Gv

Wilthorpe

A635

Northgate

Queens

Southgate

Greenfoot

Greenfoot

Granville St

Salisbury

Clarke St

HUDDERSFIELD

Hall Balk Lane

Cockerham La

Honeywell Lane

Cockerham Av

Barnsley College

Barnsley College

Barnsley Private Clinic

Walton St North

Walton St

Rowland Road

Queens Drive

Church Vw

Bond Road

Westville Rd

Kensington Rd

Pollitt St

Earnshaw Ter

Regent Gdns

Longman St

Caxton Street

Rowdene

Anfield Cl

Queens Gdns

Stanhope Gdns

Gawber

Cutty La

School St

Palm St

Haverdale

Wellfield Road

Guest St

Swift St

Victoria Crs

Hodroyd St

Western St

Surgery

E5
1 Buckden Rd
2 Darley Ter
3 Hilton St
4 Johnson St
5 Keir Ter
6 Lingard Ct
7 Newton St
8 Rock St
9 Somerset St
10 Southwell St
11 Summer St

Walton Road

Vernon

Rutland Pl

Oakham Pl

Barnsley District General Hospital

A&E

Warner Place

PO

St Matthews Infant School

Brierfield Cl

Clumber Cl

Welbeck St

Bingley St

Stock's Lane

Keir St

Summer Rd

Blackburn St

Queen's Rd

Hope Street

Arthur St

Victoria Crew

Sykes St

Victoria Road

Sackville St

Greenwood Ter

Doctors Surgery

Regent St

A635

College

Barnsley MBC

Cooper S Gallery

Falco

MBC

Mag Court

Neslia

Church St

Barnsley Co Court

Regent St

Barnsley MBC

F4
1 Burton St
2 Cavendish Rd
3 Lombard Cl
4 Wentworth St

Winter Avenue

Winter Road

St Marys C of E Junior & Infant School

Cresswell Street

Station Rd

Prospect

Chesham Rd

Crookes St

Wharncliff

High St

Westgate

Westgate

Dental Health

Peel Pde

Peel St Cen

George St

Town Hall

Market

Theatre

Kendray St

Bus Station

Eldon St

Shop

The Alhambra

DODWORTH

ROAD

Springfield Street

Doctors Surg

Rosedale Gdns

Westbourne Rd

Grosven

May Ter

Peel Sq

Shambles St

21

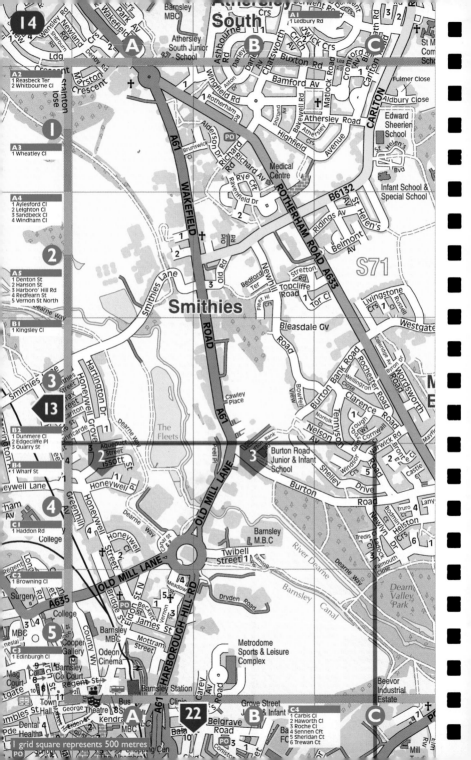

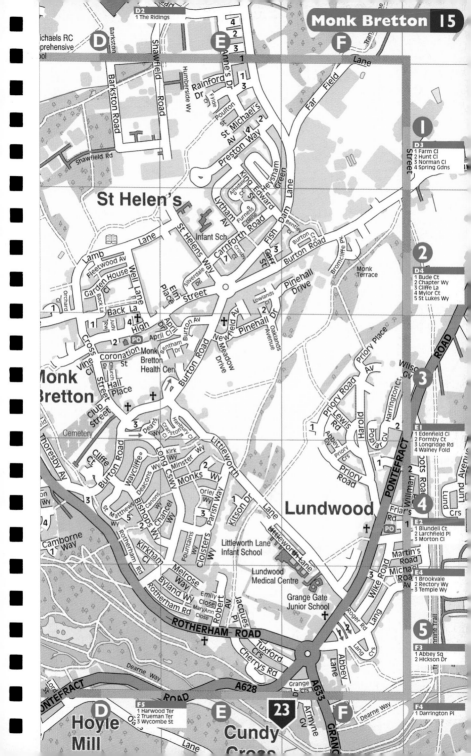

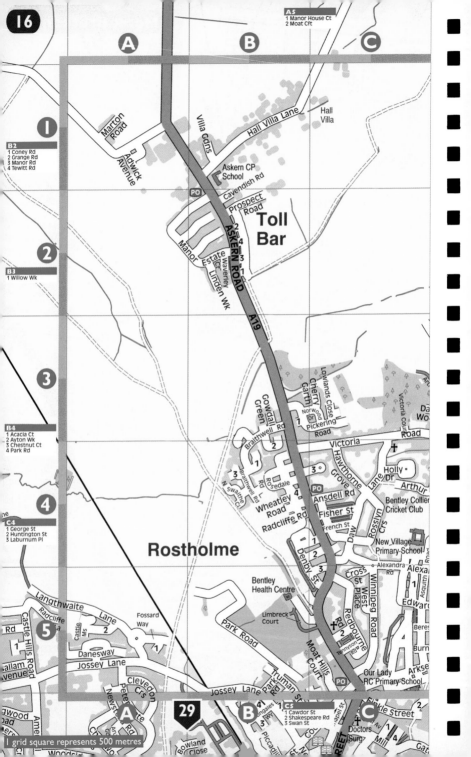

16

A5
1 Manor House Ct
2 Moat Cft

B2
1 Coney Rd
2 Grange Rd
3 Manor Rd
4 Tewitt Rd

B3
1 Willow Wk

B4
1 Acacia Ct
2 Ayton Wk
3 Chestnut Ct
4 Park Rd

C4
1 George St
2 Huntington St
3 Laburnum Pl

C5
1 Cawdor St
2 Shakespeare Rd
3 Swan St

Marton Road

Adwick Avenue

Villa Gdns

Hall Villa Lane

Hall Villa

Askern CP School

Cavendish Rd

PO

Prospect Road

Toll Bar

Manor

Estate

Waverley

Linden Wk

ASKERN ROAD

A19

Lowlands Close

Cherry Garth

Victoria Court

Da Wo

Gowdall Green

Braithwell Rd

Braithwell Rd

N Swaithe Ct

Rosedale

Norwood

Pickering Road

Victoria

Hawthorne Grove

Holly Dr

Arthur

Road

Wheatley Road

Radcliffe Rd

PO

Ansdell Rd

Fisher St

French St

Bentley Collier Cricket Club

New Village Primary School

Alexandra Rd

Alexa

Rostholme

Denby St

Cross St

Winnipeg Road

West Place

Edward

Langthwaite Lane

Radcliffe Ms

Castle Ms

Fossard Way

Bentley Health Centre

Limbreck Court

Park Road

Rd

Redbourne Rd

Tennyson Rd

Our Lady RC Primary School

Beres

Burn

Castle Hills Road

Daneway

Jossey Lane

Clevedon Crs

Newst

Peter

Jossey Lane

Truman Rd

Park Rd

PO

Finkle Street

Doctors Surg

29

A

B

C

Bowland Close

Picca

Gat

Mill

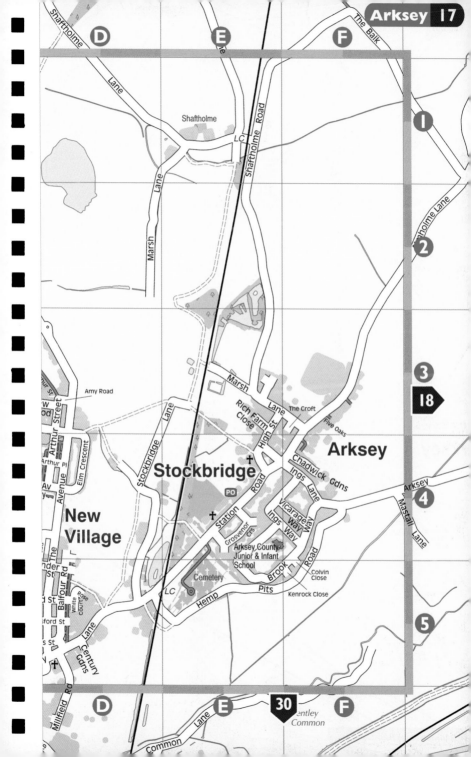

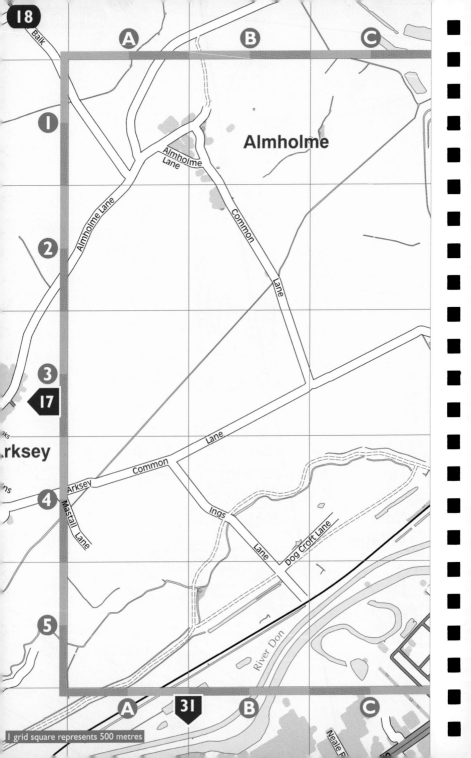

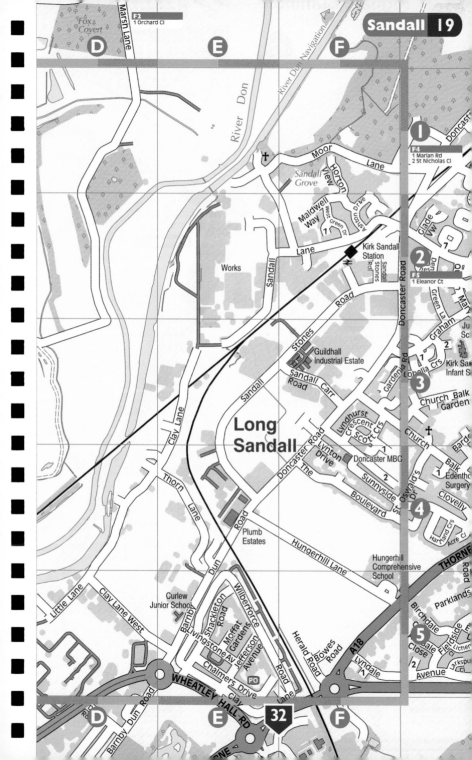

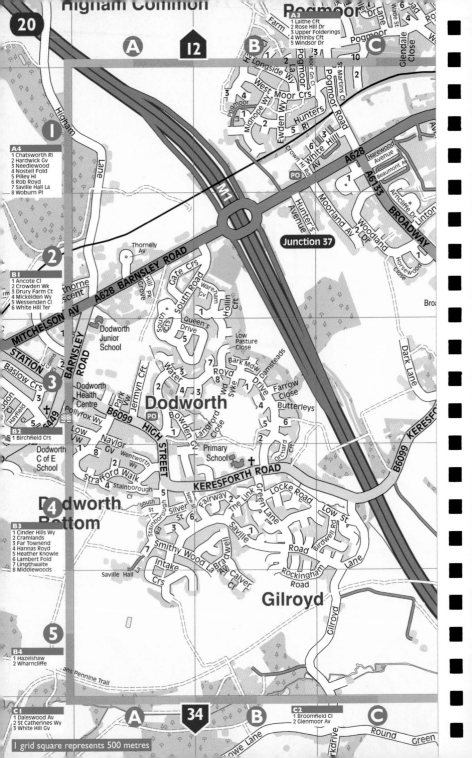

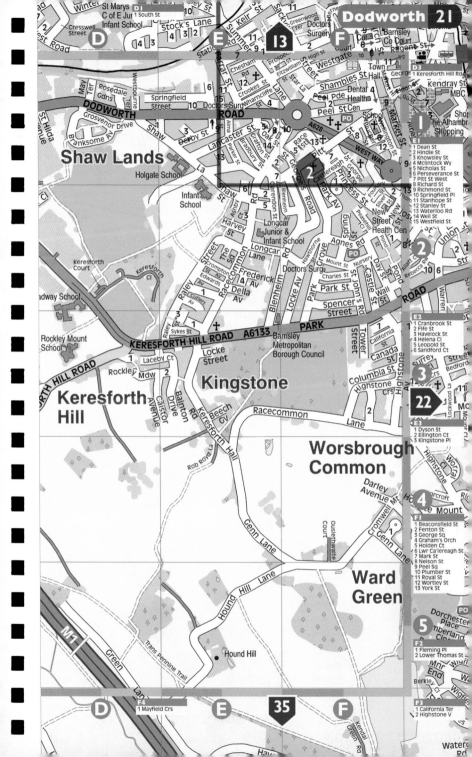

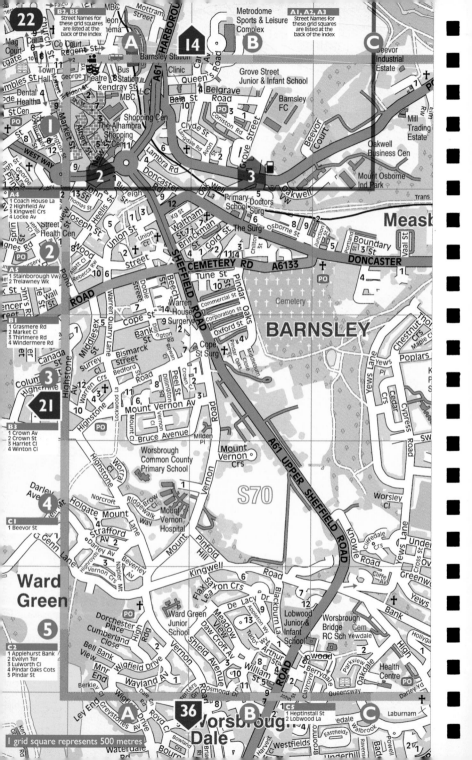

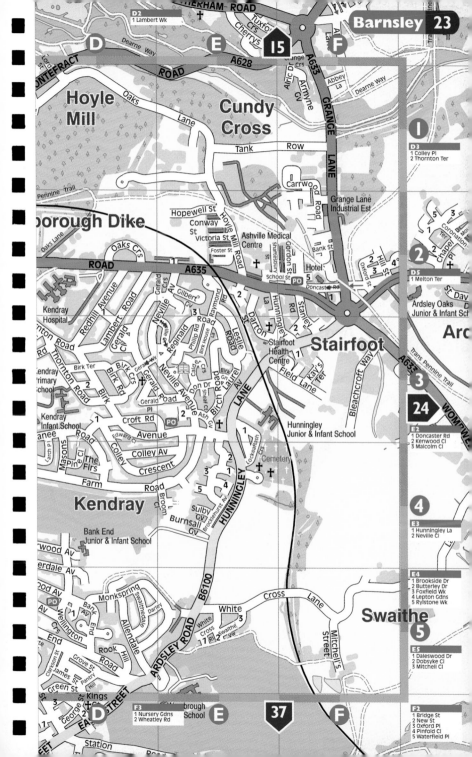

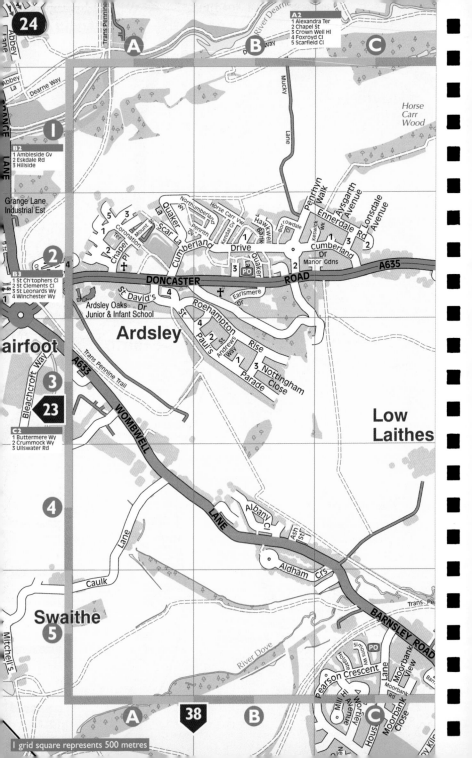

24

A   B   C

A2
1 Alexandra Ter
2 Chapel St
3 Crown Well Hl
4 Foxroyd Cl
5 Scarfield Cl

River Dearne

Mucky Lane

Horse Carr Wood

1

B2
1 Ambleside Gv
2 Eskdale Rd
3 Hillside

Grange Lane Industrial Est

Penrhyn Walk
Aysgarth Avenue
Lonsdale Avenue

Quaker La
Scar La
Cumberland
Coronation
Mount
Chapel Ter
Pl
Normumberland Wy
Horse Carr Vw
Kendal Gv
Penrith
Hawkwell Bank
Keswick Wy
Crowdale
Ennerdale Rd
Cumberland
Drive
Quaker La
Manor Gdns

2

B3
1 St Ch'tophers Cl
2 St Clements Cl
3 St Leonards Wy
4 Winchester Wy

PO

A635

DONCASTER   ROAD

St David's Dr
Ardsley Oaks Junior & Infant School

Roehampton
Rise
Earlsmere Dr

Ardsley

St Paul's St
St Andrews Way
Nottingham Close
Parade

airfoot

Bleachcroft Way
Trans Pennine Trail
A633

3

23

C2
1 Buttermere Wy
2 Crummock Wy
3 Ullswater Rd

Low Laithes

WOMBWELL

4

LANE

Albany Cl
Ash Tst
Aldham Crs

Lane

Caulk

Swaithe

5

Mitchell's

River Dove

BARNSLEY ROAD

Trans Pe

PO

Pearson Crescent
Holgate Lane
Moorbank View
Moorbank Rd
Mill Hl
Wortley Avenue
Moorbank Close
Hous

A   **38**   B   C

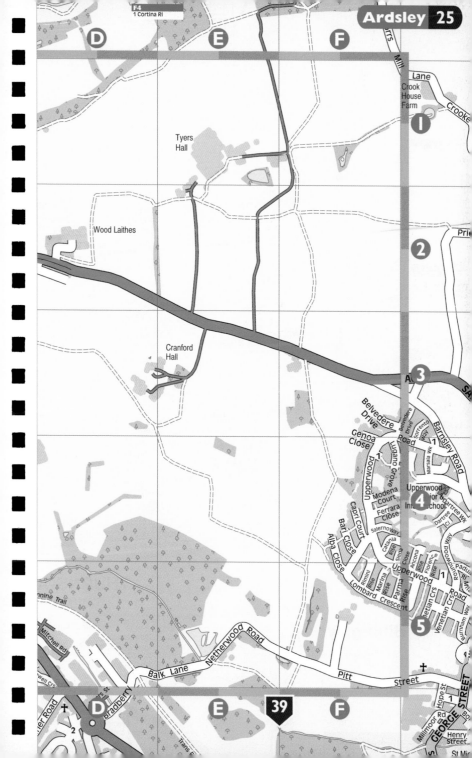

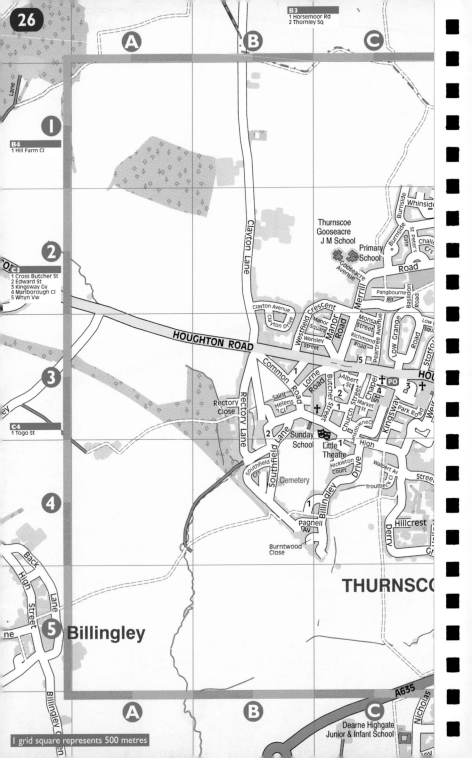

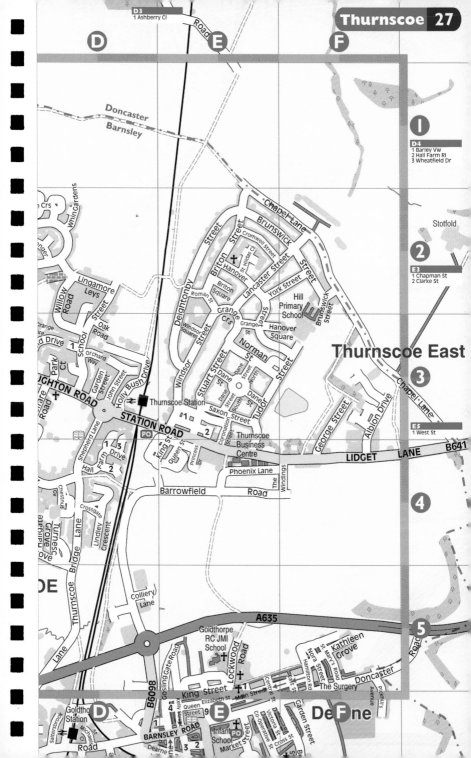

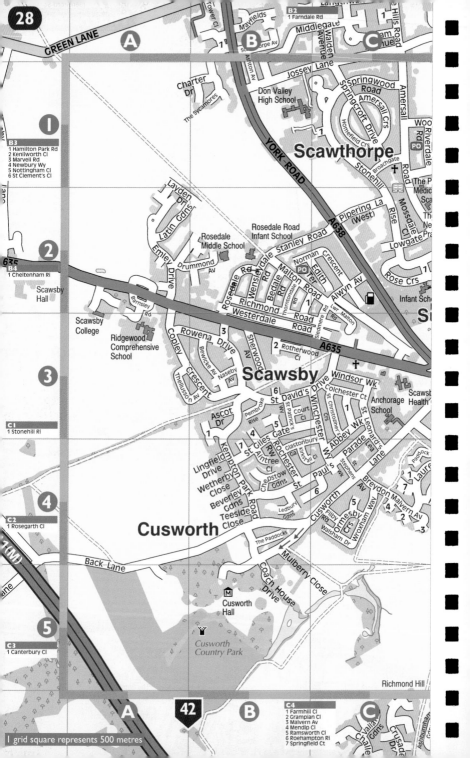

GREEN LANE

A   **B**   **C**

Tower Cl

Mayfields

B2
1 Farndale Rd

Middlegate

Walden Avenue

Langley

Hills Road

am

uel

Charter Dr

The Sycamores

Ashton Av

Skelbrooke Av

Jossey Lane

Don Valley High School

Springwood Road

Springcroft Crs

Amersall Crs

Amersall

Woo

Riverdale

Rd

PO

I

B3
1 Hamilton Park Rd
2 Kenilworth Cl
3 Marvell Rd
4 Newbury Wy
5 Nottingham Cl
6 St Clement's Cl

Scawthorpe

Homefield Crs

Stonehill

Broachgate

Road

Mossdale Cl

The P
Medic
Sca

Th
Ne
Pra

Layden Drs

Latin Gdns

Emley Drive

Rosedale Middle School

Rosedale Road Infant School

Stanley Road

Pipering La (West)

Rise

Lowgate

Rose Crs

2

635

B4
1 Cheltenham Ri

Scawsby Hall

Drummond Av

Barnsley Rd

Rosedale Rd

Wensleydale Rd

Bedale Rd

Malton Road

Norman Crescent

Edith Ter

Alwyn Av

PO

Infant Sch

S

Scawsby College

Ridgewood Comprehensive School

Copley

Rowena Drive

Bewicke Av

Thellusson Av

Naseby Av

Richmond

Westerdale

Road

Road

Thorndale Rd

Sledmere Rd

Lwr Malton Rd

A638

A635

Infant Sch

3

C1
1 Stonehill Ri

Crescent

Sherwood Av

Rotherwood Cl

Scawsby

Windsor Wk

Colchester Ct

Anchorage School

Scawsb
Health

Ascot Dr

Pembroke Rise

St David's Drive

St Patrick's Wy

St Christopher's

St Leonard's

St David's Drive

Court

Winchester Wy

Crs

Abbey Wk

Parade

Stephens Lea

Malvern Av

Laure

Paddock

4

C2
1 Rosegarth Cl

Lingfield Drive

Wetherby Close

Kempton Park Road

St Giles Gate

Aintree Cl

Rochester Wy

Chepstow Gdns

Glastonbury Gdns

Priest's Hall

St Paul's

Ledbury Gdns

Cusworth Av

Filby Rd

Ormesby Crs

Ramsworth Cl

Wroxham Wy

Breydon Av

7

5

4

2

3

5

Cusworth

Beverley Gdns

Teesdale Close

The Paddocks

Walsham Dr

C3
1 Canterbury Cl

Back Lane

Mulberry Close

Coach House Drive

Cusworth Hall

Cusworth Country Park

Richmond Hill

A   **42**   **B**   **C**

C4
1 Farmhill Cl
2 Grampian Cl
3 Malvern Av
4 Mendip Cl
5 Ramsworth Cl
6 Roehampton Ri
7 Springfield Ct

Valian
Gdns

Challe

Crusade

Ashbum

1 grid square represents 500 metres

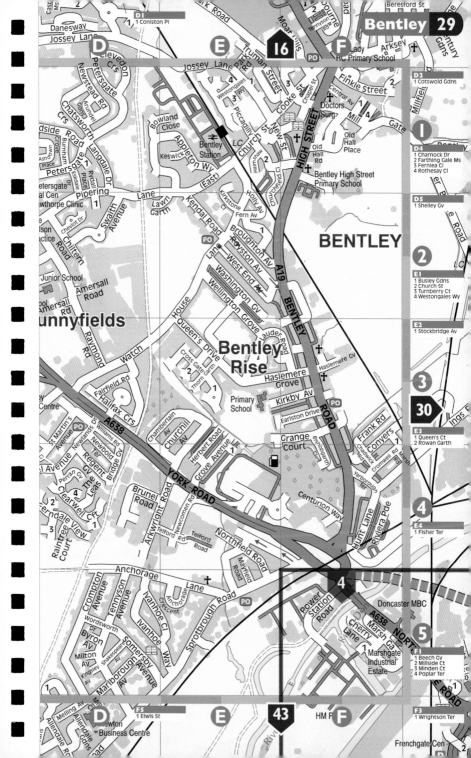

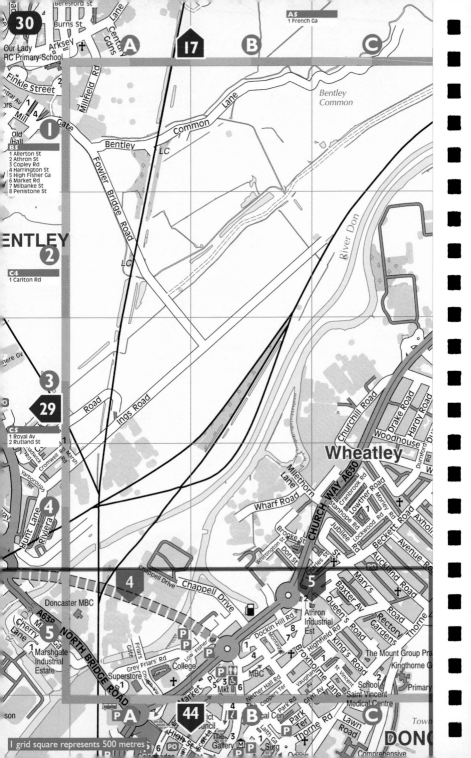

30

Beresford St
Burns St
Arksey La
Central Gdns

A

17

B

C

A5
1 French Ga

Our Lady RC Primary School

Finkle Street
Central Av
rs

Mill

4

Old Hall

1

1 Allerton St
2 Athron St
3 Copley Rd
4 Harrington St
5 High Fisher Ga
6 Market Rd
7 Milbanke St
8 Penistone St

B5

Millfield Rd

Gate

Bentley

Common

Lane

Common Lane

Bentley Common

LC

River Don

Fowler Bridge Road

LC

ENTLEY

2

C4
1 Carlton Rd

ere Gv

Ings Road

3

29

C5
1 Royal Av
2 Rutland St

o

Road

Churchill Road

Woodhouse

Drake Road
Hardy Road

yarborough
ter

Cromwell Rd
Marsh

Wheatley

arwick
Rd

Hunt Lane

Riviera

4

Wharf Road

Mexborn Lane

Stanhope Rd
Cranbrook Rd
Lowther Road
Morley Rd
Lockwood Rd

CHURCH WAY A630

Axholme

Beckett Road

Avenue Rd

Chappell Drive

Chappell Drive

Brooke St

Whitington St
Don St
Charles St

Jubilee St
St

4

Doncaster MBC

Cherry Lane

A63

M

5

NORTH BRIDGE ROAD

Marshgate Industrial Estate

Friars Gate

Grey Friars' Rd

College

Superstore

Low Fisher Ga

P

P

P

P

Market Pl

5

P

Mkt

6

5

2

Athron Industrial Est

Highfield Rd

Montagu St

Nether Hall Rd

MBC

P

Foxholme

King's Road

Queen's Road

Baxter Av

Mary's

Auckland Road

Rectory Gardens

Road

Thorne

The Mount Group Pra

Kingthorne G

P

A

44

High St

ict Council

The Gallery

M

6

PO

3

B

Leith Ct
cal Cen

Larith Ga

Coopers Ter

Park Ter
Thorne Rd

P

St Vincent

Vaughan

Glyn Av

St Vincent
Medical Centre

Saint Vincent School

Lawn Road

C

Primary

Town

DON

Comprehensive

Odeon

Surg

I grid square represents 500 metres

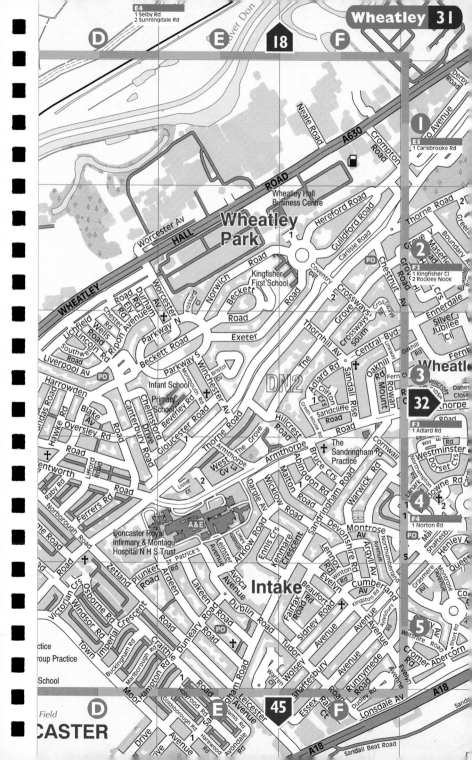

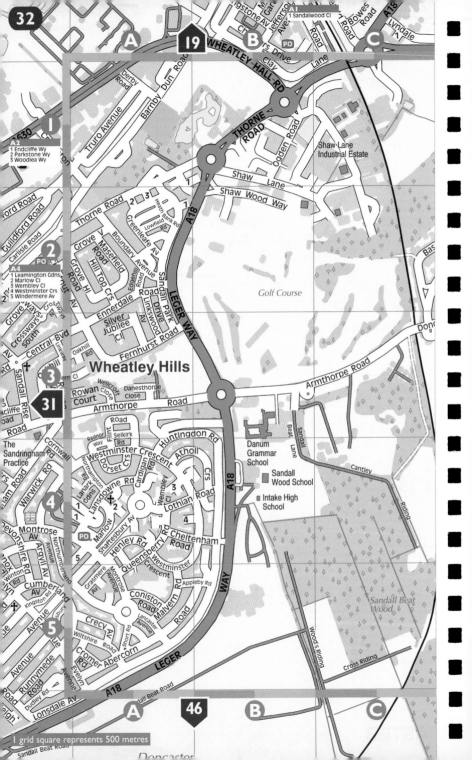

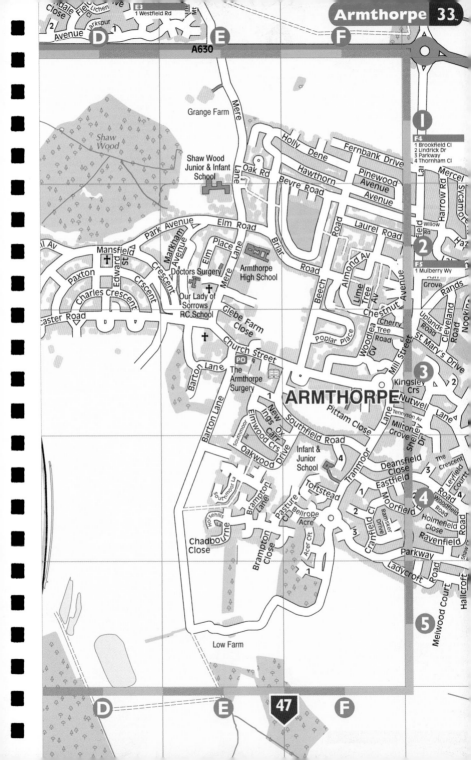

A630

Grange Farm

Shaw Wood

Shaw Wood Junior & Infant School

Holly Dene

Fernbank Drive

Oak Rd

Bevre Road

Hawthorn

Pinewood Avenue

Park Avenue

Elm Road

Laurel Road

Mansfield Avenue

Markham Crescent

Elm Place

Mere Lane

Briar Road

Almond Av

Lime Tree Av

Willow Rd

Paxton

Edward St

Crescent

Doctors Surgery

Armthorpe High School

Beech Road

Chestnut

Woodlea Gv

Rands

Charles Crescent

Caster Road

Our Lady of Sorrows RC School

Glebe Farm Close

Poplar Place

Cherry Tree Road

Uplands Road

Cleveland Road

St Mary's Drive

Nookin

Church Street

Kingsley Crs

Barton Lane

PO

The Armthorpe Surgery

ARMTHORPE

Nutwell Lane

Tennyson Av

Milton Grove

Shelley Dr

Barton Lane

New Ox

Ings Carr

Southfield Road

Pittam Close

Elmwood Crs

Oakwood

Infant & Junior School

Tranmoor Lane

Deansfield Close

Eastfield

The Crescent

Leyfield Court

Southmoor La

Southmoor

Brampton Lane

Toftstead

Moorfield

Holmefield Close

Woodfield Road

Ravenfield

Hornile

Chadbourne Close

Brampton Close

Pasture Cl

Bellrope Acre

Acer Crt

Cranfield Cl

Ramsden Drive

Parkway

Ladycroft

Melwood Court

Shaw Road

Hallcroft

Low Farm

Mercel

Harrow Rd

Sycamore

Hazel

Grove

Ash

Mill Street

Avenue

E3
1 Westfield Rd

Dale
Field
Lichen
Larkspur
Avenue

47

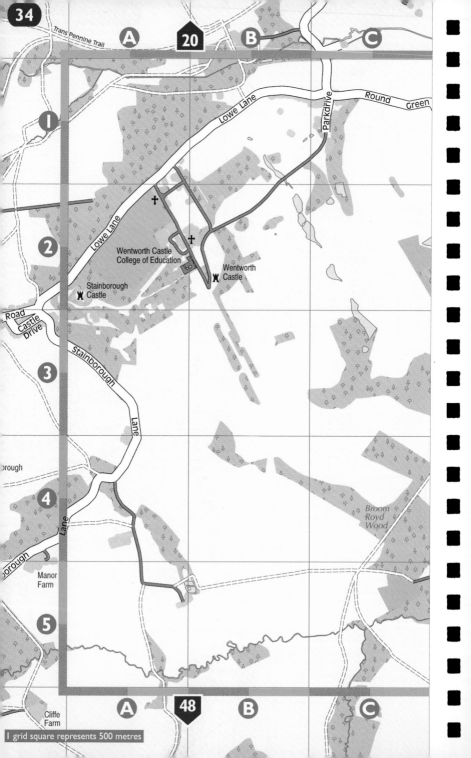

34

Trans Pennine Trail

A 20 B C

Lowe Lane

Parkdrive

Round Green

1

2

Lowe Lane

Wentworth Castle
College of Education

†

†

Wentworth
Castle

Stainborough
Castle

Road

Castle
Drive

Stainborough

3

Lane

...borough

4

Lane

Broom
Royd
Wood

Manor
Farm

5

Cliffe
Farm

A 48 B C

1 grid square represents 500 metres

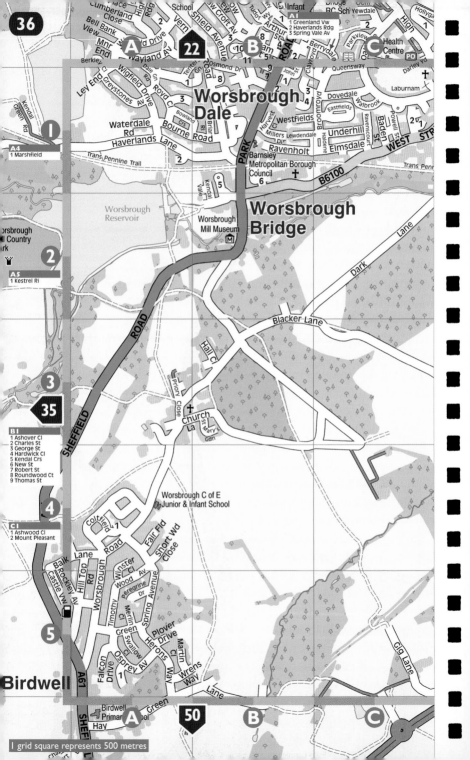

1 grid square represents 500 metres

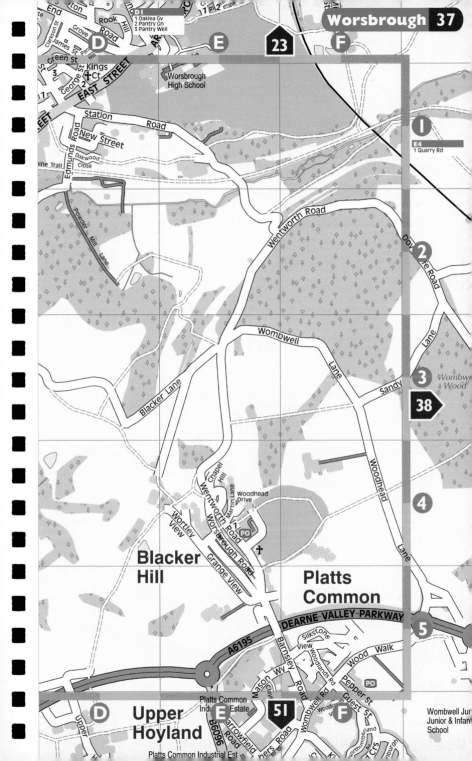

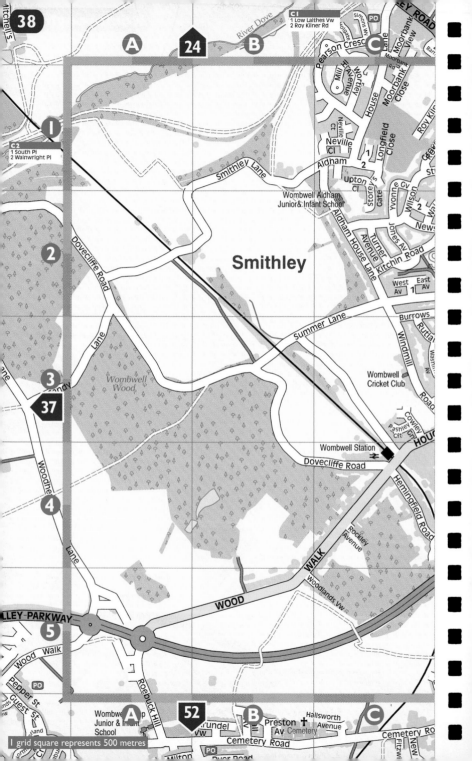

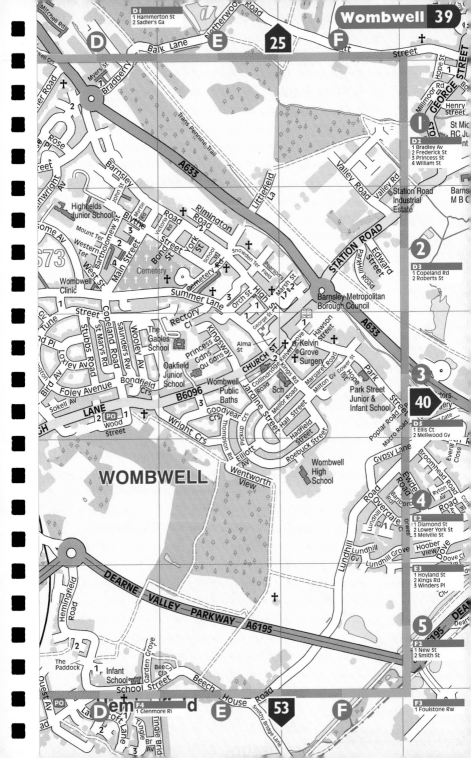

WOMBWELL

D1
1 Hammerton St
2 Sadler's Ga

D2
1 Bradley Av
2 Frederick St
3 Princess St
4 William St

D3
1 Copeland Rd
2 Roberts St

D5
1 Ellis Ct
2 Mellwood Gv

E2
1 Diamond St
2 Lower York St
3 Melville St

E3
1 Hoyland St
2 Kings Rd
3 Winders Pl

F2
1 New St
2 Smith St

F3
1 Foulstone Rw

F4
1 Glenmore Ri

Station Road Industrial Estate

Barnsley Metropolitan Borough Council

Wombwell Clinic

Highfields Junior School

Cemetery

The Gables School

Oakfield Junior School

Wombwell Public Baths

Wombwell High School

Park Street Junior & Infant School

Kelvin Grove Surgery

St Michael's RC Junior

The Paddock

Infant School

DEARNE VALLEY PARKWAY A6195

40

Pitt Street

A **B** **C** Darfi

SNAPE HILL ROAD

A1
1 Providence St

Centre
Springbank
Springfiel
Springfield
Crescent
Vicar Crs

Man La Rd
VICTORIA ROAD

Margaret St Barbara's
Verona
Havelock
Doveside

Primary School

Fern Close
Celandine Grove
Maytree Close
Larch Close
Honeysuckle Close

Aspen Grove
Alder

Low Valley

Millmoor Rd
GEORGE STREET
Hope St
Bole Close
Henry Street

St Michaels RC Junior & Infant School

STONYFORD ROAD

Ings Road

1
A3
1 Badsworth Ci
2 Reginald Rd

Valley Road
Valley Rd

Station Road Industrial Estate

Barnsley M B C

STATION ROAD

2
A4
1 Brampton Vw
2 Derwent Pl
3 Junction St
4 Medway Pl

...sley Metropolitan ...ugh Council

A633

3
Gower St
Hope St

Park S... Jun... Infan...

Everill Gate Lane

PO

Broomhill

Highgate

39

Doctors Surgery

Park Hollow

Everill Gate

B5
1 Butterfield Ct

...well

GYPSY LANE
Macro Road

Wath Road

1

WATH ROAD A633

Everill Close

Broomhead Road
Barnborough
Ewden Road

3
Junction Close

BRAMPTON ROAD

Ryton
Av
Conway
Axon

A6195

Barnsley Rotherham

4

...dale Road
Orwell
Road
Dearn...

C5
1 Melton St

4

Lundhill Grove
Hoober View

Dove Cl
Brampton Crescent

Moorbridge Crs

B6273
Derwe...

Lundhill Gv
Lundhill Grove

Grantley Close
Brendon

Dearne Va Pkwy
DEARNE VALLEY PARKWAY

Dearne Valley Parkway

A6195

Brierlow Spring
Spring
Avenue

B6089

Dearne Road
Primary School

Rother Street

Becknoll Road

Moorbridge Crs

5

Garden Drive
PO

KNOLLBECK LANE

Knollbeck Avenue
Beck Crescent

Chapel Avenue

Brampton Health Cen

Ffld
Mission Road

Cliffe Street

Brampton Street
Melton Avenue

PONTEFRACT ROAD

Milton Clo
Grov...

Knollbeck Avenue
Wyn
Grove
Wyn
...moor Cres
Ellis Cres

Doctors Surgery

BRAMPTON...

Highfield Grove

A **54** **B** **C**

Brampton Road

I grid square represents 500 metres

Brampton

Manor R...

ield

D5
1 Moorland Ct
2 Westmount Av

A635

Cliff Road

D

Road

E

Lane

F

Cathill Road

Pasture

I

A6195

Broomhill Lane

2

3

4

River

A633

5

Wath West
Industrial
Estate

Holloway
Avenue
Grove
Grove Road
Edward
Elliott
Browning
Grove
Road
Road
Moorland View
Barnsley
Tennyson
Road
2
1

MANVERS WAY

D
Burns Way
Dryden Road
Byron
Wordsworth Rd
Shakespeare
Road

E
Barnsley Road

55

F
A633

Moor Lane

Wet Moor
Lane

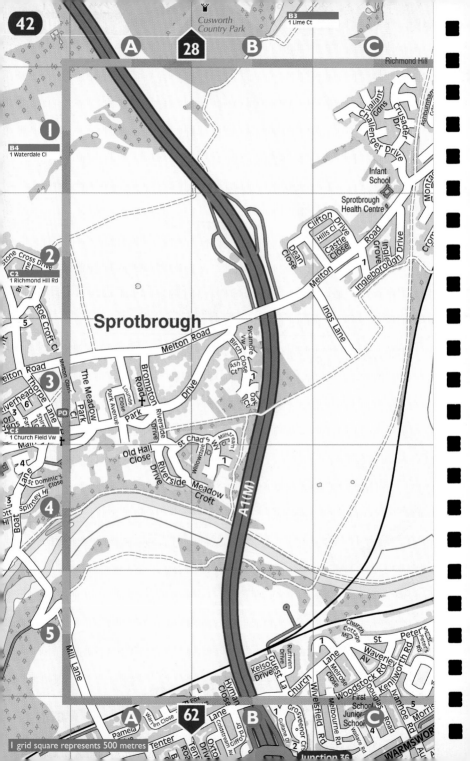

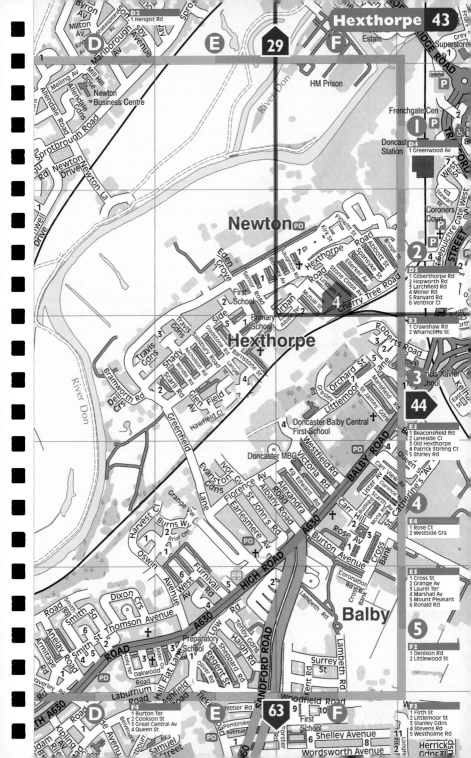

29

D2
1 Hengist Rd

D
E
F

Byron
Milton
AV

Superstore

Shakespeare
AV

Marlborough Avenue

Melling Av
King
Av

Allendale
Gdns

Newton
Business Centre

Newton Drive

HM Prison

River Don

P

P

Frenchgate Cen

I P

Doncast
Station

Newton La

D4
1 Greenwood Av

Newton PO

Eden Grove

Kirk St

Flowitt St

Hexthorpe Road

Spansyke St

Abbott St

Ellerker Av

Stone Close Av

Cherry Tree Road

Coroners
Court

P

2

4

D5
1 Gilberthorpe Rd
2 Hepworth Rd
3 Larchfield Rd
4 Milner Rd
5 Ranyard Rd
6 Ventnor Cl

First
School

Senior Road

Batley Av

Launton Rd

Urban

Aldloch Ter

Mutual St

4

E2
1 Crawshaw Rd
2 Wharncliffe St

Travis Gdns

Shady
Side

Windle Rd

Nicholson Rd

Gladstone Rd

Salisbury Road

Primary
School

Barnstone St

Langdale

Roberts Road

Orchard St

3

5

Francis Xavier
School

3

River Don

Bramworth
Dell
Crs

Scarfi Rd

Glen Field Av

Hawfield Cl

Greenfield

Littlemoor

Cresley Rd

St James Gdns

Mansfield

4

E3
1 Beaconsfield Rd
2 Laneside Cl
3 Old Hexthorpe
4 Patrick Stirling Ct
5 Shirley Rd

Doncaster Balby Central
First School

Westfield Rd

Victoria Rd

BALBY ROAD

Doncaster MBC

Evanston
Gdns

Ivor Gv

Florence Av

St John's Rd

Alexandra Rd

Albany Road

Kg Edward Rd

Carr View Av

Lister Av

Scarth Av

Clarence

St Andrine's Av

Queen St

PO

4

E4
1 Rose Ct
2 Westside Gra

Harvest Cl

Burns Wy

Briar Crc

Grange Vw

Grange Lane

Earlesmere Av

PO

HIGH ROAD

Furnivall Rd

West Av

Low Rd

Tenby Gdns

Sheppard St

Halgh Rd

Regent St

A630

Burton Avenue

Rose Av

Cross Bank

Coronation Rd

Lambeth Rd

Cart Hill

Balby

E5
1 Cross St
2 Grange Av
3 Laurel Ter
4 Marshall Av
5 Mount Pleasant
6 Ronald Rd

5

F2
1 Denison Rd
2 Littlewood St

Dixon Crs

Smith Sq

Thomson Avenue

Anelay Road

Smith St

Armitage Rd

Waverley Av

ROAD A630

Holly Ter

Oakwood Road

Preparatory
School

Oliver Rd

Ashfield Road

Laburnum Road

PO

SANDFORD ROAD

Woodfield Road

Surrey St

Kent Rd

Lambeth Rd

Herrick
Gdns

F3
1 Firth St
2 Littlemoor St
3 Stanley Gdns
4 Stevens Rd
5 Westholme Rd

D
1 Burton Ter
2 Cookson St
3 Great Central Av
4 Queen St

E
63
F

9

10

First
School

11

Shelley Avenue

Wordsworth Avenue

Samuel Street

Pembroke
Avenue

Whittier Rd

Forster Rd

PO

44

2

3

4

5

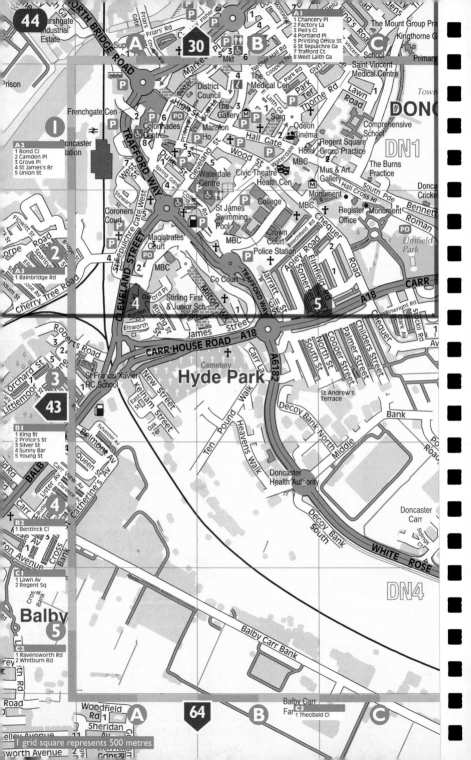

44

Marshgate
Industrial
Estate

Prison

A2
1 Bond Cl
2 Camden Pl
3 Grove Pl
4 St James's Br
5 Union St

I

2

A3
1 Bainbridge Rd

3

43

B1
1 King St
2 Prince's St
3 Silver St
4 Sunny Bar
5 Young St

BALB

4

B2
1 Bentinck Cl

C1
1 Lawn Av
2 Regent Sq

Balby

5

C2
1 Ravensworth Rd
2 Whitburn Rd

A1
1 Chancery Pl
2 Factory La
3 Peil's Cl
4 Portland Pl
5 Printing Office St
6 St Sepulchre Ga
7 Trafford Ct
8 West Laith Ga

30

A   **B**   **C**

The Mount Group Pra
Kingthorne G

Primary

Saint Vincent
Medical Centre

Comprehensive
School

DONC

DN1

Town

The Burns
Practice

Donca
Cricke

Elmfield
Park

Roman

CARR

4   **5**

Hyde Park

St Andrew's
Terrace

Bank

Doncaster
Health Authority

Doncaster
Carr

DN4

WHITE ROSE

A   **64**   **B**   **C**

Woodfield
Rd
Sheridan

Balby Carr
Far

C3
1 Theobald Cl

1 grid square represents 500 metres

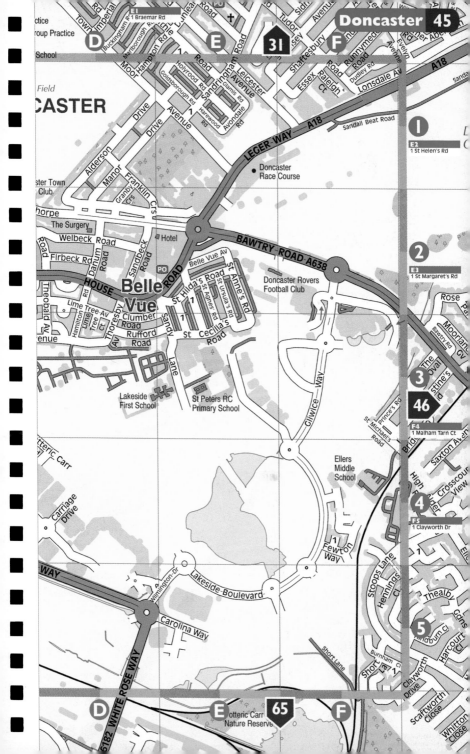

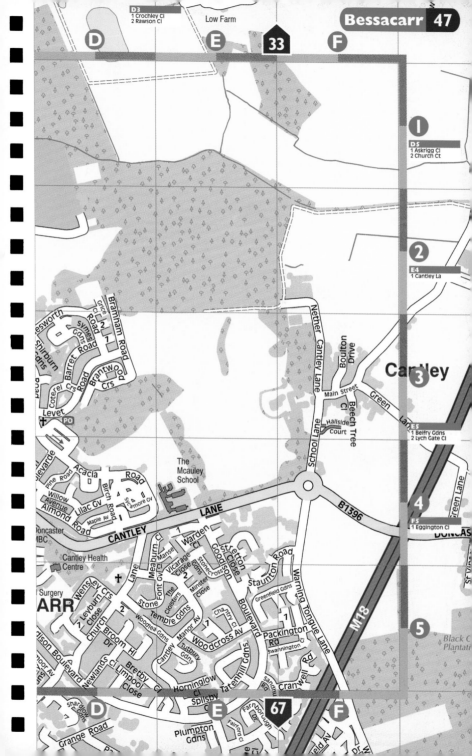

D3
1 Crochley Cl
2 Rawson Cl

Low Farm

D   **E**   33   **F**

I
D5
1 Askrigg Cl
2 Church Ct

2
E4
1 Cantley La

Bramham Road
Green Cl
Symes Gdns
Barret Road
Brantwood Crs
Shirburn Gdns
esworth
Coterel Crs
Levet
PO

Nether Cantley Lane
Bolton Drive
Cantley
Main Street
Beech Tree Ct
Green Lane

3
E5
1 Belfry Gdns
2 Lych Gate Cl

School Lane
Hallside Court

The
Mcauley
School

4
F5
1 Eggington Cl

Green Lane

Acacia Road
Pine Road
Willow Avenue
Almond Road
Birch Road
Lilac Gv
Maple Rd
Sycamore Gv
Doncaster
MBC
Boulevarde

CANTLEY LANE
B1396
DONCAS

Cantley Health
Centre

Surgery
ARR
Wensley Crs
Levburn Close
Church Dr
Broom Hl
Newlands Cl
Limpool Close
Bretby Cl
moor Av
harde
cook Cdns
Lane
Meaburn Cl
Mansel Gv
Font Cv
The cloisters
Stone
Temple Gdns
Woogiea Gdns
Cantley
Manor Av
nutbury
Gdns
Warden Cl
Vicarage Close
Stone Cross Gdns
Minster Close
Woodcross Av
Horninglow Cl
Spilsby Cl
Tatenhill Gdns

St Stretton
Goodison Close
Stone Cross
Staunton Road
Greenfield Gdns
Boulevard
cha
try cl
Packington Rd
Swannington
Warning Tongue Lane
sandhu
Cranwell Rd

M18

5
Black C
Plantati

D   **E**   67   **F**

Plumpton
Gdns

Grange Road

St V

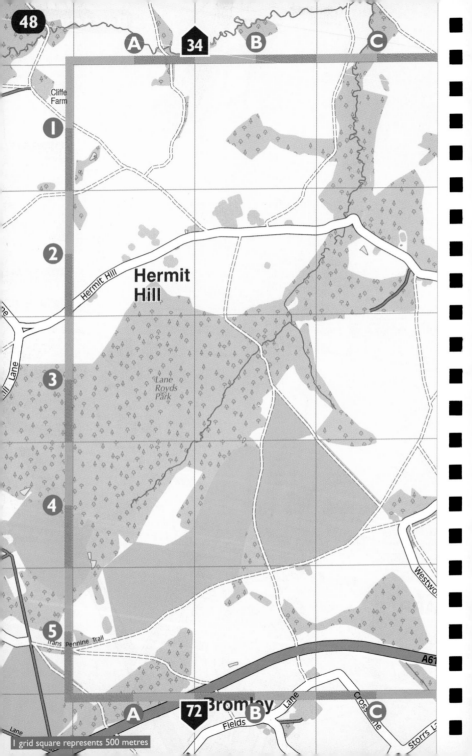

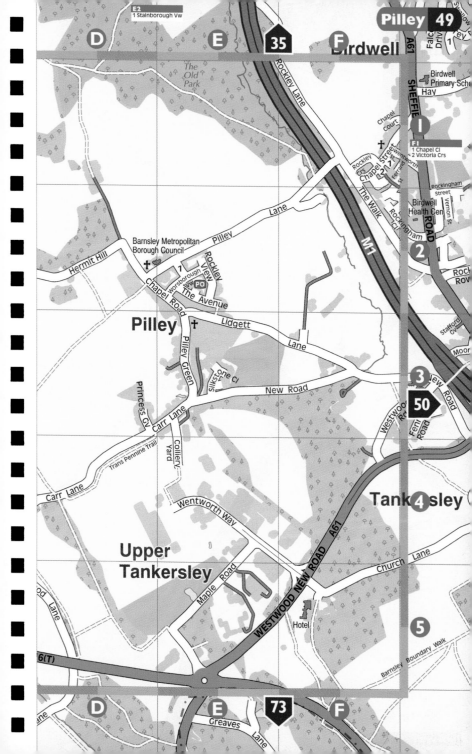

50

Birdwell

A3
1 Macnaghten Rd
2 Walker Rd

B3
1 Queens Crs

C3
1 Allott St
2 Burcroft Cl
3 Central St
4 Club St
5 Cross St
6 Queens Gdns
7 Tranmoor Ct
8 Watson St

C4
1 Steadfield Rd

Birdwell Primary School

Birdwell Health Cen

Rockingham Row

Rockingham Business Park

DEARNE VALLEY PARKWAY

A6195

Hoyland Common

Junction 36

Doctors Surg

Hoyland Common Primary School

B6096

A6135

SHEFFIELD ROAD

HOYLAND ROAD

A6135 SHEFF

New Road

Tankersley Lane

Green Lane

nkersley

Church Lane

Black Lane

M1

Bell Ground

Barnsley Boundary walk

Barnsley Boundary Walk

49

36

74

A B C

1 grid square represents 500 metres

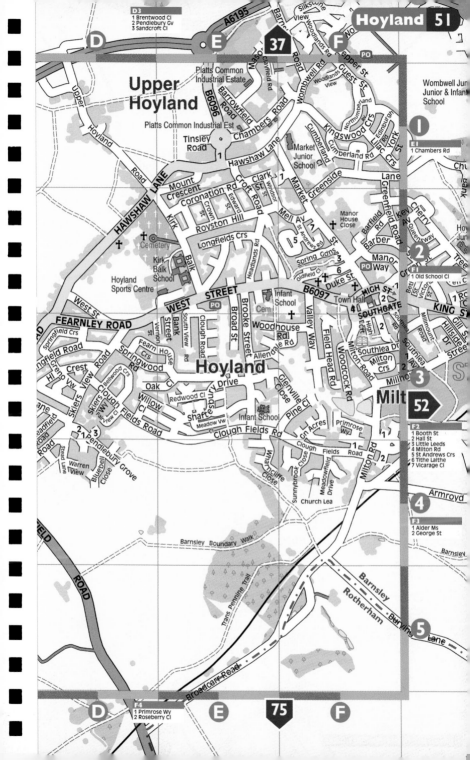

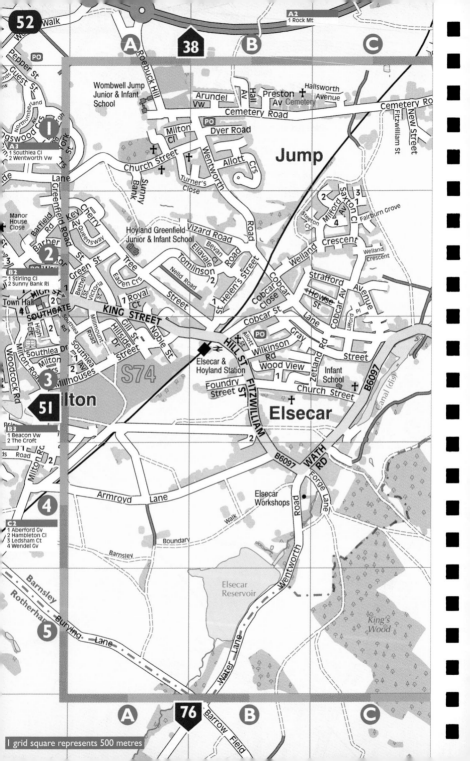

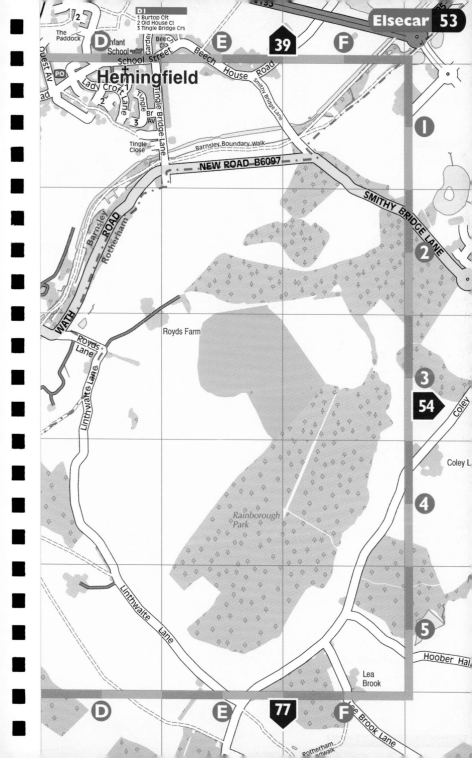

D1
1 Burtop Cft
2 Old House Cl
3 Tingle Bridge Crs

D

The Paddock

nfant School

Hemingfield

School Street

Beech House Road

PO

Lady Croft Lane

Tingle Bridge Lane

Smithy Bridge Lane

Br
AV

Tingle
Close

Barnsley Boundary Walk

NEW ROAD B6097

SMITHY BRIDGE LANE

Barnsley ROAD

Rotherham

WATH

Royds
Lane

Royds Farm

Linthwaite Lane

Coley

54

Coley L

Rainborough
Park

Linthwaite Lane

Hoober Hal

Lea
Brook

e Brook Lane

Rotherham
dwalk

39

E

F

I

2

3

4

5

D

E

77

F

54

A6195

A

40

B

B1
1 Hurley Cft
2 Westfield Rd

PONTEFRACT R

C

Milton clo

Knollbeck

Beck crescent

Wyn

moor Crescent

Ellis Crescent

Knollbeck Avenue

Doctors
Surgery

Highfield
Grove

Brampton
Road

BRAMPTON ROAD

Brampton

C1
1 Hall Cl
2 Manor Cl
3 Rainborough Ms

I

Westfield Road

Westpit Hill

2

1

Hurley
Croft

Manor Road

Fleet
Close

3

2

Brampton
Road

PACKMAN ROAD

Carnley
Street

Packman
Way

Quarry
Bank

Honister
Close

SMITHY BRIDGE LANE

2

ELSECAR ROAD

FIRTH

ROTHERHAM ROAD

Bramble Way

Brookside
Crescent

PACK

3

53

Coley Lane

Coley Lane Farm

4

Hoober
Hall

5

Lea
Brook

Hoober Hall Lane

Lee Brook

A

78

B

C

Hoo

field

I grid square represents 500 metres

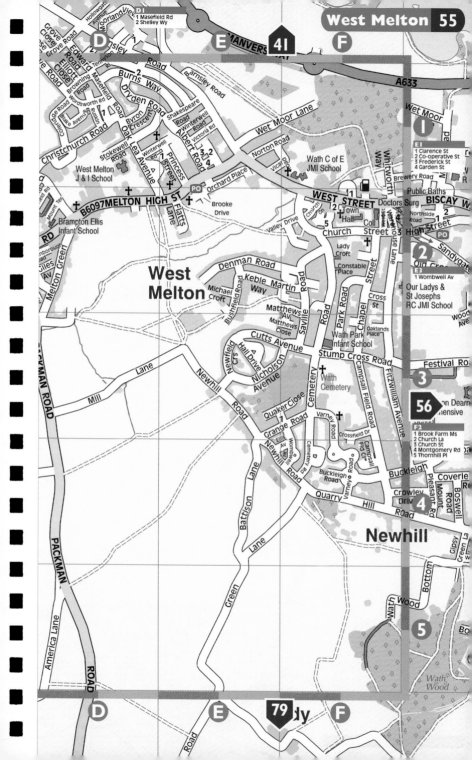

D1
1 Masefield Rd
2 Shelley Wy

D

E MANVERS WAY **41**

F

A633

Wet Moor

E1
1 Clarence St
2 Co-operative St
3 Frederick St
4 Garden St

Holloway
Moorland View
Avenue

Grove Close
Grove Road
Edward Road
Elliott Close
Browning Road
Masefield Road
Tennyson
Ainsley

Burns Way
Dryden Road
Shakespeare Road
Barnsley Road
Wet Moor Lane

Wordsworth Rd
Byron Crescent
Winterwell Road
Victoria Rd

College Road
Blake Avenue
Ruskin Road
Oak Lea Avenue
Albert Road
Norton Road
Vicar

Christchurch Road
Stokewell Road
Winterwell
Princess Street
Orchard Place

West Melton
J & I School

B6097 MELTON HIGH ST

Mount Ter
Flatts Lane

Brampton Ellis
Infant School

Valley Drive

Wath C of E
JMI School

Whitworth Way

Brewery Road

Public Baths

BISCAY W

Brooke
Drive

WEST STREET
Town
Hall
Church Street

Coll

Doctors Surg

Northside
Road

High Street

PO

Sandygate

Old Cro

E2
1 Wombwell Av

Melton Green

borough Road
Giles
AV

RD

Denman Road
Keble Martin Way
Michael Croft
Bushfield Road
Matthews AV
Matthews Close

**West
Melton**

Saville Road

Lady
Croft

Constable
Place

Cross
St

Park Road
Chapel Street

Oaklands
Place

Wath Park
Infant School

Cutts Avenue

Newfield Crs
Hall Drive
Nicholson Avenue

Stump Cross Road

Campsall Field Road
Fitzwilliam Avenue

Our Ladys &
St Josephs
RC JMI School

Wood
Ave

Festival Ro

56

on Dearn
ehensive

F1
1 Brook Farm Ms
2 Church La
3 Church St
4 Montgomery Rd
5 Thornhill Pl

Lane

Mill

Newhill Road

Quaker Close

Grange Road
Ellis Av
Wombwell Av

Cemetery Road
Wath
Cemetery

Varney Road
Crossfield Dr
Campsall Fld Gr

Da

PACKMAN ROAD

Battison Lane

Newhill Lane
Newhill Road

Buckleigh
Road

Varney Road
Quarry Hill Road

Buckleigh

Crowley
Driv

Pleasant Rd
Mount
Boswell Road
Coverie

4

Newhill

Gipsy Green La

Bo

America Lane

ROAD

Green Road

Wath Wood
Bottom

Wath Wood

5

D

E **79** dy

F

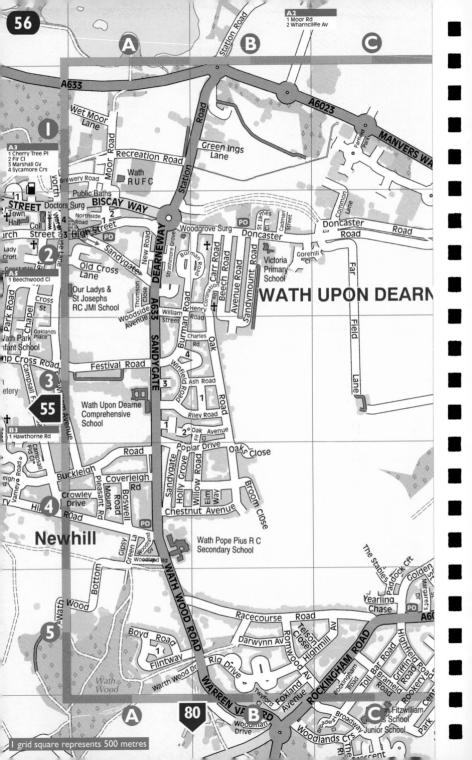

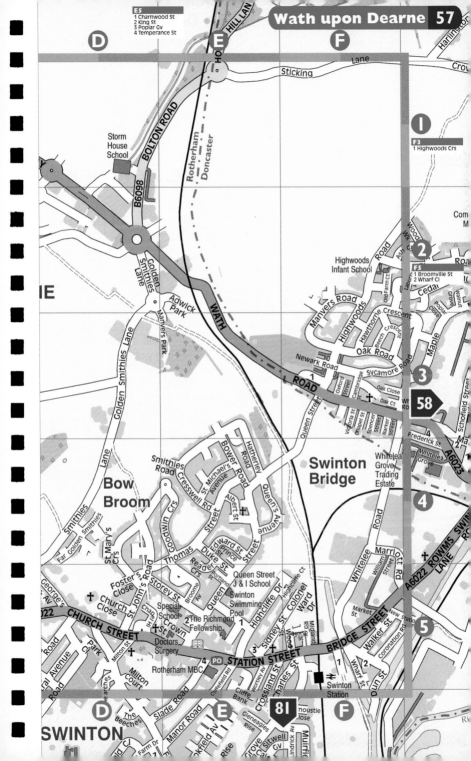

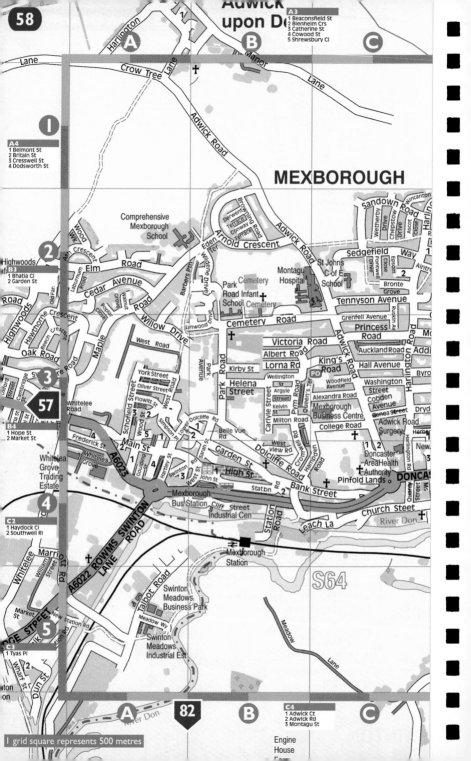

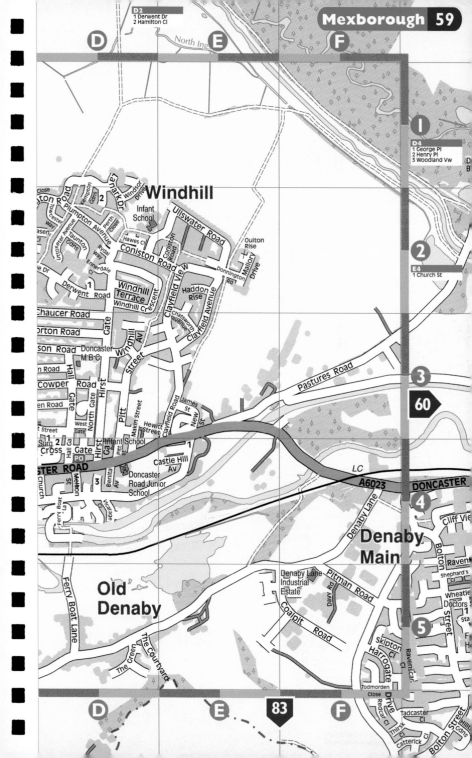

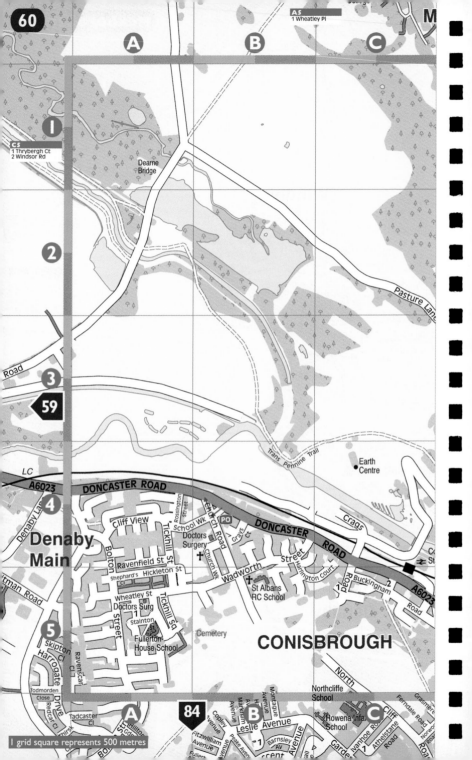

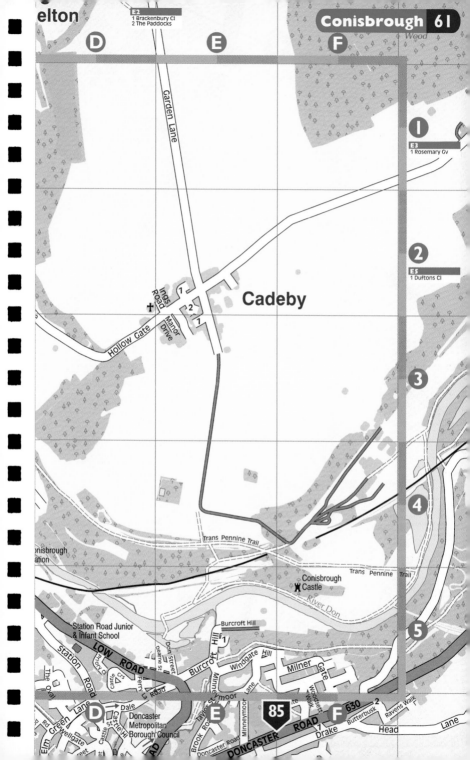

elton

D   E   F

Wood

E2
1 Brackenbury Cl
2 The Paddocks

Garden Lane

I

E3
1 Rosemary Gv

2

E5
1 Duftons Cl

Cadeby

7

Ings Road
Manor Drive

Hollow Gate

2

7

3

Trans Pennine Trail

4

Trans Pennine Trail

onisbrough
ation

Conisbrough
Castle

River Don

5

Station Road Junior
& Infant School

Burcroft Hill

Don Street

Deane St.

Ferry La.

Priory Cl

Crs

LOW   ROAD

Station Road

The Oval

Burcroft Hill

1

Minneymoor Lane

Windgate Hill

Milner Gate

Woodsets Walk

D

Dale

Castle Hill

Castle St

Doncaster
Metropolitan
Borough Council

E

Brook Road

Taylor St

Minneymoor Lane

85

Doncaster Road

F

630

DONCASTER ROAD

7 Drake

Butterbusk

2

Ravens Walk

Head

Lane

Elm Rd

Green Lane

Wellgate

Street

42

A

B

C

Junction 36

WARMSWOR

A1
1 Church Rein Cl
2 Coronation Gdns

A4
1 Boundary Cl
2 Century Ct
3 Fielders Wy
4 Johnson Ct
5 Larwood Gv

A5
1 Newbridge Gv

B1
1 Dirleton Dr
2 Grosvenor Ter

C1
1 Apostle Cl
2 Cambria Dr
3 Hyland Crs
4 Mannering Rd
5 Sandycroft Crs

C2
1 Beechcroft Rd
2 Pinewood Av
3 Whitney Cl

Warmsworth
Primary School

First
School
Junior
School

Nightingale
Primary School

Mayflower
Rd

Cemetery

Staveley Street

The
Health
Centre

HIGH ROAD A630

SHEFFIELD ROAD

A630

EDLINGTON LANE

B6376

Broomhouse Lane

Lord's Head Lane

Common Lane

Low Road West

Low Rd

Mill Lane

Pamela
Drive

Tenter

Oxton
Drive

Badsworth Road

Darrington
Drive

Stapleton Road

Oak Dale
Road

Ash Dale Road

Halt

Poplar
Grove

Park
Crs

Kennington
Grove

Grace Road

Markham Road

Granby
Road

Springfield
Rd

North Street

Wood View

Broomhouse Lane

Hotel

PO

PO

Beech
Grove

Cliff Crs

Cecil Avenue

Wigmore Av

Norbreck Rd

Sheffield Road

Lunbreck Road

Warren Close

Fox Gv

Fox
Grove

Hyman Close

Grosvenor Cr
Guisane Dr

Melbourne Rd

Wallace St

Douglas Rd

Ivanhoe Rd

Kenilworth Rd

Morri

Waverley
Av

Melrose
Close

Woodsto

Grenville

Austen

Cedar

Raleigh
Ter

Aviemore Rd

Linamoot
Close

Barrel Lane

Cedar Rd

Cedar
Rise

Woburn
Close

Cedar
Road

Sherwood
Rise

Burford
Dr

Croft

Thomas
St

Quaker
Lane

Glebe
Street

Clifford Av

JO Drfo

Coldstream Av

Guiliane Dr

Wicket
Way

Shaw

Trent St

Edgbaston
Way

Willow
Dr

Arlott Way

Volunteer

Headingley

Heaton
Gdns

Markham
Square

Lords Cl

msworth

Queens Road

Victoria Road

EDLINGTON LANE

Prin

Nelson Road

on Road

Wellington Road

Ivanhoe Road

ain Avenue

The Cl

Doctors/
Surgery

Place

Cross
Lane

Castle

Blow Hall

Stubbins Hill

Martin

oomhouse

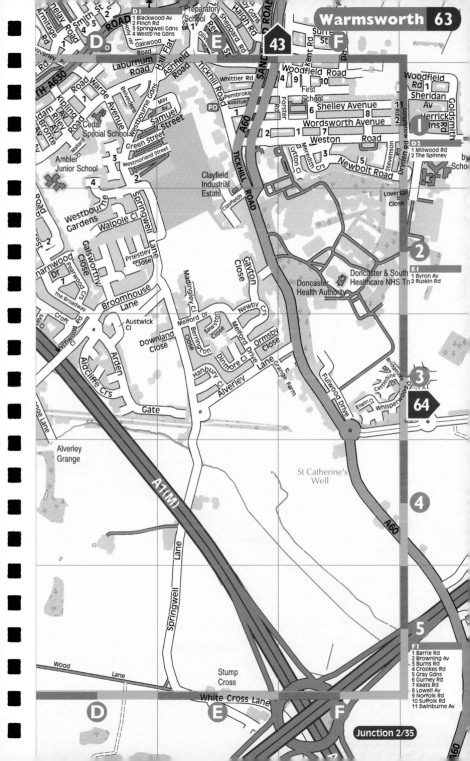

Junction 2/35

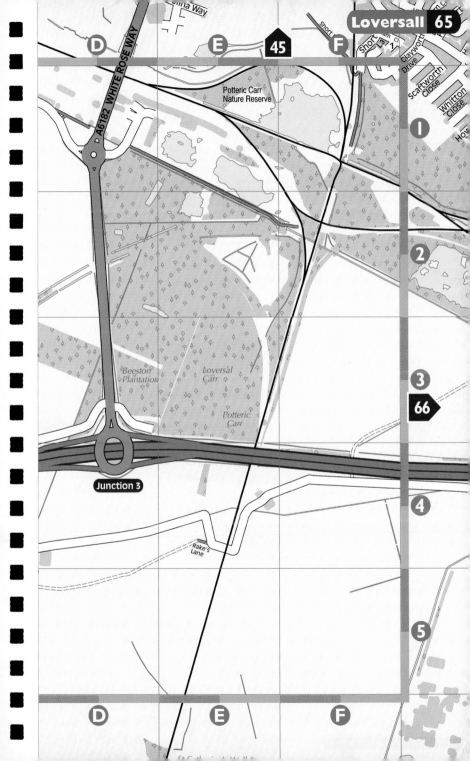

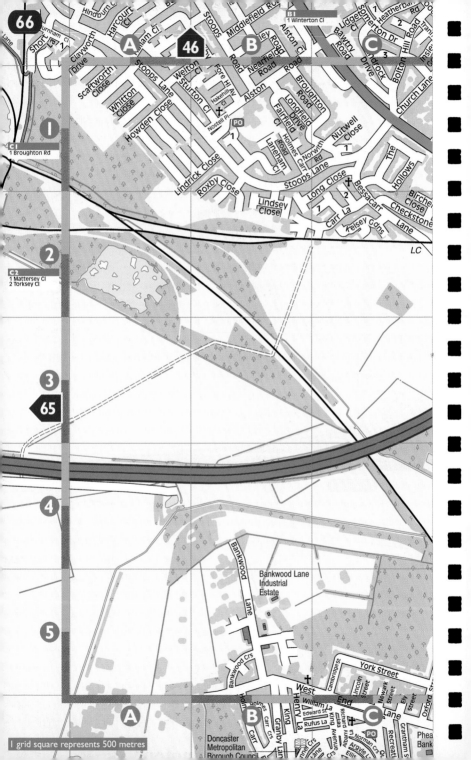

I grid square represents 500 metres

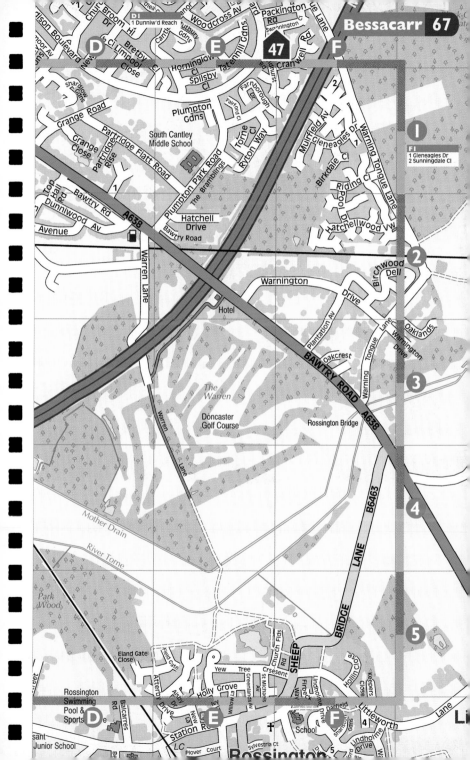

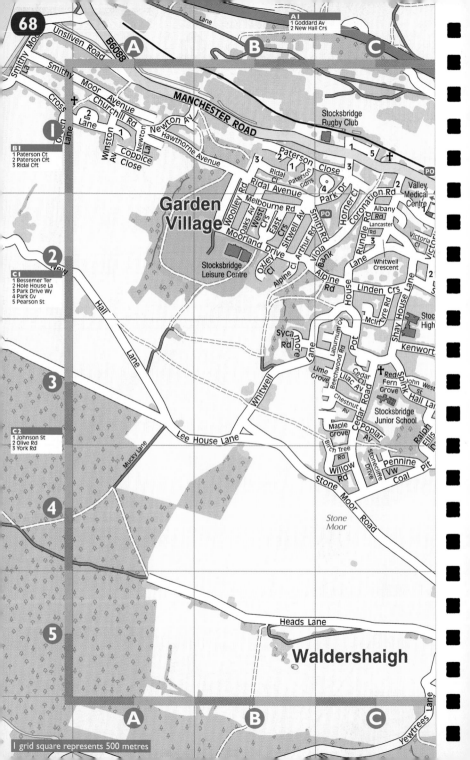

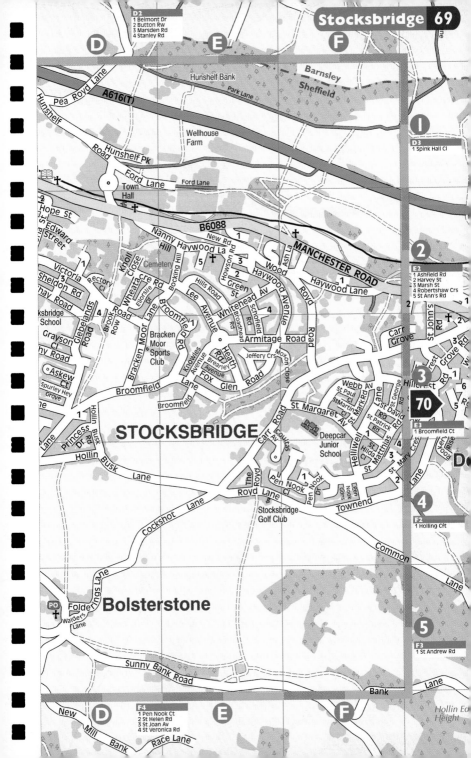

D **E** **F**

D2
1 Belmont Dr
2 Button Rw
3 Marsden Rd
4 Stanley Rd

Barnsley
Sheffield

Hunshelf Bank
Park Lane

Pea Royd Lane
A616(T)

Hunshelf

Wellhouse
Farm

Hunshelf Pk
Road

Ford Lane
Ford Lane

Town
Hall

I

D3
1 Spink Hall Cl

Hope St

Edward
Street

Nanny Haywood La
New Rd

B6088
MANCHESTER ROAD

Victoria
Close

Sheldon Rd

hay Road

Cemetery

Knoll
Close

Cre Rd

Bockhill

Hill

Green
St

Howson Rd

Wood

Ash La

Haywood Lane

2

E2
1 Ashfield Rd
2 Harvey St
3 Marsh St
4 Robertshaw Crs
5 St Ann's Rd

ksbridge
School

Grayson
Cl

hy Road

Askew
Ct

Spurley Hey
grove

Glebelands
Road

Rectory
Cl

Wheata
Cr

Ellorsle
Dr

Brook
Row

Bracken Moor Lane

Broomfield Rd

Lee
Avenue

Hills Road

Whitehead Rd

Broadhead Rd

Schofield

Haywood Av

Armitage Road

Roid

Road

Haywood Avenue

St John's
Rd

Carr
Grove

Hillcrest

Crest
Rd

Grove

3

70

E3
1 Broomfield Ct

Bracken
Moor
Sports
Club

Broomfield

Broomfield

Lane

Knowles
Avenue

Heath
Rd

Brearley
Avenue

FOX
GLEN

Jeffery Crs

Moxon
Close

St Margaret Road

Hillwell
Rd

Webb Av

St Paul
Cl

St Martins
Cl

St Mark Rd

St Patrick
Rd

St George
Rd

St David
Rd

St Margaret
Rd

St Mary Cres

St Mary
Rise

Rose
Rd

D

STOCKSBRIDGE

Hollin
Lane

Princess
Dr

Busk
Rd

Hollin Busk
Lane

Carr Road

Coultas Av

The
Royd

Royd Lane

Pen Nook
Cl

Pen Nook
Dr

Pen Nook
Gdns

Deepcar
Junior
School

St Hilda
Cl

St Matthias

Townend

Common
Lane

4

F2
1 Holling Cft

Cockshot Lane

Stocksbridge
Golf Club

Folderings Lane

Bolsterstone

PO

Walders
Lane

Sunny Bank Road

Lane

5

F3
1 St Andrew Rd

Bank
Lane

Hollin Ed
Height

D **E** **F**

F4
1 Pen Nook Ct
2 St Helen Rd
3 St Joan Av
4 St Veronica Rd

New
Mill
Bank

Race Lane

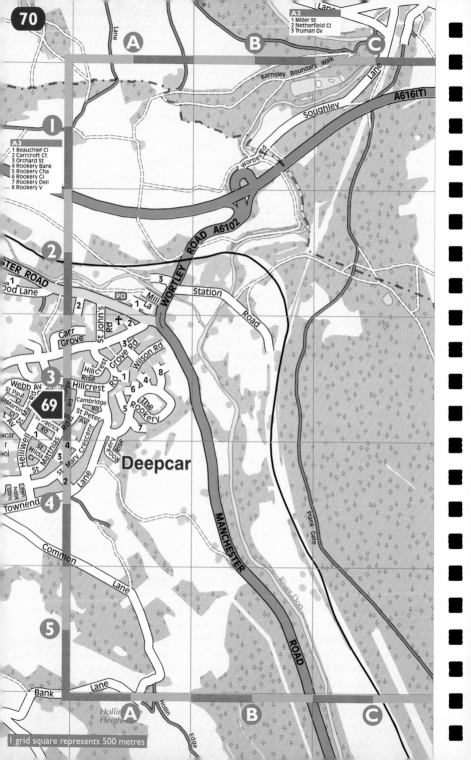

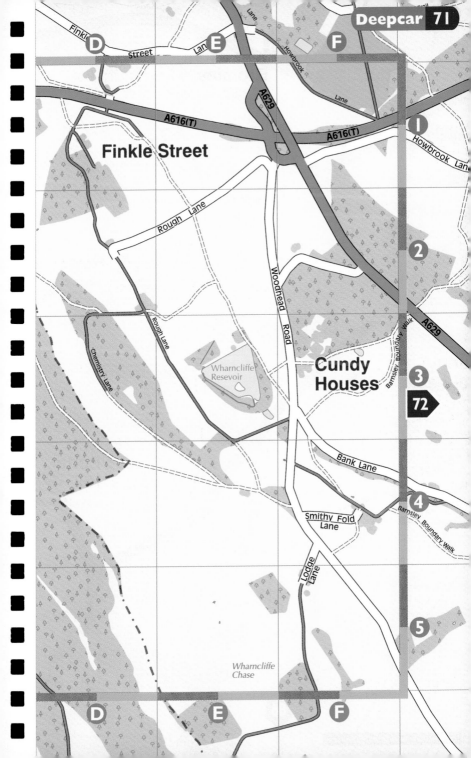

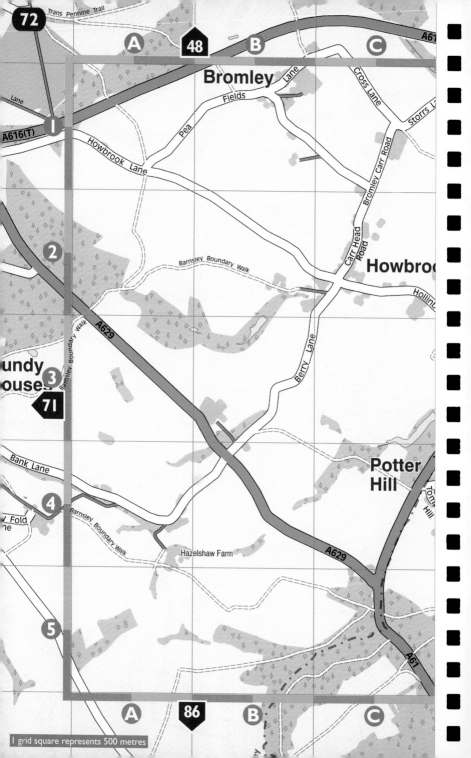

72

Trans Pennine Trail

A   **48**   **B**   **C**   A61

Bromley

Lane

Cross Lane

Fields

Pea

Storrs L

A616(T)

1

Howbrook Lane

Bromley Carr Road

2

Barnsley Boundary Walk

Carr Head Road

Howbro

Hollin

A629

Berry Lane

Barnsley Boundary Walk

undy ouses

3

71

Bank Lane

Potter Hill

4

Barnsley Boundary Walk

Tol Hill

Fold e

Hazelshaw Farm

A629

5

A61

A   **86**   **B**   **C**

1 grid square represents 500 metres

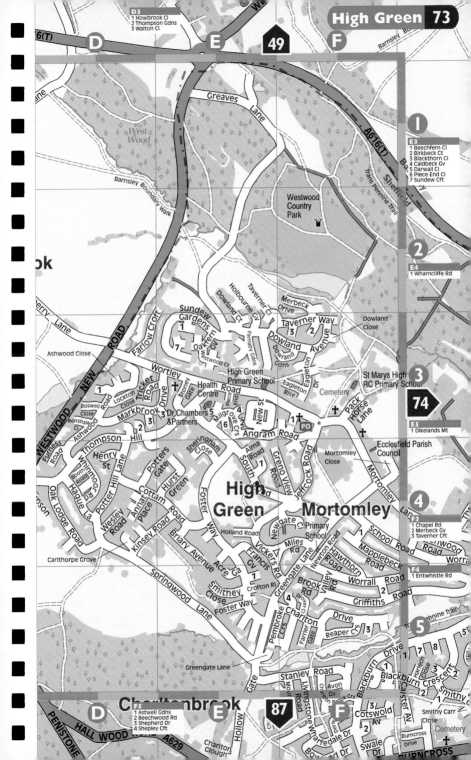

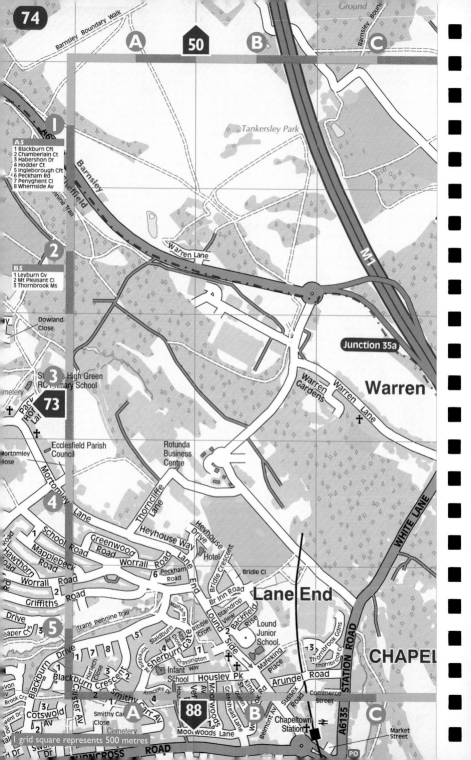

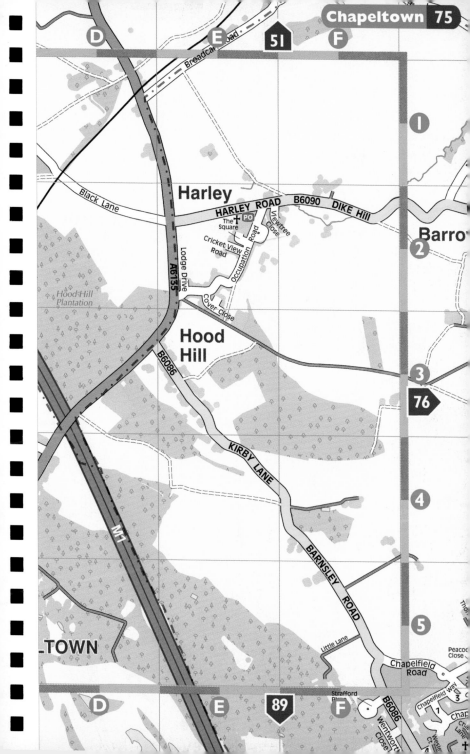

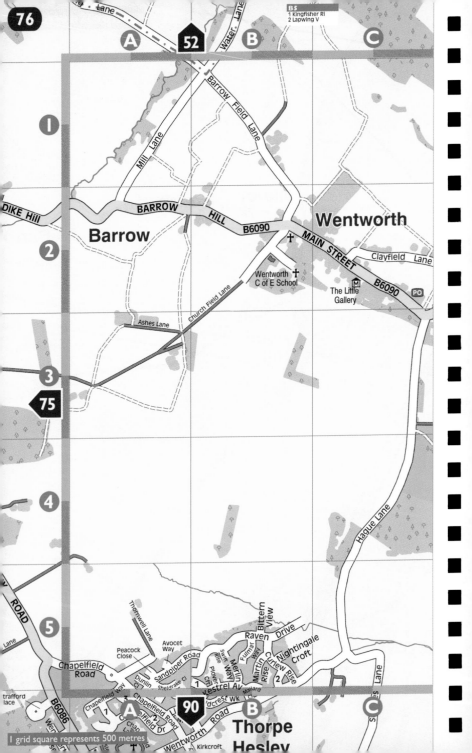

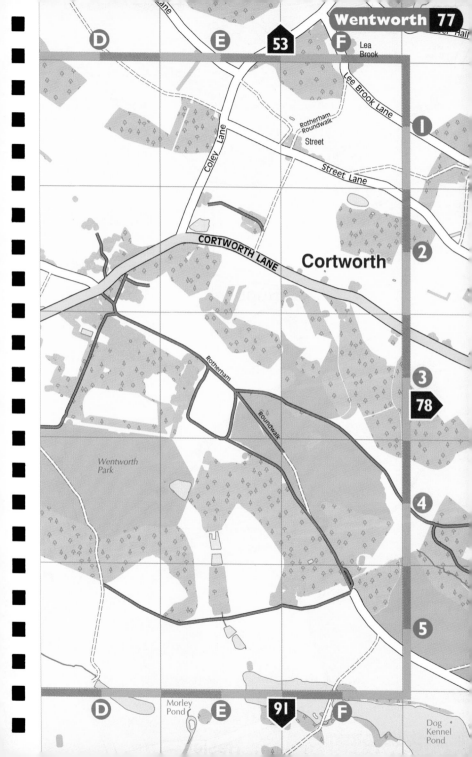

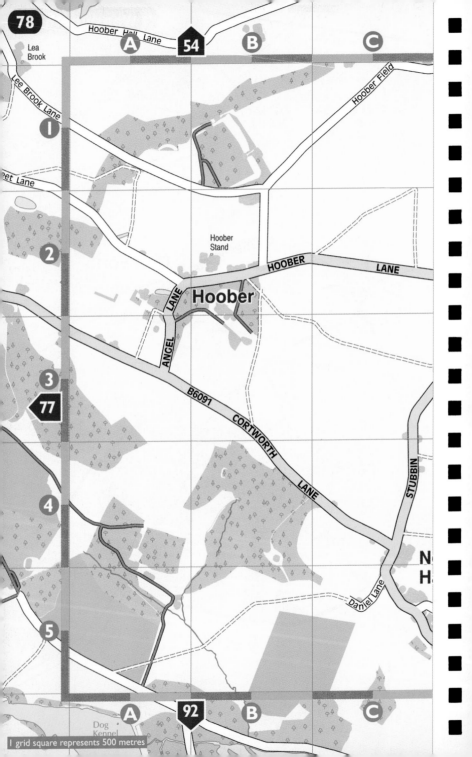

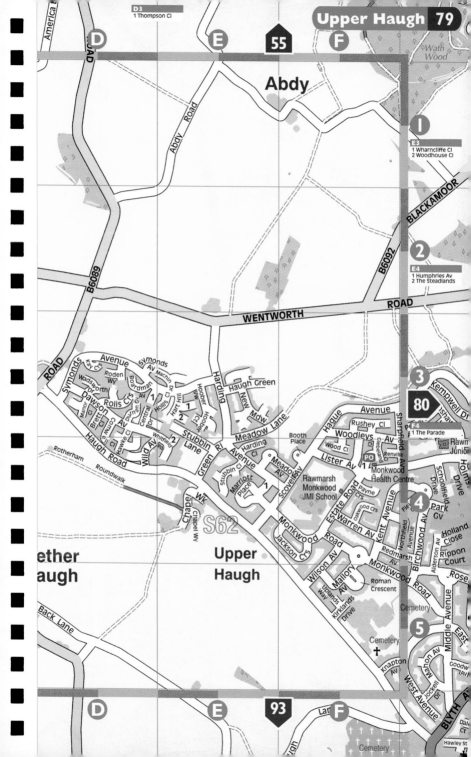

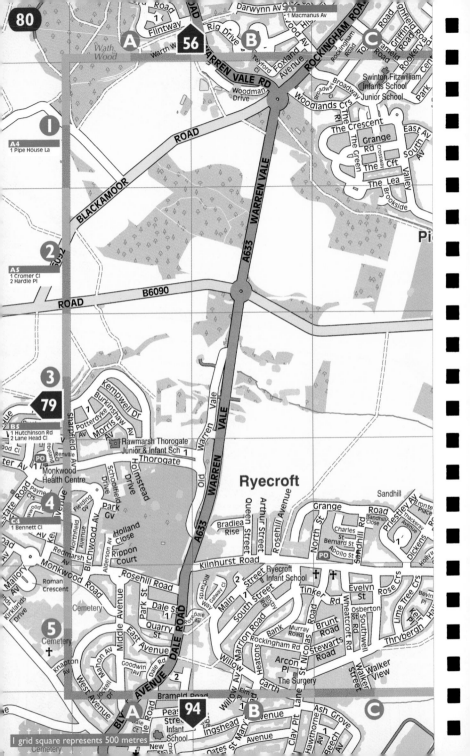

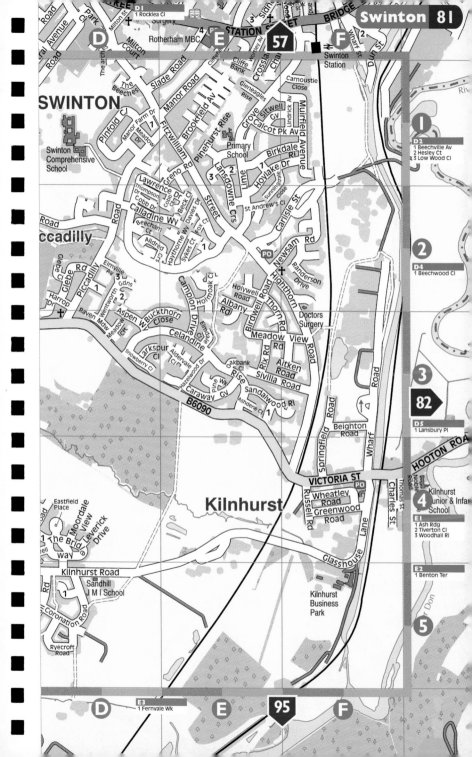

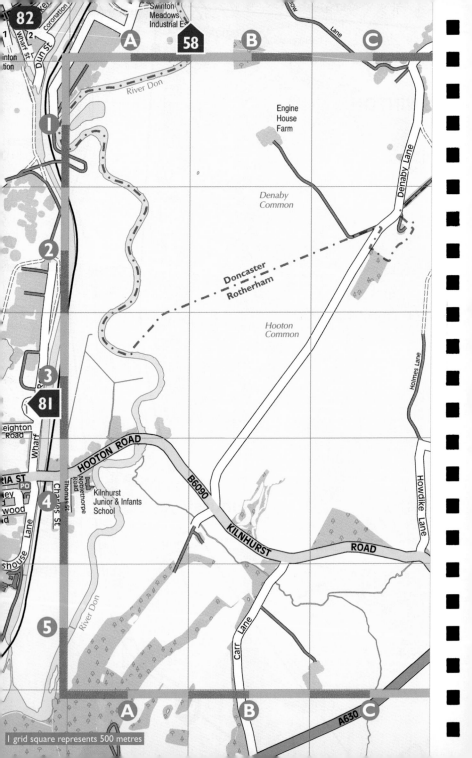

A 58 B C

1

Swinton
Meadows
Industrial E

River Don

Engine
House
Farm

Denaby Lane

Denaby
Common

2

Doncaster
Rotherham

Hooton
Common

Holmes Lane

3

81

eighton
Road

Wharf

HOOTON ROAD

Noblethorpe
Road

Thomas St

Kilnhurst
Junior & Infants
School

B6090

KILNHURST

ROAD

Howdike Lane

RIA ST

PO

ley

wood
d

Charles St

4

shouse

River Don

Carr Lane

5

A B C A630

1 grid square represents 500 metres

Dun St

Coronation

Wharf St

inton
tion

1
2

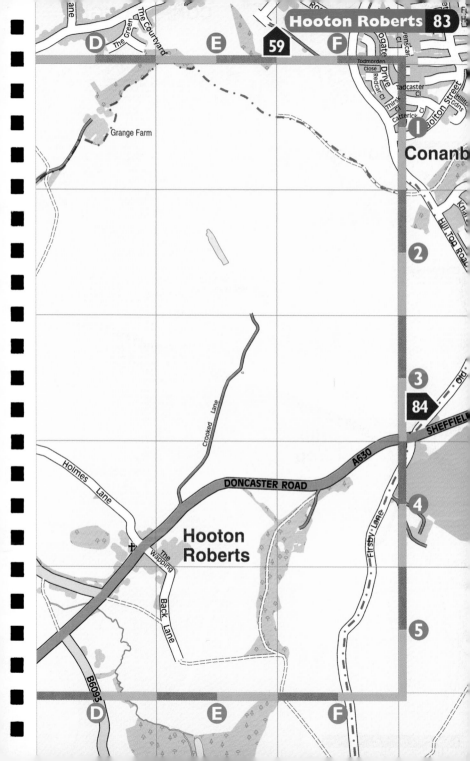

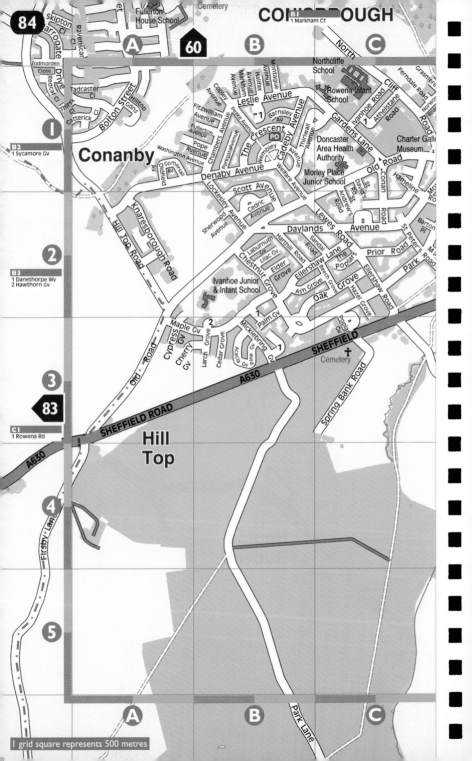

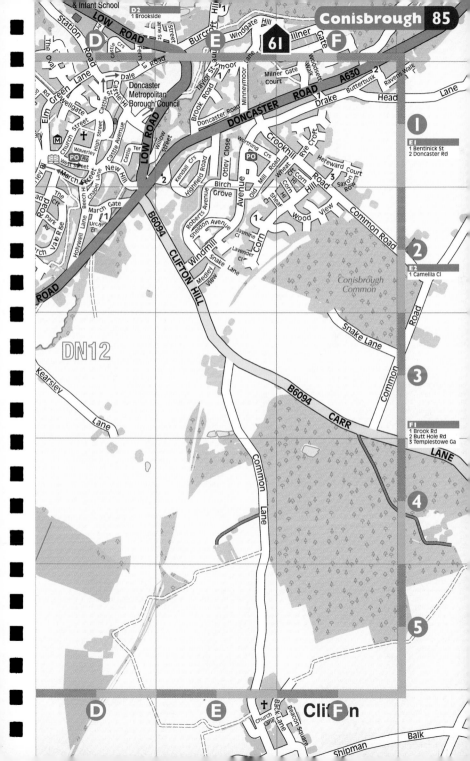

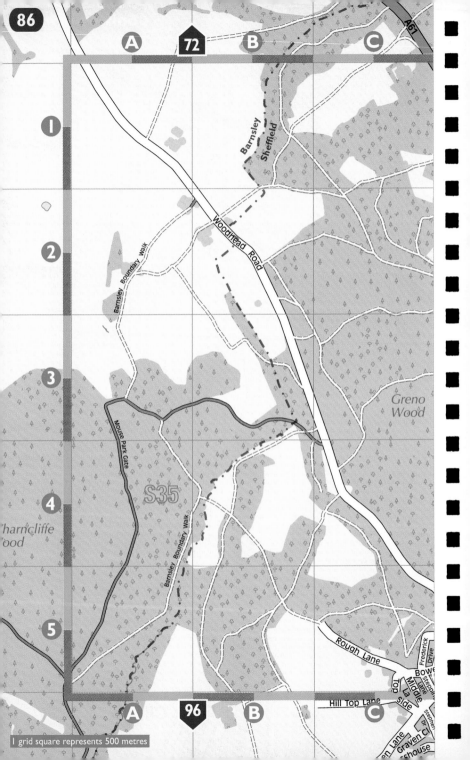

86

A   72   B   C

A61

1

Barnsley
Sheffield

Woodhead Road

2

Barnsley Boundary Walk

3

Greno
Wood

Mouse Park Gate

4

S35

harncliffe
ood

Barnsley Boundary Walk

5

Rough Lane

Frederick
Drive

Bow
top
Middle
side

Hill Top Lane

A   96   B   C

en Lane
Graven Cl
hsouse

1 grid square represents 500 metres

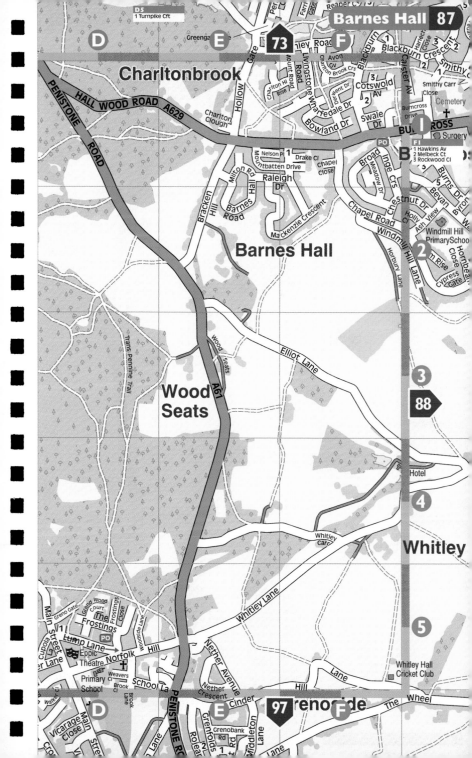

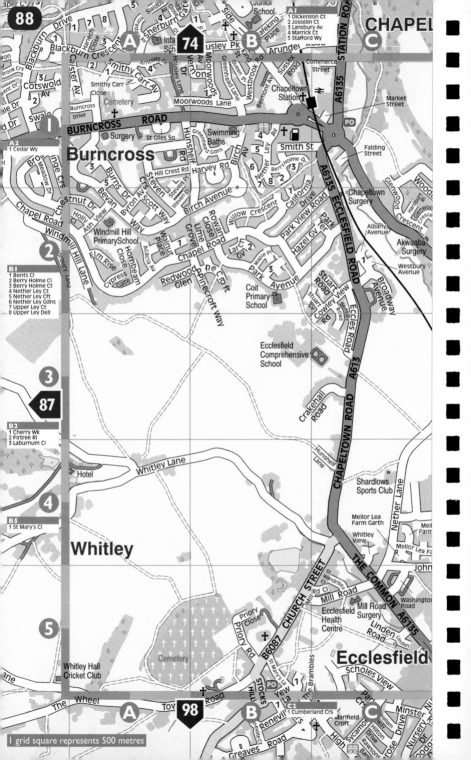

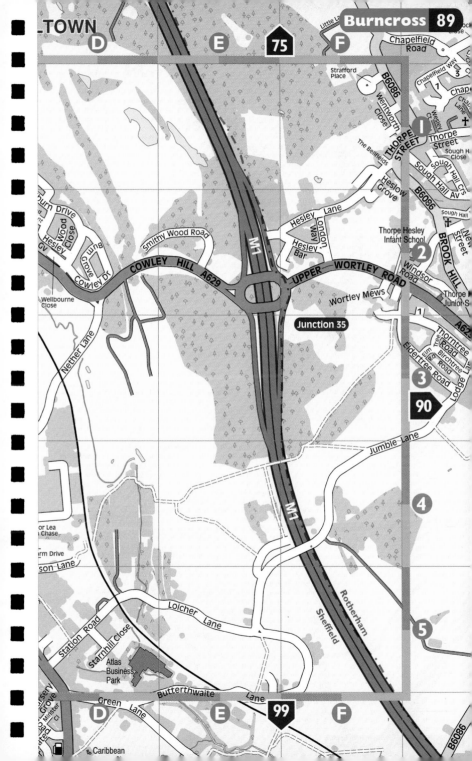

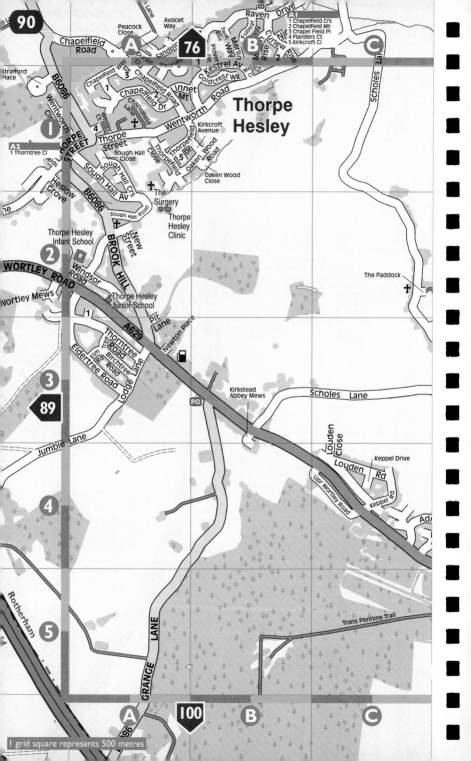

90

Chapelfield Road

Peacock Close

Avocet Way

Raven Drive

1 Chapelfield Crs
2 Chapelfield Mt
3 Chapel Field Pl
4 Flanders Ct
5 Kirkcroft Cl

76

Strafford Place

B6086

Wentworth Close

Chapelfield Way

Chapelfield Road

Chapelfield Dr

Wesley Ct

Chapelfield Lane

Chapelfield Mt

Linnet Mt

Wentworth Road

Swift Way

Dunlin

Sandpipe

Shelduck

Plover

Fulmar

Merlin Rise

Curlew Rise

Mallard Cl

Kestrel Av

Goldcrest Wk

Thorpe Hesley

Thorpe Street

THORPE STREET

A2
1 Thorntree Cl

Sough Hall Crs

Sough Hall Lane

Sough Hall Av

Sough Hall Road

Heslow Grove

B6086

The Surgery

Kirkcroft Avenue

Thorpefield Close

Thorpefield Dr

5

Oaken Wood Road

Oaken Wood Close

Thorpe Hesley Clinic

Thorpe Hesley Infant School

New Street

Windsor Road

BROOK HILL

WORTLEY ROAD

Wortley Mews

Thorpe Hesley Junior School

1

A629

Pit Lane

Newton Place

The Paddock

Thorntree Road

Birchtree Road

Eldertree Road

Elm Tree

Lodge Lane

89

Kirkstead Abbey Mews

Scholes Lane

Louden Close

Louden Rd

Keppel Drive

Keppel Rd

Jumbie Lane

PO

Rotherham

Upr Wortley Road

Trans Pennine Trail

Scholes Lane

A **100** **B** **C**

1 grid square represents 500 metres

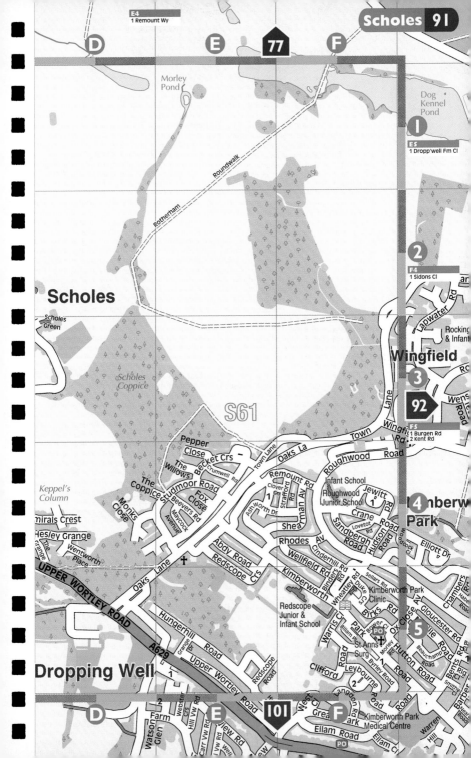

E4
1 Remount Wy

77

Morley Pond

Dog Kennel Pond

I

E5
1 Dropp'well Fm Cl

Rotherham Roundwalk

Scholes

Scholes Green

2

F4
1 Sidons Cl

Scholes Coppice

S61

Wingfield

3

92

Wens... Road

Pepper Close

Becket Crs

Crumwell Rd

Town Lane

Oaks La

Roughwood Road

Town Wingfi... Lane Rd

E5
1 Burgen Rd
2 Kent Rd

The Willows

The Coppice

Studmoor Road

Fox Close

Beevers Rd

Maycock Avenue

Ashworth Dr

Remount Rd

Clover Rd

Strafford Rd

Sherman Av

Infant School

Roughwood Junior School

Jewitt Rd

1

Keppel's Column

Monks Close

...mirals Crest

Hesley Grange

The Grange

Wentworth Place

Shea...

Rhodes Av

Crane Road

Lovetot Rd

Sandbergh Road

Hudson Rd

Woodcock...

Elliott Dr

...mberw... Park

4

Abby Road

Redscope Crs

Wellfield Rd

Cinderhill Rd

Kimberworth

Binders Rd

Sellars Rd

Due C...

Byk's Rd

Kimberworth Park Clinic

UPPER WORTLEY ROAD

A629

Oaks Lane

Hungerhill Road

Grange Dr

Upper Wortley Road

Redscope Junior & Infant School

Warris Rd

Wheaten... Rd

Park...

Billam Pl...

Bower... Rd

Morley St

PO

St Ann's Surg...

Gloucester Rd

...ville Road

Beauchamp Road

Hutton Road

5

Dropping Well

1

Watson Glen

Farm

Hill Vw Rd

Webster Crs...

Carr Vw Rd

...l Vw...

Well...

Clifford

Redscope Road

D

E

101

West Cl

Langdon Rd

Grea...

Park...

Kimberworth Park Medical Centre

Leybourne Road

Byrley Road

2

Eilam Road

PO

Eilam Cl

F

Warren Hill

Barber...

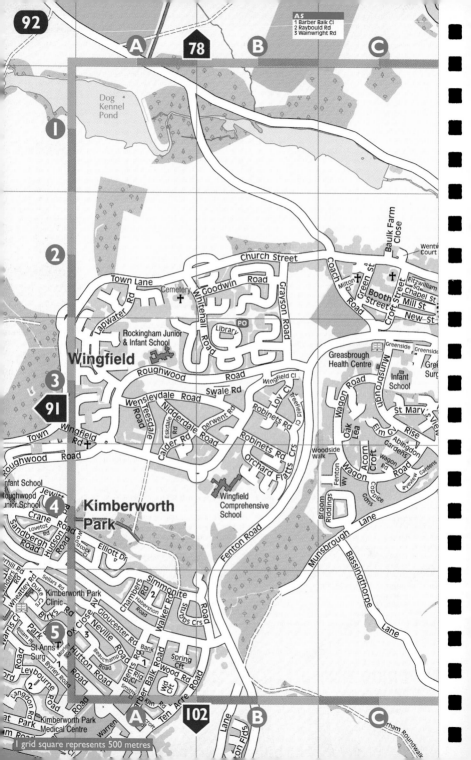

D3
1 Cross St
2 Oxford Cl

D · E · 79 · F

The Whins

Greasbrough Lane

Cemetery

Rotherham

Knapton Av

West Avenue

BLYTH AV

Hawley St

Stock's La

Goodw

1 Gateway Ct

Shopping Cen

Doctors Surg

The Surg

Rockcli

HIGH ST

Bello

Wilton

CINDER BR ROAD

Cinder

Bridge

Road

Church St

Church Rd

Church Cft

Vesey St

Fitzwi Court

Goose

Rectory

RAWMARSH HILL

Rossiter Road

MAIN ST

Harold Cft

Campbell

Greasbrough

Rotherham Roundwalk

Occupation Road

Newgate Drive

Newgate

Holm Flatt St

Gate Medical Centre

Ryan

Ashwood

Bear Tree Rd

Ann St

Morley St

Terrace Rd

2

Fran

Scrooby Drive

Scrooby Place

Scrooby Street

Firth Street

South Street

Lowfield Avenue

South Avenue

2

Providence St

POTTER HILL

PO

Cross St

Lowfield Road

Highfield Road

Munsbrough La

Greenside gery

Ash Vw

Greasbrough Road

School Lane

Infant School

Fr St

3

94

BROAD

GREAT

6

Aldw

Lic

Scrooby Lane

Lane

ROAD

B6375

TAYLORS LANE

Cornish Way

South Yorkshire Business Centre

Taylors Ct

Beale Wy

4

Mill St

Parkgate Park

Barbot Hill Road

Barbot Hall

CAR HILL

B6089

Stadium Court

MANCHAM

ROTHERHAM ROAD

The Gatewy

1 Gateway

Midland St

Stadium Way

Way

Hillside Court

Quintec Ct

B6375

Springfield Cl

Mancham Way

GREASBROUGH R

Ginhouse Lane

A633

5

Stonerow

Way

D · E · 103 · F

Eastwood

Eldon Rd

Hardwicke Rd

y Cl

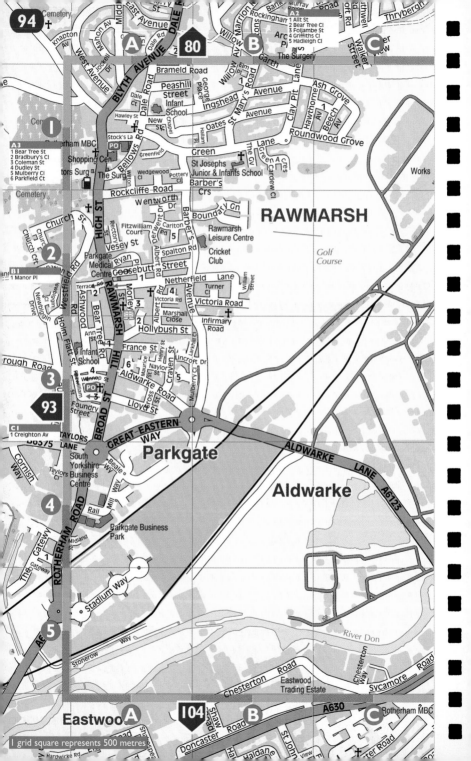

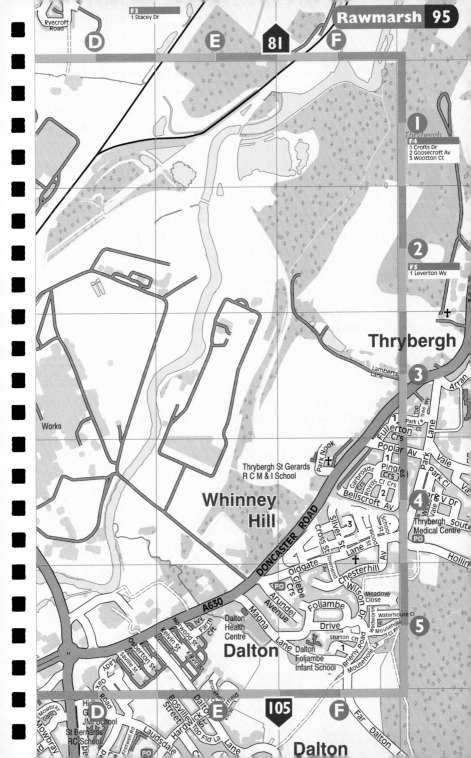

D

Ryecroft Road

F3
1 Stacey Dr

E

81

F

I
Thrybergh
F4
1 Crofts Dr
2 Goosecroft Av
3 Wootton Ct

2
F5
1 Leverton Wy

Thrybergh

3
Lamberts Lane

Arran

Top Tree Wy

Park L's Ct

Fullerton Crs

Poplar Av

Park Cl

Park Vale

Works

Park Nook

Thrybergh St Gerards
R C M & I School

Garbroads Crs

Royds Cl

Pingles Crs

Bellscroft Av

Whinney Hill

4
Thrybergh South
Medical Centre
PO

Silver St

Cross St

Townend

Oldgate

Glebe Crs

Chesterhill Av

Wilson Dr

Meadow Close

Waterhouse Cl

5

Arundel Avenue

Foljambe Drive

Wadworth

Mousehole

DONCASTER ROAD

PO

A630

Norwood St

Kelvin St

Ivy Farm Crt

Kelvin St

Magna Lane

Dalton
Dalton Health Centre

Sturton Crf

Dalton Foljambe Infant School

Brierly Road

Mousehole La

Osperton St

Saville St

Lady

Mowbray Gdns

Hill Gr

JMI School

St Bernards RC School

Fretwell Rd

Bosvillewick St

Dalton Hardwick St

Laudsdale

Brooksfield

Top Fld La

D

E

105

F

Dalton

Far Dalton

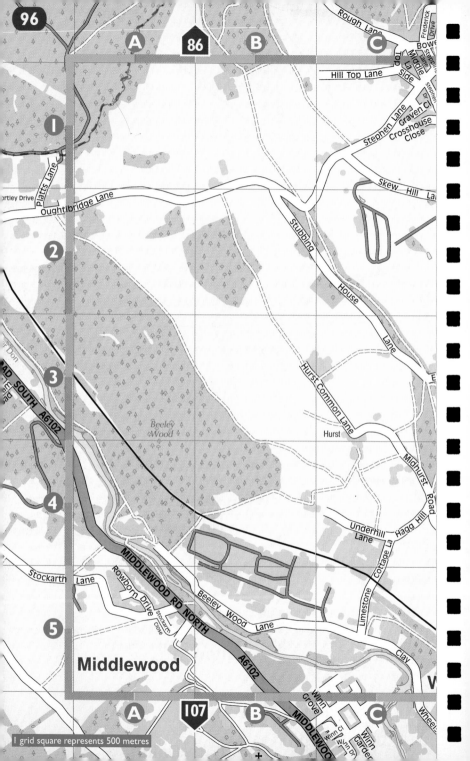

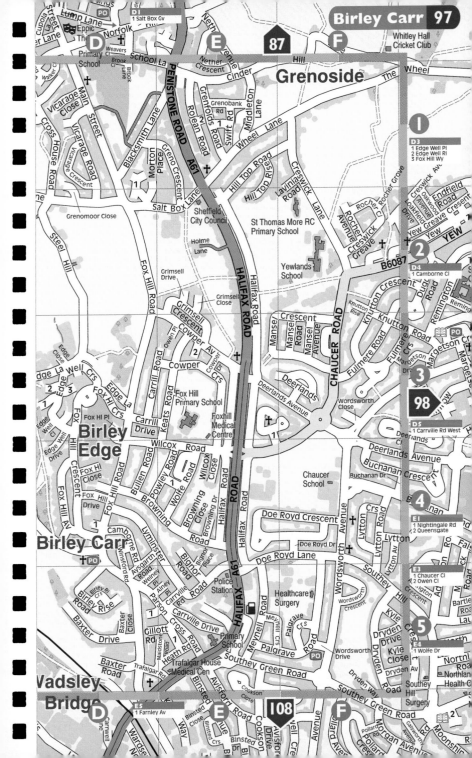

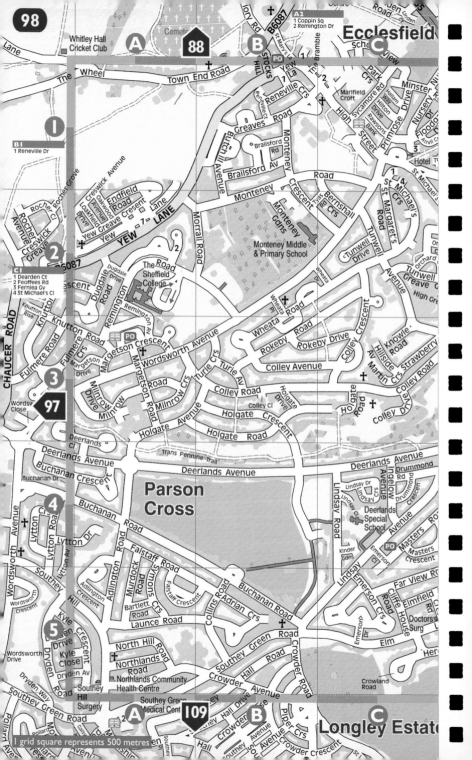

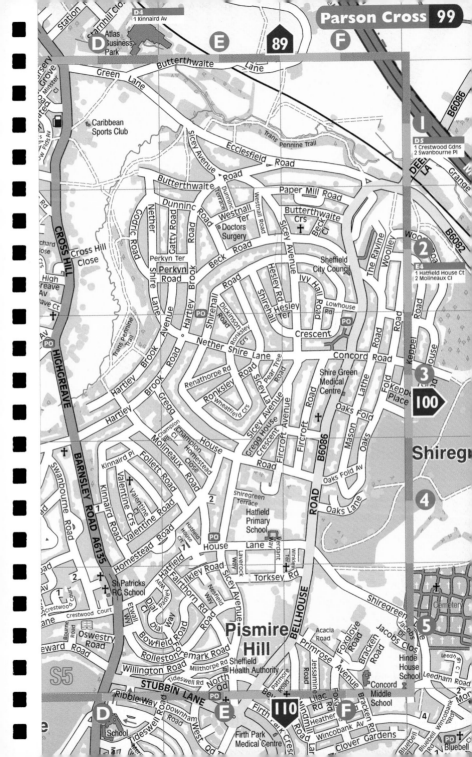

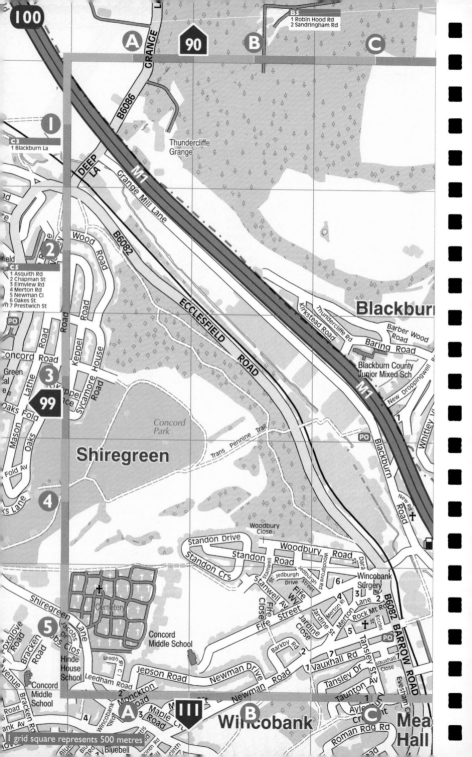

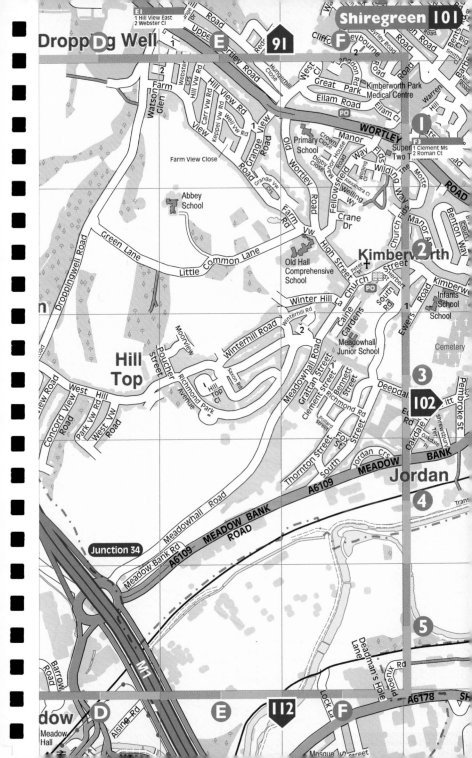

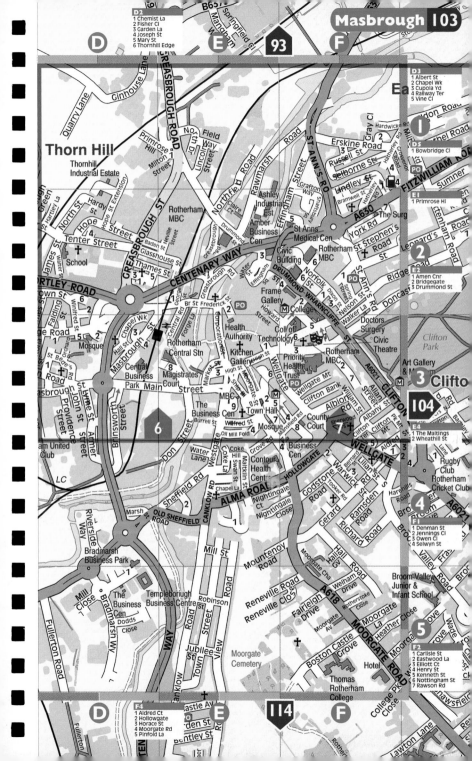

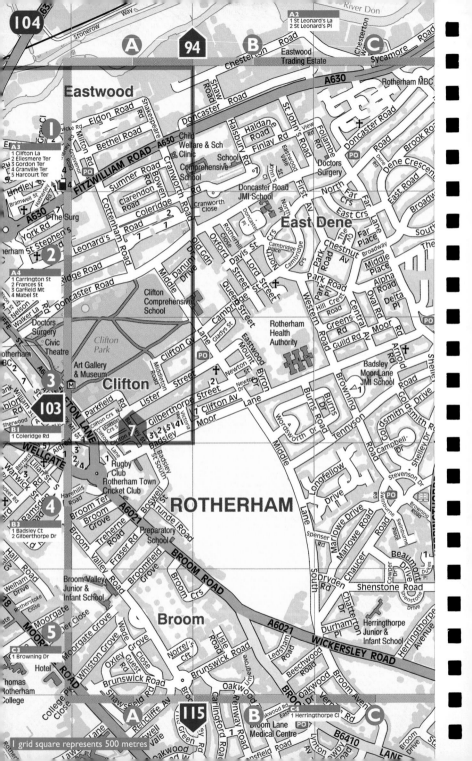

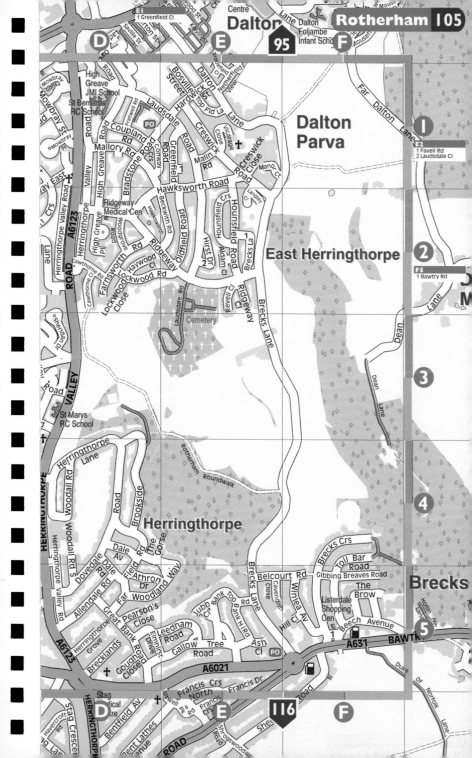

Day Hospital
A5
1 Red Oak La

Low Ash Farm **A**

B

C

Stubbing Lane

1

Loxley Chase **2**

Loxley Common

Wadsley

Merlin The

Lea Bank Farm

3

Long Lane

Rowel Lane

Hunters Gardens
Archer Ga
France Rd
Lee Rd
Phillips Road
Garland Drive
South View Rise
South Vw Cl
Woodstock Road
Cavendish Av
Keswick Close
Vale Grove
Eden Drive

Dunkerley Road

Leaton Cl

Chase Road

Hanson Road

Rodney Hill

Normandale Avenue
Auckland Avenue
Austinfield
Woodstock Road

Loxley

The Grove

LOXLEY

PO

4

Wisewood Cemetery

Lane

River

Black

Greaves

Storrs Lane

Spout La

5

Acorn Wy
Mill Wd Vw
Home Oak Wd
Drive
Robin Hood Chase
Furness Cl
Acorn Hi
High Matlock Rd
Darley
Myers Grove Lane
Ashurst Rd
Ashurst Place
Marchwood
Ashurst Cl
Ashurst Drive
Marchwood Avenue

Spout Lane

Acorn Wy
Acornwy Drive
Lomas Cl
Albanus Rdg

Nook Lane Junior School

119

Friar Cl

Clark Grove

A

B

Acorn Hi
High Matlock
Gdns
Ln
2

Webbs Av

C

Stannington

Marchwood Avenue

Spout Spinney

Hill Cl
Gr

Cliff Road
Falkland

Woodfarm

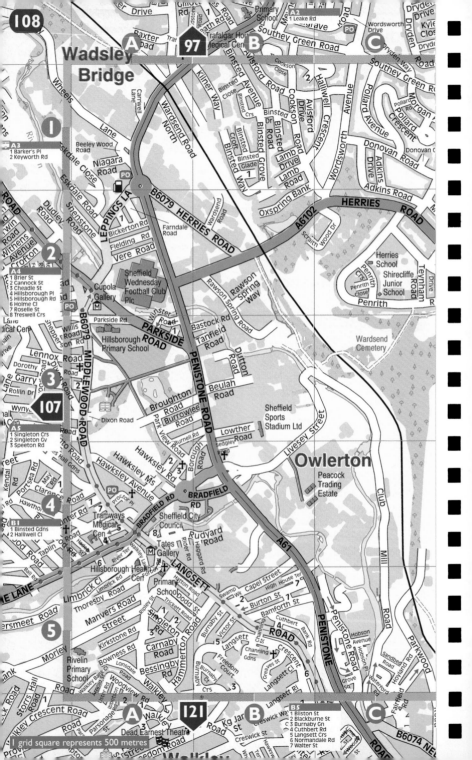

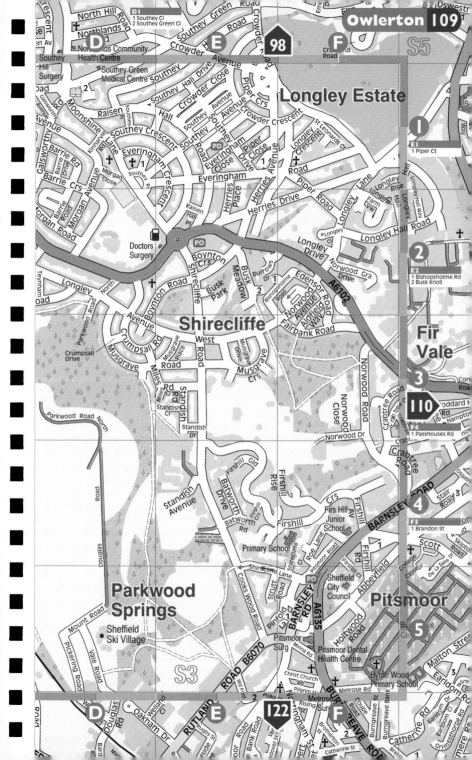

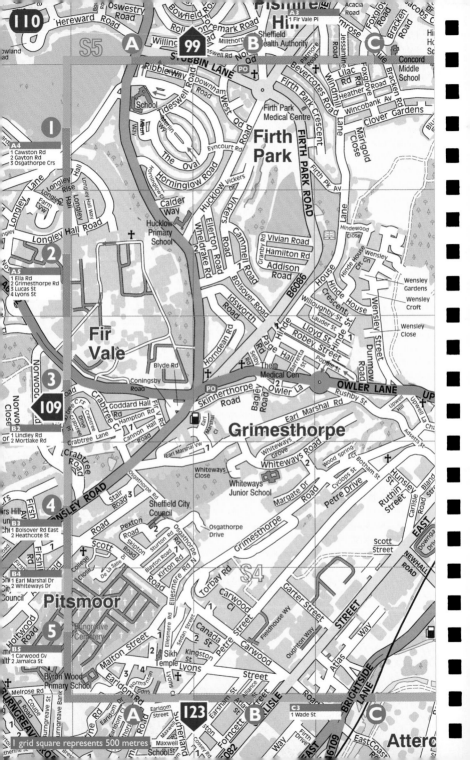

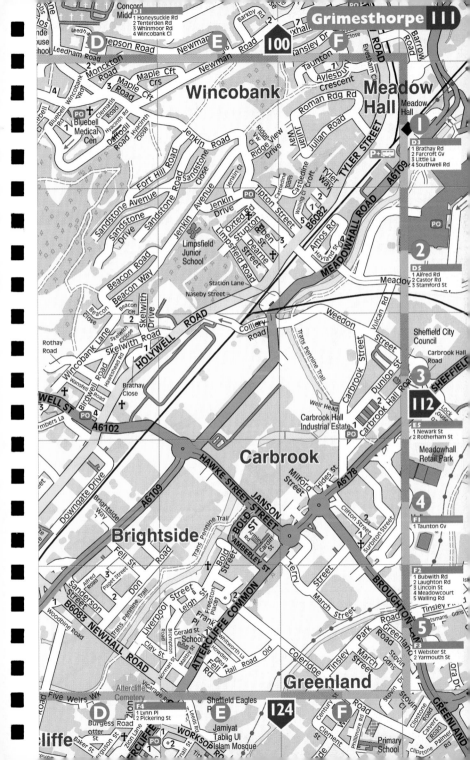

D1
1 Honeysuckle Rd
2 Tenterden Rd
3 Whinmoor Rd
4 Wincobank Cl

Concord Midd

Barkby

Leedh

Leednam Road

Monckton Road

Maple Cft

Maple Cft Crs

Maple Cft Road

Wincobank

Newman

Newman Road

Depson Road

D

E

100

Tansley Dr

F

Eversham Cl

Barrow

Aylesbu

Taunton

7

Roman Rdg Rd

Meadow Hall

Meadow Hall

Bluebell Wincobank
Daffodil Road
Clematis Road
Hyacinth Rd
Wadnth Close

Bluebell Medical Cen

Crescent

Julian Road

Julian

TYLER STREET

1

D3
1 Brathay Rd
2 Farcroft Gv
3 Little La
4 Southwell Rd

Fort Hill Road

Sandstone Road

Sandstone Close

Jenkin Road

Ridge View Drive

Ridge View

Castledine Gdns

Castledine

Marl

Tyler Way

P+

A6109

MEADOWHALL ROAD

PO

2

D5
1 Alfred Rd
2 Castor Rd
3 Stamford St

Sandstone Avenue

Sandstone Drive

Sandstone Drive

Jenkin Avenue

Jenkin Drive

Jenkin

Tipton Street

Oxted
Stupton
Eben

Deame Street

PO

B6082

5

Walling Cl

Amos Rd

Hayland St

Meadov

Beacon Way

Beacon Road

Limpsfield Junior School

Limpsfield Road

Station Lane

Naseby Street

Colliery Road

Weedon Street

Vulcan Road

Meadov

Sheffield City Council

Carbrook Hall Road

3

SHEFFIEL

Rothay Road

Beacon Lane

Beacon Close

Beacon Cft

Skelwith Close

Skelwith Drive

Skelwith Road

HOLYWELL ROAD

HOLYWELL ROAD

Carbrook Street

Dunlop Street

Carbrook Hall Road

112

Lock ouse

Wincobank Lane

Hawkshead Road

Birkwell Road

Wansfell Road

Brathay Close

Trans Pennine Trail

Weir Head

Carbrook Hall Industrial Estate

PO

E5
1 Newark St
2 Rotherham St

Meadowhall Retail Park

ELL ST

3

mbers La

PO

A6102

A6109

HAWKE STREET

JANSON STREET

BOLD ST

Carbrook

Milford street

Hides St

A6178

Clifton Street

Surbiton Street

4

F1
1 Taunton Gv

Downgate Drive

Brightside Way

Brightside Road

Trans Pennine Trail

Brightside

Fell St

Alfred Road

Paget Street

Don

Sanderson Street

B6083 NEWHALL ROAD

Woodbine Road

Trans Pennine Trail

Liverpool Street

Leigh St

Freestone Place

Frank

Bold Street

AMBERLEY ST

Cardiff St

BOLD ST

ATTERCLIFFE COMMON

Terry Street

March Street

Park Road

Greenland Road

Stovin

BROUGHTON LN

Tinsley

tsmans Gdns

F2
1 Bubwith Rd
2 Laughton Rd
3 Lincoln St
4 Meadowcourt
5 Walling Rd

5

Clay St

Gerald St

Brometon

Maltby St

Howden

Whitworth La

Hall Road

Fell Rd

Old

Coleridge

Tinsley

March Street

Stovin

Greenland Road

F5
1 Webster St
2 Yarmouth St

ora Dr

Attercliffe Cemetery

Five Weirs Wk

cliffe

Burgess Road

otter St

Baker St

Ferguson St

ZION LN

F4
1 Lynn Pl
2 Pickering St

RCLIFFE

PO

2

Vicarage Rd

Leeds Rd

WORKSOP ROAD

Sheffield Eagles R

E

124

Jamiyat Tablig Ul Islam Mosque

Greenland

Century St

Clement St

Philimore

F

Greenland Road

Clipstone Road

Calvert

Palmer

Clipstone

Primary School

GREENLAND RD

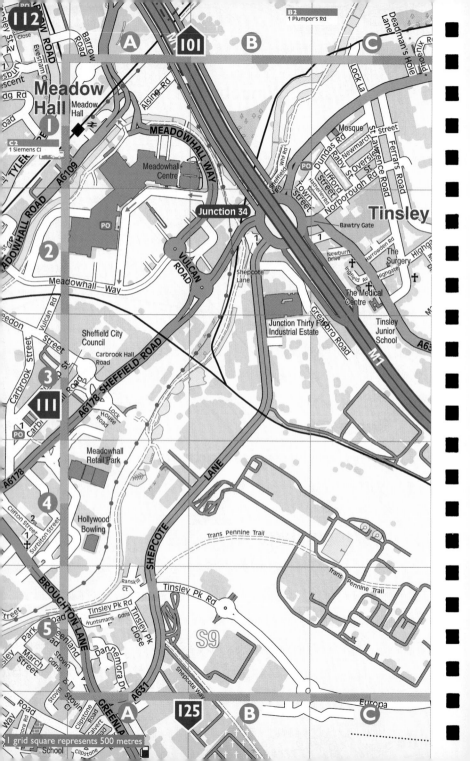

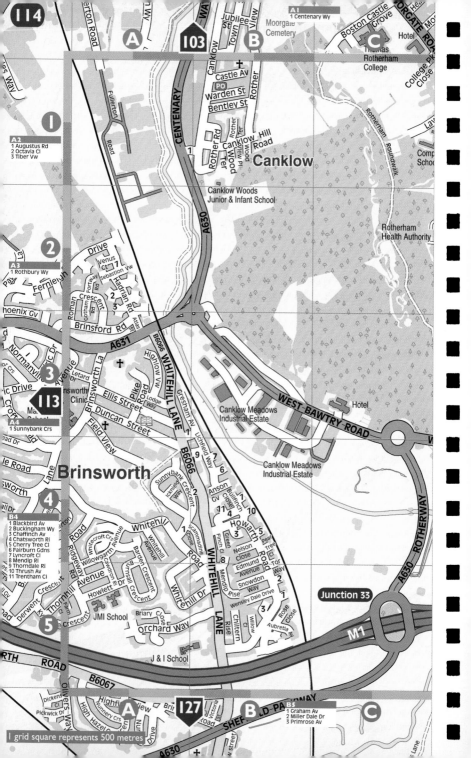

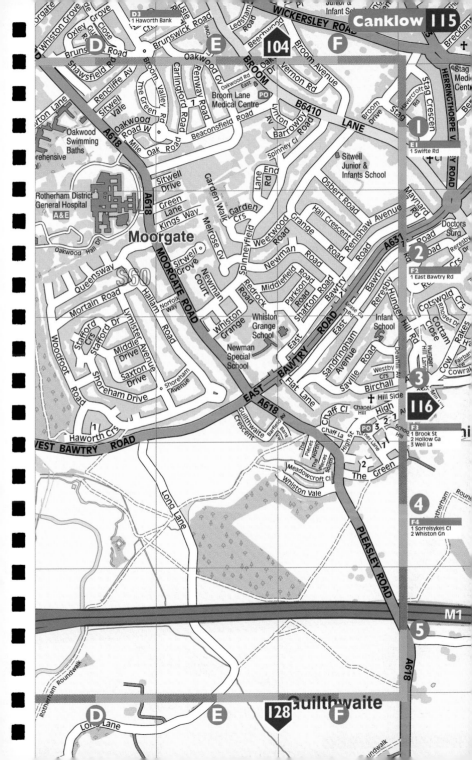

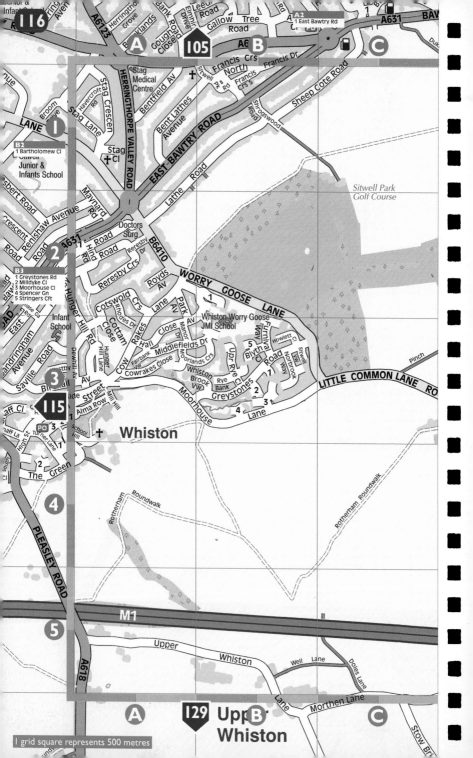

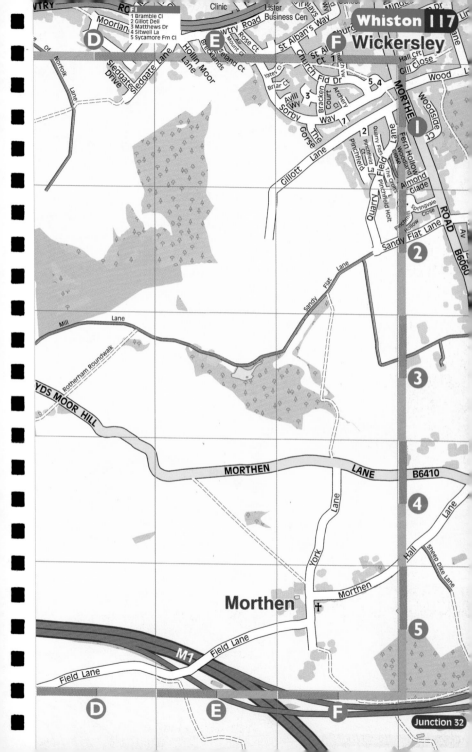

1 Bramble Cl
2 Gillot Dell
3 Matthews Dr
4 Sitwell La
5 Sycamore Fm Cl

Moorland

Sledgates Lane

Sledgate Drive

Norfolk Lane

Hollin Moor Lane

Brecklands

Bracken seland Ct

Rose Ct

St Alban's Way

Clinic

Lister Business Cen

wtrv Road

St Al Ct
Church

Yates Cl
Briar Ct

Avill WV

Sorby Way

Mount Ct

Bracken Court

Archery Way

Church Fld Dr

hatchWk

MORTHE

Hall Cft

Gill Close

Wood

Woodside

The Gorse

Gillott Lane

2
Pinchfield Ct
Pinchfield

Quarry Fld
Quarry Fld Field

Quarry La
Pinchfield Holt

Pinchfield Hollow

The Crofts

Fern Hollow

Woodland Close

Almond Glade

Springvale Close

ROAD

Av

B6060

Sandy Flat Lane

2

Sandy Flat Lane

Mill Lane

3

Rotherham Roundwalk

YDS MOOR HILL

MORTHEN **LANE** B6410

4

York Lane

Hall Lane

Sheep Dike Lane

Morthen †

Morthen

5

Morthen

M1

Field Lane

Field Lane

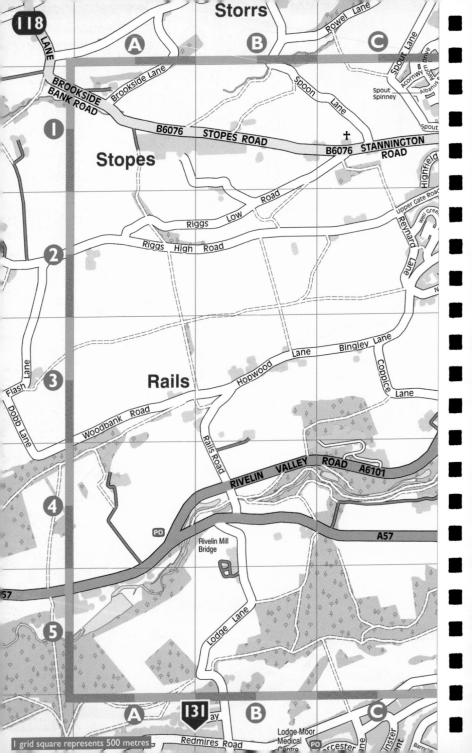

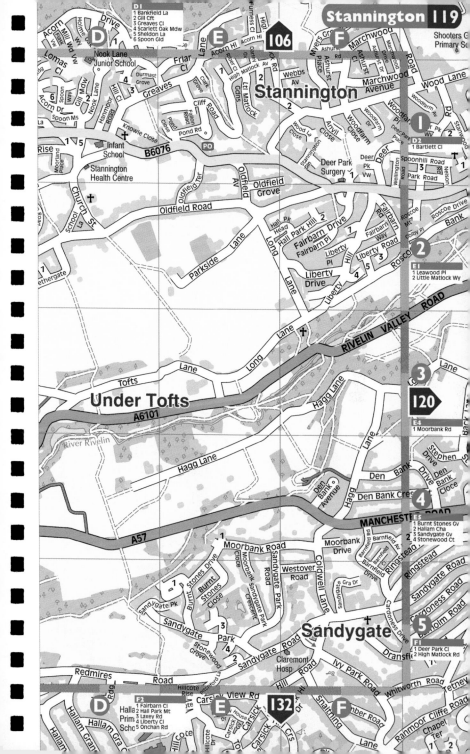

D1
1 Bankfield La
2 Gill Cft
3 Greaves Cl
4 Scarlett Oak Mdw
5 Sheldon La
6 Spoon Gld

D

E

F

106

Shooters G
Primary Sc

Acorn
Drive
Holme Bank
Lomas
Cl
Mill Wd Vw
Gill Mdw
Acorn Dr
Spoon Ms
Spoon
Rise
Nook Lane
Junior School
Friar
Cl
Durmast
Grove
Hill Cl
Hanmoor
Road
Nook Lane
Knowle Close
Infant
School
Stannington
Health Centre
Church St
Greaves
Clark
Grove
Cliff
Close
Falllon
Close
Falllon
Road
Pond Rd
Pond Rd
B6076
Oldfield Ter
Oldfield
Av
Furness Cl
Lane
Acorn Hl
Acorn Hl
High Matlock Av
Gdns
Matlock
Av
High
Lane
Ltt
River Cl
Datley
Rd
Webbs
Av
Stannington
Arzul
Close
Wood La
Close
Marchwood
Road
Ashurst
Ashurst
Rd
Marchwood
Avenue
Woodfarm
Dr
Woodfarm
Close
Wellington
Deer Park
Surgery
Deer
Pk
Vw
Deer
Park
Marchwood
Wood Lane
Woodfarm Av
Woodfarm
Rd
Pk
Vw
Deer
Park
Spoonhill Road
Park Road
Nelson
Roscoe
M7
Roscoe Drive
Bank
Colby Pl
I
D1
1 Bartlett Cl
Stannington
Oldfield Road
Parkside
Lane
Long
Lane
Lane
Hall Pk
Head
Hall Park Hill
Fairbarn
Drive
Fairbarn Pl
Liberty
Pl
Liberty
Drive
Liberty
Lane
Fairbarn
Rd
Liberty
Hill
Liberty Road
Fairbarn
Way
Roscoe
2
E1
1 Leawood Pl
2 Little Matlock Wy
RIVELIN VALLEY ROAD
Tofts
Lane
Under Tofts
A6101
River Rivelin
Hagg Lane
Hagg Lane
Long
Lane
Hagg
Lane
3
120
E4
1 Moorbank Rd
Lane
Den
Bank
Avenue
Hagg
Den Bank Cres
Stephen
Drive
Den
Bank
Drive
Den
Bank
Close
4
E5
1 Burnt Stones Gv
2 Hallam Cha
3 Sandygate Gv
4 Stonewood Ct
A57
MANCHESTER ROAD
Moorbank Road
Burnt Stones Drive
Burnt
Stones
Close
Moorbank
Close
Sandygate Park
Road
Moorbank
Sandygate Park
Crescent
Westover
Road
Coldwell Lane
Moorbank
Drive
Barnfield Av
Barnfield Rd
Barnfield
Rd
Barnfield
Drive
Ringstead
Cardoness
Gra Dr
Cardoness Drive
Ringstead Road
Sandygate Road
Denholm Road
5
F1
1 Deer Park Cl
2 High Matlock Rd
Sandygate Pk
Sandygate
Park
Stonewood
Grove
Sandygate Road
Sandygate
Claremont
Hosp
Dransfield
Ivy Park Road
Whitworth Road
Redmires
Road
Hillcote
Rise
Cattorford La
Carsick View Rd
Carsick
House
Dr
Hillcote
Dr
Carsick
Hill
Crs
Snaithing
Lane
Inber Road
Ranmoor Cliffe Road
Chapel
Ter
Retney
D
F2
1 Fairbarn Cl
2 Hall Park Mt
3 Laxey Rd
4 Liberty Cl
5 Onchan Rd
Halla
Prim
Scho
Hallam Gran
Hallam La
E
132
F

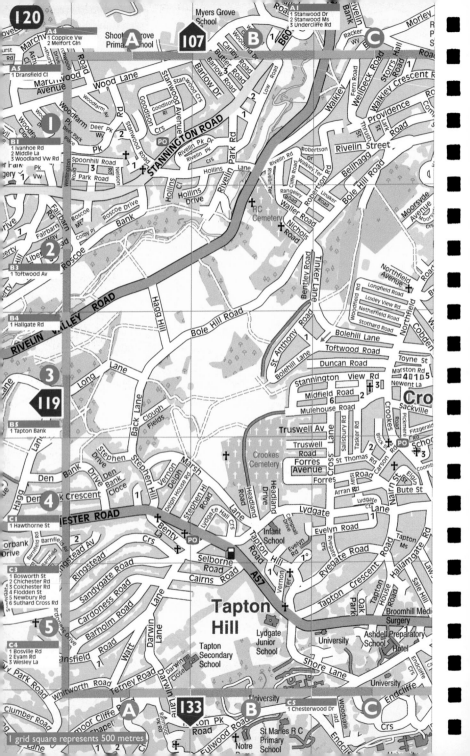

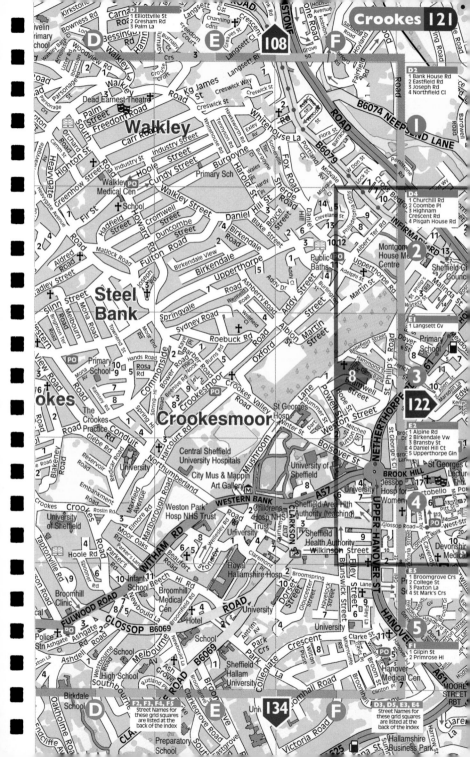

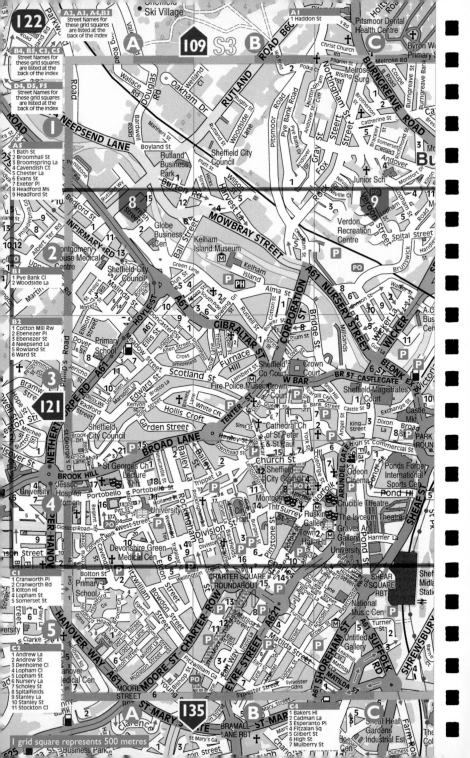

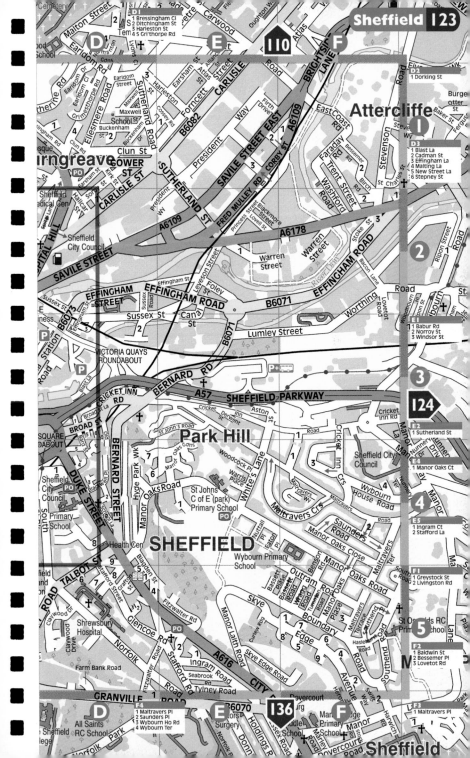

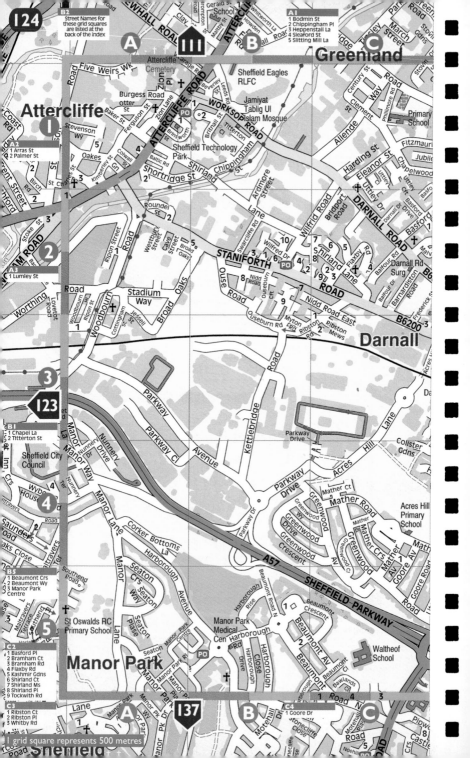

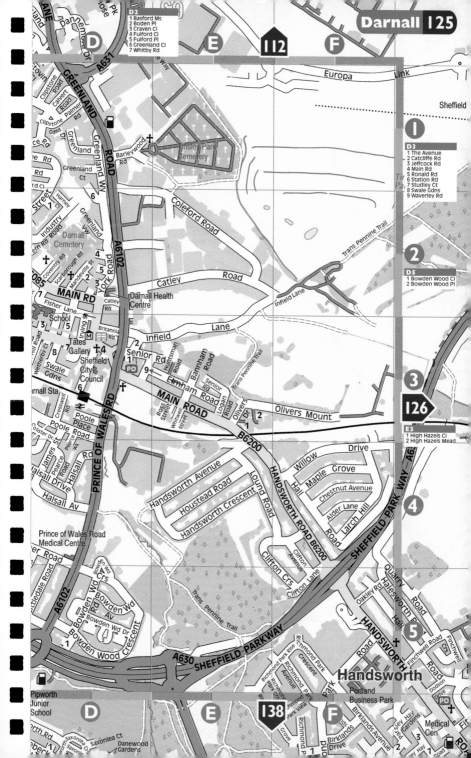

D2
1 Basford Ms
2 Boden Pl
3 Craven Cl
4 Fulford Cl
5 Fulford Pl
6 Greenland Cl
7 Whitby Rd

D   **E**   **112**   **F**

Europa   Link

Sheffield

I

D3
1 The Avenue
2 Catcliffe Rd
3 Jeffcock Rd
4 Main Rd
5 Ronald Rd
6 Station Rd
7 Studley Ct
8 Swale Gdns
9 Waverley Rd

Tinsley Park Cemetery

Trans Pennine Trail

2

D5
1 Bowden Wood Cl
2 Bowden Wood Pl

Coleford Road

GREENLAND ROAD

Clipstone
Calvert Road
Palmer Rd
Clipstone Gdns

Barleywood Rd

Greenland Ct

Greenland Way

A631

A6102

Greenland Vw

Harvey

Darnall Cemetery

Industry
Coventry Rd
Scarborough Rd
Mandeville St
York Road

MAIN RD

Fisher Lane
School

Tates Gallery

Sheffield City Council

PO   9

Darnall Sta

Catley   Road

Darnall Health Centre

Catley Rd

Infield   Lane

Infield Lane

Senior Rd
Huntsman
Bannham Road
Senior Road

Elmham Road

Logan Road

Trans Pennine Trail

Olivers   Mount

3

126

E3
1 High Hazels Cl
2 High Hazels Mead

MAIN ROAD

Ross Street
Whitwell Street

Olivers Dr

B6200

Willow   Drive

Maple   Grove

Hall

Chestnut Avenue

Alder Lane

Larch Hill

4

Prince of Wales Road Medical Centre

Handsworth Avenue

Houstead Road

Handsworth Crescent

Lound Road

HANDSWORTH ROAD B6200

Clifton Crs

Clifton Avenue

Clifton Lane

SHEFFIELD PARK WAY   A6

PRINCE OF WALES RD

A6102

James Road
Pearce Road
Pearce Wk

Halsall Drive
Halsall Av

Bowden Wd Crs
Bowden Wd Av
Bowden Wd Dr

Bowden Wood Crescent

Trans Pennine Trail

A630   SHEFFIELD PARKWAY

SHEFFIELD PARKWAY

Quarry Road

Halesworth Road

Oakley Rd

Hall

5

HANDSWORTH ROAD

Finchwell Road
Finchwell Crs

Dodson Drive

Handsworth

Portland Business Park

PO

Richmond Park Rise
Richmond Park Crescent
Richmond Park Avenue
Richmond Park Grove
Richmond Park View

Birklands Avenue
Birklands Drive

Medical Cen

Pipworth Junior School

Saxonlea Ct
Danewood Gardens

D   **E**   **138**   **F**

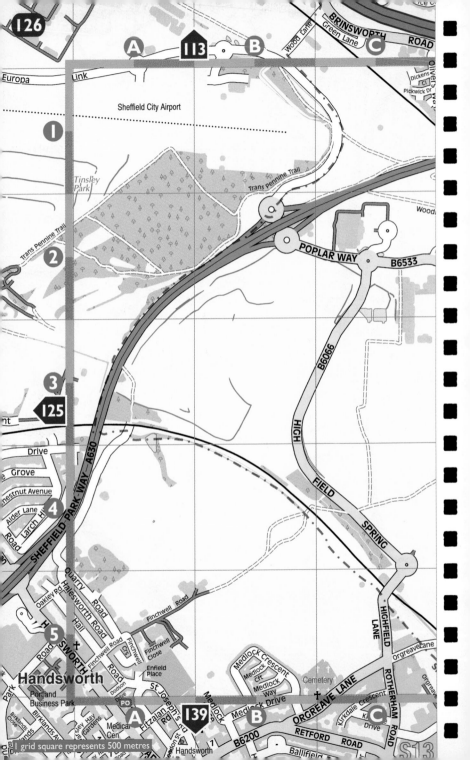

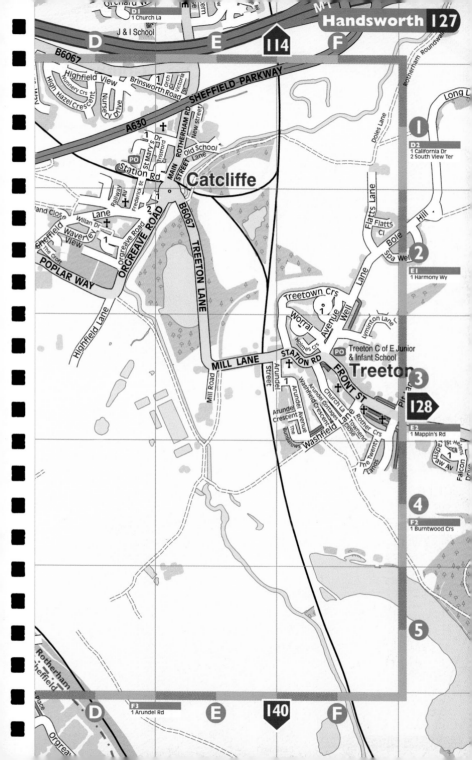

128

A   115   B   C

Guilthwaite

Long Lane

Rotherham Roundwalk

Rotherham Roundwalk

1

Flatts Lane

Flatts
Cl

Bole Hill

Well Crs

Spa House

2

Da Well

Lane

Crs

Avenue

Well

Lymington Lane

Burnt
Wood

PO   Treeton C of E Junior
& Infant School

Treeton

3

FRONT S

127

Pit Lane

Church La

Rother Crs

Townend

La Close

WOOD

St Helens
Cl

Tye Twenty
Lands

Bradshaw Av

Falcon Drive

1

LANE

B6067

4

5

AUG

A   141   B   C

West

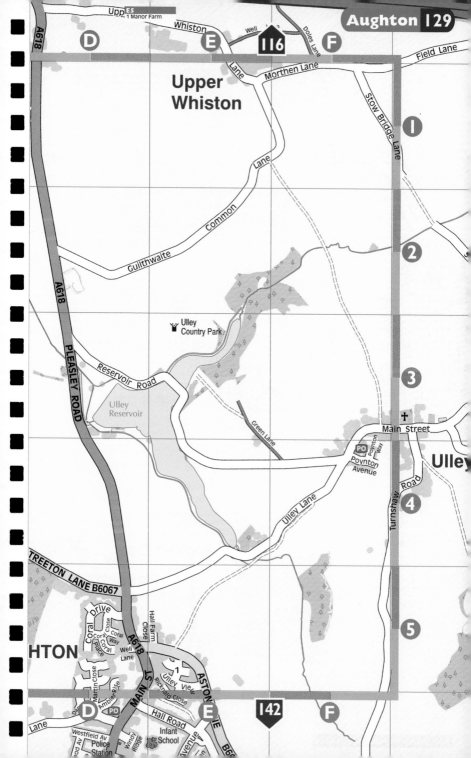

Upp **E5**
1 Manor Farm
Whiston
Well
116
Doles Lane

D **E** **F**

Field Lane

Morthen Lane

Upper Whiston

Lane

Stow Bridge Lane

I

Common Lane

2

Guilthwaite

Ulley Country Park

Reservoir Road

3

PLEASLEY ROAD

A618

Ulley Reservoir

Green Lane

Main Street

PO
Poynton Way
Poynton Avenue

Ulley

Ulley Lane

Turnshaw Road

4

5

TREETON LANE B6067

Coral Drive
Close
Coral Close
Coral Way
Coral Place
Coral

Hall Farm Close

Well Lane

Martin Close

HTON

A618

MAIN ST

Ambler Rise

PO

Ulley View

Rickdaid Close

ASTON LE B6

142

D **E** **F**

Lane

Westfield Av
Police Station

Windy Ridge

Hall Road

Infant School

Avenue

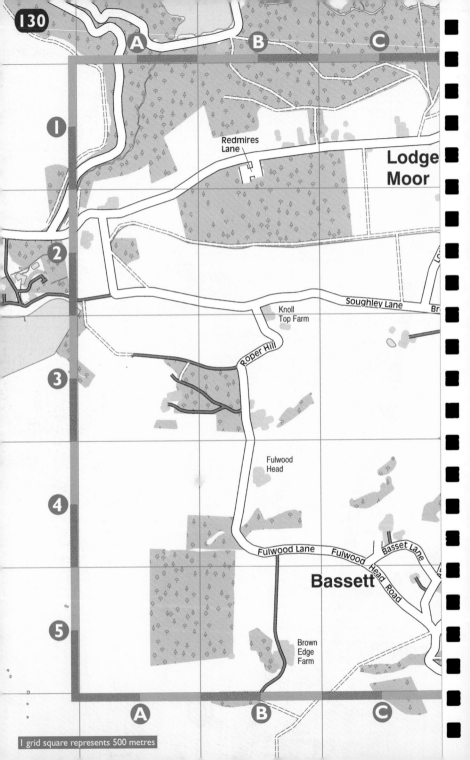

A B C

Redmires
Lane

**Lodge
Moor**

Knoll
Top Farm

Soughley Lane Br

Roper Hill

Fulwood
Head

Fulwood Lane Fulwood Head Road

Basset Lane

Bassett

Brown
Edge
Farm

A B C

I grid square represents 500 metres

1
2
3
4
5

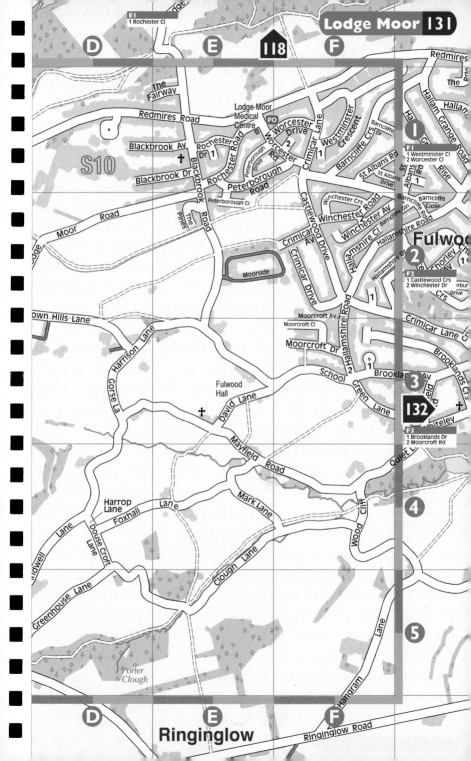

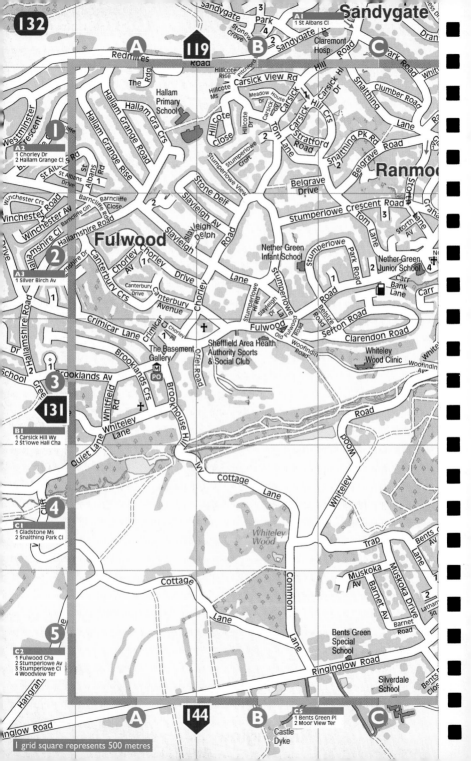

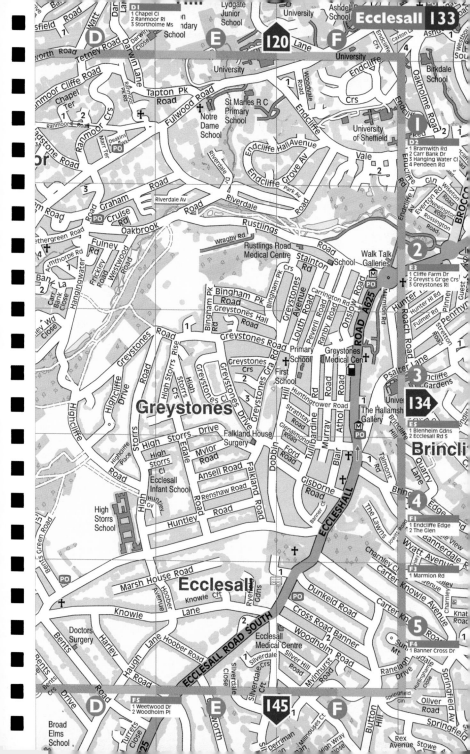

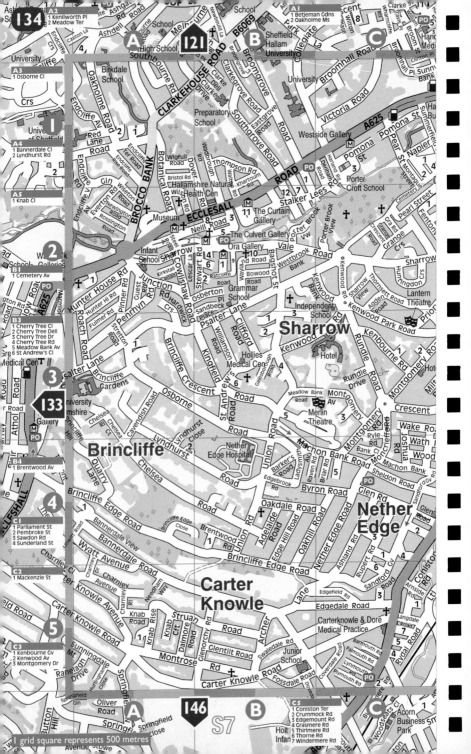

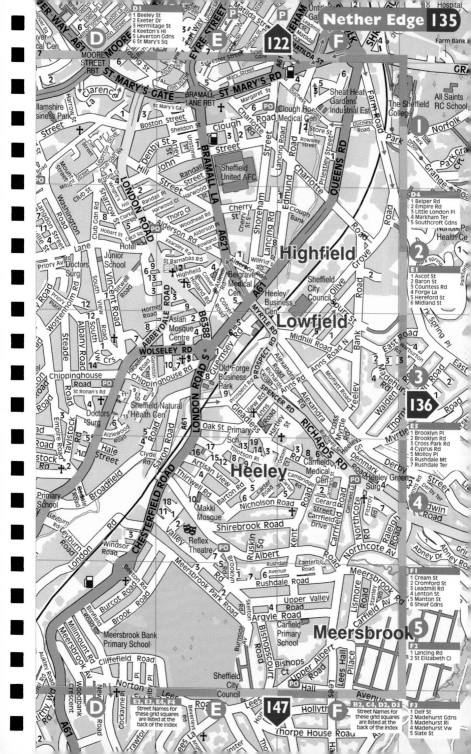

D
1 Beeley St
2 Exeter Dr
3 Hermitage St
4 Keeton's Hl
5 Leverton Gdns
6 St Mary's Sq

MOORE
STREET
RBT

ST. MARY'S-GATE

BRAMALL
LANE RBT

ST. MARY'S RD

122

MATILDA ST

Sheaf Heat
Gardens
Industrial Est

The Sheffield
College

All Saints
RC School

Norfolk

1

Boston Street

Clough
Street

PO

Clough Ho
Medical Cen

Store St

QUEENS RD

Park
Drive

Sheffield
United AFC

Highfield

Sheffield
City
Council

D4
1 Belper Rd
2 Empire Rd
3 Little London Pl
4 Markham Ter
5 Southcroft Gdns

Norfolk Pa
Health Ce

2

Junior
School

Highfield
Medical
Cen

Belgrave

E1
1 Ascot St
2 Baron St
3 Countess Rd
4 Forge La
5 Hereford St
6 Midland St

Heeley
Business
Cen

Olive
Road

ABBEYDALE ROAD

Asian
Mosque
Centre

WOLSELEY RD

MYRTLE RD

Midhill Road

Lowfield

Anns Road N

East Road

3

136

E3
1 Brooklyn Pl
2 Brooklyn Rd
3 Cross Park Rd
4 Cyprus Rd
5 Molloy Pl
6 Rushdale Mt
7 Rushdale Ter

Old Forge
Business
Park

SPENCER RD

RICHARDS RD

Sheffield Natural
Health Cen

Doctors'
Surg

LONDON ROAD S

Oak St Primary
Sch

Heeley Green
Surg

4

Artisan View

Heeley

Carfield
Medical
Cen

Makki
Mosque

Nicholson Road

Carfield
Drive

F1
1 Cream St
2 Cromford St
3 Leadmill Rd
4 Lenton St
5 Manton St
6 Sheaf Gdns

CHESTERFIELD ROAD

Reflex
Theatre

PO

Shirebrook Road

Albert

Rushdale
Avenue

Canterb'y
Road

Meersbrook

5

Rushdale Road

Carfield Av

Meersbrook
Park Road

Upper Valley
Road

Lismore
Road

F2
1 Lancing Rd
2 St Elizabeth Cl

Burcot Road

Meersbrook Bank
Primary School

Argyle
Road

Carfield
Primary
School

Meersbrook

Cliffefield Road

Norton

Sheffield
City
Council

Bishops
Ct

Upper Albert
Road

Lees Hall
Pl'ace

A61

Hollytr

Thorpe House Road

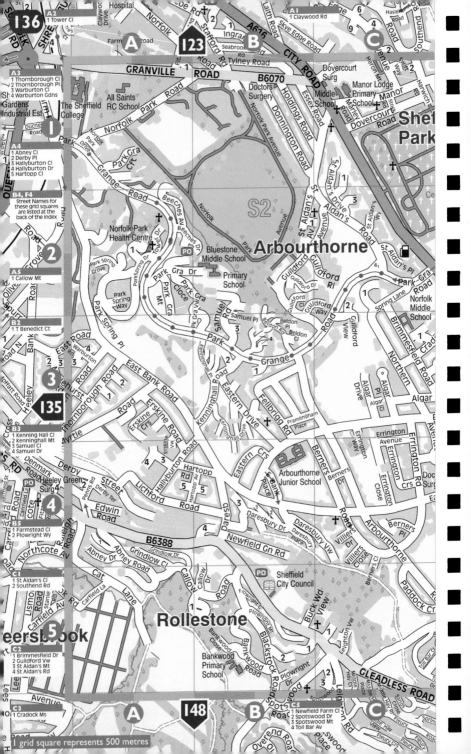

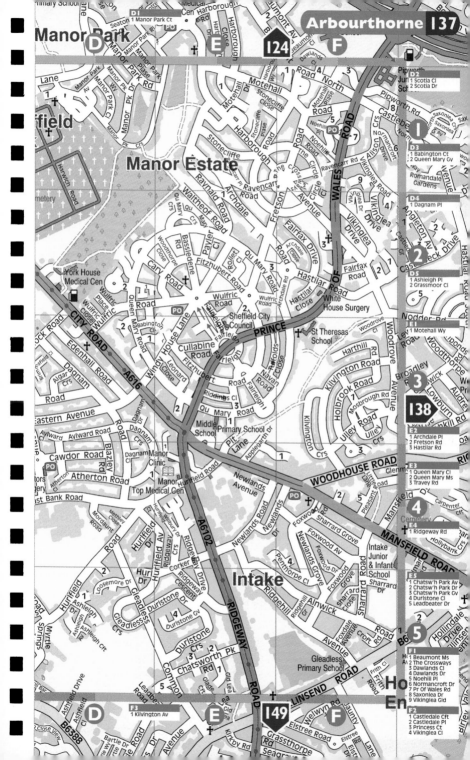

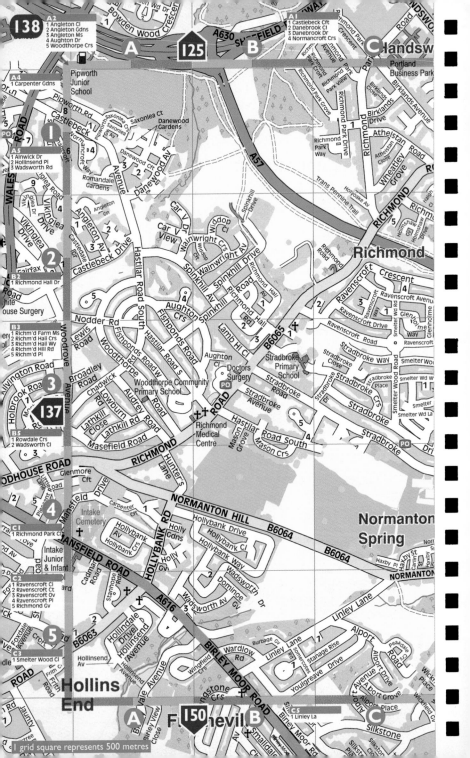

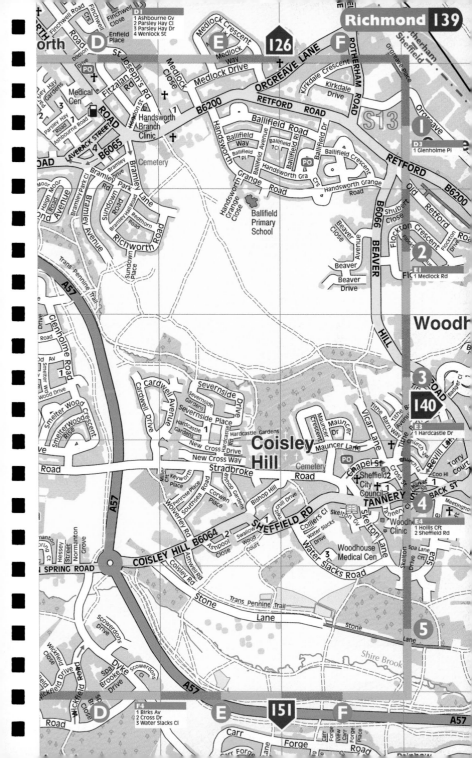

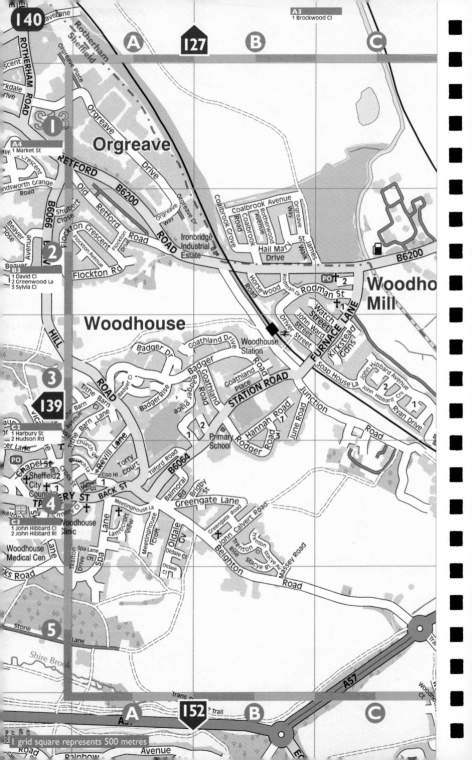

D3
1 John Hibbard Av

D   **E**   **128**   **F**

West Lane

Falconer Lane

Smallage Lane

I

Aston Comprehensive School

Westfield
Springwood Av
Gran
Hallam
Close
Aughton Avenue

Martin Close

Daniels Dr

RETFORD ROAD   SHEFFIELD ROAD

Fence

†
Aston Fence Junior & Infant School

Sheffield Road

Aston Swallownest Junior & Infant School

Chestnut Rd
Holly Ter
Oak Ter
Beech Wy

A618 AUGHTON

Anysarth Rise

2

Ale

King Street

Nursery Road

ouse

School Street

Park Street

†

Main Street

HIGH STREET

ROTHERHAM ROAD

Park Hill

Sorby Road

West Park Drive

Park Dr

3

142 ▶ Swal

CHESTERFIELD RD

Yo

Pickering

Ilkley Crs

Wetherby Drive

B6200

Soap House

Chesterfield Rd

Collingham Rd

4

Lane

River Rother

Chesterfield Road

CHESTERFIELD ROAD

A57

A57

Rotherham
Sheffield

Wragg Lane

Rotherham Road

5

Woodhouse

Pennine Trail

Woodlands Avenue

Cairns

Popular Avenue

Chestnut Avenue

Tulip Tree Close

Road

Rotherva
Close

Road

153

ouse Lane

Woodhouse Crs

Woodhouse Fern

†

Rosemary Road

Queen's

Beighton

Manvers

Lime Road

Oak Road

Elm Rd

High

Road

D   **E**   **F**

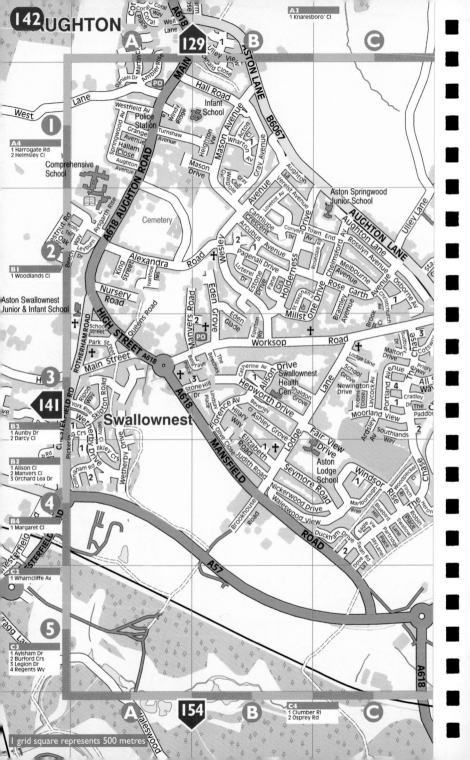

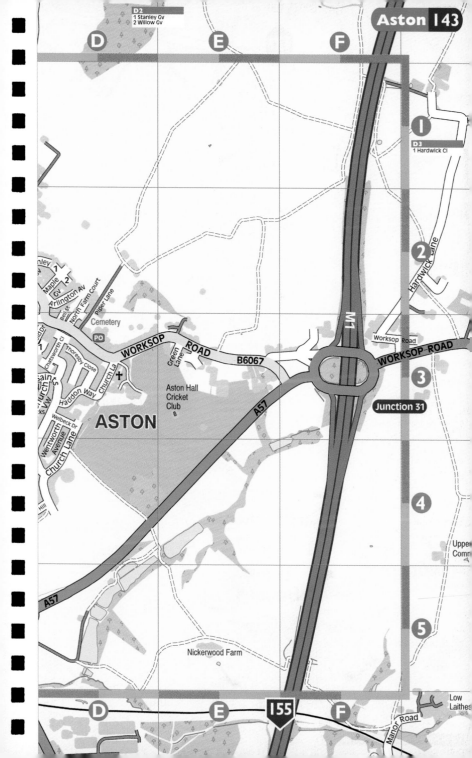

D2
1 Stanley Gv
2 Willow Gv

D   **E**   **F**

I

D3
1 Hardwick Cl

Hardwick Lane

2

Stanley
Maple
Gv
Arlington Av
Bell St
North Farm Court
Piper Lane
Cemetery
PO
Chatsworth Cl
Thoresby Close
Church La
Haddon Way
St Chad's Church
Welbeck Dr
Wentworth Avenue
Church Lane
Hill

WORKSOP   ROAD

Green Lane

B6067

Worksop Road

WORKSOP ROAD

3

Junction 31

+

ASTON

Aston Hall
Cricket
Club

A57

M1

4

Upper
Comm

A57

Nickerwood Farm

5

Low
Laithes

D   **E**   **155**   **F**

Manor Road

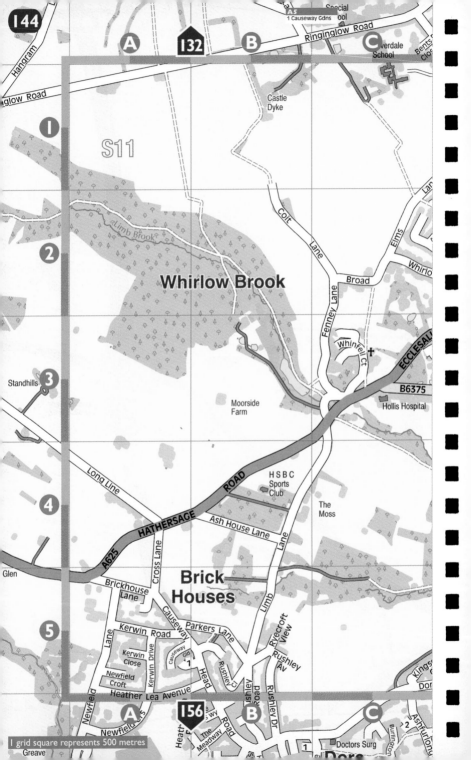

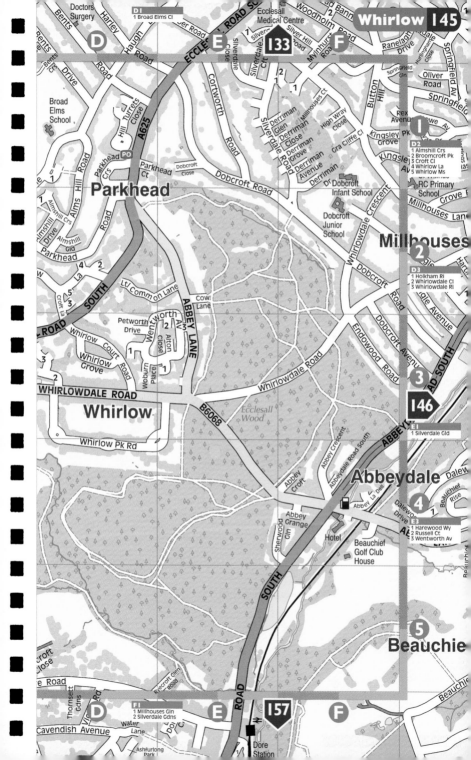

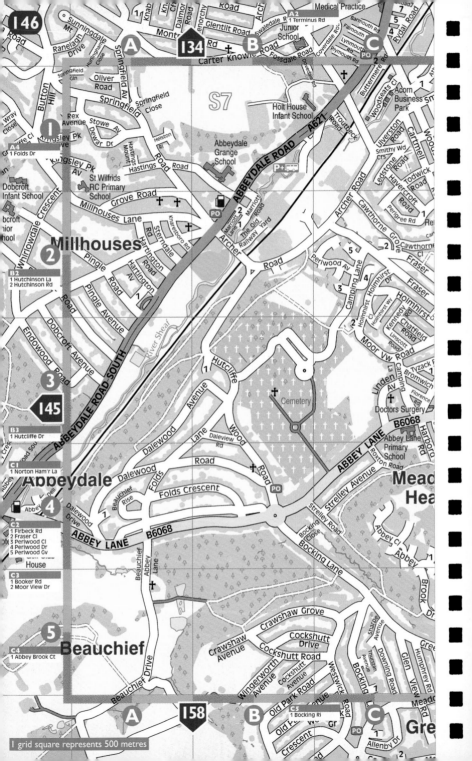

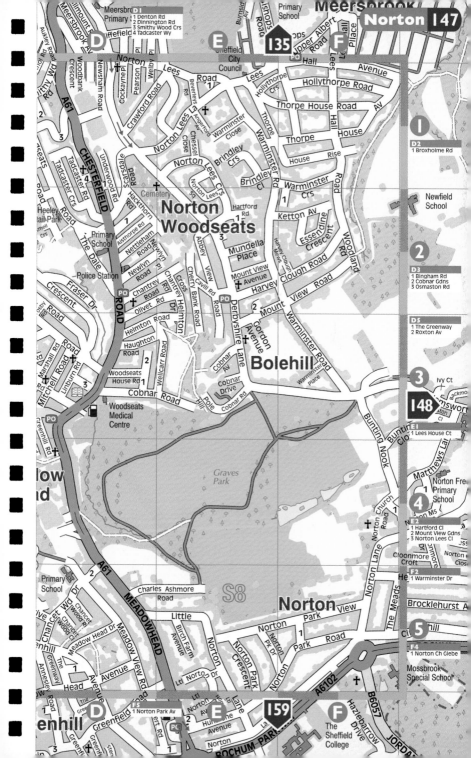

D1
1 Denton Rd
2 Dinnington Rd
3 Smithy Wood Crs
4 Tadcaster Wy

135

D2
1 Broxholme Rd

Newfield School

2

D3
1 Bingham Rd
2 Cobnar Gdns
3 Osmaston Rd

D5
1 The Greenway
2 Roxton Av

3 Ivy Ct

148

E1
1 Lees House Ct

Norton Fre Primary School

4

E2
1 Hartford Cl
2 Mount View Gdns
3 Norton Lees Cl

F2
1 Warminster Dr

Brocklehurst A

5

F4
1 Norton Ch Glebe

Mossbrook Special School

Meersbrook Primary S

Sheffield City Council

Hall

Hollythorpe Crs

Hollythorpe Road

Thorpe House Road

Thorpe House

Warminster Crs

Warminster Rd

Brindley Crs

Brindley Cl

Norton Lees Crs

Ketton Av

Essendine Crescent

Woodland Rd

Crawford Road

Warminster Close

Chessel Close

Angerford

Norton Lees La

Beverleys Rd

Lees Road

Norton Woodseats

Cemetery

Hartford Rd

Abbey View

Mundella Place

Mount View Avenue

Harvey

Mount View Road

Clough Road

Gordon Avenue

Bolehill

Warminster Road

Warminster Place

Cobnar Drive

Cobnar Rd

Pole

Cobnar Road

Graves Park

S8

Norton

Bunting Nook

Bunting Clo

Matthews La

Norton Church Road

Norton Lane

The Meads

Cloonmore Croft

Norton Clo

He

Charles Ashmore Road

Little

Norton Park Avenue

Birch Farm Avenue

Norton Park View

Norton Park Road

Norton Park Crescent

Meadow Head Dr

Meadow View Rd

Chancet Wd Dr

Chancet Wood

Primary School

A61

MEADOWHEAD

A6102

B6057

The Sheffield College

Mossbrook Special School

JORDA

ROCHUM PARK

159

Greenfield

1 Norton Park Av

Hungne Avenue

Norton

A61

CHESTERFIELD

Tadcaster Rd

Tadcaster Crs

Underwood Rd

Scarsdale Road

Hackthorn

The Dale

Primary School

Newlyn Pl

Alsthorpe Rd

Nettleham Road

Newlyn Road

Police Station

Chantrey Road

Olivet Rd

Cross Chantrey Rd

Chantrey Helmton Rd

Helmton Road

Cavill Rd

Cherry Bank Road

Fraser Dr

Crescent Road

Haughton Road

Woodseats House Rd

Wellcarr Road

Cobnar Road

Woodseats Medical Centre

Marshall Road

Mitchell Road

Heeley Retail Park

Meersbrook Cres

Newsham Road

Pearson Pl

Cokayne Pl

Welby Pl

Norton

Meersbrook Pk Rd

Meersbrook Primary S

Meersbrook

Norton

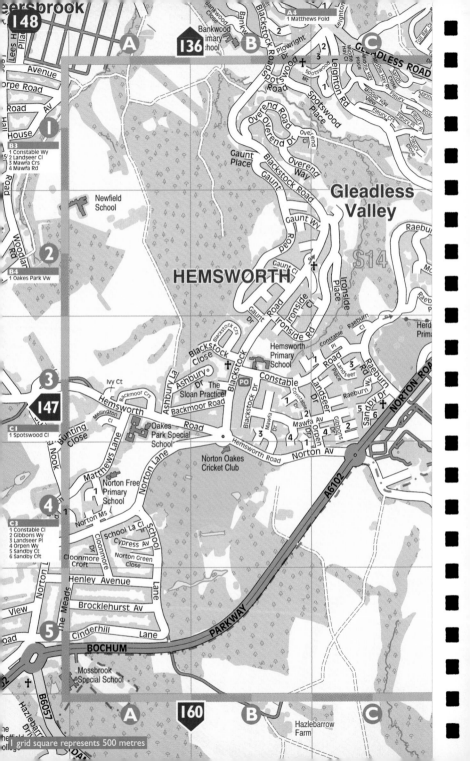

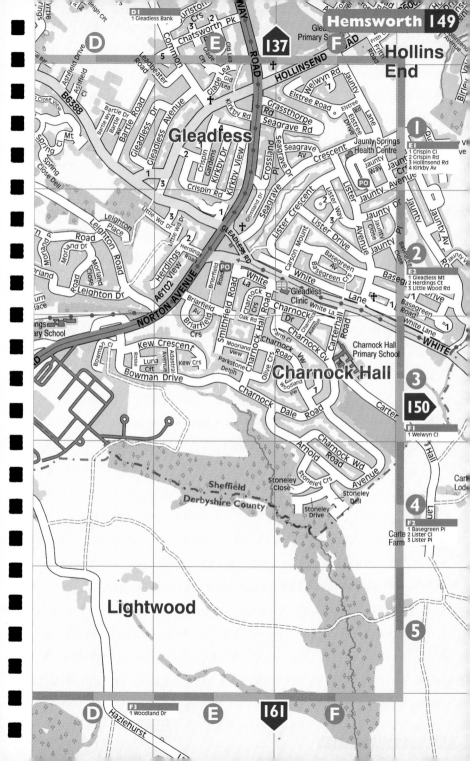

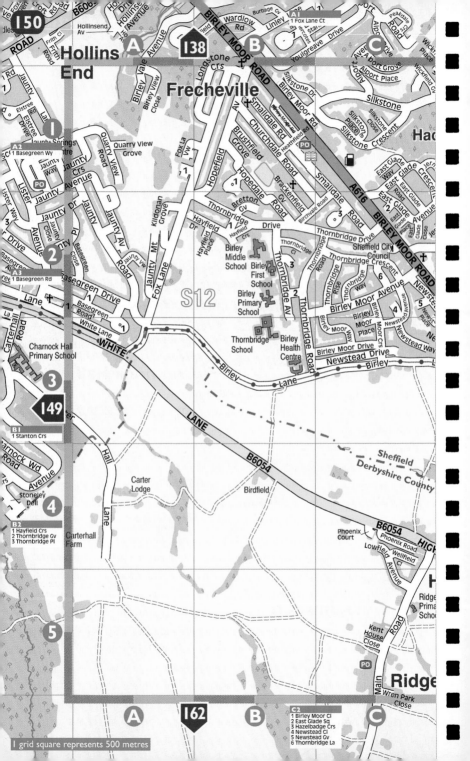

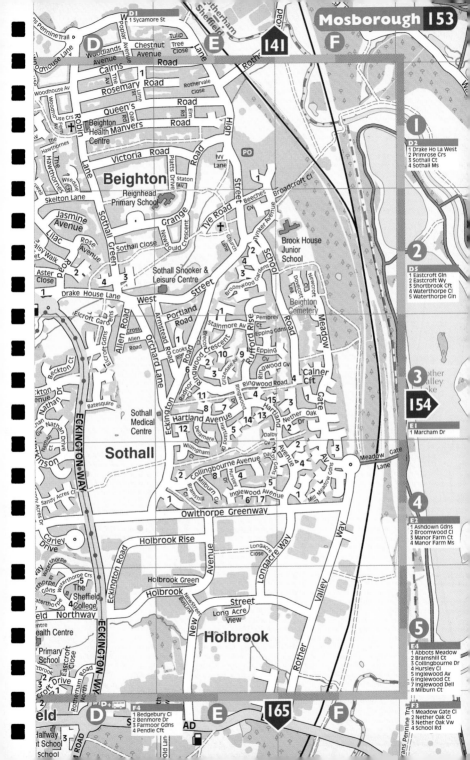

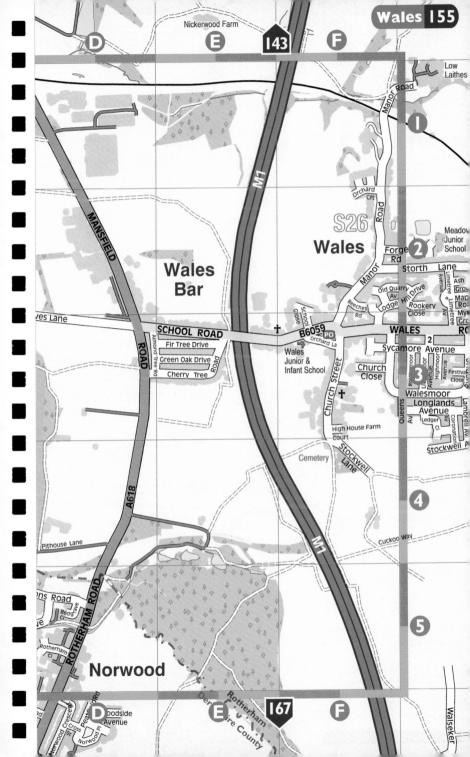

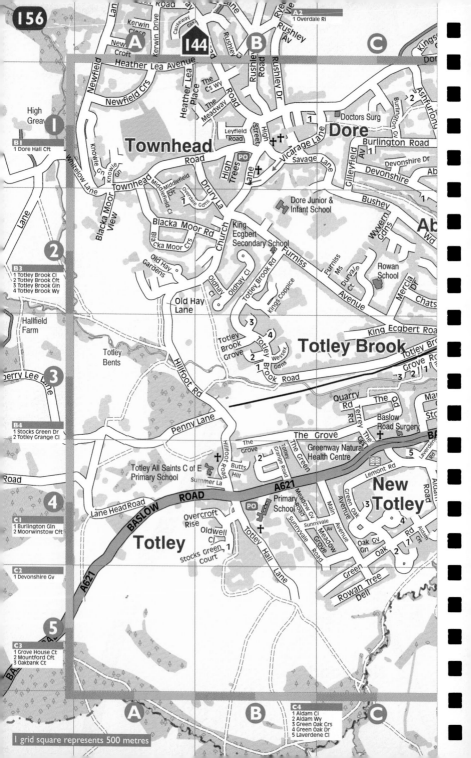

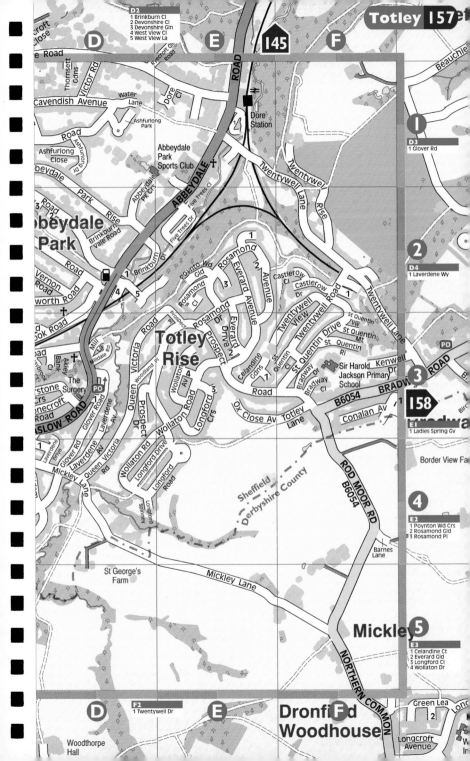

D2
1 Brinkburn Cl
2 Devonshire Gln
3 Devonshire Gln
4 West View Cl
5 West View La

D **E** **145** **F**

Beauchie

Thornsett Gdns

Ryecroft Close
Road

Victor Rd

Water
Lane

Dore
Cl

ROAD

Dore
Station

I
D3
1 Glover Rd

Cavendish Avenue

Ashfurlong
Park

Ashfurlong
Dr

Road

Abbeydale
Park Sports Club

Twentywell Lane

Twentywell Rise

Ashfurlong
Close

Abbeydale

Five Trees Cl

ABBEYDALE

Park Rise Road

Road

Brinkburn Vale Road

Brinkburn
Dr

Five Trees Dr

2
D4
1 Laverdene Wy

**bbeydale
Park**

1

Rosamond Av

Poynton Wd
Gld

Everard Avenue

Castlerow
Cl

Castlerow
Dr

Twentywell Lane

Vernon
Road

worth Road

Brinkburn

Rosamond
Cl

Rosamond
Dr

3

Avenue

Twentywell
View

Twentywell

Road

1

St Quentin
Dr

ook Road

Mill
Rd

Hilldale Rd

Prospect Rd

Everard Avenue

Everard
Drive

Celandine
Gdns

2

St
Quentin
Cl

St Quentin
Mt

St Quentin
Ri

PO

ROAD

**Totley
Rise**

Queen Victoria Road

Woodland Pl

Wollaton
Av

4

3

7

Bradway
Dr

St Quentin
Dr

Sir Harold
Jackson Primary
School

Kenwell
Dr

3
E1
1 Ladies Spring Gv

The
Surgery

Akley
Bank
Cl

onecroft
Road

PO

Glover Road

Laverdene

Prospect Dr

Wollaton Road

Longford Crs

Ox Close Av

Road

Bradway
Cl

Totley
Lane

B6054

BRADWA

158

Conalan Av

ENSLOW ROAD

1

Laverdene Av

Glover Rd

Laverdene

Queen Victoria
Rd

Wollaton Rd

Longford Drive

Longford
Road

Sheffield
Derbyshire County

ROD MOOR RD

B6054

Border View Fa

4
E2
1 Poynton Wd Crs
2 Rosamond Gld
3 Rosamond Pl

Mickley Lane

Longford
Spinney

Barnes
Lane

St George's
Farm

Mickley Lane

Mickle

5
E3
1 Celandine Ct
2 Everard Gld
3 Longford Cl
4 Wollaton Dr

D
F2
1 Twentywell Dr

E

NORTHERN COMMON

**Dronfi F d
Woodhouse**

Green Lea

2

Longcroft
Avenue

Woodthorpe
Hall

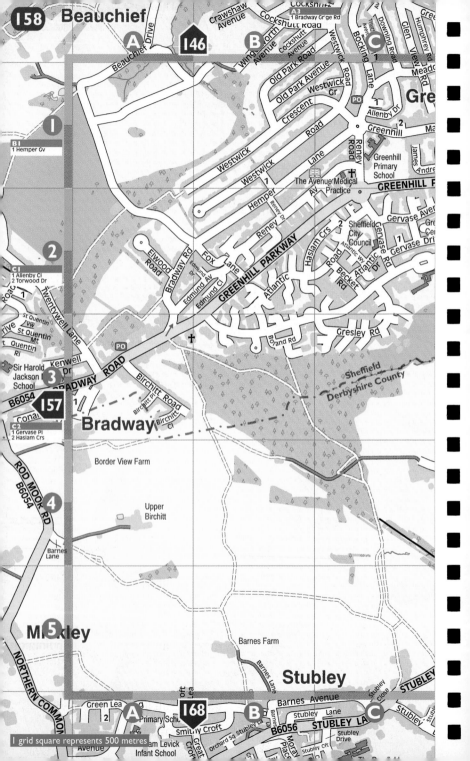

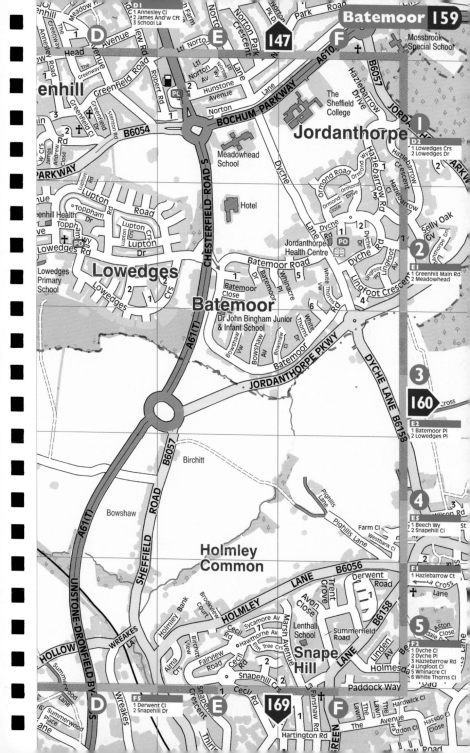

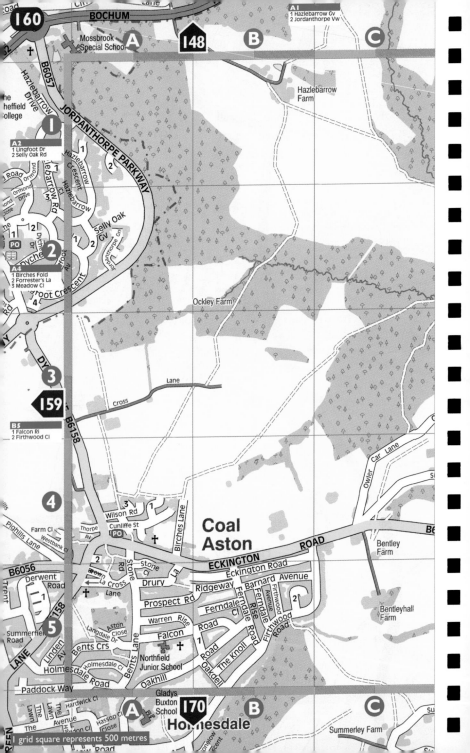

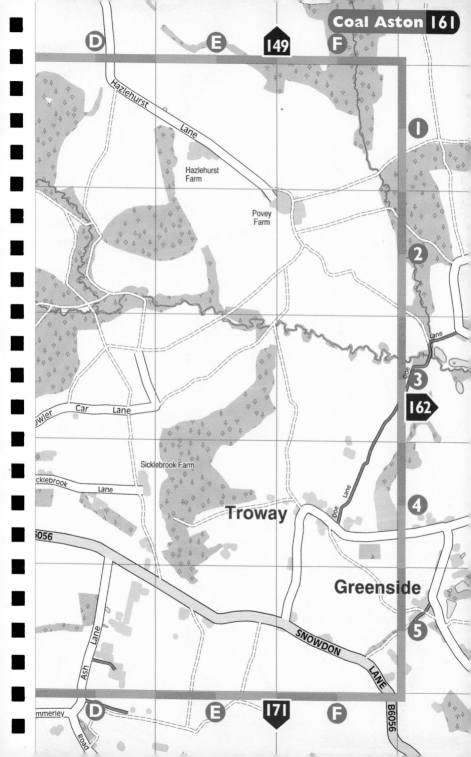

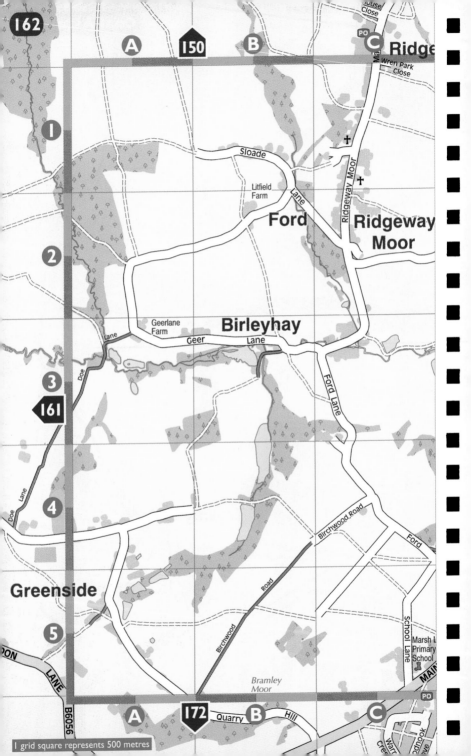

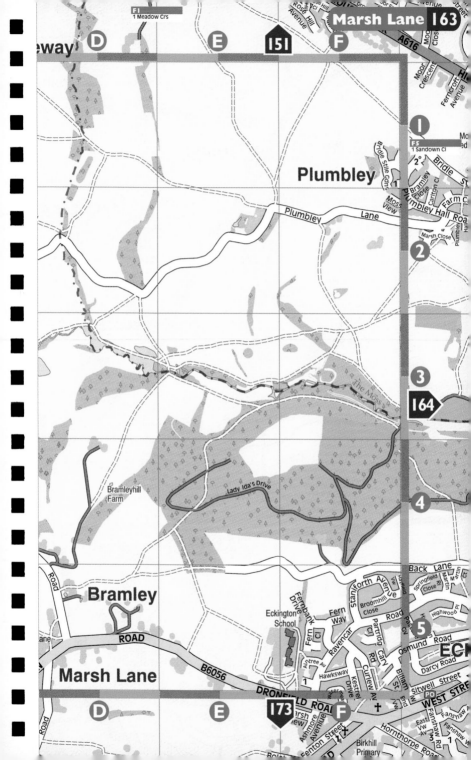

F1
1 Meadow Crs

D   **E**   151   **F**

A616

1 Sandown Cl

2°   Bridle St

Plumbley

Bridle Stile Gdns

Bramley Close

Moss View

Carlton Cl

Plumbley Hall Roa

Plumbley   Lane

Marsh Close

Plumbley Hall

Moor Crescent

Ferncroft Avenue

Hi

Mo
ed

I

F5

1

2

3

164

The Moss

4

Bramleyhill Farm

Lady Ida's Drive

Back Lane

Springfield Close

Hayfield Cl

Martin Rd

Martin Ct

Stanforth Avenue

Broomhill Close

Road

Highway

Highwood Pl

5

Bramley

Eckington School

Fernbank Drive

Fern Cl

Fern Way

Ravencar

Partridge Cl

Cary Rd

Osmund Road

Darcy Road

ECK

ROAD

B6056

Alstree Av

1

Hawksway

Kestrel Drive

Curlew Dr

Billam

End

Sitwell Street

PO

WEST STRE

Marsh Lane

D   **E**   173   Marsh View   **F**

DRONEFIELD ROAD

Ashmore Avenue

Fenton Street

Eastthorpe Vw

Fanshaw Av

Fanshaw Rd

Hornthorpe Roa

Birkhill Primary

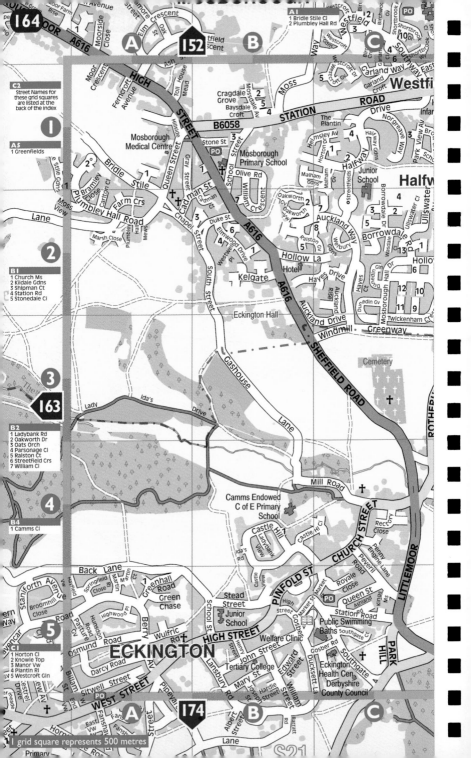

164 A616

152

A **B** **C**

Moor Farm Rise

Moorside Close

Elm Crescent

Oak

tfield scent

A1
1 Bridle Stile Cl
2 Plumbley Hall Rd

Westfield

Westcroft

Birchwoo

Shortbrook

PO

10

Ash

Toll House Mead

HIGH STREET

Moor Crescent

Fernroyd Avenue

Cragdale Grove

Baysdale Croft

Mosdale

STATION ROAD DRIVE

Moss

Garland Way

Carland Croft

Westfi

Westcroft Close

Norgreave Way

Park View Av

Bro

Sch

C2
Street Names for these grid squares are listed at the back of the index

A5
1 Greenfields

1

e Stile Gdns

Bridle Stile

Bramley Close

Carlton Cl

Farm Crs

Plumbley Hall Road

Mosborough Medical Centre

B6058

Stone St

PO

Queen Street

Hillside

Gray Street

Cadman Street

Olive Rd

William Crescent

Mosborough Primary School

The Plantin

Helmsley Av

Horton

Halfway

Malham Gdns

Streetfields

Junior School

Halfw

Infar

Malham

Oakworth Gv

Auckland Way

Borrowdale Dr

Ullswater Cl

Ullswater Rd

Oakworth Vw

Moss View

Lane

Marsh Close

Plumbley Hall Mews

Chapel Street

Duke St

Elmwood Drive

Westway Pl

South Street

Kelgate

Ralston Gv

Wevury

Borrowdale

Wasdale

Rd

Hollo

Gln

Gledhn

2

B1
1 Church Ms
2 Kildale Gdns
3 Shipman Ct
4 Station Rd
5 Stonedale Cl

A616

Hollow La

Hotel

Hayes Drive

Auckland Rise

Hayes Ct

edin Gv

Mosborough Hall Dr

Twickenham

3

163

B2
1 Ladybank Rd
2 Oakworth Dr
3 Oats Orch
4 Parsonage Cl
5 Ralston Ct
6 Streetfield Crs
7 William Cl

Thel

Lady

Ida's Drive

Eckington Hall

Auckland Drive

Windmill

Greenway

SHEFFIELD ROAD

Cemetery

ROTHERF

Gashouse Lane

Mill Road

4

B4
1 Camms Cl

Camms Endowed C of E Primary School

CHURCH STREET

Rectory Close

LITTLEMOOR

Castle Hill

Ladybank View

Ida's Rd

Castle Hi Cl

Peveril Road

Penny Engine Lane

Royale Close

5

C1
1 Horton Cl
2 Knowle Top
3 Manor Vw
4 Plantin Rl
5 Westcroft Gln

Back Lane

Stanforth Avenue

Broomhill Close

Springfield Close

Nuffield

Martin

Greenhall Road

Green Chase

Highwood Pl

Stead Street

School Road

Junior School

Pinfold St

High Street

Gosber St

Market St

Queen St

PO

Station Road

Agnland

Public Swimming Baths

southgate

PARK HILL

Road

Pasture

Berry Av

Wulfric Rd

HIGH STREET

Welfare Clinic

Gosber Rd

Southgate

Osmund Road

Darcy Road

ECKINGTON

Lansbury Rd

John Street

Edward Street

Mary St

Duckett La

William Street

Eckington Health Cen Derbyshire County Council

Sitwell Street

PO

A **WEST STREET** **174** **B** **C**

Pideval

Albert Street

Joseph Hardie Street

Bassett Rd

Lane

S21

1 grid square represents 500 metres

Primary

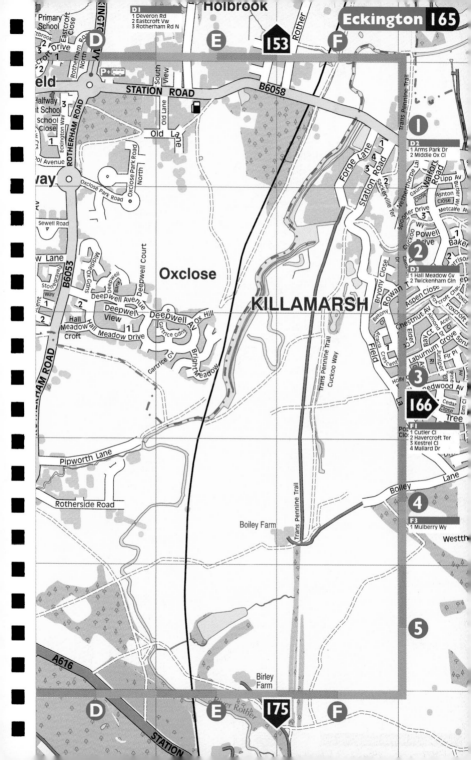

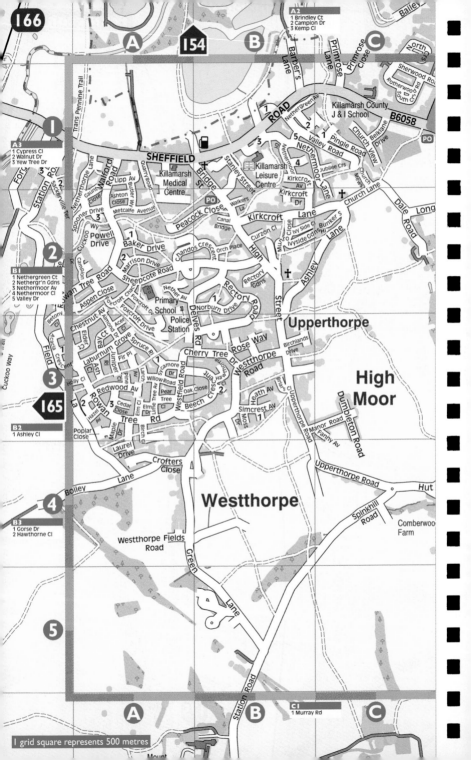

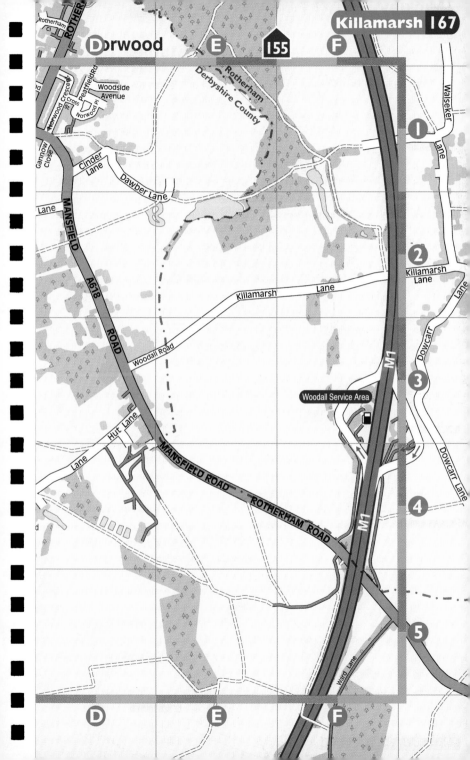

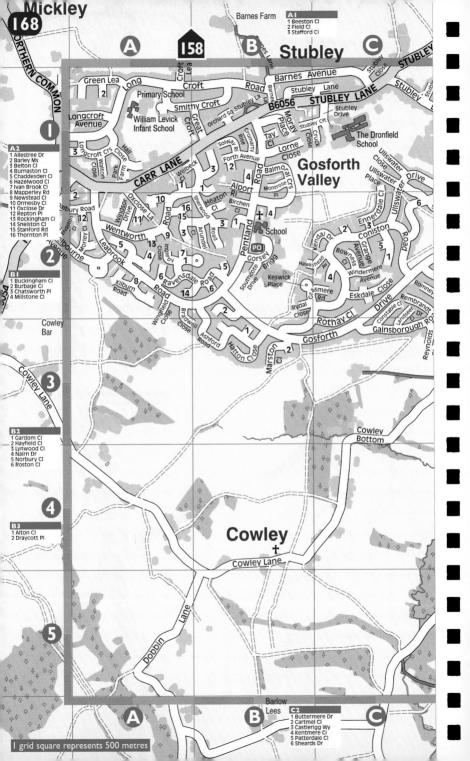

Mickley

168

158

Stubley

Gosforth Valley

The Dronfield School

Cowley Bar

Cowley

Cowley Bottom

Cowley Lane

Barlow Lees

1 grid square represents 500 metres

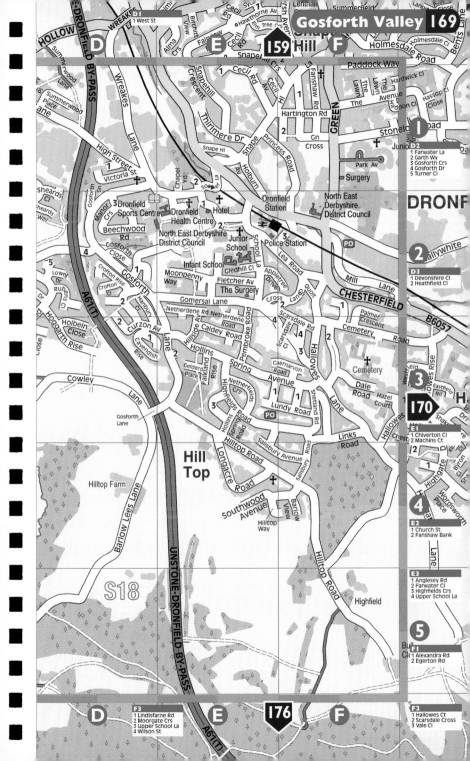

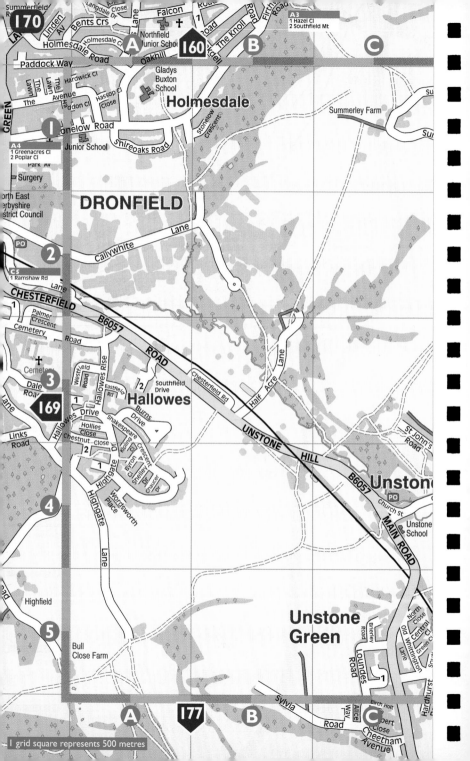

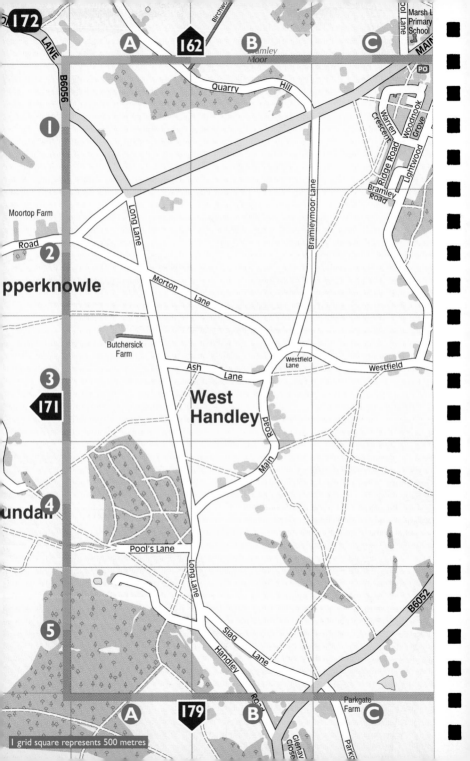

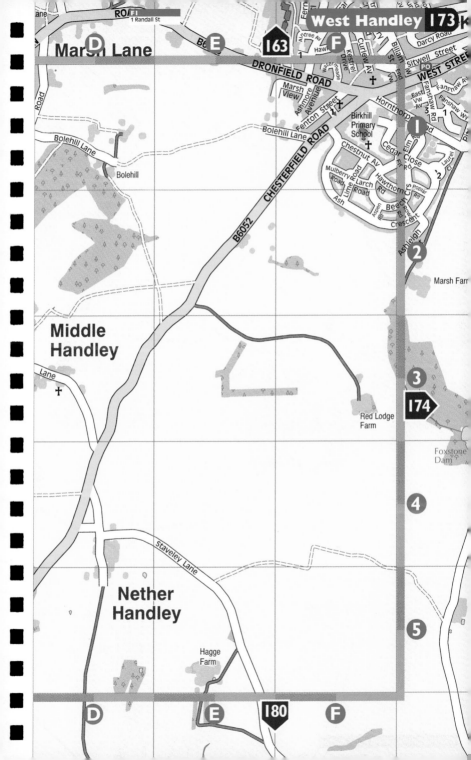

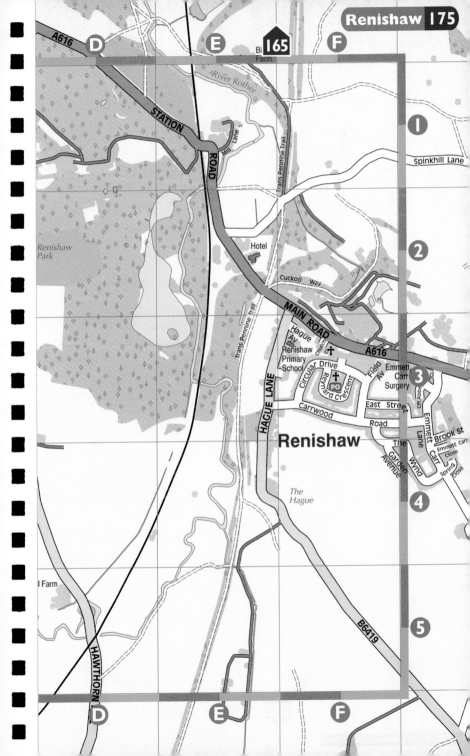

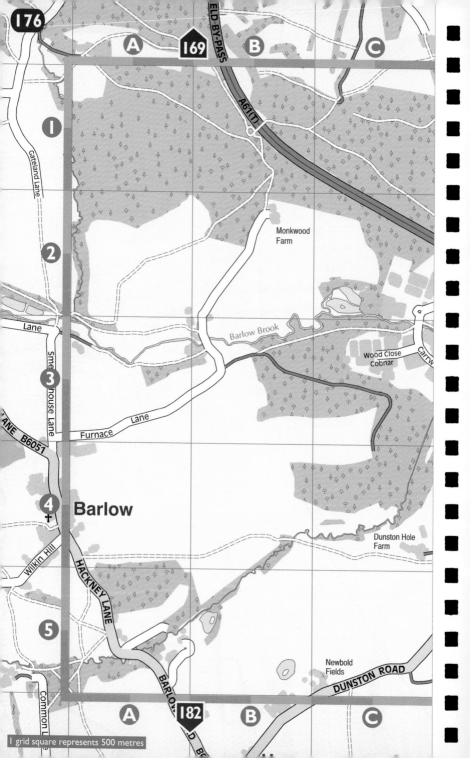

176

A
169
B
C

ELD-BY-PASS

A61(T)

1

Gateland Lane

2

Monkwood
Farm

Lane

Barlow Brook

Wood Close
Cobnar

Carr w

Sme nouse Lane

3

Furnace Lane

ANE B6051

4

✝ **Barlow**

Dunston Hole
Farm

Wilkin Hill

HACKNEY LANE

5

Newbold
Fields

Common L

DUNSTON ROAD

A
182
B
C

BARLO

1 grid square represents 500 metres

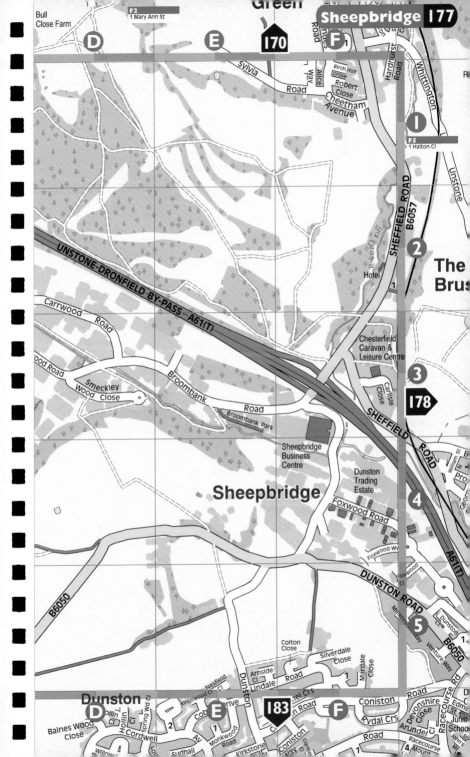

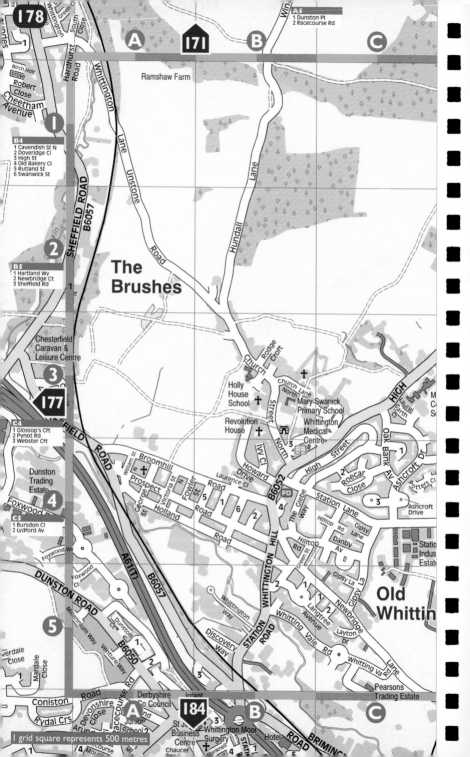

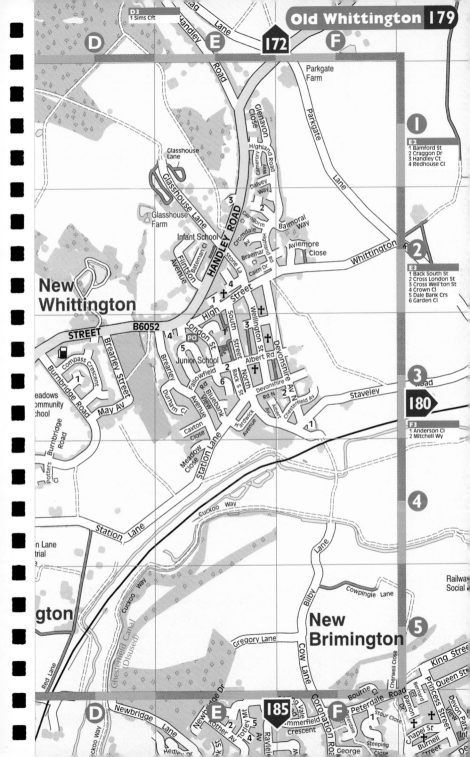

D3
1 Sims Cft

172

New
Whittington

Parkgate
Farm

Glasshouse
Lane

Glasshouse
Farm

Infant School

HANDLEY ROAD

Glenavon
Close

Highland Road

Dalvey
Way

Cairngorm
Av

Cromdale
Av

Braemar
Cl

Highland Rd

Cairn Dr

Balmoral
Way

Aviemore
Close

Whittington

Flintson
Avenue

Bateman Cl

Stone La

STREET   B6052

High Street

South Street

Wellington St

Devonshire St

London St

Brearley

PO

Junior School

Fallowfield Rd

Back S St

North

Albert Rd

Devonshire
Rd N

Chesterfield Av

Staveley

Road

180

Durham Cl

Bluebank
Avenue

Caxton
Close

Hardwick Avenue

Meadow
Close

Station Lane

Compass Crescent

Brearley Street

Burnbridge Road

May Av

Meadows
Community
School

Potters
Ct

Station Lane

Cuckoo Way

Station Lane

n Lane
ustrial

gton

Cuckoo Way

Chesterfield Canal
(Disused)

Red Lane

Gregory Lane

Bilby Lane

Cuckoo Way

Cowpingle Lane

New
Brimington

Railway
Social

Newbridge
Lane

Newbridge Dr

Rother Av

Torfey Mt

185

Rayле

mmerfield
Crescent

Coronation Road

Peterdale Road

Bourne
Dr

Cherwell Close

Stour Close

Steeping
Close

George

Chapel St

Burnell
Street

King Street

Queen St

Princess Street

Devon Park

Damon

I

E2
1 Bamford St
2 Craggon Dr
3 Handley Ct
4 Redhouse Cl

2

E3
1 Back South St
2 Cross London St
3 Cross Well'ton St
4 Crown Cl
5 Dale Bank Crs
6 Garden Cl

3

F3
1 Anderson Cl
2 Mitchell Wy

4

5

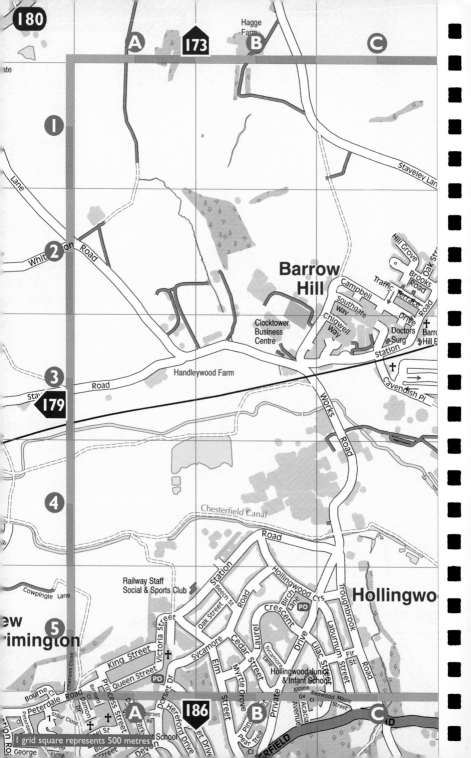

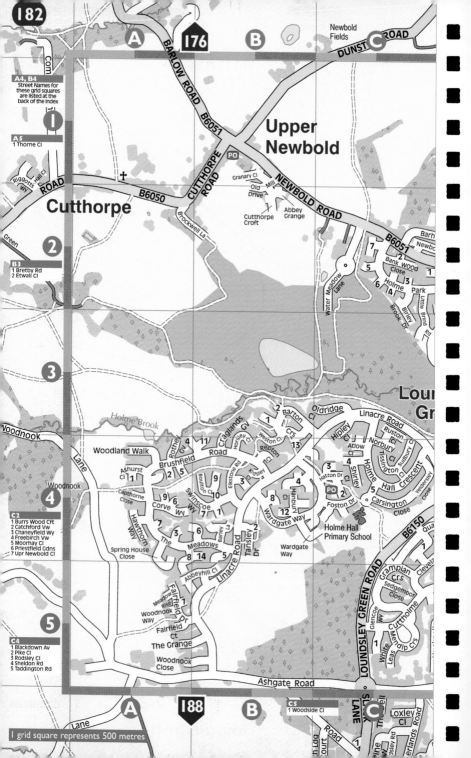

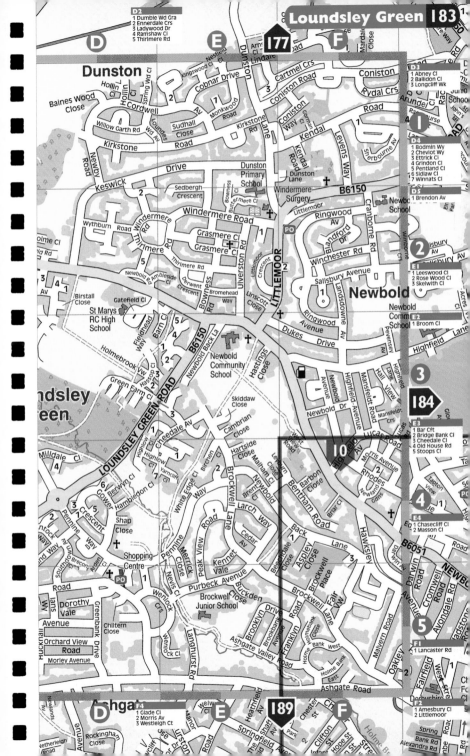

Dunston

Newbold

Loundsley Green

177

184

189

D2
1 Dumble Wd Gra
2 Ennerdale Crs
3 Ladywood Dr
4 Ramshaw Cl
5 Thirlmere Rd

D3
1 Abney Cl
2 Baildon Cl
3 Longcliff Wk

D4
1 Bodmin Wy
2 Cheviot Wy
3 Ettrick Cl
4 Grindon Cl
5 Pentland Cl
6 Sidlaw Cl
7 Winnats Cl

D5
1 Brendon Av

E1
1 Leeswood Cl
2 Rose Wood Cl
3 Skelwith Cl

E2
1 Broom Cl

E3
1 Bar Cft
2 Bridge Bank Cl
3 Cheedale Cl
4 Old House Rd
5 Stoops Cl

E4
1 Chasecliff Cl
2 Masson Cl

F1
1 Lancaster Rd

F4
1 Glade Cl
2 Morris Av
3 Westleigh Ct

1 Amesbury Cl
2 Littlemoor

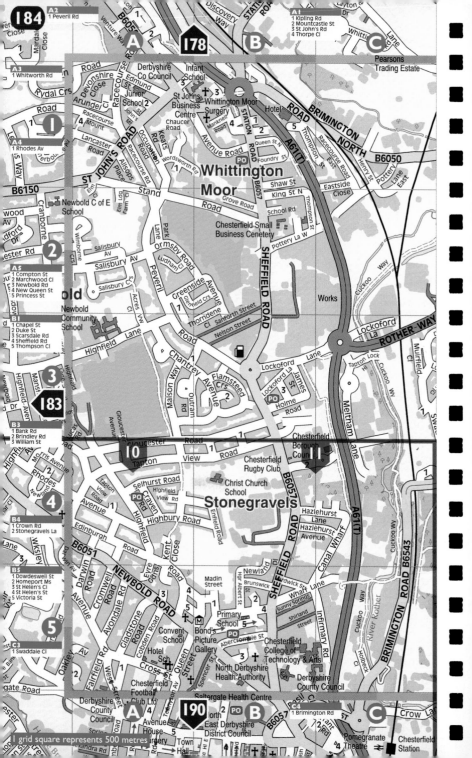

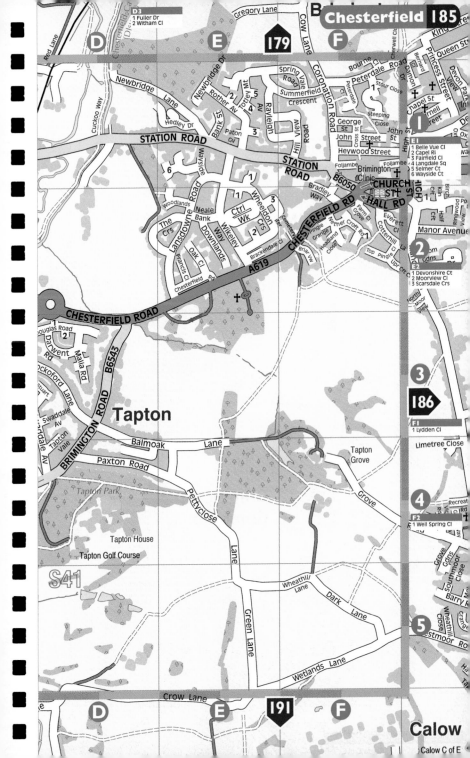

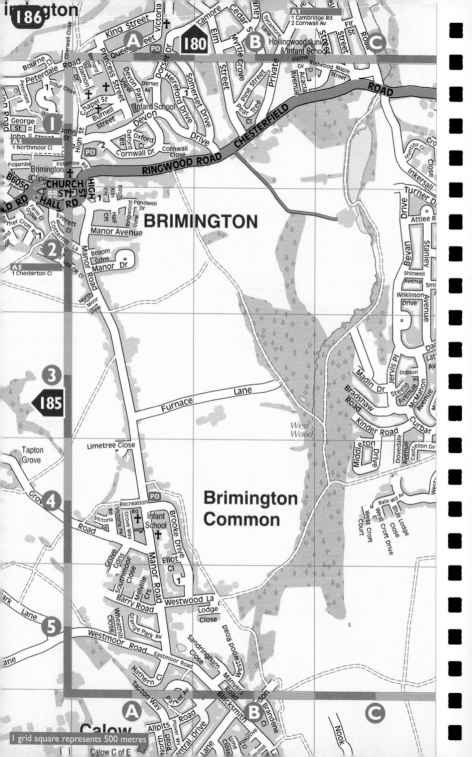

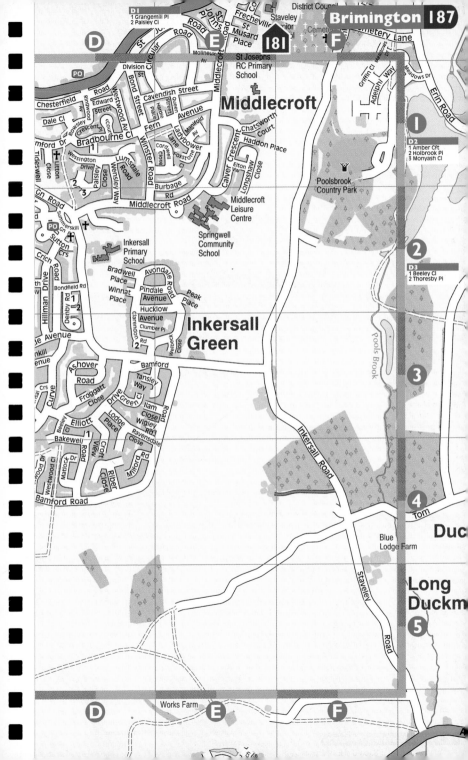

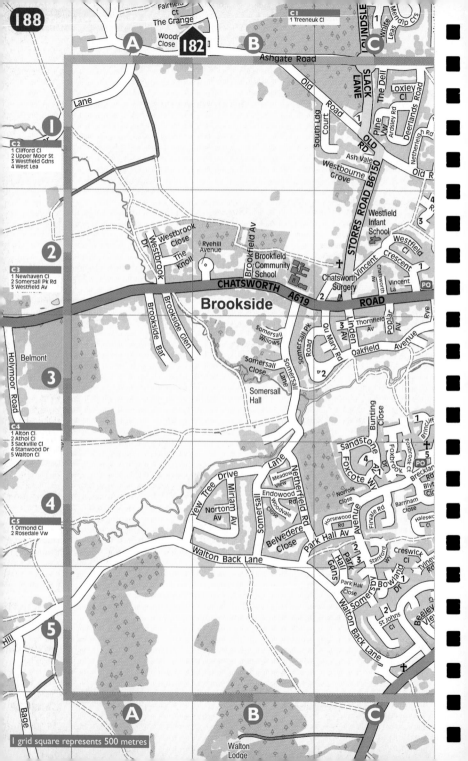

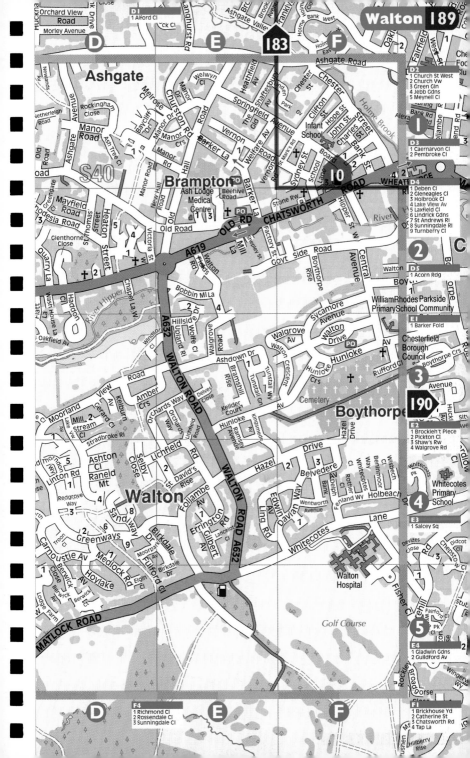

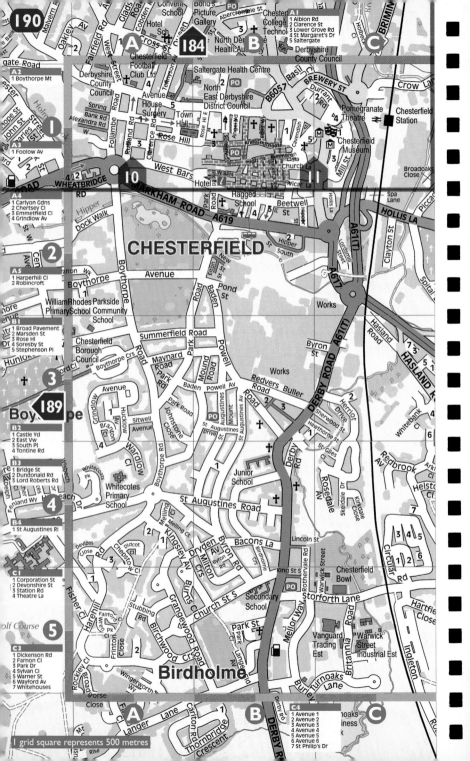

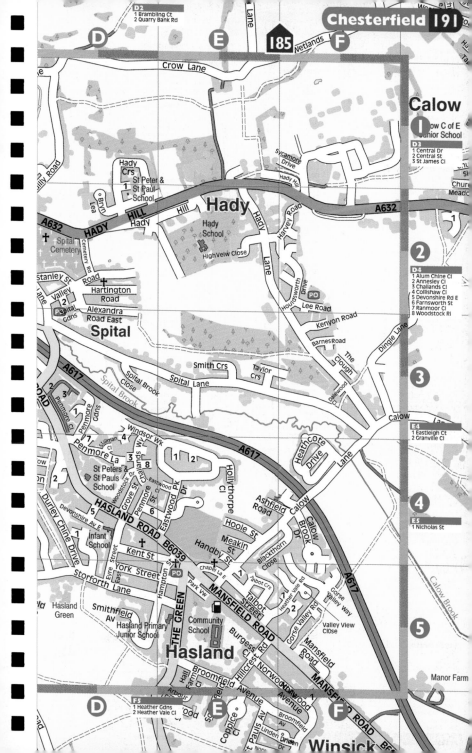

D2
1 Brambling Ct
2 Quarry Bank Rd

185 Netlands

Crow Lane

Calow

...ow C of E
...nior School

D3
1 Central Dr
2 Central St
3 St James Cl

Hady
Crs

St Peter &
St Paul
School

Bryn
Lea

A632 HADY HILL Hady Hill

Hady

Hady
School

HighVeiw Close

Harvey Road

A632

Stanley St

Spital
Cemetery

Valley
Lane

Road

Cemetery Rd

Hartington
Road

Alexandra
Road East

Spital

Houndsworth Drive

PO

Lee Road

Kenyon Road

Barnes Road

D4
1 Alum Chine Cl
2 Annesley Cl
3 Chailands Cl
4 Collishaw Cl
5 Devonshire Rd E
6 Farnsworth St
7 Ranmoor Cl
8 Woodstock Ri

A617

Spital Brook

Spital
Close

Spital Lane

Smith Crs

Taylor
Crs

The
Clough

Dingle Lane

Dalewood

Calow

Lan

Penmore Cl

Penmore Gdns

Windsor Wk

Stilman Cl

A617

E4
1 Eastleigh Ct
2 Granville Cl

Penmore La

Chailands

Eastwood St

Hollythorpe Cl

Heathcote Drive

Calow Lane

St Peters &
St Pauls
School

Grove St

Woodstock Dr

Eastwood Pk

Ashfield
Road

Calow Brook Dr

E5
1 Nicholas St

Devonshire Av E

HASLAND ROAD B6039

Hoole St

Meakin
St

Handby St

Blackthorn Close

Talbot Crs

Corse Valley Way

Durley Chine Drive

Infant
School

Kent St

York Street

PO

Chapel La E

Talbot Street

Heather Vale Rd

Corse Valley Rd

Valley View
Close

A617

Storforth Lane

Hampton St

Park Vw

MANSFIELD ROAD

Burgess Cl

Mansfield Road

Calow Brook

Hasland
Green

Smithfield
Av

Hasland Primary
Junior School

Community
School

Norwood Av

Oakwood Avenue

MANSFIELD ROAD B6

Manor Farm

Hasland

Hall Farm

Broomfield Avenue

Hillcrest Rd

Broomfield
Av

Coppice Cl

St Pauls Av

Linden
Grove

Arbour

F5
1 Heather Gdns
2 Heather Vale Cl

Winsick

Abbeydale 145 F4
Abbeydale Park 156 C2
Abdy 79 E1
Aldwarke 94 B4
Almholme 18 B1
Apperknowle 171 F2
Arbourthorne 136 B2
Ardsley 24 A3
Arksey 17 F4
Armthorpe 33 F3
Ashgate 143 D3
Aston 123 F1
Attercliffe 128 C5
Aughton 43 F5
Balby 176 A4
Barlow 87 E2
Barnes Hall 3 F3
Barnsley 22 B3
Barnsley 76 A2
Barrow 180 B2
Barrow Hill 130 B5
Bassett 159 E3
Batemoor 145 F5
Beauchief 153 D1
Beighton 45 D2
Belle Vue 29 F2
Bentley 29 E3
Bentley Rise 46 C5
Bessacarr 190 A5
Birdholme 35 F5
Birdwell 96 C4
Birley Carr 97 D3
Birley Edge 162 A3
Birleyhay 100 C2
Blackburn 37 D4
Blacker Hill 147 E3
Bolehill 69 D5
Bolsterstone 57 D4
Bow Broom 189 F3
Boythorpe 102 A2
Bradgate 158 A3
Bradway 163 D5
Bramley 54 A1
Brampton 189 E1
Brampton 144 A5
Brick Houses 111 D4
Brightside 186 A2
Brimington 186 B4
Brimington Common 134 A4
Brincliffe 72 B1
Bromley 188 B2
Brookside 104 A5
Broom 40 C3
Broomhill 178 A2
The Brushes 87 F1
Burncross 122 C1
Burngreave 61 E2
Cadeby 114 B1
Canklow 47 F3
Cantley 111 E4
Carbrook 134 B5
Carter Knowle 127 E1
Catcliffe 74 C5
Chapeltown 87 D1
Charltonbrook 149 E3
Charnock Hall 190 A2
Chesterfield 7 G6
Clifton 160 B4
Coal Aston 139 E4
Coisley Hill 84 A1
Conanby 60 B5
Conisbrough 77 F2
Cortworth 168 B4
Cowley 120 C3
Crookes 121 E3
Crookesmoor 23 E1
Cundy Cross 71 F3
Cundy Hos 28 A4
Cusworth 95 E5
Dalton 105 F1
Dalton Parva 124 C3
Darnall 70 A4
Deepcar 59 F4
Denaby Main 20 A3
Dodworth 5 H3
Doncaster 156 C1
Dore 152 B2
Drakehouse 170 A2
Dronfield 90 C5
Dropping Well 183 D1
Dunston 104 B2
East Dene 105 E2
East Herringthorpe 133 E5
Ecclesall ....

Ecclesfield 88 C5
Eckington 164 A5
Elscar 52 B3
Finkle Street 71 D1
Firth Park 110 B1
Fir Vale 110 A3
Ford 162 B2
Frecheville 150 A1
Fulwood 132 A2
Garden Village 68 A2
Gawber 12 B4
Gilroyd 20 B5
Gleadless 149 E1
Gleadless Valley 148 C2
Gosforth Valley 168 B1
Greasbrough 93 D2
Greenhill 158 C1
Greenland 111 F5
Greenside 161 F5
Grenoside 97 E1
Greystones 133 D3
Grimesthorpe 110 B3
Guilthwaite 128 C1
Hackenthorpe 150 C1
Hady 191 E2
Halfway 164 C1
Hallowes 170 A3
Handsworth 125 F5
Harley 75 E2
Hasland 191 E5
Heeley 135 E4
Hemingfield 53 D1
Hemsworth 148 A2
Hermit Hill 48 A2
Herringthorpe 105 D4
Hexthorpe 43 E3
Highfield 135 F2
High Green 73 E4
Highlane 150 C5
High Moor 166 C3
Hillsborough 107 D2
Hill Top 84 A4
Hill Top 101 D3
Hill Top 169 E4
Holbrook 153 E5
Hollingwood 137 F5
Hollins End 170 A1
Holmesdale 159 E4
Holmley Common 78 B2
Hoober 75 E3
Hood Hill 83 E4
Hooton Roberts 72 C2
Howland 51 E3
Hoyland Common 50 C2
Hoyle Mill 23 D1
Hundall 171 F4
Hyde Park 4 D6
Inkersall Green 187 E3
Intake 31 E5
Intake 137 E5
Jordanthorpe 159 F1
Jordon 101 F4
Jump 52 B1
Kendray 23 D4
Keresforth Hill 21 D3
Killamarsh 165 E2
Kilnhurst 81 E4
Kimberworth 101 F2
Kimberworth Park 92 A4
Kingstone 21 E3
Lane End 74 B5
Lightwood 149 D5
Lodge Moor 130 C1
Longley Estate 109 F1
Long Sandall 19 E3
Loundsley Green 182 C3
Loversall 12 A1
Low Barugh 159 D2
Lowedges 158 B5
Lowfield 135 E3
Low Laithes 24 C3
Low Valley 40 A1
Loxley 106 A4
Lundwood 15 F4
Malinbridge 107 E5
Manor Estate 137 D1
Manor Park 123 F5
Marsh Lane 163 D5
Masbrough 102 C2
Meadow Hall 111 F1
Meadow Head 146 C4
Measbrough Dike 22 C2
Meersbrook 135 F3

Mexborough 58 B1
Mickley 157 F5
Middlecroft 187 E1
Middle Handley 173 D3
Middlewood 96 A5
Millhouses 145 F2
Milton 51 F3
Monk Bretton 14 C3
Moorgate 115 D2
Moorhole 151 E4
Morthen 117 E5
Mortomley 73 F4
Mosborough 152 A5
Nether Edge 134 C4
Nether Handley 173 D5
Nether Haugh 78 C4
Newbold 183 F2
New Brimington 179 F5
Newhill 55 F4
Newton 43 E2
New Totley 156 C4
New Village 17 D4
New Whittington 179 D2
Normanton Spring 138 C4
Norton 147 F5
Norton Woodseats 147 E2
Norwood 155 D5
Old Denaby 59 D5
Old Whittington 179 D5
Orgreave 140 A1
Owlerton 108 B4
Owlthorpe 151 F3
Oxclose 165 E2
Parkgate 94 A4
Parkhead 145 D2
Park Hill 123 E4
Parkwood Springs 109 D5
Parson Cross 98 A4
Piccadilly 80 C2
Pilley 49 D3
Pismire Hill 99 E5
Pitsmoor 109 F5
Platts Common 37 F5
Plumbley 163 F1
Pogmoor 12 B5
Potter Hill 72 C4
Rails 118 A3
Ranmoor 132 C1
Rawmarsh 94 B2
Renishaw 175 E4
Richmond 138 C2
Ridgeway 150 C5
Ridgeway Moor 136 A5
Rollestone 16 A4
Rostholme 104 A4
Rotherham 80 B4
Ryecroft 80 B4
St Helen's 15 D2
Sandygate 119 F5
Scawsby 28 B3
Scawthorpe 28 B1
Scholes 91 D2
Sharrow 134 B3
Shaw Lands 21 D1
Sheepbridge 177 E4
Sheffield 123 D4
Sheffield Park 136 C1
Shirecliffe 109 E3
Shiregreen 100 A4
Smithies 14 A2
Smithley 38 B2
Snape Hill 159 F5
Sothall 153 D4
Spital 191 D3
Sprotbrough 42 A3
Stairfoot 23 F3
Stannington 119 E1
Steel Bank 121 D2
Stockbridge 17 D4
Stocksbridge 69 D3
Stonegravels 11 F1
Stopes 118 A1
Stubbley 158 B5
Sunnyfields 28 C3
Swaithe 142 A3
Swallownest 80 C1
Swinton 58 B4
Swinton Bridge 57 F4
Tankersley 49 F4
Tapton 185 D3
Tapton Hill 120 B5
Templeborough 102 A5
Thorn Hill 6 B3
Thorpe Hesley 90 B1

Thrybergh 95 F3
Thurnscoe 26 C5
Thurnscoe East 27 F3
Tinsley 112 C2
Toll Bar 16 B2
Totley 156 A4
Totley Brook 156 B3
Totley Rise 157 D3
Townhead 156 A1
Treeton 127 F3
Troway 161 E4
Under Tofts 119 D3
Unstone 170 C4
Unstone Green 170 B5
Upper Haugh 79 E4
Upper Hoyland 51 D1
Upper Newbold 182 B1
Upper Tankersley 49 D4
Upperthorpe 166 B3
Upper Whiston 129 E1
Wadsley 106 C2
Wadsley Bridge 96 C5
Waldershaigh 68 B5
Wales 155 F2
Wales Bar 155 E2
Walkley 121 D1
Walton 189 D4
Ward Green 21 F5
Warren 74 C3
Waterthorpe 152 B3
Wath upon Dearne 56 B2
Wentworth 76 C2
Westfield 164 C1
West Handley 172 A3
West Melton 55 D2
Westthorpe 166 B4
Wheatley 30 C4
Wheatley Hills 32 A3
Wheatley Park 31 E2
Whinney Hill 95 E4
Whirlow 145 D3
Whirlow Brook 144 A2
Whiston 116 A3
Whitley 88 A4
Whittington Moor 184 B1
Wilthorpe 13 D3
Wincobank 111 E1
Windhill 59 D2
Wingfield 91 F3
Wombwell 39 D4
Woodhouse 140 A3
Woodhouse Mill 140 C2
Wood Seats 87 E3
Worsbrough Bridge 36 B2
Worsbrough Common 21 F4
Worsbrough Dale 36 B1

USING THE STREET INDEX

Street names are listed alphabetically. Each street name is followed by its postal town or area locality, the Postcode District, the page number, and the reference to the square in which the name is found.

Abbey Brook Ct *SHEFS* S8 .... **146** C4 1

Some entries are followed by a number in a blue box. This number indicates the location of the street within the referenced grid square. The full street name is listed at the side of the map page.

GENERAL ABBREVIATIONS

ACC	ACCESS
ALY	ALLEY
AP	APPROACH
AR	ARCADE
ASS	ASSOCIATION
AV	AVENUE
BCH	BEACH
BLDS	BUILDINGS
BND	BEND
BNK	BANK
BR	BRIDGE
BRK	BROOK
BTM	BOTTOM
BUS	BUSINESS
BVD	BOULEVARD
BY	BYPASS
CATH	CATHEDRAL
CEM	CEMETERY
CEN	CENTRE
CFT	CROFT
CH	CHURCH
CHA	CHASE
CHYD	CHURCHYARD
CIR	CIRCLE
CIRC	CIRCUS
CL	CLOSE
CLFS	CLIFFS
CMP	CAMP
CNR	CORNER
CO	COUNTY
COLL	COLLEGE
COM	COMMON
COMM	COMMISSION
CON	CONVENT
COT	COTTAGE
COTS	COTTAGES
CP	CAPE
CPS	COPSE
CR	CREEK
CREM	CREMATORIUM
CRS	CRESCENT
CSWY	CAUSEWAY
CT	COURT
CTRL	CENTRAL
CTS	COURTS
CTYD	COURTYARD
CUTT	CUTTINGS
CV	COVE
CYN	CANYON
DEPT	DEPARTMENT
DL	DALE
DM	DAM
DR	DRIVE
DRO	DROVE
DRY	DRIVEWAY
DWGS	DWELLINGS
E	EAST
EMB	EMBANKMENT
EMBY	EMBASSY
ESP	ESPLANADE
EST	ESTATE
EX	EXCHANGE
EXPY	EXPRESSWAY
EXT	EXTENSION
F/O	FLYOVER
FC	FOOTBALL CLUB
FK	FORK
FLD	FIELD
FLDS	FIELDS
FLS	FALLS
FLS	FLATS
FM	FARM
FT	FORT
FWY	FREEWAY
FY	FERRY
GA	GATE
GAL	GALLERY
GDN	GARDEN
GDNS	GARDENS
GLD	GLADE
GLN	GLEN
GN	GREEN
GND	GROUND
GRA	GRANGE
GRG	GARAGE
GT	GREAT
GTWY	GATEWAY
GV	GROVE
HGR	HIGHER
HL	HILL
HLS	HILLS
HO	HOUSE
HOL	HOLLOW
HOSP	HOSPITAL
HRB	HARBOUR
HTH	HEATH
HTS	HEIGHTS
HVN	HAVEN
HWY	HIGHWAY
IMP	IMPERIAL
IN	INLET
IND EST	INDUSTRIAL ESTATE
INF	INFIRMARY
INFO	INFORMATION
INT	INTERCHANGE
IS	ISLAND
JCT	JUNCTION
JTY	JETTY
KG	KING
KNL	KNOLL
L	LAKE
LA	LANE
LDG	LODGE
LGT	LIGHT
LK	LOCK
LKS	LAKES
LNDG	LANDING
LTL	LITTLE
LWR	LOWER
MAG	MAGISTRATE
MAN	MANSIONS
MD	MEAD
MDW	MEADOWS
MEM	MEMORIAL
MKT	MARKET
MKTS	MARKETS
ML	MALL
ML	MILL
MNR	MANOR
MS	MEWS
MSN	MISSION
MT	MOUNT
MTN	MOUNTAIN
MTS	MOUNTAINS
MUS	MUSEUM
MWY	MOTORWAY
N	NORTH
NE	NORTH EAST
NW	NORTH WEST
O/P	OVERPASS
OFF	OFFICE
ORCH	ORCHARD
OV	OVAL
PAL	PALACE
PAS	PASSAGE
PAV	PAVILION
PDE	PARADE
PH	PUBLIC HOUSE
PK	PARK
PKWY	PARKWAY
PL	PLACE
PLN	PLAIN
PLNS	PLAINS
PLZ	PLAZA
POL	POLICE STATION
PR	PRINCE
PREC	PRECINCT
PREP	PREPARATORY
PRIM	PRIMARY
PROM	PROMENADE
PRS	PRINCESS
PRT	PORT
PT	POINT
PTH	PATH
PZ	PIAZZA
QD	QUADRANT
QU	QUEEN
QY	QUAY

R .....RIVER	SP .....SPUR	UPR .....UPPER
RBT .....ROUNDABOUT	SPR .....SPRING	V .....VALE
RD .....ROAD	SQ .....SQUARE	VA .....VALLEY
RDG .....RIDGE	ST .....STREET	VIAD .....VIADUCT
REP .....REPUBLIC	STN .....STATION	VIL .....VILLA
RES .....RESERVOIR	STR .....STREAM	VIS .....VISTA
RFC .....RUGBY FOOTBALL CLUB	STRD .....STRAND	VLG .....VILLAGE
RI .....RISE	SW .....SOUTH WEST	VLS .....VILLAS
RP .....RAMP	TDG .....TRADING	VW .....VIEW
RW .....ROW	TER .....TERRACE	W .....WEST
S .....SOUTH	THWY .....THROUGHWAY	WD .....WOOD
SCH .....SCHOOL	TNL .....TUNNEL	WHF .....WHARF
SE .....SOUTH EAST	TOLL .....TOLLWAY	WK .....WALK
SER .....SERVICE AREA	TPK .....TURNPIKE	WKS .....WALKS
SH .....SHORE	TR .....TRACK	WLS .....WELLS
SHOP .....SHOPPING	TRL .....TRAIL	WY .....WAY
SKWY .....SKYWAY	TWR .....TOWER	YD .....YARD
SMT .....SUMMIT	U/P .....UNDERPASS	YHA .....YOUTH HOSTEL
SOC .....SOCIETY	UNI .....UNIVERSITY	

POSTCODE TOWNS AND AREA ABBREVIATIONS

ABRD .....Abbeydale Road	DOD/DAR .....Dodworth/Darton	OWL .....Owlerton
ARMTH .....Armthorpe	DON .....Doncaster	RAW .....Rawmarsh
ATT .....Attercliffe	DONS/BSCR .....Doncaster south/ Bessacarr	RCH .....Rural Chesterfield
AU/AST/KP .....Aughton/Aston/ Kiveton Park	DRON .....Dronfield	RHAM .....Rotherham
BSLY .....Barnsley	ECC .....Ecclesall	RHAM/THRY .....Rotherham/Thrybergh
BSLYN/ROY .....Barnsley north/Royston	ECK/KIL .....Eckington/Killamarsh	SHEF .....Sheffield
BSVR .....Bolsover	FUL .....Fulwood	SHEFN .....Sheffield north
BTLY .....Bentley	GLV .....Gleadless Valley	SHEFP/MNR .....Sheffield Park/Manor
CHNE .....Chesterfield north & east	HACK/IN .....Hackenthorpe/Intake	SHEFS .....Sheffield south
CHPT/GREN .....Chapeltown/Grenoside	HAN/WDH .....Handsworth/Woodhouse	ST/HB/BR .....Stannington/ Hillsborough/Bradfield
CHSW .....Chesterfield south & west	HOY .....Hoyland	STKB/PEN .....Stocksbridge/Penistone
CONI .....Conisbrough	KIMB .....Kimberworth	STV/CWN .....Staveley/Clowne
CUD/GR .....Cudworth/Grimethorpe	MALT .....Maltby	TOT/DORE .....Totley/Dore
DARN/MH .....Darnall/Meadowhall	MEX/SWTN .....Mexborough/Swinton	WHHL .....Wheatley Hills
DEARNE .....Wath upon Dearne/ Bolton upon Dearne	MOS .....Mosborough	WMB/DAR .....Wombwell/Darfield
	NROS/TKH .....New Rossington/Tickhill	

Abb - Ald

Index - streets

A

Abbey Brook Ct SHEFS S8 ...146 C4 🔲
Abbey Brook Dr SHEFS S8 ...146 C4
Abbey CI SHEFS S8 ...146 C4
Abbey Crs ABRD S7 ...145 F4
Abbey Cft ABRD S7 ...145 F4
Abbeydale Park Crs
  TOT/DORE S17 ...157 D2
Abbeydale Park Ri TOT/DORE S17 ...156 C1
Abbeydale Rd SHEFS S8 ...135 D3
  SHEFS S8 ...146 B2
Abbeydale Rd South SHEFS S8 ...145 F4
  TOT/DORE S17 ...157 E2
Abbeyfield Rd ATT S4 ...109 F5
  RCH S42 ...182 B2
Abbey Gv BSLYN/ROY S71 ...15 F3
Abbeyhill CI CHSW S40 ...182 A5
Abbey La BSLYN/ROY S71 ...15 F5
  BSLYN/ROY S71 ...23 F1
  ECC S11 ...145 E2
  SHEFS S8 ...146 C4
Abbey Lane Dell SHEFS S8 ...145 F4
Abbey Sq BSLYN/ROY S71 ...15 F3 🔲
Abbey View Rd SHEFS S8 ...147 E2
Abbey Wk BTLY DN5 ...28 C4
Abbots Meadow MOS S20 ...153 E4 🔲
Abbott St DONS/BSCR DN4 ...4 B5
Abdy Rd KIMB S61 ...91 E4
  RAW S62 ...79 E1
Abercorn Rd WHHL DN2 ...32 A5
Abercrombie St CHNE S41 ...11 E4
Aberford Gv HOY S74 ...52 C2 🔲
Abingdon Gdns KIMB S61 ...92 C3
Abingdon Rd WHHL DN2 ...31 F4
Abney CI CHSW S40 ...183 D3 🔲
  SHEFS S8 ...136 A4 🔲
Abney Dr SHEFS S8 ...136 A4
Abney Rd SHEFS S8 ...136 A4
Acacia Av CHPT/GREN S35 ...88 A2
  STV/CWN S43 ...186 B1
Acacia Ct BTLY DN5 ...16 B4 🔲
Acacia Crs ECK/KIL S21 ...165 F3
Acacia Gv CONI DN12 ...84 B3
Acacia Rd DONS/BSCR DN4 ...47 D4
  SHEFN S5 ...99 F5
Acer CI ECK/KIL S21 ...166 A3
Acer Cft ARMTH DN3 ...33 F4
Ackworth Dr DARN/MH S9 ...113 D3 🔲
Acorn Cft KIMB S61 ...92 C4
Acorn Dr ST/HB/BR S6 ...106 A5

ST/HB/BR S6 ...118 C1
ST/HB/BR S6 ...119 D1
Acorn HI ST/HB/BR S6 ...106 B5
Acorn Rdg CHSW S40 ...189 D5 🔲
Acorn St OWL S3 ...8 C2
Acorn Wy ST/HB/BR S6 ...118 C1
Acre Ga CHPT/GREN S35 ...73 E4
Acres Hill La DARN/MH S9 ...124 C3
Acres Hill Rd DARN/MH S9 ...124 C3
Acres View CI CHNE S41 ...184 A2
Acton CI AU/AST/KP S26 ...142 B1
Adastral Av HACK/IN S12 ...149 E3
Addison Rd MEX/SWTN S64 ...58 C3
  SHEFN S5 ...110 B2
Addy CI ST/HB/BR S6 ...121 F2
Addy Dr ST/HB/BR S6 ...121 F2
Addy St ST/HB/BR S6 ...121 F3
Adelaide Rd ECC S11 ...134 B4
Adelphi St ST/HB/BR S6 ...8 A2
Adelphi Wy STV/CWN S43 ...187 F1
Adkins Dr SHEFN S5 ...108 C1
Adkins Rd SHEFN S5 ...108 C1
Adlard Rd WHHL DN2 ...31 F3 🔲
Adlington Crs SHEFN S5 ...98 A5
Adlington Rd SHEFN S5 ...98 A5
Admirals Crest KIMB S61 ...90 C4
Adrian Crs SHEFN S5 ...98 B5
Adsetts St ATT S4 ...110 C3
Adwick Av BTLY DN5 ...16 A1
Adwick Ct MEX/SWTN S64 ...58 C4 🔲
Adwick Pk DEARNE S63 ...57 E2
Adwick Rd MEX/SWTN S64 ...58 A1
  MEX/SWTN S64 ...58 C4 🔲
Agden Rd ABRD S7 ...134 C2
Agnes Rd BSLY S70 ...21 F2
Ainsdale Ct BSLYN/ROY S71 ...15 E2
Ainsley Rd FUL S10 ...121 D3 🔲
Ainsty Rd ABRD S7 ...135 D3 🔲
Aintree Av DONS/BSCR DN4 ...46 B2
  ECK/KIL S21 ...163 F5
Aintree CI BTLY DN5 ...28 B4
Aintree Dr MEX/SWTN S64 ...58 C2
Aire CI CHPT/GREN S35 ...74 A5
Airedale Rd ST/HB/BR S6 ...107 E2
Aireton Rd BSLY S70 ...2 B4
Aisby Dr NROS/TKH DN11 ...67 E5
Aisthorpe Rd SHEFS S8 ...147 D2
Aitken Rd MEX/SWTN S64 ...81 E3
Aizlewood Rd SHEFS S8 ...135 D3 🔲
Akley Bank CI TOT/DORE S17 ...157 D3
Alba CI WMB/DAR S73 ...25 F4
Albanus Rdg ST/HB/BR S6 ...118 C1
Albany Av CHPT/GREN S35 ...88 C2
Albany CI WMB/DAR S73 ...24 B4

Albany Rd ABRD S7 ...135 D3
  DONS/BSCR DN4 ...43 E4
  MEX/SWTN S64 ...81 E2
  STKB/PEN S36 ...68 C2
Albany St RHAM/THRY S65 ...7 F6
Albert Av STV/CWN S43 ...179 E3
Albert Rd DEARNE S63 ...55 E1
  HACK/IN S12 ...151 F2
  MEX/SWTN S64 ...58 B3
  RAW S62 ...94 A2
  SHEFS S8 ...135 E4
  STV/CWN S43 ...179 E3
Albert St BSLY S70 ...2 D5
  DEARNE S63 ...26 C5
  ECK/KIL S21 ...174 B1
  MEX/SWTN S64 ...57 E4
  RHAM S60 ...6 A5
Albert Terrace Rd ST/HB/BR S6 ...8 A2
Albion Dr DEARNE S63 ...27 F3
Albion Rd CHSW S40 ...10 D5
  RHAM/THRY S65 ...7 E6
Albion St ST/HB/BR S6 ...121 F3
Albion Ter DONS/BSCR DN4 ...43 F5
Alcester Rd ABRD S7 ...135 D3 🔲
Aldam CI RHAM/THRY S65 ...105 E2
  TOT/DORE S17 ...156 C4 🔲
Aldam Cft TOT/DORE S17 ...156 C4
Aldam Rd DONS/BSCR DN4 ...62 C1
  TOT/DORE S17 ...156 C4
Aldam Wy TOT/DORE S17 ...156 C4 🔲
Aldbury CI BSLYN/ROY S71 ...14 C1
Aldcliffe Crs DONS/BSCR DN4 ...63 D3
Aldene Av ST/HB/BR S6 ...107 D3
Aldene CI ST/HB/BR S6 ...107 D3
Aldene Rd ST/HB/BR S6 ...107 D2
Alder Gv DONS/BSCR DN4 ...43 E5
  WMB/DAR S73 ...40 A1
Alder La DARN/MH S9 ...125 F4
Alder Ms HOY S74 ...51 F3 🔲
Alderney Rd SHEFP/MNR S2 ...135 E3 🔲
Alderson Av RAW S62 ...80 A5
Alderson Dr BSLYN/ROY S71 ...14 B1
  WHHL DN2 ...45 D1
Alderson PI SHEFP/MNR S2 ...135 E2
Alderson Rd SHEFP/MNR S2 ...135 D2
Alderson Rd North
  SHEFP/MNR S2 ...135 E2 🔲
Aldervale CI MEX/SWTN S64 ...81 E3
Aldesworth Rd DONS/BSCR DN4 ...46 C3
Aldfield Wy SHEFN S5 ...109 F5
Aldham Crs WMB/DAR S73 ...24 B4
Aldham House La WMB/DAR S73 ...24 C2
Aldred CI ECK/KIL S21 ...154 C5
Aldred Ct RHAM/THRY S65 ...103 F4 🔲

Aldred Rd *FUL* S10 ... 121 D2
Aldred St *RHAM/THRY* S65 ... 103 F4
Aldwarke La *RHAM/THRY* S65 ... 94 B4
  RHAM/THRY S65 ... 105 D2
Aldwarke Rd *RAW* S62 ... 94 A3
Alexander St *BTLY* DN5 ... 16 C5
Alexandra Cl *KIMB* S61 ... 101 F1
Alexandra Rd *AU/AST/KP* S26 ... 142 A2
  BTLY DN5 ... 16 C5
  DONS/BSCR DN4 ... 43 F4
  DRON S18 ... 169 F1
  MEX/SWTN S64 ... 58 C3
  SHEFP/MNR S2 ... 135 E3
Alexandra Rd East *CHNE* S41 ... 191 D3
Alexandra Rd West *CHSW* S40 ... 10 C5
Alexandra St *BSLYN/ROY* S71 ... 24 A2
Alford Cl *CHSW* S40 ... 189 D1
Alfred Rd *DARN/MH* S9 ... 111 D5
Algar Cl *SHEFP/MNR* S2 ... 136 C3
Algar Dr *SHEFP/MNR* S2 ... 137 D3
Algar Dr *SHEFP/MNR* S2 ... 136 C3
Algar Pl *SHEFP/MNR* S2 ... 136 C3
Algar Rd *SHEFP/MNR* S2 ... 136 C3
Alice Rd *KIMB* S61 ... 102 C2
Alice Wy *DRON* S18 ... 177 F1
Alison Cl *AU/AST/KP* S26 ... 142 B3
Alison Crs *SHEFP/MNR* S2 ... 137 F1
Alison Dr *AU/AST/KP* S26 ... 142 B3
Allan St *RHAM/THRY* S65 ... 7 F6
Allatt Cl *BSLY* S70 ... 22 A2
Alldred Crs *MEX/SWTN* S64 ... 81 D2
Allenby Cl *SHEFS* S8 ... 158 C1
Allenby Dr *SHEFS* S8 ... 158 C1
Allendale *BSLY* S70 ... 23 D5
Allendale Gdns *BTLY* DN5 ... 43 D1
Allendale Rd *BTLY* DN5 ... 43 D1
  DOD/DAR S75 ... 13 F3
  HOY S74 ... 51 E3
  RHAM/THRY S65 ... 105 D5
Allende Wy *DARN/MH* S9 ... 124 C1
Allen Rd *MOS* S20 ... 153 D3
Allen St *OWL* S3 ... 8 C3
Allerton St *DON* DN1 ... 5 E2
Allestree Dr *DRON* S18 ... 168 A2
Alliance St *ATT* S4 ... 123 E1
Allott Crs *HOY* S74 ... 52 B1
Allott St *HOY* S74 ... 50 C3
  HOY S74 ... 52 B3
All Saints Wy *AU/AST/KP* S26 ... 142 C3
Allsops Pl *CHNE* S41 ... 184 A1
Allt St *RAW* S62 ... 94 A2
Alma Crs *DRON* S18 ... 159 E5
Alma Rd *CHPT/GREN* S35 ... 73 E4
  RHAM S60 ... 103 E4
Alma Rw *RHAM* S60 ... 116 A3
Alma St *BSLY* S70 ... 2 A5
  OWL S3 ... 8 D2
  WMB/DAR S73 ... 39 E3
Almholme La *BTLY* DN5 ... 18 A1
Almond Av *ARMTH* DN3 ... 33 F2
Almond Dr *ECK/KIL* S21 ... 166 A3
Almond Rd *DONS/BSCR* DN4 ... 47 D4
Almond Tree Rd *AU/AST/KP* S26 ... 155 D3
Almshill Crs *ECC* S11 ... 145 D2
Almshill Dr *ECC* S11 ... 145 D2
Almshill Gld *ECC* S11 ... 145 D2
Alms Hill Rd *ECC* S11 ... 145 D2
Alney Rd *ST/HB/BR* S6 ... 97 E5
Alnwick Dr *HACK/IN* S12 ... 138 A5
Alnwick Rd *HACK/IN* S12 ... 137 F5
Alpha Rd *RHAM/THRY* S65 ... 104 C2
Alpine Cl *STKB/PEN* S36 ... 68 B2
Alpine Gv *STV/CWN* S43 ... 180 B5
Alpine Rd *ST/HB/BR* S6 ... 121 E2
  STKB/PEN S36 ... 68 B2
Alport Av *HACK/IN* S12 ... 150 C1
Alport Cl *HACK/IN* S12 ... 138 C5
Alport Dr *HACK/IN* S12 ... 138 C5
Alport Pl *HACK/IN* S12 ... 150 C1
Alport Ri *DRON* S18 ... 168 B1
Alport Rd *HACK/IN* S12 ... 138 C5
Alric Dr *BSLYN/ROY* S71 ... 23 F1
  RHAM S60 ... 113 F3
Alsing Rd *DARN/MH* S9 ... 112 A1
Alston Cl *DONS/BSCR* DN4 ... 46 B5
Alston Rd *DONS/BSCR* DN4 ... 66 B2
Alton Cl *CHSW* S40 ... 188 C4
  DRON S18 ... 168 B3
  ECC S11 ... 145 E3
Alum Chine Cl *CHNE* S41 ... 191 D4
Alverley La *DONS/BSCR* DN4 ... 63 E3
Alwyn Av *BTLY* DN5 ... 28 C2
Amber Crs *CHSW* S40 ... 189 D3
Amber Cft *STV/CWN* S43 ... 187 D2
Amberley St *DARN/MH* S9 ... 111 E4
Ambler Ri *AU/AST/KP* S26 ... 142 A1
Ambleside Cl *CHNE* S41 ... 183 D2
  MOS S20 ... 164 C2
  RHAM S60 ... 113 E3
Ambleside Gv *BSLYN/ROY* S71 ... 24 B2
Amen Cnr *RHAM* S60 ... 6 C4
America La *DEARNE* S63 ... 55 D5
Amersall Crs *BTLY* DN5 ... 28 C1
Amersall Rd *BTLY* DN5 ... 28 C1
Amesbury Cl *CHNE* S41 ... 183 F2

Amos Rd *DARN/MH* S9 ... 111 F2
Amy Rd *BTLY* DN5 ... 17 D3
Anchorage Crs *BTLY* DN5 ... 29 E5
Anchorage La *BTLY* DN5 ... 29 D5
Ancote Cl *DOD/DAR* S75 ... 20 B1
Anderson Cl *STV/CWN* S43 ... 179 F3
Andover Dr *OWL* S3 ... 122 B1
Andover St *OWL* S3 ... 122 B1
Andrew La *OWL* S3 ... 9 G2
Andrews Pl *KIMB* S61 ... 102 B1
Andrew St *OWL* S3 ... 9 G2
Andwell La *FUL* S10 ... 130 C5
Anelay Rd *DONS/BSCR* DN4 ... 43 D5
Anfield Rd *DONS/BSCR* DN4 ... 46 C5
Angel La *RAW* S62 ... 78 A2
Angel St *SHEF* S1 ... 9 F4
Angel Yd *CHSW* S40 ... 11 E6
Angerford Av *SHEFS* S8 ... 147 E1
Angleton Av *SHEFP/MNR* S2 ... 138 A2
Angleton Cl *SHEFP/MNR* S2 ... 138 A2
Angleton Gdns *SHEFP/MNR* S2 ... 138 A2
Angleton Gn *SHEFP/MNR* S2 ... 138 A2
Angleton Ms *SHEFP/MNR* S2 ... 138 A2
Angram Rd *CHPT/GREN* S35 ... 73 E3
Annat Pl *CHPT/GREN* S35 ... 73 D4
Annesley Cl *CHNE* S41 ... 191 D4
  SHEFS S8 ... 159 D1
Annesley Rd *SHEFS* S8 ... 147 D5
Anns Rd *SHEFP/MNR* S2 ... 135 E3
Anns Rd North *SHEFP/MNR* S2 ... 135 F3
Ann St *RAW* S62 ... 94 A3
Ansdell Rd *BTLY* DN5 ... 16 C4
Ansell Rd *ECC* S11 ... 133 E4
Anson Gv *RHAM* S60 ... 114 B4
Anson St *SHEFP/MNR* S2 ... 9 H5
Ansten Crs *DONS/BSCR* DN4 ... 46 C5
Antrim Av *FUL* S10 ... 121 E5
Anvil Cl *ST/HB/BR* S6 ... 119 F1
Anvil Crs *CHPT/GREN* S35 ... 98 C1
Apley Rd *DON* DN1 ... 5 F6
Apollo St *RAW* S62 ... 80 C4
Apostle Cl *DONS/BSCR* DN4 ... 62 C1
Appleby Rd *WHHL* DN2 ... 32 A5
Applegarth Cl *HAN/WDH* S13 ... 137 F4
Applegarth Dr *HACK/IN* S12 ... 137 E4
Applehurst Bank *BSLY* S70 ... 22 C2
Appleton Wy *BSLY* S70 ... 22 B5
  BTLY DN5 ... 29 E1
Appletree Dr *DRON* S18 ... 169 E2
April Cl *BSLYN/ROY* S71 ... 15 D3
April Dr *BSLYN/ROY* S71 ... 15 E3
Aqueduct St *BSLYN/ROY* S71 ... 2 D1
Arbourthorne Rd *SHEFP/MNR* S2 ... 136 C4
Archdale Cl *SHEFP/MNR* S2 ... 137 F2
Archdale Pl *SHEFP/MNR* S2 ... 137 E2
Archdale Rd *SHEFP/MNR* S2 ... 137 E1
Archer Ga *ST/HB/BR* S6 ... 106 B3
Archer La *ABRD* S7 ... 134 B5
Archer Rd *SHEFS* S8 ... 146 B2
Archery Cl *MALT* S66 ... 117 F1
Archibald St *ABRD* S7 ... 134 C4
Arcon Pl *RAW* S62 ... 80 B5
Arcubus Av *AU/AST/KP* S26 ... 142 B2
Ardeen Rd *WHHL* DN2 ... 31 E5
Arden Cl *CHSW* S40 ... 183 D5
Arden Ga *DONS/BSCR* DN4 ... 63 D3
Ardmore St *DARN/MH* S9 ... 124 B2
Ardsley Av *AU/AST/KP* S26 ... 142 C4
Ardsley Cl *MOS* S20 ... 151 D3
Ardsley Dr *MOS* S20 ... 151 D3
Ardsley Gv *MOS* S20 ... 151 D3
Ardsley Rd *BSLY* S70 ... 23 D5
  CHSW S40 ... 188 C1
Argyle Rd *SHEFS* S8 ... 135 C5
Argyle St *MEX/SWTN* S64 ... 58 B3
Argyll Av *WHHL* DN2 ... 31 F4
Arklow Cl *CHNE* S41 ... 190 C4
Arklow Rd *WHHL* DN2 ... 31 E5
Arksey Common La *BTLY* DN5 ... 17 F4
Arksey La *BTLY* DN5 ... 16 D5
Arkwright Rd *BTLY* DN5 ... 29 D5
Arley St *SHEFP/MNR* S2 ... 135 E1
Arlington Av *AU/AST/KP* S26 ... 143 E1
Arlott Wy *CONI* DN12 ... 62 A4
Armer St *RHAM* S60 ... 6 A6
Armitage Rd *DONS/BSCR* DN4 ... 43 D5
  STKB/PEN S36 ... 69 E3
Armley Rd *DARN/MH* S9 ... 111 E4
Armroyd La *HOY* S74 ... 52 A4
Arms Park Dr *MOS* S20 ... 165 D2
Armstead Rd *MOS* S20 ... 153 D2
Armthorpe La *WHHL* DN2 ... 31 E4
Armthorpe Rd *ECC* S11 ... 133 D2
  WHHL DN2 ... 31 E4
Armyne Gv *BSLYN/ROY* S71 ... 23 F1
Arncliffe Dr *BSLY* S70 ... 20 C1
  CHPT/GREN S35 ... 88 A1
Arnold Av *HACK/IN* S12 ... 149 F4
Arnold Crs *MEX/SWTN* S64 ... 58 B2
Arnold Rd *RHAM/THRY* S65 ... 104 C3
Arnold St *ST/HB/BR* S6 ... 121 D1
Arnside Cl *CHNE* S41 ... 177 E5
Arnside Rd *SHEFS* S8 ... 134 C5
Arran Rd *FUL* S10 ... 120 C4

Arras St *DARN/MH* S9 ... 124 A2
Arthington St *SHEFS* S8 ... 135 E4
Arthur Av *BTLY* DN5 ... 16 C4
Arthur Pl *BTLY* DN5 ... 16 C4
Arthur Rd *STKB/PEN* S36 ... 68 B2
Arthur St *BSLY* S70 ... 22 B5
  BTLY DN5 ... 16 C3
  RAW S62 ... 80 B4
Artisan Vw *SHEFS* S8 ... 135 E4
Arundel Av *RHAM* S60 ... 127 F3
  RHAM/THRY S65 ... 95 E5
Arundel Cl *CHNE* S41 ... 184 A1
  DRON S18 ... 168 B2
Arundel Cottages *RHAM* S60 ... 127 F3
Arundel Crs *RHAM* S60 ... 127 E3
Arundel Gdns *BTLY* DN5 ... 29 D1
Arundel Ga *SHEF* S1 ... 9 F5
  SHEF S1 ... 9 F6
Arundel La *SHEF* S1 ... 122 C5
Arundel Rd *CHPT/GREN* S35 ... 74 B5
  RHAM S60 ... 127 F3
  RHAM/THRY S65 ... 104 A4
Arundel St *RHAM* S60 ... 127 E3
  SHEF S1 ... 122 B5
Arundel Vw *HOY* S74 ... 52 B1
Ascot Av *DONS/BSCR* DN4 ... 46 B3
Ascot Cl *MEX/SWTN* S64 ... 58 C2
Ascot Dr *BTLY* DN5 ... 28 B3
Ascot St *SHEFP/MNR* S2 ... 135 E1
Ashberry Cl *DEARNE* S63 ... 27 D3
Ashberry Rd *ST/HB/BR* S6 ... 121 E2
Ashbourne Cl *CHSW* S40 ... 182 B4
Ashbourne Gv *HAN/WDH* S13 ... 139 D1
Ashbourne Rd *HAN/WDH* S13 ... 139 D1
Ashburnham Gdns *BTLY* DN5 ... 42 C1
Ashbury Dr *SHEFS* S8 ... 148 A3
Ashbury La *SHEFS* S8 ... 148 A3
Ashby Ct *BSLY* S70 ... 21 E2
Ash Cl *ECK/KIL* S21 ... 166 E5
  RHAM/THRY S65 ... 105 E5
Ash Ct *BTLY* DN5 ... 42 B3
Ash Crs *ECK/KIL* S21 ... 173 F2
  MEX/SWTN S64 ... 57 F2
Ashcroft Dr *CHNE* S41 ... 178 C4
Ashdell *ECC* S11 ... 121 D5
Ashdell La *ECC* S11 ... 121 D5
Ashdell Rd *ECC* S11 ... 121 D5
Ashdene Ct *MEX/SWTN* S64 ... 81 E3
Ashdown Dr *CHSW* S40 ... 189 E3
Ashdown Gdns *MOS* S20 ... 153 E2
Ashdown Pl *BTLY* DN5 ... 28 C1
Asher Rd *ABRD* S7 ... 135 D2
Ashes La *RAW* S62 ... 76 A3
Ashfield Cl *DOD/DAR* S75 ... 13 D4
  HACK/IN S12 ... 149 D1
Ashfield Dr *HACK/IN* S12 ... 149 D1
Ashfield Rd *CHNE* S41 ... 191 E4
  DONS/BSCR DN4 ... 63 E1
  STKB/PEN S36 ... 69 E2
Ashford Rd *DRON* S18 ... 168 B3
  ECC S11 ... 134 B2
Ashfurlong Cl *TOT/DORE* S17 ... 157 D1
Ashfurlong Dr *TOT/DORE* S17 ... 157 D1
Ashfurlong Pk *TOT/DORE* S17 ... 157 D1
Ashfurlong Rd *TOT/DORE* S17 ... 156 C1
Ashgate Av *CHSW* S40 ... 189 D1
Ashgate Cl *ECC* S11 ... 121 D5
Ashgate La *FUL* S10 ... 121 D5
Ashgate Rd *CHSW* S40 ... 10 A4
  ECC S11 ... 121 D5
Ashgate Valley Rd *CHSW* S40 ... 183 E5
Ash Gv *BSLY* S70 ... 23 E3
  CONI DN12 ... 84 B2
  FUL S10 ... 121 E5
  RAW S62 ... 94 B1
Ash House La *TOT/DORE* S17 ... 144 B4
Ashland Rd *ABRD* S7 ... 134 C5
  ECK/KIL S21 ... 164 C5
Ash La *DRON* S18 ... 166 E5
  ECK/KIL S21 ... 172 A3
  STKB/PEN S36 ... 69 F2
Ashleigh Av *HACK/IN* S12 ... 137 D5
Ashleigh Ct *ECK/KIL* S21 ... 174 A2
Ashleigh Cft *HACK/IN* S12 ... 137 D5
Ashleigh Dr *HACK/IN* S12 ... 137 D5
Ashleigh Pl *HACK/IN* S12 ... 137 D5
Ashley Cl *ECK/KIL* S21 ... 166 B2
Ashley Gv *AU/AST/KP* S26 ... 142 B3
Ashley La *ECK/KIL* S21 ... 166 B2
Ashmore Av *ECK/KIL* S21 ... 173 F1
Ashover Cl *BSLY* S70 ... 36 B1
Ashover Rd *STV/CWN* S43 ... 187 D3
Ashpool Cl *HAN/WDH* S13 ... 139 E4
Ash Rdg *MEX/SWTN* S64 ... 81 E1
Ash Rd *DEARNE* S63 ... 56 A3
Ash St *MOS* S20 ... 164 A1
  ST/HB/BR S6 ... 121 F1
  WMB/DAR S73 ... 24 B4
Ashton Cl *CHSW* S40 ... 189 D4
  ECK/KIL S21 ... 166 A2
Ashton Dr *ARMTH* DN3 ... 19 F2
Ash Tree Cl *CHSW* S40 ... 189 D1
Ashurst Cl *RCH* S42 ... 182 A4
  ST/HB/BR S6 ... 106 C5
Ashurst Dr *ST/HB/BR* S6 ... 106 C5

Ashurst Pl *ST/HB/BR* S6 .... 106 C5
Ashurst Rd *ST/HB/BR* S6 .... 106 C5
Ash V *CHSW* S40 .... 188 C1
Ash Vw *CHPT/GREN* S35 .... 88 A2
  KIMB S61 .... 92 C3
Ashwell Rd *HAN/WDH* S13 .... 139 E4
Ashwood Cl *BSLY* S70 .... 36 C1 🔢
  CHPT/GREN S35 .... 73 D3
Ashwood Rd *CHPT/GREN* S35 .... 73 D3
  RAW S62 .... 94 A2
Ashworth Dr *KIMB* S61 .... 91 E4
Askern Rd *BTLY* DN5 .... 16 B2
Askew Ct *STKB/PEN* S36 .... 69 D3
Askrigg Cl *DONS/BSCR* DN4 .... 47 D5 🔢
Asline Rd *RHAM/THRY* S2 .... 135 E2
Aspen Cl *ECK/KIL* S21 .... 166 A2
Aspen Gv *WMB/DAR* S73 .... 40 B1
Aspen Rd *ECK/KIL* S21 .... 173 F2
Aspen Wy *MEX/SWTN* S64 .... 81 D3
Aspley Cl *CHSW* S40 .... 10 A3
Asquith Rd *DN5* 16 C5
  DARN/MH S9 .... 100 C5 🔢
Aster Cl *SHEFP/MNR* S2 .... 153 D2
Aston Cl *DRON* S18 .... 160 A5
Aston Dr *BSLYN/ROY* S71 .... 14 B1
Aston La *AU/AST/KP* S26 .... 129 E5
Aston St *SHEFP/MNR* S2 .... 123 E3
Astwell Gdns *CHPT/GREN* S35 .... 73 F5 🔢
Athelstan Cl *HAN/WDH* S13 .... 138 C1
Athelstan Rd *CONI* DN12 .... 84 C1
Athelstan Rd *HAN/WDH* S13 .... 138 C1
Athersley Cs *BSLYN/ROY* S71 .... 14 B1
Athersley Gdns *MOS* S20 .... 151 E3
Athersley Rd *BSLYN/ROY* S71 .... 14 B1
Atherton Cl *SHEFP/MNR* S2 .... 137 D3
Atherton Rd *SHEFP/MNR* S2 .... 137 D3
Athol Cl *CHSW* S40 .... 188 C4 🔢
Atholl Crs *WHHL* DN2 .... 32 A4
Athol Rd *SHEFS* S8 .... 146 C1
Athron Dr *RHAM/THRY* S65 .... 105 D5
Athron St *DON* DN1 .... 5 F1 🔢
Atkin Pl *SHEFP/MNR* S2 .... 135 E2 🔢
Atlantic Dr *SHEFS* S8 .... 158 C2
Atlantic Rd *SHEFS* S8 .... 158 B2
Atlantic Wy *SHEFS* S8 .... 158 C2
Atlas St *ATT* S4 .... 123 E1
  RHAM S60 .... 114 A3
Atlas Wy *ATT* S4 .... 110 C5
Atlow Cl *CHSW* S40 .... 182 C4
Attenborough Rd *NROS/TKH* DN11 .... 67 E5
Attercliffe Common *DARN/MH* S9 .... 111 E5
Attercliffe Rd *DARN/MH* S9 .... 124 A1
Attlee Rd *STV/CWN* S43 .... 186 C2
Aubretia Av *RHAM* S60 .... 114 B5
Auckland Av *ST/HB/BR* S6 .... 106 C4
Auckland Dr *MOS* S20 .... 164 B2
Auckland Ri *MOS* S20 .... 164 C2
Auckland Rd *DON* DN1 .... 30 C4
  MEX/SWTN S64 .... 58 C3
Auckland Wy *MOS* S20 .... 164 C2
Audrey Rd *HAN/WDH* S13 .... 138 A3
Aughton Av *AU/AST/KP* S26 .... 142 A1
Aughton Cl *HAN/WDH* S13 .... 138 B3
Aughton Crs *HAN/WDH* S13 .... 138 B3
Aughton Dr *HAN/WDH* S13 .... 138 A2 🔢
Aughton Rd *AU/AST/KP* S26 .... 142 A2
Augustus Rd *RHAM* S60 .... 114 A2 🔢
Aukley Rd *SHEFS* S8 .... 135 D5
Aunby Dr *AU/AST/KP* S26 .... 142 B2 🔢
Austen Av *DONS/BSCR* DN4 .... 62 C1
Austin Cl *ST/HB/BR* S6 .... 106 C4
Austin Ct *ST/HB/BR* S6 .... 106 C3
Austwick Cl *DONS/BSCR* DN4 .... 63 D3
Avenue 1 *CHNE* S41 .... 190 C4 🔢
Avenue 2 *CHNE* S41 .... 190 C4 🔢
Avenue 3 *CHNE* S41 .... 190 C4 🔢
Avenue 4 *CHNE* S41 .... 190 C4 🔢
Avenue 5 *CHNE* S41 .... 190 C4 🔢
Avenue 6 *CHNE* S41 .... 190 C4 🔢
Avenue Cl *CHNE* S41 .... 184 B1
  DEARNE S63 .... 56 B2
  WHHL DN2 .... 30 C4
The Avenue *BTLY* DN5 .... 17 D5
  DARN/MH S9 .... 125 D3 🔢
  DOD/DAR S75 .... 49 E2
  DONS/BSCR DN4 .... 46 A3
  DRON S18 .... 169 F1
  MOS S20 .... 153 D1
Aviemore Cl *STV/CWN* S43 .... 179 F2
Aviemore Rd *DONS/BSCR* DN4 .... 62 C1
Avill Wy *MALT* S66 .... 117 F1
Avisford Dr *SHEFN* S5 .... 108 B1
Avisford Rd *SHEFN* S5 .... 97 E5
Avoca Av *WHHL* DN2 .... 31 E5
Avocet Wy *KIMB* S61 .... 76 A5
Avon Cl *DRON* S18 .... 159 F5
  WMB/DAR S73 .... 40 A4
Avondale Rd *CHSW* S40 .... 10 C4
  KIMB S61 .... 102 B2
  ST/HB/BR S6 .... 107 F4 🔢
  STV/CWN S43 .... 187 D2
  WHHL DN2 .... 45 E1
Avon Gv *CHPT/GREN* S35 .... 73 F5
Avon Mt *KIMB* S61 .... 102 B2
Avon St *BSLYN/ROY* S71 .... 3 F6
Axholme Rd *WHHL* DN2 .... 30 C4
Aylesbury Crs *DARN/MH* S9 .... 111 F1
Aylesbury Rd *WHHL* DN2 .... 31 F5
Aylesford Cl *BSLYN/ROY* S71 .... 2 D1
Aylsham Dr *AU/AST/KP* S26 .... 142 C3 🔢
Aylward Cl *SHEFP/MNR* S2 .... 137 D3
Aylward Rd *SHEFP/MNR* S2 .... 137 D3
Aysgarth Av *BSLYN/ROY* S71 .... 24 C2
Aysgarth Ri *AU/AST/KP* S26 .... 142 A2
Aysgarth Rd *ST/HB/BR* S6 .... 97 D5
Ayton Wk *BTLY* DN5 .... 16 B4 🔢

B

Babington Cl *SHEFP/MNR* S2 .... 137 D3
Babington Ct *SHEFP/MNR* S2 .... 137 D3 🔢
Babur Rd *ATT* S4 .... 123 E1 🔢
Backfield Ri *CHPT/GREN* S35 .... 74 B5
Backfields *SHEF* S1 .... 8 D6
Back La *BSLYN/ROY* S71 .... 15 D2
  BTLY DN5 .... 28 A4
  DRON S18 .... 171 D2
  ECK/KIL S21 .... 164 A5
  FUL S10 .... 120 A3
  RAW S62 .... 79 D5
  RHAM/THRY S65 .... 83 E5
Backmoor Crs *SHEFS* S8 .... 148 A3
Backmoor Rd *SHEFS* S8 .... 148 A3
Back Rd *DRON* S18 .... 171 D2
Back South St *STV/CWN* S43 .... 179 E3 🔢
Back St *HAN/WDH* S13 .... 140 A4
Bacon La *DARN/MH* S9 .... 123 F2
Bacons La *CHSW* S40 .... 190 B4
Baden Powell Av *CHSW* S40 .... 190 A3
Baden Powell Rd *CHSW* S40 .... 190 B2
Baden St *BSLY* S70 .... 36 C1
  RHAM S60 .... 6 B3
Badger Cl *HAN/WDH* S13 .... 140 A3
Badger Dr *HAN/WDH* S13 .... 140 A3
Badger La *SHEF* S1 .... 8 C5
Badger Pl *HAN/WDH* S13 .... 140 A3
Badger Ri *HAN/WDH* S13 .... 140 A3
Badsley Ct *RHAM/THRY* S65 .... 7 H6 🔢
  RHAM/THRY S65 .... 104 B3 🔢
Badsley Moor La *RHAM/THRY* S65 .... 104 A4
Badsley St *RHAM/THRY* S65 .... 7 G6
Badsley St South
  RHAM/THRY S65 .... 104 A4
Badsworth Cl *WMB/DAR* S73 .... 40 A3 🔢
Badsworth Rd *DONS/BSCR* DN4 .... 62 A2
Bagley Rd *ATT* S4 .... 110 B3
Bagshaw's La *HACK/IN* S12 .... 137 F4 🔢
Bagshot St *ECC* S11 .... 134 B2
Bahram Rd *DONS/BSCR* DN4 .... 46 A4 🔢
Bailey Cl *ECK/KIL* S21 .... 154 C5
Bailey La *SHEF* S1 .... 8 C5
Bailey St *SHEF* S1 .... 8 C5
Bainbridge Rd *DONS/BSCR* DN4 .... 44 A3 🔢
Baines Wood Cl *CHNE* S41 .... 183 D1
Bainton Dr *BSLY* S70 .... 21 E3
Bakehouse La *DOD/DAR* S75 .... 12 B4
Baker Dr *ECK/KIL* S21 .... 166 A2
Bakers Hl *SHEF* S1 .... 9 F5
Bakers La *SHEF* S1 .... 8 C4
Baker St *DARN/MH* S9 .... 124 A1
Bakewell Rd *BSLYN/ROY* S71 .... 14 B1
  STV/CWN S43 .... 187 D4
Bala St *BSLYN/ROY* S71 .... 3 E5
Balby Carr Bank *DONS/BSCR* DN4 .... 44 B5
Balby Rd *DONS/BSCR* DN4 .... 43 F4
Baldwin St *DARN/MH* S9 .... 123 F2 🔢
Balfour Dr *DARN/MH* S9 .... 124 C2
Balfour Rd *BTLY* DN5 .... 17 D5
  DARN/MH S9 .... 124 C2
Balk La *BSLY* S70 .... 35 F4
  RHAM S60 .... 113 G2
Balldon Cl *CHSW* S40 .... 183 D5 🔢
Ballfield Av *HAN/WDH* S13 .... 139 E1
Ballfield Cl *HAN/WDH* S13 .... 139 E1
Ballfield Crs *HAN/WDH* S13 .... 139 F1
Ballfield Dr *HAN/WDH* S13 .... 139 F1
Ballfield Pl *HAN/WDH* S13 .... 139 E1
Ballfield Ri *HAN/WDH* S13 .... 139 F1
Ballfield Rd *HAN/WDH* S13 .... 139 E1
Ballfield Wy *HAN/WDH* S13 .... 139 E1
Ball Rd *ST/HB/BR* S6 .... 107 F5
Ball St *OWL* S3 .... 8 C2
Balmain Dr *ST/HB/BR* S6 .... 107 F3
Balmain Rd *ST/HB/BR* S6 .... 107 F3
Balm Gn *SHEF* S1 .... 8 D5
Balmoak La *CHNE* S41 .... 185 D4
Balmoral Crs *DRON* S18 .... 168 B1
Balmoral Rd *HAN/WDH* S13 .... 140 A4
Balmoral Wy *STV/CWN* S43 .... 179 F2
Baltic Rd *DARN/MH* S9 .... 124 A1
Bamford Av *BSLYN/ROY* S71 .... 14 B1
Bamford Cl *STV/CWN* S43 .... 187 D3
Bamford St *STV/CWN* S43 .... 179 E2 🔢
Bamforth St *ST/HB/BR* S6 .... 108 B5
Bank Cl *ABRD* S7 .... 134 C4
  KIMB S61 .... 92 A5
Bank End Av *BSLY* S70 .... 23 D5
Bank End Rd *BSLY* S70 .... 22 C5
Bankfield La *ST/HB/BR* S6 .... 119 D1 🔢
Bankfield Rd *ST/HB/BR* S6 .... 107 E5
Bank House Rd *FUL* S10 .... 121 D2 🔢
Banka La *CHPT/GREN* S35 .... 71 F4
Bank Rd *CHNE* S41 .... 184 B3 🔢
Bank St *BSLY* S70 .... 22 A3
  BSLYN/ROY S71 .... 10 B6
  CHSW S40 .... 10 B6
  HOY S74 .... 51 E3
  MEX/SWTN S64 .... 58 B4
  SHEF S1 .... 9 F4
  STV/CWN S43 .... 185 E1
Bank Top Rd *RHAM/THRY* S65 .... 105 E5
Bank Vw *RHAM* S60 .... 115 F3
Bank Wood Cl *CHSW* S40 .... 182 C2
Bankwood Cl *SHEFS* S8 .... 136 B5
Bankwood Crs *NROS/TKH* DN11 .... 66 B5
Bankwood La *NROS/TKH* DN11 .... 66 B4
Bankwood Rd *SHEFP/MNR* S2 .... 136 B5
Banner Ct *ECC* S11 .... 133 F4
Banner Cross Dr *ECC* S11 .... 133 F4 🔢
Bannerdale Cl *ECC* S11 .... 134 A1 🔢
Bannerdale Rd *ECC* S11 .... 134 A4
Bannerdale Vw *ECC* S11 .... 134 A4
Bannham Rd *DARN/MH* S9 .... 125 E3
Barber Balk Cl *KIMB* S61 .... 92 A5 🔢
Barber Balk Rd *KIMB* S61 .... 102 A1
Barber Crs *ST/HB/BR* S6 .... 121 E3 🔢
Barber Pl *FUL* S10 .... 121 E3 🔢
Barber Rd *FUL* S10 .... 121 E3
Barber's Av *RAW* S62 .... 94 A2
Barber's Crs *RAW* S62 .... 94 A1
Barber's La *ECK/KIL* S21 .... 154 B5
Barbers Pth *MEX/SWTN* S64 .... 58 A2
Barber St *HOY* S74 .... 51 F2
Barber Wood Rd *KIMB* S61 .... 100 C3
Barbon Cl *CHSW* S40 .... 10 A1
Barbot Hill Rd *KIMB* S61 .... 93 D4
Bar Cft *CHSW* S40 .... 183 E5 🔢
Barcroft *DOD/DAR* S75 .... 12 B3 🔢
Barden Crs *RHAM* S60 .... 114 A4
Barden Dr *DOD/DAR* S75 .... 12 C4
Bardolf Rd *DONS/BSCR* DN4 .... 46 C3
Bard St *SHEFP/MNR* S2 .... 9 H4
Bardwell Rd *OWL* S3 .... 122 A1
Barfield Av *RHAM* S60 .... 115 E3
Barfield Rd *HOY* S74 .... 51 F2
Barholme Cl *CHNE* S41 .... 182 C2
Barholm Rd *FUL* S10 .... 120 A5
Bari Cl *WMB/DAR* S73 .... 25 F4
Baring Rd *KIMB* S61 .... 100 C3
Barkby Rd *DARN/MH* S9 .... 100 B5
Barker Fold *CHSW* S40 .... 189 E1 🔢
Barker La *CHSW* S40 .... 189 E1
Barker's Pl *ST/HB/BR* S6 .... 108 A3 🔢
Barker's Pool *SHEF* S1 .... 8 D6
Barker's Rd *ECC* S11 .... 134 B4
Barker St *MEX/SWTN* S64 .... 57 F3
Bark Mdw *DOD/DAR* S75 .... 20 B3
Barlborough Rd *BSLYN/ROY* S71 .... 15 D1
Barlborough Rd *WMB/DAR* S73 .... 39 F4
Barlby Gv *HACK/IN* S12 .... 152 A2
Barley La *CHSW* S40 .... 182 B4
Barley Ms *DRON* S18 .... 168 A2 🔢
Barley Vw *DEARNE* S63 .... 27 D4 🔢
Barleywood Rd *DARN/MH* S9 .... 125 D1
Barlow Dr *ST/HB/BR* S6 .... 120 B1
Barlow Lees La *DRON* S18 .... 169 D4
Barlow Rd *CHNE* S41 .... 176 A5
  ST/HB/BR S6 .... 107 E5
  STV/CWN S43 .... 181 F4 🔢
Barlow Vw *DRON* S18 .... 169 F4
Barmouth Rd *ABRD* S7 .... 134 C5
Barnard Av *DRON* S18 .... 160 B5
Barnardiston Rd *DARN/MH* S9 .... 124 C2
Barnby Dun Rd *WHHL* DN2 .... 32 A1
Barncliffe Cl *FUL* S10 .... 132 A2
Barncliffe Crs *FUL* S10 .... 131 F1
Barncliffe Dr *FUL* S10 .... 131 F1
Barncliffe Gln *FUL* S10 .... 131 F2
Barncliffe Rd *FUL* S10 .... 132 A2
Barn Cl *CHSW* S40 .... 183 D3
Barnes Av *DRON* S18 .... 168 B1
Barnes Ct *SHEFP/MNR* S2 .... 122 C5
Barnes Hall Rd *CHPT/GREN* S35 .... 87 E2
Barnes La *DRON* S18 .... 157 F4
  DRON S18 .... 158 B5
  DRON S18 .... 168 B1
Barnes Rd *CHNE* S41 .... 191 F3
Barnet Av *ECC* S11 .... 132 C5
Barnet Rd *ECC* S11 .... 132 C5
Barnfield Av *FUL* S10 .... 119 F4
Barnfield Cl *FUL* S10 .... 119 F5
  STV/CWN S43 .... 181 F4
Barnfield Dr *FUL* S10 .... 119 F5
Barnfield Rd *FUL* S10 .... 119 F5
Barnham Cl *CHSW* S40 .... 188 C4
Barnsdale Av *MOS* S20 .... 151 E3
Barnsley Av *CONI* DN12 .... 84 B1
Barnsley Boundary Wk
  CHPT/GREN S35 .... 70 B1
  CHPT/GREN S35 .... 86 A5
  HOY S74 .... 52 A4

WMB/DAR S73 .... 53 E1
Barnsley Rd ATT S4 .... 109 F4
  BTLY DN5 .... 28 A2
  DEARNE S63 .... 41 D5
  DEARNE S63 .... 55 E1
  DOD/DAR S75 .... 20 A2
  HOY S74 .... 37 E5
  KIMB S61 .... 75 F4
  OWL S3 .... 109 F5
  SHEFN S5 .... 99 D4
  WMB/DAR S73 .... 24 C5
  WMB/DAR S73 .... 39 D1
Barnstone St DONS/BSCR DN4 .... 43 E3
Barnwell Crs WMB/DAR S73 .... 24 C5
Baron St SHEFS S1 .... 135 E1
Barrack Rd DRON S18 .... 171 E2
Barratt Rd ECK/KIL S21 .... 174 B1
Barrel La DONS/BSCR DN4 .... 62 B1
Barret Rd DONS/BSCR DN4 .... 47 D3
Barretta St ATT S4 .... 110 B3
Barrie Crs SHEFN S5 .... 109 D1
Barrie Dr SHEFN S5 .... 109 D1
Barrie Rd DONS/BSCR DN4 .... 63 F1
  SHEFN S5 .... 109 D2
Barrowby Rd RHAM S60 .... 115 E1
Barrow Field La RAW S62 .... 76 B1
Barrowfield Rd DEARNE S63 .... 27 E4
  HOY S74 .... 51 E1
Barrow Hl RAW S62 .... 76 A2
Barrow Rd DARN/MH S9 .... 100 C5
  DARN/MH S9 .... 101 D5
Barry Rd STV/CWN S43 .... 186 A5
Bartholomew Cl RHAM S60 .... 116 B2
Bartholomew St WMB/DAR S73 .... 39 D2
Bartle Av HACK/IN S12 .... 149 D1
Bartle Dr HACK/IN S12 .... 149 D1
Bartle Rd HACK/IN S12 .... 149 D1
Bartlett Cl ST/HB/BR S6 .... 119 D2
Bartlett Rd SHEFN S5 .... 98 A5
Bartle Wy HACK/IN S12 .... 149 D1
Barton Crs CHSW S40 .... 182 B3
Barton La ARMTH DN3 .... 33 E3
Barton Pl CONI DN12 .... 84 C2
Barton Rd SHEFS S8 .... 135 E4
Basegreen Av HACK/IN S12 .... 149 F2
Basegreen Cl HACK/IN S12 .... 150 A2
Basegreen Crs HACK/IN S12 .... 149 F2
Basegreen Dr HACK/IN S12 .... 149 F2
Basegreen Rd HACK/IN S12 .... 149 F2
Basegreen Wy HACK/IN S12 .... 150 A3
Basford Cl DARN/MH S9 .... 124 C2
Basford Dr DARN/MH S9 .... 124 C2
Basford Ms DARN/MH S9 .... 125 D2
Basford Pl DARN/MH S9 .... 124 C2
Basford St DARN/MH S9 .... 124 C2
Basil Av ARMTH DN3 .... 32 C2
Basil Cl CHNE S41 .... 11 F4
Basildon Rd DEARNE S63 .... 26 C2
Baslow Rd TOT/DORE S17 .... 156 A4
Bassett La FUL S10 .... 130 C4
Bassett Pl SHEFP/MNR S2 .... 123 E5
Bassett Rd SHEFP/MNR S2 .... 123 F5
Bassingthorpe La KIMB S61 .... 92 C4
Bassledene Rd SHEFP/MNR S2 .... 137 E2
Bastock Rd ST/HB/BR S6 .... 108 B3
Bateman Cl STV/CWN S43 .... 179 E2
Batemoor Cl SHEFS S8 .... 159 E2
Batemoor Dr SHEFS S8 .... 159 E2
Batemoor Pl SHEFS S8 .... 159 E2
Batemoor Rd SHEFS S8 .... 159 E2
Batesquire Rd CHSW S40 .... 153 D5
Bate Wood Av STV/CWN S43 .... 186 C4
Bath St OWL S3 .... 122 A5
Battison La DEARNE S63 .... 55 E4
Batt St SHEFP/MNR S2 .... 135 E2
Batworth Dr ATT S4 .... 109 E4
Batworth Rd SHEFN S5 .... 109 E4
Baulk Farm Cl RAW S62 .... 92 C2
Bawtry Ga DARN/MH S9 .... 112 C2
Bawtry Rd DARN/MH S9 .... 113 D3
  DONS/BSCR DN4 .... 45 E2
  DONS/BSCR DN4 .... 67 D2
  RHAM S60 .... 113 F3
  RHAM/THRY S65 .... 105 F5
Baxter Av DON DN1 .... 5 G1
Baxter Cl ST/HB/BR S6 .... 97 D5
Baxter Dr ST/HB/BR S6 .... 97 D5
Baxter Ga DON DN1 .... 4 D3
Baxter Rd ST/HB/BR S6 .... 97 D5
Baycliff Dr CHSW S40 .... 189 D1
Bay Ct ECK/KIL S21 .... 166 A5
Baysdale Cft MOS S20 .... 164 B1
Beacon Cl DARN/MH S9 .... 111 D2
Beacon Cft DARN/MH S9 .... 111 D2
Beacon Rd DARN/MH S9 .... 111 D2
Beaconsfield Rd
  DONS/BSCR DN4 .... 43 E3
  RHAM S60 .... 115 E1
Beaconsfield St MEX/SWTN S64 .... 58 B3
Beacon Vw HOY S74 .... 52 B3
Beacon Wy DARN/MH S9 .... 111 D2
Beale Wy RAW S62 .... 94 A4
Bear Tree Cl RAW S62 .... 94 A2
Bear Tree Rd RAW S62 .... 94 A2

Bear Tree St RAW S62 .... 94 A3
Beauchamp Rd KIMB S61 .... 92 A5
Beauchief Abbey La SHEFS S8 .... 146 A5
Beauchief Cl STKB/PEN S36 .... 70 A3
Beauchief Dr SHEFS S8 .... 158 A1
Beauchief Ri SHEFS S8 .... 146 A4
Beaufort Rd FUL S10 .... 121 E4
  WHHL DN2 .... 31 F5
Beaumont Av BSLY S70 .... 20 C1
  SHEFP/MNR S2 .... 124 B5
Beaumont Cl SHEFP/MNR S2 .... 124 C5
Beaumont Crs SHEFP/MNR S2 .... 124 B5
Beaumont Dr RHAM/THRY S65 .... 104 C4
Beaumont Ms SHEFP/MNR S2 .... 137 F1
Beaumont Rd North
  SHEFP/MNR S2 .... 124 B5
Beaumont St HOY S74 .... 50 C3
Beaumont Wy SHEFP/MNR S2 .... 124 B5
Beaver Av HAN/WDH S13 .... 139 F2
Beaver Cl HAN/WDH S13 .... 139 F2
Beaver Dr HAN/WDH S13 .... 139 F2
Beaver Hill Rd HAN/WDH S13 .... 139 F2
Beck Cl MEX/SWTN S64 .... 81 E2
  SHEFN S5 .... 99 F2
Becket Crs KIMB S61 .... 91 E4
Becket Rd SHEFS S8 .... 158 C2
Beckett Rd DON DN1 .... 30 C4
  WHHL DN2 .... 31 G4
Becknoll Rd WMB/DAR S73 .... 40 B5
Beck Rd SHEFN S5 .... 99 E2
Beckton Av MOS S20 .... 152 C3
Beckton Cl MOS S20 .... 153 D3
Beckton Gv MOS S20 .... 152 C3
Beckwith Rd RHAM/THRY S65 .... 105 D2
Bedale Rd BTLY DN5 .... 28 B2
  SHEFS S8 .... 135 D4
Bedford St BSLY S70 .... 22 A3
  ST/HB/BR S6 .... 8 B1
Bedford Ter BSLYN/ROY S71 .... 14 B2
Bedgebury Cl MOS S20 .... 153 F4
Bedgrave Cl ECK/KIL S21 .... 155 D5
Beecham Cl MEX/SWTN S64 .... 81 D2
Beech Av RAW S62 .... 94 C1
  RHAM/THRY S65 .... 105 F5
Beech Cl WMB/DAR S73 .... 39 D5
Beech Crs ECK/KIL S21 .... 166 A3
  ECK/KIL S21 .... 173 F2
  MEX/SWTN S64 .... 57 G5
Beechcroft Rd DONS/BSCR DN4 .... 62 C2
Beechdale Cl CHSW S40 .... 183 E5
Beeches Dr SHEFP/MNR S2 .... 136 A2
Beeches Dr SHEFP/MNR S2 .... 136 A2
Beeches Gv MOS S20 .... 153 E2
Beeches Rd AU/AST/KP S26 .... 155 F2
The Beeches AU/AST/KP S26 .... 142 B5
  MEX/SWTN S64 .... 81 D1
Beechfern Cl CHPT/GREN S35 .... 73 E3
Beechfield Rd DON DN1 .... 5 F6
Beech Gv BSLY S70 .... 21 E3
  BTLY DN5 .... 29 F1
  CONI DN12 .... 84 C2
  DONS/BSCR DN4 .... 62 A1
Beech Hl CONI DN12 .... 85 D2
Beech Hill Rd FUL S10 .... 121 D5
Beech House Rd WMB/DAR S73 .... 39 E5
Beech Rd ARMTH DN3 .... 33 F2
  DEARNE S63 .... 56 B2
Beech St BSLY S70 .... 22 A2
  STV/CWN S43 .... 180 B5
Beech Tree Cl ARMTH DN3 .... 47 F3
Beechville Av MEX/SWTN S64 .... 81 D2
Beech Wy AU/AST/KP S26 .... 141 F2
Beechwood Cl DEARNE S63 .... 56 A5
  RAW S62 .... 81 D4
Beechwood Rd CHPT/GREN S35 .... 73 F5
  DRON S18 .... 169 D2
  RHAM/THRY S65 .... 104 B5
  ST/HB/BR S6 .... 107 F4
  STKB/PEN S36 .... 68 C3
Beehive Rd CHSW S40 .... 189 D2
  FUL S10 .... 121 E3
Beeley Cl STV/CWN S43 .... 187 D3
Beeley St SHEFP/MNR S2 .... 135 D1
Beeley Vw CHSW S40 .... 188 C5
Beeley Wood La ST/HB/BR S6 .... 96 B5
Beeley Wood Rd ST/HB/BR S6 .... 108 A1
Beeston Cl DRON S18 .... 168 A1
Beeton Rd SHEFS S8 .... 135 D5
Beet St OWL S3 .... 8 B5
Beetwell St CHSW S40 .... 190 B4
Beever La DOD/DAR S75 .... 12 B4
Beevers Rd KIMB S61 .... 91 E4
Beevor Ct BSLYN/ROY S71 .... 14 C5
Beevor St BSLYN/ROY S71 .... 22 C1
Beighton Rd HACK/IN S12 .... 151 F2
  HAN/WDH S13 .... 140 B4
  MEX/SWTN S64 .... 81 F3
Beighton Rd East MOS S20 .... 152 A2
Belcourt Rd RHAM/THRY S65 .... 105 E5
Beldon Cl SHEFP/MNR S2 .... 136 B3
Beldon Pl SHEFP/MNR S2 .... 136 B3
Beldon Rd SHEFP/MNR S2 .... 136 B3
Belfry Gdns DONS/BSCR DN4 .... 47 E5

Belgrave Dr FUL S10 .... 132 B1
Belgrave Pl AU/AST/KP S26 .... 142 A3
Belgrave Rd BSLYN/ROY S71 .... 3 F5
  FUL S10 .... 132 C1
Belgrave Sq SHEFP/MNR S2 .... 135 E2
Belklane Dr ECK/KIL S21 .... 166 C1
Bell Bank Vw BSLY S70 .... 22 A5
Bellefield St OWL S3 .... 8 A3
Belle Vue Av DONS/BSCR DN4 .... 45 E2
Belle Vue Cl STV/CWN S43 .... 185 E1
Belle Vue Rd MEX/SWTN S64 .... 58 B4
The Bellfields KIMB S61 .... 89 F1
Bellhagg Rd ST/HB/BR S6 .... 120 C1
Bellhouse Rd SHEFN S5 .... 99 F5
Bellows Rd RAW S62 .... 94 A1
Bellrope Acre ARMTH DN3 .... 33 F4
Bellscroft Av RHAM/THRY S65 .... 95 F4
Bells Sq SHEF S1 .... 8 D5
Bell St AU/AST/KP S26 .... 143 D5
Bellwood Crs HOY S74 .... 51 D3
Belmont Av BSLYN/ROY S71 .... 14 C2
  CHPT/GREN S35 .... 88 B1
  DONS/BSCR DN4 .... 44 A3
Belmont Dr STKB/PEN S36 .... 69 D2
Belmont St KIMB S61 .... 102 B3
  MEX/SWTN S64 .... 58 A4
Belper Rd SHEFS S8 .... 135 D4
Belridge Cl DOD/DAR S75 .... 12 C3
Belsize Rd ECC S11 .... 132 B2
Belton Cl DRON S18 .... 168 A2
Belvedere DONS/BSCR DN4 .... 63 D1
Belvedere Av CHSW S40 .... 189 F4
Belvedere Cl RCH S42 .... 188 B4
Belvedere Dr WMB/DAR S73 .... 25 F3
Ben Cl ST/HB/BR S6 .... 107 D3
Beninmoor Wy CHSW S40 .... 189 F4
Benita Av MEX/SWTN S64 .... 59 D4
Ben La ST/HB/BR S6 .... 107 D5
Benmore Dr MOS S20 .... 153 F4
Bennett Cl RAW S62 .... 80 C4
Bennett St KIMB S61 .... 101 F3
  SHEFP/MNR S2 .... 135 D2
Benson Rd SHEFP/MNR S2 .... 123 F5
Bentfield Av RHAM/THRY S65 .... 116 A1
Bentham Dr BSLYN/ROY S71 .... 15 E3
Bentham Rd CHSW S40 .... 10 A1
Bentinck Cl DON DN1 .... 5 E6
Bentinck St CONI DN12 .... 85 E1
Bent Lathes Av RHAM S60 .... 116 A1
Bentley Av DONS/BSCR DN4 .... 43 E2
Bentley Cl BSLYN/ROY S71 .... 15 F2
Bentley Common La BTLY DN5 .... 30 A1
Bentley Rd BTLY DN5 .... 29 F2
  CHPT/GREN S35 .... 88 C2
  FUL S10 .... 120 B2
Bentley St RHAM S60 .... 114 B1
Benton Ter MEX/SWTN S64 .... 81 E2
Benton Wy KIMB S61 .... 102 A2
Bents Cl CHPT/GREN S35 .... 88 B1
  ECC S11 .... 132 C5
Bents Crs DRON S18 .... 160 A5
  ECC S11 .... 145 D1
Bents Dr ECC S11 .... 132 C5
Bents Green Av ECC S11 .... 132 C4
Bents Green Pl ECC S11 .... 132 C5
Bents Green Rd ECC S11 .... 133 D5
Bents La DRON S18 .... 160 A5
Bents Rd ECC S11 .... 133 D5
  KIMB S61 .... 92 A5
Benty La FUL S10 .... 120 A4
Beresford St BTLY DN5 .... 16 C5
Berkley Cl BSLY S70 .... 22 A5
Bernard Cl STV/CWN S43 .... 180 A5
Bernard Rd ATT S4 .... 123 E3
  SHEFP/MNR S2 .... 123 E3
Bernard St RAW S62 .... 80 C4
  RHAM/THRY S65 .... 103 F4
  SHEFP/MNR S2 .... 123 D3
Berners Cl SHEFP/MNR S2 .... 136 C5
Berners Dr SHEFP/MNR S2 .... 136 C4
Berners Pl SHEFP/MNR S2 .... 136 C4
Berners Rd SHEFP/MNR S2 .... 136 B4
Berneslai Cl BSLY S70 .... 2 B4
Berneslai Ct BSLY S70 .... 2 B4
Bernshall Crs SHEFN S5 .... 98 C2
Berresford Rd ECC S11 .... 134 B2
Berrington Cl DONS/BSCR DN4 .... 63 E3
Berry Av ECK/KIL S21 .... 164 A5
Berrydale BSLY S70 .... 22 B5
Berry Holme Cl CHPT/GREN S35 .... 88 B1
Berry Holme Ct CHPT/GREN S35 .... 88 B1
Berry Holme Dr CHPT/GREN S35 .... 88 B1
Berry La CHPT/GREN S35 .... 72 B3
Berwick Av CHSW S40 .... 189 D4
Berwick Cl CHSW S40 .... 189 D4
Berwick Ct CHSW S40 .... 189 D5
Berwick Wy CHSW S40 .... 189 D4
Bessacarr La DONS/BSCR DN4 .... 61 D5
Bessemer Pl DARN/MH S9 .... 123 F2
Bessemer Rd DARN/MH S9 .... 123 F2
Bessemer Ter STKB/PEN S36 .... 68 C1
Bessemer Wy RHAM S60 .... 102 B4
Bessingby Rd ST/HB/BR S6 .... 108 A5
Bethel Rd RHAM/THRY S65 .... 7 G2
Bethel St HOY S74 .... 52 A2

Betjeman Gdns *ECC* S11 ..... **134** A1 🔲
Betony Cl *ECK/KIL* S21 ..... **165** F3
Beulah Rd *ST/HB/BR* S6 ..... **108** B3
Bevan Cl *HOY* S74 ..... **52** B2
Bevan Dr *STV/CWN* S43 ..... **186** C2
Bevan Wy *CHPT/GREN* S35 ..... **88** A2
Bevercotes Rd *SHEFN* S5 ..... **110** B1
Beverley Av *BSLY* S70 ..... **22** A4
Beverley Cl *AU/AST/KP* S26 ..... **142** B3
Beverley Gdns *BTLY* DN5 ..... **28** B4
Beverley Rd *WHHL* DN2 ..... **31** E3
Beverleys Rd *SHEFS* S8 ..... **147** E1
Beverley St *DARN/MH* S9 ..... **124** B1
Bevin Pl *RAW* S62 ..... **80** C5
Bevre Rd *ARMTH* DN3 ..... **33** E1
Bewicke Av *BTLY* DN5 ..... **28** B3
Bhatia Cl *MEX/SWTN* S64 ..... **58** B3 🔲
Bickerton Rd *ST/HB/BR* S6 ..... **108** A4
Bierlow Cl *WMB/DAR* S73 ..... **40** B4
Bignor Pl *ST/HB/BR* S6 ..... **97** E5
Bignor Rd *HAN/WDH* S13 ..... **97** E4
Bilby La *STV/CWN* S43 ..... **179** F5
Billam Pl *KIMB* S61 ..... **91** F5
Billam St *ECK/KIL* S21 ..... **165** F5
Billingley Dr *DEARNE* S63 ..... **26** C4
Bilston St *ST/HB/BR* S6 ..... **108** B5 🔲
Binders Rd *KIMB* S61 ..... **91** F5
Binfield Rd *SHEFS* S8 ..... **135** D5
Bingham Park Crs *ECC* S11 ..... **133** E2
Bingham Park Rd *ECC* S11 ..... **133** E3
Bingham Rd *SHEFS* S8 ..... **147** D3 🔲
Bingley La *ST/HB/BR* S6 ..... **118** C3
Bingley St *DOD/DAR* S75 ..... **13** E5
Binsted Av *SHEFN* S5 ..... **97** E5
Binsted Cl *SHEFN* S5 ..... **108** B1
Binsted Crs *SHEFN* S5 ..... **108** B1
Binsted Cft *SHEFN* S5 ..... **108** B1
Binsted Dr *SHEFN* S5 ..... **108** B1
Binsted Gdns *SHEFN* S5 ..... **108** B1 🔲
Binsted Gld *SHEFN* S5 ..... **108** B1
Binsted Gv *SHEFN* S5 ..... **108** B1
Binsted Rd *SHEFN* S5 ..... **108** B1
Binsted Wy *SHEFN* S5 ..... **108** B1
Birchall Av *RHAM* S60 ..... **115** F3
Birch Av *CHPT/GREN* S35 ..... **88** A2
Birch Cl *BTLY* DN5 ..... **42** B3
  ECK/KIL S21 ..... **166** A3
Birchen Cl *CHSW* S40 ..... **183** E4
  DONS/BSCR DN4 ..... **66** C2
  DRON S18 ..... **168** B2
Birches Fold *DRON* S18 ..... **160** A4 🔲
Birches La *DRON* S18 ..... **160** A4
Birch Farm Av *SHEFS* S8 ..... **147** E5
Birchfield Crs *DOD/DAR* S75 ..... **20** B2 🔲
Birchfield Wk *DOD/DAR* S75 ..... **12** C5 🔲
Birch Gv *CONI* DN12 ..... **85** E1
Birch Holt Gv *DRON* S18 ..... **177** F1
Birchitt Cl *TOT/DORE* S17 ..... **158** A3
Birchitt Pl *TOT/DORE* S17 ..... **158** A3
Birchitt Rd *TOT/DORE* S17 ..... **158** A3
Birchitt Vw *DRON* S18 ..... **159** E5
Birch Kiln Cft *STV/CWN* S43 ..... **186** A1
Birchlands Dr *ECK/KIL* S21 ..... **166** B3
Birch La *STV/CWN* S43 ..... **180** B5
Birch Rd *BSLY* S70 ..... **23** E5
  DARN/MH S9 ..... **123** F1
  DONS/BSCR DN4 ..... **47** D4
Birchtree Rd *KIMB* S61 ..... **90** A3
Birch Tree Rd *STKB/PEN* S36 ..... **68** C3
Birchvale Rd *HACK/IN* S12 ..... **150** B2
Birchwood Av *RAW* S62 ..... **80** A5
Birchwood Cl *MOS* S20 ..... **152** C5 🔲
Birchwood Crs *CHSW* S40 ..... **190** A5
Birchwood Cft *MOS* S20 ..... **152** C5
Birchwood Dell *DONS/BSCR* DN4 ..... **67** F2
Birchwood Gdns *MOS* S20 ..... **152** C5 🔲
Birchwood Gv *MOS* S20 ..... **152** C5
Birchwood Ri *MOS* S20 ..... **152** C5 🔲
Birchwood Rd *ECK/KIL* S21 ..... **162** B5
Birchwood Vw *MOS* S20 ..... **152** C5
Birchwood Wy *MOS* S20 ..... **152** C5 🔲
Bird Av *WMB/DAR* S73 ..... **39** D3
Birdholme Crs *CHSW* S40 ..... **190** B4
Birdwell Rd *ATT* S4 ..... **111** D3
  DOD/DAR S75 ..... **20** B4
  MEX/SWTN S64 ..... **81** E3
Birk Av *BSLY* S70 ..... **23** D3
Birkbeck Ct *CHPT/GREN* S35 ..... **73** E3 🔲
Birk Crs *BSLY* S70 ..... **23** D3
Birkdale Cl *DONS/BSCR* DN4 ..... **67** F1
Birkdale Dr *CHSW* S40 ..... **189** D4
Birkdale Ri *MEX/SWTN* S64 ..... **81** E1
Birkendale *ST/HB/BR* S6 ..... **121** E2
Birkendale Rd *ST/HB/BR* S6 ..... **121** E2
Birkendale Vw *ST/HB/BR* S6 ..... **121** E2 🔲
Birk Gn *BSLY* S70 ..... **23** E3
Birk House La *BSLY* S70 ..... **23** E3
Birklands Av *HAN/WDH* S13 ..... **138** C3
Birklands Cl *HAN/WDH* S13 ..... **138** C1
Birklands Dr *HAN/WDH* S13 ..... **138** C1
Birk Rd *BSLY* S70 ..... **23** D3
Birks Av *HAN/WDH* S13 ..... **139** F4 🔲
Birks Rd *KIMB* S61 ..... **91** F5
Birk Ter *BSLY* S70 ..... **23** D3
Birley Brook Dr *CHSW* S40 ..... **182** C2

Birley La *HACK/IN* S12 ..... **150** B3
Birley Moor Av *HACK/IN* S12 ..... **150** C2
Birley Moor Cl *HACK/IN* S12 ..... **150** C2 🔲
Birley Moor Crs *HACK/IN* S12 ..... **150** C2
Birley Moor Dr *HACK/IN* S12 ..... **150** C3
Birley Moor Pl *HACK/IN* S12 ..... **150** C3
Birley Moor Rd *HACK/IN* S12 ..... **138** B5
Birley Moor Wy *HACK/IN* S12 ..... **150** C2
Birley Rise Crs *ST/HB/BR* S6 ..... **97** D5
Birley Rise Rd *ST/HB/BR* S6 ..... **97** D5
Birley Spa Dr *HACK/IN* S12 ..... **151** F1
Birley Spa La *HACK/IN* S12 ..... **151** D1
Birley Vale Av *HACK/IN* S12 ..... **150** A1
Birley Vale Cl *HACK/IN* S12 ..... **150** A1
Birstall Cl *CHSW* S40 ..... **183** D2
Bisby Rd *RAW* S62 ..... **80** B5
Biscay Wy *DEARNE* S63 ..... **56** A2
Bishopdale Ct *MOS* S20 ..... **151** E4 🔲
Bishopdale Dr *HACK/IN* S12 ..... **151** E5 🔲
Bishopdale Ri *HACK/IN* S12 ..... **151** E5
Bishop Gdns *HAN/WDH* S13 ..... **139** F3
Bishopgarth Cl *BTLY* DN5 ..... **29** F5
Bishop Hl *HAN/WDH* S13 ..... **139** E4
Bishops Ct *SHEFS* S8 ..... **135** E5
Bishopscourt Rd *SHEFS* S8 ..... **135** E5
Bishopsholme Rd *SHEFN* S5 ..... **109** E2 🔲
Bishop St *SHEF* S1 ..... **122** A5
Bishops Wy *BSLYN/ROY* S71 ..... **15** D4
Bismarck St *BSLY* S70 ..... **22** A3
Bittern Vw *KIMB* S61 ..... **76** B5
Blacka Moor Crs *TOT/DORE* S17 ..... **156** A2
Blackamoor Rd *RAW* S62 ..... **80** A2
Blacka Moor Rd *TOT/DORE* S17 ..... **156** A2
Blacka Moor Vw *TOT/DORE* S17 ..... **156** A2
Blackbird Av *RHAM* S60 ..... **114** B4 🔲
Blackbrook Av *FUL* S10 ..... **131** D1
Blackbrook Dr *FUL* S10 ..... **131** D1
Blackbrook Rd *FUL* S10 ..... **131** E1
Blackburn Crs *CHPT/GREN* S35 ..... **73** F5
Blackburn Cft *CHPT/GREN* S35 ..... **74** A5 🔲
Blackburn Dr *CHPT/GREN* S35 ..... **87** F1
Blackburne St *ST/HB/BR* S6 ..... **108** B5 🔲
Blackburn La *BSLY* S70 ..... **22** B5
  DOD/DAR S75 ..... **13** E5
  KIMB S61 ..... **100** C3
Blackburn Rd *KIMB* S61 ..... **100** C3
Blackburn St *BSLY* S70 ..... **22** B5 🔲
Blackdown Av *CHSW* S40 ..... **182** C4 🔲
  MOS S20 ..... **152** B3
Blacker La *BSLY* S70 ..... **36** B3
Black Hill Rd *RHAM/THRY* S65 ..... **105** E5
Black La *HOY* S74 ..... **50** A4
  ST/HB/BR S6 ..... **106** B5
Blackmoor Crs *RHAM* S60 ..... **113** F3
Blackmore St *ATT* S4 ..... **123** E2
Blacksmith La *CHPT/GREN* S35 ..... **97** D1
Blackstock Cl *SHEFS* S8 ..... **148** B3
Blackstock Crs *GLV* S14 ..... **148** B3
Blackstock Dr *SHEFS* S8 ..... **148** B3
Blackstock Rd *SHEFP/MNR* S2 ..... **136** B5
  SHEFS S8 ..... **148** B3
Blackthorn Cl *CHNE* S41 ..... **191** E5
  CHPT/GREN S35 ..... **73** E3 🔲
Blackwell Cl *SHEFP/MNR* S2 ..... **123** D4 🔲
Blackwell Pl *SHEFP/MNR* S2 ..... **9** H5
Blackwood Av *DONS/BSCR* DN4 ..... **63** D1 🔲
Blagden St *SHEFP/MNR* S2 ..... **123** D4
Blair Athol Rd *ECC* S11 ..... **133** F4
Blake Av *DEARNE* S63 ..... **55** D1
  WHHL DN2 ..... **31** D3
Blake Grove Rd *ST/HB/BR* S6 ..... **121** F2 🔲
Blakeney Rd *FUL* S10 ..... **121** D4
Blake St *ST/HB/BR* S6 ..... **121** E2
Blandford Dr *CHNE* S41 ..... **183** F2
Bland La *ST/HB/BR* S6 ..... **107** D3
Bland St *ATT* S4 ..... **110** C4
Blast La *ATT* S4 ..... **9** H4
  SHEFP/MNR S2 ..... **9** H4
Blaxton Cl *MOS* S20 ..... **151** E3
Blayton Rd *ATT* S4 ..... **110** A5
Blazley Rd *SHEFP/MNR* S2 ..... **137** D4
Bleachcroft Wy *BSLY* S70 ..... **23** F5
Bleasdale Gv *BSLYN/ROY* S71 ..... **14** B3
Blenheim Av *BSLY* S70 ..... **21** F2
Blenheim Crs *MEX/SWTN* S64 ..... **58** A3 🔲
Blenheim Gdns *ECC* S11 ..... **133** E5 🔲
Blenheim Rd *BSLY* S70 ..... **21** E3
Blonk St *OWL* S3 ..... **9** G3
Blucher St *BSLY* S70 ..... **2** C6
Bluebank Vw *CHNE* S41 ..... **179** E3
Bluebell Cl *HOY* S74 ..... **51** D4
  SHEFN S5 ..... **110** C1
Bluebell Rd *SHEFN* S5 ..... **111** D1
Bluebird Hl *AU/AST/KP* S26 ..... **142** C4
Blue Boy St *OWL* S3 ..... **8** C3
Blue Lodge Cl *STV/CWN* S43 ..... **186** C4
Blundell Cl *BSLYN/ROY* S71 ..... **15** E2 🔲
Blyde Rd *SHEFN* S5 ..... **110** A3
Blyth Av *RAW* S62 ..... **94** A1
Blyth Cl *CHSW* S40 ..... **188** B1
  RHAM S60 ..... **116** B3
Blythe St *WMB/DAR* S73 ..... **39** D2
Boardman Av *RAW* S62 ..... **79** D3
Bobbin Mill La *CHSW* S40 ..... **189** E2
Bochum Pkwy *SHEFS* S8 ..... **148** A5

Bocking Cl *SHEFS* S8 ..... **146** B4
Bocking Hl *STKB/PEN* S36 ..... **69** E2
Bocking La *SHEFS* S8 ..... **146** B4
Bocking Ri *SHEFS* S8 ..... **146** C5 🔲
Boden La *SHEF* S1 ..... **8** C5
Bodmin Ct *BSLYN/ROY* S71 ..... **14** C4
Bodmin St *DARN/MH* S9 ..... **124** A1 🔲
Bodmin Wy *CHSW* S40 ..... **183** D4 🔲
Boiley La *ECK/KIL* S21 ..... **165** F4
Boland Rd *TOT/DORE* S17 ..... **158** B3
Bold St *DARN/MH* S9 ..... **111** E4
Bole Cl *WMB/DAR* S73 ..... **40** A1
Bole Hl *RHAM* S60 ..... **127** F2
Bolehill La *ECK/KIL* S21 ..... **173** D1
  FUL S10 ..... **120** B3
Bole Hill Rd *FUL* S10 ..... **120** A3
Bolsover Rd *SHEFN* S5 ..... **110** B2
Bolsover Rd East *ATT* S4 ..... **110** B3 🔲
Bolsover St *OWL* S3 ..... **121** F4
Bolton Hill Rd *DONS/BSCR* DN4 ..... **66** C1
Bolton St *DEARNE* S63 ..... **57** D1
Bolton St *CONI* DN12 ..... **84** A1
  OWL S3 ..... **122** A5
Bond Cl *DON* DN1 ..... **4** C6
Bondfield Crs *WMB/DAR* S73 ..... **39** D3
Bondfield Rd *STV/CWN* S43 ..... **187** D2
Bond Rd *DOD/DAR* S75 ..... **13** E4
Bond St *STV/CWN* S43 ..... **187** D1
  WMB/DAR S73 ..... **39** D2
Bonet La *RHAM* S60 ..... **113** E3
Booker Rd *SHEFS* S8 ..... **146** C3 🔲
Booth Cl *MOS* S20 ..... **152** B3
Booth Cft *MOS* S20 ..... **152** B3
Booth Pl *RAW* S62 ..... **79** F3
Booth Rd *CHPT/GREN* S35 ..... **73** D4
Booth St *HOY* S74 ..... **51** F2 🔲
  KIMB S61 ..... **92** C2
Borough Rd *ST/HB/BR* S6 ..... **108** B4
Borrowdale Av *MOS* S20 ..... **164** C2 🔲
Borrowdale Cl *BSLYN/ROY* S71 ..... **24** B2
  MOS S20 ..... **164** C2 🔲
Borrowdale Dr *MOS* S20 ..... **164** C1
Borrowdale Rd *MOS* S20 ..... **164** C2
Boston Castle Gv *RHAM* S60 ..... **103** F5
Boston St *SHEFP/MNR* S2 ..... **135** D1
Bosville Rd *FUL* S10 ..... **120** C4
Bosville St *RHAM/THRY* S65 ..... **105** E1
Boswell Cl *CHPT/GREN* S35 ..... **73** D3
  DONS/BSCR DN4 ..... **46** A5
Boswell St *RHAM/THRY* S65 ..... **104** A4
Bosworth St *FUL* S10 ..... **120** C3 🔲
Botanical Rd *FUL* S10 ..... **134** A1
Botham St *ATT* S4 ..... **110** C4
The Boulevard *ARMTH* DN3 ..... **19** F4
Boulton Cl *RCH* S42 ..... **182** B4
Boulton Dr *ARMTH* DN3 ..... **47** E5
Boundary Av *WHHL* DN2 ..... **32** A2
Boundary Cl *CONI* DN12 ..... **62** A4 🔲
Boundary Gn *RAW* S62 ..... **94** A2
Boundary Rd *SHEFP/MNR* S2 ..... **123** F5
Boundary St *BSLY* S70 ..... **22** C2
Boundary Wk *RHAM* S60 ..... **113** E4
Bourne Cl *STV/CWN* S43 ..... **185** F1
Bourne Rd *BSLY* S70 ..... **36** A1
  SHEFN S5 ..... **99** D5
Bowbridge Cl *RHAM* S60 ..... **103** D5 🔲
Bowden Gv *DOD/DAR* S75 ..... **20** A3
Bowden Wood Av *DARN/MH* S9 ..... **125** D5
Bowden Wood Cl *DARN/MH* S9 ..... **125** D5
Bowden Wood Crs *DARN/MH* S9 ..... **125** D5
Bowden Wood Dr *DARN/MH* S9 ..... **125** D5
Bowden Wood Pl *DARN/MH* S9 ..... **125** D5 🔲
Bowden Wood Rd *DARN/MH* S9 ..... **125** D5
Bowdon St *SHEF* S1 ..... **122** A5
Bowen Rd *RHAM/THRY* S65 ..... **7** H2
Bower Cl *KIMB* S61 ..... **91** F5
Bower La *CHPT/GREN* S35 ..... **86** C5
Bower Rd *FUL* S10 ..... **121** E3
  MEX/SWTN S64 ..... **57** E4
Bower Spring *OWL* S3 ..... **9** E3
Bower St *OWL* S3 ..... **9** E3
Bowes Rd *ARMTH* DN3 ..... **19** F5
Bowfell Vw *BSLYN/ROY* S71 ..... **14** B3
Bowfield Rd *SHEFN* S5 ..... **99** D5
Bowland Cl *BTLY* DN5 ..... **29** D1
Bowland Crs *BSLY* S70 ..... **36** A1
Bowland Dr *CHPT/GREN* S35 ..... **87** F1
  CHSW S40 ..... **188** C5
Bowlease Gdns *DONS/BSCR* DN4 ..... **46** C4
Bowling Green St *OWL* S3 ..... **8** D3
Bowman Cl *CHSW* S40 ..... **149** D5
Bowman Dr *HACK/IN* S12 ..... **149** D5
Bowness Cl *CHNE* S41 ..... **183** E2
  DRON S18 ..... **168** C2
Bowness Rd *CHNE* S41 ..... **183** E2
  ST/HB/BR S6 ..... **108** A5
Bowood Rd *ECC* S11 ..... **134** B2
Bowshaw Av *SHEFS* S8 ..... **159** E3
Bowshaw Cl *SHEFS* S8 ..... **159** E3
Bowshaw Vw *SHEFS* S8 ..... **159** E3
Boyce St *ST/HB/BR* S6 ..... **121** E2
Boyd Rd *DEARNE* S63 ..... **56** A5
Boyland St *OWL* S3 ..... **122** A1

Boynton Crs *SHEFN* S5 .... 109 E2
Boynton Rd *SHEFN* S5 .... 109 D3
Boythorpe Av *CHSW* S40 .... 189 F2
Boythorpe Crs *CHSW* S40 .... 190 A3
Boythorpe Mt *CHSW* S40 .... 190 A2 🔟
Boythorpe Ri *CHSW* S40 .... 189 F2
Boythorpe Rd *CHSW* S40 .... 190 A2
Brackenbury Cl *BTLY* DN5 .... 61 E2 🔟
Bracken Ct *MALT* S66 .... 117 F1
Brackendale Cl *STV/CWN* S43 ...... 185 E2
Brackenfield Gv *HACK/IN* S12 ...... 150 B1
Bracken Hl *CHPT/GREN* S35 .... 87 E2
Bracken Moor La *STKB/PEN* S36 .... 69 D3
Bracken Rd *SHEFN* S5 .... 99 F5
    SHEFN S5 .... 110 C1
Brackley St *OWL* S3 .... 122 C1
Bradberry Balk La *WMB/DAR* S73 ... 39 D1
Bradbourne Cl *STV/CWN* S43 .... 187 D1
Bradbury's Cl *RAW* S62 .... 94 A3 🔟
Bradbury St *BSLY* S70 .... 2 A6
    SHEFS S8 .... 135 E4 🔟
Bradfield Rd *ST/HB/BR* S6 .... 108 A4
Bradgate Cl *KIMB* S61 .... 102 A2
Bradgate Ct *KIMB* S61 .... 102 A2
Bradgate La *KIMB* S61 .... 102 A2
Bradgate Pl *KIMB* S61 .... 102 B1
Bradgate Pl *KIMB* S61 .... 102 B2
Bradlea Ri *RAW* S62 .... 80 B4
Bradley Av *WMB/DAR* S73 .... 39 D2 🔟
Bradley St *FUL* S10 .... 120 C2
Bradley Wy *STV/CWN* S43 .... 185 F2
Bradmarsh Wy *RHAM* S60 .... 103 D5
Bradshaw Av *RHAM* S60 .... 128 A3
Bradshaw Cl *DOD/DAR* S75 .... 12 B5 🔟
Bradshaw Rd *STV/CWN* S43 .... 186 C3
Bradshaw Wy *RHAM* S60 .... 128 A4 🔟
Bradstone Rd *RHAM/THRY* S65 .... 105 D2
Bradway Cl *TOT/DORE* S17 .... 157 F3
Bradway Dr *TOT/DORE* S17 .... 157 F3
Bradway Grange Rd
    TOT/DORE S17 .... 158 A3 🔟
Bradway Rd *TOT/DORE* S17 .... 157 F3
Bradwell Av *DOD/DAR* S75 .... 20 B5
Bradwell Cl *DRON* S18 .... 168 A2
Bradwell Pl *STV/CWN* S43 .... 187 D2
Bradwell St *SHEFP/MNR* S2 .... 135 E1
Braemar Cl *STV/CWN* S43 .... 179 E2
Braemar Rd *WHHL* DN2 .... 45 E1 🔟
Braemore Rd *ST/HB/BR* S6 .... 107 E3
Brailsford Av *SHEFN* S5 .... 98 B1
Brailsford Rd *SHEFN* S5 .... 98 B1
Braithwell Rd *BTLY* DN5 .... 16 B4
Bramall La *SHEFP/MNR* S2 .... 135 E1
Bramble Cl *MALT* S66 .... 117 F1 🔟
The Brambles *CHPT/GREN* S35 .... 98 B1
Bramble Wy *DEARNE* S63 .... 54 C2
Brambling Cl *CHNE* S41 .... 191 D2 🔟
The Bramblings *DONS/BSCR* DN4 .. 67 E2
Brameld Rd *MEX/SWTN* S64 .... 56 C5
    RAW S62 .... 94 A1
Bramham Ct *DARN/MH* S9 .... 124 C2 🔟
Bramham Rd *DARN/MH* S9 .... 124 C2 🔟
    DONS/BSCR DN4 .... 47 D2
Bramley Av *AU/AST/KP* S26 .... 142 C3
    HAN/WDH S13 .... 139 D3
Bramley Cl *MOS* S20 .... 164 A2
Bramley Dr *HAN/WDH* S13 .... 139 D1
Bramley Hall Rd *HAN/WDH* S13 ... 139 D2
Bramley La *HAN/WDH* S13 .... 139 D1
Bramleymoor La *ECK/KIL* S21 ..... 172 C2
Bramley Park Cl *HAN/WDH* S13 ... 139 D1
Bramley Park Rd *HAN/WDH* S13 ... 139 D1
Brampton Cl *ARMTH* DN3 .... 33 E5
Brampton Ct *MOS* S20 .... 151 E3
Brampton Crs *WMB/DAR* S73 ...... 40 A4
Brampton La *ARMTH* DN3 .... 33 E4
Brampton Rd *DEARNE* S63 .... 54 C1
    WMB/DAR S73 .... 40 A4
Brampton Vw *WMB/DAR* S73 ...... 40 A4 🔟
Bramshill Cl *MOS* S20 .... 153 E4
Bramshill Ct *MOS* S20 .... 153 E4 🔟
Bramshill Ri *CHSW* S40 .... 189 E3
Bramwell St *OWL* S3 .... 8 A4
    RHAM/THRY S65 .... 7 F3
Bramwith Rd *ECC* S11 .... 133 D2 🔟
Bramworth Rd *DONS/BSCR* DN4 ... 43 D3
Brandeth Rd *ST/HB/BR* S6 .... 121 F2 🔟
Brandon St *OWL* S3 .... 109 F5 🔟
Brandreth Cl *ST/HB/BR* S6 .... 121 F2 🔟
Branksome Av *BSLY* S70 .... 21 D1
Bransby St *ST/HB/BR* S6 .... 121 E2 🔟
Branton Cl *CHSW* S40 .... 190 A3
Brantwood Crs *DONS/BSCR* DN4 .. 47 D3
Brathay Cl *ATT* S4 .... 111 D3
Brathay Rd *ATT* S4 .... 111 D3 🔟
Bray St *DARN/MH* S9 .... 124 B2 🔟
Brearley Av *CHNE* S41 .... 179 E3
    STKB/PEN S36 .... 69 E3
Brearley St *CHNE* S41 .... 179 D3
Breckland Rd *CHSW* S40 .... 188 C4
Brecklands *RHAM/THRY* S65 .... 105 D5
Breck La *ECK/KIL* S21 .... 174 A3
Brecks Crs *RHAM/THRY* S65 .... 105 F4

Brecks La *RHAM/THRY* S65 .... 105 E2
Brecon Cl *CHSW* S40 .... 183 D4
    MOS S20 .... 153 E3
Brendon Av *CHSW* S40 .... 183 D5 🔟
Brendon Cl *WMB/DAR* S73 .... 40 A4
Brent Cl *CHSW* S40 .... 183 E4
Brentwood Av *ECC* S11 .... 134 B4 🔟
Brentwood Rd *ECC* S11 .... 134 B4
Bressingham Cl *ATT* S4 .... 123 D1 🔟
Bressingham Rd *ATT* S4 .... 122 C1
Bretby Cl *DONS/BSCR* DN4 .... 47 D5
Bretby Rd *CHSW* S40 .... 182 B3 🔟
Brett Cl *RAW* S62 .... 79 D3
Bretton Cl *CHSW* S40 .... 182 B4 🔟
Bretton Gv *HACK/IN* S12 .... 150 B2
Brewery Rd *DEARNE* S63 .... 55 F1
Brewery St *CHNE* S41 .... 11 D5
Breydon Av *BTLY* DN5 .... 28 C4
Briar Cl *MALT* S66 .... 117 E1
Briar Cft *DONS/BSCR* DN4 .... 43 E4
Briardene Cl *RCH* S42 .... 182 A4 🔟
Briarfield Av *HACK/IN* S12 .... 149 E3
Briarfield Crs *HACK/IN* S12 .... 149 E3
Briar Ri *BSLY* S70 .... 36 B1
Briar Rd *ABRD* S7 .... 134 C4
    ARMTH DN3 .... 33 E2
Briars Cl *ECK/KIL* S21 .... 166 B3
Briar Vw *STV/CWN* S43 .... 185 F2
Briary Av *CHPT/GREN* S35 .... 73 E4
Briary Cl *RHAM* S60 .... 114 A5
Brickhouse La *TOT/DORE* S17 ..... 144 A5
Brickhouse Yd *CHSW* S40 .... 10 A6
Brick St *FUL* S10 .... 120 C3
Bridby St *HAN/WDH* S13 .... 140 A4
Bridge Bank Cl *CHSW* S40 .... 183 E3 🔟
Bridgegate *RHAM* S60 .... 6 D4
Bridge Gv *BTLY* DN5 .... 29 D4
Bridge Inn Rd *CHPT/GREN* S35 ... 74 B5
Bridgelake Dr *DONS/BSCR* DN4 ... 63 F3
Bridge Rd *DONS/BSCR* DN4 .... 46 A4
Bridge St *BSLY* S70 .... 23 F2 🔟
    BSLYN/ROY S71 .... 2 D2
    CHSW S40 .... 190 B3 🔟
    DONS/BSCR DN4 .... 4 B5
    ECK/KIL S21 .... 166 B1
    MEX/SWTN S64 .... 57 F5
    OWL S3 .... 9 E2
    RHAM S60 .... 6 C4
Bridle Cl *CHPT/GREN* S35 .... 74 B5
Bridle Crs *CHPT/GREN* S35 .... 74 B5
Bridle Stile *MOS* S20 .... 164 A1
Bridle Stile La *MOS* S20 .... 164 A1 🔟
Bridle Stile Gdns *MOS* S20 .... 163 F1
The Bridleway *RAW* S62 .... 81 D4
Bridport Rd *DARN/MH* S9 .... 124 C2
Brier Cl *MOS* S20 .... 152 B4
Brierfield Cl *DOD/DAR* S75 .... 13 D5
Brierfield Rd *HACK/IN* S12 .... 149 E2
Brierley Cl *STV/CWN* S43 .... 181 F5
Brierley Rd *DONS/BSCR* DN4 ...... 46 B5
    DRON S18 .... 170 C5
Brierly Rd *RHAM/THRY* S65 .... 95 F5
Brier St *ST/HB/BR* S6 .... 108 A4 🔟
Bright Meadow *MOS* S20 .... 165 E3
Brightmore Dr *OWL* S3 .... 8 A5
Brighton Terrace Rd *FUL* S10 ..... 121 D5
Brightside La *DARN/MH* S9 .... 123 F1
Brightside Wy *ATT* S4 .... 111 D4
Brimington Rd *CHNE* S41 .... 11 H4
Brimington Rd North *CHNE* S41 .. 184 B1
Brimmesfield Dr
    pj*SHEFP/MNR* S2 .... 136 C2 🔟
Brimmesfield Rd *SHEFP/MNR* S2 .. 136 C3
Brimmsfield Cl *SHEFP/MNR* S2 .... 137 D3
Brincliffe St *BSLY* S70 .... 22 A2
Brincliffe Cl *CHSW* S40 .... 188 C3
Brincliffe Crs *ECC* S11 .... 134 A3
Brincliffe Edge Cl *ECC* S11 .... 134 A4
Brincliffe Edge Rd *ECC* S11 .... 133 F4
Brincliffe Gdns *ECC* S11 .... 134 A3
Brincliffe Hi *ECC* S11 .... 133 F3
Brindley Cl *SHEFS* S8 .... 147 E1
Brindley Ct *ECK/KIL* S21 .... 166 A2 🔟
Brindley Crs *SHEFS* S8 .... 147 E1
Brindley Rd *CHNE* S41 .... 184 B3 🔟
Brinkburn Cl *TOT/DORE* S17 ...... 157 D2 🔟
Brinkburn Dr *TOT/DORE* S17 ...... 157 D2
Brinkburn Vale Rd *TOT/DORE* S17 . 157 D2
Brinsford Rd *RHAM* S60 .... 114 A3
Brinsworth Hall Av *RHAM* S60 .... 113 F4
Brinsworth Hall Crs *RHAM* S60 ... 113 F4
Brinsworth Hall Dr *RHAM* S60 .... 113 F4
Brinsworth Hall Gv *RHAM* S60 .... 113 F4
Brinsworth La *RHAM* S60 .... 113 F4
Brinsworth Rd *RHAM* S60 .... 113 E4
    RHAM S60 .... 113 F5
    RHAM S60 .... 121 D1
Brinsworth St *DARN/MH* S9 .... 124 A1
    RHAM S60 .... 103 D4
Bristol Gv *WHHL* DN2 .... 31 E3
Bristol Rd *ECC* S11 .... 134 A1
Britain St *MEX/SWTN* S64 .... 58 A4 🔟
Britannia Cl *BSLY* S70 .... 22 A2 🔟
Britannia Rd *CHSW* S40 .... 190 C5

Brixworth ... (DARN/MH S9) 125 D3
Britland Cl *DOD/DAR* S75 .... 12 B5 🔟
Britnall St *DARN/MH* S9 .... 124 B1
Briton Sq *DEARNE* S63 .... 27 E2
Briton St *DEARNE* S63 .... 27 E2
Brittain St *SHEF* S1 .... 122 C5 🔟
Broachgate *BTLY* DN5 .... 28 C1
Broadcarr Rd *HOY* S74 .... 75 E1
Broadcroft Cl *MOS* S20 .... 153 E2
Broad Elms Cl *ECC* S11 .... 145 D1 🔟
Broad Elms La *ECC* S11 .... 144 C2
Broadfield Rd *SHEFS* S8 .... 135 D4
Broadgate House Cl *KIMB* S61 .... 102 B2 🔟
Broadgorse Cl *CHSW* S40 .... 190 A5
Broadhead Rd *STKB/PEN* S36 ...... 69 E2
Broad Inge Crs *CHPT/GREN* S35 ... 87 F1
Broadlands Av *MOS* S20 .... 151 E3
Broadlands Cl *MOS* S20 .... 151 F3
Broadlands Cft *MOS* S20 .... 151 F3 🔟
Broadlands Ri *HACK/IN* S12 .... 151 F3 🔟
Broad La *SHEF* S1 .... 8 B5
Broad Lane Ct *SHEF* S1 .... 8 B5 🔟
Bradley Rd *HAN/WDH* S13 .... 137 F3
Broad Oaks *DARN/MH* S9 .... 124 A2
Broad Pavement *CHSW* S40 .... 11 F6
Broad St *HOY* S74 .... 51 E2
    RAW S62 .... 94 A3
    SHEF S1 .... 9 G4
    SHEFP/MNR S2 .... 9 H4
Broad Street La *SHEFP/MNR* S2 ... 9 H4
Broadway *BSLY* S70 .... 20 C2
    MEX/SWTN S64 .... 80 C1
    RHAM S60 .... 113 F5
    RHAM/THRY S65 .... 104 C2
Broadway Av *CHPT/GREN* S35 .... 88 C2
Broadway Cl *MEX/SWTN* S64 ...... 80 C1
Broadway East *RHAM/THRY* S65 .. 104 C2
The Broadway *DONS/BSCR* DN4 ... 63 D2
Brocco Bank *ECC* S11 .... 134 A2
Brocco Cl *OWL* S3 .... 8 C4
Brocco St *OWL* S3 .... 8 C4
Brockfield Cl *BSLY* S70 .... 22 B5 🔟
Brockiehurst Av *BSLY* S70 .... 23 E4
    SHEFS S8 .... 148 A5
Brockiehurst Piece *CHSW* S40 .... 189 E2 🔟
Brockwell La *CHSW* S40 .... 183 E4
    RCH S42 .... 182 A2
Brockwell Pl *CHSW* S40 .... 10 A3
Brockwood Cl *HAN/WDH* S13 ...... 140 A3 🔟
Bromcliffe Pk *BSLYN/ROY* S71 .... 15 F2
Bromehead Wy *CHNE* S41 .... 183 E2
Brompton Rd *BTLY* DN5 .... 42 A3
    DARN/MH S9 .... 111 E5
Bromwich Rd *SHEFS* S8 .... 146 C3
Bronte Av *DONS/BSCR* DN4 .... 63 D1
Bronte Cl *BSLYN/ROY* S71 .... 14 C4
Bronte Gv *MEX/SWTN* S64 .... 58 C2
Bronte Pl *RAW* S62 .... 80 C4
Brookbank Av *CHSW* S40 .... 183 E5
Brook Cl *AU/AST/KP* S26 .... 142 C3
    CHPT/GREN S35 .... 87 D5
Brook Dr *OWL* S3 .... 8 B4
Brooke Dr *DEARNE* S63 .... 55 E2
    STV/CWN S43 .... 186 A4
Brooke St *DON* DN1 .... 30 B4
    HOY S74 .... 51 E2
Brook Farm Ms *DEARNE* S63 ...... 55 F2 🔟
Brookfield Av *CHSW* S40 .... 188 B2
    MEX/SWTN S64 .... 81 E1
Brookfield Cl *ARMTH* DN3 .... 33 F4 🔟
    RHAM/THRY S65 .... 95 E5
Brookfield Rd *SHEFS* S8 .... 135 D3 🔟
Brook Hl *KIMB* S61 .... 90 A2
    OWL S3 .... 8 A5
Brookhouse Cl *HACK/IN* S12 ...... 151 F2
Brookhouse Dr *HACK/IN* S12 ...... 151 F2
Brookhouse Hi *ECC* S11 .... 132 A3
Brookhouse Rd *AU/AST/KP* S26 ... 142 B4
Brooklands Av *FUL* S10 .... 131 F3
Brooklands Crs *FUL* S10 .... 132 A3
Brooklands Dr *FUL* S10 .... 131 F3 🔟
Brook La *CHPT/GREN* S35 .... 97 D1
    HACK/IN S12 .... 151 F2
    OWL S3 .... 8 A5
Brooklyn Dr *CHSW* S40 .... 183 E5
Brooklyn Pl *SHEFS* S8 .... 135 E5 🔟
Brooklyn Rd *SHEFS* S8 .... 135 E5 🔟
Brook Rd *CHPT/GREN* S35 .... 73 F5
    CONI DN12 .... 85 F1 🔟
    RHAM/THRY S65 .... 104 C1
    SHEFS S8 .... 135 D5
Brook Rw *STKB/PEN* S36 .... 69 D3
Brookside *CONI* DN12 .... 85 D2 🔟
    MEX/SWTN S64 .... 80 C2
    RHAM/THRY S65 .... 105 D4
Brookside Bar *CHSW* S40 .... 188 A2
Brookside Cl *HACK/IN* S12 .... 151 F2
Brookside Crs *DEARNE* S63 .... 54 C3
Brookside Dr *BSLY* S70 .... 23 E4 🔟
Brookside Gln *CHSW* S40 .... 188 A2
Brookside La *ST/HB/BR* S6 .... 118 A1
Brooks Rd *STV/CWN* S43 .... 180 C2
Brook St *RHAM* S60 .... 115 F3 🔟
Brookvale *BSLYN/ROY* S71 .... 15 E4 🔟

Brookview Ct *DRON* S18 .... 159 E5
Brook Wy *BTLY* DN5 .... 17 E5
Broom Av *RHAM/THRY* S65 .... 104 C5
Broombank Pk *DRON* S18 .... 177 E3
Broombank Rd *DRON* S18 .... 177 E3
Broom Cl *BSLY* S70 .... 23 E4
   CHNE S41 .... 183 E2 🔢
   DEARNE S63 .... 56 B4
   ECC S11 .... 135 D1
Broom Crs *RHAM/THRY* S65 .... 104 A5
Broomcroft Pk *ECC* S11 .... 145 D2 🔢
Broom Dr *RHAM* S60 .... 115 F1
Broome Av *RHAM/SWTN* S64 .... 57 E5
Broomfield Av *CHNE* S41 .... 191 E5
Broomfield Cl *BSLY* S70 .... 20 C2 🔢
Broomfield Ct *STKB/PEN* S36 ...... 69 E3 🔢
Broomfield Gv *RHAM/THRY* S65 .. 104 A5
   STKB/PEN S36 .... 69 D3
Broomfield La *DEARNE* S63 .... 69 D3
Broomfield Rd *FUL* S10 .... 121 C5
   STKB/PEN S36 .... 69 E2
Broom Gdns *STV/CWN* S43 .... 186 A2
Broom Gn *OWL* S3 .... 122 A5
Broom Gv *RHAM/THRY* S65 .... 104 A4
Broomgrove Crs *FUL* S10 .... 121 E5 🔢
Broomgrove La *FUL* S10 .... 121 E5
Broomgrove Rd *FUL* S10 .... 121 E5
Broomhall Pl *FUL* S10 .... 121 F5
Broomhall Rd *FUL* S10 .... 134 C1
Broomhall St *OWL* S3 .... 122 A5 🔢
Broomhead Rd *WMB/DAR* S73 ..... 40 A4
Broomhill Cl *ECK/KIL* S21 .... 163 F5
Broom Hill Dr *DONS/BSCR* DN4 ... 47 D5
Broomhill La *DEARNE* S63 .... 41 D2
Broomhill Rd *CHNE* S41 .... 178 A4
Broomhouse La *CONI* DN12 .... 62 A5
   DONS/BSCR DN4 .... 63 D2
Broom La *RHAM/THRY* S65 .... 104 B5
Broom Riddings *KIMB* S61 .... 92 C4
Broom Rd *RHAM/THRY* S65 .... 104 A4
Broomroyd *BSLY* S70 .... 36 C1
Broomspring Cl *OWL* S3 .... 121 F5 🔢
Broomspring La *FUL* S10 .... 121 F5 🔢
   OWL S3 .... 122 A5 🔢
Broom St *FUL* S10 .... 121 F5
Broom Ter *RHAM/THRY* S65 .... 104 A5
Broom Valley Rd *RHAM* S60 .... 104 A5
   RHAM/THRY S65 .... 103 F4
Broomville St *MEX/SWTN* S64 ..... 57 F5 🔢
Broomwood Cl *MOS* S20 .... 153 E2 🔢
Broomwood Gdns *MOS* S20 .... 153 E2
Brotherton St *OWL* S3 .... 122 C1
Broughton Av *BTLY* DN5 .... 29 E2
Broughton La *DARN/MH* S9 .... 111 F5
Broughton Rd *DONS/BSCR* DN4 ... 66 C1 🔢
   ST/HB/BR S6 .... 108 A3
Brow Cl *BSLY* S70 .... 22 A4
Brow Crs *MOS* S20 .... 164 C1
Brownell St *OWL* S3 .... 8 B4
Brown Hills La *FUL* S10 .... 130 C2
Browning Av *DONS/BSCR* DN4 .... 63 F1 🔢
Browning Cl *BSLYN/ROY* S71 ...... 14 C2 🔢
   ST/HB/BR S6 .... 97 E4
Browning Dr *RHAM/THRY* S65 ... 104 C3 🔢
   ST/HB/BR S6 .... 97 E4
Browning Rd *DEARNE* S63 .... 55 D1
   MEX/SWTN S64 .... 58 B2
   RHAM/THRY S65 .... 104 C3
   ST/HB/BR S6 .... 97 E4
Brown La *DRON* S18 .... 160 A5
Brown St *RHAM* S60 .... 102 C2
   SHEF S1 .... 122 C5
The Brow *RHAM/THRY* S65 .... 105 F5
Broxholme La *DON* DN1 .... 5 F2
Broxholme Rd *SHEFS* S8 .... 147 D2 🔢
Bruce Av *BSLY* S70 .... 22 A4
Bruce Crs *WHHL* DN2 .... 31 F4
Bruce Rd *ECC* S11 .... 134 B2 🔢
Brunel Rd *BTLY* DN5 .... 29 D4
Brunswick Cl *BSLYN/ROY* S71 ..... 14 A1
Brunswick Rd *OWL* S3 .... 9 G1
   RHAM S60 .... 104 A5
Brunswick St *CHNE* S41 .... 11 E3
   DEARNE S63 .... 55 D1
Brunt Rd *RAW* S62 .... 80 C5
Brushfield Gv *HACK/IN* S12 .... 150 D1
Brushfield Rd *RCH* S42 .... 182 A1
Bryn Lea *CHNE* S41 .... 191 D2
Bryony Cl *ECK/KIL* S21 .... 165 F2
Bubup Hl *NROS/TKH* DN11 .... 64 A5
Bubwith Rd *DARN/MH* S9 .... 111 F2 🔢
Buchanan Crs *SHEFN* S5 .... 97 F4
Buchanan Dr *SHEFN* S5 .... 97 F4
Buchanan Rd *SHEFN* S5 .... 98 A4
Buckden Cl *CHSW* S40 .... 183 E5
Buckden Rd *BSLY* S70 .... 2 A4
Buckenham St *ATT* S4 .... 123 D1
Buckingham Cl *DRON* S18 .... 168 B1 🔢
Buckingham Rd *CONI* DN12 .... 60 C5
   WHHL DN2 ....
Buckingham Wy *RHAM* S60 .... 114 B4 🔢
Buckleigh Rd *DEARNE* S63 .... 55 F5
Buckley Ct *BSLY* S70 .... 22 A2 🔢
Buckthorn Cl *MEX/SWTN* S64 ..... 81 D3

Buck Wood Vw *SHEFP/MNR* S2 .. 136 B5
Bude Ct *BSLYN/ROY* S71 .... 15 D4 🔢
Bude Rd *DONS/BSCR* DN4 .... 43 F4
Bullen Rd *ST/HB/BR* S6 .... 97 D4
Bullfinch Cl *RHAM* S60 .... 114 B4
The Bungalows *RHAM* S60 .... 127 F5
Bunker S HI *ECK/KIL* S21 .... 166 C2
Bunting Cl *CHSW* S40 .... 188 C3
   SHEFS S8 .... 147 F4
Bunting Nook *SHEFS* S8 .... 147 F3
Burbage Cl *DRON* S18 .... 168 B1 🔢
Burbage Gv *HACK/IN* S12 .... 138 B5
Burbage Rd *STV/CWN* S43 .... 187 D2
Burcot Rd *SHEFS* S8 .... 135 D5
Burcroft Cl *HOY* S74 .... 50 C3 🔢
Burden Cl *DON* DN1 .... 4 C6
Burford Av *DONS/BSCR* DN4 .... 62 C2
Burford Crs *AU/AST/KP* S26 ...... 142 C3 🔢
Burgen Rd *KIMB* S61 .... 91 F5 🔢
Burgess Cl *CHNE* S41 .... 191 E5
Burgess Rd *DARN/MH* S9 .... 124 A1
Burgess St *SHEF* S1 .... 8 D6
Burgoyne Cl *ST/HB/BR* S6 .... 121 E1
Burgoyne Rd *ST/HB/BR* S6 .... 121 E1
Burkinshaw Av *RAW* S62 .... 80 A3
Burleigh Ct *BSLY* S70 .... 2 D6 🔢
Burley Cl *DON* DN1 .... 11 F6
Burley St *CHSW* S40 .... 190 B5
Burlington Ar *BSLY* S70 .... 2 D5 🔢
Burlington Ct *ST/HB/BR* S6 .... 121 F2 🔢
Burlington Gln *TOT/DORE* S17 ... 156 C1 🔢
Burlington Gv *TOT/DORE* S17 ..... 156 C1
Burlington Rd *TOT/DORE* S17 ..... 156 C1
Burlington St *CHSW* S40 .... 11 F6
   ST/HB/BR S6 .... 121 F2
Burman Rd *DEARNE* S63 .... 56 A2
Burnaby Cl *ST/HB/BR* S6 .... 108 B5
Burnaby Crs *ST/HB/BR* S6 .... 108 B5
Burnaby Gn *ST/HB/BR* S6 .... 108 B5 🔢
Burnaby St *DON* DN1 .... 4 C5 🔢
   ST/HB/BR S6 .... 108 B5
Burnaston Cl *DRON* S18 .... 168 A2 🔢
Burnbridge Rd *CHNE* S41 .... 179 D3
Burncross Dr *CHPT/GREN* S35 .... 88 A1 🔢
Burncross Rd *CHPT/GREN* S35 .... 87 F1
Burnell Rd *ST/HB/BR* S6 .... 108 A4
Burnell St *STV/CWN* S43 .... 186 A1
Burngreave Bank *ATT* S4 .... 122 C1
Burngreave Rd *ATT* S4 .... 109 F5
Burngreave St *ATT* S4 .... 122 C1
Burn Gv *CHPT/GREN* S35 .... 89 D2
Burnham Cl *DONS/BSCR* DN4 ..... 45 F5
Burnham Dr *BTLY* DN5 .... 29 D1
Burnsall Crs *RHAM* S60 .... 114 A4
Burnsall Gv *BSLY* S70 .... 23 E4
Burns Cl *CHSW* S40 .... 190 A5
Burns Dr *CHPT/GREN* S35 .... 88 A1
   DRON S18 .... 170 A3
   RHAM/THRY S65 .... 104 C3
Burnside *DEARNE* S63 .... 26 C2
Burnside Av *SHEFS* S8 .... 135 E5
Burns Rd *DONS/BSCR* DN4 .... 63 F1 🔢
   RHAM/THRY S65 .... 104 B3
   ST/HB/BR S6 .... 121 E5
Burns St *BTLY* DN5 .... 16 C5
Burns Wy *DEARNE* S63 .... 55 D1
   DONS/BSCR DN4 .... 43 E4
Burnt Stones Cl *FUL* S10 .... 119 E5
Burnt Stones Dr *FUL* S10 .... 119 E5
Burnt Stones Gv *FUL* S10 .... 119 E5 🔢
Burnt Tree La *OWL* S3 .... 8 B2
Burntwood Cl *DEARNE* S63 .... 26 B4
Burntwood Crs *RHAM* S60 .... 127 F2 🔢
Burrell St *RAW* S62 .... 6 C6
Burrowlee Rd *ST/HB/BR* S6 ...... 108 A3
Burrows Dr *SHEFN* S5 .... 109 E2
Burrows Gv *WMB/DAR* S73 .... 38 C3
Burrs Wood Cft *CHSW* S40 .... 182 C2 🔢
Bursdon Cl *CHNE* S41 .... 178 C5 🔢
Burton Av *BSLYN/ROY* S71 .... 15 E3
   DONS/BSCR DN4 .... 43 F4
Burton Bank Rd *BSLYN/ROY* S71 .. 3 F1
Burton Crs *BSLYN/ROY* S71 .... 15 F2
Burtonlees Ct *DONS/BSCR* DN4 .. 46 C5 🔢
Burton Rd *BSLYN/ROY* S71 .... 15 D4
   OWL S3 .... 8 C1
Burton St *BSLYN/ROY* S71 .... 2 C1
   ST/HB/BR S6 .... 108 B5
Burton Ter *DONS/BSCR* DN4 .... 43 F4 🔢
Burtop Cft *WMB/DAR* S73 .... 53 D1 🔢
Burying La *RAW* S62 .... 51 F5
Bushey Wood Rd *TOT/DORE* S17 .. 156 C2
Bushfield Rd *DEARNE* S63 .... 55 F3
Busk Knoll *SHEFN* S5 .... 109 E2 🔢
Busk Meadow *SHEFN* S5 .... 109 E2
Busk Pk *SHEFN* S5 .... 109 E2
Busley Gdns *BTLY* DN5 .... 29 E1 🔢
Butcher St *DEARNE* S63 .... 26 C3
Butchill Av *SHEFN* S5 .... 98 B1
Bute St *FUL* S10 .... 120 C4
Butler Rd *ST/HB/BR* S6 .... 107 E5
Butler Wy *ECK/KIL* S21 .... 166 A1
Butterbusk *CONI* DN12 .... 85 F1
Butterfield Ct *WMB/DAR* S73 ..... 40 B5 🔢
Butterley Dr *BSLY* S70 .... 23 E4 🔢

Butterleys *DOD/DAR* S75 .... 20 B3
Buttermere Cl *CHNE* S41 .... 183 E2
Buttermere Dr *DRON* S18 .... 168 C2 🔢
Buttermere Rd *SHEFS* S8 .... 146 C1
Buttermere Wy *BSLYN/ROY* S71 . 24 C2 🔢
Butterthwaite Crs *SHEFN* S5 ...... 99 F2
Butterthwaite La *CHPT/GREN* S35 .. 99 D1
Butterthwaite Rd *SHEFN* S5 .... 99 D1
Butterton Dr *CHSW* S40 .... 182 B4 🔢
Butt Hole Rd *CONI* DN12 .... 85 F1 🔢
Button Hl *ECC* S11 .... 145 F1
Button Rw *STKB/PEN* S36 .... 69 D2 🔢
Butts Hl *TOT/DORE* S17 .... 156 B4
Byland Wy *BSLYN/ROY* S71 .... 15 D5
Byrley Rd *KIMB* S61 .... 91 F5
Byron Av *BTLY* DN5 .... 29 D5
   CHPT/GREN S35 .... 88 A2
   DONS/BSCR DN4 .... 63 E1 🔢
Byron Cl *DRON* S18 .... 170 A4
Byron Crs *DEARNE* S63 .... 55 D1
Byron Dr *BSLYN/ROY* S71 .... 14 C3
   RHAM/THRY S65 .... 104 B3
Byron Rd *ABRD* S7 .... 134 B4
   CHSW S40 .... 190 B4
   MEX/SWTN S64 .... 58 C3
   MOS S20 .... 153 E3 🔢
Byron St *CHSW* S40 .... 190 B3

C

Cadeby Av *CONI* DN12 .... 84 B1
Cadman Ct *MOS* S20 .... 164 B2
Cadman La *SHEF* S1 .... 9 E6
Cadman Rd *HACK/IN* S12 .... 138 A5
Cadman St *ATT* S4 .... 123 D3 🔢
   DEARNE S63 .... 56 B2
   MOS S20 .... 164 A2
Caernarvon Cl *CHSW* S40 .... 189 D3 🔢
Caernarvon Rd *DRON* S18 .... 169 E3
Caine Gdns *KIMB* S61 .... 101 F3
Cairn Dr *STV/CWN* S43 .... 179 E2
Cairngorm Cl *STV/CWN* S43 ...... 179 E2
Cairns Rd *FUL* S10 .... 120 A5
   MOS S20 .... 153 D1
Caister Av *CHPT/GREN* S35 .... 74 A5
Caistor Av *BSLY* S70 .... 21 D3
Calcot Park Av *MEX/SWTN* S64 .... 81 E1
Caldbeck Gv *CHPT/GREN* S35 ..... 73 E3 🔢
Calder Cl *BSLY* S70 .... 23 E4
Calder Rd *KIMB* S61 .... 92 A4
Calder Wy *SHEFN* S5 .... 110 A2
Caldey Rd *DRON* S18 .... 169 E3
California Crs *BSLY* S70 .... 22 A3 🔢
California Dr *CHPT/GREN* S35 ..... 88 B2
   RHAM S60 .... 127 D2 🔢
California St *BSLY* S70 .... 21 F3
California Ter *BSLY* S70 .... 21 F3 🔢
Calladine Wy *MEX/SWTN* S64 ..... 81 D2
Callow Dr *SHEFP/MNR* S2 .... 136 B5
Callow Mt *SHEFS* S8 .... 136 A5 🔢
Callow Pl *SHEFP/MNR* S2 .... 136 A5
Callywhite La *DRON* S18 .... 170 A2
Calner Cft *MOS* S20 .... 153 F3
Calow Brook Dr *CHNE* S41 .... 191 F4
Calow La *BSVR* S44 .... 191 F3
   CHNE S41 .... 191 F4
Calver Cl *DOD/DAR* S75 .... 20 B5
Calver Crs *STV/CWN* S43 .... 187 E2
Calvert Rd *DARN/MH* S9 .... 125 D1
Camborne Cl *ST/HB/BR* S6 .... 97 D4 🔢
Camborne Rd *ST/HB/BR* S6 .... 97 D4
Camborne Wy *BSLYN/ROY* S71 .... 15 D4
Cambria Dr *DONS/BSCR* DN4 ..... 62 C1 🔢
Cambrian Cl *CHSW* S40 .... 183 E3
Cambridge Crs *RHAM/THRY* S65 .. 104 B2
Cambridge Pl *RHAM/THRY* S65 ... 104 B2
Cambridge Rd *SHEFS* S8 .... 135 F4
   STKB/PEN S36 .... 70 A3
   STV/CWN S43 .... 186 A1 🔢
Cambridge St *MEX/SWTN* S64 ..... 57 F3
   NROS/TKH DN11 .... 66 C5
   RHAM/THRY S65 .... 104 B3
   SHEF S1 .... 8 D6
   SHEF S1 .... 122 B5 🔢
Camdale Ri *HACK/IN* S12 .... 151 D4
Camdale Vw *HACK/IN* S12 .... 151 D4
Camden Pl *DON* DN1 .... 4 D5 🔢
Camellia Cl *CONI* DN12 .... 82 E2 🔢
Cammerway *STV/CWN* S43 .... 179 E1
Cammell Rd *SHEFN* S5 .... 110 B2
Camms Cl *ECK/KIL* S21 .... 164 B4 🔢
Camm St *ST/HB/BR* S6 .... 121 D1
Campbell Dr *RHAM/THRY* S65 ... 104 C4
   STV/CWN S43 .... 180 C2
Campbell St *RAW* S62 .... 93 D2
Camping La *SHEFS* S8 .... 146 C2
Campion Dr *ECK/KIL* S21 .... 166 A2 🔢
   MEX/SWTN S64 .... 81 E2
Campo La *SHEF* S1 .... 8 D5
Campsall Dr *FUL* S10 .... 120 B4
Campsall Field Cl *DEARNE* S63 .... 55 F4
Campsall Field Rd *DEARNE* S63 ... 55 F3
Canada St *ATT* S4 .... 110 B5

BSLY S70 .... 21 F3
Canal Br ECK/KIL S21 .... 166 B2
Canal St ATT S4 .... 123 E3
  BSLYN/ROY S71 .... 3 E2
Canal Whf CHNE S41 .... 11 C3
Canklow Hill Rd RHAM S60 ...... 114 B1
Canklow Rd RHAM S60 .... 103 E4
Canning St SHEF S1 .... 8 C6
Cannock St ST/HB/BR S6 .... 108 A4 ⊞
Cannon Hall Rd SHEFN S5 ...... 110 A4
Cannon Wy DOD/DAR S75 .... 12 A2
Canons Wy BSLYN/ROY S71 ...... 15 D4
Canterbury Av FUL S10 .... 132 A2
Canterbury Cl BTLY DN5 .... 28 C3 ⊞
Canterbury Crs FUL S10 .... 132 A2
Canterbury Dr FUL S10 .... 132 A2
Canterbury Rd SHEFS S8 .... 135 F5
  WHHL DN2 .... 31 D3
Cantilupe Crs AU/AST/KP S26 .. 142 B2
Cantley La DONS/BSCR DN4 .... 46 B3
  DONS/BSCR DN4 .... 47 E4 ⊞
Cantley Manor Ri DONS/BSCR DN4.. 47 E5
Cantley Riding WHHL DN2 .... 32 C4
Capel Ri STV/CWN S43 .... 185 E1 ⊞
Capel St ST/HB/BR S6 .... 108 E3
Capri Ct WMB/DAR S73 .... 25 F4
Capthorne Cl RCH S42 .... 182 A4
Caraway Cl HAN/WDH S13 ...... 81 E3
Carbis Cl BSLYN/ROY S71 .... 14 C4 ⊞
Carbrook Hall Rd DARN/MH S9 .. 111 F3
Carbrook St DARN/MH S9 .... 111 F3
Cardew Cl RAW S62 .... 94 B1
Cardiff St DARN/MH S9 .... 111 E4
Cardigan Rd DARN DN2 .... 32 A4
Cardoness Dr FUL S10 .... 119 F5
Cardoness Rd FUL S10 .... 120 A5
Cardwell Av HAN/WDH S13 ...... 139 D3
Cardwell Dr HAN/WDH S13 ...... 139 D3
Carey Av BSLYN/ROY S71 .... 3 F5
Carfield Av SHEFS S8 .... 135 F5
Carfield La SHEFS S8 .... 136 A5
Car HI KIMB S61 .... 93 D4
Carisbrooke Rd WHHL DN2 ...... 31 E5 ⊞
Carlby Rd ST/HB/BR S6 .... 107 E5
Carley Dr MOS S20 .... 153 D4
Carlingford Rd RHAM S60 .... 104 B5
Carlin St HAN/WDH S13 .... 138 C5
Carlisle Cl CHNE S41 .... 177 E3
Carlisle Rd ATT S4 .... 110 C4
  WHHL DN2 .... 31 F2
Carlisle St ATT S4 .... 9 H1
  MEX/SWTN S64 .... 81 E2
  RHAM/THRY S65 .... 7 E4
Carlisle St East ATT S4 .... 123 E1
Carlthorpe Crs CHPT/GREN S35 .. 73 D4
Carlton Av RHAM/THRY S65 .... 104 A4
Carlton Cl MOS S20 .... 164 A2
Carlton Rd BSLYN/ROY S71 ...... 14 C1
  RAW S62 .... 94 A2
  ST/HB/BR S6 .... 107 F2
  WHHL DN2 .... 30 C4 ⊞
Carlton St BSLYN/ROY S71 .... 13 F3
Carlyle St MEX/SWTN S64 .... 58 B3
Carlyon Gdns OWL S3 .... 190 A4 ⊞
Carnaby Rd ST/HB/BR S6 .... 108 A5
Carnarvon St ST/HB/BR S6 ...... 121 F2 ⊞
Carnforth Rd BSLYN/ROY S71 .. 15 E2
Carnley St DEARNE S63 .... 54 C2
Carnoustie Av CHSW S40 .... 189 D4
Carnoustie Cl MEX/SWTN S64 .. 81 F1
Carolina Wy DONS/BSCR DN4 .. 45 E5
Carpenter Cft HACK/IN S12 .... 138 A4
Carpenter Gdns HACK/IN S12 .. 138 A4 ⊞
Carr Bank Cl ECC S11 .... 133 D2
Carr Bank La ECC S11 .... 132 C2
Carr Cl RHAM S60 .... 113 E4
Carrcroft Ct STKB/PEN S36 ...... 70 A5 ⊞
Carrfield Dr SHEFS S8 .... 135 F4
Carrfield La SHEFP/MNR S2 .... 135 F4
Carrfield Rd SHEFS S8 .... 135 F4
Carrfield St SHEFP/MNR S2 .... 135 F4
Carr Forge Cl HACK/IN S12 .... 151 E1
Carr Forge La HACK/IN S12 .... 151 E1
Carr Forge Mt HACK/IN S12 .... 151 E1
Carr Forge Pl HACK/IN S12 .... 151 E1
Carr Forge Rd HACK/IN S12 .... 151 E1
Carr Forge Ter HACK/IN S12 .... 151 E1
Carr Forge Vw HACK/IN S12 .... 151 F1
Carr Gv STKB/PEN S36 .... 69 F3
Carr Head Rd CHPT/GREN S35 .. 72 C2
Carrill Dr ST/HB/BR S6 .... 97 D3
Carrill Rd ST/HB/BR S6 .... 97 D3
Carrington Av DOD/DAR S75 .... 13 F3
Carrington Rd ECC S11 .... 133 F2
Carrington St DOD/DAR S75 .... 2 A2
  RHAM/THRY S65 .... 104 A4 ⊞
Carr La CHPT/GREN S35 .... 85 F3
  CONI DN12 .... 85 F3
  DOD/DAR S75 .... 49 D3
  DON DN1 .... 44 B3

DONS/BSCR DN4 .... 66 C2
DRON S18 .... 168 A1
RHAM/THRY S65 .... 82 B5
Carr Rd DEARNE S63 .... 56 B2
  ST/HB/BR S6 .... 121 D1
  STKB/PEN S36 .... 69 E4
Carr St BSLYN/ROY S71 .... 15 E2
Carr View Av DONS/BSCR DN4 .. 43 F4
Carr View Rd KIMB S61 .... 101 E1
Carville Dr ST/HB/BR S6 .... 97 E5
Carville Rd ST/HB/BR S6 .... 97 E5
Carville Rd West ST/HB/BR S6 .. 97 D5 ⊞
Carwell La ST/HB/BR S6 .... 108 A1
Carwood Rd BSLY S70 .... 23 F1
  DRON S18 .... 176 C3
  ECK/KIL S21 .... 175 F3
Carsick Gv FUL S10 .... 132 B1
Carsick Hill Crs FUL S10 .... 132 B1
Carsick Hill Cr FUL S10 .... 132 C1
Carsick Hill Rd FUL S10 .... 132 B1
Carsick Hill Wy FUL S10 .... 132 B1 ⊞
Carsick View Rd FUL S10 .... 132 B1
Carsington Cl CHSW S40 .... 182 B1
Carson Mt HACK/IN S12 .... 149 F2
Carson Rd FUL S10 .... 120 C4
Carter Hall La HACK/IN S12 .... 149 F3
Carterhall Rd HACK/IN S12 .... 149 F3
Carter Knowle Av ECC S11 ...... 133 F5
Carter Knowle Rd ECC S11 ...... 133 F5
Carter Lodge Av HACK/IN S12 .. 151 E1
Carter Lodge Dr HACK/IN S12 .. 151 F1
Carter Lodge Pl HACK/IN S12 .. 151 F1
Carter Lodge Ri HACK/IN S12 .. 151 F1
Carter Pl SHEFS S8 .... 135 F4
Carter Rd SHEFS S8 .... 135 E4
Cartmel Cl DRON S18 .... 168 C2 ⊞
Cartmel Crs CHNE S41 .... 183 E1
Cartmel Crs SHEFS S8 .... 146 C1
Cartmell Rd SHEFS S8 .... 146 C1
Car Vale Dr SHEFP/MNR S2 .... 138 A2
Car Vale Vw SHEFP/MNR S2 .... 138 A2
Carver La SHEF S1 .... 8 D5
Carver St SHEF S1 .... 8 D6
Carwood Cl ATT S4 .... 110 B5
Carwood Gv ATT S4 .... 110 B5 ⊞
Carwood Rd ATT S4 .... 110 B5
Cary Rd ECK/KIL S21 .... 163 F5
  SHEFP/MNR S2 .... 137 D2
Castell Crs DONS/BSCR DN4 .... 46 C3
Castle Av CONI DN12 .... 85 D1
  RHAM S60 .... 114 B1
Castlebeck Av SHEFP/MNR S2 .. 137 F1
Castlebeck Cft SHEFP/MNR S2 .. 138 A1 ⊞
Castlebeck Dr SHEFP/MNR S2 .. 138 A2
Castle Cl BSLYN/ROY S71 .... 14 C4
  BTLY DN5 .... 42 C2
Castle Crs CONI DN12 .... 61 D5
Castledale Cft SHEFP/MNR S2 .. 137 F2 ⊞
Castledale Gv SHEFP/MNR S2 .. 137 F2 ⊞
Castledale Pl SHEFP/MNR S2 .. 137 F2 ⊞
Castledine Ct DONS/BSCR DN4 .. 63 F3
Castledine Cft DARN/MH S9 .... 111 F2
Castledine Gdns DARN/MH S9 .. 111 F2
Castlegate OWL S3 .... 9 F4
Castle Gn SHEF S1 .... 9 F4
Castle HI CONI DN12 .... 85 D1
  ECK/KIL S21 .... 164 B4
Castle Hill Av MEX/SWTN S64 .. 59 D4
Castle Hill Cl ECK/KIL S21 ...... 164 B4
Castle Ms BTLY DN5 .... 16 A5
Castlereagh St BSLY S70 .... 2 B6
Castlerigg Wy DRON S18 .... 168 C2 ⊞
Castlerow Cl TOT/DORE S17 .... 157 E3
Castlerow Dr TOT/DORE S17 .... 157 F2
Castle St BSLY S70 .... 21 F2
  CONI DN12 .... 85 D1
  SHEF S1 .... 9 F4
Castle Ter CONI DN12 .... 85 D1
Castleton Gv STV/CWN S43 ...... 184 B4
Castle Vw BSLY S70 .... 35 F5
  ECK/KIL S21 .... 164 B5
Castlewood Crs FUL S10 .... 131 F2 ⊞
Castlewood Dr FUL S10 .... 131 F2
Castor Rd DARN/MH S9 .... 111 D5 ⊞
Catania Ri WMB/DAR S73 .... 25 D4
Catchford Vw CHSW S40 .... 182 C2 ⊞
Catcliffe Rd DARN/MH S9 .... 125 D3
Catherine Rd ATT S4 .... 122 C1
Catherine St CHSW S40 .... 10 B6
  DON DN1 .... 5 E5
  MEX/SWTN S64 .... 58 A3 ⊞
  OWL S3 .... 122 C1
  RHAM/THRY S65 .... 7 E5
Cathill Rd WMB/DAR S73 .... 41 D1
Cat La SHEFS S8 .... 136 A5
Catley Rd DARN/MH S9 .... 125 D2
Cattal St DARN/MH S9 .... 124 B2 ⊞
Catterick Cl CONI DN12 .... 83 F1
Cauldon Dr CHSW S40 .... 182 B4 ⊞
Caulk La BSLY S70 .... 24 A5
Causeway Gdns TOT/DORE S17 .. 144 A5 ⊞
Causeway Gld TOT/DORE S17 .. 144 A5

Causeway Head Rd
  TOT/DORE S17 .... 144 A5
The Causeway TOT/DORE S17 .. 156 B1
Cavendish Av ST/HB/BR S6 ...... 106 C3
  TOT/DORE S17 .... 156 C1
Cavendish Cl OWL S3 .... 122 A5 ⊞
Cavendish Ct OWL S3 .... 122 A5 ⊞
Cavendish Pl STV/CWN S43 .... 180 C3
Cavendish Ri DRON S18 .... 169 D3
Cavendish Rd BTLY DN5 .... 16 B2
  DOD/DAR S75 .... 2 A1
  ECC S11 .... 134 A3
  KIMB S61 .... 102 B3
Cavendish St CHSW S40 .... 11 F6
  OWL S3 .... 8 B6
  STV/CWN S43 .... 187 D1
Cavendish St North CHNE S41 .. 178 B4 ⊞
Cave St DARN/MH S9 .... 124 A2
Cavill Rd SHEFS S8 .... 147 E2
Cawdor Rd SHEFP/MNR S2 .... 137 D4
Cawdor St BTLY DN5 .... 16 C5 ⊞
Cawdron Ri RHAM S60 .... 114 A4
Cawley Pl BSLYN/ROY S71 ...... 14 B3
Cawston Rd ATT S4 .... 110 A4 ⊞
Cawthorne Cl RHAM/THRY S65 .. 105 D2
  SHEFS S8 .... 146 C2
Cawthorne Gv SHEFS S8 .... 146 C2
Cawthorne Rd RHAM/THRY S65 .. 105 D2
Caxton Cl CHNE S41 .... 179 E3
Caxton La ECC S11 .... 120 C5
Caxton Rd ECC S11 .... 121 D5 ⊞
Caxton St BSLY S70 .... 2 C3
Cecil Av DONS/BSCR DN4 .... 62 A2
  DRON S18 .... 169 E1
Cecil Rd DRON S18 .... 159 E5
  DRON S18 .... 169 E1
Cecil Sq SHEFP/MNR S2 .... 135 D2
Cedar Av CHNE S41 .... 183 E4
  MEX/SWTN S64 .... 58 A2
Cedar Cl DONS/BSCR DN4 ...... 62 C2
  ECK/KIL S21 .... 166 A3
  ECK/KIL S21 .... 173 F1
  STKB/PEN S36 .... 68 C3
Cedar Crs BSLY S70 .... 22 C3
Cedar Gv CONI DN12 .... 84 B3
Cedar Rd DONS/BSCR DN4 ...... 62 C1
  STKB/PEN S36 .... 68 C3
Cedar St STV/CWN S43 .... 180 B5
Cedar Wy CHPT/GREN S35 ...... 88 A2 ⊞
Cedric Av CONI DN12 .... 84 B2
Celandine Ct TOT/DORE S17 .... 157 E3 ⊞
Celandine Gdns TOT/DORE S17 .. 157 E3
Celandine Gv WMB/DAR S73 .. 40 B1
Celandine Ri MEX/SWTN S64 .. 81 E3
Cemetery Av ECC S11 .... 134 B1 ⊞
Cemetery La STV/CWN S43 ...... 181 F5
Cemetery Rd BSLY S70 .... 191 D2
  CHNE S41 .... 191 D2 ⊞
  DEARNE S63 .... 55 F3
  DRON S18 .... 169 F3
  ECC S11 .... 134 C2
  HOY S74 .... 52 B1
  MEX/SWTN S64 .... 58 B3
  WMB/DAR S73 .... 39 E2
Cemetery Ter STV/CWN S43 .... 185 F2
Centenary Wy RHAM S60 .... 6 A1
  RHAM S60 .... 114 A3 ⊞
Central Av BTLY DN5 .... 29 F1
  CHSW S40 .... 189 D2
  MEX/SWTN S64 .... 80 C1
  RHAM/THRY S65 .... 104 C2
Central Bvd WHHL DN2 .... 31 F3
Central Cl DRON S18 .... 170 C5
Central Dr CHNE S41 .... 191 D5 ⊞
  RAW S62 .... 79 D3
Central Rd RHAM S60 .... 6 C5
Central St CHNE S41 .... 191 D3 ⊞
  DEARNE S63 .... 27 E5
  HOY S74 .... 50 C3 ⊞
Central Wk STV/CWN S43 .... 185 E2
Centurion Wy BTLY DN5 .... 29 F4
Century Ct CONI DN12 .... 62 A4 ⊞
Century Gdns BTLY DN5 .... 17 D5
Century Dr BTLY DN5 .... 29 F4
Century Gn MOS S20 .... 152 C5 ⊞
Century Vw DARN/MH S9 .... 124 C3
Century Vw RHAM S60 .... 113 E4
Chadbourne Cl ARMTH DN3 .... 33 E4
Chaddesden Cl DRON S18 ...... 168 A2 ⊞
Chadwick Gdns BTLY DN5 ...... 17 F4
Chadwick Rd BTLY DN5 .... 29 F4
  HAN/WDH S13 .... 138 A3
Chaff Cl RHAM S60 .... 115 F3 ⊞
Chaffinch Av RHAM S60 .... 114 B4 ⊞
Chaff La RHAM S60 .... 115 F3
Challands Cl CHNE S41 .... 191 D4 ⊞
Challands Wy CHNE S41 .... 191 D4
Challenger Crs DEARNE S63 .... 26 C2
Challenger Dr BTLY DN5 .... 42 C1
Chaloner Gn MOS S20 .... 152 C5 ⊞
Chaloner Wy MOS S20 .... 152 C5
Chalmers Dr WHHL DN2 .... 19 E5
Chamberlain Av BTLY DN5 ...... 29 E5
Chamberlain Ct CHPT/GREN S35 .. 74 A3 ⊞
Chambers Av CONI DN12 .... 84 B1
Chambers La ATT S4 .... 110 C3
Chambers Rd HOY S74 .... 51 E1 ⊞

KIMB S61 .... 92 A5
Champion Cl *SHEFN* S5 .... 99 E3
Champion Rd *SHEFN* S5 .... 99 D3
Chancel Wy *BSLYN/ROY* S71 .... 15 D4
Chancery Pl *DON* DN1 .... 4 D4 ▣
Chancet Wood Cl *SHEFS* S8 .... 147 D5
Chancet Wood Dr *SHEFS* S8 .... 147 D5
Chancet Wood Ri *SHEFS* S8 .... 147 D5
Chandos Crs *ECK/KIL* S21 .... 166 A2
Chandos St *FUL* S10 .... 121 D5 ▣
Chaneyfield Wy *CHSW* S40 .... 182 C2 ▣
Channing Gdns *ST/HB/BR* S6 ..... 108 B5
Channing St *ST/HB/BR* S6 .... 108 B5
Chantrey Av *CHNE* S41 .... 184 A3
Chantrey Rd *SHEFS* S8 .... 147 D2
Chantry Cl *DONS/BSCR* DN4 .... 47 E5
Chapel Av *WMB/DAR* S73 .... 40 B5
Chapel Cl *BSLY* S70 .... 49 F1 ▣
CHPT/GREN S35 .... 87 F1
FUL S10 .... 133 D1 ▣
Chapel Ct *BSLY* S70 .... 49 F1
Chapelfield Crs *KIMB* S61 .... 90 A1 ▣
Chapelfield Dr *KIMB* S61 .... 90 A1
Chapelfield La *KIMB* S61 .... 90 A1
Chapelfield Mt *KIMB* S61 .... 90 A1 ▣
Chapel Field Pl *KIMB* S61 .... 90 A1 ▣
Chapelfield Pl *KIMB* S61 .... 75 F5
KIMB S61 .... 90 A1
Chapelfield Wy *KIMB* S61 .... 90 A1
Chapel Hl *HOY* S74 .... 37 E4
RHAM S60 .... 57 D5
RHAM S60 .... 115 F3
Chapel La *CONI* DN12 .... 85 D2
DARN/MH S9 .... 124 B1 ▣
DEARNE S63 .... 27 E2
DRON S18 .... 171 E2
RHAM S60 .... 103 E4
Chapel La East *CHNE* S41 .... 191 E5
Chapel La West *CHSW* S40 .... 189 D2
Chapel Pl *BSLYN/ROY* S71 .... 24 A2
Chapel Rd *CHPT/GREN* S35 .... 73 F3 ▣
CHPT/GREN S35 .... 87 F2
DOD/DAR S75 .... 94 A5
Chapel St *BSLY* S70 .... 49 F1
BSLYN/ROY S71 .... 24 A2 ▣
BTLY DN5 .... 29 F1
CHNE S41 .... 184 B1 ▣
DEARNE S63 .... 26 C3
DEARNE S63 .... 55 F3
HAN/WDH S13 .... 139 F4
HOY S74 .... 50 C3
KIMB S61 .... 92 C2
MEX/SWTN S64 .... 57 F3
MOS S20 .... 164 A2
RAW S62 .... 94 A1
STV/CWN S43 .... 186 A1
Chapel Ter *FUL* S10 .... 133 D1
Chapeltown Rd *CHPT/GREN* S35 . 88 C4
Chapel Wk *RAW* S62 .... 79 E4
RHAM S60 .... 6 A5
SHEF S1 .... 9 E5
Chapel Wy *RAW* S62 .... 79 E4
Chapelwood Rd *DARN/MH* S9 .... 124 C1
Chapel Yd *DRON* S18 .... 169 E1
Chapman St *DARN/MH* S9 .... 100 C5 ▣
DEARNE S63 .... 27 E3 ▣
Chappell Dr *BTLY* DN5 .... 4 D1
Chapter Wy *BSLYN/ROY* S71 ...... 15 D4 ▣
Charles Ashmore Rd *SHEFS* S8 . 147 D5
Charles Crs *ARMTH* DN3 .... 33 D2
Charles La *SHEF* S1 .... 9 E6
Charles Rd *DEARNE* S63 .... 56 A3
Charles St *BSLY* S70 .... 21 F2
BSLY S70 .... 36 B1 ▣
CHSW S40 .... 10 B6
DON DN1 .... 5 F1
MEX/SWTN S64 .... 81 E1
RAW S62 .... 80 C4
SHEF S1 .... 9 E5
Charlotte La *SHEF* S1 .... 8 B6 ▣
Charlotte Rd *SHEF* S1 .... 135 E1
SHEFP/MNR S2 .... 135 F1
Charlton Brook Crs
CHPT/GREN S35 .... 73 F3
Charlton Clough *CHPT/GREN* S35 87 E1
Charlton Dr *CHPT/GREN* S35 ..... 73 F5
Charlton Hill Ri *CHPT/GREN* S35 .. 87 E1
Charnley Av *ECC* S11 .... 134 A5
Charnley Cl *ECC* S11 .... 133 F4
Charnley Dr *ECC* S11 .... 134 A5
Charnley Ri *ECC* S11 .... 134 A5
Charnock Av *HACK/IN* S12 .... 149 F3
Charnock Crs *HACK/IN* S12 .... 149 E2
Charnock Dale Rd *HACK/IN* S12 . 149 E3
Charnock Dr *BTLY* DN5 .... 29 D4 ▣
HACK/IN S12 .... 149 E2
Charnock Gv *HACK/IN* S12 .... 149 F3
Charnock Hall Rd *HACK/IN* S12 . 149 F3
Charnock View Rd *HACK/IN* S12 . 149 F3
Charnock Wood Rd *HACK/IN* S12 149 F3
Charnwood Ct *MOS* S20 .... 153 E3 ▣
Charnwood Dr *DONS/BSCR* DN4 . 62 C2
Charnwood Gv *MOS* S20 .... 102 A3
Charnwood St *MEX/SWTN* S64 . 57 E5 ▣
Charter Dr *BTLY* DN5 .... 28 A1

Charter Rw *SHEF* S1 .... 122 A5
Charter Square Rbt *SHEF* S1 ..... 122 B5
Chasecliff Cl *CHSW* S40 .... 183 E4 ▣
Chase Rd *ST/HB/BR* S6 .... 106 B4
The Chase *AU/AST/KP* S26 .... 142 C4
Chatfield Rd *SHEFS* S8 .... 146 C3
Chatham St *OWL* S3 .... 9 E1
RHAM/THRY S65 .... 7 E5
Chatsworth Av *CHSW* S40 .... 188 C2
MEX/SWTN S64 .... 59 E3
Chatsworth Cl *AU/AST/KP* S26 . 143 D3
Chatsworth Ct *STV/CWN* S43 ... 187 E1
Chatsworth Crs *BTLY* DN5 .... 29 D1
Chatsworth Park Av
HACK/IN S12 .... 137 E5 ▣
Chatsworth Park Dr
HACK/IN S12 .... 137 E5 ▣
Chatsworth Park Gv
HACK/IN S12 .... 137 E5 ▣
Chatsworth Park Rd *HACK/IN* S12 137 E5
Chatsworth Pl *DRON* S18 .... 168 B1 ▣
Chatsworth Ri *DOD/DAR* S75 ...... 20 A4 ▣
Chatsworth Rd *BSLYN/ROY* S71 . 14 B1 ▣
CHSW S40 .... 10 A6
KIMB S61 .... 102 C3 ▣
TOT/DORE S17 .... 156 C2
Chatterton Dr *RHAM/THRY* S65 104 C5
Chaucer Cl *SHEFN* S5 .... 97 E3 ▣
Chaucer Dr *DRON* S18 .... 170 A4
Chaucer Rd *CHNE* S41 .... 184 A1
MEX/SWTN S64 .... 58 C3
RHAM/THRY S65 .... 104 C5
SHEFN S5 .... 97 F3
Cheadle St *ST/HB/BR* S6 .... 108 A4 ▣
Cheapside *BSLY* S70 .... 2 D5
Checkstone Av *DONS/BSCR* DN4 66 C2
Cheedale Av *CHSW* S40 .... 183 E4
Cheedale Cl *CHSW* S40 .... 183 E3 ▣
Cheetham Av *DRON* S18 .... 177 F1
Chelmsford Av *AU/AST/KP* S26 . 142 C2
Chelmsford Dr *WHHL* DN2 .... 31 D3
Chelsea Ct *ECC* S11 .... 134 A3
Chelsea Ri *ECC* S11 .... 134 A3
Chelsea Rd *ECC* S11 .... 134 A4
Cheltenham Ri *BTLY* DN5 .... 28 B4 ▣
Cheltenham Rd *WHHL* DN2 .... 32 A4
Chemist La *RHAM* S60 .... 6 B4 ▣
Chemistry La *CHPT/GREN* S35 ... 71 D3
Chepstow Cl *CHSW* S40 .... 190 A4
Chepstow Dr *MEX/SWTN* S64 .... 58 C2
Chepstow Gdns *BTLY* DN5 .... 28 B4
Chequer Av *DONS/BSCR* DN4 ...... 5 C6
Chequer Rd *DON* DN1 .... 5 F5
Cherry Bank Rd *SHEFS* S8 .... 147 E2
Cherry Garth *BTLY* DN5 .... 16 C3
Cherry Gv *CONI* DN12 .... 84 A3
Cherry La *BTLY* DN5 .... 4 B1
Cherrys Rd *BSLYN/ROY* S71 .... 15 E5
Cherry St *SHEFP/MNR* S2 .... 135 E2
Cherry St South *SHEFP/MNR* S2 135 E2
Cherry Tree Cl *ECC* S11 .... 134 B3 ▣
RHAM S60 .... 114 B4 ▣
Cherry Tree Dell *ECC* S11 .... 134 B3 ▣
Cherry Tree Dr *ABRD* S7 .... 134 B3 ▣
ECK/KIL S21 .... 166 A3
Cherry Tree Pl *DEARNE* S63 .... 56 A3 ▣
Cherry Tree Rd *ABRD* S7 .... 134 B3 ▣
ARMTH DN3 .... 33 F3
AU/AST/KP S26 .... 155 E3
DONS/BSCR DN4 .... 4 B6
Cherry Tree St *HOY* S74 .... 52 A2
Cherry Wk *CHPT/GREN* S35 .... 88 B2 ▣
Chertsey Cl *CHSW* S40 .... 190 A4 ▣
Cherwell Cl *STV/CWN* S43 .... 179 F5
Chesham Rd *BSLY* S70 .... 2 A5
Chessel Cl *SHEFS* S8 .... 147 E1
Chesterfield Rd *STV/CWN* S43 . 179 F3
Chesterfield Rd *AU/AST/KP* S26 141 F3
CHNE S41 .... 185 D3
DRON S18 .... 169 F2
ECK/KIL S21 .... 173 E2
SHEFS S8 .... 135 D4
STV/CWN S43 .... 185 F2
STV/CWN S43 .... 186 B1
STV/CWN S43 .... 187 D1
Chesterfield Rd South *SHEFS* S8 159 E2
Chesterhill Av *RHAM/THRY* S65 95 F5
Chester La *SHEF* S1 .... 122 A5 ▣
Chester Rd *WHHL* DN2 .... 31 D2
Chester St *CHSW* S40 .... 10 A5 ▣
SHEF S1 .... 8 C6
Chesterton Cl *STV/CWN* S43 ..... 186 A5 ▣
Chesterton Rd *DONS/BSCR* DN4 . 64 A1 ▣
RHAM/THRY S65 .... 7 H1
Chesterton Wy *RHAM/THRY* S65 94 C5
Chesterwood Dr *FUL* S10 .... 120 C5 ▣
Chestnut Av *ARMTH* DN3 .... 33 F3
DARN/MH S9 .... 125 F4
DEARNE S63 .... 56 A4
ECK/KIL S21 .... 165 F3
ECK/KIL S21 .... 173 E1
MOS S20 .... 141 D5
RHAM/THRY S65 .... 104 C3
STKB/PEN S36 .... 68 C3

Chestnut Cl *DRON* S18 .... 169 F3
Chestnut Ct *BSLY* S70 .... 22 A3 ▣
BTLY DN5 .... 16 B4 ▣
Chestnut Crs *BSLY* S70 .... 22 C5
Chestnut Dr *CHPT/GREN* S35 ..... 87 F2
Chestnut Gv *CONI* DN12 .... 84 B2
DEARNE S63 .... 27 D4
Chestnut Rd *AU/AST/KP* S26 .... 141 F2
Cheviot Dr *BTLY* DN5 .... 29 D2
Cheviot Wy *CHSW* S40 .... 183 D4 ▣
Chichester Rd *FUL* S10 .... 120 C3 ▣
Chigwell Wy *STV/CWN* S43 .... 180 C3
Childers St *DONS/BSCR* DN4 .... 44 C3
Chiltern Cl *CHSW* S40 .... 183 D5
Chiltern Ri *RHAM* S60 .... 114 B5
Chiltern Rd *BTLY* DN5 .... 29 D2
ST/HB/BR S6 .... 107 F4
Chilton St *BSLY* S70 .... 22 B2
Chinley St *DARN/MH* S9 .... 124 B2 ▣
Chippingham Pl *DARN/MH* S9 ... 124 A1 ▣
Chippingham St *DARN/MH* S9 ... 124 B1
Chippinghouse Rd *ABRD* S7 ..... 135 D3
SHEFS S8 .... 135 D3
Chiverton Cl *DRON* S18 .... 169 E1 ▣
Chorley Av *FUL* S10 .... 132 A2
Chorley Dr *FUL* S10 .... 132 A3
Chorley Pl *FUL* S10 .... 132 A3
Chorley Rd *FUL* S10 .... 132 B2
Christchurch Av *AU/AST/KP* S26 142 C2
Christchurch Rd *DEARNE* S63 .... 55 D1
Christ Church Rd *DON* DN1 .... 5 F2
OWL S3 .... 109 F5
Church Av *RAW* S62 .... 93 F2
Church Cl *AU/AST/KP* S26 .... 155 F3
ECK/KIL S21 .... 175 F3
MEX/SWTN S64 .... 57 D5
Church Cottage Ms
DONS/BSCR DN4 .... 42 C5
Church Ct *DONS/BSCR* DN4 ...... 47 D5 ▣
Church Cft *RAW* S62 .... 93 F2
Churchdale Rd *HACK/IN* S12 ..... 150 B1
Churchfield *BSLY* S70 .... 2 B4
Churchfield Cl *BTLY* DN5 .... 29 E2
Church Field La *RAW* S62 .... 76 A3
Church Flds *KIMB* S61 .... 101 F2
Church Fields Rd *NROS/TKH* DN11 67 F5
Church Field Vw
DONS/BSCR DN4 .... 42 C5
Church Gn *DEARNE* S63 .... 55 F2
Church Gv *BSLYN/ROY* S71 .... 15 D3
Churchill Av *BTLY* DN5 .... 29 E4
Churchill Rd *FUL* S10 .... 121 D4 ▣
STKB/PEN S36 .... 68 A1
WHHL DN2 .... 30 C3
Church La *AU/AST/KP* S26 .... 143 D3
BSLY S70 .... 2 C2
BSLY S70 .... 2 C4
BSLY S70 .... 36 A3
CHSW S40 .... 11 F6
DEARNE S63 .... 55 F2 ▣
DONS/BSCR DN4 .... 47 D5
DONS/BSCR DN4 .... 62 B1
DONS/BSCR DN4 .... 66 C1
ECK/KIL S21 .... 166 C2
HACK/IN S12 .... 152 A2
HAN/WDH S13 .... 139 F4
HOY S74 .... 49 F5
MOS S20 .... 153 E2
RHAM S60 .... 127 D1 ▣
RHAM S60 .... 127 F5
TOT/DORE S17 .... 156 B2
Church La North *CHNE* S41 .... 178 B3
Church Lea *HOY* S74 .... 51 F4
Church Ms *ECK/KIL* S21 .... 166 C1
MEX/SWTN S64 .... 59 D4
MOS S20 .... 164 B1 ▣
Church Rein Cl *DONS/BSCR* DN4 62 A1 ▣
Church Rd *CONI* DN12 .... 60 B4
Church St *ARMTH* DN3 .... 33 E3
AU/AST/KP S26 .... 155 F3
BSLY S70 .... 2 C3
BTLY DN5 .... 29 E1 ▣
CHPT/GREN S35 .... 88 B5
CONI DN12 .... 84 C3
DEARNE S63 .... 26 C3
DEARNE S63 .... 55 F2 ▣
DOD/DAR S75 .... 12 B4
DON DN1 .... 4 D2
DRON S18 .... 169 E2 ▣
DRON S18 .... 170 C4
ECK/KIL S21 .... 164 C4
HOY S74 .... 52 A1
HOY S74 .... 52 B3
KIMB S61 .... 92 B2
KIMB S61 .... 101 F2
MEX/SWTN S64 .... 58 C4
MEX/SWTN S64 .... 59 E4 ▣
RAW S62 .... 93 F2
SHEF S1 .... 9 E5
ST/HB/BR S6 .... 119 D2
STV/CWN S43 .... 181 F4
STV/CWN S43 .... 185 F2
Church St North *CHNE* S41 ...... 178 B3

Church St South *CHSW* S40 .... **190** B5
Church St West *CHSW* S40 ...... **189** D2 🔟
Church Vw *AU/AST/KP* S26 ...... **142** C3
  CHSW S40 .... **189** D2 🔟
  DOD/DAR S75 .... **13** D4
  DON DN1 .... **4** D2
  ECK/KIL S21 .... **166** C1
  HAN/WDH S13 .... **140** A4
  HOY S74 .... **50** C3
Church Wk *CONI* DN12 .... **60** B4
Church Wy *CHNE* S41 .... **11** F6
  DON DN1 .... **30** C4
Churston Rd *CHSW* S40 .... **189** E1
Cinder Bridge Rd *RAW* S62 .... **93** D2
Cinder Hill La *CHPT/GREN* S35 ...... **97** E1
Cinderhill La *SHEFS* S8 .... **148** A5
Cinderhill Rd *KIMB* S61 .... **91** F4
Cinder Hills Wy *DOD/DAR* S75 ...... **20** B3 🔟
Cinder La *ECK/KIL* S21 .... **167** D1
Circle Cl *SHEFP/MNR* S2 .... **137** F2
The Circle *SHEFP/MNR* S2 .... **137** F1
Circular Dr *ECK/KIL* S21 .... **175** F3
Circular Rd *CHNE* S41 .... **190** C4
  STV/CWN S43 .... **187** D1
City Rd *SHEFP/MNR* S2 .... **123** E5
Claire Ct *RHAM* S60 .... **6** D3
Clanricarde St *BSLYN/ROY* S71 ..... **2** C1
Clara Pl *KIMB* S61 .... **102** A3
Clarell Gdns *DONS/BSCR* DN4 ..... **46** C3
Claremont Crs *FUL* S10 .... **121** E4 🔟
Claremont Pl *FUL* S10 .... **121** E4
Claremont St *KIMB* S61 .... **102** A3
Clarence Av *DONS/BSCR* DN4 ...... **43** F4
Clarence La *SHEFP/MNR* S2 ...... **135** D1
Clarence Rd *BSLYN/ROY* S71 ..... **14** C3
  CHSW S40 .... **10** D6
  ST/HB/BR S6 .... **107** F4
Clarence St *CHSW* S40 .... **10** C6
  DEARNE S63 .... **55** E1 🔟
Clarendon Rd *ECC* S11 .... **132** C3
  RHAM/THRY S65 .... **7** G3
  STV/CWN S43 .... **187** D2
Clarendon St *BSLY* S70 .... **2** A6
Clark Av *DONS/BSCR* DN4 .... **5** H6
Clarke Dell *FUL* S10 .... **134** B1
Clarke Dr *FUL* S10 .... **134** B1
Clarkegrove Rd *FUL* S10 .... **121** E5
Clarkehouse Rd *FUL* S10 .... **134** A1
Clarke Sq *SHEFP/MNR* S2 .... **135** D2
Clarke St *DEARNE* S63 .... **27** E3 🔟
  DOD/DAR S75 .... **2** A1
  FUL S10 .... **121** F5
Clark Gv *ST/HB/BR* S6 .... **119** E1
Clarkson St *BSLY* S70 .... **23** D5
  FUL S10 .... **121** F4
Clark St *HOY* S74 .... **51** F4
Claycliffe Av *DOD/DAR* S75 .... **12** A3
Claycliffe Rd *DOD/DAR* S75 ...... **12** A2
Clayfield Av *MEX/SWTN* S64 .... **59** E3
Clayfield La *RAW* S62 .... **76** C2
Clayfield Rd *MEX/SWTN* S64 .... **59** E3
Clayfields *DONS/BSCR* DN4 .... **63** E2
Clayfield Vw *MEX/SWTN* S64 .... **59** E3
Clay La *SHEF* S1 .... **122** B5 🔟
  WHHL DN2 .... **19** E4
  WHHL DN2 .... **32** B1
Clay La West *WHHL* DN2 .... **19** D5
Clay Pit La *RAW* S62 .... **94** B1
Clayroyd *BSLY* S70 .... **36** B1
Clay St *DARN/MH* S9 .... **111** D5
Clayton Av *DEARNE* S63 .... **26** B2
Clayton Crs *MOS* S20 .... **152** C3
Clayton Dr *DEARNE* S63 .... **26** B3
Clayton Hollow *MOS* S20 .... **152** C3
Clayton La *DEARNE* S63 .... **26** B2
Clayton St *CHNE* S41 .... **190** C2
Clay Wheels La *ST/HB/BR* S6 ..... **96** C5
Claywood Dr *SHEFP/MNR* S2 .... **123** D5
Claywood Rd *SHEFP/MNR* S2 .. **136** A1 🔟
Clayworth Dr *DONS/BSCR* DN4 ... **45** F5 🔟
Clearwell Cft *BTLY* DN5 .... **29** D4
Cleeve Hill Gdns *MOS* S20 .... **152** B3
Clematis Rd *SHEFN* S5 .... **111** D1
Clement Ms *KIMB* S61 .... **101** F3 🔟
Clementson Rd *FUL* S10 .... **121** D3 🔟
Clement St *DARN/MH* S9 .... **124** C1
  KIMB S61 .... **101** F3
Clevedon Crs *BTLY* DN5 .... **16** A5
Cleveland St *DON* DN1 .... **4** C6
  ST/HB/BR S6 .... **121** F2
Cleveland Wy *CHSW* S40 .... **182** C5
Cliff Crs *DONS/BSCR* DN4 .... **62** A1
Cliffe Av *BSLY* S70 .... **22** C5
Cliffe Bank *MEX/SWTN* S64 .... **81** E1
Cliffe Ct *BSLYN/ROY* S71 .... **15** D4
Cliffedale Crs *BSLY* S70 .... **22** C4
Cliffe Farm Dr *ECC* S11 .... **133** E3 🔟
Cliffefield Rd *MEX/SWTN* S64 ...... **81** E1
  SHEFS S8 .... **135** D5
Cliffe House Rd *SHEFN* S5 .... **98** C5
Cliffe La *BSLYN/ROY* S71 .... **15** D4 🔟
Cliffe Rd *ST/HB/BR* S6 .... **120** B2
  WMB/DAR S73 .... **40** C5
Clifford Cl *CHSW* S40 .... **188** C2 🔟
Clifford Rd *ECC* S11 .... **134** B3

  KIMB S61 .... **91** F5
Cliff Rd *ST/HB/BR* S6 .... **119** E1
  WMB/DAR S73 .... **41** D1
Cliff St *ECC* S11 .... **135** D1
  MEX/SWTN S64 .... **58** B4
Cliff Vw *CONI* DN12 .... **60** A4
Clifton Av *DARN/MH* S9 .... **125** F4
  RHAM/THRY S65 .... **104** B3
Clifton Bank *RHAM/THRY* S65 .... **7** F4
Clifton Crs *DARN/MH* S9 .... **125** E4
  WHHL DN2 .... **31** F3
Clifton Crs North *RHAM/THRY* S65 ..... **7** G6
Clifton Crs South *RHAM/THRY* S65 ..... **7** G6
Clifton Dr *BTLY* DN5 .... **42** B2
Clifton Gv *RHAM/THRY* S65 .... **7** H5
Clifton Hl *CONI* DN12 .... **85** E2
Clifton La *DARN/MH* S9 .... **125** F5
  RHAM/THRY S65 .... **7** F6
Clifton Mt *RHAM/THRY* S65 .... **7** F6
Clifton St *BSLY* S70 .... **22** B2 🔟
  CHSW S40 .... **10** A6
  DARN/MH S9 .... **111** F4
Clifton Ter *RHAM/THRY* S65 .... **7** F6
Clinton Pl *FUL* S10 .... **134** C1
Clipstone Gdns *DARN/MH* S9 ... **125** D1
Clipstone Rd *DARN/MH* S9 .... **125** D1
The Cloisters *DONS/BSCR* DN4 ..... **47** E5
Cloisters Wy *BSLYN/ROY* S71 ..... **15** E5
Cloonmore Cft *SHEFS* S8 .... **147** F4
Cloonmore Dr *SHEFS* S8 .... **148** A4
Clough Bank *KIMB* S61 .... **102** C2
  SHEFP/MNR S2 .... **135** F2
Clough Flds *FUL* S10 .... **120** A3
Clough Fields Rd *HOY* S74 .... **51** D3
Clough Gn *KIMB* S61 .... **102** C2
Clough La *ECC* S11 .... **135** E5
Clough Rd *HOY* S74 .... **51** E3
  KIMB S61 .... **102** C2
  SHEF S1 .... **135** E1
Clough St *KIMB* S61 .... **102** C2
The Clough *CHNE* S41 .... **191** F3
Clover Gdns *SHEFN* S5 .... **110** C1
Clover Gn *KIMB* S61 .... **91** E4
Club Garden Rd *ECC* S11 .... **135** D2
Club Garden Wk *ECC* S11 .... **135** D1
Club Mill Rd *ST/HB/BR* S6 .... **108** C4
Club St *BSLYN/ROY* S71 .... **15** D3
  ECC S11 .... **135** D2
  HOY S74 .... **50** C3 🔟
Clumber Pl *STV/CWN* S43 .... **187** D3
Clumber Ri *AU/AST/KP* S26 .... **142** C4 🔟
Clumber Rd *DONS/BSCR* DN4 ..... **45** D3
  FUL S10 .... **132** C1
Clumber St *DOD/DAR* S75 .... **13** E5
Clun Rd *ATT* S4 .... **123** D1
Clun St *ATT* S4 .... **123** D1
Clyde Rd *SHEFS* S8 .... **135** D4
Clyde St *BSLYN/ROY* S71 .... **3** E6
Coach House Dr *BTLY* DN5 .... **28** B3
Coach House La *BSLY* S70 .... **22** A4 🔟
The Coach Houses *FUL* S10 .... **121** E3 🔟
Coach Rd *KIMB* S61 .... **92** C2
Coalbrook Av *HAN/WDH* S13 ..... **140** B2
Coalbrook Gv *HAN/WDH* S13 .... **140** B2
Coalbrook Rd *HAN/WDH* S13 .... **140** B2
Coal Pit La *STKB/PEN* S36 .... **68** C4
Coalpit Rd *CONI* DN12 .... **59** F5
Coates St *SHEFP/MNR* S2 .... **123** D5 🔟
Cobb Ct *MEX/SWTN* S64 .... **81** E2
Cobb Dr *MEX/SWTN* S64 .... **81** D2
Cobcar Av *HOY* S74 .... **52** C3
Cobcar Cl *HOY* S74 .... **52** B2
Cobcar La *HOY* S74 .... **52** B3
Cobcar St *HOY* S74 .... **52** B3
Cobden Av *MEX/SWTN* S64 .... **58** C3
Cobden Pl *FUL* S10 .... **121** D3 🔟
Cobden Rd *CHSW* S40 .... **10** D4
Cobden View Rd *FUL* S10 .... **120** C3
Cobnar Av *SHEFS* S8 .... **147** E3
Cobnar Dr *CHNE* S41 .... **183** E1
  SHEFS S8 .... **147** E3
Cobnar Gdns *SHEFS* S8 .... **147** D3 🔟
Cobnar Rd *SHEFS* S8 .... **147** D3
Cockayne Pl *SHEFS* S8 .... **147** D1
Cockerham Av *DOD/DAR* S75 .... **2** B2
Cockerham La *DOD/DAR* S75 .... **2** B1
Cockshot La *STKB/PEN* S36 .... **69** D4
Cockshutt Av *SHEFS* S8 .... **146** B5
Cockshutt Dr *SHEFS* S8 .... **146** B5
Cockshutt Rd *SHEFS* S8 .... **146** B5
Coisley Hl *HAN/WDH* S13 .... **139** D5
Coisley Rd *HAN/WDH* S13 .... **139** E4
Coit La *ECC* S11 .... **144** B2
Coke Hl *RHAM* S60 .... **103** E4
Coke La *RHAM* S60 .... **103** E4
Colby Pl *ST/HB/BR* S6 .... **120** A2
Colchester Ct *BTLY* DN5 .... **28** C3
Colchester Rd *FUL* S10 .... **120** B3
Coldstream Av *DONS/BSCR* DN4 .... **62** B1
Coldwell La *FUL* S10 .... **119** F4
Coleford Rd *DARN/MH* S9 .... **125** D1
Coleman St *RAW* S62 .... **94** A3 🔟
Coleridge Av *BSLYN/ROY* S71 ..... **14** C3
Coleridge Rd *DARN/MH* S9 .... **111** F5
  DEARNE S63 .... **55** D1

Rham/Thry S65 .... **7** H3
RHAM/THRY S65 .... **104** B1 🔟
Coley La *RAW* S62 .... **77** E1
Colister Dr *DARN/MH* S9 .... **124** C3
Colister Gdns *DARN/MH* S9 ...... **124** C4
College Av *STV/CWN* S43 .... **181** E5
College Park Cl *RHAM* S60 .... **114** C1
College Rd *DON* DN1 .... **4** D5
  MEX/SWTN S64 .... **58** C3
  RHAM S60 .... **6** A5
College St *FUL* S10 .... **121** E5 🔟
  RHAM/THRY S65 .... **6** D5
Collegiate Crs *FUL* S10 .... **134** B1
Colley Av *BSLY* S70 .... **23** D4
  SHEFN S5 .... **98** B3
Colley Cl *SHEFN* S5 .... **98** B3
Colley Crs *BSLY* S70 .... **23** D4
  SHEFN S5 .... **98** C3
Colley Dr *SHEFN* S5 .... **98** C3
Colley Pl *BSLY* S70 .... **23** D3 🔟
Colley Rd *SHEFN* S5 .... **98** B3
Colliers Cl *HAN/WDH* S13 .... **139** F4
Colliery Rd *ATT* S4 .... **111** E3
Colliery Yd *DOD/DAR* S75 .... **49** E4
Collin Av *ST/HB/BR* S6 .... **107** E3
Collindridge Rd *WMB/DAR* S73 ... **39** E3
Collingbourne Av *MOS* S20 ...... **153** E4
Collingbourne Dr *MOS* S20 .... **153** E4 🔟
Collingham Rd *AU/AST/KP* S26 ... **142** A4
Collins Rd *SHEFN* S5 .... **98** B5
Collishaw Cl *CHNE* S41 .... **191** D4 🔟
Colonel Ward Dr *MEX/SWTN* S64 ... **57** F5
Colster Cl *DOD/DAR* S75 .... **12** B5
Coltfield *BSLY* S70 .... **36** A4
Colton Cl *CHNE* S41 .... **177** F5
Columbia St *BSLY* S70 .... **21** F3
Colver Rd *SHEFP/MNR* S2 .... **135** E2
Colvin Cl *BTLY* DN5 .... **17** F5
Colwall St *DARN/MH* S9 .... **124** A1
Commerce St *CHPT/GREN* S35 .... **88** B1
Commercial St *BSLY* S70 .... **22** B2
  SHEF S1 .... **9** G5
Common La *BTLY* DN5 .... **18** B2
  CONI DN12 .... **85** E4
  DEARNE S63 .... **56** C2
  DONS/BSCR DN4 .... **62** B2
  ECC S11 .... **132** B5
  STKB/PEN S36 .... **69** F4
Common Rd *CONI* DN12 .... **85** F2
  CONI DN12 .... **85** F3
  DEARNE S63 .... **26** B3
Commonside *FUL* S10 .... **121** D3
The Common *CHPT/GREN* S35 ..... **88** C4
Compass Crs *CHNE* S41 .... **179** D3
Compton St *CHSW* S40 .... **10** C4
  ST/HB/BR S6 .... **120** C1
Conalan Av *TOT/DORE* S17 ...... **157** F3
Conan Rd *CONI* DN12 .... **84** C1
Concord Rd *SHEFN* S5 .... **99** F3
Concord View Rd *KIMB* S61 ...... **101** D4
Conduit La *FUL* S10 .... **121** D3 🔟
Conduit Rd *FUL* S10 .... **121** D3
Coney Rd *BTLY* DN5 .... **16** B2 🔟
Congress St *SHEF* S1 .... **8** C5 🔟
Coningsby Rd *SHEFN* S5 .... **110** A3
Coniston Pl *BTLY* DN5 .... **29** D1 🔟
Coniston Rd *BSLYN/ROY* S71 .... **3** F5
  CHNE S41 .... **183** E1
  DRON S18 .... **168** C2
  MEX/SWTN S64 .... **59** D2
  SHEFS S8 .... **134** C5
  WHHL DN2 .... **32** A5
Coniston Ter *SHEFS* S8 .... **134** C5 🔟
Coniston Wy *CHNE* S41 .... **183** F1
Constable Cl *DRON* S18 .... **168** C3
  GLV S14 .... **148** C3 🔟
Constable Dr *SHEFS* S8 .... **148** B3
Constable Pl *DEARNE* S63 .... **55** F2
  GLV S14 .... **148** C3
Constable Rd *SHEFS* S8 .... **148** B3
Constable Wy *SHEFS* S8 .... **148** B3 🔟
Convent Gv *DONS/BSCR* DN4 ..... **46** B4
Convent Pl *OWL* S3 .... **8** B6 🔟
Convent Wk *OWL* S3 .... **8** B6
Conway Crs *RHAM/THRY* S65 ... **105** D1
Conway Pl *WMB/DAR* S73 .... **40** A4
Conway St *BSLY* S70 .... **23** E2
Conway Ter *MEX/SWTN* S64 ...... **58** B2
Conyers Dr *AU/AST/KP* S26 ..... **142** B2
Conyers Rd *BTLY* DN5 .... **29** F4
Coo Hl *HAN/WDH* S13 .... **140** A4
Cooke St *BTLY* DN5 .... **29** E1
Cookson Cl *SHEFN* S5 .... **97** E5
Cookson Rd *SHEFN* S5 .... **108** B1
Cookson St *DONS/BSCR* DN4 ..... **43** F4 🔟
Cooks Rd *MOS* S20 .... **153** G3
Cooks Wood Rd *OWL* S3 .... **109** E5
Coombe Pl *FUL* S10 .... **121** D4 🔟
Coombe Rd *FUL* S10 .... **120** C4
Co-operative St *DEARNE* S63 ... **55** E1 🔟
Coopers Ter *DON* DN1 .... **5** F3
Cooper St *DONS/BSCR* DN4 .... **44** C3
Copeland Rd *WMB/DAR* S73 .... **39** D3 🔟
Cope St *BSLY* S70 .... **22** A3

Copley Av CONI DN12............... 84 B1
Copley Crs BTLY DN5............... 28 A3
Copley Pl KIMB S61.................. 102 B2
Copley Rd DON DN1.................... 5 E2
Copper Cl BSLY S70.................. 22 A2 3
Copper Cl OWL S3......................... 8 D3
Coppice Av DOD/DAR S75............ 12 C3
Coppice Cl STKB/PEN S36............ 68 A1
Coppice Gdns KIMB S61.............. 92 C4
Coppice La ST/HB/BR S6............ 118 C3
The Coppice KIMB S61................ 91 D4
Coppice Vw FUL S10............... 120 A4 9
Coppicewood Ct DONS/BSCR DN4.... 64 A3
Coppin Sq SHEFN S5.............. 98 A2 1
Coral Cl AU/AST/KP S26............ 129 D5
Coral Dr AU/AST/KP S26............ 129 D5
Coral Pl AU/AST/KP S26............ 129 D5
Coral Wy AU/AST/KP S26............ 129 D5
Corby St ATT S4...................... 123 E1
Cordwell Av CHNE S41............... 183 D1
Cordwell Cl STV/CWN S43........... 187 E1
Corker Bottoms La
    SHEFP/MNR S2.................. 124 A4
Corker Rd HACK/IN S12.............. 137 E4
Cornfield Cl CHSW S40............. 182 B4 3
Corn Hi CONI DN12.................... 85 E2
Cornish Cl OWL S3....................... 8 C1
Cornish Wy RAW S62.................. 80 C4
Cornwall Av STV/CWN S43.......... 186 A1 2
Cornwall Cl BSLYN/ROY S71.......... 14 C5
    STV/CWN S43..................... 186 A1
Cornwall Dr STV/CWN S43.......... 186 A1
Cornwall Rd WHHL DN2.............. 31 F4
Cornwell Cl RAW S62................. 79 D3
Coronation Br RHAM S60............ 102 C3
Coronation Gdns
    DONS/BSCR DN4................. 62 A1 8
Coronation Rd DEARNE S63........ 56 B2
    DONS/BSCR DN4................. 43 F5
    HOY S74............................ 51 F2
    MEX/SWTN S64................... 57 F5
    RAW S62........................... 81 D5
    STKB/PEN S36.................... 68 C2
    STV/CWN S43.................... 185 F1
Coronation St BSLYN/ROY S71..... 15 D3
    DEARNE S63...................... 27 E4
Coronation Ter BSLYN/ROY S71.... 24 A2
Corporation St BSLY S70............. 22 B3
    CHNE S41.......................... 11 G5
    OWL S3............................... 9 E3
    RHAM S60.......................... 6 C5
Cortina Ri WMB/DAR S73............ 25 F4 5
Cortworth La RAW S62............... 77 E2
Cortworth Rd ECC S11.............. 145 E5
Corve Wy RCH S42.................. 182 A4
Corwen Pl HAN/WDH S13........... 139 E4
Cossey Rd ATT S4.................... 123 D1
Coterel Crs DONS/BSCR DN4........ 47 D3
Cotleigh Av HACK/IN S12........... 151 E2
Cotleigh Cl HACK/IN S12.......... 151 E2 6
Cotleigh Crs HACK/IN S12.......... 151 E2
Cotleigh Dr HACK/IN S12........... 151 E2
Cotleigh Gdns HACK/IN S12........ 151 E2
Cotleigh Pl HACK/IN S12.......... 151 E2 7
Cotleigh Rd HACK/IN S12.......... 151 E2
Cotleigh Wy HACK/IN S12.......... 151 E2
Cotswold Av CHPT/GREN S35........ 87 F1
Cotswold Cl DOD/DAR S75.......... 12 C5 2
Cotswold Crs RHAM S60............ 116 A2
Cotswold Dr AU/AST/KP S26....... 142 C3
Cotswold Gdns BTLY DN5........... 29 D2 1
Cotswold Rd ST/HB/BR S6......... 107 F3
Cottage La ECC S11................ 132 A5
Cottam Cl RHAM S60............... 116 A3
Cottam Rd CHPT/GREN S35.......... 73 E4
Cottenham Rd RHAM/THRY S65..... 7 F3
Cotterhill La STV/CWN S43......... 185 F2
Cottesmore Cl DOD/DAR S75....... 13 D4 1
Cottingham St DARN/MH S9....... 124 A3
Cotton Mill Rw OWL S3................ 9 E3
Cotton St OWL S3........................ 9 E3
Coultas Av STKB/PEN S36........... 69 E3
Countess Rd SHEF S1............... 135 E3 8
County Wy BSLY S70.................. 2 D3
Coupe Rd ATT S4.................... 122 C1
Coupland Rd RHAM/THRY S65..... 105 D1
Court Cl ECC S11.................... 145 D2 3
Court Pl STV/CWN S43............. 187 E1
The Courtyard CONI DN12......... 59 D5
Coventry Gv WHHL DN2............ 31 F2
Coventry Rd DARN/MH S9......... 125 D2
Cover Cl RAW S62..................... 75 E2
Coverdale Rd ABRD S7............. 134 C5
Coverleigh Rd DEARNE S63........ 56 A4
Cow La ECC S11.................... 145 E2
    STV/CWN S43.................. 179 F5
Cowley Bottom DRON S18......... 168 C3
Cowley Dr CHPT/GREN S35......... 89 D2
Cowley Gdns MOS S20............. 152 C5
Cowley Gn WMB/DAR S73........... 38 C3
Cowley Hi CHPT/GREN S35......... 89 D2
Cowley La DRON S18............... 169 D3
Cowley View Rd CHPT/GREN S35... 88 C3
Cowlishaw Rd ECC S11............. 134 A2
Cowood St MEX/SWTN S64......... 58 A3 4

Cowper Av ST/HB/BR S6............ 97 E3
Cowper Crs ST/HB/BR S6........... 97 E3
Cowper Dr RHAM/THRY S65........ 104 C5
    ST/HB/BR S6...................... 97 E3
Cowper Rd MEX/SWTN S64......... 59 D3
Cowpingle La STV/CWN S43....... 179 F5
Cowrakes Cl RHAM S60............ 116 A3
Cow Rakes La RHAM S60........... 116 A3
Cox Pl ST/HB/BR S6................ 107 D3
Cox Rd ST/HB/BR S6............... 107 D4
Crabtree Cl SHEFN S5.............. 110 A3
Crabtree Crs SHEFN S5............ 110 A3
Crabtree Dr SHEFN S5............. 110 A3
Crabtree La SHEFN S5............. 109 F4
Crabtree Pl SHEFN S5............. 109 F3
Crabtree Rd SHEFN S5............. 109 F3
Cradley Dr AU/AST/KP S26........ 142 C5
Cradock Ms SHEFP/MNR S2....... 136 C3 1
Cradock Rd SHEFP/MNR S2........ 136 C3
Cragdale Gv MOS S20.............. 164 B1
Craggon Dr STV/CWN S43......... 179 E2 3
Craglands Gv RCH S42............. 182 B4
Crags Rd CONI DN12................ 60 C4
Craithie Rd WHHL DN2.............. 31 D5
Crakehall Rd CHPT/GREN S35..... 88 B3
Cramlands DOD/DAR S75............ 20 B3 8
Cranborne Rd CHNE S41.......... 183 F2
Cranbrook Rd DON DN1............. 30 C4
Cranbrook St BSLY S70.............. 21 D1
Crane Dr KIMB S61.................. 101 F2
Crane Rd KIMB S61.................. 91 F4
Cranfield Cl ARMTH DN3............ 33 F4
Cranford Ct MOS S20.............. 151 E3 2
Cranford Dr HACK/IN S12......... 151 E2
Cranston Cl BSLYN/ROY S71........ 15 E3
Cranwell Rd DONS/BSCR DN4...... 67 F1
Cranworth Pl OWL S3.............. 122 C1 3
Cranworth Rd OWL S3.............. 122 C1 6
    RHAM/THRY S65.................... 7 H2
Craven Cl DARN/MH S9............ 125 D2 3
    DONS/BSCR DN4................. 46 C4 3
Craven Rd CHNE S41................ 10 D1
Craven St OWL S3...................... 8 B3
    RAW S62............................ 94 A3
Craven Wood Cl DOD/DAR S75..... 12 B4
Crawford Rd SHEFS S8............ 147 D1
Crawshaw Av SHEFS S8............ 146 B5
Crawshaw Gv SHEFS S8............ 146 B5
Crawshaw Rd DONS/BSCR DN4.... 43 E2 1
Cream St SHEFP/MNR S2.......... 135 F1 1
Crecy Av WHHL DN2.................. 32 A5
Creighton Av RAW S62.............. 94 C1 1
Crescent Rd ABRD S7............. 134 C3
The Crescent CONI DN12............ 84 B1
    DOD/DAR S75..................... 12 C3
    MEX/SWTN S64................... 80 C1
    STV/CWN S43.................. 185 E2
    TOT/DORE S17................... 156 C3
Cresswell Rd DARN/MH S9........ 125 D3
    MEX/SWTN S64..................... 57 F4
Cresswell St DOD/DAR S75......... 11 D4
    MEX/SWTN S64.................. 58 A4 3
Crest Rd SHEFN S5.................. 98 C5
Crestwood Ct SHEFN S5............ 99 D5
Crestwood Gdns SHEFN S5........ 99 D5 3
Creswick Av SHEFN S5.............. 98 A2
Creswick Cl CHSW S40............. 188 C4
    RHAM/THRY S65................. 105 E1
Creswick Greave SHEFN S5........ 97 F2
Creswick La CHPT/GREN S35....... 97 F1
Creswick Rd RHAM/THRY S65..... 105 E1
Creswick Rd ST/HB/BR S6........ 121 E1
Creswick Wy ST/HB/BR S6........ 121 E1
Crich Rd STV/CWN S43............ 187 D2
Cricket Inn Crs SHEFP/MNR S2... 123 F3
Cricket Inn Rd SHEFP/MNR S2.... 123 D3
Cricket View Rd RAW S62............ 75 F2
Crimicar Av FUL S10............... 131 F2
Crimicar Cl FUL S10............... 132 A3
Crimicar Dr FUL S10............... 131 F2
Crimicar La FUL S10............... 131 F1
Crispin Cl HACK/IN S12........... 149 E1 1
Crispin Gdns HACK/IN S12........ 149 E1
Crispin Rd HACK/IN S12.......... 149 E1 2
Crochley Cl DONS/BSCR DN4....... 47 D3 1
Croft Cl ECC S11................... 145 D2 3
Crofters Cl ECC S11............... 145 D2
Croft Lea DRON S18................ 168 A1
Crofton Av ST/HB/BR S6........... 107 F2
Crofton Cl DRON S18.............. 169 D2
Crofton Ri CHPT/GREN S35......... 73 E5
    DRON S18......................... 169 D2
Croft Rd BSLY S70................... 23 D3
    DONS/BSCR DN4................. 62 C2
    HACK/IN S12..................... 137 F5
    HOY S74............................ 50 C3
    RHAM S60.......................... 113 F3
Crofts Dr RHAM/THRY S65......... 95 F4 1
The Crofts MALT S66................... 6 D6 2
    RHAM S60............................ 95 F4
Croft St BSLY S70.................. 22 B5 3
    KIMB S61........................... 92 C3
The Croft BTLY DN5................. 17 F3

CONI DN12.......................... 85 D2
    HOY S74............................ 52 B3 8
    MEX/SWTN S64.................. 80 C1
    RHAM S60......................... 127 D2
Croft Vw STV/CWN S43............ 187 D4
Cromarty Ri DRON S18............ 168 B1
Cromdale Av STV/CWN S43....... 187 E1
Cromer Cl RAW S62................. 80 A5 1
Cromer Rd WHHL DN2............... 32 A5
Cromford Av BSLYN/ROY S71...... 14 C1
Cromford Dr STV/CWN S43....... 186 C1
Cromford St SHEFP/MNR S2..... 135 F1 8
Crompton Av BSLY S70.............. 21 E2
    BTLY DN5........................... 29 D5
Crompton Rd WHHL DN2............ 31 F1
Cromwell Dr BTLY DN5.............. 42 C2
Cromwell Mt BSLY S70.............. 21 F4
Cromwell Rd BTLY DN5.............. 29 F4
    CHSW S40.......................... 10 C3
    MEX/SWTN S64.................. 58 B4
Cromwell St DEARNE S63.......... 27 E2
    ST/HB/BR S6...................... 121 D2
Crooked La CONI DN12.............. 83 E4
Crookes FUL S10.................... 120 C3
Crookesmoor Dr ST/HB/BR S6.... 121 E3 1
Crookesmoor Rd FUL S10.......... 121 E3
Crookes Rd DONS/BSCR DN4...... 63 F1 1
    FUL S10........................... 121 D4
Crookes St BSLY S70................... 2 A5
Crookes Valley Rd FUL S10....... 121 E3
Crookhill Rd CONI DN12............ 85 E1
Crosby Ct BSLYN/ROY S71.......... 15 E2
Crosby Rd SHEFS S8................ 146 C3
Cross Allen Rd MOS S20........... 153 D5
Cross Bank DONS/BSCR DN4....... 43 E5 8
Cross Bedford St ST/HB/BR S6..... 8 A1
Cross Burgess St SHEF S1........... 8 D6
Cross Butcher St DEARNE S63.... 26 C3 6
Cross Chantrey Rd SHEFS S8...... 147 E2
Crosscourt Vw DONS/BSCR DN4... 46 A4
Cross Dr HAN/WDH S13............ 139 F4 3
Crossfield Dr DEARNE S63.......... 55 F3
Cross Ga BTLY DN5.................. 29 E3
Crossgate DEARNE S63............. 27 D4
Cross Ga MEX/SWTN S64.......... 59 D4
Cross Hill CHPT/GREN S35......... 99 D2
Cross Hill Cl CHPT/GREN S35...... 99 D2
Crosshouse Cl CHPT/GREN S35.... 96 C1
Cross House Rd CHPT/GREN S35... 97 D1
Cross Keys La HOY S74............. 50 B2
Cross La CHPT/GREN S35............ 72 C1
    DRON S18......................... 160 A5
    DRON S18......................... 169 E2
    FUL S10........................... 120 C4
    SHEFS S8......................... 160 A3
    TOT/DORE S17................... 144 A5
Cross London St STV/CWN S43... 179 E3 2
Cross Myrtle Rd SHEFP/MNR S2.. 135 F1 3
Cross Park Rd SHEFS S8.......... 135 E5 3
Cross Riding DONS/BSCR DN4..... 32 C5
Cross Road Banner ECC S11...... 133 F5
Cross Smithfield OWL S3............. 8 C5
Cross South St KIMB S61.......... 93 D3
Cross St BSLY S70.................. 22 C5
    BSLYN/ROY S71.................. 15 D3
    BTLY DN5........................... 16 C5
    CHSW S40.......................... 10 C4
    DEARNE S63....................... 55 F2
    DOD/DAR S75...................... 2 A1
    DONS/BSCR DN4................. 43 E5 8
    ECK/KIL S21...................... 167 D1
    HAN/WDH S13.................... 139 F4
    HOY S74............................ 50 C3 8
    KIMB S61........................... 93 D3 8
    KIMB S61........................... 102 B3
    RAW S62........................... 94 A3
    RHAM/THRY S65................. 95 F4
    STV/CWN S43.................... 185 F1
Cross Turner St SHEFP/MNR S2.. 122 C5 2
Crossway MEX/SWTN S64.......... 80 C1
Crossways WHHL DN2............... 31 F2
Crossways North WHHL DN2....... 31 F2
Crossways South WHHL DN2....... 31 F3
The Crossways SHEFP/MNR S2... 137 F1 2
Cross Wellington St
    STV/CWN S43.................... 179 E3 8
Crowden Wk DOD/DAR S75.......... 20 B1 3
Crowder Av SHEFN S5............... 98 B5
Crowder Cl SHEFN S5.............. 109 E1
Crowder Crs SHEFN S5............ 109 E1
Crowder Rd SHEFN S5............... 98 B5
Crowland Rd SHEFN S5............. 98 C5
Crow La CHNE S41.................. 11 C5
    DRON S18......................... 170 C4
Crowley Dr DEARNE S63............ 51 F4
Crown Av BSLY S70.................. 22 B3 1
Crown Cl BSLY S70.................. 22 A3
    CHNE S41......................... 179 E3 2
    KIMB S61.......................... 101 F2
Crown Hill Rd DOD/DAR S75....... 20 B1
Crownhill Rd RHAM S60........... 113 E3
Crown Pl SHEFP/MNR S2............. 9 H5

Crown Rd *CHNE* S41 .... 11 E1
Crown St *BSLY* S70 .... 22 B3 🔲
　HOY S74 .... 51 E2
　MEX/SWTN S64 .... 57 E5
Crown Well HI *BSLYN/ROY* S71 ... 24 A2 🔲
Crowther PI *SHEFP/MNR* S2 ..... 135 D2 🔲
Crow Tree La *MEX/SWTN* S64 ..... 58 A1
Croydon St *ECC* S11 .... 135 D2 🔲
Cruck CI *DRON* S18 .... 168 C1
Cruise Rd *ECC* S11 .... 133 D2
Crummock Rd *SHEFS* S8 .... 134 C5 🔲
Crummock Wy *BSLYN/ROY* S71 ... 24 C2 🔲
Crumpsall Dr *DARN/MH* S9 ..... 109 D3
Crumpsall Rd *SHEFN* S5 .... 109 D3
Crumwell Rd *KIMB* S61 .... 91 E4
Crusader Dr *BTLY* DN5 .... 42 C1
Cuckoo Wy *ECK/KIL* S21 .... 165 F5 🔲
　STV/CWN S43 .... 185 D1
Cullabine Rd *SHEFP/MNR* S2 ..... 137 E3
Cumberland Av *WHHL* DN2 ..... 31 F5
Cumberland CI *BSLY* S70 .... 22 A5
　HOY S74 .... 51 F1
Cumberland Crs *CHPT/GREN* S35 ... 88 C2 🔲
Cumberland Dr *BSLYN/ROY* S71 ... 24 A2
Cumberland Rd *HOY* S74 .... 51 F1
Cumberland Wy *SHEF* S1 ..... 122 B5 🔲
Cundy St *ST/HB/BR* S6 .... 121 D2
Cunliffe St *DRON* S18 .... 160 A4
Cunningham Rd *DON* DN1 .... 5 F6
Cupola *OWL* S3 .... 8 D3
Cupola La *CHPT/GREN* S35 .... 87 D5
Cupola Yd *RHAM* S60 .... 6 B5
Curbar Curve *STV/CWN* S43 ..... 186 C3
Curlew Av *ECK/KIL* S21 .... 163 F5
Curlew Rdg *SHEFP/MNR* S2 ..... 123 E5
Curlew Ri *KIMB* S61 .... 76 B5
Curzon Av *DRON* S18 .... 169 D3
Curzon CI *ECK/KIL* S21 .... 166 B2
Cusworth La *BTLY* DN5 .... 28 C4
Cuthbert Bank Rd *ST/HB/BR* S6 ... 108 B5 🔲
Cuthbert Rd *ST/HB/BR* S6 ..... 108 B5 🔲
Cutler CI *ECK/KIL* S21 .... 165 F1 🔲
Cutlers Av *BSLY* S70 .... 21 E2
Cuttholme Rd *CHSW* S40 .... 182 C5
Cutthorpe Cft *RCH* S42 .... 182 B2
Cutthorpe Rd *RCH* S42 .... 182 A2
Cutts Av *DEARNE* S63 .... 55 E3
Cutts Ter *SHEFS* S8 .... 135 D3 🔲
Cutty La *DOD/DAR* S75 .... 13 E4
Cyclops St *ATT* S4 .... 110 C4
Cypress Av *SHEFS* S8 .... 148 A4
Cypress CI *ECK/KIL* S21 .... 166 A3 🔲
Cypress Ga *CHPT/GREN* S35 ..... 88 A2
Cypress Gv *CONI* DN12 .... 84 A3
Cypress Rd *BSLY* S70 .... 22 C3
Cyprus Rd *SHEFS* S8 .... 135 E5 🔲

D

Dade Av *STV/CWN* S43 .... 186 C3
Daffodil Rd *SHEFN* S5 .... 111 D1
Dagnam CI *SHEFP/MNR* S2 ..... 137 D4
Dagnam Crs *SHEFP/MNR* S2 ..... 137 D3
Dagnam Dr *SHEFP/MNR* S2 ..... 137 D3
Dagnam PI *SHEFP/MNR* S2 ..... 137 D4 🔲
Dagnam Rd *SHEFP/MNR* S2 ..... 137 D3
Daisy Bank *OWL* S3 .... 8 A3
Daisy Wk *MOS* S20 .... 152 C2
　OWL S3 .... 8 B4
Dalby Gdns *MOS* S20 .... 153 E4
Dalby Gv *MOS* S20 .... 153 E3
Dale Av *RHAM/THRY* S65 .... 105 D4
Dale Bank Crs *CHNE* S41 ..... 179 E3 🔲
Dale CI *STV/CWN* S43 .... 187 D1
Dale Ct *RAW* S62 .... 94 A1
Dale Green Rd *BSLY* S70 .... 22 A5
Dale Rd *CONI* DN12 .... 85 D1
　DRON S18 .... 169 F3
　ECK/KIL S21 .... 166 C2
　RAW S62 .... 80 A5
　RHAM/THRY S65 .... 105 D4
Dale St *RAW* S62 .... 80 A5
Daleswood Av *BSLY* S70 ..... 20 C1 🔲
Daleswood Dr *BSLY* S70 .... 23 E5 🔲
The Dale *SHEFS* S8 .... 147 D2
Daleview Rd *SHEFS* S8 .... 146 B3
Dalewood Av *SHEFS* S8 .... 146 A4
Dalewood CI *CHNE* S41 .... 191 F3
Dalewood Dr *SHEFS* S8 .... 145 F4
Dalewood Rd *SHEFS* S8 .... 146 A4
Dalmore Rd *ECC* S11 .... 134 A5
Dalton Ct *SHEFS* S8 .... 135 D3 🔲
Dalton La *RHAM/THRY* S65 ..... 105 F1
Dalvey Wy *STV/CWN* S43 .... 179 E2
Damer St *FUL* S10 .... 121 E4 🔲
Damon Dr *STV/CWN* S43 .... 186 A1
Damsteads *DOD/DAR* S75 .... 20 B3
Danby Av *CHNE* S41 .... 178 C4
Danebrook CI *SHEFP/MNR* S2 ..... 138 A1 🔲
Danebrook Dr *SHEFP/MNR* S2 ..... 138 A1 🔲
Danesthorpe CI *WHHL* DN2 ..... 32 A3
Dane St *DEARNE* S63 .... 27 E3
Dane St North *DEARNE* S63 .... 27 E3

Dane St South *DEARNE* S63 .... 27 E3
Danesway *BTLY* DN5 .... 16 A5
Danethorpe Wy *CONI* DN12 ..... 84 B3 🔲
Danewood Av *SHEFP/MNR* S2 ..... 138 A2
Danewood Cft *SHEFP/MNR* S2 ..... 138 A1
Danewood Gdns *SHEFP/MNR* S2 ..... 138 A1
Daniel HI *ST/HB/BR* S6 .... 121 F2
Daniel CI *ST/HB/BR* S6 .... 121 F2 🔲
Daniel Hill Ct *ST/HB/BR* S6 ..... 121 E2 🔲
Daniel Hill St *ST/HB/BR* S6 ..... 121 E2 🔲
Daniel Hill Ter *ST/HB/BR* S6 ..... 121 F2 🔲
Daniel La *RAW* S62 .... 78 C5
Daniels Dr *AU/AST/KP* S26 ..... 142 A1
Dannemora Dr *DARN/MH* S9 ..... 112 A5
Danum Dr *RHAM/THRY* S65 .... 7 H4
Danum Rd *DONS/BSCR* DN4 ..... 45 D2
Dara St *DARN/MH* S9 .... 100 C4
Darcy CI *AU/AST/KP* S26 ..... 142 B2 🔲
Darcy Rd *ECK/KIL* S21 .... 164 A5
Daresbury Dr *SHEFP/MNR* S2 ..... 136 B4
Daresbury PI *SHEFP/MNR* S2 ..... 136 B4
Daresbury Rd *SHEFP/MNR* S2 ..... 136 B4
Daresbury Vw *SHEFP/MNR* S2 ..... 136 B4
Darfield Av *MOS* S20 .... 151 D3
Darfield CI *MOS* S20 .... 151 D3 🔲
Dargle Av *CHSW* S40 .... 31 E4
Dark La *BSLY* S70 .... 20 C3
　BSLY S70 .... 36 C2
　CHNE S41 .... 185 F5
Darley *BSLY* S70 .... 23 D5
Darley Av *BSLY* S70 .... 21 F4
　BSLYN/ROY S71 .... 14 B1
Darley CI *BSLYN/ROY* S71 ..... 14 B1
　STV/CWN S43 .... 181 F4 🔲
Darley Gv *ST/HB/BR* S6 .... 106 B5
Darley Ter *DOD/DAR* S75 ..... 13 E5 🔲
Darley Yd *BSLY* S70 .... 36 C1
Darnall Dr *DARN/MH* S9 .... 124 C2
Darnall Rd *DARN/MH* S9 .... 124 C2
Darrington Dr *DONS/BSCR* DN4 ..... 62 B2
Darrington PI *BSLYN/ROY* S71 ..... 15 F4 🔲
Darton St *BSLY* S70 .... 23 E2
Dart Sq *OWL* S3 .... 121 F3
Darwall St *CHPT/GREN* S35 ..... 73 E5 🔲
Darwent Rd *CHNE* S41 .... 185 D3
Darwin Av *CHSW* S40 .... 10 B2
Darwin CI *FUL* S10 .... 120 A5
Darwin La *FUL* S10 .... 120 A5
Darwin Rd *CHSW* S40 .... 10 C3
　ST/HB/BR S6 .... 107 F2
Darwynn Av *MEX/SWTN* S64 ..... 56 B5
Davian Wy *CHSW* S40 .... 189 F4
David CI *HAN/WDH* S13 ..... 140 B3 🔲
David La *FUL* S10 .... 131 E3
Davies Dr *MEX/SWTN* S64 ..... 81 E2
Davis St *RHAM/THRY* S65 ..... 104 B2
Davy Rd *CONI* DN12 .... 59 F5
Dawber La *ECK/KIL* S21 .... 167 D1
Daw Croft Av *BSLY* S70 .... 22 B5
Dawlands CI *SHEFP/MNR* S2 ..... 137 F1 🔲
Dawlands Dr *SHEFP/MNR* S2 ..... 137 F1 🔲
Daw La *BTLY* DN5 .... 16 C4
Dawson Av *RAW* S62 .... 79 D3
Daw Wd *BTLY* DN5 .... 16 C3
Daylands Av *CONI* DN12 .... 84 B2
Day St *BSLY* S70 .... 21 F2
Deacons Wy *BSLYN/ROY* S71 ..... 15 D4
Deadman's Hole La *DARN/MH* S9 ... 101 F5
Deakins Wk *FUL* S10 .... 133 D1
Dean CI *BTLY* DN5 .... 42 B2
Deane Field Vw *MOS* S20 ..... 152 B3 🔲
Deanhead Ct *MOS* S20 ..... 151 E3 🔲
Deanhead Dr *MOS* S20 .... 151 D3
Dean La *RHAM/THRY* S65 ..... 105 F3
Deansfield CI *ARMTH* DN3 ..... 33 F4
Dean St *BSLY* S70 .... 21 E1 🔲
Deans Wy *BSLYN/ROY* S71 ..... 15 D3
Dearden St *CHPT/GREN* S35 ..... 98 C1 🔲
Dearne Br *BTLY* DN5 .... 60 A1
Dearne CI *WMB/DAR* S73 ..... 40 A4
Dearne Hall Fold *DOD/DAR* S75 ... 12 A1
Dearne Hall Rd *DOD/DAR* S75 ..... 12 A1
Dearne Rd *WMB/DAR* S73 ..... 40 B5
Dearne St *CONI* DN12 .... 61 D5
　DARN/MH S9 .... 111 E2
Dearne Valley Pkwy
　WMB/DAR S73 .... 39 D5
Dearneway *DEARNE* S63 .... 56 A2
Dearney Vw *DOD/DAR* S75 ..... 13 E3 🔲
Deben CI *CHSW* S40 .... 189 D4 🔲
Decoy Bank North
　DONS/BSCR DN4 .... 44 B3
Decoy Bank South
　DONS/BSCR DN4 .... 44 B4
Deepdale CI *STV/CWN* S43 ..... 181 F5
Deepdale Rd *KIMB* S61 .... 101 F3
Deep La *SHEFN* S5 .... 100 A1
Deepwell Av *MOS* S20 .... 165 D2
Deepwell Bank *MOS* S20 ..... 165 D2
Deepwell Ct *MOS* S20 .... 165 D2
Deepwell Vw *MOS* S20 .... 165 D2
Deerlands Av *SHEFN* S5 .... 97 F3
Deerlands CI *SHEFN* S5 .... 97 F3
Deerlands Mt *SHEFN* S5 .... 97 F3
Deerlands Rd *CHSW* S40 .... 188 C1
Deer Park PI *ST/HB/BR* S6 ..... 119 F1 🔲

Deer Park PI *ST/HB/BR* S6 ..... 119 F1
Deer Park Ri *ST/HB/BR* S6 ..... 119 F1
Deer Park Vw *ST/HB/BR* S6 ..... 119 F1
Deer Park Wy *ST/HB/BR* S6 ..... 120 A1
Deightonby St *DEARNE* S63 ..... 57 D3
De Lacy Dr *BTLY* DN5 .... 22 B5
Delamere CI *MOS* S20 .... 153 E5
De La Salle Dr *ATT* S4 .... 110 A5
Delf St *SHEFP/MNR* S2 ..... 135 F3 🔲
Della Av *BSLY* S70 .... 21 E2
Dell Crs *DONS/BSCR* DN4 ..... 43 D3
The Dell *CHSW* S40 .... 188 C1
Delph Bank *CHSW* S40 .... 189 F4
Delph House Rd *FUL* S10 ..... 120 A4
Delta PI *RHAM/THRY* S65 ..... 104 C2
Delves Av *CHSW* S40 .... 189 E3
　HACK/IN S12 .... 152 A1
Delves CI *CHSW* S40 .... 189 E3
　HACK/IN S12 .... 152 A1
Delves Dr *HACK/IN* S12 .... 152 A2
Delves La *AU/AST/KP* S26 ..... 154 B3
Delves PI *HACK/IN* S12 .... 151 F2
Delves Rd *ECK/KIL* S21 .... 166 A2
　HACK/IN S12 .... 152 A1
Delves Ter *HACK/IN* S12 ..... 152 A2 🔲
Denaby Av *CONI* DN12 .... 84 B1
Denaby La *CONI* DN12 .... 82 C2
Den Bank Av *FUL* S10 .... 119 F4
Den Bank CI *FUL* S10 .... 120 A4
Den Bank Crs *FUL* S10 .... 119 F4
Den Bank Dr *FUL* S10 .... 119 F4
Denby Rd *STV/CWN* S43 ..... 187 D3
Denby St *BTLY* DN5 .... 16 B4
　SHEFP/MNR S2 .... 135 D1
Dene Crs *RHAM/THRY* S65 ..... 104 C1
Dene La *OWL* S3 .... 122 A5
Dene Rd *RHAM/THRY* S65 ..... 104 C1
Denham Rd *FUL* S10 .... 134 C1
Denholme CI *OWL* S3 .... 9 F1
Denison Ct *BSLY* S70 .... 22 A2 🔲
Denison Rd *DONS/BSCR* DN4 ..... 4 A5
Denman Rd *DEARNE* S63 ..... 55 E2
Denman St *RHAM/THRY* S65 ..... 7 F2
Denmark Rd *SHEFP/MNR* S2 ..... 135 F4
Dent La *MOS* S20 .... 153 D5
Denton Rd *SHEFS* S8 .... 147 D1 🔲
Denton St *BSLYN/ROY* S71 ..... 3 E5
Derby PI *SHEFP/MNR* S2 ..... 136 A4 🔲
Derby Rd *CHSW* S40 .... 190 B3
　WHHL DN2 .... 32 A1
Derbyshire La *SHEFS* S8 .... 147 D3
Derby St *BSLY* S70 .... 21 E1
　SHEFP/MNR S2 .... 135 F4
Derby Ter *SHEFP/MNR* S2 ..... 136 A4
Derriman Av *ECC* S11 .... 145 F1
Derriman CI *ECC* S11 .... 145 F1
Derriman Dr *ECC* S11 .... 145 F1
Derriman Gln *ECC* S11 .... 145 F1
Derriman Gv *ECC* S11 .... 145 F1
Derry Gv *DEARNE* S63 .... 26 C4
Derwent CI *DRON* S18 .... 159 F5 🔲
Derwent Crs *CHNE* S41 .... 183 E2
　RHAM S60 .... 113 F5
Derwent Dr *CHPT/GREN* S35 ..... 87 F1
　MEX/SWTN S64 .... 59 D2 🔲
　RAW S62 .... 94 A2
Derwent PI *WMB/DAR* S73 ..... 40 A4 🔲
Derwent Rd *DRON* S18 .... 159 F5
　KIMB S61 .... 91 E4
　MEX/SWTN S64 .... 59 D2
Derwent St *SHEFP/MNR* S2 ..... 123 E3
Derwent Ter *MEX/SWTN* S64 ..... 58 B2
Derwent Wy *DEARNE* S63 ..... 40 C5
Deveron Rd *MOS* S20 .... 165 D1 🔲
Devizes CI *CHSW* S40 .... 190 A4
Devon Dr *STV/CWN* S43 .... 186 A1
Devon Park Vw *STV/CWN* S43 ..... 186 A1
Devonshire Av East *CHNE* S41 ..... 191 D4
Devonshire Av North
　STV/CWN S43 .... 179 E3
Devonshire CI *CHNE* S41 ..... 184 A1
　DRON S18 .... 169 D3 🔲
　STV/CWN S43 .... 181 F4 🔲
　TOT/DORE S17 .... 157 D2 🔲
Devonshire Ct *STV/CWN* S43 ..... 185 E2 🔲
Devonshire Dr *DOD/DAR* S75 ..... 13 E3
　TOT/DORE S17 .... 156 C1
Devonshire Gln *TOT/DORE* S17 ..... 157 D2 🔲
Devonshire Gv *TOT/DORE* S17 ..... 156 C2 🔲
Devonshire La *SHEF* S1 .... 8 C6
Devonshire Rd *TOT/DORE* S17 ..... 156 C1
　WHHL DN2 .... 31 F4
Devonshire Rd East *CHNE* S41 ..... 191 D4
Devonshire Rd North
　STV/CWN S43 .... 179 E3
Devonshire St *CHNE* S41 .... 11 F5
　KIMB S61 .... 102 C3 🔲
　SHEF S1 .... 8 B6
　STV/CWN S43 .... 181 F4
Dewar Dr *ABRD* S7 .... 146 A1
Dewhill Av *RHAM* S60 .... 115 F3
Dial CI *SHEFS* S8 .... 99 D5
Dial House Rd *ST/HB/BR* S6 ..... 107 E4
Dial Wy *SHEFS* S8 .... 99 D5
Diamond St *WMB/DAR* S73 ..... 39 E2 🔲
Dickens CI *RHAM* S60 .... 126 C1

Dickenson Ct *CHPT/GREN* S35 .... 88 A1 **1**
Dickenson Rd *CHNE* S41 .... 190 C3 **1**
Dickens Rd *RAW* S62 .... 80 C4
Dickinson Pl *BSLY* S70 .... 22 A3 **3**
Dickinson Rd *BSLY* S70 .... 22 A3 **1**
  SHEFN S5 .... 99 E2
Didcot Cl *CHSW* S40 .... 190 A4
Digby Cl *KIMB* S61 .... 101 F1
Dike Hl *RAW* S62 .... 75 F2
Dikelands Mt *CHPT/GREN* S35 .... 73 E5 **1**
Dillington Rd *BSLY* S70 .... 22 A3
Dillington Sq *BSLY* S70 .... 22 A3
Dingle La *CHNE* S41 .... 191 F5 **3**
Dinmore Cl *DONS/BSCR* DN4 .... 63 E3
Dinnington Rd *SHEFS* S8 .... 147 D1 **3**
Dirleton Dr *DONS/BSCR* DN4 .... 62 B1 **1**
Discovery Wy *CHNE* S41 .... 178 B5
Ditchingham St *ATT* S4 .... 123 D1 **2**
Division La *SHEF* S1 .... 8 D6
Division St *SHEF* S1 .... 8 C6
  STV/CWN S43 .... 187 D1
Dixon Crs *DONS/BSCR* DN4 .... 43 D5
Dixon La *SHEF* S1 .... 9 G4
Dixon Rd *ST/HB/BR* S6 .... 107 F3
Dixon St *OWL* S3 .... 8 C1
  RHAM/THRY S65 .... 7 E4
Dobbin Hl *ECC* S11 .... 133 E4
Dobbin La *DRON* S18 .... 168 A5
Dobcroft Av *ABRD* S7 .... 145 F3
Dobcroft Cl *ECC* S11 .... 145 E1
Dobcroft Rd *ECC* S11 .... 145 E1
Dobie St *BSLY* S70 .... 22 A3
Dobson Pl *STV/CWN* S43 .... 186 C3
Dobsyke Cl *BSLY* S70 .... 23 E5 **1**
Dockin Hill Rd *DON* DN1 .... 5 F2
Dock Wk *CHSW* S40 .... 190 A2
Dodds Cl *RHAM* S60 .... 103 D5
Dodd St *ST/HB/BR* S6 .... 108 A5
Dodson Dr *HAN/WDH* S13 .... 126 A5
Dodsworth St *MEX/SWTN* S64 .... 58 A4 **1**
Dodworth Rd *BSLY* S70 .... 21 D1
Doe La *ECK/KIL* S21 .... 161 F4
  SHEFS S8 .... 162 A3
Doe Royd Crs *SHEFN* S5 .... 97 E4
Doe Royd Dr *SHEFN* S5 .... 97 F4
Doe Royd La *SHEFN* S5 .... 97 E5
Dog Croft La *BTLY* DN5 .... 18 B5
Dolcliffe Rd *MEX/SWTN* S64 .... 58 B4
Doles La *RHAM* S60 .... 116 C5
  RHAM S60 .... 127 F1
Domine La *RHAM* S60 .... 6 C5
Dominoe Gv *HACK/IN* S12 .... 138 D5
Don Av *ST/HB/BR* S6 .... 107 E1
Doncaster Ga *RHAM/THRY* S65 .... 6 D5
Doncaster Pl *RHAM/THRY* S65 .... 104 D2
Doncaster Rd *ARMTH* DN3 .... 19 F4
  ARMTH DN3 .... 32 C3
  BSLY S70 .... 3 E6
  BSLY S70 .... 22 C2
  BSLY S70 .... 23 E2 **1**
  BSLYN/ROY S71 .... 23 F2
  CONI DN12 .... 60 A3
  CONI DN12 .... 85 E1 **3**
  DEARNE S63 .... 27 F5
  DEARNE S63 .... 56 B2
  DEARNE S63 .... 56 C2
  MEX/SWTN S64 .... 58 C4
  RHAM/THRY S65 .... 7 F5
  RHAM/THRY S65 .... 95 E5
Doncaster St *OWL* S3 .... 8 C2
Don Dr *BSLY* S70 .... 23 E3
Donetsk Wy *HACK/IN* S12 .... 151 E2
Donnington Rd *MEX/SWTN* S64 .... 59 E2
  SHEFP/MNR S2 .... 136 B1
Donovan Cl *SHEFN* S5 .... 108 C1
Donovan Rd *SHEFN* S5 .... 108 C1
Don Rd *DARN/MH* S9 .... 111 D3
Don St *CONI* DN12 .... 61 E5
  DON DN1 .... 30 B4
  RHAM S60 .... 103 E4
Dorchester Pl *BSLY* S70 .... 22 A3
Dore Cl *TOT/DORE* S17 .... 157 E1
Dore Hall Cft *TOT/DORE* S17 .... 156 B1 **1**
Dore Rd *TOT/DORE* S17 .... 144 C5
Dorking St *ATT* S4 .... 9 H1
Dorothy Rd *ST/HB/BR* S6 .... 107 F3
Dorothy V *CHSW* S40 .... 183 D5
Dorset Av *STV/CWN* S43 .... 186 A1
Dorset Crs *BSLY* S70 .... 22 A3
Dorset Dr *STV/CWN* S43 .... 186 A1
Dorset St *FUL* S10 .... 121 F5
Douglas Rd *CHNE* S41 .... 184 C3
  DONS/BSCR DN4 .... 42 C5
  OWL S3 .... 109 D5
  OWL S3 .... 122 A1
Douse Croft La *FUL* S10 .... 131 D4
Dovecliffe Rd *WMB/DAR* S73 .... 37 F2
Dove Cl *WMB/DAR* S73 .... 40 A4
Dovecott Lea *MOS* S20 .... 153 F2
Dovedale *BSLY* S70 .... 36 C1
Dovedale Av *STV/CWN* S43 .... 186 A1
Dovedale Rd *ABRD* S7 .... 134 B5
  RHAM/THRY S65 .... 105 D5
Dove La *AU/AST/KP* S26 .... 142 C5

Dovercourt Rd *KIMB* S61 .... 102 B2
  SHEFP/MNR S2 .... 136 C1
Doveridge Cl *CHNE* S41 .... 178 B4 **1**
Dove Rd *WMB/DAR* S73 .... 40 A4
Dover Rd *FUL* S10 .... 134 A1
Dover St *OWL* S3 .... 8 A3
Dowdeswell St *CHNE* S41 .... 11 E3
Dowland Av *CHPT/GREN* S35 .... 73 F3
Dowland Cl *CHPT/GREN* S35 .... 73 F3
Dowland Ct *CHPT/GREN* S35 .... 73 E2
Dowland Gdns *CHPT/GREN* S35 .... 73 E3
Downgate Dr *ATT* S4 .... 110 C4
Downham Rd *SHEFN* S5 .... 110 B1
Downing La *OWL* S3 .... 8 B2 **1**
Downing Rd *SHEFS* S8 .... 146 C5
Downland Cl *DONS/BSCR* DN4 .... 63 D3
Downlands *STV/CWN* S43 .... 185 E2
Down's Rw *RHAM* S60 .... 6 D6
Drake *CHPT/GREN* S35 .... 87 F1
Drake Head La *CONI* DN12 .... 85 F1
Drake House Crs *MOS* S20 .... 152 B2
Drake House La *MOS* S20 .... 153 D2
Drake House La West *MOS* S20 .... 153 D2 **1**
Drake House Wy *MOS* S20 .... 152 C2
Drake Rd *WHHL* DN2 .... 30 C5
Dransfield Cl *FUL* S10 .... 120 A5 **1**
Dransfield Rd *FUL* S10 .... 119 F5
Draycott Pl *DRON* S18 .... 168 B3 **3**
Driver St *HAN/WDH* S13 .... 140 B3
The Drive *ST/HB/BR* S6 .... 107 F2
Dronfield Rd *ECK/KIL* S21 .... 173 E1
Droppingwell Farm Cl *KIMB* S61 ... 91 E5 **3**
Droppingwell Rd *KIMB* S61 .... 101 D2
Drover Cl *CHPT/GREN* S35 .... 73 F5
Drummond Av *BTLY* DN5 .... 28 A2
Drummond Crs *SHEFN* S5 .... 98 C4
Drummond Rd *SHEFN* S5 .... 98 C4
Drummond St *RHAM* S60 .... 6 D3
Drury Farm Ct *DOD/DAR* S75 .... 20 B1 **3**
Drury La *DRON* S18 .... 160 A5
  TOT/DORE S17 .... 156 B1
Dryden Av *CHSW* S40 .... 190 A4
  SHEFN S5 .... 97 F5
Dryden Dr *SHEFN* S5 .... 97 F5
Dryden Rd *BSLYN/ROY* S71 .... 3 F3
  DEARNE S63 .... 55 D1
  DONS/BSCR DN4 .... 64 A1
  MEX/SWTN S64 .... 58 C3
  RHAM/THRY S65 .... 104 C5
  SHEFN S5 .... 97 F5
Dublin Rd *WHHL* DN2 .... 31 D2
Duchess Rd *SHEFP/MNR* S2 .... 135 F1
Duckham Dr *AU/AST/KP* S26 .... 142 C4
Ducksett La *ECK/KIL* S21 .... 164 B5
Dudley Rd *ST/HB/BR* S6 .... 107 F2
  WHHL DN2 .... 45 F1
Dudley St *RAW* S62 .... 94 A3 **3**
Duftons Cl *CONI* DN12 .... 61 E5 **3**
Dugdale Dr *SHEFN* S5 .... 98 A2
Dugdale Rd *SHEFN* S5 .... 98 A2
Duke Crs *BSLY* S70 .... 22 A2 **3**
  KIMB S61 .... 91 F5
Duke La *SHEF* S1 .... 122 B5
Duke of Norfolk La *MALT* S66 .... 105 F5
Dukes Dr *CHNE* S41 .... 183 F3
Dukes Pl *RHAM/THRY* S65 .... 104 C5
Duke St *BSLY* S70 .... 22 A2 **3**
  CHNE S41 .... 184 B1 **1**
  DON DN1 .... 4 D4
  HOY S74 .... 51 E3 **1**
  MEX/SWTN S64 .... 57 E4
  MOS S20 .... 164 B2
  STV/CWN S43 .... 181 F4
Dumbleton Rd *ECK/KIL* S21 .... 166 A4
Dumble Wood Gra *CHSW* S40 .... 183 D2 **3**
Duncan Rd *FUL* S10 .... 120 C3
Duncan St *RHAM* S60 .... 114 A4
Duncombe St *ST/HB/BR* S6 .... 121 E2
Dundas Rd *DARN/MH* S9 .... 112 C1
  WHHL DN2 .... 30 C4
Dundonald Rd *CHSW* S40 .... 190 B3 **1**
Dunedin Gln *MOS* S20 .... 164 C2
Dunedin Gv *MOS* S20 .... 164 C2
Dunella Dr *ST/HB/BR* S6 .... 107 F3
Dunella Pl *ST/HB/BR* S6 .... 107 E3
Dunella Rd *ST/HB/BR* S6 .... 107 E3
Dun Flds *OWL* S3 .... 8 C2
Dunkeld Rd *ECC* S11 .... 133 F5
Dunkerley Rd *ST/HB/BR* S6 .... 106 B3
Dun La *OWL* S3 .... 8 C2
Dunleary Rd *WHHL* DN2 .... 31 E5
Dunlin Cl *KIMB* S61 .... 76 A5
Dunlop St *DARN/MH* S9 .... 111 F3
Dunmere Cl *BSLYN/ROY* S71 .... 14 B2 **1**
Dunmow Rd *ATT* S4 .... 110 C3
Dunninc Rd *SHEFN* S5 .... 99 E2
Dunninc Ter *SHEFN* S5 .... 99 E2
Dunniwood Av *DONS/BSCR* DN4 .... 67 D2
Dunniwood Reach
  DONS/BSCR DN4 .... 67 D1 **1**
Dunston Ct *CHNE* S41 .... 178 A5
Dunston La *CHNE* S41 .... 183 F1
Dunston Pl *CHNE* S41 .... 178 A5 **1**

Dunston Rd *CHNE* S41 .... 176 C5
Dun St *MEX/SWTN* S64 .... 81 F1
  OWL S3 .... 8 C2
Durham Cl *CHNE* S41 .... 179 E3
Durham La *FUL* S10 .... 121 F4
Durham Pl *RHAM/THRY* S65 .... 104 C5
Durham Rd *FUL* S10 .... 121 F4 **3**
  WHHL DN2 .... 31 D2
Durley Chine Dr *CHNE* S41 .... 191 D4
Durlstone Cl *HACK/IN* S12 .... 137 E5 **3**
Durlstone Crs *HACK/IN* S12 .... 137 E5
Durlstone Dr *HACK/IN* S12 .... 137 D5
Durlstone Gv *HACK/IN* S12 .... 137 E5
Durmast Gv *ST/HB/BR* S6 .... 119 D1
Durnan Gv *RAW* S62 .... 79 D3
Durnford Rd *WHHL* DN2 .... 30 C4
Durrant Rd *CHNE* S41 .... 11 F5
Durvale Ct *TOT/DORE* S17 .... 156 C5
Dutton Rd *ST/HB/BR* S6 .... 108 B3
Dyche Cl *SHEFS* S8 .... 159 F2 **1**
Dyche Dr *SHEFS* S8 .... 159 F2
Dyche La *SHEFS* S8 .... 159 E1
Dyche Pl *SHEFS* S8 .... 159 F2 **1**
Dyche Rd *SHEFS* S8 .... 159 F2
Dycott Rd *KIMB* S61 .... 102 A2 **1**
Dyer Rd *HOY* S74 .... 52 B1
Dykes Hall Gdns *ST/HB/BR* S6 .... 107 F4
Dykes Hall Pl *ST/HB/BR* S6 .... 107 F3
Dykes Hall Rd *ST/HB/BR* S6 .... 107 E4
Dykes La *ST/HB/BR* S6 .... 107 E4
Dyke Vale Av *HACK/IN* S12 .... 151 E1
Dyke Vale Cl *HACK/IN* S12 .... 151 E1
Dyke Vale Pl *HACK/IN* S12 .... 151 E1
Dyke Vale Rd *HACK/IN* S12 .... 139 D5
Dyke Vale Wy *HACK/IN* S12 .... 151 D1
Dykewood Dr *ST/HB/BR* S6 .... 107 D1
Dyson Pl *ECC* S11 .... 134 B2 **3**
Dyson St *BSLY* S70 .... 21 E3 **1**

E

Eaden Crs *HOY* S74 .... 52 A2
Eagleton Dr *CHPT/GREN* S35 .... 73 F3
Eagleton Ri *CHPT/GREN* S35 .... 73 F3
Eagle Vw *AU/AST/KP* S26 .... 142 C4
Eaming Vw *BSLYN/ROY* S71 .... 3 G2
Earldom Cl *ATT* S4 .... 123 D1
Earldom Dr *ATT* S4 .... 123 D1
Earldom Rd *ATT* S4 .... 110 A5
Earldom St *ATT* S4 .... 123 D1
Earlesmere Av *DONS/BSCR* DN4 .... 43 E4
Earl Marshal Cl *ATT* S4 .... 110 B3
Earl Marshal Dr *ATT* S4 .... 110 B4 **1**
Earl Marshal Rd *ATT* S4 .... 110 B3
Earl Marshal Vw *ATT* S4 .... 110 A4
Earlsmere Dr *BSLYN/ROY* S71 .... 24 B2
Earlston Dr *BTLY* DN5 .... 29 F3
Earl St *SHEF* S1 .... 122 B5
Earl Wy *SHEF* S1 .... 122 B5
Earnshaw Ter *DOD/DAR* S75 .... 2 A2
Earsham St *ATT* S4 .... 123 D1
Easedale Cl *RCH* S42 .... 182 A4 **3**
East Av *MEX/SWTN* S64 .... 80 C1
  RAW S62 .... 80 A5
  WMB/DAR S73 .... 38 C2
East Bank Cl *SHEFP/MNR* S2 .... 136 B4 **1**
East Bank Pl *SHEFP/MNR* S2 .... 136 B4
East Bank Rd *SHEFP/MNR* S2 .... 136 A3
East Bank Vw *SHEFP/MNR* S2 .... 136 B4 **3**
East Bank Wy *SHEFP/MNR* S2 .... 136 B4 **3**
East Bawtry Rd *RHAM* S60 .... 115 F2 **3**
  RHAM S60 .... 116 A1
  RHAM S60 .... 116 A2 **3**
East Coast Rd *DARN/MH* S9 .... 123 F1
East Crs *RHAM/THRY* S65 .... 104 C2
  STKB/PEN S36 .... 68 B2
Eastcroft Cl *MOS* S20 .... 153 D5
Eastcroft Dr *MOS* S20 .... 164 C1
Eastcroft Gln *MOS* S20 .... 153 D5 **3**
Eastcroft Vw *MOS* S20 .... 165 D1 **3**
Eastcroft Wy *MOS* S20 .... 153 D5 **3**
Eastern Av *SHEFP/MNR* S2 .... 136 C3
Eastern Crs *SHEFP/MNR* S2 .... 136 B4
Eastern Dr *SHEFP/MNR* S2 .... 136 B3
Eastfield Pl *RAW* S62 .... 81 D4
Eastfield Rd *ARMTH* DN3 .... 33 F4
  DRON S18 .... 170 A3
  FUL S10 .... 121 D2 **3**
Eastfields *BSLY* S70 .... 36 C1
Eastgate *BSLY* S70 .... 2 C4
East Glade Av *HACK/IN* S12 .... 150 C2
East Glade Cl *HACK/IN* S12 .... 150 C2
East Glade Crs *HACK/IN* S12 .... 150 C1
East Glade Pl *HACK/IN* S12 .... 150 C1
East Glade Rd *HACK/IN* S12 .... 150 C1
East Glade Sq *HACK/IN* S12 .... 150 C2 **3**
East Glade Wy *HACK/IN* S12 .... 150 C1
Eastgrove Rd *FUL* S10 .... 134 B1
East Laith Ga *DON* DN1 .... 5 F3
Eastleigh Ct *CHNE* S41 .... 191 E4 **3**
Eastmoor Rd *STV/CWN* S43 .... 186 A5
East Pde *SHEF* S1 .... 9 E5
East Rd *RHAM/THRY* S65 .... 104 C2

SHEFP/MNR S2....135 F3
Eastside Cl CHNE S41....184 C2
East St BSLY S70....37 D1
  DEARNE S63....27 F5
  DON DN1....44 A3
  ECK/KIL S21....175 F2
East Vw CHSW S40....190 B2
East View Av ECK/KIL S21....174 A1
Eastwood Cl CHNE S41....191 D4
Eastwood Mt RHAM/THRY S65....7 E5
Eastwood Park Dr CHNE S41....191 E4
Eastwood Rd ECC S11....134 B2
Eastwood V RHAM/THRY S65....104 B1
Eaton Pl SHEFP/MNR S2....123 E4
Ebenezer Pl OWL S3....8 D2
Ebenezer St OWL S3....8 D2
Eben St DARN/MH S9....111 E2
Ecclesall Rd ECC S11....133 F3
Ecclesall Rd South ECC S11....133 E5
Ecclesfield Rd CHPT/GREN S35....88 C2
  DARN/MH S9....100 A2
  SHEFN S5....99 E1
Eccles St DARN/MH S9....100 C5
Eckington Rd DRON S18....160 B5
  MOS S20....153 D5
Edale Rd ECC S11....133 E4
  KIMB S61....101 F3
Eden Dr ST/HB/BR S6....106 C4
Edenfield Cl BSLYN/ROY S71....15 E1
Eden Gld AU/AST/KP S26....142 B3
Eden Gv AU/AST/KP S26....142 B2
  DONS/BSCR DN4....43 E2
Edenhall Rd SHEFP/MNR S2....137 D3
Edensor Rd SHEFN S5....100 F2
Eden Ter MEX/SWTN S64....58 B2
Edenthorpe Dell HACK/IN S12....151 F3
Edenthorpe Gv MOS S20....152 A3
Edgbaston Wy CONI DN12....62 A4
Edgebrook Rd ECC S11....134 B4
Edgecliffe Pl BSLYN/ROY S71....14 B2
Edge Cl ST/HB/BR S6....97 D3
Edgedale Rd ABRD S7....134 C5
Edgefield Rd ABRD S7....134 C5
Edge Hill Rd ABRD S7....134 B4
Edgehill Rd WHHL DN2....32 A2
Edge La ST/HB/BR S6....96 C3
Edgemount Rd ABRD S7....134 C5
Edge Well Cl ST/HB/BR S6....97 D3
Edge Well Crs ST/HB/BR S6....97 D3
Edge Well Dr ST/HB/BR S6....97 D4
Edge Well Pl ST/HB/BR S6....97 D3
Edge Well Ri ST/HB/BR S6....97 D3
Edinburgh Cl BSLYN/ROY S71....14 C5
  HOY S74....51 F1
Edith Ter BTLY DN5....28 B2
Edlington La DONS/BSCR DN4....62 A2
Edmonton Cl DOD/DAR S75....12 B5
Edmund Av RHAM S60....114 B5
  TOT/DORE S17....158 A2
Edmund Cl TOT/DORE S17....158 A2
Edmund Dr TOT/DORE S17....158 A2
Edmund Rd SHEFP/MNR S2....135 F2
Edmunds Rd BSLY S70....37 D1
Edmund St CHNE S41....184 A1
Edward Cl BSLY S70....23 D3
Edward Rd DEARNE S63....41 D5
Edward St ARMTH DN3....33 D2
  BTLY DN5....16 C5
  DEARNE S63....26 C3
  ECK/KIL S21....164 B5
  HOY S74....51 E2
  MEX/SWTN S64....57 E4
  OWL S3....8 B4
  STKB/PEN S36....69 D2
  STV/CWN S43....187 D1
  WMB/DAR S73....39 F2
Edwin Av CHSW S40....189 E4
Edwin Rd SHEFP/MNR S2....136 A4
Effingham La ATT S4....9 H3
Effingham Rd ATT S4....123 D2
  DARN/MH S9....123 F2
Effingham Sq RHAM S60....6 D4
Effingham St ATT S4....9 H2
  RHAM/THRY S65....7 E3
Egerton Cl SHEF S1....122 A5
Egerton La OWL S3....122 A5
Egerton Rd AU/AST/KP S26....142 B3
  DRON S18....169 F1
Egerton St OWL S3....122 A5
Eggington Cl ARMTH DN3....47 F5
Eilam Cl KIMB S61....101 F1
Eilam Rd KIMB S61....101 F1
Ekin St RHAM S60....102 B5
Eland Gate Cl NROS/TKH DN11....67 D5
Elcroft Gdns MOS S20....153 D2
Elder Ct ECK/KIL S21....166 A5
Elder Gv CONI DN12....84 B2
Eldertree Rd KIMB S61....90 A3
Elder Wy CHSW S40....11 F6
Eldon Rd RHAM/THRY S65....7 G1
Eldon St BSLY S70....2 C5
  SHEF S1....8 C6

Eldon St North BSLY S70....2 D4
Eleanor Ct ARMTH DN3....19 F5
Eleanor St DARN/MH S9....124 C1
Elgin Cl CHSW S40....189 D5
Elgin St FUL S10....120 C4
Eliot Cl STV/CWN S43....186 A4
Elizabeth Rd AU/AST/KP S26....142 B3
Elkstone Rd CHSW S40....182 B4
Ella Rd ATT S4....110 A5
Ellavale HOY S74....52 B2
Ellenbro Rd ST/HB/BR S6....107 F4
Ellen Tree Cl RHAM S60....113 F4
Ellerker Av DONS/BSCR DN4....4 B6
Ellers Av DONS/BSCR DN4....46 A4
Ellers Crs DONS/BSCR DN4....46 A4
Ellers Dr DONS/BSCR DN4....46 A4
Ellershaw La CONI DN12....84 B2
Ellershaw Rd CONI DN12....84 C2
Ellers Rd DONS/BSCR DN4....46 A4
Ellerton Gdns DONS/BSCR DN4....46 C3
Ellerton Rd SHEFN S5....110 B3
Ellesmere Rd ATT S4....110 A5
  ATT S4....123 D1
Ellesmere Rd North ATT S4....110 A4
Ellesmere Ter RHAM/THRY S65....7 H6
Ellington Ct BSLY S70....21 E3
Ellin St SHEF S1....135 E1
Elliot La CHPT/GREN S35....87 F3
Elliot Rd ST/HB/BR S6....121 E3
Elliott Av WMB/DAR S73....39 E4
Elliott Cl DEARNE S63....55 D1
Elliott Ct RHAM/THRY S65....7 E4
Elliott Dr KIMB S61....92 A4
  STV/CWN S43....187 D3
Elliottville St ST/HB/BR S6....121 D1
Ellis Av DEARNE S63....55 E4
Ellis Ct WMB/DAR S73....39 E3
Ellis Crs WMB/DAR S73....54 B1
Ellisons Rd ECK/KIL S21....154 C5
Ellison St OWL S3....8 A3
  RHAM S60....114 A3
Eliorslie Dr STKB/PEN S36....69 D2
Elm Cl CHNE S41....184 C1
  ECK/KIL S21....166 A3
Elm Crs BTLY DN5....17 D4
  MOS S20....152 A5
Elmdale Cl MEX/SWTN S64....81 E3
Elm Dr ECK/KIL S21....166 A3
Elmfield Av WHHL DN2....98 C5
Elmfield Rd DON DN1....5 F6
Elm Green La CONI DN12....85 D1
Elm Gv KIMB S61....92 C3
Elmham Rd DARN/MH S9....125 E3
  DONS/BSCR DN4....46 C3
Elmhirst Dr RHAM/THRY S65....105 D5
Elm La SHEFN S5....98 C5
Elm Lodge Farm Cl CHNE S41....184 A2
Elmore Rd FUL S10....121 D4
Elm Pl ARMTH DN3....33 E2
  BSLYN/ROY S71....15 E2
  RAW S62....94 B1
Elm Ri CHPT/GREN S35....88 A2
Elm Rd ARMTH DN3....33 E2
  ECK/KIL S21....174 A1
  MEX/SWTN S64....58 A2
  MOS S20....153 E1
Elm Rw BSLYN/ROY S71....22 C1
Elmsdale BSLY S70....36 C1
Elm St HOY S74....50 C3
  STV/CWN S43....180 B5
Elm Tree Crs DRON S18....159 E5
Elm Tree Rd KIMB S61....90 A3
Elmview Rd DARN/MH S9....100 C5
Elmville Av MEX/SWTN S64....81 D2
Elm Wy DEARNE S63....56 B4
Elmwood Crs ARMTH DN3....33 E3
Elmwood Dr MOS S20....164 B2
Elsecar Rd RAW S62....54 A3
Elstree Dr HACK/IN S12....149 F1
Elstree Rd HACK/IN S12....149 F1
Elsworth Cl DON DN1....44 A3
Elton St CHSW S40....190 B2
Elton Vw STV/CWN S43....187 E1
Elwin Ct DONS/BSCR DN4....63 F3
Elwis St BTLY DN5....4 B3
Elwood Rd TOT/DORE S17....158 A2
Ely Rd WHHL DN2....31 D2
Embankment Rd FUL S10....121 D4
Emerson Cl SHEFN S5....98 C4
Emerson Crs SHEFN S5....98 C5
Emerson Dr SHEFN S5....98 C5
Emily Cl BSLYN/ROY S71....15 E5
Emley Dr BTLY DN5....28 A2
Emmetfield Cl CHSW S40....190 A4
Empire Rd ABRD S7....135 D5
  SHEFS S8....135 D4
Endcliffe Av ECC S11....133 F1
Endcliffe Crs ECC S11....133 F1
Endcliffe Edge FUL S10....133 F1
Endcliffe Glen Rd ECC S11....134 A1
Endcliffe Grove Av FUL S10....133 E1
Endcliffe Hall Av FUL S10....133 E1
Endcliffe Rise Rd ECC S11....134 A1
Endcliffe Terrace Rd ECC S11....134 A1

Endcliffe Vale Av ECC S11....134 A2
Endcliffe Vale Rd FUL S10....133 F1
Endcliffe Wy WHHL DN2....32 A2
Endfield Rd SHEFN S5....98 A2
Endowood Rd ABRD S7....145 F3
  CHSW S40....188 B4
Enfield Pl HAN/WDH S13....126 A5
Enfield Rd CHNE S41....11 E2
Ennerdale Av MOS S20....164 C2
Ennerdale Cl DRON S18....168 C2
  MEX/SWTN S64....59 D2
Ennerdale Crs CHNE S41....183 D2
Ennerdale Dr MOS S20....164 C2
Ennerdale Rd BSLYN/ROY S71....24 C2
  WHHL DN2....32 A3
Ennis Crs WHHL DN2....31 E4
Entwhistle Rd CHPT/GREN S35....73 F4
Epping Gdns MOS S20....153 E3
Epping Gv MOS S20....153 E3
Epsom Cl MEX/SWTN S64....58 C2
Epsom Rd DONS/BSCR DN4....46 B2
Errington Av SHEFP/MNR S2....136 C3
Errington Cl SHEFP/MNR S2....136 C4
Errington Crs SHEFP/MNR S2....136 C4
Errington Rd CHSW S40....189 E4
  SHEFP/MNR S2....136 C3
Errington Wy SHEFP/MNR S2....136 C3
Erskine Crs SHEFP/MNR S2....136 A3
Erskine Rd RHAM/THRY S65....7 E2
  SHEFP/MNR S2....136 A3
Erskine Vw SHEFP/MNR S2....136 A4
Eskdale Cl DRON S18....168 C2
  ST/HB/BR S6....107 F1
Eskdale Dr BTLY DN5....29 D1
Eskdale Rd BSLYN/ROY S71....24 B2
  KIMB S61....92 A3
  ST/HB/BR S6....107 F1
Esperanto Pl SHEF S1....9 F5
Essendine Crs SHEFS S8....147 F2
Essex Av WHHL DN2....45 F1
Essex Rd BSLY S70....22 A3
  SHEFP/MNR S2....136 B1
Estate Rd RAW S62....79 F4
Estone Dr AU/AST/KP S26....142 B2
Ettrick Cl CHSW S40....183 D4
Etwall Cl CHSW S40....182 B3
Etwall Wy SHEFN S5....99 D5
Europa Link DARN/MH S9....125 F1
Evans St OWL S3....122 A5
Evanston Gdns DONS/BSCR DN4....43 E4
Evelyn Av WHHL DN2....31 F5
Evelyn Rd FUL S10....120 B4
Evelyn St RAW S62....80 C5
Evelyn Ter BSLY S70....22 C2
Everard Av TOT/DORE S17....157 E2
Everard Dr TOT/DORE S17....157 E2
Everard Gld TOT/DORE S17....157 E3
Everett Cl STV/CWN S43....185 F2
Everill Cl WMB/DAR S73....40 A4
Everill Gate La WMB/DAR S73....40 A3
Everingham Cl SHEFN S5....109 E1
Everingham Crs SHEFN S5....109 F1
Everingham Rd DONS/BSCR DN4....46 C3
  SHEFN S5....109 E1
Everton Rd ECC S11....134 A2
Evesham Cl DARN/MH S9....100 C5
Ewden Rd WMB/DAR S73....40 A4
Ewden Wy DOD/DAR S75....20 B1
Ewers Rd KIMB S61....102 A3
Ewood Dr DONS/BSCR DN4....46 C4
Exchange Pl ATT S4....9 G4
Exchange St SHEF S1....9 G4
Exeter Dr OWL S3....135 D1
Exeter Pl OWL S3....122 A5
Exeter Rd WHHL DN2....31 E3
Exeter Wy OWL S3....121 F5
Exley Av ST/HB/BR S6....121 E1
Eyam Rd FUL S10....120 C4
Eyncourt Rd SHEFN S5....110 B1
Eyre Gdns CHNE S41....10 D3
Eyre La SHEF S1....122 B5
Eyre St SHEF S1....135 E1
Eyre St East CHNE S41....191 D5

F

Factory La DON DN1....4 C3
Factory St CHSW S40....189 E2
Fairbank Rd SHEFN S5....109 F3
Fairbank Vw RHAM S60....116 A3
Fairbarn Cl ST/HB/BR S6....119 F2
Fairbarn Dr ST/HB/BR S6....119 F2
Fairbarn Pl ST/HB/BR S6....119 F2
Fairbarn Rd ST/HB/BR S6....119 F2
Fairbarn Wy ST/HB/BR S6....119 F2
Fairburn Gdns RHAM S60....114 B4
Fairburn Gv HOY S74....52 C2
Fairfax Dr SHEFP/MNR S2....137 F2
Fairfax Rd SHEFP/MNR S2....137 F2
  WHHL DN2....31 F5
Fair Fld BSLY S70....36 A4
Fairfield Cl DONS/BSCR DN4....66 B1
  STV/CWN S43....185 E1

Fairfield Ct *CHSW* S40 .... 182 A5
Fairfield Dr *CHSW* S40 .... 182 A5
Fairfield Rd *BTLY* DN5 .... 29 D3
  CHSW S40 .... 10 C5
  OWL S3 .... 121 F1
Fairford Cl *CHSW* S40 .... 190 A5
  DONS/BSCR DN4 .... 67 E1
Fairleigh *SHEFP/MNR* S2 .... 137 E2
Fairleigh Dr *RHAM* S60 .... 103 F5
Fairmount Gdns *HACK/IN* S12 .. 151 E2 ▣
Fairthorn Rd *SHEFN* S5 .... 99 E5
Fair Vw *CHSW* S40 .... 10 A3
Fairview Cl *HOY* S74 .... 51 D3
Fair View Dr *AU/AST/KP* S26 .... 142 B3
Fairview Rd *DRON* S18 .... 159 E5
Fairway *DOD/DAR* S75 .... 20 B4
The Fairway *FUL* S10 .... 131 E1
Falcon Dr *BSLY* S70 .... 36 A5
  RHAM S60 .... 128 A4
Falconer La *HAN/WDH* S13 .... 141 D1
Falcon Ri *DRON* S18 .... 160 B5 ▣
Falcon Rd *DRON* S18 .... 160 A5
Falcon St *BSLY* S70 .... 2 C4
Falding St *CHPT/GREN* S35 .... 88 C1
  RHAM S60 .... 6 A5
Falkland Rd *DRON* S18 .... 169 E3
Falkland Rd *ECC* S11 .... 133 E4
Fallon Rd *ST/HB/BR* S6 .... 119 E1
Fallowfield Rd *CHNE* S41 .... 179 E3
Falmouth Cl *BSLYN/ROY* S71 .... 14 C5
Falmouth Rd *ABRD* S7 .... 134 C5
Falstaff Crs *SHEFN* S5 .... 98 A5
Falstaff Rd *SHEFN* S5 .... 98 A4
Fane Crs *AU/AST/KP* S26 .... 142 B2
Fanny Av *ECC/KIL* S21 .... 166 C3
Fanshaw Bank *DRON* S18 .... 169 E2 ▣
Fanshaw Dr *ECK/KIL* S21 .... 174 A1 ▣
Fanshaw Rd *DRON* S18 .... 169 F1
  ECK/KIL S21 .... 174 A1
Fanshaw Wy *ECK/KIL* S21 .... 174 A1
Faraday Rd *DARN/MH* S9 .... 123 F1
Faranden Rd *DARN/MH* S9 .... 124 B2 ▣
Far Crs *RHAM/THRY* S65 .... 104 C2
Farcroft Gv *ATT* S4 .... 111 D3 ▣
Far Dalton La *RHAM/THRY* S65.. 105 F1
Far Field La *BSLYN/ROY* S71 .... 15 F1
  DEARNE S63 .... 56 C2
Farfield Pk *DEARNE* S63 .... 56 C1
Far Field Rd *RHAM/THRY* S65 .... 105 D5
Fargate *SHEF* S1 .... 9 E5
Far Golden Smithies
  MEX/SWTN S64 .... 57 D4
Farish Pl *SHEFP/MNR* S2 .... 135 F4 ▣
Far La *RHAM/THRY* S65 .... 104 C2
  ST/HB/BR S6 .... 107 F3
Farlow Cft *CHPT/GREN* S35 .... 73 F3
Farm Bank Rd *SHEFP/MNR* S2 .. 123 D5
Farm View Rd *KIMB* S61 .... 101 E3
Farm View La *HACK/IN* S12 ..... 151 F2 ▣
  KIMB S61 .... 101 D1
Farm View Rd *HACK/IN* S12 ...... 151 F2
Farm View Gdns *HACK/IN* S12 .. 151 F2
Farm View Rd *KIMB* S61 .... 101 D1
Farnaby Gdns *CHPT/GREN* S35... 73 E3
Farnborough Dr *DONS/BSCR* DN4 .. 67 F4 ▣
Farndale Rd *BTLY* DN5 .... 28 B2 ▣
  ST/HB/BR S6 .... 108 A2
  STV/CWN S43 .... 181 F2
Farnley Av *ST/HB/BR* S6 .... 97 E5 ▣
Farnon Cl *CHNE* S41 .... 190 C3 ▣
Farnsworth Rd *RHAM/THRY* S65 .. 105 D2
Farnsworth St *CHNE* S41 .... 191 D4 ▣
Far Pl *RHAM/THRY* S65 .... 104 C2
Farrar Rd *SHEFS* S8 .... 135 D3 ▣
Farrar St *BSLY* S70 .... 2 A5
Farrier Ga *CHPT/GREN* S35 .... 73 F5
Farrow Cl *DOD/DAR* S75 .... 20 B3
Farthing Gale Ms *BTLY* DN5 .... 29 D3 ▣
Far Townend *DOD/DAR* S75 .... 20 B3 ▣
Far View Rd *SHEFN* S5 .... 98 C5
Farwater Cl *DRON* S18 .... 169 E3 ▣
Farwater La *DRON* S18 .... 169 D2 ▣
Favell Rd *OWL* S3 .... 8 A5
  RHAM/THRY S65 .... 105 F2 ▣
Fawcett St *OWL* S3 .... 8 A3
Fearnehough St *DARN/MH* S9 .. 124 B2 ▣
Fearn House Crs *HOY* S74 .... 51 D3
Fearnley Rd *HOY* S74 .... 51 D3
Fellbrigg Rd *SHEFP/MNR* S2 .... 136 B3
Fellowsfield Wy *KIMB* S61 .... 101 F2
Fell Rd *DARN/MH* S9 .... 111 E5
Fell St *DARN/MH* S9 .... 111 D4

Fenland Wy *CHSW* S40 .... 189 F4
Fenney La *ECC* S11 .... 144 C3
Fenn Rd *DOD/DAR* S75 .... 50 A3
Fenton Cft *KIMB* S61 .... 102 B1
Fenton Flds *KIMB* S61 .... 102 B1
Fenton Rd *KIMB* S61 .... 92 B4
Fenton St *BSLY* S70 .... 2 B5 ▣
  ECK/KIL S21 .... 175 F1
  KIMB S61 .... 102 A2
Fentonville St *ECC* S11 .... 134 C2
Fenton Wy *KIMB* S61 .... 102 A1
Feoffees Rd *CHPT/GREN* S35 ..... 98 C1 ▣
Ferguson St *DARN/MH* S9 .... 124 A1
Ferham Cl *KIMB* S61 .... 102 B3
Ferham Park Av *KIMB* S61 ...... 102 B3 ▣
Ferham Rd *KIMB* S61 .... 102 B3
Fern Av *BTLY* DN5 .... 29 E2
  MOS S20 .... 153 D1
  STV/CWN S43 .... 187 D1
Fernbank Dr *ARMTH* DN3 .... 33 F1
  ECK/KIL S21 .... 165 F5
Fern Cl *ECK/KIL* S21 .... 165 F5
  WHHL DN2 .... 31 F3
  WMB/DAR S73 .... 40 B1
Ferncroft Av *MOS* S20 .... 164 A1
Ferndale Cl *DRON* S18 .... 160 B5
Ferndale Ri *DRON* S18 .... 160 B5
Ferndale Rd *CONI* DN12 .... 84 C1
  DRON S18 .... 160 B5
Ferndale Vw *BTLY* DN5 .... 28 C4
Fernhurst Rd *WHHL* DN2 .... 32 A3
Fernlea Cl *BTLY* DN5 .... 29 D4 ▣
Fernlea Gv *CHPT/GREN* S35 .... 98 C1 ▣
Fernleigh Dr *RHAM* S60 .... 113 F2
Fern Rd *ST/HB/BR* S6 .... 120 C1
Fernvale Wk *MEX/SWTN* S64 ... 81 E3 ▣
Fern Wy *ECK/KIL* S21 .... 163 F5
Ferrand St *BSLY* S70 .... 49 F1
Ferrara Cl *WMB/DAR* S73 .... 25 F4
Ferrars Cl *DARN/MH* S9 .... 113 D2
Ferrars Dr *DARN/MH* S9 .... 113 D3
Ferrars Rd *DARN/MH* S9 .... 112 C1
Ferrars Wy *DARN/MH* S9 .... 113 D3
Ferrers Rd *WHHL* DN2 .... 31 D4
Ferriby Rd *ST/HB/BR* S6 .... 107 F2
Ferry Boat La *MEX/SWTN* S64 .... 59 D4
Ferry La *CONI* DN12 .... 61 D5
Festival Rd *DEARNE* S63 .... 56 A3
Fewton Wy *DONS/BSCR* DN4 ...... 45 F4
Field Av *ECK/KIL* S21 .... 175 E3
Field Cl *DRON* S18 .... 168 A1 ▣
Fielders Wy *CONI* DN12 .... 62 A4 ▣
Field Ga *NROS/TKH* DN11 .... 67 E5
Field Head Rd *HOY* S74 .... 51 F3
Fieldhead Rd *SHEFP/MNR* S2 ... 135 E3 ▣
Fieldhouse Wy *ATT* S4 .... 110 B5
Fielding Gv *RAW* S62 .... 80 A4
Fielding Rd *ST/HB/BR* S6 .... 108 A2
Field La *BSLY* S70 .... 23 F3
  ECK/KIL S21 .... 165 F3
  RHAM S60 .... 117 D5
Field Vw *RHAM* S60 .... 114 A3
Field Wy *RHAM* S60 .... 6 C2
Fife Cl *DARN/MH* S9 .... 100 B5
Fife St *BSLY* S70 .... 21 E2 ▣
  DARN/MH S9 .... 100 B5
Fife Wy *DARN/MH* S9 .... 100 B5
Filby Rd *BTLY* DN5 .... 28 A5
Filey La *OWL* S3 .... 121 F5
Finch Ri *AU/AST/KP* S26 .... 142 C4
Finch Rd *DONS/BSCR* DN4 .... 63 D1 ▣
Finchwell Cl *HAN/WDH* S13 ...... 126 A5
Finchwell Crs *HAN/WDH* S13 ..... 126 A5
Finchwell Rd *HAN/WDH* S13 ..... 126 A5
Findon Crs *ST/HB/BR* S6 .... 107 E4
Findon Pl *ST/HB/BR* S6 .... 107 E4 ▣
Findon St *ST/HB/BR* S6 .... 107 E4
Finkle St *BTLY* DN5 .... 29 F1
Finlay Rd *RHAM/THRY* S65 .... 104 B1
Finlay St *OWL* S3 .... 8 A3
First Av *RHAM/THRY* S65 .... 104 B1
The Firs *BSLY* S70 .... 23 D4
Fir St *FUL* S10 .... 120 C3
  STV/CWN S43 .... 180 C5
Firth Dr *ATT* S4 .... 123 E1
Firth Park Av *SHEFN* S5 .... 110 B1
Firth Park Crs *SHEFN* S5 .... 110 B1
Firth Park Rd *SHEFN* S5 .... 110 B1

Firth Rd *DEARNE* S63 .... 54 C2
Firth St *DONS/BSCR* DN4 .... 43 F3 ▣
  KIMB S61 .... 93 D3
Firthwood Av *DRON* S18 .... 160 B5
Firthwood Cl *DRON* S18 .... 160 B5 ▣
Firthwood Rd *DRON* S18 .... 160 B5
Fir Tree Dr *AU/AST/KP* S26 .... 155 E3
Firtree Ri *CHPT/GREN* S35 .... 88 B2 ▣
Fir Vale Pl *SHEFN* S5 .... 110 A3 ▣
Firvale Rd *CHSW* S40 .... 188 C4
Fir Vale Rd *SHEFN* S5 .... 110 A3
Fisher Cl *CHSW* S40 .... 189 F5
  RHAM S60 .... 6 A5
Fisher La *DARN/MH* S9 .... 125 D2
Fisher St *BTLY* DN5 .... 16 C4
Fisher Ter *BTLY* DN5 .... 29 E4 ▣
Fishponds Rd *HAN/WDH* S13 .... 138 A2
Fishponds Rd West
  HAN/WDH S13 .... 138 A3
Fitzalan Rd *HAN/WDH* S13 .... 139 D1
Fitzalan Sq *SHEF* S1 .... 9 F5
Fitzgerald Rd *FUL* S10 .... 120 C3
Fitzhubert Rd *SHEFP/MNR* S2 .. 137 E2
Fitzmaurice Rd *DARN/MH* S9 .. 124 C1
Fitzroy Rd *SHEFP/MNR* S2 .... 135 F4
Fitzwalter Rd *SHEFP/MNR* S2 .. 123 E5
  SHEFP/MNR S2 .... 136 A1
Fitzwilliam Av *CONI* DN12 .... 84 A1
  DEARNE S63 .... 55 F3
Fitzwilliam Ct *RAW* S62 .... 94 A2
Fitzwilliam Ga *SHEF* S1 .... 122 A5
Fitzwilliam Rd *RAW/THRY* S65 ... 7 F3
Fitzwilliam Sq *RAW* S62 .... 92 C2
Fitzwilliam St *BSLY* S70 .... 2 A5
  HOY S74 .... 50 C3
  HOY S74 .... 52 B3
  MEX/SWTN S64 .... 81 D1
  RAW S62 .... 94 A3
  SHEF S1 .... 122 A5
  WMB/DAR S73 .... 52 C1
Five Oaks *BTLY* DN5 .... 17 F3
Five Trees Cl *TOT/DORE* S17 ..... 157 E3
Five Trees Dr *TOT/DORE* S17 ..... 157 E2
Five Weirs Wk *DARN/MH* S9 .... 124 A1
Flamsteed Crs *CHNE* S41 .... 184 B3
Flanders Ct *KIMB* S61 .... 90 A1 ▣
Flask Vw *ST/HB/BR* S6 .... 106 A5
Flat La *RHAM* S60 .... 115 F3
Flatt St *SHEF* S1 .... 9 F5
Flatts Cl *RHAM* S60 .... 127 F2
Flatts La *DEARNE* S63 .... 55 E2
  RHAM S60 .... 127 F2
Flaxby Rd *DARN/MH* S9 .... 124 C2 ▣
Flax Lea *BSLY* S70 .... 22 B5
Fleet Cl *DEARNE* S63 .... 54 B1
Fleet Hill Crs *BSLYN/ROY* S71 ... 14 B2
Fleetwood Av *BSLYN/ROY* S71 ... 15 D2
Fleming Pl *BSLY* S70 .... 21 F2 ▣
Fletcher Av *DRON* S18 .... 169 E2
Fleury Cl *GLV* S14 .... 148 C1
Fleury Crs *GLV* S14 .... 148 C1
Fleury Pl *GLV* S14 .... 148 C1
Fleury Ri *GLV* S14 .... 148 C1
Fleury Rd *GLV* S14 .... 148 C1
Flint Rd *WHHL* DN2 .... 32 A4
Flintson Av *CHNE* S41 .... 179 E2
Flintway *DEARNE* S63 .... 56 A5
Flockton Av *HAN/WDH* S13 ...... 139 F2
Flockton Crs *HAN/WDH* S13 ..... 139 F2
Flockton Dr *HAN/WDH* S13 ...... 140 A2
Flockton Rd *HAN/WDH* S13 ...... 140 A2
Flodden St *FUL* S10 .... 120 C3
Floodgate Dr *CHPT/GREN* S35 .. 98 C1
Flora St *ST/HB/BR* S6 .... 121 F1
Florence Av *AU/AST/KP* S26 ..... 142 B3
  DONS/BSCR DN4 .... 43 E4
Florence Rd *KIMB* S61 .... 102 C3 ▣
  SHEFS S8 .... 146 C3
Flowitt St *DONS/BSCR* DN4 .... 4 A5
  MEX/SWTN S64 .... 58 C3
Flowright Ct *SHEFP/MNR* S2 .... 136 B5
Folderings La *STKB/PEN* S36 ...... 69 D5
Folds Crs *SHEFS* S8 .... 146 A4 ▣
Folds Dr *SHEFS* S8 .... 146 A4
Folds La *SHEFS* S8 .... 146 A4
Foley Av *WMB/DAR* S73 .... 39 D3
Foley St *ATT* S4 .... 123 E2
Foljambe Av *CHSW* S40 .... 189 E4
Foljambe Dr *RHAM/THRY* S65 ... 95 F5
Foljambe Rd *CHSW* S40 .... 10 C6
  RHAM/THRY S65 .... 104 C3
  STV/CWN S43 .... 185 F1
Foljambe St *RAW* S62 .... 94 A2 ▣
Follett Rd *SHEFN* S5 .... 99 D4
Fontwell Dr *MEX/SWTN* S64 ...... 58 C2
Foolow Av *CHSW* S40 .... 190 A3 ▣
Forbes Rd *ST/HB/BR* S6 .... 108 A5
Ford La *HACK/IN* S12 .... 162 C3
  STKB/PEN S36 .... 69 D1
Ford Rd *ECC* S11 .... 133 F4
  ECK/KIL S21 .... 162 C4
Fore Hill Av *DONS/BSCR* DN4 ..... 66 B1
Foremark Rd *SHEFN* S5 .... 99 E5
Forest Ri *DONS/BSCR* DN4 .... 62 C2
Forge La *ECK/KIL* S21 .... 165 F1

HOY S74 .... 52 B4
RHAM S60 .... 6 C5
SHEF S1 .... 135 E1
Forge Rd AU/AST/KP S26 ...... 155 F2
Formby Ct BSLYN/ROY S71 ..... 15 E1
Forncett St ATT S4 .... 123 E1
Fornham St SHEFP/MNR S2 .... 122 C5
Forres Av FUL S10 .... 120 B4
Forres Rd FUL S10 .... 120 C4
Forrester's La DRON S18 .... 160 A4
Forster Rd DONS/BSCR DN4 ..... 63 F1
Forth Av DRON S18 .... 168 B1
Fort Hill Rd DARN/MH S9 .... 111 D2
Fortway Rd RHAM S60 .... 114 A2
Fossard Cl WHHL DN2 .... 31 E3
Fossard Wy BTLY DN5 .... 16 A5
Fossdale Rd ABRD S7 .... 134 B5
Foster's Cl MEX/SWTN S64 ...... 57 D5
Foster St BSLY S70 .... 23 E2
Foston Dr CHSW S40 .... 182 C4
Foulstone Rw WMB/DAR S73 ... 39 F3
Foundry St BSLY S70 .... 21 F2
  CHNE S41 .... 184 B1
  HOY S74 .... 52 B3
  RAW S62 .... 94 A3
Fountains Wy BSLYN/ROY S71 ... 15 E4
Four Wells Dr HACK/IN S12 ..... 151 E2
Fowler Bridge Rd BTLY DN5 ..... 30 A1
Fowler St CHNE S41 .... 178 A4
Foxbrook Cl RCH S42 .... 182 A4
Foxbrook Ct CHSW S40 .... 188 C3
Foxbrook Dr CHSW S40 .... 188 C4
Fox Cl KIMB S61 .... 91 E4
Foxcote Wy CHSW S40 .... 188 C4
Fox Ct MEX/SWTN S64 .... 81 E2
Foxcroft Cha ECK/KIL S21 .... 166 A2
Foxcroft Dr ECK/KIL S21 .... 166 A2
Foxcroft Gv ECK/KIL S21 .... 166 A2
Foxfield Wk BSLY S70 .... 23 E4
Fox Glen Rd STKB/PEN S36 ...... 69 E3
Foxglove Rd SHEFS S5 .... 99 F5
Fox Gv DONS/BSCR DN4 .... 62 A1
Foxhall La FUL S10 .... 131 D4
Fox Hill Av ST/HB/BR S6 .... 97 D4
Fox Hill Cl ST/HB/BR S6 .... 97 D4
Fox Hill Crs ST/HB/BR S6 .... 97 D3
Fox Hill Dr ST/HB/BR S6 .... 97 D4
Fox Hill Pl ST/HB/BR S6 .... 97 D3
Fox Hill Rd ST/HB/BR S6 .... 97 D2
Fox Hill Wy ST/HB/BR S6 .... 97 D3
Foxland Av MEX/SWTN S64 ...... 80 B1
Fox La HACK/IN S12 .... 150 A2
  TOT/DORE S17 .... 158 B2
Fox Lane Ct HACK/IN S12 ...... 150 A1
Fox Lane Vw HACK/IN S12 ..... 150 A1
Fox Rd ST/HB/BR S6 .... 120 C1
Foxroyd Cl BSLYN/ROY S71 ...... 24 A2
Foxstone Cl STV/CWN S43 ...... 187 E1
Fox St KIMB S61 .... 101 F3
  OWL S3 .... 122 C1
Foxwood Av HACK/IN S12 ...... 137 F4
Foxwood Cl CHNE S41 .... 177 F5
Foxwood Dr HACK/IN S12 ...... 137 F4
Foxwood Gv HACK/IN S12 ...... 137 F5
Foxwood Rd CHNE S41 .... 177 F4
  HACK/IN S12 .... 137 F4
Foxwood Wy CHNE S41 .... 177 F4
Framlingham Pl SHEFP/MNR S2 .. 136 B3
France Rd ST/HB/BR S6 .... 106 B3
Frances St DON DN1 .... 5 E3
  RHAM/THRY S65 .... 104 A4
France St RAW S62 .... 94 A3
Francis Cl STV/CWN S43 .... 185 E2
Francis Crs North
  RHAM/THRY S65 .... 116 B1
Francis Crs South
  RHAM/THRY S65 .... 116 B1
Francis Dr RHAM/THRY S65 .... 116 B1
Francis Gv CHPT/GREN S35 ...... 73 E4
Franklin Rd CHSW S40 .... 10 A4
Franklyn Rd CHSW S40 .... 10 A4
Frank Pl DARN/MH S9 .... 111 E5
Frank Rd BTLY DN5 .... 29 F3
Fraser Cl SHEFS S8 .... 146 C2
Fraser Crs SHEFS S8 .... 146 C2
Fraser Dr SHEFS S8 .... 147 D2
Fraser Rd RHAM/THRY S65 .... 104 A4
  SHEFS S8 .... 146 C2
Frecheville St STV/CWN S43 ... 181 E5
Frederick Av BSLY S70 .... 21 E2
Frederick Dr CHPT/GREN S35 ... 86 C5
Frederick St DARN/MH S9 ...... 124 C3
  DEARNE S63 .... 55 E1
  MEX/SWTN S64 .... 58 A3
  RHAM S60 .... 6 C4
  RHAM S60 .... 127 D2
  WMB/DAR S73 .... 39 D2
Frederic Pl BSLY S70 .... 22 A3
Fred Mulley Rd ATT S4 .... 123 E2
Freebirch Vw CHSW S40 .... 182 C2
Freedom Ct ST/HB/BR S6 .... 108 B5
Freedom Rd ST/HB/BR S6 ...... 121 D1
Freeman St BSLY S70 .... 22 A2
Freemans Yd BSLY S70 .... 3 E6

Freeston Pl DARN/MH S9 .... 111 E5
French Ga DON DN1 .... 4 C2
French St BTLY DN5 .... 16 C4
Fretson Rd SHEFP/MNR S2 .... 137 E2
Fretwell Rd RHAM/THRY S65 .. 105 D1
Friar Cl ST/HB/BR S6 .... 119 E1
Friars Ga BTLY DN5 .... 4 D1
Friar's Rd BSLYN/ROY S71 .... 15 F4
Frickley Rd ECC S11 .... 133 D2
Frinton Cl CHSW S40 .... 190 A5
Frith Cl HACK/IN S12 .... 137 F5
Frith Rd HACK/IN S12 .... 137 F5
Froggatt Cl STV/CWN S43 ...... 187 D3
Froggatt La SHEF S1 .... 122 B5
Front St RHAM S60 .... 127 F3
Frostings Cl CHPT/GREN S35 .... 87 D5
The Frostings CHPT/GREN S35 . 87 D5
Fulford Cl CHSW S40 .... 189 D4
  DARN/MH S9 .... 125 D2
Fulford Pl DARN/MH S9 .... 125 D2
Fuller Dr CHNE S41 .... 185 D3
Fullerton Av CONI DN12 .... 84 A1
Fullerton Crs RHAM/THRY S65 . 95 F4
Fullerton Dr RHAM S60 .... 113 F4
Fullerton Rd RHAM S60 .... 103 D5
  RHAM S60 .... 114 A1
Fulmar Wy KIMB S61 .... 76 B5
Fulmer Cl BSLYN/ROY S71 .... 14 C1
Fulmere Crs SHEFN S5 .... 97 F3
Fulmere Rd SHEFN S5 .... 97 F3
Fulmer Rd ECC S11 .... 134 A3
Fulney Rd ECC S11 .... 133 D2
Fulton Rd FUL S10 .... 121 D2
Fulwood Cha FUL S10 .... 132 C2
Fulwood Dr DONS/BSCR DN4 ... 63 F3
Fulwood Head Rd FUL S10 ..... 130 C4
Fulwood La FUL S10 .... 130 B4
Fulwood Rd ECC S11 .... 121 D5
  ECC S11 .... 132 B3
  FUL S10 .... 133 E1
Furnace Hl OWL S3 .... 8 D3
Furnace La DRON S18 .... 176 A3
  HAN/WDH S13 .... 140 B3
  STV/CWN S43 .... 186 A3
Furness Cl ST/HB/BR S6 .... 106 B5
Furness Dene BSLYN/ROY S71 . 15 E2
Furness Rd CHPT/GREN S35 .... 73 D4
Furniss Av TOT/DORE S17 ...... 156 B2
Furniss Ms TOT/DORE S17 ..... 156 C2
Furnivall Rd DONS/BSCR DN4 .. 43 E4
Furnival St SHEF S1 .... 122 B5
Furnival Wy RHAM S60 .... 116 B3
Fylde Cl BSLYN/ROY S71 .... 15 E1

G

Gainsborough Rd ABRD S7 ..... 134 B3
  DRON S18 .... 168 C3
Gainsborough Wy BSLYN/ROY S71 .. 3 H1
Galley Dr MOS S20 .... 152 B4
Gallow Tree Rd RHAM/THRY S65 .. 105 E5
Galsworthy Av SHEFN S5 .... 109 D1
Galsworthy Cl DONS/BSCR DN4 .. 63 D2
Galsworthy Rd SHEFN S5 .... 109 D1
Galway Cl RAW S62 .... 80 B5
Gamston Rd SHEFS S8 .... 135 D3
Gannow Cl ECK/KIL S21 .... 167 D1
Ganton Rd ST/HB/BR S6 .... 107 F2
Garbroads Crs RHAM/THRY S65 . 95 F4
Garden Av ECK/KIL S21 .... 175 F4
Garden Cl STV/CWN S43 .... 179 E3
Garden Crs RHAM S60 .... 115 E2
Garden Dr WMB/DAR S73 .... 40 B5
Garden Gv WMB/DAR S73 .... 39 D5
Garden House Cl BSLYN/ROY S71 . 15 D2
Gardenia Rd ARMTH DN3 .... 19 F3
Garden La BTLY DN5 .... 61 E1
  RHAM S60 .... 6 B4
Gardens La CONI DN12 .... 84 A1
The Gardens DONS/BSCR DN4 .. 46 B5
Garden St DEARNE S63 .... 27 D3
  DEARNE S63 .... 55 E1
  KIMB S61 .... 102 C2
  MEX/SWTN S64 .... 58 B3
  MEX/SWTN S64 .... 58 B3
  SHEF S1 .... 8 C4
Garden Wk RHAM S60 .... 115 E1
Gardom Cl DRON S18 .... 168 B2
Garfield Mt RHAM/THRY S65 .. 104 A4
Garland Cl MOS S20 .... 164 C1
Garland Cft MOS S20 .... 164 C1
Garland Dr ST/HB/BR S6 .... 106 B3
Garland Mt MOS S20 .... 152 C5
Garland Wy MOS S20 .... 164 C1
Garry Rd ST/HB/BR S6 .... 107 F3
Garter St ATT S4 .... 110 B5
Garth Cl DARN/MH S9 .... 124 B2
Garth Wy DRON S18 .... 169 D2
Gartrice Gdns MOS S20 .... 165 E3
Gartrice Gv MOS S20 .... 165 D3
Gashouse La MOS S20 .... 164 B3
Gate Crs DOD/DAR S75 .... 20 A2

Gatefield Cl CHSW S40 .... 183 D2
Gatefield Rd ABRD S7 .... 134 C4
Gateway Cl RAW S62 .... 93 F4
Gateway Ct RAW S62 .... 93 F4
The Gateway RAW S62 .... 93 F5
Gatty Rd SHEFN S5 .... 99 E2
Gaunt Cl ECK/KIL S21 .... 166 A2
  GLV S14 .... 148 B2
Gaunt Dr GLV S14 .... 148 B1
Gaunt Pl GLV S14 .... 148 B1
Gaunt Rd GLV S14 .... 148 B1
Gaunt Wy GLV S14 .... 148 B2
Gawber Rd DOD/DAR S75 .... 13 D4
Gayton Cl DONS/BSCR DN4 ..... 63 C2
Gayton Rd ATT S4 .... 110 A4
Geer La HACK/IN S12 .... 162 A3
Gelderd Pl DRON S18 .... 169 E3
Gell St OWL S3 .... 122 A5
Genn La BSLY S70 .... 21 E4
Genoa Cl WMB/DAR S73 .... 25 F3
Genoa St MEX/SWTN S64 .... 58 C3
George Pl MEX/SWTN S64 .... 59 D4
  RAW S62 .... 94 B1
George Sq BSLY S70 .... 2 C6
George St BSLY S70 .... 2 C6
  BSLY S70 .... 36 B1
  BSLY S70 .... 37 D1
  BTLY DN5 .... 16 C4
  CHNE S41 .... 178 A4
  DEARNE S63 .... 27 F4
  HOY S74 .... 51 F3
  RHAM S60 .... 6 C4
  SHEF S1 .... 9 F5
  STV/CWN S43 .... 181 F3
  WMB/DAR S73 .... 39 E3
  WMB/DAR S73 .... 40 A1
George Yd BSLY S70 .... 2 C5
Gerald Cl BSLY S70 .... 23 D3
Gerald Crs BSLY S70 .... 23 D3
Gerald Pl BSLY S70 .... 23 D3
Gerald Rd BSLY S70 .... 23 D3
Gerald St DARN/MH S9 .... 111 E5
Gerald Wk BSLY S70 .... 23 D3
Gerard Cl CHSW S40 .... 189 D3
  SHEFP/MNR S2 .... 135 F4
Gerard Rd RHAM S60 .... 103 F4
Gerard St SHEFS S8 .... 135 F4
Gervase Av SHEFS S8 .... 158 C2
Gervase Dr SHEFS S8 .... 158 C2
Gervase Pl SHEFS S8 .... 158 C2
Gervase Rd SHEFS S8 .... 158 C2
Gibbing Greaves Rd
  RHAM/THRY S65 .... 105 F3
Gibbons Dr SHEFS S8 .... 148 C3
Gibbons Wy SHEFS S8 .... 148 C3
Gibraltar St OWL S3 .... 8 D3
Gifford Dr DONS/BSCR DN4 ..... 62 B1
Gifford Rd SHEFP/MNR S2 ..... 135 E3
Gig La HOY S74 .... 36 C5
Gilbert Av CHSW S40 .... 189 D4
Gilbert Gv BSLY S70 .... 23 E2
Gilberthorpe Dr
  RHAM/THRY S65 .... 104 B3
Gilberthorpe Rd
  DONS/BSCR DN4 .... 43 D5
Gilberthorpe St RHAM/THRY S65 .. 7 H6
Gilbert St SHEFP/MNR S2 .... 9 G5
Giles Av DEARNE S63 .... 55 D2
Gill Cft ST/HB/BR S6 .... 119 D1
Gilleyfield Av TOT/DORE S17 ... 156 C1
Gill Mdw ST/HB/BR S6 .... 119 D1
Gillot Dell MALT S66 .... 117 F1
Gillott La MALT S66 .... 117 F1
Gillott Rd ST/HB/BR S6 .... 97 D5
Gill St DON DN1 .... 5 F6
  HOY S74 .... 52 A3
Gilpin La ST/HB/BR S6 .... 8 A1
Gilpin St ST/HB/BR S6 .... 8 A1
  ST/HB/BR S6 .... 121 F1
Gilroyd La DOD/DAR S75 .... 20 C5
Ginhouse La KIMB S61 .... 6 B1
Gipsy Green La DEARNE S63 .... 56 A4
Gipsy La CHNE S41 .... 178 C4
  DRON S18 .... 171 E2
Gisborne Rd ECC S11 .... 133 F4
Glade Cl CHSW S40 .... 10 A2
Glade Cft HACK/IN S12 .... 137 E5
Glade Lea HACK/IN S12 .... 149 E1
The Glade CHSW S40 .... 189 E1
Gladstone Ms FUL S10 .... 132 C1
Gladstone Rd CHSW S40 .... 10 C4
  DONS/BSCR DN4 .... 43 E3
  FUL S10 .... 132 C1
Gladwin Gdns CHSW S40 .... 189 E4
Gladys St RHAM/THRY S65 ..... 104 B3
Glamis Rd WHHL DN2 .... 45 E1
Glasshouse La CHNE S41 .... 179 E1
  MEX/SWTN S64 .... 81 F4
  STV/CWN S43 .... 179 E1
Glasshouse St RHAM S60 .... 6 B4
Glastonbury Ga BTLY DN5 .... 28 B4
Gleadless Av HACK/IN S12 ...... 149 D1
Gleadless Bank HACK/IN S12 .. 149 D1
Gleadless Common HACK/IN S12 .. 137 D5
Gleadless Ct SHEFP/MNR S2 .. 135 F4

Gleadless Crs *HACK/IN* S12 .... 137 D5
Gleadless Dr *HACK/IN* S12 .... 149 D1
Gleadless Mt *HACK/IN* S12 ...... 149 E2 🗓
Gleadless Rd *HACK/IN* S12 .... 136 C5
  HACK/IN S12 .... 149 E2
  SHEFP/MNR S2 .... 136 B4 🗓
  SHEFS S8 .... 135 E3
  SHEFS S8 .... 135 E4 🗓
Glebe Cl *MEX/SWTN* S64............... 81 D2
Glebe Crs *RHAM/THRY* S65 .... 95 F5
Glebe Farm Cl *ARMTH* DN3 .... 33 E3
Glebeland Cl *RAW* S62 .... 79 F3
Glebelands Rd *STKB/PEN* S36 ...... 69 D3
Glebe Rd *FUL* S10 .... 121 D3
  MEX/SWTN S64............................ 81 D2
Glebe St *DONS/BSCR* DN4 .... 62 B1
The Glebe Wy *CHNE* S41 .... 178 B4
Gledhill Cl *DRON* S18...................... 169 E2
Glenalmond Rd *ECC* S11 .... 133 F3
Glenavon Cl *STV/CWN* S43 .... 179 E1
Glencoe Dr *SHEFP/MNR* S2 .... 123 D5 🗓
Glencoe Pl *SHEFP/MNR* S2 .... 123 D5 🗓
Glencoe Rd *SHEFP/MNR* S2........... 123 D5
Glencoe Wy *CHSW* S40 .... 182 C5
Glendale Cl *DOD/DAR* S75 .... 20 F2
Gleneagles Cl *CHSW* S40 .... 189 D4 🗓
Gleneagles Dr *ARMTH* DN3 .... 67 F1 🗓
  DONS/BSCR DN4............................ 67 F1
Gleneagles Ri *MEX/SWTN* S64....... 81 E1
Glen Field Av *DONS/BSCR* DN4 ..... 43 F3
Glenfield Crs *CHSW* S41 .... 184 A2
Glenholme Dr *HAN/WDH* S13 .... 138 C3
Glenholme Pl *HAN/WDH* S13 ..... 139 D3 🗓
Glenholme Rd *HAN/WDH* S13 ..... 139 D3
Glenholme Wy *HAN/WDH* S13 ..... 138 C2
Glenmoor Av *BSLY* S70 .... 20 C2 🗓
Glenmore Cft *HACK/IN* S12 .... 137 F4
Glenmore Ri *WMB/DAR* S73 .... 39 F4 🗓
Glenorchy Rd *ABRD* S7 .... 134 B5
Glen Rd *ABRD* S7 .... 134 C4
The Glen *ECC* S11 .... 133 F1 🗓
Glenthorne Cl *CHSW* S40 .... 189 D2
Glentilt Rd *ABRD* S7 .... 134 B5
Glen View Rd *SHEFS* S8 .... 146 C5
Glenville Cl *HOY* S74 .... 51 E1
Glenwood Crs *CHPT/GREN* S35...... 88 C1
Gliwice Wy *DONS/BSCR* DN4 .... 45 F3
Glossop Rd *FUL* S10 .... 121 D5
  OWL S3 .... 8 A6
Glossop's Cft *CHNE* S41 .... 178 C4 🗓
Gloucester Cl *CHNE* S41 .... 184 A3
Gloucester Crs *FUL* S10 .... 121 F5 🗓
Gloucester Rd *CHNE* S41 .... 10 C1
  KIMB S61 .... 92 A5
  WHHL DN2 .... 31 E4
Gloucester St *FUL* S10 .... 121 F5
Glover Rd *SHEFP/MNR* S2 .... 135 E3 🗓
  TOT/DORE S17 .... 157 D3 🗓
Glumangate *CHSW* S40 .... 11 E5
Glyn Av *DON* DN1 .... 5 F1
Goathland Dr *HAN/WDH* S13..... 140 A3
Goathland Pl *HAN/WDH* S13 ..... 140 B3
Goathland Rd *HAN/WDH* S13 ..... 140 B3
Goddard Av *STKB/PEN* S36 .... 68 A1 🗓
Goddard Hall Rd *SHEFN* S5 .... 110 A3
Godric Dr *SHEFN* S60 .... 113 F3
Godric Gn *RHAM* S60 .... 113 F3
Godric Rd *SHEFN* S5 .... 99 D2
Godstone Rd *RHAM* S60 .... 103 F4
Goldcrest Wk *KIMB* S61 .... 90 B1
Gold Cft *BSLY* S70 .... 22 B2 🗓
Golden Smithies La
  MEX/SWTN S64............................ 56 C5
Goldsborough Rd *WHHL* DN2 ...... 45 E1
Goldsmith Dr *RHAM/THRY* S65 .. 104 C3
Goldsmith Rd *DONS/BSCR* DN4 ... 64 A1
  RHAM/THRY S65........................... 104 C3
Gold St *BSLY* S70 .... 22 B2
Gomersal La *DRON* S18.................. 169 E2
Gomersall Av *CONI* DN12 .... 84 A1
Goodison Bvd *DONS/BSCR* DN4 .... 46 C5
Goodison Crs *ST/HB/BR* S6 .... 120 A1
Goodison Ri *ST/HB/BR* S6 .... 120 A1
Goodwin Av *RAW* S62 .... 80 A5
Goodwin Crs *MEX/SWTN* S64 .... 57 E4
Goodwin Rd *KIMB* S61 .... 92 B2
  SHEFS S8 .... 135 E4 🗓
Goodyear Crs *WMB/DAR* S73 .... 39 E3
Goore Av *DARN/MH* S9 .... 124 C5
Goore Dr *DARN/MH* S9 .... 124 C4 🗓
Goore Rd *DARN/MH* S9 .... 124 C5
Gooseacre Av *DEARNE* S63 .... 26 C2
Goosebutt St *RAW* S62 .... 94 A2
Goosecroft Av *RHAM/THRY* S65 ... 95 F4
Gordon Av *SHEFS* S8 .... 147 E3
Gordon Rd *ECC* S11 .... 134 B2 🗓
Gordon St *BSLY* S70 .... 23 F2
  DON DN1 .... 4 C4
Gordon Ter *RHAM/THRY* S65 .... 7 H6 🗓
Gorehill Cl *DEARNE* S63 .... 56 B2
Gorman Cl *CHNE* S41 .... 183 F1
Gorse Dr *ECK/KIL* S21 .... 166 B3 🗓
Gorse La *FUL* S10 .... 131 D3
The Gorse *MALT* S66 .... 117 F1
  RHAM/THRY S65........................... 105 D4

Gorse Valley Rd *CHNE* S41............ 191 F5
Gorse Valley Wy *CHNE* S41 .... 191 F5
Gorsey Brigg *DRON* S18................. 168 B2
Gosber Rd *ECK/KIL* S21................. 164 B5
Gosber St *ECK/KIL* S21 .... 164 B5
Gosforth Cl *DRON* S18 .... 169 D2
Gosforth Dr *DRON* S18 .... 169 D2 🗓
Gosforth Crs *DRON* S18 .... 169 D2 🗓
Gosforth Gn *DRON* S18 .... 169 D2
Gosforth La *DRON* S18 .... 169 D2
Gotham Rd *RHAM* S60 .... 114 A3
Goudhurst Rd *RHAM/THRY* S65... 105 D5
Goulding St *MEX/SWTN* S64 .... 58 A4
Gowdall Gn *BTLY* DN5..................... 16 B3
Gower Cl *CHSW* S40 .... 183 D4
Gower St *ATT* S4 .... 123 D1
  WMB/DAR S73 .... 39 F3
Goyt Side Rd *CHSW* S40 .... 189 E2
Grace Rd *CONI* DN12 .... 62 A4
Grafton St *BSLY* S70 .... 2 A6
  SHEFP/MNR S2 .... 123 D5
Grafton Wy *RHAM/THRY* S65 .... 7 E3
Graham Av *RHAM* S60 .... 114 B5 🗓
Graham Rd *ECC* S11 .... 133 D2
  FUL S10 .... 132 C2
Graham's Orch *BSLY* S70 .... 2 C5
Grampian Cl *BTLY* DN5 .... 28 C4 🗓
  DOD/DAR S75 .... 12 C5 🗓
Grampian Crs *CHSW* S40 .... 182 C5
Granary Cl *RCH* S42........................ 182 B1
Granby Crs *WHHL* DN2 .... 45 D2
Granby Rd *CONI* DN12 .... 62 A5
  SHEFS S8 .... 110 B2
Grange Av *AU/AST/KP* S26 .... 142 A1
  DONS/BSCR DN4........................ 43 E5 🗓
  DRON S18 .... 168 C2
Grange Cliffe Cl *ECC* S11 .... 145 F1
Grange Cl *DONS/BSCR* DN4 .... 67 D1
Grange Ct *BTLY* DN5 .... 29 E3
Grange Crs *BSLYN/ROY* S71 .... 15 F5
  DEARNE S63 .... 27 E3
  ECC S11 .... 134 C2
Grange Crescent Rd *ECC* S11 ..... 134 C2
Grange Dr *KIMB* S61 .... 91 E5
Grange Farm *DONS/BSCR* DN4 ..... 63 E3
Grange La *BSLYN/ROY* S71 .... 23 F1
  DONS/BSCR DN4............................ 62 C3
  RHAM S60 .... 100 A1
  RHAM S60 .... 113 E1
Grange Mill La *SHEFN* S5 .... 100 A1
Grangemill Pl *STV/CWN* S43 ...... 187 D1 🗓
Grange Park Av *STV/CWN* S43 ... 186 A5
Grange Rd *BTLY* DN5 .... 16 B2 🗓
  DEARNE S63 .... 55 E3
  DONS/BSCR DN4............................ 63 D3
  ECC S11 .... 134 C2
  MEX/SWTN S64............................ 80 C1
  MOS S20 .... 153 E2
  RAW S62 .... 80 B4
  RHAM S60 .... 115 F2
Grange St *DEARNE* S63................... 27 E3
The Grange *CHSW* S40 .... 182 A5
  KIMB S61 .... 91 D4
Grange Vw *DONS/BSCR* DN4 .... 43 E4
  HOY S74 .... 37 E4
Grange View Crs *KIMB* S61 .... 101 F1
Grange View Rd *KIMB* S61 .... 101 E1
Grangewood Rd *CHSW* S40......... 190 A5
Grantley Cl *WMB/DAR* S73 .... 40 A5
Granville Cl *CHNE* S41 .... 191 E4 🗓
Granville Rd *SHEFP/MNR* S2 .... 136 A1
Granville St *DOD/DAR* S75 .... 13 E4
  SHEFP/MNR S2 .... 122 C5 🗓
Granville Ter *RHAM/THRY* S65 ...... 7 H6
Grasmere Av *WHHL* DN2 .... 32 A5
Grasmere Cl *CHNE* S41 .... 183 E2
Grasmere Rd *BSLYN/ROY* S71 .... 3 F5
  CONI DN12 .... 84 C1
  DRON S18 .... 168 C2
  SHEFS S8 .... 134 C5 🗓
Grassdale Vw *HACK/IN* S12 .... 151 D2
Grassington Cl *HACK/IN* S12 ...... 151 F2 🗓
Grassington Dr *HACK/IN* S12 ...... 151 E2
Grassington Wy *CHPT/GREN* S35 .. 74 A5
Grassmoor Cl *HACK/IN* S12 .... 137 D5 🗓
Grassthorpe Rd *HACK/IN* S12 .... 149 E1
Grattan St *KIMB* S61 .... 101 F3
Graven Cl *CHPT/GREN* S35 .... 96 C1
Gray Av *AU/AST/KP* S26 .... 142 B1
Gray Cl *RHAM/THRY* S65 .... 7 F2
Gray Gdns *DONS/BSCR* DN4 .... 63 F1 🗓
Grays Ct *CONI* DN12 .... 60 B4
Grayson Cl *STKB/PEN* S36 .... 69 D3
Grayson Rd *KIMB* S61 .... 92 B2
Gray St *HOY* S74 .... 52 B3
  MOS S20 .... 164 A1
  OWL S3 .... 122 C1
Greasbro Rd *DARN/MH* S9 .... 112 B2
Greasbrough La *RAW* S62 .... 93 E1
Greasbrough Rd *KIMB* S61 .... 6 C1
  RAW S62 .... 93 F3
  RHAM S60 .... 6 C2
Greasbrough St *RHAM* S60 .... 6 B3
Great Bank Rd *RHAM/THRY* S65 .. 105 D5

Great Central Av
  DONS/BSCR DN4............................ 43 F4 🗓
Great Cft *DRON* S18 .... 168 B1
Great Eastern Wy *RAW* S62........... 94 A4
Great Park Rd *KIMB* S61 .... 101 F1
Greaves Cl *ST/HB/BR* S6 .... 119 D1 🗓
Greaves Fold *DOD/DAR* S75 .... 12 C5 🗓
Greaves La *CHPT/GREN* S35 .... 73 E1
  ST/HB/BR S6................................ 106 C5
  ST/HB/BR S6................................ 119 D1
Greaves Rd *KIMB* S61 .... 102 B2
  SHEFN S5 .... 98 B1
Greaves St *ST/HB/BR* S6 .... 108 B5
Green Acres *HOY* S74 .... 51 F3
  RAW S62 .... 94 A1
Greenacres Cl *DRON* S18............. 170 A4 🗓
Greenbank Dr *CHSW* S40 .... 183 D5
Green Boulevarde
  DONS/BSCR DN4............................ 46 C4
Green Cha *ECK/KIL* S21................. 164 A5
Green Cl *DRON* S18 .... 170 C5
Green Cross *DRON* S18................. 169 F1
Green Crest *CHSW* S40................. 183 D3
Greenfield *RAW* S62 .... 94 A1
Greenfield Cl *RHAM/THRY* S65 .. 105 F1 🗓
  SHEFS S8 .... 159 D1
Greenfield Dr *SHEFS* S8 .... 159 D1
Greenfield Gdns *DONS/BSCR* DN4 ... 47 E5
Greenfield La *DONS/BSCR* DN4 .... 43 E3
Greenfield Rd *HOY* S74 .... 51 F1
  RHAM/THRY S65........................... 105 E1
  SHEFS S8 .... 159 D1
Greenfields *ECK/KIL* S21 .... 164 A5 🗓
Green Finch Cl *RHAM* S60 .... 114 B4
Greenfoot Cl *DOD/DAR* S75 .... 13 E4
Greenfoot La *DOD/DAR* S75 .... 13 E4
Greengate Cl *CHSW* S40 .... 189 D2
Greengate La *CHPT/GREN* S35 ..... 73 E5
  HAN/WDH S13 .... 140 A4
Greengate Rd *HAN/WDH* S13 .... 140 B4
Green Gln *DRON* S18 .... 189 D2 🗓
Greenhall Rd *ECK/KIL* S21 .... 164 A5
Greenhead Gdns *CHPT/GREN* S35 . 88 B1
Greenhead La *CHPT/GREN* S35 ..... 74 B5
Greenhill Av *BSLYN/ROY* S71 .... 2 C1
  SHEFS S8 .... 146 C5
Greenhill Main Rd *SHEFS* S8 ..... 159 E1 🗓
Greenhill Pkwy *SHEFS* S8 .... 158 C2
Greenhill Rd *SHEFS* S8 .... 146 C5
Greenhouse La *FUL* S10 .... 131 D5
Green House Rd *WHHL* DN2 .... 31 F3
Greenhow St *FUL* S10 .... 121 D2
Green Ings La *DEARNE* S63 .... 56 B1
Greenland Cl *DARN/MH* S9 .... 125 D2
Greenland Ct *DARN/MH* S9 .... 125 D1
Greenland Dr *DARN/MH* S9 .... 125 D1
Greenland Rd *DARN/MH* S9 .... 125 D1
Greenlands Av *NROS/TKH* DN11 .. 67 E5
Greenland Vw *BSLY* S70 .... 36 A1 🗓
  DARN/MH S9.................................. 125 D2
Greenland Wy *DARN/MH* S9 .... 125 D1
Green La *ARMTH* DN3 .... 47 F3
  AU/AST/KP S26 .... 129 E3
  AU/AST/KP S26 .... 143 E3
  CHNE S41 .... 185 E5
  CHPT/GREN S35 .... 99 D1
  DEARNE S63 .... 55 E5
  DOD/DAR S75 .... 20 B4
  DOD/DAR S75 .... 21 D5
  DRON S18 .... 169 F1
  ECK/KIL S21 .... 166 A4
  HOY S74 .... 50 B4
  KIMB S61 .... 101 D2
  OWL S3 .... 8 C2
  RAW S62 .... 94 A1
  RHAM S60 .... 113 F5
  RHAM S60 .... 115 E2
Green Lea *DRON* S18 .... 168 A1
Greenleafe Av *WHHL* DN2 .... 32 A1
Green Oak Av *TOT/DORE* S17 ..... 156 C4
Green Oak Crs *TOT/DORE* S17 ... 156 C4 🗓
Green Oak Dr *AU/AST/KP* S26 .... 155 E3
  TOT/DORE S17 .... 156 C4 🗓
Green Oak Rd *TOT/DORE* S17 ..... 156 C5
Greenock St *ST/HB/BR* S6 .... 107 F4 🗓
Green Ri *RAW* S62 .... 79 E4
Greenside *KIMB* S61 .... 92 C5
Greenside Av *CHNE* S41 .... 184 A2
Greenside La *HOY* S74 .... 51 F2
Greenside Ms *HACK/IN* S12 .... 151 F2 🗓
Green Spring Av *BSLY* S70 .... 36 A5
Greens Rd *RHAM/THRY* S65......... 104 C3
Green St *BSLY* S70 .... 37 D1
  CHNE S41 .... 10 C6
  DONS/BSCR DN4............................ 63 D1
  HOY S74 .... 52 A2
  KIMB S61 .... 92 C2
  STKB/PEN S36................................ 69 E2
The Green *CHNE* S41 .... 191 E5
  CONI DN12 .... 59 D5
  MEX/SWTN S64............................ 80 C1
  RHAM S60 .... 115 D1
  TOT/DORE S17 .... 156 B4

Greenways *CHSW* S40 .... 189 D4
The Greenway *SHEFS* S8 .... 147 D5 🄳
Greenwood Av *BSLY* S70 .... 22 C5
  DARN/MH S9 .... 124 B4
  DONS/BSCR DN4 .... 43 D4 🄳
Greenwood Cl *DARN/MH* S9 .... 124 C4
Greenwood Crs *DARN/MH* S9 ..... 124 C4
Greenwood Dr *DARN/MH* S9 .... 124 B4
Greenwood La *HAN/WDH* S13 .... 140 D3 🄳
Greenwood Rd *CHPT/GREN* S35... 74 A4
  DARN/MH S9 .... 124 C4
  MEX/SWTN S64 .... 81 F4
Greenwood Ter *BSLY* S70 .... 2 B4
Greenwood Wy *DARN/MH* S9 ..... 124 B4
Gregg House Crs *SHEFS* S5 .... 99 E4
Gregg House Rd *SHEFN* S5 .... 99 D3
Gregory La *STV/CWN* S43 .... 179 E5
Gregory Rd *SHEFS* S8 .... 135 E4 🄳
Grend Wood Ct *CHPT/GREN* S35 ... 87 D5
Grenfell Av *MEX/SWTN* S64 .... 58 C3
Grenfolds Rd *CHPT/GREN* S35 ..... 97 E1
Grenobank Rd *CHPT/GREN* S35 ... 97 E1
Greno Crs *CHPT/GREN* S35 .... 87 D5
Grenomoor Cl *CHPT/GREN* S35.... 97 D2
Greno Rd *MEX/SWTN* S64 .... 81 E2
Greno Vw *HOY* S74 .... 51 D5
Greno View Rd *CHPT/GREN* S35 ... 73 E4
Grenville Pl *DOD/DAR* S75 .... 13 D4 🄳
Grenville Rd *DONS/BSCR* DN4 ..... 62 C1
Gresham Av *RHAM* S60 .... 114 A3
Gresham Rd *ST/HB/BR* S6 .... 121 D1 🄳
Gresley Rd *DONS/BSCR* DN4 .... 43 F3
  SHEFS S8 .... 158 C3
Grey Friars' Rd *DON* DN1 .... 4 C2
Greystock St *ATT* S4 .... 123 F1 🄳
Greystones Av *BSLY* S70 .... 36 A1
  ECC S11 .... 133 F3
Greystones Cl *ECC* S11 .... 133 E3
Greystones Crs *ECC* S11 .... 133 E3
Greystones Dr *ECC* S11 .... 133 E3
Greystones Grange Crs *ECC* S11 ... 133 E3 🄳
Greystones Grange Rd *ECC* S11 ... 133 E3
Greystones Hall Rd *ECC* S11 ..... 133 E3
Greystones Ri *ECC* S11 .... 133 E3 🄳
Greystones Rd *ECC* S11 .... 133 D3
  RHAM S60 .... 116 B3 🄳
Grice Cl *DONS/BSCR* DN4 .... 47 D2
Griffin Cl *STV/CWN* S43 .... 187 F1
Griffin Rd *MEX/SWTN* S64 .... 58 C5
Griffiths Cl *RAW* S62 .... 94 A2 🄳
Griffiths Rd *CHPT/GREN* S35 .... 73 F5
Grimesthorpe Rd *ATT* S4 .... 110 A5 🄳
  ATT S4 .... 110 B4
  ATT S4 .... 123 D1
Grimsell Cl *ST/HB/BR* S6 .... 97 E2
Grimsell Crs *ST/HB/BR* S6 .... 97 E2
Grimsell Dr *ST/HB/BR* S6 .... 97 E2
Grindlow Av *CHSW* S40 .... 190 A4 🄳
Grindlow Cl *SHEFS* S8 .... 136 A4
Grindlow Dr *SHEFP/MNR* S2 ..... 136 A4
Grindon Cl *CHSW* S40 .... 183 D4 🄳
Grizedale Av *MOS* S20 .... 153 E3
Grizedale Cl *MOS* S20 .... 153 E3 🄳
Grosvenor Crs *BTLY* DN5 .... 17 E4
  DONS/BSCR DN4 .... 62 B1
Grosvenor Dr *BSLY* S70 .... 21 D1
Grosvenor Rd *RHAM/THRY* S65 ..... 7 F2
Grosvenor Sq *SHEFP/MNR* S2 ... 135 D2 🄳
Grosvenor Ter *DONS/BSCR* DN4 ... 62 B1
Grouse Cft *ST/HB/BR* S6 .... 121 D1
Grove Av *BTLY* DN5 .... 29 E4
  ST/HB/BR S6 .... 107 E2
Grove Cl *DEARNE* S63 .... 41 D5
Grove Gdns *STV/CWN* S43 .... 186 A5
Grove Hill Rd *WHHL* DN2 .... 31 F2
Grove House Ct *TOT/DORE* S17 ... 156 C3 🄳
Grove Pl *DON* DN1 .... 4 D5
Grove Rd *ABRD* S7 .... 146 A2
  CHNE S41 .... 184 B2
  DEARNE S63 .... 40 C5
  RHAM S60 .... 103 E4
  STKB/PEN S36 .... 70 A3
  STV/CWN S43 .... 185 F4
  TOT/DORE S17 .... 156 C3
Grove Sq *ST/HB/BR* S6 .... 108 C5
Grove St *BSLY* S70 .... 23 D5
  BSLYN/ROY S71 .... 3 F6
  CHNE S41 .... 191 D4
The Grove *RAW* S62 .... 94 B1
  RHAM/THRY S65 .... 104 C2
  ST/HB/BR S6 .... 106 C4
  TOT/DORE S17 .... 156 B3
  WHHL DN2 .... 31 E4
Grove V *WHHL* DN2 .... 32 A2
Grove Wy *STV/CWN* S43 .... 186 A4
Guernsey Rd *SHEFP/MNR* S2 ... 135 E3 🄳
Guest La *DONS/BSCR* DN4 .... 42 B5
Guest Rd *DOD/DAR* S75 .... 2 A2
  ECC S11 .... 134 A2
  RHAM S60 .... 104 A5
Guest St *HOY* S74 .... 51 F1
Guildford Av *CHSW* S40 .... 189 E4 🄳
  SHEFP/MNR S2 .... 136 B2
Guildford Cl *SHEFP/MNR* S2 ..... 136 B2

Guildford Dr *SHEFP/MNR* S2..... 136 B2
Guildford Ri *SHEFS* S8 .... 136 B2
Guildford Rd *WHHL* DN2 .... 31 F2
Guildford Vw *SHEFP/MNR* S2 ... 136 C2 🄳
Guildford Wy *SHEFP/MNR* S2 ... 136 B3
Guild Rd *RHAM/THRY* S65 .... 104 C3
Guilthwaite Common La
  AU/AST/KP S26 .... 129 D2
Guilthwaite Crs *RHAM* S60 .... 115 E3
Gullane Dr *DONS/BSCR* DN4 .... 62 B1
Gun La *OWL* S3 .... 9 F3
Gurney Dr *DONS/BSCR* DN4 .... 63 F1 🄳
Gypsy La *WMB/DAR* S73 .... 39 F4

H

Habershon Dr *CHPT/GREN* S35 ... 74 A5 🄳
Habershon Rd *KIMB* S61 .... 92 A5
Hackness La *RAW* S62 .... 113 F3
Hackney La *DRON* S18 .... 176 A4
Hackthorn Rd *SHEFS* S8 .... 147 D2
Haddon Cl *CHSW* S40 .... 189 D2
  DRON S18 .... 169 F1
Haddon Pl *STV/CWN* S43 .... 187 E1
Haddon Ri *MEX/SWTN* S64 .... 59 E2
Haddon Rd *BSLYN/ROY* S71 .... 14 C1 🄳
Haddon St *OWL* S3 .... 122 A1 🄳
Haddon Wy *AU/AST/KP* S26 ..... 143 D3
Haden St *ST/HB/BR* S6 .... 108 A4
Hadfield St *FUL* S10 .... 121 D2
  WMB/DAR S73 .... 39 F4
Hadleigh Cl *RAW* S62 .... 94 A2 🄳
Hadrian Rd *RHAM* S60 .... 114 A2
Hady Crs *CHNE* S41 .... 191 D1
Hady Hl *CHNE* S41 .... 191 D2
Hady La *CHNE* S41 .... 191 D1
Haggard Rd *ST/HB/BR* S6 .... 108 B4
Hagg Hl *FUL* S10 .... 120 A2
  ST/HB/BR S6 .... 96 C4
Hagg La *FUL* S10 .... 119 E4
Hague Av *ECK/KIL* S21 .... 175 F3
  RAW S62 .... 79 F3
Hague La *CHPT/GREN* S35 .... 73 D4
  ECK/KIL S21 .... 175 E3
  KIMB S61 .... 76 C4
Haigh Moor Cl *HAN/WDH* S13 ... 138 C2
Haigh Moor Rd *HAN/WDH* S13 ... 139 D2
Haigh Rd *DONS/BSCR* DN4 .... 43 E5
Hail Mary Dr *HAN/WDH* S13 ..... 140 D3
Hakehill Cl *DONS/BSCR* DN4 .... 66 B1
Halcyon Cl *HACK/IN* S12 .... 151 E2
Haldane Rd *RHAM/THRY* S65 ... 104 B1
Haldene *BSLY* S70 .... 36 C1
Hale St *SHEFS* S8 .... 135 D4
Halesworth Cl *CHSW* S40 .... 188 C4
Halesworth Rd *HAN/WDH* S13 ... 125 F5
Half Acre La *DRON* S18 .... 170 B3
Half Cft *STV/CWN* S43 .... 186 A2
Halfway Dr *MOS* S20 .... 164 C1
Halfway Gdns *MOS* S20 .... 164 C1
Halifax Av *CONI* DN12 .... 84 B1
Halifax Crs *BTLY* DN5 .... 29 D3
Halifax Rd *CHPT/GREN* S35 .... 97 E2
  SHEFN S5 .... 97 E4
  ST/HB/BR S6 .... 97 E5
Halifax St *BSLYN/ROY* S71 .... 13 F3
Hallam Cha *STV/CWN* S43 .... 119 E5 🄳
Hallam Cl *AU/AST/KP* S26.......... 142 A1
  DONS/BSCR DN4 .... 46 A5
Hallamgate Rd *FUL* S10 .... 120 C5
Hallam Grange Cl *FUL* S10 .... 132 A2 🄳
Hallam Grange Crs *FUL* S10 ..... 132 A1
Hallam Grange Ri *FUL* S10 .... 132 A1
Hallam Grange Rd *FUL* S10 .... 132 A1
Hallam La *SHEF* S1 .... 122 D5 🄳
Hallam Pl *RAW* S62 .... 94 B1
Hallam Rd *RHAM* S60 .... 115 D2
Hallamshire Cl *FUL* S10 .... 131 F2
Hallamshire Dr *FUL* S10 .... 131 F2
Hallamshire Rd *FUL* S10 .... 131 F2
Hallam Wy *CHPT/GREN* S35...... 98 C1
Hall Av *HOY* S74 .... 52 B1
  MEX/SWTN S64 .... 58 C3
Hall Balk La *DOD/DAR* S75 .... 2 A1
  DONS/BSCR DN4 .... 64 B3
  NROS/TKH DN11 .... 64 A4
Hallcar St *ATT* S4 .... 9 H1
Hall Cl *BSLY* S70 .... 36 B3
  DEARNE S63 .... 54 C1 🄳
  DRON S18 .... 168 A1
Hall Close Av *RHAM* S60 .... 116 A3
Hall Crs *RHAM* S60 .... 115 F2
Hall Dr *DEARNE* S63 .... 55 E3
Hall Farm Cl *AU/AST/KP* S26 ... 129 E5
  CHNE S41 .... 191 E5
Hall Farm Dr *DEARNE* S63 .... 27 D4
Hall Farm Ri *DEARNE* S63 .... 27 D4 🄳
Hall Flat La *DONS/BSCR* DN4 ..... 63 E1
Hallgate *DEARNE* S63 .... 27 D4
Hall Ga *DON* DN1 .... 4 D5
  MEX/SWTN S64 .... 59 D3
Hallgate Rd *FUL* S10 .... 120 B4 🄳

Hall Gv *RHAM* S60 .... 103 F4
Halliwell Cl *SHEFN* S5 .... 108 B1 🄳
Halliwell Crs *SHEFN* S5 .... 108 C1
Hall La *STV/CWN* S43 .... 181 D2
Hall Meadow Cft *MOS* S20 .... 165 D3
Hall Meadow Dr *MOS* S20 .... 165 D3
Hall Meadow Gv *MOS* S20 .... 165 D3 🄳
Hallowes Ct *DRON* S18 .... 169 F2 🄳
Hallowes Dr *DRON* S18 .... 169 F3
Hallowes La *DRON* S18 .... 169 F3
Hallowes Ri *DRON* S18 .... 170 A3
Hallowmoor Rd *ST/HB/BR* S6 ... 107 E4
Hall Park Head *ST/HB/BR* S6 ... 119 E2
Hall Park Hl *ST/HB/BR* S6 .... 119 F2
Hall Park Mt *ST/HB/BR* S6 .... 119 F2 🄳
Hall Pl *BSLYN/ROY* S71 .... 15 D3
Hall Rd *AU/AST/KP* S26 .... 142 B1
  DARN/MH S9 .... 125 F4
  HAN/WDH S13 .... 125 F5
  RHAM S60 .... 103 F3
  STV/CWN S43 .... 185 F2
Hall Road Old *DARN/MH* S9 ..... 111 E5
Hallside Ct *ARMTH* DN3 .... 47 F3
Hall St *HOY* S74 .... 51 F2 🄳
  RHAM S60 .... 6 B5
  WMB/DAR S73 .... 39 F4
Hallsworth Av *HOY* S74 .... 52 B1
Hall Vw *CHNE* S41 .... 183 F3
Hall Villa La *BTLY* DN5................. 16 B1
Hall Wood Rd *CHPT/GREN* S35 ... 98 C1
Hallyburton Cl *SHEFP/MNR* S2 ... 136 A4 🄳
Hallyburton Dr *SHEFP/MNR* S2 ... 136 A4 🄳
Hallyburton Rd *SHEFP/MNR* S2 ... 136 A4
Halmshaw *BTLY* DN5 .... 29 E1
Halsall Av *DARN/MH* S9 .... 125 D4
Halsall Dr *DARN/MH* S9 .... 124 C4
Halsall Rd *DARN/MH* S9 .... 125 D4
Halsbury Rd *RHAM/THRY* S65 ... 104 B1
Halton Cl *CHNE* S41 .... 177 F5 🄳
Halton Ct *HACK/IN* S12 .... 152 A2
Hambledon Cl *CHSW* S40 .... 183 D4
Hambleton Cl *DOD/DAR* S75 ..... 12 C5 🄳
  HOY S74 .... 52 C2 🄳
Hameline Rd *CONI* DN12 .... 84 C1
Hamilton Cl *MEX/SWTN* S64 ..... 59 D2 🄳
Hamilton Park Rd *BTLY* DN5 ..... 28 B3 🄳
Hamilton Rd *DEARNE* S63 .... 27 F5
  DONS/BSCR DN4 .... 45 D3
  SHEFN S5 .... 110 B2
Hammerton Rd *ST/HB/BR* S6 ... 108 A5
Hammerton St *WMB/DAR* S73 ... 39 D1 🄳
Hammond St *OWL* S3 .... 8 A3
Hampden Rd *MEX/SWTN* S64 ..... 58 B4
Hampton Rd *SHEFN* S5 .... 110 A3
  WHHL DN2 .... 45 D1
Hampton St *CHNE* S41 .... 191 E4
Hanbury Cl *BSLYN/ROY* S71 .... 15 E3
  CHSW S40 .... 182 B4
  DONS/BSCR DN4 .... 63 E3
  DRON S18 .... 169 D2
Handby St *CHNE* S41 .... 191 E4
Handley Ct *STV/CWN* S43 .... 179 E2 🄳
Handley Rd *ECK/KIL* S21 .... 172 B5
  STV/CWN S43 .... 179 E2
Handley St *OWL* S3 .... 9 C2
Hands Rd *FUL* S10 .... 121 D3
Handsworth Av *DARN/MH* S9 ... 125 D4
Handsworth Crs *DARN/MH* S9 ... 125 E4
Handsworth Grange Cl
  HAN/WDH S13 .... 139 E2
Handsworth Grange Crs
  HAN/WDH S13 .... 139 E1
Handsworth Grange Rd
  HAN/WDH S13 .... 139 E1
Handsworth Rd *DARN/MH* S9 ... 125 E4
Hanging Water Cl *FUL* S10 .... 133 D2 🄳
Hangingwater Rd *ECC* S11 .... 133 D3
Hanley Cl *HACK/IN* S12 .... 151 F2
Hanmoor Rd *ST/HB/BR* S6 .... 119 D1
Hannah Rd *HAN/WDH* S13 .... 140 B3
Hannas Royd *DOD/DAR* S75 ..... 20 B3 🄳
Hanover Sq *DEARNE* S63 .... 27 E3
  OWL S3 .... 121 F5
Hanover St *DEARNE* S63 .... 27 E2
  OWL S3 .... 121 F5 🄳
Hanover Wy *OWL* S3 .... 121 F5
Hanson Rd *ST/HB/BR* S6 .... 106 B4
Hanson St *BSLY* S70 .... 2 D5 🄳
Harbord Rd *SHEFS* S8 .... 146 C3
Harborough Av *SHEFP/MNR* S2 ... 124 A4
  SHEFP/MNR S2 .... 137 E1
Harborough Cl *SHEFP/MNR* S2 ... 124 B5
Harborough Dr *SHEFP/MNR* S2 ... 124 B5
Harborough Hill Rd
  BSLYN/ROY S71 .... 3 E3 🄳
Harborough Ri *SHEFP/MNR* S2 ... 124 B5
Harborough Rd *SHEFP/MNR* S2 ... 124 B5
Harborough Wy *SHEFP/MNR* S2 ... 137 E1
Harbury St *HAN/WDH* S13 .... 140 C2 🄳
Harcourt Cl *DONS/BSCR* DN4 ..... 46 A5
Harcourt Crs *FUL* S10 .... 121 E4 🄳
Harcourt Ri *CHPT/GREN* S35 ..... 88 C2
Harcourt Rd *FUL* S10 .... 121 E4
Harcourt Ter *RHAM/THRY* S65 ..... 7 H6
Hardcastle Dr *HAN/WDH* S13 ... 139 E3 🄳

Hardcastle Gdns HAN/WDH S13 ...... 139 E3
Hardcastle Rd HAN/WDH S13 ...... 139 E4
Harden Cl DOD/DAR S75 ...... 12 B5
Hardhurst Rd DRON S18 ...... 177 F1
Hardie Pl RAW S62 ...... 80 A5 🔢
  STV/CWN S43 ...... 187 E1
Hardie St ECK/KIL S21 ...... 174 B1
Harding Av RAW S62 ...... 79 E3
Harding Cl RAW S62 ...... 79 E4
Harding St DARN/MH S9 ...... 124 C1
Hardwick Av CHNE S41 ...... 179 E5
Hardwick Cl AU/AST/KP S26 ...... 143 D3 🔢
  BSLY S70 ...... 36 B1 🔢
  DRON S18 ...... 169 F1
Hardwick Crs ECC S11 ...... 134 A2
Hardwicke Rd RHAM/THRY S65 ...... 7 F2
Hardwick Gv DOD/DAR S75 ...... 20 A4 🔢
Hardwick St CHNE S41 ...... 11 F3
  RHAM/THRY S65 ...... 105 E1
Hardy Pl ST/HB/BR S6 ...... 121 E2
Hardy Rd WHHL DN2 ...... 30 C3
Hardy St KIMB S61 ...... 6 A3
Harefield Rd ECC S11 ...... 134 B2 🔢
Harehill Rd CHSW S40 ...... 190 A5
Harehills Rd RHAM/THRY S65 ...... 103 F4
Harewood Av BSLY S70 ...... 20 C1
Harewood Rd WHHL DN2 ...... 45 E1
Harewood Wy ECC S11 ...... 145 E3 🔢
Harland Rd FUL S10 ...... 134 C1
Harlech Cl CHPT/GREN S35 ...... 74 A5
Harleston St ATT S4 ...... 123 D1 🔢
Harley Rd ECC S11 ...... 133 D5
  RAW S62 ...... 75 E2
Harlington Ct CONI DN12 ...... 60 B4
Harlington Rd MEX/SWTN S64 ...... 58 C3
Harmer La SHEF S1 ...... 9 F6
Harmony Wy RHAM S60 ...... 127 E3 🔢
Harney Cl DARN/MH S9 ...... 125 D2
Harold Av BSLYN/ROY S71 ...... 15 F3
Harold Cft RAW S62 ...... 93 D2
Harold St ST/HB/BR S6 ...... 121 E1
Harperhill Cl CHSW S40 ...... 190 A5 🔢
Harriet Cl BSLY S70 ...... 22 B3 🔢
Harrington Cl BSLYN/ROY S71 ...... 15 F3
Harrington Rd SHEFP/MNR S2 ...... 135 E2 🔢
Harrington St DON DN1 ...... 5 E2
Harrison La FUL S10 ...... 131 D3
Harrison Rd ST/HB/BR S6 ...... 107 F5
Harrison St KIMB S61 ...... 102 B4
Harris Rd ST/HB/BR S6 ...... 107 F2
Harrogate Dr CONI DN12 ...... 59 F5
Harrogate Rd AU/AST/KP S26 ...... 142 A4 🔢
Harrop Dr MEX/SWTN S64 ...... 58 C3
Harrop La FUL S10 ...... 131 D4
Harrowden Rd DARN/MH S9 ...... 112 C2
  WHHL DN2 ...... 31 D3
Harrow St ECC S11 ...... 135 D1
Harry Firth Cl DARN/MH S9 ...... 124 B2 🔢
Harry Rd DOD/DAR S75 ...... 37 F2
Hartfield Cl CHNE S41 ...... 190 C5
Hartford Cl SHEFS S8 ...... 147 E2 🔢
Hartford Rd SHEFS S8 ...... 147 E2
Hart Hl RAW S62 ...... 79 E3
Harthill Rd CONI DN12 ...... 84 B2
  HAN/WDH S13 ...... 137 F3
Hartington Av ABRD S7 ...... 146 A2
Hartington Cl KIMB S61 ...... 102 B3
Hartington Dr BSLYN/ROY S71 ...... 14 A3
Hartington Rd ABRD S7 ...... 146 A2
  CHNE S41 ...... 191 D2
  DRON S18 ...... 169 F1
  KIMB S61 ...... 102 B3
Hartland Av MOS S20 ...... 153 E3 🔢
Hartland Ct MOS S20 ...... 153 E3 🔢
Hartland Dr MOS S20 ...... 153 E3
Hartland Wy CHNE S41 ...... 178 B5 🔢
Hartley Brook Av SHEFN S5 ...... 99 D3
Hartley Brook Rd SHEFN S5 ...... 99 D3
Hartley La KIMB S61 ...... 6 A3
Hartley St MEX/SWTN S64 ...... 58 A4
  SHEFP/MNR S2 ...... 135 E3
Hartopp Av SHEFP/MNR S2 ...... 136 A4
Hartopp Cl SHEFP/MNR S2 ...... 136 A4 🔢
Hartopp Dr SHEFP/MNR S2 ...... 136 B4 🔢
Hartopp Rd SHEFP/MNR S2 ...... 136 A4
Harts Head SHEF S1 ...... 9 E4
Hartside Cl CHSW S40 ...... 183 E4
Harvest Cl BSLY S70 ...... 36 B1
  DONS/BSCR DN4 ...... 43 D4
Harvest La OWL S3 ...... 122 B1
Harvest Wy CHSW S40 ...... 182 B4 🔢
Harvey Clough Ms SHEFS S8 ...... 147 E2
Harvey Clough Rd SHEFS S8 ...... 147 E2
Harvey Rd CHNE S41 ...... 191 F2
  CHPT/GREN S35 ...... 88 B1
Harvey St BSLY S70 ...... 21 E2
  STKB/PEN S36 ...... 69 E2 🔢
Harwell Rd SHEFS S8 ...... 135 D3
Harwich Rd SHEFP/MNR S2 ...... 136 C1
Harwood Cl SHEFP/MNR S2 ...... 135 D2
Harwood Dr MOS S20 ...... 152 B4
Harwood Gdns MOS S20 ...... 152 C4
Harwood St SHEFP/MNR S2 ...... 135 E2
Harwood Ter BSLYN/ROY S71 ...... 15 F3 🔢
Haslam Crs SHEFS S8 ...... 158 C2 🔢

Hasland Rd CHNE S41 ...... 190 C3
Haslehurst Rd SHEFP/MNR S2 ...... 123 F5
Haslemere Gv BTLY DN5 ...... 29 E3
Hassop Cl CHSW S40 ...... 183 D3
  DRON S18 ...... 170 A1
Hastilar Cl SHEFP/MNR S2 ...... 137 F2
Hastilar Rd SHEFP/MNR S2 ...... 137 E2 🔢
Hastilar Rd South HAN/WDH S13 ...... 138 A3
  SHEFP/MNR S2 ...... 138 A2
Hastings Cl CHSW S40 ...... 183 E3
Hastings Mt ABRD S7 ...... 146 A1
Hastings Rd ABRD S7 ...... 146 A1
Hatchell Dr DONS/BSCR DN4 ...... 67 E2
Hatchellwood Vw
  DONS/BSCR DN4 ...... 67 F2
Hatfield House Ct SHEFN S5 ...... 99 E4 🔢
Hatfield House Cft SHEFN S5 ...... 99 E4
Hatfield House La SHEFN S5 ...... 99 D5
Hatherley Rd DARN/MH S9 ...... 112 B1
  MEX/SWTN S64 ...... 57 E4
  RHAM/THRY S65 ...... 7 F2
Hathern Cl STV/CWN S43 ...... 186 A5
Hathersage Rd TOT/DORE S17 ...... 144 A4
Hatton Cl DRON S18 ...... 168 B3
Hatton Dr CHSW S40 ...... 182 C4
Hatton Rd ST/HB/BR S6 ...... 108 A5
Haugh Gn RAW S62 ...... 79 E3
Haugh La RAW S62 ...... 79 D3
Haughton Rd SHEFS S8 ...... 147 D3
Havelock St BSLY S70 ...... 21 E2 🔢
  FUL S10 ...... 121 F5
Havercroft Rd RHAM S60 ...... 116 A1
  SHEFS S8 ...... 146 C1
Havercroft Ter ECK/KIL S21 ...... 165 F1 🔢
Haverdale Ri DOD/DAR S75 ...... 13 E4
Haverlands La BSLY S70 ...... 35 E1
Haverlands Rdg BSLY S70 ...... 36 A1 🔢
Hawes Cl MEX/SWTN S64 ...... 59 D2
Hawfield Cl DONS/BSCR DN4 ...... 43 E3
Hawke Cl RAW S62 ...... 79 D4
Hawke Rd WHHL DN2 ...... 31 D4
Hawke St DARN/MH S9 ...... 111 E4
Hawkins Av CHPT/GREN S35 ...... 87 F1 🔢
Hawkshead Av DRON S18 ...... 168 B2
Hawkshead Rd ATT S4 ...... 111 D3
Hawksley Av CHSW S40 ...... 10 B2
  ST/HB/BR S6 ...... 108 A4
Hawksley Ms ST/HB/BR S6 ...... 108 A4
Hawksley Rd ST/HB/BR S6 ...... 108 A4
Hawksway ECK/KIL S21 ...... 163 F5
Hawkwell Rd RHAM/THRY S65 ...... 105 D2
Hawksworth Rd RHAM/THRY S65 ...... 105 D2
  ST/HB/BR S6 ...... 121 E1
Hawkwell Bank BSLYN/ROY S71 ...... 24 B2
Hawley St DRON S18 ...... 171 E2
  RAW S62 ...... 94 A1
  SHEF S1 ...... 8 D4
Haworth Bank RHAM S60 ...... 115 D3 🔢
Haworth Cl BSLYN/ROY S71 ...... 14 C4 🔢
Haworth Crs RHAM S60 ...... 115 D3
Hawshaw La HOY S74 ...... 51 D2
Hawson St WMB/DAR S73 ...... 39 F3
Hawthorn Av ARMTH DN3 ...... 33 F1
  MOS S20 ...... 152 B4
Hawthorne Av DRON S18 ...... 159 E5
  RAW S62 ...... 94 B1
  STKB/PEN S36 ...... 68 A5
Hawthorne Cl ECK/KIL S21 ...... 166 B3 🔢
Hawthorne Crs MEX/SWTN S64 ...... 57 F3
Hawthorne Gv BTLY DN5 ...... 16 C4
Hawthorne Rd DEARNE S63 ...... 56 B3 🔢
The Hawthornes MOS S20 ...... 153 D1
Hawthorne St BSLY S70 ...... 21 F2
  CHSW S40 ...... 190 B3
  ST/HB/BR S6 ...... 120 C1 🔢
Hawthorn Gv CONI DN12 ...... 84 B3 🔢
Hawthorn Hl STV/CWN S43 ...... 175 D5
Hawthorn Rd CHPT/GREN S35 ...... 73 F4
  ECK/KIL S21 ...... 173 F1
  ST/HB/BR S6 ...... 107 F4
Hawthorn Wy RCH S42 ...... 182 A4
Haxby Cl HAN/WDH S13 ...... 138 C3
Haxby Pl HAN/WDH S13 ...... 138 C4
Haxby St HAN/WDH S13 ...... 138 C5
Haybrook Ct TOT/DORE S17 ...... 156 C2
Haydock Cl MEX/SWTN S64 ...... 58 C2 🔢
Hayes Ct MOS S20 ...... 164 C2
Hayes Cft BSLY S70 ...... 2 D6
Hayes Dr MOS S20 ...... 164 B2
Hayfield Cl DRON S18 ...... 168 B2 🔢
Hayfield Crs HACK/IN S12 ...... 150 B2 🔢
Hayfield Dr HACK/IN S12 ...... 150 A2
Hayfield Pl HACK/IN S12 ...... 150 B2
Hayfield Vw ECK/KIL S21 ...... 163 F5
Hayford Wy STV/CWN S43 ...... 181 F5
Hay Green La BSLY S70 ...... 50 A1
Hayland St DARN/MH S9 ...... 111 F2
Haymarket SHEF S1 ...... 9 F4
Haythorne Wy MEX/SWTN S64 ...... 81 E2
Haywood Av STKB/PEN S36 ...... 69 E2
Haywood Cl RHAM/THRY S65 ...... 105 D2
Haywood La STKB/PEN S36 ...... 69 E2
Hazel Av ECK/KIL S21 ...... 166 A3
Hazelbadge Crs HACK/IN S12 ...... 150 C2 🔢

Hazel Cl DRON S18 ...... 170 A3 🔢
Hazel Ct DRON S18 ...... 169 F3
Hazel Dr CHSW S40 ...... 189 E4
Hazel Gv CHPT/GREN S35 ...... 88 B2
  CONI DN12 ...... 84 C2
Hazel Rd ECK/KIL S21 ...... 174 A1 🔢
Hazelshaw DOD/DAR S75 ...... 20 B4 🔢
Hazelwood Cl DRON S18 ...... 168 A2 🔢
Hazelwood Dr MEX/SWTN S64 ...... 81 E3
Hazlebarrow Cl SHEFS S8 ...... 159 F1
Hazlebarrow Ct SHEFS S8 ...... 159 F1 🔢
Hazlebarrow Crs SHEFS S8 ...... 159 F1
Hazlebarrow Dr SHEFS S8 ...... 159 F1
Hazlebarrow Gv SHEFS S8 ...... 160 A1 🔢
Hazlebarrow Rd SHEFS S8 ...... 159 F2 🔢
Hazlehurst Av CHNE S41 ...... 11 F2
Hazlehurst La CHNE S41 ...... 11 F2
  SHEFS S8 ...... 161 D1
Headford Gdns OWL S3 ...... 122 A5
Headford La OWL S3 ...... 122 A5
Headford Ms OWL S3 ...... 122 A5 🔢
Headford St OWL S3 ...... 122 A5 🔢
Headingley Wy CONI DN12 ...... 62 A4
Headland Cl STV/CWN S43 ...... 185 F2
Headland Dr FUL S10 ...... 120 B4
Headland Rd FUL S10 ...... 120 B4
Headlands Rd HOY S74 ...... 51 E2
Heads La STKB/PEN S36 ...... 68 B5
Heath Av ECK/KIL S21 ...... 166 B3
Heath Bank Rd WHHL DN2 ...... 32 A2
Heathcote Dr CHNE S41 ...... 191 F4
Heathcote St ATT S4 ...... 110 B3 🔢
Heatherbank Rd DONS/BSCR DN4 ... 46 C5
Heather Cl RHAM S60 ...... 103 F5
Heather Gdns CHNE S41 ...... 191 F5 🔢
Heather Knowle DOD/DAR S75 ...... 20 B5 🔢
Heather Lea Av TOT/DORE S17 ...... 156 A1
Heather Lea Pl TOT/DORE S17 ...... 156 A1
Heather Rd SHEFN S5 ...... 110 C1
Heather Vale Cl CHNE S41 ...... 191 F5 🔢
Heather Vale Rd CHNE S41 ...... 191 E5
Heatherfield Av CHSW S40 ...... 189 E1
Heathfield Cl DRON S18 ...... 169 D3 🔢
Heathfield Rd HACK/IN S12 ...... 150 B1
Heath Rd ST/HB/BR S6 ...... 97 E5
  STKB/PEN S36 ...... 69 E3
Heaton Cl DRON S18 ...... 168 B2
Heaton Gdns CONI DN12 ...... 62 A5
Heatons Bank RAW S62 ...... 80 B5
Heaton St CHSW S40 ...... 189 D2
Heavens Wk DONS/BSCR DN4 ...... 44 B3
Heavygate Av FUL S10 ...... 121 D2
  ST/HB/BR S6 ...... 121 D1
Heavygate Rd ST/HB/BR S6 ...... 121 D1
Hedley Dr STV/CWN S43 ...... 185 E1
Heeley Bank Rd SHEFP/MNR S2 ...... 135 F4
Heeley Gn SHEFP/MNR S2 ...... 135 F4
Heelis St BSLY S70 ...... 22 A2
Heighton Vw AU/AST/KP S26 ...... 142 A2 🔢
Helena Cl BSLY S70 ...... 21 E2 🔢
Helena St MEX/SWTN S64 ...... 58 B3
Helensburgh Cl DOD/DAR S75 ...... 13 D5 🔢
Helliwell La STKB/PEN S36 ...... 69 F4
Helmsley Av MOS S20 ...... 164 B1
Helmsley Cl AU/AST/KP S26 ...... 142 A4 🔢
Helmton Dr SHEFS S8 ...... 147 E2
Helmton Rd SHEFS S8 ...... 147 D3
Helston Cl CHNE S41 ...... 190 C4
Helston Crs BSLYN/ROY S71 ...... 14 C4
Helston Ri ABRD S7 ...... 146 A1
Hemingfield Rd WMB/DAR S73 ...... 38 C4
Hemper Gv SHEFS S8 ...... 158 B1 🔢
Hemper La SHEFS S8 ...... 158 B2
Hemp Pits Rd BTLY DN5 ...... 17 E5
Hemsworth Rd SHEFS S8 ...... 148 A3
Hendon St HAN/WDH S13 ...... 139 D1
Hengist Rd BTLY DN5 ...... 43 D2 🔢
Henley Av SHEFS S8 ...... 147 F5
Henley Grove Rd KIMB S61 ...... 102 C2
Henley La KIMB S61 ...... 102 B1
Henley Ri KIMB S61 ...... 102 C2
Henley Rd WHHL DN2 ...... 32 A4
Henley Wy KIMB S61 ...... 102 B2
Hennings Cl DONS/BSCR DN4 ...... 45 F5
Henry La NROS/TKH DN11 ...... 66 B5
Henry Pl MEX/SWTN S64 ...... 59 D2 🔢
Henry Rd DEARNE S63 ...... 56 A2
Henry St BSLY S70 ...... 22 B5 🔢
  CHNE S41 ...... 184 C1
  CHPT/GREN S35 ...... 73 D4
  ECK/KIL S21 ...... 164 B5
  OWL S3 ...... 8 B2
  RAW S62 ...... 94 A3
  RHAM/THRY S65 ...... 7 F4
  WMB/DAR S73 ...... 40 A1
Henshall St BSLY S70 ...... 22 B2 🔢
Heppenstall La DARN/MH S9 ...... 124 A1 🔢
Heptinstall St BSLY S70 ...... 22 C5 🔢
Hepworth Dr AU/AST/KP S26 ...... 142 B3 🔢
Hepworth Rd DONS/BSCR DN4 ...... 43 D5 🔢
Herald Rd ARMTH DN3 ...... 19 F5
Herbert Rd ABRD S7 ...... 134 C2 🔢
  BTLY DN5 ...... 29 E4
Herbert St KIMB S61 ...... 101 F2
  MEX/SWTN S64 ...... 58 C3

Herdings Ct HACK/IN S12 .... 149 E2
Herdings Rd HACK/IN S12 .... 149 E2
Herdings Vw HACK/IN S12 .... 149 E2
Hereford Dr STV/CWN S43 .... 186 A1
Hereford Rd WHHL DN2 .... 31 F2
Hereford St SHEF S1 .... 135 E1
Hereward Ct CONI DN12 .... 85 F1
Hereward Rd SHEFN S5 .... 98 C5
Hermitage St SHEF/MNR S2 .... 135 D1
Hermit La DOD/DAR S75 .... 12 A5
Heron Hl AU/AST/KP S26 .... 142 C4
Heron Mt SHEFP/MNR S2 .... 123 F5
Herons Wy BSLY S70 .... 36 A5
Herrick Gdns DONS/BSCR DN4 .... 64 A1
Herries Av SHEFN S5 .... 109 E2
Herries Dr SHEFN S5 .... 109 E2
Herries Pl SHEFN S5 .... 109 E2
Herries Rd SHEFN S5 .... 108 C2
  SHEFN S5 .... 109 F2
  ST/HB/BR S6 .... 108 A2
Herringthorpe Av
  RHAM/THRY S65 .... 104 C5
Herringthorpe Cl
  RHAM/THRY S65 .... 104 C4
Herringthorpe Gv
  RHAM/THRY S65 .... 105 D5
Herringthorpe La
  RHAM/THRY S65 .... 105 D4
Herringthorpe Valley Rd
  RHAM/THRY S65 .... 105 D1
  RHAM/THRY S65 .... 116 A1
Herriot Dr CHSW S40 .... 190 C3
Herschell Rd SHEFS S8 .... 135 D3
Hesley Bar KIMB S61 .... 89 F2
Hesley Ct MEX/SWTN S64 .... 81 D2
Hesley Gra KIMB S61 .... 90 C4
Hesley Gv CHPT/GREN S35 .... 89 D2
Hesley La KIMB S61 .... 89 F2
Hesley Rd SHEFN S5 .... 99 E3
Hesley Ter SHEFN S5 .... 99 E3
Heslow Gv KIMB S61 .... 89 F1
Hessey St HAN/WDH S13 .... 139 D4
Hessle Rd ST/HB/BR S6 .... 107 F2
Hewitt St MEX/SWTN S64 .... 59 D3
Hexthorpe Rd DONS/BSCR DN4 .... 4 B5
Heyhouse Dr CHPT/GREN S35 .... 74 B4
Heyhouse Wy CHPT/GREN S35 .... 74 A4
Heysham Gn BSLYN/ROY S71 .... 15 F2
Heywood St STV/CWN S43 .... 185 F1
Hibberd Pl ST/HB/BR S6 .... 107 E4
Hickleton Ct DEARNE S63 .... 26 C4
Hickleton St CONI DN12 .... 60 A5
Hickmott Rd ECC S11 .... 134 B2
Hickson Dr BSLYN/ROY S71 .... 15 F3
Hicks St OWL S3 .... 122 B1
Hides St DARN/MH S9 .... 111 F4
High Alder Rd DONS/BSCR DN4 .... 46 A4
Highbury Av DONS/BSCR DN4 .... 46 C4
Highbury Rd CHNE S41 .... 10 D2
Highcliffe Dr ECC S11 .... 133 D3
  MEX/SWTN S64 .... 57 F5
Highcliffe Pl ECC S11 .... 133 D4
Highcliffe Rd ECC S11 .... 133 D5
High Cft HOY S74 .... 51 F3
Higher Albert St CHNE S41 .... 11 E3
Highfield Av BSLY S70 .... 22 A4
  BSLYN/ROY S71 .... 14 B1
Highfield Gv DEARNE S63 .... 54 B1
Highfield La CHNE S41 .... 183 F3
  HAN/WDH S13 .... 126 C5
  RHAM S60 .... 127 D3
Highfield Pl SHEFP/MNR S2 .... 135 E2
Highfield Ri ST/HB/BR S6 .... 118 C2
Highfield Rd CHNE S41 .... 10 D2
  CONI DN12 .... 85 E2
  DON DN1 .... 5 F2
  KIMB S61 .... 93 D4
  MEX/SWTN S64 .... 56 C5
Highfields Crs DRON S18 .... 169 E3
High Field Spring HAN/WDH S13 .... 126 B3
Highfields Rd DRON S18 .... 169 E3
Highfield Vw RHAM S60 .... 127 D1
Highfield View Rd CHNE S41 .... 10 D1
High Fisher Ga DON DN1 .... 5 E2
Highgate DARN/MH S9 .... 112 C2
  DEARNE S63 .... 40 C3
Highgate Dr DRON S18 .... 170 A4
Highgate La DRON S18 .... 170 A4
Highgreave SHEFN S5 .... 99 D3
High Greave Av SHEFN S5 .... 99 D2
High Greave Ct SHEFN S5 .... 98 C2
High Greave Pl RHAM/THRY S65 .... 105 D2
High Greave Rd RHAM/THRY S65 ...... 105 D2
High Hazel Crs RHAM S60 .... 127 D1
High Hazels Cl DARN/MH S9 .... 125 E3
High Hazels Md DARN/MH S9 .... 125 E3
High House Farm Ct
  AU/AST/KP S26 .... 155 F3
High House Ter ST/HB/BR S6 .... 108 B5
Highland STV/CWN S43 .... 179 E1
High La HACK/IN S12 .... 150 C4
Highlow Cl CHSW S40 .... 183 D4

Highlow Vw RHAM S60 .... 114 A3
High Matlock Av ST/HB/BR S6 .... 119 E1
High Matlock Rd ST/HB/BR S6 .... 119 F1
Highmill Av MEX/SWTN S64 .... 56 B5
Hignam Crescent Rd FUL S10 .... 121 D4
High Rdg BSLY S70 .... 22 A5
High Rd DONS/BSCR DN4 .... 43 E5
  DONS/BSCR DN4 .... 62 A1
Highroyds BSLY S70 .... 22 A5
Highstone Av BSLY S70 .... 21 F3
Highstone Crs BSLY S70 .... 21 F3
Highstone La BSLY S70 .... 22 A3
Highstone Rd BSLY S70 .... 22 A4
Highstone V BSLY S70 .... 21 F3
High Storrs Cl ECC S11 .... 133 D4
High Storrs Crs ECC S11 .... 133 E3
High Storrs Dr ECC S11 .... 133 D4
High Storrs Ri ECC S11 .... 133 E3
High Storrs Rd ECC S11 .... 133 D3
High St AU/AST/KP S26 .... 142 A2
  BSLY S70 .... 2 B4
  BSLY S70 .... 22 C5
  BSLYN/ROY S71 .... 15 D3
  BTLY DN5 .... 29 F1
  BTLY DN5 .... 29 F1
  CHNE S41 .... 178 B4
  CHPT/GREN S35 .... 73 E2
  CHSW S40 .... 11 E6
  CONI DN12 .... 85 D1
  DEARNE S63 .... 26 C4
  DEARNE S63 .... 56 A2
  DOD/DAR S75 .... 20 A3
  DON DN1 .... 4 D3
  DRON S18 .... 169 D1
  DRON S18 .... 171 E2
  ECK/KIL S21 .... 164 B5
  ECK/KIL S21 .... 166 B2
  HOY S74 .... 51 F2
  KIMB S61 .... 101 F2
  MEX/SWTN S64 .... 58 B4
  MOS S20 .... 153 E1
  MOS S20 .... 164 A1
  RAW S62 .... 94 A2
  RHAM S60 .... 6 D5
  RHAM S60 .... 115 F3
  SHEF S1 .... 9 F4
  STV/CWN S43 .... 179 E3
  STV/CWN S43 .... 181 F4
  STV/CWN S43 .... 186 A4
  TOT/DORE S17 .... 156 B1
  WMB/DAR S73 .... 39 E2
High Street La SHEFP/MNR S2 .... 9 H5
Highthorn Rd MEX/SWTN S64 .... 57 F3
Highton St FUL S10 .... 121 D1
High Trees TOT/DORE S17 .... 156 D1
High View Cl CHNE S41 .... 191 E2
Highwood Pl ECK/KIL S21 .... 164 A5
Highwoods Crs MEX/SWTN S64 .... 57 F3
Highwoods Rd MEX/SWTN S64 .... 57 F3
High Wray Cl ECC S11 .... 145 F1
Hilary Wy AU/AST/KP S26 .... 142 B3
Hill Cl RHAM/THRY S65 .... 105 E3
  ST/HB/BR S6 .... 119 D1
Hillcote Cl FUL S10 .... 132 B1
Hillcote Dr FUL S10 .... 132 B1
Hillcote Mt FUL S10 .... 132 B1
Hillcote Ri FUL S10 .... 132 B1
Hillcrest DEARNE S63 .... 26 C4
Hill Crest HOY S74 .... 51 D3
Hillcrest Ri STKB/PEN S36 .... 70 A3
Hillcrest Rd CHNE S41 .... 191 E5
Hill Crest Rd CHPT/GREN S35 .... 88 A1
  RHAM/THRY S65 .... 104 C2
Hillcrest Rd STKB/PEN S36 .... 70 A3
  WHHL DN2 .... 31 E3
Hill Farm Cl DEARNE S63 .... 26 B4
Hillfoot Rd TOT/DORE S17 .... 156 A3
Hill Gv STV/CWN S43 .... 180 C2
Hillman Dr STV/CWN S43 .... 187 D3
Hill Park Gv DOD/DAR S75 .... 20 A2
Hillsborough Pl ST/HB/BR S6 .... 108 A4
Hillsborough Rd DONS/BSCR DN4 ...... 46 C4
  ST/HB/BR S6 .... 108 A4
Hills Cl BTLY DN5 .... 42 C2
Hillside BSLYN/ROY S71 .... 24 B2
  MOS S20 .... 164 A1
Hill Side RHAM S60 .... 115 F3
Hillside Av DRON S18 .... 169 E3
  SHEFN S5 .... 98 C3
Hillside Ct KIMB S61 .... 93 E5
Hillside Dr CHSW S40 .... 189 D4
  HOY S74 .... 52 A3
Hills Rd STKB/PEN S36 .... 69 E2
Hill St BSLYN/ROY S71 .... 23 F2
  HOY S74 .... 52 B3
  SHEFP/MNR S2 .... 135 D1
Hill Top Cl KIMB S61 .... 101 E3
  RHAM S60 .... 113 E3
Hill Top Crs MOS S20 .... 152 B4
  WHHL DN2 .... 32 A2
Hilltop Gdns CONI DN12 .... 84 A1
Hill Top La CHPT/GREN S35 .... 96 C1
  DOD/DAR S75 .... 12 C4
Hill Top Ri CHPT/GREN S35 .... 97 E2
Hill Top Rd BSLY S70 .... 36 A5

Hilltop Rd CHNE S41 .... 178 C4
Hill Top Rd CHPT/GREN S35 .... 97 E2
  CONI DN12 .... 84 A2
Hilltop Rd DRON S18 .... 169 E3
Hilltop Wy DRON S18 .... 169 E4
Hill Turrets Cl ECC S11 .... 145 D1
Hill Vw East KIMB S61 .... 101 E1
Hill View Rd KIMB S61 .... 101 E1
  STV/CWN S43 .... 185 F1
Hilton Dr CHPT/GREN S35 .... 98 C1
Hilton St DOD/DAR S75 .... 13 E5
Hindburn Cl DONS/BSCR DN4 .... 46 A5
Hinde House La ATT S4 .... 110 C2
Hinde House Crt ATT S4 .... 110 C2
Hinde House La ATT S4 .... 110 B3
Hinde St ATT S4 .... 110 C3
Hindewood Cl ATT S4 .... 110 C2
Hindle St BSLY S70 .... 2 A6
Hind Rd RHAM S60 .... 116 A3
Hipley Cl CHSW S40 .... 182 C4
Hipper St CHSW S40 .... 190 B2
Hipper St South CHSW S40 .... 190 B2
Hipper St West CHSW S40 .... 189 F2
Hirst Common La ST/HB/BR S6 .... 96 B3
Hirst Dr RHAM/THRY S65 .... 105 E2
Hirst Ga MEX/SWTN S64 .... 59 D3
Hobart St ECC S11 .... 135 D2
Hobson Av ST/HB/BR S6 .... 108 C5
Hobson Pl ST/HB/BR S6 .... 108 C5
Hodder Ct CHPT/GREN S35 .... 74 A5
Hodgson St OWL S3 .... 122 A5
Hoggarth Ri DRON S18 .... 169 D2
Holbeach Dr CHSW S40 .... 189 F4
Holbeck Cl CHNE S41 .... 11 G4
Holbein Cl DRON S18 .... 169 D3
Holberry Cl FUL S10 .... 121 F5
Holberry Gdns FUL S10 .... 121 F5
Holbourne Gv CHPT/GREN S35 .... 73 E2
Holbrook Av MOS S20 .... 153 D5
Holbrook Cl CHSW S40 .... 189 D4
Holbrook Dr HAN/WDH S13 .... 137 F4
Holbrook Ri MOS S20 .... 153 D5
Holbrook Pl STV/CWN S43 .... 187 D2
Holbrook Ri MOS S20 .... 153 D4
Holbrook Rd HAN/WDH S13 .... 137 F3
Holburn Av DRON S18 .... 169 E1
Holden Ct BSLY S70 .... 2 B6
Holderness Dr AU/AST/KP S26 .... 142 B2
Holdings Rd SHEFP/MNR S2 .... 136 B1
Hole House La STKB/PEN S36 .... 68 C1
Holgate WMB/DAR S73 .... 24 C5
Holgate Av SHEFN S5 .... 98 A3
Holgate Crs SHEFN S5 .... 98 B3
Holgate Dr SHEFN S5 .... 98 B3
Holgate Mt BSLY S70 .... 22 A4
Holgate Rd SHEFN S5 .... 98 B3
Holkham Ri ECC S11 .... 145 D3
Holland Cl RAW S62 .... 80 A4
Holland Pl SHEFP/MNR S2 .... 135 E2
Holland Rd CHNE S41 .... 178 A4
  CHPT/GREN S35 .... 73 E4
  SHEFP/MNR S2 .... 135 E2
Holland St SHEF S1 .... 8 C5
Hollens Wy RCH S42 .... 182 A4
Hollies Cl DRON S18 .... 170 A3
Hollinberry La CHPT/GREN S35 .... 72 C2
Hollin Busk La STKB/PEN S36 .... 69 D4
Hollin Busk Rd STKB/PEN S36 .... 69 D3
Hollin Cl CHNE S41 .... 183 D1
  NROS/TKH DN11 .... 67 F5
Hollin Cft DOD/DAR S75 .... 20 B2
Hollindale Dr HACK/IN S12 .... 138 A5
Holling Cft STKB/PEN S36 .... 69 F2
Hollingwood Crs STV/CWN S43 .... 180 B5
Hollins Cl ST/HB/BR S6 .... 120 A2
Hollins Dr ST/HB/BR S6 .... 120 A2
Hollinsend Av HACK/IN S12 .... 138 A5
Hollinsend Pl HACK/IN S12 .... 138 A5
Hollinsend Rd HACK/IN S12 .... 149 E1
Hollins La ST/HB/BR S6 .... 120 B1
Hollins Spring Av DRON S18 .... 169 E3
Hollins Spring Rd DRON S18 .... 169 E3
Hollis Cl RAW S62 .... 79 D3
Hollis Cft HAN/WDH S13 .... 139 E4
  SHEF S1 .... 8 C4
Hollis La CHNE S41 .... 190 C2
Hollowdene DOD/DAR S75 .... 12 C4
Hollow Ga BTLY DN5 .... 29 E2
  CHPT/GREN S35 .... 87 E1
Hollowgate RHAM S60 .... 103 F4
Hollow Ga RHAM S60 .... 115 F3
Hollowgate RHAM/THRY S65 .... 103 F4
Hollowgate Av DEARNE S63 .... 41 D5
Hollow La MOS S20 .... 164 B2
The Hollows DONS/BSCR DN4 .... 66 C1
Holly Av BTLY DN5 .... 29 E2
Hollybank Av HACK/IN S12 .... 138 A4
Hollybank Cl HACK/IN S12 .... 138 B4
Hollybank Crs HACK/IN S12 .... 138 A4
Hollybank Dr HACK/IN S12 .... 138 A4
Hollybank Rd HACK/IN S12 .... 138 A5
Hollybank Wy HACK/IN S12 .... 138 B4
Holly Bush Dr DEARNE S63 .... 27 D3
Hollybush St RAW S62 .... 94 A3
Holly Cl CHPT/GREN S35 .... 88 A2

ECK/KIL S21.................................. 165 F3
Holly Dene ARMTH DN3 .... 33 E1
Holly Dr BTLY DN5 .... 16 C4
Holly Gdns HACK/IN S12 .... 138 A4
Hollygate BSLY S70 .... 22 C5
Holly Gv DEARNE S63 .... 56 A4
HACK/IN S12 .... 138 A4
Holly La SHEF S1 .... 8 D5 🖪
Holly St SHEF S1 .... 8 D5
Holly Ter AU/AST/KP S26 .... 141 F2
DONS/BSCR DN4 .... 43 D5
Hollythorpe Cl CHNE S41 .... 191 E4
Hollythorpe Crs SHEFS S8 .... 147 E1
Hollythorpe Rd SHEFS S8 .... 147 F1
Hollywell Cl RAW S62 .... 80 C5
Holmbeck CHSW S40 .... 10 A4
Holme Bank East CHSW S40 .... 10 A4
Holmebank Vw CHSW S40 .... 10 A4
Holme Bank West CHSW S40 .... 10 A4
Holmebrook Vw CHSW S40 .... 183 D3
Holme Cl ST/HB/BR S6 .... 108 A4 🖪
Holme Hall Crs CHSW S40 .... 182 C4
Holme La CHPT/GREN S35 .... 97 E2
ST/HB/BR S6 .... 107 F5
Holme Oak Wy ST/HB/BR S6......... 106 A5
Holme Park Av CHSW S40 .... 182 C2
Holme Rd CHNE S41 .... 184 B3
Holmes Carr Rd DONS/BSCR DN4... 66 B3
NROS/TKN DN11 .... 66 B5
Holmes Crs RHAM S60 .... 127 F3
Holmesdale Cl DRON S18 .... 160 A5
Holmesdale Rd DRON S18 .... 159 F5
Holmes La CONI DN12 .... 85 D2
KIMB S61 .... 102 C3
The Holmes DON DN1 .... 5 F1
Holme Wood Gdns
DONS/BSCR DN4 .... 46 C5 🖪
Holm Flatt St RAW S62 .... 93 F3
Holmhirst Cl SHEFS S8 .... 146 C3
Holmhirst Dr SHEFS S8 .... 146 C2
Holmhirst Rd SHEFS S8 .... 146 C2
Holmhirst Wy SHEFS S8 .... 146 C3
Holmley Bank DRON S18 .... 159 E5
Holmley La DRON S18 .... 159 E5
Holmoak Cl MEX/SWTN S64 .... 81 E2
Holmshaw Dr HAN/WDH S13 .... 138 C2
Holmshaw Gv HAN/WDH S13 .... 138 C2
Holtwood Rd ATT S4 .... 109 F5
Holyoake Av HAN/WDH S13 .... 138 C1
Holyrood Rd WHHL DN2 .... 45 E1
Holywell La CONI DN12 .... 85 D2
Holywell Rd ATT S4 .... 111 D3
MEX/SWTN S64 .... 81 E2
Holywell St CHNE S41 .... 11 F5
Homefield Crs BTLY DN5 .... 28 C1
Homeport Ms CHNE S41 .... 11 F3
Homestead Dr SHEFN S5 .... 99 E4
Homestead Dr RAW S62 .... 80 A4
RHAM S60 .... 113 F3
Homestead Rd SHEFN S5 .... 99 D5
Honeysuckle Cl WMB/DAR S73 .... 40 B1
Honeysuckle Rd SHEFN S5 .... 111 D1 🖪
Honeywell Cl BSLY/ROY S71 .... 2 D2
Honeywell Gv BSLY/ROY S71 .... 14 A3
Honeywell La DOD/DAR S75 .... 2 B1
Honeywell Pl BSLY/ROY S71 .... 2 D1
Honeywell St BSLY/ROY S71 .... 2 D1
Honister Cl DEARNE S63 .... 54 B1
Hoober Av ECC S11 .... 133 E5
Hoober Ct RAW S62 .... 79 E3
Hoober Fld RAW S62 .... 78 C1
Hoober Hall La RAW S62 .... 54 A5
Hoober La RAW S62 .... 78 B2
Hoober Rd ECC S11 .... 133 E5
Hoober St DEARNE S63 .... 54 C2
Hoober Vw RAW S62 .... 79 E3
WMB/DAR S73 .... 40 A4
Hoole La FUL S10 .... 121 D5 🖪
Hoole Rd FUL S10 .... 121 D4
Hoole St CHNE S41 .... 191 E4
ST/HB/BR S6 .... 121 D1
Hooton Rd MEX/SWTN S64 .... 82 A4
Hopedale Rd HACK/IN S12 .... 150 B1
Hopefield Av HACK/IN S12 .... 150 B1
Hope St CHSW S40 .... 10 A6
DOD/DAR S75 .... 13 E5
MEX/SWTN S64 .... 58 B4 🖪
OWL S3 .... 8 A4
RHAM S60 .... 6 A3
STKB/PEN S36 .... 69 D2
WMB/DAR S73 .... 39 F3
Hope Street Extension RHAM S60..... 6 B3
Hopewell St BSLY S70 .... 23 E2
Hopwood La ST/HB/BR S6 .... 118 B3
Hopwood St BSLY S70 .... 2 B3
Horace St RHAM/THRY S65 .... 103 F4 🖪
Horbury La CHPT/GREN S35 .... 87 F2
Hornbeam Cl CHPT/GREN S35 .... 88 C2
Hornby St BSLY S70 .... 22 A3 🖪
Horndean Rd SHEFN S5 .... 110 B3
Hornby Cl STKB/PEN S36 .... 68 C2
Horner Rd SHEFS S8 .... 135 D3
Horninglow Cl DONS/BSCR DN4 ...... 67 E1
SHEFN S5 .... 110 A1
Horninglow Rd SHEFN S5 .... 110 A1

Hornthorpe Rd ECK/KIL S21 .... 173 F1
Horse Carr Vw BSLY/ROY S71 .... 24 B2
Horsehills La ARMTH DN3 .... 33 E4
Horsemoor Rd DEARNE S63 .... 26 B3 🖪
Horsewood Cl BSLY S70 .... 20 C2
Horsewood Rd CHSW S40 .... 188 C4
HAN/WDH S13 .... 140 B2
Horsley Cl CHSW S40 .... 182 B4
Horton Cl MOS S20 .... 164 C1 🖪
Horton Dr MOS S20 .... 164 C1
Horton Rd ARMTH DN3 .... 19 F1
Hough La WMB/DAR S73 .... 38 C4
Houghton Rd DEARNE S63 .... 26 A3
Houldsworth Dr CHNE S41 .... 191 F2
Hound Hill La DOD/DAR S75 .... 21 E5
MEX/SWTN S64 .... 57 E1
Hounsfield Crs RHAM/THRY S65 ... 105 E2
Hounsfield La OWL S3 .... 8 A4
Hounsfield Rd OWL S3 .... 8 A5
RHAM/THRY S65 .... 105 E2
Housley La CHPT/GREN S35 .... 74 A5
Housley Pk CHPT/GREN S35 .... 74 B5
Houstead Rd DARN/MH S9 .... 125 E4
Howard Dr CHNE S41 .... 178 B4
Howard La SHEF S1 .... 122 C5
Howard Rd ST/HB/BR S6 .... 121 D2
Howard St BSLY S70 .... 22 A3 🖪
RHAM/THRY S65 .... 6 D4
SHEF S1 .... 122 C5
Howarth Rd RHAM S60 .... 116 B1
Howbrook Cl CHPT/GREN S35 .... 73 D3 🖪
Howbrook La CHPT/GREN S35 .... 72 A1
Howden Cl DONS/BSCR DN4 .... 66 A1
Howden Rd DARN/MH S9 .... 111 E5
Howdike La CONI DN12 .... 82 C4
Howlett Cl RHAM S60 .... 16 B3
Howlett Dr RHAM S60 .... 114 A5
Howse St HOY S74 .... 52 B2
Howson Rd STKB/PEN S36 .... 69 E2
Hoylake Av CHSW S40 .... 189 D5
Hoylake Dr MEX/SWTN S64 .... 81 E2
Hoyland Av HOY S74 .... 50 C5
OWL S3 .... 108 C5
Hoyland St WMB/DAR S73 .... 39 E3 🖪
Hoyle Mill Rd BSLY S70 .... 23 E2
Hoyle St OWL S3 .... 8 C3
Hucklow Av CHSW S40 .... 190 A3
STV/CWN S43 .... 187 D2
Hucklow Rd SHEFN S5 .... 110 B2
Hucknall Av CHSW S40 .... 183 D5
Huddersfield Rd DOD/DAR S75 ...... 13 D3 🖪
KIMB S61 .... 91 F4
Hudson Rd HAN/WDH S13 .... 140 C2 🖪
Humberside Wy BSLY/ROY S71 .... 15 E1
Humphrey Rd SHEFS S8 .... 146 C5
Humphries Av RAW S62 .... 79 E4 🖪
Hundall La CHNE S41 .... 178 B2
DRON S18 .... 171 D4
Hungerhill Cl KIMB S61 .... 101 E1
Hungerhill La ARMTH DN3 .... 19 E4
Hunger Hill La RHAM S60 .... 116 A3
Hungerhill Rd KIMB S61 .... 91 E5
Hunger Hill Rd RHAM S60 .... 115 F2
Hunloke Av CHSW S40 .... 189 E3
Hunloke Crs CHSW S40 .... 189 F3
Hunningley La BSLY S70 .... 23 E3 🖪
BSLY S70 .... 23 E4
Hunsdon Rd ECK/KIL S21 .... 164 A5
Hunshelf La CHPT/GREN S35 .... 88 C4
Hunshelf Pk STKB/PEN S36 .... 69 D1
Hunshelf Rd CHPT/GREN S35 .... 88 A1
STKB/PEN S36 .... 68 C1
Hunsley St ATT S4 .... 110 C4
Hunstone Av SHEFS S8 .... 159 E1
Hunt Cl BSLY/ROY S71 .... 15 D3 🖪
Hunter Hill Rd ECC S11 .... 134 A3
Hunter House Rd ECC S11 .... 133 F3
Hunter Rd ST/HB/BR S6 .... 107 F4
Hunter's Av BSLY S70 .... 20 B2
Hunters Gdns ST/HB/BR S6 .... 106 B3
Hunter's La HAN/WDH S13 .... 138 A4
Hunters Ri DOD/DAR S75 .... 20 B1
Huntingdon Crs ECC S11 .... 134 C2
Huntingdon Rd WHHL DN2 .... 32 A4
Huntington St BTLY DN5 .... 16 C4 🖪
Huntingtower Rd ECC S11 .... 133 F3
Hunt La BTLY DN5 .... 29 F4
Huntley Cl STV/CWN S43 .... 186 C1
Huntley Gv ECC S11 .... 133 D4
Huntley Rd ECC S11 .... 133 E4
Huntsman Rd DARN/MH S9 .... 137 F4
STV/CWN S43 .... 181 F4
Huntsmans Gdns DARN/MH S9 .... 112 A5
Hunt St HOY S74 .... 50 C3
Hurl Dr HACK/IN S12 .... 137 D5
Hurley Cft DEARNE S63 .... 54 B1 🖪
Hurlfield Av HACK/IN S12 .... 137 E5
Hurlfield Ct HACK/IN S12 .... 137 D4
Hurlfield Dr HACK/IN S12 .... 137 D4
Hurlfield Rd HACK/IN S12 .... 137 D5
Hurlingham Cl ABRD S7 .... 146 A1
Hursley Cl MOS S20 .... 153 E4 🖪
Hursley Dr MOS S20 .... 153 E4
Hurst Gn CHPT/GREN S35 .... 73 E4
Hutchinson La SHEFS S8 .... 146 B2 🖪

Hutchinson Rd RAW S62 .... 80 B5 🖪
SHEFS S8 .... 146 B2 🛛
Hutcliffe Dr SHEFS S8 .... 146 B3 🖪
Hutcliffe Wood Rd SHEFS S8 .... 146 B3
Hut La ECK/KIL S21 .... 166 C4
Hutton Rd KIMB S61 .... 91 F5
Hyacinth Cl DARN/MH S9 .... 111 D1
Hyacinth Rd SHEFN S5 .... 111 D1
Hyde Park Wk SHEFP/MNR S2 ..... 123 D4
Hyland Crs DONS/BSCR DN4 .... 62 C1 🖪
Hyman Cl DONS/BSCR DN4 .... 42 B5

I

Ians Wy CHSW S40 .... 183 D5
Ibbotson Rd ST/HB/BR S6 .... 121 D1
Ickles Wy RHAM S60 .... 102 C5
Icknield Wy RHAM S60 .... 114 A4
Ida's Rd ECK/KIL S21 .... 164 B4
Idsworth Rd SHEFN S5 .... 110 B2
Ilam Cl STV/CWN S43 .... 187 D3
Ilkley Crs AU/AST/KP S26 .... 142 A4
Ilkley Rd SHEFN S5 .... 99 E5
Imperial Crs WHHL DN2 .... 31 D5
Industry Rd DARN/MH S9 .... 125 D2
Industry St ST/HB/BR S6 .... 121 D1
Infield La DARN/MH S9 .... 125 D3
Infirmary Rd CHNE S41 .... 11 G3
OWL S3 .... 8 B2
RAW S62 .... 94 B3
ST/HB/BR S6 .... 121 F1
Ingelow Av SHEFN S5 .... 98 C4
Ingfield Av DARN/MH S9 .... 112 C2
Ingleborough Cft
CHPT/GREN S35 .... 74 A5 🖪
Ingleborough Dr BTLY DN5 .... 42 C2
Ingleby Cl DRON S18 .... 168 A2
Ingle Gv BTLY DN5 .... 42 C2
Ingleton Rd CHNE S41 .... 190 C5
Inglewood Av MOS S20 .... 153 E4 🖪
Inglewood Ct MOS S20 .... 153 E4
Inglewood Dell MOS S20 .... 153 E4 🖪
Ingram Ct SHEFP/MNR S2 .... 123 E5 🖪
Ingram Rd SHEFP/MNR S2 .... 123 E5
Ingshead Av RAW S62 .... 94 B1
Ings La BTLY DN5 .... 18 B4
BTLY DN5 .... 18 B4
BTLY DN5 .... 42 C2
Ings Rd BTLY DN5 .... 30 A3
BTLY DN5 .... 61 E2
WMB/DAR S73 .... 40 B1
Ings Wy BTLY DN5 .... 17 E4
Inkersall Dr MOS S20 .... 152 C5
Inkersall Green Rd STV/CWN S43 ... 186 C1
Inkersall Rd STV/CWN S43 .... 187 F3
Innovation Wy DOD/DAR S75 .... 13 D3
Insley Gdns DONS/BSCR DN4 .... 46 C5
Intake Crs DOD/DAR S75 .... 20 A4
Intake La DOD/DAR S75 .... 12 C5
Ironside Cl GLV S14 .... 148 B3
Ironside Pl GLV S14 .... 148 C2
Ironside Rd GLV S14 .... 148 B3
Irving St DARN/MH S9 .... 125 D3
Irwell Gdns DONS/BSCR DN4 .... 46 B2 🖪
Islay St FUL S10 .... 120 C4
Issott St BSLY/ROY S71 .... 2 D1
Ivan Brook Cl DRON S18 .... 168 A2 🖪
Ivanhoe Cl BTLY DN5 .... 29 D5
Ivanhoe Ms AU/AST/KP S26 .... 142 A4
Ivanhoe Rd CONI DN12 .... 84 C1
DONS/BSCR DN4 .... 42 C5
ST/HB/BR S6 .... 120 B1 🖪
Ivanhoe Wy BTLY DN5 .... 29 D5
Ivor Gv DONS/BSCR DN4 .... 43 E4
Ivy Cl CHNE S41 .... 178 B4
Ivy Cottage La ECC S11 .... 132 A4
Ivy Ct SHEFS S8 .... 148 A3
Ivy Dr FUL S10 .... 121 E3 🖪
Ivy Farm Cft RHAM/THRY S65 .... 95 E5
Ivy Gv FUL S10 .... 121 E3 🛛
Ivy Hall Rd SHEFN S5 .... 99 F2
Ivy La MOS S20 .... 153 E1
Ivy Park Rd FUL S10 .... 119 F5
Ivy Side Cl ECK/KIL S21 .... 166 B2
Ivyside Gdns ECK/KIL S21 .... 166 B2

J

Jackson Crs RAW S62 .... 79 E4
Jacobs Cl SHEFN S5 .... 99 F5
Jacobs Dr SHEFN S5 .... 99 F5
Jacques Pl BSLY/ROY S71 .... 15 E5
Jamaica St ATT S4 .... 110 B5 🖪
James Andrew Cl SHEFS S8 .... 159 D1
James Andrew Crs SHEFS S8 .... 158 C1
James Andrew Cft SHEFS S8 .... 159 D1 🖪
James St BSLY S70 .... 23 D5
BSLY/ROY S71 .... 3 E3
CHNE S41 .... 184 B3
DARN/MH S9 .... 125 D4

MEX/SWTN S64.................... 59 E3
RHAM S60............................. 6 A4
Janson St DARN/MH S9............. 111 E4
Jardine Cl DARN/MH S9............. 100 B5
Jardine St DARN/MH S9............. 100 C5
WMB/DAR S73....................... 39 E3
Jarratt St DON DN1........................ 5 F6
Jarrow Rd ECC S11.................... 134 B2 ⑤
Jasmine Av MOS S20................. 153 D2
Jasmine Cl CONI DN12............... 85 E2
Jaunty Av HACK/IN S12............. 149 F2
Jaunty Cl HACK/IN S12.............. 149 F2
Jaunty Crs HACK/IN S12............ 149 F1
Jaunty Dr HACK/IN S12.............. 149 F2
Jaunty La HACK/IN S12.............. 149 F2
Jaunty Mt HACK/IN S12............. 150 A2
Jaunty Pl HACK/IN S12............... 149 F2
Jaunty Rd HACK/IN S12............. 150 A2
Jaunty Vw HACK/IN S12............. 150 A2
Jaunty Wy HACK/IN S12............ 149 F1
Jay La AU/AST/KP S26............... 142 C4
Jebb Gdns CHSW S40................ 189 D2 ④
Jedburgh Dr DARN/MH S9.......... 100 B5
Jedburgh St DARN/MH S9........... 100 B5
Jeffcock Rd CHPT/GREN S35....... 73 F4
DARN/MH S9....................... 125 D3 ③
Jefferson Av WHHL DN2............. 19 E5
Jeffery Crs STKB/PEN S36.......... 69 E3
Jeffery St SHEFP/MNR S2........... 135 F4 ④
Jenkin Av DARN/MH S9.............. 111 E2
Jenkin Cl DARN/MH S9............... 111 E1
Jenkin Dr DARN/MH S9............... 111 E2
Jenkin Rd DARN/MH S9............... 111 E1
Jennings Cl RHAM/THRY S65......... 7 F2
Jepson Rd SHEFN S5................. 100 A5
Jericho St OWL S3...................... 8 A3
Jermyn Av HACK/IN S12............. 150 C1
Jermyn Cl HACK/IN S12.............. 151 D2
Jermyn Crs HACK/IN S12............ 151 D2
Jermyn Cft DOD/DAR S75........... 20 A3
Jermyn Dr HACK/IN S12.............. 151 D2
Jermyn Wy HACK/IN S12............. 150 C2
Jersey Rd SHEFP/MNR S2........... 135 E3 ⑤
Jervis Pl STV/CWN S43............... 186 C3
Jessamine Rd SHEFN S5............. 99 F5
Jessell St DARN/MH S9............... 124 A2
Jessop St SHEF S1.................... 122 B5 ⑦
Jewitt Rd KIMB S61.................... 91 F4
Jockell Dr RAW S62.................... 94 A1
John Calvert Rd HAN/WDH S13.... 140 B4
John Hibbard Av HAN/WDH S13 .. 141 D3 ⑤
John Hibbard Cl HAN/WDH S13 ... 140 C5 ⑥
John Hibbard Crs HAN/WDH S13 .. 140 C3
John Hibbard Ri HAN/WDH S13 ... 140 C3 ④
Johnson Ct CONI DN12................ 62 A4 ⑤
Johnson La CHPT/GREN S35......... 88 C5
OWL S3............................... 9 F3 ⑥
Johnson St DOD/DAR S75........... 13 E5 ④
OWL S3............................... 9 F2
STKB/PEN S36...................... 68 C2 ①
Johnstone Cl CHSW S40............. 190 A3
John St BSLY S70..................... 22 A2
BSLY S70............................. 22 B5 ⑧
CHSW S40........................... 10 A6
DEARNE S63......................... 27 D5
DOD/DAR S75....................... 13 E5 ④
ECK/KIL S21......................... 164 B5
MEX/SWTN S64..................... 58 B4
RHAM S60............................. 6 A6
SHEFP/MNR S2..................... 135 E1
STV/CWN S43....................... 185 F1
WMB/DAR S73....................... 39 D2
John Ward St HAN/WDH S13....... 140 B3
John West St STKB/PEN S36........ 68 C3
Joiner St OWL S3....................... 9 F3
Jones Av WMB/DAR S73.............. 38 C2
Jordan Crs KIMB S61................. 101 F4
Jordanthorpe Gn SHEFS S8......... 160 A2
Jordanthorpe Pkwy SHEFS S8..... 159 E3
Jordanthorpe Vw SHEFS S8........ 160 A1 ⑥
Josephine Rd KIMB S61.............. 102 B3
Joseph Rd FUL S10.................... 121 D2 ⑥
Joseph St BSLY S70.................... 21 F2
ECK/KIL S21......................... 164 B5
RHAM S60............................. 6 A3
Joshua Rd ABRD S7................... 134 C3
Josselin Ct CHPT/GREN S35........ 88 A1 ②
Jossey La BTLY DN5................... 28 B1
Jowitt Rd ECC S11..................... 133 F4
Jubb Cl RHAM/THRY S65............. 105 E5
Jubilee Crs ECK/KIL S21............. 166 C1
Jubilee Rd DARN/MH S9............. 124 C3
DON DN1.............................. 30 C4
Jubilee St RHAM S60................. 103 E5
Judith Rd AU/AST/KP S26........... 142 B4
Judy Row BSLYN/ROY S71........... 15 D3
Julian Rd DARN/MH S9............... 111 F1
Julian Wy DARN/MH S9............... 111 F1
Jumble La KIMB S61................... 89 F4
Junction Cl WMB/DAR S73.......... 40 A4
Junction Rd ECC S11.................. 134 A2
HAN/WDH S13...................... 140 B3
Junction St BSLY S70................. 22 C2
WMB/DAR S73....................... 40 A4 ③
June Rd HAN/WDH S13............... 140 B4
Juniper Ri ECK/KIL S21............... 166 A3

K

Kashmir Gdns DARN/MH S9 ...... 124 C2 ⑤
Kathleen Gv DEARNE S63............ 27 F5
Kay Crs RAW S62....................... 79 D3
Kaye Pl FUL S10....................... 121 E3
Kay's Ter BSLY S70.................... 23 F3
Kay St HOY S74........................ 50 C3
Kearsley La CONI DN12.............. 84 C3
Kearsley Rd SHEFP/MNR S2....... 135 E2
Keats Rd CHNE S41................... 184 A1
DONS/BSCR DN4.................... 63 F1 ⑧
ST/HB/BR S6......................... 97 E3
Keble Martin Wy DEARNE S63..... 55 E2
Keepers Cl NROS/TKH DN11........ 67 F5
Keeton's Hl SHEFP/MNR S2....... 135 D1 ⑥
Keilder Ct CHSW S40................. 189 E3
Keir Pl RAW S62....................... 80 C5
Keir St BSLY S70........................ 2 A4
Keir Ter BSLY S70....................... 2 A4
Kelburn Av CHSW S40............... 189 D3
Kelgate MOS S20...................... 164 B2
Kelham Island OWL S3................. 8 D2
Kelham St DON DN1................... 44 A3
Kelsey Gdns DONS/BSCR DN4...... 66 C2
Kelsey Ter BSLY S70.................. 22 A3 ⑧
Kelso Dr DONS/BSCR DN4.......... 42 B5
Kelvin Gv WMB/DAR S73............. 39 F3
Kelvin St MEX/SWTN S64........... 58 B3
RHAM/THRY S65.................... 95 E5
Kemp Cl ECK/KIL S21................ 166 A2 ⑤
Kempton Gdns MEX/SWTN S64.... 59 D2
Kempton Park Rd BTLY DN5........ 28 B4
Kempwell Dr RAW S62................ 80 B5
Kenbourne Gv ABRD S7............. 134 C3 ④
Kenbourne Rd ABRD S7.............. 134 C3
Kendal Crs BSLY S70.................. 36 B1 ⑥
CONI DN12........................... 85 E1
Kendal Dr DRON S18.................. 168 C2
Kendal Green Rd BSLY S70.......... 35 F1
Kendal Rd BSLYN/ROY S71.......... 24 B2
BTLY DN5............................. 29 E2
CHNE S41............................ 183 F1
ST/HB/BR S6........................ 107 F4
Kendal V BSLY S70.................... 36 B1
Kendray St BSLY S70................... 2 D5
Kenilworth Cl BTLY DN5............. 28 B3 ②
Kenilworth Pl ECC S11................ 134 A2 ①
Kenilworth Rd DONS/BSCR DN4... 42 C5
Kenmare Crs WHHL DN2............. 31 E5
Kennedy Rd SHEFS S8............... 146 C3
Kenneth St RHAM/THRY S65......... 7 E3
Kennet V CHSW S40.................. 188 E5
Kenning Hall Ct SHEFP/MNR S2 .. 136 B3 ⑥
Kenninghall Dr SHEFP/MNR S2 .. 136 B3
Kenninghall Mt SHEFP/MNR S2 .. 136 B3 ⑦
Kenninghall Pl SHEFP/MNR S2 .. 136 B3
Kenninghall Rd SHEFP/MNR S2 .. 136 B3
Kennington Gv CONI DN12.......... 62 A4
Kenrock Cl BTLY DN5................. 17 F5
Kensington Rd DOD/DAR S75...... 13 E4
Kent Av RAW S62...................... 79 F4
Kent Cl CHNE S41..................... 10 D2
Kent House Cl HACK/IN S12........ 150 C5
Kentmere Cl DRON S18.............. 168 C2 ④
Kent Rd DONS/BSCR DN4........... 63 F1
KIMB S61............................. 91 F5 ②
SHEFS S8............................ 135 F4
Kent St CHNE S41..................... 191 D4
Kenwell Dr TOT/DORE S17......... 157 F3
Kenwood Av ABRD S7................ 134 C3 ⑧
Kenwood Bank ECC S11.............. 134 B2
Kenwood Cl BSLY S70................. 23 F2 ⑥
Kenwood Park Rd ABRD S7.......... 134 C2
Kenwood Rd ABRD S7................ 134 C2
ECC S11.............................. 134 C2
Kenworthy Rd BSLY S70............. 22 A3 ⑩
STKB/PEN S36...................... 68 C3
Kenyon Gv CHNE S41................. 191 E3
Kenyon St OWL S3...................... 8 B4
Keppel Dr KIMB S61.................. 90 C4
Keppel Pl SHEFN S5.................. 99 F3
Keppel Rd KIMB S61.................. 90 C4
SHEFN S5............................ 100 A3
Keppel View Rd KIMB S61........... 101 E1
Keresforth Cl BSLY S70.............. 21 D2
Keresforth Ct BSLY S70.............. 21 D2
Keresforth Hall Rd BSLY S70....... 21 E3
Keresforth Hill Rd BSLY S70........ 21 D3 ⑥
Keresforth Rd DOD/DAR S75....... 20 A4
Kerwin Cl TOT/DORE S17........... 144 A5
Kerwin Dr TOT/DORE S17........... 144 A5
Kerwin Rd TOT/DORE S17........... 144 A5
Kestrel Av KIMB S61.................. 90 B1
Kestrel Cl ECK/KIL S21............... 165 F1 ⑥
Kestrel Dr ECK/KIL S21............... 165 F5
Kestrel Gn SHEFP/MNR S2......... 123 F5 ⑧
Kestrel Ri BSLY S70.................... 36 A5 ⑥
Keswick BTLY DN5.................... 29 E1
Keswick Cl ST/HB/BR S6............ 106 C4
Keswick Crs RHAM S60.............. 113 F5
Keswick Dr CHNE S41................ 183 D2
Keswick Pl DRON S18................ 168 B2
Keswick Wk BSLYN/ROY S71....... 24 C2
Kettlebridge Rd DARN/MH S9..... 124 B4
Ketton Av SHEFS S8.................. 147 E2
Ketton Wk DOD/DAR S75........... 13 D4 ⑧
Kew Crs HACK/IN S12................ 149 D3
Key Av HOY S74........................ 51 F2
Keyworth Pl HAN/WDH S13........ 139 E4
Keyworth Rd ST/HB/BR S6......... 108 A3 ⑧
Khartoum Rd ECC S11............... 134 B2
Kidsley Cl CHSW S40................ 182 B4
Kilburn Rd DRON S18................ 168 A2
Kildale Gdns MOS S20............... 164 B1 ⑥
Kildonan Gv HAN/WDH S13........ 150 A2
Killamarsh La ECK/KIL S21.......... 167 E2
Kilner Wy SHEFN S5.................. 108 B1
Kilnhurst Rd CONI DN12............. 82 A4
RAW S62.............................. 80 B5
RHAM/THRY S65.................... 82 B4
Kiln Rd KIMB S61..................... 102 A1
Kilton Hl OWL S3...................... 122 C1 ⑧
Kilton Pl OWL S3......................... 9 G1
Kilvington Av HAN/WDH S13....... 137 F3 ①
Kilvington Crs HAN/WDH S13 ..... 137 F3
Kilvington Rd HAN/WDH S13....... 137 F3
Kimberley St DARN/MH S9.......... 124 A1
Kimberworth Park Rd KIMB S61.... 91 F5
KIMB S61............................. 102 A2 ⑧
Kimberworth Rd KIMB S61.......... 102 A2
Kinder Gdns SHEFN S5............... 98 C4
Kinder Rd STV/CWN S43............. 186 C3
King Eggbert Rd TOT/DORE S17... 156 C3
King Edward Rd DONS/BSCR DN4.... 43 F4
King Edward St BSLYN/ROY S71.... 15 E1
Kingfield Rd ECC S11................ 134 B3
Kingfisher Cl WHHL DN2............. 31 F2 ⑥
Kingfisher Ri KIMB S61.............. 76 B5 ⑥
King James St ST/HB/BR S6........ 121 E1
Kings Coppice TOT/DORE S17...... 156 B2
Kings Ct BSLY S70.................... 37 D1
Kingscroft Cl TOT/DORE S17....... 144 C5
Kingsley Av BTLY DN5................ 29 D5
CHSW S40............................ 190 A4
Kingsley Cl BSLYN/ROY S71......... 14 B1 ⑥
Kingsley Crs ARMTH DN3............ 33 F3
Kingsley Park Av ABRD S7.......... 145 F1
Kingsley Park Gv ECC S11........... 145 F1
Kingsmede Av CHSW S40........... 189 E3
Kings Ms ECK/KIL S21............... 164 C5
King's Rd DON DN1..................... 5 G2
MEX/SWTN S64..................... 58 C3
WMB/DAR S73....................... 39 E3 ②
Kingstone Pl BSLY S70............... 21 E3 ⑤
Kingston Rd WHHL DN2.............. 31 F5
Kingston St ATT S4.................... 110 A5
King St AU/AST/KP S26.............. 142 A2
BSLY S70............................. 22 A2
CHPT/GREN S35.................... 74 B5
DEARNE S63......................... 27 E4
DON DN1.............................. 5 F3 ⑥
HOY S74.............................. 52 A2
MEX/SWTN S64..................... 57 E5 ②
SHEF S1.............................. 9 F4
STV/CWN S43....................... 180 A5
King St North CHNE S41............ 184 B2
King St South CHSW S40............ 190 B5
Kings Wy RHAM S60.................. 115 G2
Kingsway DEARNE S63............... 26 C3
WMB/DAR S73....................... 39 E3
Kingsway Gv DEARNE S63.......... 26 C3 ⑧
Kingswood Av MOS S20............. 151 E3
Kingswood Cl CHNE S41............. 183 E1
MOS S20............................. 151 E3 ④
Kingswood Crs HOY S74............. 51 F1
Kingswood Cft MOS S20............. 151 E3 ⑤
Kingswood Gv MOS S20............. 151 E3
Kingwell Crs BSLY S70............... 22 A4 ⑧
Kingwell Cft BSLY S70............... 22 B5 ⑥
Kingwell Ms BSLY S70............... 22 B5 ⑦
Kingwell Rd BSLY S70................ 22 B5
Kinharvie Rd SHEFN S5.............. 109 D1
Kinnaird Av SHEFN S5................ 99 D4 ⑥
Kinnaird Pl SHEFN S5................ 99 D4
Kinnaird Rd SHEFN S5............... 99 D4
Kinsey Rd CHPT/GREN S35......... 73 D4
Kipling Av DONS/BSCR DN4........ 63 D1
Kipling Cl DRON S18.................. 170 A4
Kipling Rd CHNE S41................ 184 A1 ⑥
Kirby La KIMB S61..................... 75 E4
Kirby St MEX/SWTN S64............. 58 B3
Kirk Balk HOY S74..................... 51 E2
Kirkby Av BTLY DN5................... 29 E3
HACK/IN S12........................ 149 E5 ①
Kirkby Dr HACK/IN S12............... 149 E1
Kirkby Rd HACK/IN S12............... 149 E1
Kirkby Vw HACK/IN S12.............. 149 E2
Kirkcroft Av ECK/KIL S21............. 166 B1
KIMB S61............................. 90 B1
Kirkcroft Cl KIMB S61................. 90 A1 ⑧
Kirkcroft Dr ECK/KIL S21............ 166 B2
Kirkcroft La ECK/KIL S21............. 166 B2
Kirkdale Cl CHSW S40............... 190 C4
Kirkdale Crs HAN/WDH S13......... 139 F1
Kirkdale Dr HAN/WDH S13.......... 139 F1
Kirkham Cl BSLYN/ROY S71......... 15 D4
Kirklands Dr RAW S62................ 79 F5

Kirkstall Cl *BTLY* DN5 .... 28 B4
RHAM S60 .... 113 E3
Kirkstall Rd *ECC* S11 .... 134 A2
Kirkstead Abbey Ms *KIMB* S61 .... 90 B3
Kirkstead Gdns *HAN/WDH* S13 .... 140 C3
Kirkstead Rd *KIMB* S61 .... 100 B2
Kirkstone Cl *BTLY* DN5 .... 29 E1
Kirkstone Rd *CHNE* S41 .... 183 D1
ST/HB/BR S6 .... 108 A5
Kirk St *ATT* S4 .... 123 D1
DONS/BSCR DN4 .... 4 A5
Kirk Wy *BSLYN/ROY* S71 .... 15 E4
Kirton Rd *ATT* S4 .... 110 A5
Kitchin Rd *WMB/DAR* S63 .... 38 C2
Kitson Dr *BSLYN/ROY* S71 .... 15 E4
Knab Cl *ECC* S11 .... 134 A5
Knab Cft *ECC* S11 .... 134 A5
Knab Ri *ECC* S11 .... 134 A5
Knab Rd *ECC* S11 .... 134 A5
Knapton Av *RAW* S62 .... 79 F5
Knaresboro Rd *ABRD* S7 .... 146 A2
Knaresborough Cl
AU/AST/KP S26 .... 142 A3
Knaresborough Rd *CONI* DN12 .... 84 C3
Knavesmire Gdns
DONS/BSCR DN4 .... 46 B2
Knifesmithgate *CHSW* S40 .... 11 E6
Knollbeck Av *WMB/DAR* S73 .... 40 B5
Knoll Beck Crs *WMB/DAR* S73 .... 40 B5
Knollbeck La *WMB/DAR* S73 .... 40 B5
Knoll Cl *STKB/PEN* S36 .... 69 D2
The Knoll *CHSW* S40 .... 188 A2
DRON S18 .... 160 B5
Knowle Cl *ST/HB/BR* S6 .... 119 D1
Knowle Cft *ECC* S11 .... 133 E5
Knowle Gn *TOT/DORE* S17 .... 156 A1
Knowle La *ECC* S11 .... 133 D5
Knowle Rd *BSLY* S70 .... 22 C4
SHEFS S5 .... 98 C3
Knowles Av *STKB/PEN* S36 .... 69 E3
Knowle Top *MOS* S20 .... 164 C1
Knowsley St *BSLY* S70 .... 21 E3
Knutton Crs *SHEFN* S5 .... 97 F3
Knutton Ri *SHEFN* S5 .... 97 F2
Knutton Rd *SHEFN* S5 .... 97 F3
Kyle Cl *SHEFN* S5 .... 97 F5
Kyle Crs *SHEFN* S5 .... 97 F5
Kynance Crs *RHAM* S60 .... 113 F5

L

Laburnam *BSLY* S70 .... 36 C1
Laburnum Cl *CHPT/GREN* S35 .... 88 B2
Laburnum *CONI* DN12 .... 84 B2
ECK/KIL S21 .... 166 A3
STKB/PEN S36 .... 68 C3
Laburnum Pl *BTLY* DN5 .... 16 C4
Laburnum Rd *DONS/BSCR* DN4 .... 63 D1
MEX/SWTN S64 .... 58 A2
Laburnum St *STV/CWN* S43 .... 180 C5
Laceby Ct *BSLY* S70 .... 21 D3
Ladies Spring Gv *TOT/DORE* S17 .... 157 E1
Ladock Cl *BSLYN/ROY* S71 .... 3 H2
Ladybank Rd *MOS* S20 .... 164 B2
Ladybank Vw *ECK/KIL* S21 .... 164 B4
Ladybower La *STV/CWN* S43 .... 187 F1
Lady Cft *DEARNE* S63 .... 55 F2
Lady Croft La *WMB/DAR* S73 .... 53 D1
Ladycroft Rd *ARMTH* DN3 .... 33 F5
Lady Ida's Dr *ECK/KIL* S21 .... 163 E4
MOS S20 .... 164 A3
Lady Oak Rd *RHAM/THRY* S65 .... 95 D5
Lady's Br *OWL* S3 .... 9 F3
Ladysmith Av *ABRD* S7 .... 134 B4
Ladywood Dr *CHSW* S40 .... 183 D2
Laird Av *ST/HB/BR* S6 .... 107 E3
Laird Dr *ST/HB/BR* S6 .... 107 E3
Laird Rd *ST/HB/BR* S6 .... 107 E3
Laithe Cft *DOD/DAR* S75 .... 20 A3
Lakeen Rd *WHHL* DN2 .... 31 E1
Lakeside Bvd *DONS/BSCR* DN4 .... 45 E5
Lake View Av *CHSW* S40 .... 189 D4
Lambcroft Vw *HAN/WDH* S13 .... 140 A4
Lamb Dr *SHEFN* S5 .... 108 B1
Lambert Fold *DOD/DAR* S75 .... 20 B3
Lambert Rd *BSLY* S70 .... 23 D3
Lamberts La *RHAM/THRY* S65 .... 9 F5
Lambert St *OWL* S3 .... 8 C3
Lambert Wk *BSLY* S70 .... 23 D2
Lambeth Rd *DONS/BSCR* DN4 .... 43 F5
Lamb Hill Cl *HAN/WDH* S13 .... 138 B3
Lamb La *BSLYN/ROY* S71 .... 15 D2
Lambra Rd *BSLY* S70 .... 3 E6
Lamb Rd *SHEFN* S5 .... 108 B1
Lanark Dr *MEX/SWTN* S64 .... 59 D1
Lanark Gdns *WHHL* DN2 .... 32 A4
Lancaster Av *WHHL* DN2 .... 32 A5
Lancaster Ga *BSLY* S70 .... 2 C4
Lancaster Rd *CHNE* S41 .... 183 F1
STKB/PEN S36 .... 68 C2
Lancaster St *BSLY* S70 .... 21 E1
DEARNE S63 .... 27 E2

OWL S3 .... 8 C1
Lancelot Cl *CHSW* S40 .... 189 E4
Lancing Rd *SHEFP/MNR* S2 .... 135 E2
SHEFP/MNR S2 .... 135 F1
SHEFP/MNR S2 .... 135 F2
Landsdowne Av *CHNE* S41 .... 183 F2
Landseer Cl *DRON* S18 .... 168 C3
SHEFS S8 .... 148 B3
Landseer Dr *SHEFS* S8 .... 148 B3
Landseer Pl *GLV* S14 .... 148 C3
Lane End *CHPT/GREN* S35 .... 74 A4
Lane End Rd *RHAM* S60 .... 115 E1
Laneham Cl *DONS/BSCR* DN4 .... 66 B1
Lane Head Cl *RAW* S62 .... 80 B5
Lane Head Cl *RAW* S62 .... 80 B5
Lane Head Rd *TOT/DORE* S17 .... 156 A4
Laneside Cl *DONS/BSCR* DN4 .... 43 E3
The Lanes *RHAM/THRY* S65 .... 104 C2
Lang Av *BSLYN/ROY* S71 .... 15 F5
Lang Crs *BSLYN/ROY* S71 .... 15 F5
Langdale Cl *RCH* S42 .... 182 A4
Langdale Dr *BTLY* DN5 .... 29 D1
DRON S18 .... 160 A5
Langdale Rd *BSLYN/ROY* S71 .... 3 F6
SHEFS S8 .... 134 C5
Langdale Sq *STV/CWN* S43 .... 185 E1
Langdon Dr *KIMB* S61 .... 101 F1
Langdon St *ECC* S11 .... 135 D2
Langer Field Av *CHSW* S40 .... 190 B5
Langer St *DONS/BSCR* DN4 .... 43 E3
Langford Cl *DOD/DAR* S75 .... 20 B3
Langhurst Rd *CHSW* S40 .... 183 E5
Langley Cl *CHSW* S40 .... 182 B4
RHAM/THRY S65 .... 105 E2
Langsett Av *ST/HB/BR* S6 .... 107 E2
Langsett Cl *ST/HB/BR* S6 .... 108 B5
Langsett Crs *ST/HB/BR* S6 .... 108 B5
Langsett Gv *ST/HB/BR* S6 .... 121 E1
Langsett Ri *ST/HB/BR* S6 .... 121 E1
Langsett Rd *ST/HB/BR* S6 .... 108 A4
Langtree Av *CHNE* S41 .... 178 B5
Lansbury Av *CHPT/GREN* S35 .... 88 A1
Lansbury Pl *RAW* S62 .... 81 D5
Lansbury Rd *ECK/KIL* S21 .... 164 B5
Lansdowne Cl *DEARNE* S63 .... 26 C4
Lansdowne Crs *STV/CWN* S43 .... 185 F2
Lansdowne Rd *STV/CWN* S43 .... 185 E2
WHHL DN2 .... 32 A4
Lanyon Wy *BSLYN/ROY* S71 .... 15 E4
Lapwater Rd *KIMB* S61 .... 92 A3
Lapwing V *KIMB* S61 .... 76 B5
Larch Av *ECK/KIL* S21 .... 166 A3
The Larches *MEX/SWTN* S64 .... 81 D1
Larchfield Pl *BSLYN/ROY* S71 .... 15 E2
Larchfield Rd *DONS/BSCR* DN4 .... 43 D5
Larch Gv *CHPT/GREN* S35 .... 88 B2
CONI DN12 .... 84 B3
Larch Hl *DARN/MH* S9 .... 125 F4
Larch Pl *BSLY* S70 .... 23 D4
Larch Rd *ECK/KIL* S21 .... 173 F1
Larch Wy *CHSW* S40 .... 183 E4
Larkhill Cl *RAW* S62 .... 80 A4
Larkspur Cl *MEX/SWTN* S64 .... 81 D3
Lark St *ST/HB/BR* S6 .... 120 C1
Larwood Gv *CONI* DN12 .... 62 A4
Latham Sq *ECC* S11 .... 132 C5
Lathe Rd *RHAM* S60 .... 116 A2
Lathkill Av *STV/CWN* S43 .... 186 C3
Lathkill Cl *HAN/WDH* S13 .... 138 A3
Lathkill Rd *HAN/WDH* S13 .... 138 A3
Latin Gdns *BTLY* DN5 .... 28 A2
Lauder Rd *BTLY* DN5 .... 29 E3
Lauder St *ATT* S4 .... 110 B3
Laudsdale Cl *RHAM/THRY* S65 .... 105 E2
Laudsdale Rd *RHAM/THRY* S65 .... 105 D1
Laughton Rd *DARN/MH* S9 .... 111 F2
DONS/BSCR DN4 .... 4 A5
Launce Rd *SHEFN* S5 .... 98 A5
Laurel Av *BSLY* S70 .... 23 E3
BTLY DN5 .... 28 C4
Laurel Cl *ECK/KIL* S21 .... 174 A1
Laurel Crs *STV/CWN* S43 .... 180 B5
Laurel Dr *ECK/KIL* S21 .... 166 A3
Laurel Garth Cl *CHNE* S41 .... 178 C3
Laurel Rd *ARMTH* DN3 .... 33 F2
Laurel Ter *DONS/BSCR* DN4 .... 43 E3
Laurence Cl *CHNE* S41 .... 178 B4
Lavender Cl *CONI* DN12 .... 85 E2
Laverack St *HAN/WDH* S13 .... 139 D1
Laverdene Av *TOT/DORE* S17 .... 157 D3
Laverdene Cl *TOT/DORE* S17 .... 156 C4
Laverdene Dr *TOT/DORE* S17 .... 157 D4
Laverdene Rd *TOT/DORE* S17 .... 156 C4
Laverdene Wy *TOT/DORE* S17 .... 157 D3
Laverock Wy *SHEFN* S5 .... 99 E4
Lavinia Rd *CHPT/GREN* S35 .... 97 D3
Lawn Av *DON* DN1 .... 5 G3
Lawn Garth *BTLY* DN5 .... 29 D2
Lawn Rd *DON* DN1 .... 5 G3
The Lawns *ECC* S11 .... 133 F4
The Lawn *DRON* S18 .... 169 F1
Lawrence Dr *MEX/SWTN* S64 .... 81 D1
Lawson Rd *FUL* S10 .... 120 C5
Lawton La *RHAM* S60 .... 114 C1
Laxey Rd *ST/HB/BR* S6 .... 119 F2
Laxfield Cl *CHSW* S40 .... 189 D4

Laycock Av *AU/AST/KP* S26 .... 142 C3
Layden Dr *BTLY* DN5 .... 28 A1
Layton Dr *CHNE* S41 .... 178 C5
Leabrook Rd *DRON* S18 .... 168 A2
Leach La *MEX/SWTN* S64 .... 58 B4
Leadbeater Dr *HACK/IN* S12 .... 137 E5
Leadbeater Rd *HACK/IN* S12 .... 137 D5
Leader Rd *ST/HB/BR* S6 .... 107 F3
Leadmill Rd *SHEF* S1 .... 122 C5
SHEFP/MNR S2 .... 135 F1
Leadmill St *SHEF* S1 .... 122 C5
Leake Rd *ST/HB/BR* S6 .... 108 A2
Leamington Gdns *WHHL* DN2 .... 32 A4
WHHL DN2 .... 32 A4
Leamington St *FUL* S10 .... 121 D3
Lea Rd *DRON* S18 .... 169 E2
Lease Gate Rd *RHAM* S60 .... 115 F2
The Leas *BTLY* DN5 .... 29 D4
The Lea *MEX/SWTN* S64 .... 80 C2
MOS S20 .... 152 B3
Leaton Cl *ST/HB/BR* S6 .... 106 B3
Leavy Greave *FUL* S10 .... 8 A6
Leavygreave Rd *OWL* S3 .... 8 A5
Leawood Pl *ST/HB/BR* S6 .... 119 E1
Ledbury Gdns *BTLY* DN5 .... 28 B4
Ledbury Rd *BSLYN/ROY* S71 .... 14 A1
Ledsham Ct *HOY* S74 .... 52 C2
Ledsham Rd *RHAM/THRY* S65 .... 104 B5
Ledstone Rd *SHEFS* S8 .... 146 C1
Lee Av *STKB/PEN* S36 .... 69 D2
Lee Brook La *RAW* S62 .... 77 F1
Lee Cft *SHEF* S1 .... 8 D4
Leedham Cl *SHEFN* S5 .... 100 A5
Leedham Rd *RHAM/THRY* S65 .... 105 D5
SHEFN S5 .... 100 A5
Leeds Rd *DARN/MH* S9 .... 124 B1
Lee House La *STKB/PEN* S36 .... 68 A3
Lee Rd *CHNE* S41 .... 191 F2
ST/HB/BR S6 .... 106 B3
Lees Hall Av *SHEFS* S8 .... 147 E1
Lees Hall Pl *SHEFS* S8 .... 135 F5
Lees Hall Rd *SHEFS* S8 .... 135 F5
Lees House Ct *SHEFS* S8 .... 147 E1
Leeswood Cl *CHNE* S41 .... 183 E1
Leger Wy *DONS/BSCR* DN4 .... 32 A5
DONS/BSCR DN4 .... 32 A5
WHHL DN2 .... 32 A2
Legion Dr *AU/AST/KP* S26 .... 142 C3
Leicester Av *WHHL* DN2 .... 45 E1
Leigh St *DARN/MH* S9 .... 111 E5
Leighton Cl *BSLYN/ROY* S71 .... 2 D2
Leighton Dr *GLV* S14 .... 149 D2
Leighton Pl *GLV* S14 .... 149 D2
Leighton Rd *GLV* S14 .... 136 C5
Leighton Vw *SHEFP/MNR* S2 .... 136 C5
Leinster Av *WHHL* DN2 .... 31 E4
Lemont Rd *TOT/DORE* S17 .... 156 C4
Lennox Rd *ST/HB/BR* S6 .... 107 F3
WHHL DN2 .... 31 F4
Lenton St *SHEFP/MNR* S2 .... 135 F1
Leonard Cl *SHEFP/MNR* S2 .... 137 D3
Leopold St *BSLY* S70 .... 21 E2
SHEF S1 .... 8 D5
Leppings La *ST/HB/BR* S6 .... 108 A2
Lepton Gdns *BSLY* S70 .... 23 E4
Lescar La *ECC* S11 .... 134 A2
Leslie Av *CONI* DN12 .... 84 B1
Leslie Rd *BSLY* S70 .... 23 E3
ST/HB/BR S6 .... 107 E3
Letard Dr *RHAM* S60 .... 114 A3
Levens Wy *CHNE* S41 .... 183 F1
Leverick Dr *RAW* S62 .... 81 D4
Leverton Dr *ECC* S11 .... 134 A3
Leverton Gdns *SHEFP/MNR* S2 .... 135 D1
Leverton Wy *RHAM/THRY* S65 .... 95 F5
Leveson St *ATT* S4 .... 123 D1
Levet Rd *DONS/BSCR* DN4 .... 47 D3
Lewdendale *BSLY* S70 .... 36 B1
Lewes Rd *CONI* DN12 .... 84 C2
Lewis Rd *BSLYN/ROY* S71 .... 15 F3
HAN/WDH S13 .... 138 A3
Leybourne Rd *KIMB* S61 .... 91 F5
Leyburn Cl *CHSW* S40 .... 183 E4
DONS/BSCR DN4 .... 47 D5
Leyburn Dr *AU/AST/KP* S26 .... 142 A2
Leyburn Gv *CHPT/GREN* S35 .... 74 B5
Leyburn Rd *SHEFS* S8 .... 135 D4
Ley End *BSLY* S70 .... 36 A1
Leyfield Rd *TOT/DORE* S17 .... 156 B1
The Leylands *DOD/DAR* S75 .... 12 B3
Leys Cl *DONS/BSCR* DN4 .... 63 D3
Liberty Cl *ST/HB/BR* S6 .... 119 F2
Liberty Dr *ST/HB/BR* S6 .... 119 F2
Liberty Hl *ST/HB/BR* S6 .... 119 F2
Liberty Pl *ST/HB/BR* S6 .... 119 F2
Liberty Rd *ST/HB/BR* S6 .... 119 F2
Library Cl *KIMB* S61 .... 92 B3
Lichfield Rd *DONS/BSCR* DN4 .... 189 D4
WHHL DN2 .... 31 D5
Lichfield Wy *RHAM* S60 .... 114 B3
Lichford Rd *SHEFP/MNR* S2 .... 136 A4
Lidget Cl *DONS/BSCR* DN4 .... 46 C5
Lidget La *DEARNE* S63 .... 27 F4
Lidgett La *DOD/DAR* S75 .... 49 E3
Liffey Av *WHHL* DN2 .... 31 E4

Lifford Pl *HOY* S74.................................... 52 C3
Lifford Rd *WHHL* DN2............................. 31 D4
Lifford St *DARN/MH* S9 .... 112 C1
Lightwood Rd *ECK/KIL* S21 .... 172 C1
Lilac Av *STKB/PEN* S36 .... 68 C3
Lilac Crs *HOY* S74..................................... 51 F1
Lilac Gv *CONI* DN12 .... 84 B2
    DONS/BSCR DN4 .... 47 D4
Lilac Rd *MOS* S20 .... 153 D2
    SHEFN S5 .... 110 C1
Lilac St *STV/CWN* S43 .... 180 B5
Lilian St South *RHAM/THRY* S65 ...... 103 F4
Limb La *TOT/DORE* S17.......................... 144 C4
Limbreck Cl *BTLY* DN5 .... 16 B5
Limbrick Cl *ST/HB/BR* S6 .... 107 F5
Limbrick Rd *ST/HB/BR* S6 .... 108 A5
Lime Av *STV/CWN* S43 .... 181 F5
Lime Ct *BTLY* DN5 .... 42 B5 🛈
Lime Gv *CHPT/GREN* S35 .... 88 B2
    MEX/SWTN S64...................................... 81 E2
Limegrove *RHAM* S60............................ 104 B5
Lime Gv *STKB/PEN* S36 .... 68 B3
Lime Rd *ECK/KIL* S21 .... 173 F2
Limes Av *DOD/DAR* S75 .... 12 C4
Limestone Cottage La
    ST/HB/BR S6 .... 96 C5
Lime St *MOS* S20 .... 153 D1
    ST/HB/BR S6 .... 121 F1
Limesway *DOD/DAR* S75 .... 12 C4
Lime Tree Av *ARMTH* DN3 .... 33 F2
    DONS/BSCR DN4 .... 5 H6
    ECK/KIL S21 .... 166 A3
Limetree Cl *STV/CWN* S43 .... 186 A4
Lime Tree Ct *DONS/BSCR* DN4 .... 46 D3
Lime Tree Crs *RAW* S62........................ 80 C5
Limpool Cl *DONS/BSCR* DN4 .... 47 D5
Limpsfield Rd *DARN/MH* S9 .... 111 E2
Linacre Rd *CHSW* S40 .... 182 B5
Linaker Rd *ST/HB/BR* S6 .... 120 C2
Linburn Rd *SHEFS* S8 .... 147 D3
Lincoln Rd *WHHL* DN2 .... 31 D3
Lincoln St *CHSW* S40........................... 190 B4
    DARN/MH S9 .... 111 F2 🛈
    RHAM S60 .... 6 C2
Lincroft Dr *RAW* S62.............................. 94 A3
Lindale Rd *CHNE* S41 .... 183 E1
The Lindales *DOD/DAR* S75 .... 13 D5 🛈
Linden Av *CHSW* S40 .... 188 C3
    DRON S18 .... 159 F5
    SHEFS S8 .... 146 C3
Linden Ct *CHPT/GREN* S35 .... 88 C5
Linden Crs *SHEFN* S5 .... 98 C5
Linden Park Gv *CHSW* S40 .... 10 A5
Linden Rd *CHPT/GREN* S35 .... 88 C5
    DEARNE S63 .... 56 C2
Linden Wk *BTLY* DN5 .... 16 B2
Lindholme Dr *NROS/TKH* DN11........... 67 F5
Lindholme Gdns *MOS* S20 .... 152 A3 🛈
Lindisfarne Rd *DRON* S18 .... 169 F5 🛈
Lindley Crs *DEARNE* S63....................... 27 D4
Lindley Rd *SHEFS* S8 .... 110 B2 🛈
Lindley St *RHAM/THRY* S65 .... 7 E1
Lindrick Av *MEX/SWTN* S64 .... 81 F1
Lindrick Cl *DONS/BSCR* DN4 .... 66 A2
Lindrick Dr *ARMTH* DN3 .... 33 F4 🛈
Lindrick Gdns *CHSW* S40 .... 189 D4 🛈
Lindsay Av *SHEFN* S5 .... 98 C5
Lindsay Cl *SHEFN* S5 .... 98 C4
Lindsay Crs *SHEFN* S5 .... 98 C4
Lindsay Dr *SHEFN* S5 .... 98 C4
Lindsay Pl *AU/AST/KP* S26 .... 142 B3
Lindsay Rd *SHEFN* S5 .... 98 C4
Lindsey Cl *DONS/BSCR* DN4.................. 66 B2
Lindum St *DONS/BSCR* DN4.................... 4 A6
Lingamore Leys *DEARNE* S63 .... 27 D2
Lingard St *DOD/DAR* S75 .... 2 A3 🛈
Lingard St *DOD/DAR* S75....................... 2 A2
Lingfield Dr *BTLY* DN5 .... 28 B4
Lingfoot Av *SHEFS* S8 .... 159 F2
Lingfoot Cl *SHEFS* S8 .... 159 F2 🛈
Lingfoot Crs *SHEFS* S8 .... 159 F2
Lingfoot Dr *SHEFS* S8 .... 160 A2 🛈
Lingfoot Pl *SHEFS* S8 .... 159 F2
Lingmoor Cl *DONS/BSCR* DN4 .... 62 C1
Ling Rd *CHSW* S40 .... 189 E4
Lingthwaite *DOD/DAR* S75 .... 20 B3 🛈
Links Rd *DRON* S18 .... 169 F3
Linkswood Av *WHHL* DN2 .... 32 A2
The Link *DOD/DAR* S75........................ 20 B4
Linkway *WHHL* DN2 .... 31 F3
Linley La *HACK/IN* S12 .... 138 C5 🛈
Linnet Mt *KIMB* S61 .... 90 A1
Linscott Cl *CHNE* S41 .... 183 E2
Linscott Rd *SHEFS* S8 .... 146 C3
Linthwaite La *HOY* S74........................ 53 D3
    RAW S62 .... 53 D5
Linton Cl *BSLY* S70................................ 20 C2
Linton Rd *CHSW* S40 .... 189 D4
Lipp Av *ECK/KIL* S21 .... 166 A1
Lisle Rd *RHAM/THRY* S65 .... 104 B5
Lismore Rd *SHEFS* S8 .... 135 F5
Lister Av *DONS/BSCR* DN4 .... 43 F4
    HACK/IN S12 .... 149 F1
    RAW S62 .... 79 F4
Lister Cl *HACK/IN* S12 .... 149 F2 🛈

Lister Ct *WHHL* DN2 .... 31 E4
Lister Crs *HACK/IN* S12 .... 149 F2
Lister Dr *HACK/IN* S12 .... 149 F2
Lister La *OWL* S3 .... 8 B2
Lister Pl *HACK/IN* S12 .... 149 F2 🛈
Lister Rd *ST/HB/BR* S6 .... 121 D1
Lister St *RHAM/THRY* S65 .... 7 H6
Lister Wy *HACK/IN* S12 .... 149 F1
Little Brind Rd *CHSW* S40 .... 182 C2
Little Common La *ECC* S11 .... 145 D2
    KIMB S61 .... 101 E2
    RHAM S60 .... 116 C3
Littledale Rd *DARN/MH* S9 .... 124 C5
Littlefield La *WMB/DAR* S73 .... 39 E2
Little La *ATT* S4 .... 111 D3 🛈
    HACK/IN S12 .... 137 F4
    KIMB S61 .... 75 F5
    WHHL DN2 .... 19 D5
Little Leeds *HOY* S74........................ 51 F2 🛈
Little London Pl *SHEFS* S8 .... 135 D4 🛈
Little London Rd *SHEFS* S8 .... 135 D4
Little Matlock Gdns *ST/HB/BR* S6 .. 119 E1
Little Matlock Wy *ST/HB/BR* S6 ... 119 E1 🛈
Littlemoor *CHNE* S41 .... 183 E2
    CHNE S41 .... 183 F2 🛈
    ECK/KIL S21 .... 164 C4
Littlemoor Crs *CHNE* S41 .... 183 E2
Littlemoor La *DONS/BSCR* DN4.......... 43 F3
Littlemoor St *DONS/BSCR* DN4 ..... 43 F3 🛈
Little New Cl *DOD/DAR* S75 .... 12 C4 🛈
Little Norton Av *SHEFS* S8 .... 159 E1
Little Norton Cl *SHEFS* S8 .... 147 E5
Little Norton Dr *SHEFS* S8 .... 147 E5
Little Norton La *SHEFS* S8 .... 147 E5
Little Norton Wy *SHEFS* S8 .... 159 E1
Little Wood Dr *GLV* S14 .... 149 D2
Little Wood Rd *GLV* S14 .... 149 E2 🛈
Littlewood St *DONS/BSCR* DN4 .... 4 A6
Littleworth La *BSLYN/ROY* S71 .... 15 E4
Litton Cl *STV/CWN* S43 .... 187 D1
Liverpool Av *WHHL* DN2...................... 31 D3
Liverpool St *DARN/MH* S9................. 111 D5
Livesey St *ST/HB/BR* S6 .... 108 B4
Livingstone Av *WHHL* DN2 .... 19 E5
Livingstone Crs *BSLYN/ROY* S71 ...... 14 C2
Livingstone Rd *CHPT/GREN* S35....... 73 F5
Livingston Rd *DARN/MH* S9 .... 123 F1 🛈
Lloyd St *ATT* S4 .... 110 B3
    RAW S62 .... 94 A3
Loakfield Dr *SHEFN* S5 .... 98 A2
Lobwood *BSLY* S70.................................. 22 B5
Lobwood La *BSLY* S70....................... 22 C5 🛈
Lockeafiash Crs *BSLY* S70 .... 23 E4
Locke Av *BSLY* S70.................................. 21 F5
    BSLY S70 .... 22 A4 🛈
Locke Rd *DOD/DAR* S75 .... 20 B4
Lockesley Av *CONI* DN12 .... 84 B1
Lock St *BSLY* S70 .... 21 E3
Lock House Rd *DARN/MH* S9 .... 112 A3
Lock La *DARN/MH* S9 .... 112 C1
Lockoford La *CHNE* S41 .... 184 B3
Lock St *ST/HB/BR* S6 .... 121 F1
Lockton Cl *CHPT/GREN* S35 .... 73 D3
Lockwood Cl *RHAM/THRY* S65 .... 105 D3
Lockwood La *BSLY* S70 .... 22 A3
Lockwood Rd *DEARNE* S63 .... 27 E5
    DON DN1 .... 30 C4
    RHAM/THRY S65 .... 105 D2
Lodge Cl *STV/CWN* S43 .... 186 B5
Lodge Dr *RAW* S62 .... 79 F2
Lodge Farm Cl *CHSW* S40 .... 189 D5
Lodge Hill Dr *AU/AST/KP* S26 .... 155 F5
Lodge La *AU/AST/KP* S26 .... 142 B4
    CHPT/GREN S35 .... 71 F5
    FUL S10 .... 118 B5
    KIMB S61 .... 90 A1
Lodge Moor Rd *FUL* S10 .... 130 C2
Lodge Pl *STV/CWN* S43........................ 187 D3
Lodge Wy *RHAM* S60 .... 114 A3
Logan Rd *DARN/MH* S9 .... 125 E3
Loicher La *CHPT/GREN* S35 .... 89 E5
Lomas Cl *ST/HB/BR* S6 .... 106 A5
Lombard Cl *DOD/DAR* S75 .... 2 B1
Lombard St *WMB/DAR* S73 .... 25 F5
London Rd *SHEFP/MNR* S2 .... 135 D1
London Rd North *SHEFS* S8 .... 135 E3
London St *CHNE* S41 .... 179 E3
London Wy *KIMB* S61 .... 89 F2
Longacre Rd *DRON* S18 .... 169 E4
Long Acre Vw *MOS* S20 .... 153 E5
Longacre Wy *MOS* S20 .... 153 E5
Longcar La *BSLY* S70.............................. 21 E2
Long Cswy *BSLYN/ROY* S71 .... 15 D5
Longcliff Wk *CHSW* S40 .... 183 D3 🛈
Longcroft Cl *DONS/BSCR* DN4 .... 66 B2
Longcroft Dr *DRON* S18 .... 168 A1
Long Croft Rd *DRON* S18 .... 168 A1
Longfellow Dr *RHAM/THRY* S65 ...... 104 C4
Longfellow Rd *DONS/BSCR* DN4 .... 64 A1
Longfield Cl *WMB/DAR* S73 .... 38 C1
Longfield Dr *DONS/BSCR* DN4 .... 66 B1
Longfield Rd *FUL* S10 .... 120 C2
Longfields Crs *HOY* S74.................... 51 E2 🛈
Longford Cl *TOT/DORE* S17 .... 157 E3
Longford Crs *TOT/DORE* S17............ 157 E3

Longford Dr *TOT/DORE* S17 .... 157 D4
Longford Rd *TOT/DORE* S17 .... 157 D4
Longford Spinney *TOT/DORE* S17 .. 157 D4
Long La *ECK/KIL* S21 .... 166 C2
    ECK/KIL S21 .... 172 A2
    FUL S10 .... 120 A3
    RHAM S60 .... 128 A1
    ST/HB/BR S6 .... 106 A3
    ST/HB/BR S6 .... 119 E2
Longley Av West *SHEFN* S5 .... 109 D2
Longley Cl *SHEFN* S5 .... 109 F2
Longley Crs *SHEFN* S5 .... 109 F1
Longley Dr *SHEFN* S5 .... 109 F2
Longley Farm Vw *SHEFN* S5 .... 109 F2
Longley Hall Gv *SHEFN* S5 .... 110 A2
Longley Hall Ri *SHEFN* S5 .... 109 F2
Longley Hall Rd *SHEFN* S5 .... 109 F2
Longley Hall Wy *SHEFN* S5 .... 110 A1
Longley La *SHEFN* S5 .... 109 F2
Long Line *ECC* S11 .... 144 A4
Longman Rd *BSLY* S70 .... 2 C2
Longridge Rd *BSLYN/ROY* S71 ...... 15 E1 🛈
Long Shambles *CHSW* S40 .... 11 F6
Longshaw Cl *STV/CWN* S43 .... 187 C2
Longside Wy *DOD/DAR* S75 .... 12 B5
Longstone Crs *HACK/IN* S12 .... 150 B1
Lonsdale Av *BSLYN/ROY* S71 .... 24 C2
    WHHL DN2 .... 45 F1
Lonsdale Rd *ST/HB/BR* S6 .... 108 A5
Loosemore Dr *HACK/IN* S12 .... 137 D5
Lopham Cl *OWL* S3 .... 9 G1
Lopham St *OWL* S3 .... 122 C1 🛈
Lord Roberts Rd *CHSW* S40 .... 190 B3 🛈
Lords Cl *DONS/BSCR* DN12................... 62 A3
Lord's Head La *DONS/BSCR* DN4 .... 62 B3
Lordsmill St *CHNE* S41 .... 11 G6
Lord St *BSLYN/ROY* S71 .... 15 D5
    RHAM/THRY S65................................ 104 B2
Lorna Rd *MEX/SWTN* S64 .... 58 B3
Lorne Cl *DRON* S18 .... 168 B1
Lorne Rd *DEARNE* S63 .... 26 B3
Lothian Rd *WHHL* DN2......................... 32 A4
Louden Cl *KIMB* S61 .... 90 C4
Louden Rd *KIMB* S61 .... 90 C4
Lounde Cl *BTLY* DN5 .... 28 C2
Loundes Rd *DRON* S18 .... 170 C5
Loundes Wood Av *CHNE* S41 .... 183 D1
Lound Rd *DARN/MH* S9 .... 125 E4
Lound Side *CHPT/GREN* S35 .... 74 B5
Loundsley Green Rd *CHSW* S40 ...... 182 C5
Louth Rd *ECC* S11 .... 133 F3
Lovell St *ATT* S4 .... 123 E2
Loversall Cl *DONS/BSCR* DN4 .... 63 F2
Love St *OWL* S3 .... 9 E3
Lovetot Av *AU/AST/KP* S26 .... 142 B2
Lovetot Rd *DARN/MH* S9 .... 123 F2 🛈
    KIMB S61 .... 91 F4
Lowburn Rd *HAN/WDH* S13................ 138 A3
Lowedges Crs *SHEFS* S8 .... 159 D2 🛈
Lowedges Dr *SHEFS* S8 .... 159 D2 2️⃣
Lowedges Pl *SHEFS* S8 .... 159 E2 2️⃣
Lowedges Rd *SHEFS* S8 .... 159 D2
Lowe La *DOD/DAR* S75........................ 34 A2
Lowell Av *DONS/BSCR* DN4 .... 63 F1 🛈
Lower Castlereagh St *BSLY* S70 .... 2 C6
Lower Dolcliffe Rd *MEX/SWTN* S64 .. 58 A3
Lower Grove Rd *DRON* S18 .... 10 D6
Lower Malton Rd *BTLY* DN5 .... 28 C2
Lower Thomas St *BSLY* S70 .... 21 F2 🛈
Lower York St *WMB/DAR* S73 .... 39 E2
Lowfield Av *HACK/IN* S12................... 150 C4
    KIMB S61 .... 93 D3
Lowfield Rd *WHHL* DN2......................... 32 A2
Low Fisher Ga *DON* DN1 .... 4 D2
Lowgate *BTLY* DN5 .... 28 C2
Low Grange Rd *DEARNE* S63 .... 26 C3
Low Grange Sq *DEARNE* S63 .... 26 C3
Lowhouse Rd *SHEFN* S5 .... 99 F2
Low Laithes Vw *WMB/DAR* S73 .... 38 C1 🛈
Lowlands Cl *BSLYN/ROY* S71 .... 15 E2
    BTLY DN5 .... 16 C3
Low La *KIMB* S61 .... 102 B1
Low Pasture Cl *DOD/DAR* S75............. 20 B3
Low Pavement *CHSW* S40 .... 11 E6
Low Rd *CONI* DN12 .... 61 D5
    DONS/BSCR DN4 .... 43 E5
    ST/HB/BR S6 .... 120 B1
Low Rd East *DONS/BSCR* DN4 .... 62 B1
Low Rd West *DONS/BSCR* DN4........... 62 A2
Lowry Dr *DRON* S18 .... 169 D2
Low St *DOD/DAR* S75 .... 20 C4
Lowther Rd *DON* DN1 .... 30 C4
    ST/HB/BR S6 .... 108 B3
Low Wood Cl *MEX/SWTN* S64 .... 81 D2 🛈
Loxley Av *WMB/DAR* S73 .... 39 D3
Loxley Cl *CHSW* S40 .... 188 C1
Loxley Rd *ST/HB/BR* S6 .... 106 C4
Loxley View Rd *FUL* S10 .... 120 C2
Loy Cl *KIMB* S61 .... 92 B3
Lucas Rd *CHNE* S41 .... 10 B1
Lucas St *ATT* S4 .... 110 A5 🛈
Ludham Cl *CHNE* S41 .... 184 A2
Lugano Gv *WMB/DAR* S73 .... 25 F4
Luke La *ST/HB/BR* S6 .... 107 D3

Lulworth Cl *BSLY* S70 .... 22 C2 🇨
Lumley St *ATT* S4 .... 123 E3
  DARN/MH S9 .... 124 A3 🇨
Lump La *CHPT/GREN* S35 .... 87 D5
Lumsdale Rd *STV/CWN* S43 .... 187 D1
Luna Cft *HACK/IN* S12 .... 149 D3
Lunbreck Rd *DONS/BSCR* DN4 .... 62 A2
Lundhill Cl *WMB/DAR* S73 .... 39 F4
Lundhill Gv *WMB/DAR* S73 .... 39 F5
Lundhill Rd *WMB/DAR* S73 .... 39 F5
Lundwood Cl *MOS* S20 .... 152 A3 🇨
Lundwood Dr *MOS* S20 .... 152 A3
Lundwood Gv *MOS* S20 .... 152 A3
Lundy Rd *DRON* S18 .... 169 E3
Lupton Crs *SHEFS* S8 .... 159 D2
Lupton Dr *SHEFS* S8 .... 159 D2
Lupton Rd *SHEFS* S8 .... 159 D2
Luterel Dr *AU/AST/KP* S26 .... 142 B2
Lych Gate Cl *DONS/BSCR* DN4 .... 47 E3 🇨
Lydden Cl *STV/CWN* S43 .... 185 F1 🇨
Lydford Av *CHNE* S41 .... 178 C5 🇨
Lydgate Ct *FUL* S10 .... 120 C4
Lydgate Hall Crs *FUL* S10 .... 120 B4
Lydgate La *FUL* S10 .... 120 B4
Lyme St *RHAM* S60 .... 6 A6
Lyminster Rd *ST/HB/BR* S6 .... 97 C3
Lyminton La *RHAM* S60 .... 127 F3
Lymister Av *RHAM* S60 .... 115 D3
Lyncroft Cl *RHAM* S60 .... 114 B4 🇨
Lyndale Av *ARMTH* DN3 .... 19 F5
Lyndhurst Cl *ECC* S11 .... 134 A4
Lyndhurst Crs *ARMTH* DN3 .... 19 F3
Lyndhurst Rd *ECC* S11 .... 134 A4 🇨
Lynmouth Rd *ABRD* S7 .... 134 C5
Lynn Pl *DARN/MH* S9 .... 111 F4 🇨
Lynton Av *RHAM* S60 .... 115 E1
Lynton Dr *ARMTH* DN3 .... 19 F3
Lynton Rd *ECC* S11 .... 134 B2 🇨🇨
Lynwood Cl *DRON* S18 .... 168 B2 🇨
Lynwood Dr *MEX/SWTN* S64 .... 58 A3
Lyons Cl *ATT* S4 .... 110 A5
Lyons St *ATT* S4 .... 110 A5 🇨
Lytham Av *BSLYN/ROY* S71 .... 15 E2
Lytton Av *SHEFN* S5 .... 97 F5
Lytton Cl *DONS/BSCR* DN4 .... 63 F1
Lytton Crs *SHEFN* S5 .... 97 F4
Lytton Dr *SHEFN* S5 .... 97 F4
Lytton Rd *SHEFN* S5 .... 97 F4

M

Mabel St *RHAM/THRY* S65 .... 104 A4 🇨
Machin Dr *RAW* S62 .... 79 D3
Machins Ct *DRON* S18 .... 169 E1 🇨
Machon Bank *ABRD* S7 .... 134 C4
Machon Bank Rd *ECC* S11 .... 134 B4
Mackenzie Crs *CHPT/GREN* S35 .... 87 E2
  FUL S10 .... 121 F5 🇨
Mackenzie St *ECC* S11 .... 134 C2 🇨
Macmanus Av *RAW* S62 .... 80 A3 🇨
Macnaghten Rd *DOD/DAR* S75 .... 50 A3 🇨
Macro Rd *WMB/DAR* S73 .... 39 F4
Madehurst Gdns
  SHEFP/MNR S2 .... 135 F3 🇨
Madehurst Ri *SHEFP/MNR* S2 .... 135 F3 🇨
Madehurst Rd *SHEFP/MNR* S2 .... 135 F3 🇨
Madehurst Vw *SHEFP/MNR* S2 .... 135 F3 🇨
Madin Dr *STV/CWN* S43 .... 186 C3
Madingley Cl *DONS/BSCR* DN4 .... 63 E2
Madin St *CHNE* S41 .... 11 E3
Mafeking Pl *CHPT/GREN* S35 .... 74 B5
Magna La *RHAM/THRY* S65 .... 95 E5
Magpie Gv *SHEFP/MNR* S2 .... 123 F5 🇨
Mahon Av *RAW* S62 .... 80 A5
Maidstone Rd *ST/HB/BR* S6 .... 97 E5
Maidwell Wy *ARMTH* DN3 .... 19 F2
Main Av *TOT/DORE* S17 .... 156 C4
Main Rd *DARN/MH* S9 .... 125 D2
  DARN/MH S9 .... 125 E3 🇨
  DRON S18 .... 170 C4
  ECC/KIL S21 .... 162 C5
  ECC/KIL S21 .... 172 B4
  ECC/KIL S21 .... 175 F2
  HACK/IN S12 .... 162 C1
Main St *ARMTH* DN3 .... 47 F3
  AU/AST/KP S26 .... 129 F3
  AU/AST/KP S26 .... 142 A1
  AU/AST/KP S26 .... 142 A3
  CHPT/GREN S35 .... 97 D1
  HACK/IN S12 .... 151 F1
  KIMB S61 .... 93 D3
  MEX/SWTN S64 .... 58 A4
  RAW S62 .... 76 B2
  RAW S62 .... 80 B5
  RHAM S60 .... 6 B6
  RHAM S60 .... 127 E1
  WMB/DAR S73 .... 39 D2
Makin St *MEX/SWTN* S64 .... 59 D3
Malcolm Cl *BSLY* S70 .... 23 E2 🇨
Malham Cl *CHSW* S40 .... 183 E4
Malham Gdns *MOS* S20 .... 164 B1

Malham Gv *MOS* S20 .... 164 C1
Malham Pl *CHPT/GREN* S35 .... 74 A5
Malham Tarn Ct
  DONS/BSCR DN4 .... 45 F4 🇨
Malia Rd *CHNE* S41 .... 185 D3
Malinda St *OWL* S3 .... 8 B2
Malin Rd *RHAM/THRY* S65 .... 105 F1
  ST/HB/BR S6 .... 107 E5
Malkin St *CHNE* S41 .... 11 C5
Mallard Cl *DONS/BSCR* DN4 .... 63 D1
  KIMB S61 .... 90 B1
Mallard Dr *ECK/KIL* S21 .... 165 F1 🇨
Mallory Av *RAW* S62 .... 79 F5
Mallory Dr *MEX/SWTN* S64 .... 59 E2
Mallory Rd *RHAM/THRY* S65 .... 105 D1
Malson Wy *CHNE* S41 .... 184 A3
Maltby St *DARN/MH* S9 .... 111 E5
Malthouse Rd *BSLYN/ROY* S71 .... 3 E6 🇨
Malting La *ATT* S4 .... 9 H5
The Maltings *RHAM* S60 .... 103 E4 🇨
Maitkiln St *RHAM* S60 .... 105 E4
Malton Dr *AU/AST/KP* S26 .... 142 C5
Malton St *ATT* S4 .... 110 A5
Maltravers Cl *SHEFP/MNR* S2 .... 123 F5 🇨
Maltravers Crs *SHEFP/MNR* S2 .... 123 E4
Maltravers Pl *SHEFP/MNR* S2 .... 123 F3 🇨
  SHEFP/MNR S2 .... 123 F4 🇨
Maltravers Rd *SHEFP/MNR* S2 .... 123 F4
Maltravers Ter *SHEFP/MNR* S2 .... 123 F5
Maltravers Wy *SHEFP/MNR* S2 .... 123 E4
Malvern Av *BTLY* DN5 .... 28 C4 🇨
Malvern Cl *DOD/DAR* S75 .... 12 C5 🇨
Malvern Rd *CHSW* S40 .... 10 B4
  DARN/MH S9 .... 124 C2
  WHHL DN2 .... 32 A5
Manchester Rd *FUL* S10 .... 119 F4
  STKB/PEN S36 .... 68 A1
  STKB/PEN S36 .... 70 B4
Mandeville St *DARN/MH* S9 .... 125 D2 🇨
Mangham Rd *KIMB* S61 .... 93 E5
Mangham Wy *KIMB* S61 .... 93 E5
Manifold Av *STV/CWN* S43 .... 187 E1
Manknell Rd *CHNE* S41 .... 184 B1
Mannering Rd *DONS/BSCR* DN4 .... 62 C1 🇨
Manners St *OWL* S3 .... 122 A1
Manor Ap *KIMB* S61 .... 102 A2
Manor Cl *STV/CWN* S43 .... 186 A2
Manor Cl *DEARNE* S63 .... 54 C1 🇨
  RAW S62 .... 79 D3
Manor Ct *RHAM/THRY* S65 .... 105 E1
Manor Crs *CHSW* S40 .... 189 E1
  DRON S18 .... 169 D2
  RHAM S60 .... 113 F4
Manor Dr *BTLY* DN5 .... 61 E3
  CHSW S40 .... 189 E1
  RHAM S60 .... 113 F4
  STV/CWN S43 .... 186 A2
  WHHL DN2 .... 45 D1
Manor End *BSLY* S70 .... 22 A5
Manor Est *BTLY* DN5 .... 16 A2
Manor Farm *AU/AST/KP* S26 .... 129 E5 🇨
Manor Farm Ct *MOS* S20 .... 153 E2 🇨
Manor Farm Dr *MEX/SWTN* S64 .... 81 D1
Manor Farm Ms *MOS* S20 .... 153 E2 🇨
Manor Flds *KIMB* S61 .... 101 F1
Manor Gdns *BSLYN/ROY* S71 .... 24 B2
Manor House Cl *HOY* S74 .... 51 F2
Manor House Ct *BTLY* DN5 .... 16 A5 🇨
Manor House Rd *KIMB* S61 .... 101 F1
Manor Laith Rd *SHEFP/MNR* S2 .... 123 E5
Manor Oaks Cl *SHEFP/MNR* S2 .... 123 F4
Manor Oaks Ct *SHEFP/MNR* S2 .... 123 E4 🇨
Manor Oaks Dr *SHEFP/MNR* S2 ...... 123 D4 🇨
Manor Oaks Gdns
  SHEFP/MNR S2 .... 123 D4 🇨
Manor Oaks Pl *SHEFP/MNR* S2 .... 123 F5
Manor Oaks Rd *SHEFP/MNR* S2 .... 123 D4
Manor Park Av *SHEFP/MNR* S2 .... 137 D1
Manor Park Centre
  SHEFP/MNR S2 .... 124 B5 🇨
Manor Park Cl *SHEFP/MNR* S2 .... 137 D1
Manor Park Ct *SHEFP/MNR* S2 .... 137 D1 🇨
Manor Park Crs *SHEFP/MNR* S2 .... 137 D1
Manor Park Dr *SHEFP/MNR* S2 .... 137 D1
Manor Park Pl *SHEFP/MNR* S2 .... 124 A5
Manor Park Ri *SHEFP/MNR* S2 .... 124 A5
Manor Park Rd *SHEFP/MNR* S2 .... 124 A5
Manor Park Wy *SHEFP/MNR* S2 .... 137 D1
Manor Pl *RAW* S62 .... 94 B1 🇨
Manor Rd *AU/AST/KP* S26 .... 155 F1
  BTLY DN5 .... 16 B2 🇨
  CHSW S40 .... 189 D1
  DEARNE S63 .... 26 C3
  DEARNE S63 .... 54 B1
  ECK/KIL S21 .... 166 B3
  MEX/SWTN S64 .... 81 E1
  RHAM S60 .... 113 F4
  STV/CWN S43 .... 186 A2
Manor Sq *DEARNE* S63 .... 26 B3
Manor Vw *MOS* S20 .... 164 C1 🇨
Manor Wy *HOY* S74 .... 51 F2
  SHEFP/MNR S2 .... 123 F4

Manse Cl *DONS/BSCR* DN4 .... 47 E4
Mansel Av *SHEFN* S5 .... 97 F3
Mansel Crs *SHEFN* S5 .... 97 F3
Mansel Rd *SHEFN* S5 .... 97 F3
Mansfeldt Crs *CHNE* S41 .... 183 D1
Mansfeldt Rd *CHNE* S41 .... 183 F3
Mansfield Crs *ARMTH* DN3 .... 33 D2
Mansfield Rd *AU/AST/KP* S26 .... 142 B4
  AU/AST/KP S26 .... 155 D2
  CHNE S41 .... 191 E5
  DONS/BSCR DN4 .... 43 F3
  ECK/KIL S21 .... 167 D2
  HACK/IN S12 .... 137 F4
Manton St *SHEFP/MNR* S2 .... 135 F1 🇨
Manvers Cl *AU/AST/KP* S26 .... 142 B3 🇨
Manvers Rd *AU/AST/KP* S26 .... 142 B3
  MEX/SWTN S64 .... 57 F3
  MOS S20 .... 153 D1
  ST/HB/BR S6 .... 108 A5
  STV/CWN S43 .... 186 B5
Manvers Wy *DEARNE* S63 .... 41 E5
  DEARNE S63 .... 56 C1
Maple Av *DONS/BSCR* DN4 .... 47 D4
Maplebeck Dr *DARN/MH* S9 .... 112 C2
Maplebeck Rd *DARN/MH* S9 .... 112 C3
Maple Cl *BSLY* S70 .... 22 C3
Maple Croft Crs *SHEFN* S5 .... 111 D1
Maple Croft Rd *SHEFN* S5 .... 111 D1
Maple Dr *ECK/KIL* S21 .... 166 A3
Maple Gv *AU/AST/KP* S26 .... 143 D2
  CONI DN12 .... 84 A3
  DARN/MH S9 .... 125 F4
  STKB/PEN S36 .... 68 C3
Maple Pl *CHPT/GREN* S35 .... 88 B2
Maple Rd *DOD/DAR* S75 .... 49 E5
  MEX/SWTN S64 .... 58 A3
Maple St *STV/CWN* S43 .... 186 C1
Mapperley Rd *DRON* S18 .... 168 A2 🇨
Mappin's Rd *RHAM* S60 .... 127 E2 🇨
Mappin St *SHEF* S1 .... 8 B5
Mapplebeck Rd *CHPT/GREN* S35 .... 73 F4
Marcham Dr *MOS* S20 .... 153 E1 🇨
March Ga *CONI* DN12 .... 85 D2
March St *CONI* DN12 .... 85 D1
  DARN/MH S9 .... 111 F3
March Vale Ri *CONI* DN12 .... 84 C2
Marchwood Av *ST/HB/BR* S6 .... 119 F1
Marchwood Rd *CHSW* S40 .... 10 B4
Marchwood Dr *ST/HB/BR* S6 .... 106 C5
Marchwood Rd *ST/HB/BR* S6 .... 106 C5
Mardale Cl *CHNE* S41 .... 177 F5
Marden Rd *ABRD* S7 .... 134 C4 🇨
Margaret Cl *AU/AST/KP* S26 .... 142 B4 🇨
Margaret Rd *WMB/DAR* S73 .... 39 F3
Margaret St *SHEF* S1 .... 135 E1
Margate Dr *ATT* S4 .... 110 B4
Margetson Crs *SHEFN* S5 .... 98 A3
Margetson Dr *SHEFN* S5 .... 97 F3
Margetson Rd *SHEFN* S5 .... 98 A3
Marian Rd *ARMTH* DN3 .... 19 F4 🇨
Marigold Cl *SHEFN* S5 .... 110 C1
Marina Ri *WMB/DAR* S73 .... 25 F5
Marion Rd *ST/HB/BR* S6 .... 107 F2
Markbrook Dr *CHPT/GREN* S35 .... 73 F2
Market Cl *BSLYN/ROY* S71 .... 3 F6
Market Hl *BSLY* S70 .... 2 C5
Market Pl *DON* DN1 .... 5 E3
Market Rd *DON* DN1 .... 5 E2
Market Sq *HAN/WDH* S13 .... 140 A4 🇨
Market St *BSLY* S70 .... 2 C5
  CHPT/GREN S35 .... 88 C1
  DEARNE S63 .... 26 C3
  ECK/KIL S21 .... 164 B5
  HAN/WDH S13 .... 140 A4 🇨
  HOY S74 .... 51 F1
  MEX/SWTN S64 .... 57 F5
  MEX/SWTN S64 .... 58 B4 🇨
  RHAM S60 .... 6 C5
  STV/CWN S43 .... 181 F4
Markham Av *ARMTH* DN3 .... 33 E2
  CONI DN12 .... 84 B1 🇨
Markham Cl *CONI* DN12 .... 84 B1 🇨
Markham Sq *CONI* DN12 .... 62 A5
Markham Ter *SHEFS* S8 .... 135 D4 🇨
Mark La *FUL* S10 .... 131 E4
Mark St *BSLY* S70 .... 2 B6
Marlborough Av *BTLY* DN5 .... 43 D1
Marlborough Cl *DEARNE* S63 .... 26 C3 🇨
Marlborough Ri *AU/AST/KP* S26 .... 142 C4
Marlborough Rd *FUL* S10 .... 121 D4
  WHHL DN2 .... 31 D5
Marlcliffe Rd *ST/HB/BR* S6 .... 107 C2
Marley Rd *SHEFP/MNR* S2 .... 136 C1
Marlfield Cft *CHPT/GREN* S35 .... 98 C1
Marlow Cl *WHHL* DN2 .... 32 A4 🇨
Marlowe Dr *RHAM/THRY* S65 .... 104 C4
Marlowe Rd *RHAM/THRY* S65 .... 104 C4
Marlow Rd *WHHL* DN2 .... 32 A4
Marmion Rd *ECC* S11 .... 133 F2
Marples Cl *SHEFS* S8 .... 135 D3 🇨
Marples Dr *SHEFS* S8 .... 135 D3 🇨🇨
Marrick Ct *CHPT/GREN* S35 .... 88 A1 🇨
Marrion Rd *RAW* S62 .... 80 B5

Marriott La *SHEFS* S8 ...... 146 B2
Marriott Pl *RAW* S62 ...... 79 E4
Marriott Rd *MEX/SWTN* S64 ...... 57 F4
  SHEFS S8 ...... 146 B2
Marrison Dr *ECK/KIL* S21 ...... 166 A2
Marr Ter *FUL* S10 ...... 133 D1
Marsden La *OWL* S3 ...... 8 B4
Marsden Rd *STKB/PEN* S36 ...... 69 D2 3
Marsden St *CHSW* S40 ...... 11 E5
Marshall Av *DONS/BSCR* DN4 ...... 43 E5 1
Marshall Cl *RAW* S62 ...... 94 A2
Marshall Gv *DEARNE* S63 ...... 56 A3 3
Marshall Rd *SHEFS* S8 ...... 147 D3
Marsh Av *DRON* S18 ...... 159 F5
Marsh Cl *MOS* S20 ...... 164 A2
Marshfield *BSLY* S70 ...... 36 A4 1
Marsh Ga *BTLY* DN5 ...... 4 B1
Marsh House Rd *ECC* S11 ...... 133 D5
Marsh La *BTLY* DN5 ...... 17 D2
  FUL S10 ...... 120 A4
Marsh Rd *BTLY* DN5 ...... 29 F4
Marsh St *RHAM* S60 ...... 103 D4
  STKB/PEN S36 ...... 69 E3 3
  WMB/DAR S73 ...... 39 E2
Marsh Vw *ECK/KIL* S21 ...... 173 F1
Marston Cl *DRON* S18 ...... 168 B3
Marston Crs *BSLYN/ROY* S71 ...... 14 A1
Marstone Crs *TOT/DORE* S17 ...... 156 C3
Marston Rd *FUL* S10 ...... 120 C3
Martin Cl *AU/AST/KP* S26 ...... 142 A1
  BSLY S70 ...... 36 A5
Martin Ct *ECK/KIL* S21 ...... 164 A5
Martin Crs *SHEFN* S5 ...... 98 C3
Martin La *HOY* S74 ...... 37 E4
Martin Ri *ECK/KIL* S21 ...... 164 A5
  KIMB S61 ...... 76 B5
Martin's Rd *BSLYN/ROY* S71 ...... 15 F4
Martin St *ST/HB/BR* S6 ...... 8 A2
  ST/HB/BR S6 ...... 121 F3
Marton Rd *BTLY* DN5 ...... 16 A1
Marvell Rd *BTLY* DN5 ...... 28 B5 3
Mary Ann Cl *BSLYN/ROY* S71 ...... 15 E5
Mary Ann St *DRON* S18 ...... 177 F2 7
Mary's Pl *DOD/DAR* S75 ...... 12 C5 7
Mary St *ECK/KIL* S21 ...... 164 B5
  RHAM S60 ...... 6 B4
  SHEF S1 ...... 135 E1
Masbrough St *RHAM* S60 ...... 6 B5
  RHAM S60 ...... 102 C3
Masefield Rd *DEARNE* S63 ...... 55 D1 6
  HAN/WDH S13 ...... 138 A3
  WHHL DN2 ...... 32 A2
Masham Ct *DONS/BSCR* DN4 ...... 46 C4 2
Mason Av *AU/AST/KP* S26 ...... 142 B1
Mason Crs *HAN/WDH* S13 ...... 138 B3
Mason Dr *AU/AST/KP* S26 ...... 142 A1
Mason Gv *HAN/WDH* S13 ...... 138 B4
Mason Lathe Rd *SHEFN* S5 ...... 99 F4
Masons Wy *BSLY* S70 ...... 23 E4
Mason Wy *HOY* S74 ...... 51 E1
Massey Rd *HAN/WDH* S13 ...... 140 B5
Masson Cl *CHSW* S40 ...... 183 E4 2
Mastall La *BTLY* DN5 ...... 17 F4
Masters Crs *SHEFN* S5 ...... 98 C4
Masters Rd *SHEFN* S5 ...... 98 C4
Mather Av *DARN/MH* S9 ...... 124 C5
Mather Ct *DARN/MH* S9 ...... 124 C4
Mather Crs *DARN/MH* S9 ...... 124 C4
Mather Dr *DARN/MH* S9 ...... 124 C4
Mather Rd *DARN/MH* S9 ...... 124 C4
Matilda La *SHEF* S1 ...... 122 C5
Matilda St *SHEF* S1 ...... 122 B5 5
Matlock Dr *STV/CWN* S43 ...... 187 D4
Matlock Rd *BSLYN/ROY* S71 ...... 14 C1
  FUL S10 ...... 121 D2
Mattersey Cl *DONS/BSCR* DN4 ...... 66 C2 1
Matthews Av *DEARNE* S63 ...... 55 E2
Matthews Cl *DEARNE* S63 ...... 55 E3
Matthews Dr *MALT* S66 ...... 117 F1 3
Matthews Fold *SHEFS* S8 ...... 148 A4 1
Matthews La *SHEFS* S8 ...... 148 A4
Matthew St *OWL* S3 ...... 8 C3
Mauncer Crs *HAN/WDH* S13 ...... 139 F3
Mauncer Dr *HAN/WDH* S13 ...... 139 F3
Mauncer La *HAN/WDH* S13 ...... 139 F4
Maun Wy *SHEFN* S5 ...... 110 A1
Maurice St *RAW* S62 ...... 94 A3
Mawfa Av *SHEFS* S8 ...... 148 B3
Mawfa Crs *SHEFS* S8 ...... 148 B3 3
Mawfa Dr *SHEFS* S8 ...... 148 B3
Mawfa Rd *SHEFS* S8 ...... 148 B3 3
Maxfield Rd *DOD/DAR* S75 ...... 12 A3
Maxey Pl *SHEFS* S8 ...... 135 E4 5
Maxfield Av *FUL* S10 ...... 121 D4
Maxwell St *ATT* S4 ...... 123 D1
Maxwell Wy *ATT* S4 ...... 123 D1
May Av *CHNE* S41 ...... 179 D3
  DONS/BSCR DN4 ...... 63 E1
Maycock Av *KIMB* S61 ...... 91 E4
May Day Gn *BSLY* S70 ...... 2 D5
Mayfield *BSLYN/ROY* S71 ...... 14 C3
Mayfield Crs *BSLY* S70 ...... 21 F4 1
Mayfield Rd *BTLY* DN5 ...... 29 E4
  CHSW S40 ...... 189 D2

FUL S10 ...... 131 E3
Mayflower Rd *DONS/BSCR* DN4 ...... 62 A2
Maynard Rd *CHSW* S40 ...... 190 A5
  RHAM S60 ...... 116 A1
May Rd *ST/HB/BR* S6 ...... 107 F4
May Ter *BSLY* S70 ...... 21 D1
May Tree Cl *MOS* S20 ...... 152 C4
  WMB/DAR S73 ...... 40 B1
Maytree Cl *WMB/DAR* S73 ...... 152 C4 1
May Tree Cft *MOS* S20 ...... 152 C4
May Tree La *MOS* S20 ...... 152 C4
Mcintyre Rd *STKB/PEN* S36 ...... 68 C3
Mclintock Wy *BSLY* S70 ...... 2 A5
Mcmahon Av *STV/CWN* S43 ...... 186 C3
Meaburn Cl *DONS/BSCR* DN4 ...... 47 D5
Meadow Av *RAW* S62 ...... 79 E4
Meadow Bank Av *ABRD* S7 ...... 134 B3 5
Meadowbank Cl *KIMB* S61 ...... 102 B3 2
Meadow Bank Rd *ABRD* S7 ...... 134 B3
  DARN/MH S9 ...... 101 D5
  KIMB S61 ...... 101 E4
Meadow Cl *CHNE* S41 ...... 179 E4
  DRON S18 ...... 160 A4 3
  RHAM/THRY S65 ...... 95 F5
Meadowcourt *DARN/MH* S9 ...... 111 F2 7
Meadowcroft Cl *RHAM* S60 ...... 163 F1 1
Meadow Cft *BTLY* DN5 ...... 42 A4
  DRON S18 ...... 81 D3
  MEX/SWTN S64 ......
Meadowcroft Cl *RHAM* S60 ...... 115 F4
Meadowcroft Gdns *MOS* S20 ...... 152 C5 7
Meadowcroft Gld *MOS* S20 ...... 152 C5 7
Meadowcroft Ri *MOS* S20 ...... 152 C5 5
Meadow Dr *BSLYN/ROY* S71 ...... 15 E3
  CHPT/GREN S35 ...... 87 F1
  MEX/SWTN S64 ...... 81 D1
Meadowfield Dr *HOY* S74 ...... 51 F4
Meadow Gate Av *MOS* S20 ...... 153 F2
Meadow Gate Cl *MOS* S20 ...... 153 F3 1
Meadow Gate La *MOS* S20 ...... 153 F4
Meadow Gv *TOT/DORE* S17 ...... 156 C4
Meadow Grove Rd *TOT/DORE* S17 ... 156 B4
Meadowhall Rd *DARN/MH* S9 ...... 111 F2
  KIMB S61 ...... 101 E4
Meadowhall Wy *DARN/MH* S9 ...... 112 A1 1
Meadow Head *SHEFS* S8 ...... 159 E1 2
Meadow Head Av *SHEFS* S8 ...... 158 C1
Meadow Head Dr *SHEFS* S8 ...... 147 D5
Meadow House Dr *FUL* S10 ...... 132 B1
Meadow La *MEX/SWTN* S64 ...... 58 B5
  RAW S62 ...... 79 E4
Meadow Ri *CHSW* S40 ...... 182 A5
The Meadows *RCH* S42 ...... 182 A4
Meadow St *BSLYN/ROY* S71 ...... 3 E3
  KIMB S61 ...... 102 B3
  OWL S3 ...... 8 B4
Meadow Ter *ECC* S11 ...... 134 A2 2
The Meadow *BTLY* DN5 ...... 42 A3
Meadow Vw *BSLY* S70 ...... 22 B5
  CHSW S40 ...... 188 B4
Meadow View Cl *HOY* S74 ...... 51 E5
Meadow View Rd *MEX/SWTN* S64 ... 81 E3
  SHEFS S8 ...... 147 D5
Meadow Wy *MEX/SWTN* S64 ...... 58 A5
The Meads *SHEFS* S8 ...... 147 F5
The Meadway *TOT/DORE* S17 ...... 156 B1
Meakin St *CHNE* S41 ...... 191 E4
Medley Vw *CONI* DN12 ...... 85 E2
Medlock Cl *HAN/WDH* S13 ...... 126 B5
Medlock Crs *HAN/WDH* S13 ...... 126 B5
Medlock Cft *HAN/WDH* S13 ...... 126 B5
Medlock Dr *HAN/WDH* S13 ...... 139 E1
Medlock Rd *CHSW* S40 ...... 189 D4
  HAN/WDH S13 ...... 139 E1 1
Medlock Wy *HAN/WDH* S13 ...... 126 B5
Medway Cl *DOD/DAR* S75 ...... 12 A2
Medway Pl *WMB/DAR* S73 ...... 40 A4 1
Meersbrook Av *SHEFS* S8 ...... 135 D5
Meersbrook Park Rd *SHEFS* S8 ... 135 E4
Meersbrook Rd *SHEFS* S8 ...... 135 F5
Meetinghouse Cft *HAN/WDH* S13 ... 140 A4
Meetinghouse La *HAN/WDH* S13 ... 140 A4
  SHEF S1 ...... 9 E4
Melbeck Ct *CHPT/GREN* S35 ...... 87 F1 1
Melbourne Av *AU/AST/KP* S26 ...... 142 C2
  FUL S10 ...... 121 D5
Melbourne Rd *DONS/BSCR* DN4 ...... 62 C1
  STKB/PEN S36 ...... 68 C2
Melbourn Rd *FUL* S10 ...... 121 D2
Melford Dr *DONS/BSCR* DN4 ...... 63 E5
Melfort Gln *FUL* S10 ...... 120 A4 1
Mell Av *HOY* S74 ...... 51 E2
Melling Av *BTLY* DN5 ...... 43 D1
Melling Cl *CHSW* S40 ...... 190 A4
Melling Ct *CHSW* S40 ...... 190 A4
Mellington Cl *SHEFS* S8 ...... 148 A3
Mellor Lea Farm Cha
  CHPT/GREN S35 ...... 88 C4
Mellor Lea Farm Dr
  CHPT/GREN S35 ...... 88 C4
Mellor Lea Farm Garth
  CHPT/GREN S35 ...... 88 C4
Mellor Rd *WMB/DAR* S73 ...... 39 F3
Mellor Wy *CHSW* S40 ...... 190 B5
Mellwood Gv *WMB/DAR* S73 ...... 39 D5 3
Melrose Cl *CHSW* S40 ...... 189 D1
  DONS/BSCR DN4 ...... 42 C5

Melrose Gv *RHAM* S60 ...... 115 E2
Melrose Rd *ATT* S4 ...... 122 C1
Melrose Wy *BSLYN/ROY* S71 ...... 15 E5
Meltham La *CHNE* S41 ...... 184 C3
Meltham Av *WMB/DAR* S73 ...... 40 C5
Melton Gn *DEARNE* S63 ...... 55 D2
Melton Gv *HACK/IN* S12 ...... 151 E3
Melton High St *DEARNE* S63 ...... 55 D2
Melton Rd *BTLY* DN5 ...... 42 B2
Melton St *MEX/SWTN* S64 ...... 59 D4
  WMB/DAR S73 ...... 40 C5 1
Melton Ter *BSLY* S70 ...... 23 D5 1
Melville Crs *STV/CWN* S43 ...... 186 A5
Melville St *WMB/DAR* S73 ...... 39 E2 3
Melvinia Crs *DOD/DAR* S75 ...... 13 E3
Mendip Cl *BTLY* DN5 ...... 28 C4 1
  DOD/DAR S75 ...... 12 C5 5
Mendip Crs *CHSW* S40 ...... 182 C5
Mendip Ri *RHAM* S60 ...... 114 B4 1
Merbeck Dr *CHPT/GREN* S35 ...... 73 F2
Merbeck Gv *CHPT/GREN* S35 ...... 73 F3 3
Mercaston Cl *CHSW* S40 ...... 182 B4 3
Mercia Dr *TOT/DORE* S17 ...... 156 C2
Meredith Crs *DONS/BSCR* DN4 ...... 63 F1
Meredith Rd *ST/HB/BR* S6 ...... 107 F4
Mere La *ARMTH* DN3 ...... 33 E2
Merlin Cl *BSLY* S70 ...... 36 A5
Merlin Wy *KIMB* S61 ...... 76 B5
  SHEFN S5 ...... 110 A1
Merrick Cl *CHSW* S40 ...... 183 E4
Merrill Rd *DEARNE* S63 ...... 26 C2
Merton La *DARN/MH* S9 ...... 100 C5
Merton Ri *DARN/MH* S9 ...... 100 C5
Merton Rd *DARN/MH* S9 ...... 100 C4 1
Metcalfe Av *ECK/KIL* S21 ...... 166 A2
Methley Cl *SHEFP/MNR* S2 ...... 137 D4
Meynell Cl *CHSW* S40 ...... 189 D2 5
Meynell Crs *SHEFN* S5 ...... 97 E5
Meynell Rd *SHEFN* S5 ...... 97 E5
Michael Cft *DEARNE* S63 ...... 55 D2
Michael Rd *BSLYN/ROY* S71 ...... 15 F5
Mickelden Wy *DOD/DAR* S75 ...... 20 B1 1
Micklebring Gv *CONI* DN12 ...... 84 B3
Mickley La *TOT/DORE* S17 ...... 157 D4
Middle Av *RAW* S62 ...... 80 A5
Middle Bank *DONS/BSCR* DN4 ...... 44 C4
Middleburn Cl *BSLY* S70 ...... 22 B3
Middlecliff Cl *MOS* S20 ...... 152 C4
Middlecliff Ct *MOS* S20 ...... 152 C4 2
Middlecliff Ri *MOS* S20 ...... 152 C4
Middlecroft Rd *STV/CWN* S43 ...... 187 D2
Middle Dr *RHAM* S60 ...... 115 D3
Middlefield Cl *TOT/DORE* S17 ...... 156 A1
Middlefield Cft *TOT/DORE* S17 ...... 156 A2
Middlefield Rd *DONS/BSCR* DN4 ... 46 B5
  RHAM S60 ...... 115 E2
Middlefields Dr *RHAM* S60 ...... 116 A3
Middle Hay Cl *HACK/IN* S12 ...... 136 C5
Middle Hay Pl *HACK/IN* S12 ...... 136 C5
Middle Hay Ri *HACK/IN* S12 ...... 136 C5
Middle Hay Vw *GLV* S14 ...... 148 C1
Middle La *CHPT/GREN* S35 ...... 86 C5
  RHAM/THRY S65 ...... 7 H4
  ST/HB/BR S6 ...... 120 B1 1
Middle La South *RHAM/THRY* S65 ... 104 B3
Middle Ox Cl *MOS* S20 ...... 165 D2 3
Middle Ox Gdns *MOS* S20 ...... 165 D2
Middle Pl *RHAM/THRY* S65 ...... 104 C2
Middlesex St *BSLY* S70 ...... 22 A3
Middle Shambles *CHSW* S40 ...... 11 E5
Middleton Dr *STV/CWN* S43 ...... 186 C4
Middleton La *CHPT/GREN* S35 ...... 97 E1
Middleton Rd *RHAM/THRY* S65 ...... 7 H5
Middlewood Rd *ST/HB/BR* S6 ...... 107 E1
Middlewood Rd North
  CHPT/GREN S35 ...... 96 A4
Middlewoods *DOD/DAR* S75 ...... 20 B3 1
Midfield Rd *FUL* S10 ...... 120 B3
Midhill Rd *SHEFP/MNR* S2 ...... 135 F3
Midhope Wy *DOD/DAR* S75 ...... 20 B1
Midhurst Rd *ST/HB/BR* S6 ...... 96 C4
Midland Rd *KIMB* S61 ...... 102 B3
  MEX/SWTN S64 ...... 57 F5
Midland St *BSLY* S70 ...... 2 D5
  RAW S62 ...... 93 F4
  SHEF S1 ...... 135 E1 1
Midvale Av *ST/HB/BR* S6 ...... 121 F1
Midvale Cl *ST/HB/BR* S6 ...... 121 F2
Milbanke St *DON* DN1 ...... 5 F1
Milburn Ct *MOS* S20 ...... 153 E4 3
Milburn Gv *MOS* S20 ...... 153 E4
Milden Pl *BSLY* S70 ...... 22 B3
Milden Rd *ST/HB/BR* S6 ...... 107 E2
Mile Oak Rd *RHAM* S60 ...... 115 D1
Miles Cl *SHEFN* S5 ...... 109 E3
Miles Rd *CHPT/GREN* S35 ...... 73 F4
  SHEFN S5 ...... 109 D3
Milethorn La *DON* DN1 ...... 30 B4
Milford Av *HOY* S74 ...... 52 C2
Milford Rd *STV/CWN* S43 ...... 187 D4
Milford St *DARN/MH* S9 ...... 111 F4
Milgrove Crs *CHPT/GREN* S35 ...... 73 E3 3
Mill Cl *RHAM* S60 ...... 103 D5
Mill Ct *BSLY* S70 ...... 22 B5 1
Milldale Cl *CHSW* S40 ...... 183 D4

Milldale Rd TOT/DORE S17............157 D3
Milldyke Cl RHAM S60............116 B3 2
Millennium Wy CHNE S41............177 F5
Miller Cft HAN/WDH S13............139 E4
Miller Dale Dr RHAM S60............114 B5 2
Miller Rd SHEFS S8............135 D3 1
Millers Dl BSLY S70............36 B1
Miller St STKB/PEN S36............70 A2 1
Millfield Rd BTLY DN5............50 A1
Mill Ga BTLY DN5............29 F1
Mill Gn STV/CWN S43............181 E4
Mill Hl RHAM S60............116 A3
  WMB/DAR S73............38 C1
Mill Hill Cl BTLY DN5............43 D1
Millhouses Ct ECC S11............145 F1
Millhouses Gln ECC S11............145 F1 3
Millhouses La ABRD S7............146 A2
Millhouses St HOY S74............51 F3
Mill La CHSW S40............189 E2
  DEARNE S63............55 D3
  DRON S18............169 F2
  ECK/KIL S21............175 E1
  RAW S62............76 A1
  RHAM S60............127 E3
  STKB/PEN S36............70 A2
  TOT/DORE S17............157 D3
Mill Meadow Gdns MOS S20............153 F4
Millmoor La RHAM S60............102 C3
Millmoor Rd WMB/DAR S73............40 A1
Millmount Rd HOY S74............72 A2
  SHEFS S8............135 D5
Mill Rd CHPT/GREN S35............88 C5
  ECK/KIL S21............164 B4
  RHAM S60............127 E3
Mill Road Cl CHPT/GREN S35............88 B5
Millsands OWL S3............9 F3
Millside Ct BTLY DN5............29 F1 3
Millstone Cl DRON S18............168 B1 1
Millstone Dr AU/AST/KP S26............142 B3
Millstream Cl BTLY DN5............42 B3
Mill Stream Cl CHSW S40............189 D3
Mill St ARMTH DN3............33 F1
  CHNE S41............11 G6
  KIMB S61............92 C2
  RHAM S60............103 E4
Millthorpe Rd SHEFN S5............99 E5
Millwood Rd DONS/BSCR DN4............63 D2 1
Mill Wood Vw ST/HB/BR S6............106 A5
Milner Ga CONI DN12............61 F5
Milner Gate Ct CONI DN12............85 E1
Milner Rd DONS/BSCR DN4............43 D5 1
Milnes St BSLY S70............22 B2
Milnrow Crs SHEFN S5............98 A3
Milnrow Dr SHEFN S5............98 A3
Milnrow Rd SHEFN S5............98 A3
Milton Av BTLY DN5............29 D5
Milton Cl DEARNE S63............40 C5
  HOY S74............52 A1
  KIMB S61............92 C2
Milton Ct MEX/SWTN S64............57 D5
  HOY S74............51 F3
Milton Crs CHSW S40............190 B4
  HOY S74............51 F3
Milton Gv ARMTH DN3............33 F3
  WMB/DAR S73............122 A5
Milton La SHEF S1............122 A5
Milton Rd ABRD S7............134 C3
  CHPT/GREN S35............87 E1
  HOY S74............51 F2 3
  HOY S74............51 F3
  MEX/SWTN S64............58 B3
  RHAM/THRY S65............7 G2
Milton St MEX/SWTN S64............57 D5
  OWL S3............122 A5
  RHAM S60............6 B2
Milton Wk DON DN1............4 D5
Minden Ct BTLY DN5............29 F1 3
Minna Rd OWL S3............109 F5
Minneymoor Hl CONI DN12............61 E5
Minneymoor La CONI DN12............85 E1
Minster Cl CHPT/GREN S35............99 D1
  DONS/BSCR DN4............47 E5
Minster Rd CHPT/GREN S35............98 C1
Minster Wy BSLYN/ROY S71............15 E4
Minto Rd ST/HB/BR S6............107 F3
Miriam Av RCH S42............188 B4
Mission Fld WMB/DAR S73............40 B5
Mitchell Cl BSLY S70............23 E5 3
Mitchell Rd SHEFS S8............147 D3
  WMB/DAR S73............25 D5
Mitchell's St BSLY S70............23 F5
Mitchell St OWL S3............8 A4
Mitchell Wy STV/CWN S43............179 F3 3
Moat Cft BTLY DN5............16 A5 2
Moat Hills Ct BTLY DN5............16 B5
Modena Ct WMB/DAR S73............25 F4
Moffat Gdns WHHL DN2............19 E5
Moffatt Rd SHEFP/MNR S2............135 F3
Molineaux Cl SHEFN S5............99 E4 3
Molineaux Rd SHEFN S5............99 D3
Molineux Av STV/CWN S43............181 E5
Molloy Pl SHEFS S8............135 E5 3
Molloy St SHEFS S8............135 E4 7
Mona Av FUL S10............121 D3
Mona Rd DONS/BSCR DN4............43 F4
  FUL S10............121 D2

Monckton Rd SHEFN S5............111 D1
Moncrieffe Rd ABRD S7............134 C4
Monks Cl KIMB S61............91 D4
Monkspring BSLY S70............23 D5
Monks Wy BSLYN/ROY S71............15 E4
Monk Ter BSLYN/ROY S71............15 F2
Monkwood Rd CHNE S41............183 E1
  RAW S62............79 E4
Monmouth Rd WHHL DN2............31 E3
Monmouth St OWL S3............121 F5 3
Monsal Crs STV/CWN S43............186 C3
Monsal St DEARNE S63............26 C3
Montague Av CONI DN12............60 B5
Montague St DON DN1............5 F1
  ECC S11............134 C1
Montagu Rd BTLY DN5............42 C2
Monteney Crs SHEFN S5............98 B1
Monteney Gdns SHEFN S5............98 B2
Monteney Rd SHEFN S5............98 B2
Montfort Dr OWL S3............122 C1
Montgomery Av ABRD S7............134 C3
Montgomery Dr ABRD S7............134 C3 3
  DEARNE S63............55 F2 3
Montgomery Terrace Rd OWL S3............8 B2
Montrose Av WHHL DN2............31 F4
Montrose Pl DRON S18............168 B1
Montrose Rd ECC S11............134 A5
Monyash Cl STV/CWN S43............187 D2 3
Moonpenny Wy DRON S18............169 E2
Moonshine La SHEFN S5............109 D1
Moorbank Cl DOD/DAR S75............13 D5 3
  FUL S10............119 E4
  WMB/DAR S73............38 C1
Moorbank Dr FUL S10............119 F4
Moorbank Rd FUL S10............119 E4 3
  WMB/DAR S73............24 C5
Moorbank Vw WMB/DAR S73............24 C5
Moorbridge Crs WMB/DAR S73............40 C4
Moor Crs MOS S20............164 A1
Moorcroft Av FUL S10............131 F2
Moorcroft Cl FUL S10............131 F3
Moorcroft Dr FUL S10............131 F3
Moorcroft Rd FUL S10............131 F3 3
Moordale Vw RAW S62............81 D4
Moor End Rd FUL S10............121 D3
Moore St SHEFP/MNR S2............122 A5
Moore Street Rtt OWL S3............122 A5
Moor Farm Av MOS S20............151 F5
Moor Farm Garth MOS S20............152 A5 3
Moor Farm Rl MOS S20............151 F5
Moorfield Dr ARMTH DN3............33 F4
Moorgate Av FUL S10............121 E3 3
  RHAM S60............103 F5
Moorgate Cha RHAM S60............103 F4
Moorgate Crs DRON S18............169 F3 3
Moorgate Gv RHAM S60............103 F5
Moorgate La RHAM S60............103 F5
Moorgate Rd RHAM S60............103 F4 3
Moor Green Cl DOD/DAR S75............12 B5 3
Moorhay Cl CHSW S40............182 C2 3
Moor Head SHEF S1............122 B5 3
Moorhouse Cl RHAM S60............116 B3 3
Moorhouse La RHAM S60............116 A3
Moorland Av BSLY S70............20 C2
Moorland Ct DEARNE S63............41 D5 1
Moorland Dr STKB/PEN S36............68 B2
Moorland Gv DONS/BSCR DN4............46 A3
Moorland Pl ST/HB/BR S6............119 D1
Moorlands Crs RHAM S60............116 A3
Moorland Vw AU/AST/KP S26............142 C3
  DEARNE S63............41 D5
  DRON S18............171 E2 3
  HACK/IN S12............149 E3
Moorland View Rd CHSW S40............189 D3
Moor La ARMTH DN3............19 F1
  BSLY S70............50 A3
Moor Oaks Rd FUL S10............121 D4
Moorpark Av CHSW S40............189 D4
Moor Rd DEARNE S63............56 A2 1
  RHAM/THRY S65............56 A5
Moorside FUL S10............131 E2
Moorside Cl MOS S20............152 A5
Moorsyde Av FUL S10............120 C2
Moorsyde Crs FUL S10............120 C2
Moorthorpe Gdns MOS S20............151 E3
Moorthorpe Gn HACK/IN S12............151 D3
Moorthorpe Wy MOS S20............151 E3
  MOS S20............152 A3
Moortop Rd DRON S18............171 F2
Moor Va MOS S20............151 D3
Moor Valley Cl HACK/IN S12............151 E4
Moorview Cl STV/CWN S43............185 E2 3
Moorview Dr SHEFS S8............146 C3 3
Moor View Rd SHEFS S8............146 C3
Moor View Ter ECC S11............132 C5 3
Moorwinstow Cft
  TOT/DORE S17............156 C1 3
Moorwoods Av CHPT/GREN S35............74 B5 3
Moorwoods La CHPT/GREN S35............88 A1
Moray Pl DRON S18............168 B1
Mordaunt Rd SHEFP/MNR S2............137 D4

Morgan Av SHEFN S5............108 C1
Morgan Cl SHEFN S5............109 D1
Morgan Rd SHEFN S5............108 C2
Morland Cl GLV S14............149 D2
Morland Dr GLV S14............149 D2
Morland Pl GLV S14............149 D2
Morland Rd GLV S14............148 C2
Morley Av CHSW S40............183 D5
Morley Cl DRON S18............168 A2
Morley Pl CONI DN12............84 C2
Morley Rd KIMB S61............91 F5
  WHHL DN2............30 C4
Morley St RAW S62............94 A2
  ST/HB/BR S6............107 F5
Morpeth St OWL S3............8 B3
  RHAM/THRY S65............7 E4 1
Morrall Rd SHEFN S5............98 A2
Morris Av CHNE S41............10 B1
  RAW S62............80 A3
Morris Dr CHNE S41............10 B1
Morris Rd DONS/BSCR DN4............62 C1
Mortain Rd RHAM S60............115 D3
Morthen Hall La MALT S66............117 F5
Morthen La MALT S66............117 E4
  RHAM S60............129 E1
Morthen Rd MALT S66............117 E4
Mortlake Rd SHEFN S5............110 B2 3
Mortomley Cl CHPT/GREN S35............73 F4
Mortomley La CHPT/GREN S35............73 F4
Morton Cl BSLYN/ROY S71............15 E2 3
Morton La ECK/KIL S21............172 A2
Morton Pl CHPT/GREN S35............97 D1
Morton Rd MEX/SWTN S64............58 C3
Mosborough Hall Dr MOS S20............164 C3
Mosborough Moor MOS S20............151 F5
Mosbrough Rd HAN/WDH S13............137 F3
Mossdale Av MOS S20............164 B1
Mossdale Cl BTLY DN5............28 C2
Moss Dr ECK/KIL S21............166 B3
Moss Gv HACK/IN S12............152 B1
Moss Vw MOS S20............163 F2
Moss Wy HACK/IN S12............152 B2
  MOS S20............164 B1
Motehall Dr SHEFP/MNR S2............137 E1
Motehall Pl SHEFP/MNR S2............137 F1
Motehall Rd SHEFP/MNR S2............137 E1
Motehall Wy SHEFP/MNR S2............137 E1 3
The Motte KIMB S61............102 A1
Mottram St BSLYN/ROY S71............2 D4
Mound Rd CHSW S40............190 B3
Mountbatten Dr CHPT/GREN S35............87 E1
Mountcastle St CHNE S41............184 A1 3
Mount Cl BSLY S70............22 A3
Mount Crs HOY S74............51 E2
Mountenov Rd RHAM S60............105 E5
Mountford Cft TOT/DORE S17............156 C3 3
Mount Pleasant BSLY S70............36 C1 2
  DONS/BSCR DN4............43 E5 3
Mount Pleasant Cl
  CHPT/GREN S35............74 B5 3
Mount Pleasant Rd DEARNE S63............56 A4
  KIMB S61............102 C2
  SHEFP/MNR S2............135 D2 3
Mount Rd CHPT/GREN S35............73 F5
  OWL S3............109 D5
Mount St BSLY S70............21 F2
  BSLYN/ROY S71............24 A2
  ECC S11............135 D1
  KIMB S61............102 C2
Mount Ter DEARNE S63............55 D2
  WMB/DAR S73............39 D2
Mount Vernon Av BSLY S70............22 A3
Mount Vernon Crs BSLY S70............22 B4
Mount Vernon Rd BSLY S70............22 B4
Mount View Av BSLY S70............147 E2
Mount View Gdns SHEFS S8............147 E2 3
Mount View Rd SHEFS S8............147 E3
Mousehole Cl RHAM/THRY S65............95 F5
Mousehole La RHAM/THRY S65............95 F5
Mouse Park Ga CHPT/GREN S35............86 A3
Mowbray Gdns RHAM/THRY S65............105 D3
Mowbray Pl RHAM/THRY S65............105 D1
Mowbray St OWL S3............8 D1
  RHAM/THRY S65............104 C3
Moxon Cl STKB/PEN S36............69 E3
Mucky La BSLYN/ROY S71............24 B1
  STKB/PEN S36............68 A4
Muirfield Av DONS/BSCR DN4............67 F1
  MEX/SWTN S64............81 F1
Muirfield Cl CHNE S41............184 C3
Mulberry Cl BTLY DN5............28 B4
  RAW S62............94 A3 3
Mulberry Rd ECK/KIL S21............173 F1
Mulberry St SHEF S1............5 F5
Mulberry Wy ARMTH DN3............33 F5 3
  ECK/KIL S21............165 F3 3
Mulehouse Rd FUL S10............120 B3
Mundella Pl SHEFS S8............147 E2
Munro Cl ECK/KIL S21............166 B2
Munsbrough La KIMB S61............93 D4
  KIMB S61............93 D4
Munsbrough Ri KIMB S61............92 C3
Murdock Rd SHEFN S5............98 A5
Murrayfield Dr MOS S20............164 C2 3
Murray Rd ECC S11............133 F4

ECK/KIL S21 .... 166 C1
RAW S62 .... 80 B5
Musard Pl STV/CWN S43 .... 181 E5
Musgrave Crs SHEFN S5 .... 109 E3
Musgrave Dr SHEFN S5 .... 109 E3
Musgrave Rd SHEFN S5 .... 109 E3
Musgrave Rd SHEFN S5 .... 109 D3
Mushroom La FUL S10 .... 121 E4
Muskoka Av ECC S11 .... 132 C5
Muskoka Dr ECC S11 .... 132 C4
Mutual St DONS/BSCR DN4 .... 4 A6
Myers Grove La ST/HB/BR S6 .... 106 C5
ST/HB/BR S6 .... 107 D5
Myers St WMB/DAR S73 .... 39 D1
Mylnhurst Rd ECC S11 .... 145 F1
Mylor Cl BSLYN/ROY S71 .... 15 D4
Mylor Rd ECC S11 .... 133 E4
Myrtle Gv STV/CWN S43 .... 180 B5
Myrtle Rd SHEFP/MNR S2 .... 135 E2
WMB/DAR S73 .... 39 D2
Myrtle Springs HACK/IN S12 .... 137 D5
Myrtle St DOD/DAR S75 .... 13 D5
Myton Rd DARN/MH S9 .... 124 B3

N

Nairn Dr DRON S18 .... 168 B2
Nairn St FUL S10 .... 120 C4
Nanny HI STKB/PEN S36 .... 69 D2
Napier Mt BSLY S70 .... 22 A4
Napier St ECC S11 .... 134 C1
Naseby Av BTLY DN5 .... 28 B3
Naseby St DARN/MH S9 .... 111 E2
Nathan Ct MOS S20 .... 153 D4
Nathan Dr MOS S20 .... 153 D3
Nathan Gv MOS S20 .... 152 C3
Navan Rd SHEFP/MNR S2 .... 137 E3
Naylor Gv DOD/DAR S75 .... 20 A3
Naylor St RAW S62 .... 94 A3
Neale Bank STV/CWN S43 .... 185 E2
Neale Rd WHHL DN2 .... 31 F1
Nearcroft Rd KIMB S61 .... 102 A1
Nearfield Rd DONS/BSCR DN4 .... 66 B1
Needham Wy ECC S11 .... 134 A5
Needlewood DOD/DAR S75 .... 20 A4
Neepsend La OWL S3 .... 121 F1
Neild Rd HOY S74 .... 52 A2
Neill Rd ECC S11 .... 134 A2
Nelson Av BSLYN/ROY S71 .... 14 B3
Nelson Cl RHAM S60 .... 114 B4
Nelson Pl CHPT/GREN S35 .... 87 E1
Nelson Rd ST/HB/BR S6 .... 120 A1
Nelson St BSLY S70 .... 2 C6
CHNE S41 .... 184 B3
RHAM/THRY S65 .... 7 F5
Nesfield Cl CHNE S41 .... 183 E1
Nesfield Wy SHEFN S5 .... 99 E5
Nether Av CHPT/GREN S35 .... 87 E5
ECK/KIL S21 .... 166 A2
Nether Cantley La ARMTH DN3 .... 47 F2
Nether Crs CHPT/GREN S35 .... 87 E5
Nether Croft Rd STV/CWN S43 .... 185 F2
Netherdene Rd DRON S18 .... 169 E2
Nether Edge Rd ABRD S7 .... 134 C5
Netherfield Cl STKB/PEN S36 .... 70 A2
Netherfield La RAW S62 .... 94 A2
Netherfield Rd CHSW S40 .... 188 B4
FUL S10 .... 120 C2
Netherfields Crs DRON S18 .... 169 E3
Netherfield Vw RHAM/THRY S65 .... 105 E1
Nethergate ST/HB/BR S6 .... 118 C2
Nethergreen Av ECK/KIL S21 .... 166 B1
Nethergreen Ct ECK/KIL S21 .... 166 B1
Nethergreen Gdns ECK/KIL S21 .... 166 B1
Nethergreen Rd ECC S11 .... 132 C2
Nether Hall Rd DON DN1 .... 5 E3
Nether La CHPT/GREN S35 .... 88 C4
Netherleigh Rd CHSW S40 .... 188 C1
Nether Ley Av CHPT/GREN S35 .... 88 B1
Nether Ley Ct CHPT/GREN S35 .... 88 B1
Nether Ley Cft CHPT/GREN S35 .... 88 B1
Nether Ley Gdns CHPT/GREN S35 .... 88 B1
Nethermoor Av ECK/KIL S21 .... 166 B1
Nethermoor Cl ECK/KIL S21 .... 166 B1
Nethermoor Dr ECK/KIL S21 .... 166 B1
Nethermoor La ECK/KIL S21 .... 166 B1
Nether Oak Cl MOS S20 .... 153 F2
Nether Oak Dr MOS S20 .... 153 F2
Nether Oak Vw MOS S20 .... 153 F3
Nether Shire La SHEFN S5 .... 99 D2
Netherthorpe La ECK/KIL S21 .... 166 A2
Netherthorpe Pl OWL S3 .... 8 B2
Netherthorpe Rd OWL S3 .... 8 A4
Netherthorpe St OWL S3 .... 8 B1
Netherwood Rd WMB/DAR S73 .... 25 E5
Nettleham Rd SHEFS S8 .... 147 D2
Neville Av BSLY S70 .... 23 D3
Neville Cl BSLY S70 .... 23 E2
WMB/DAR S73 .... 38 C1
Neville Ct WMB/DAR S73 .... 38 C1
Neville Crs BSLY S70 .... 23 E3
Neville Dr OWL S3 .... 122 C1

Neville Rd KIMB S61 .... 92 A5
Neville St RHAM S60 .... 6 C4
Nevis Cl CHSW S40 .... 183 E5
Newark Rd MEX/SWTN S64 .... 57 F3
Newark St DARN/MH S9 .... 111 E5
New Beetwell St CHSW S40 .... 11 E6
Newbiggin Cl RAW S62 .... 93 F2
Newbiggin Dr RAW S62 .... 93 F2
Newbold Av CHNE S41 .... 183 F5
Newbold Back La CHSW S40 .... 183 E3
Newbold Dr CHSW S40 .... 183 E3
Newbold Rd CHNE S41 .... 10 D3
CHNE S41 .... 182 C2
RCH S42 .... 182 B1
Newbold Ter BTLY DN5 .... 29 D3
Newbolt Rd DONS/BSCR DN4 .... 63 F1
Newbould Crs MOS S20 .... 153 E2
Newbould La FUL S10 .... 121 D5
Newbridge Cl CHNE S41 .... 178 B5
Newbridge Dr STV/CWN S43 .... 185 E3
Newbridge Gv CONI DN12 .... 62 A5
Newbridge La CHNE S41 .... 178 C5
STV/CWN S43 .... 185 D1
Newburn Dr DARN/MH S9 .... 112 C2
Newbury Rd FUL S10 .... 120 C3
Newbury Wy BTLY DN5 .... 28 B3
Newby Crs DONS/BSCR DN4 .... 63 E2
Newby Rd CHNE S41 .... 183 D5
Newcastle St SHEF S1 .... 8 C5
Newcomen Rd BTLY DN5 .... 29 E4
Newcroft Cl MOS S20 .... 153 F2
New Cross Dr HAN/WDH S13 .... 139 E4
New Cross Wy HAN/WDH S13 .... 139 E4
New Droppingwell Rd KIMB S61 .... 100 C3
Newent La FUL S10 .... 120 C3
Newfield Av BSLYN/ROY S71 .... 15 E3
Newfield Crs DEARNE S63 .... 55 E3
TOT/DORE S17 .... 156 A1
Newfield Cft TOT/DORE S17 .... 144 A5
Newfield Farm Cl
SHEFP/MNR S2 .... 136 C5
Newfield Green Rd
SHEFP/MNR S2 .... 136 B4
Newfield La TOT/DORE S17 .... 156 A1
Newgate Cl CHPT/GREN S35 .... 73 E4
New Hall Crs STKB/PEN S36 .... 68 A1
Newhall Rd ATT S4 .... 110 C3
New Hall Rd CHSW S40 .... 189 D2
Newhall Rd DARN/MH S9 .... 111 D5
Newhaven Cl CHSW S40 .... 188 C3
New HI CONI DN12 .... 85 D1
Newhill Rd BSLYN/ROY S71 .... 14 B2
DEARNE S63 .... 55 E3
New Ings ARMTH DN3 .... 33 E3
Newington Dr AU/AST/KP S26 .... 142 C3
Newington Rd ECC S11 .... 134 A2
Newland Dl CHNE S41 .... 11 F3
Newland Gdns CHNE S41 .... 10 B1
Newlands Av CHSW S40 .... 189 D1
HACK/IN S12 .... 137 E4
Newlands Cl DONS/BSCR DN4 .... 67 D1
HACK/IN S12 .... 137 E4
Newlands Dr BTLY DN5 .... 29 D3
HACK/IN S12 .... 137 E4
Newlands Gv HACK/IN S12 .... 137 F4
Newlands Rd HACK/IN S12 .... 137 E4
Newlyn Dr BSLYN/ROY S71 .... 3 H2
Newlyn Pl SHEFS S8 .... 147 D2
Newlyn Rd SHEFS S8 .... 147 D2
Newman Cl DARN/MH S9 .... 100 C5
Newman Ct RHAM S60 .... 115 E2
Newman Dr DARN/MH S9 .... 100 B5
Newman Rd DARN/MH S9 .... 111 E1
RHAM S60 .... 115 E2
Newmarch St DARN/MH S9 .... 112 C1
Newmarket Rd DONS/BSCR DN4 .... 46 B2
New Mdw RAW S62 .... 79 E3
New Queen St CHNE S41 .... 10 D3
New DEARNE S63 .... 56 A2
DOD/DAR S75 .... 49 E3
DOD/DAR S75 .... 50 A4
DRON S18 .... 171 E2
HOY S74 .... 53 E1
KIMB S61 .... 100 C4
STKB/PEN S36 .... 69 E2
Newsam Rd MEX/SWTN S64 .... 81 E2
Newsham Rd SHEFS S8 .... 135 D5
Newsome Av WMB/DAR S73 .... 38 C2
New Station Rd MEX/SWTN S64 .... 57 F5
Newstead Cl DRON S18 .... 168 A2
HACK/IN S12 .... 150 C2
Newstead Dr HACK/IN S12 .... 150 C3
Newstead Gv HACK/IN S12 .... 150 C2
Newstead Pl HACK/IN S12 .... 150 C3
Newstead Ri HACK/IN S12 .... 150 C3
Newstead Rd BTLY DN5 .... 16 A5
HACK/IN S12 .... 150 C3
Newstead Wy HACK/IN S12 .... 150 C3
New St BSLY S70 .... 2 D6
BSLY S70 .... 21 F2
BSLY S70 .... 36 B1
BSLY S70 .... 37 D1
BSLYN/ROY S71 .... 23 F2
BTLY DN5 .... 29 E1
CHPT/GREN S35 .... 73 E3

CHSW S40 .... 190 B2
DOD/DAR S75 .... 20 A4
DON DN1 .... 44 A3
KIMB S61 .... 90 A2
KIMB S61 .... 92 C2
MEX/SWTN S64 .... 59 E5
MOS S20 .... 153 E5
RAW S62 .... 94 A1
RHAM S60 .... 127 E1
SHEF S1 .... 9 E4
WMB/DAR S73 .... 39 F2
WMB/DAR S73 .... 52 C5
New Street Bus Link MOS S20 .... 153 E5
New Street La SHEFP/MNR S2 .... 9 H4
Newton Av STKB/PEN S36 .... 68 A1
Newton Dr BTLY DN5 .... 43 D1
RHAM/THRY S65 .... 104 B3
Newton La BTLY DN5 .... 43 D1
SHEF S1 .... 122 B5
STKB/PEN S36 .... 68 A1
Newton Pl HACK/IN S12 .... 90 A3
Newton Rd CHPT/GREN S35 .... 73 F5
Newton St BSLY S70 .... 2 A5
RHAM/THRY S65 .... 104 B3
New Wortley Rd KIMB S61 .... 102 C2
Niagara Rd ST/HB/BR S6 .... 108 A1
Nicholas St BSLY S70 .... 2 A6
CHNE S41 .... 191 E5
Nicholson Av DEARNE S63 .... 55 E3
Nicholson Pl SHEFS S8 .... 135 F4
Nicholson Rd DONS/BSCR DN4 .... 43 E3
SHEFS S8 .... 135 E4
Nichols Rd ST/HB/BR S6 .... 120 B3
Nickerwood Dr AU/AST/KP S26 .... 142 B4
Nidderdale Rd KIMB S61 .... 92 A3
Nidd Rd DARN/MH S9 .... 124 B2
Nidd Rd East DARN/MH S9 .... 124 B2
Nightingale Cl RHAM S60 .... 103 E4
Nightingale Ct RHAM S60 .... 103 E4
Nightingale La STKB/PEN S36 .... 76 B5
Nightingale Rd CHPT/GREN S35 .... 97 E1
Nile St FUL S10 .... 121 D5
Ninian Gv DONS/BSCR DN4 .... 46 C4
Noble St HOY S74 .... 52 A3
Nodder Rd HAN/WDH S13 .... 138 A3
Noehill Pl SHEFP/MNR S2 .... 137 F1
Noehill Rd SHEFP/MNR S2 .... 137 F1
Nook La ST/HB/BR S6 .... 119 D1
The Nook FUL S10 .... 121 E3
Nora St DEARNE S63 .... 27 F5
Norborough Rd DARN/MH S9 .... 112 C2
WHHL DN2 .... 31 D4
Norbreck Av RHAM S60 .... 116 B3
Norbreck Wy RHAM S60 .... 116 B3
Norburn Dr ECK/KIL S21 .... 166 B2
Norbury Cl CHSW S40 .... 182 C4
DRON S18 .... 168 B2
Norcroft BSLY S70 .... 22 A4
Norfolk Cl BSLYN/ROY S71 .... 14 C3
CHSW S40 .... 188 C4
Norfolk HI CHPT/GREN S35 .... 87 D5
Norfolk La SHEF S1 .... 9 E6
Norfolk Park Av SHEFP/MNR S2 .... 136 B2
Norfolk Park Dr SHEFP/MNR S2 .... 136 A1
Norfolk Park Rd SHEFP/MNR S2 .... 136 A1
Norfolk Rd DONS/BSCR DN4 .... 63 F1
SHEFP/MNR S2 .... 123 D5
Norfolk Rw SHEF S1 .... 9 E5
Norfolk St RHAM/THRY S65 .... 7 E4
SHEF S1 .... 9 E6
Norfolk Wy RHAM S60 .... 115 E2
Norgreave Wy MOS S20 .... 164 C1
Norman Cl BSLY S70 .... 22 B5
BSLYN/ROY S71 .... 15 D3
Norman Crs BTLY DN5 .... 28 B2
Normancroft Crs
SHEFP/MNR S2 .... 138 A1
Normancroft Dr
SHEFP/MNR S2 .... 137 F1
Normancroft Wy SHEFP/MNR S2 .... 137 F1
Normandale Av ST/HB/BR S6 .... 106 B4
Normandale Rd ST/HB/BR S6 .... 108 B5
Norman St DARN/MH S9 .... 111 E5
DEARNE S63 .... 27 E3
Normanton Gdns ATT S4 .... 110 A5
Normanton Gv HAN/WDH S13 .... 139 D4
Normanton HI HACK/IN S12 .... 138 A4
Normanton Spring Ct
HAN/WDH S13 .... 138 C4
Normanton Spring Rd
HAN/WDH S13 .... 138 C5
Normanville Av RHAM S60 .... 113 F5
Norrel's Cft RHAM S60 .... 104 A5
Norris Rd ST/HB/BR S6 .... 107 F4
Norroy St ATT S4 .... 123 E1
Northampton Rd WHHL DN2 .... 32 A4
North Bridge Rd BTLY DN5 .... 9 E1
North Church St SHEF S1 .... 9 E4
North Cliff Rd CONI DN12 .... 60 C5
North Cl DRON S18 .... 170 C5
Northcote Av SHEFS S8 .... 135 F4
Northcote Rd SHEFS S8 .... 135 F4
North Crs ECK/KIL S21 .... 154 C5
RHAM/THRY S65 .... 104 B2
North Dr KIMB S61 .... 6 C2

Northern Av *SHEFP/MNR* S2.......... 136 C3
Northern Common *DRON* S18 ...... 157 F5
North Farm Ct *AU/AST/KP* S26 ...... 143 D3
Northfield Av *FUL* S10 .... 120 C2
  RAW S62 .... 80 A4
Northfield Cl *FUL* S10 .... 121 D2 🔢
Northfield Rd *BTLY* DN5................... 4 A2
  BTLY DN5....................................... 29 E4
  FUL S10 .... 120 C3
  RHAM S60 .... 6 C5
Northgate *DOD/DAR* S75 .... 13 D4
North Ga *MEX/SWTN* S64............... 59 D3
North Hill Rd *SHEFN* S5 .... 98 A5
Northlands Rd *SHEFN* S5 .... 98 A5
Northmoor Cl *STV/CWN* S43 .... 186 A2 🔢
North Moor Vw *STV/CWN* S43 .... 186 A2
North Pitt St *KIMB* S61 .... 102 A3
North Pl *DOD/DAR* S75 .... 12 C4
  RHAM/THRY S65 .... 104 B2
North Qd *SHEFN* S5........................ 99 E5
North Rd *RHAM/THRY* S65............. 104 C2
Northside Rd *DEARNE* S63.............. 56 A2
North St *CONI* DN12 .... 62 A5
  DONS/BSCR DN4.......................... 44 B3
  KIMB S61 .... 6 A3
  MEX/SWTN S64............................ 57 F5
  RAW S62 .... 80 C4
North Swaithe Cl *BTLY* DN5............ 16 B4
Northumberland Av *HOY* S74......... 51 F1
  WHHL DN2...................................... 31 F1
Northumberland Rd *FUL* S10........ 121 D4
Northumberland Wy
  BSLYN/ROY S71 .... 24 A2
Norton Av *HACK/IN* S12 .... 149 D3
  RCH S42.. 188 B4
  SHEFS S8 .... 148 B4
Norton Church Glebe *SHEFS* S8 .. 147 E4 🔢
Norton Church Rd *SHEFS* S8.......... 147 F4
Norton Green Cl *SHEFS* S8............ 148 A4
Norton Hammer La *SHEFS* S8 ...... 146 C1 🔢
Norton La *SHEFS* S8........................ 147 F5
  SHEFS S8 .... 159 E1
Norton Lees Cl *SHEFS* S8.............. 147 E2 🔢
Norton Lees Crs *SHEFS* S8............ 147 E1
Norton Lees La *SHEFS* S8.............. 147 D1
Norton Lees Rd *SHEFS* S8............. 135 D5
Norton Lees Sq *SHEFS* S8............. 147 E1
Norton Ms *SHEFS* S8...................... 148 A4
Norton Park Av *SHEFS* S8.............. 147 F5 🔢
Norton Park Crs *SHEFS* S8............ 147 E5
Norton Park Dr *SHEFS* S8.............. 147 E5
Norton Park Rd *SHEFS* S8............. 159 E1
Norton Park Vw *SHEFS* S8............. 147 E5
Norton Rd *DEARNE* S63.................. 55 E1
  SHEFS S8 .... 148 C3
  WHHL DN2...................................... 31 F4 🔢
Norwich Rd *WHHL* DN2.................. 31 E2
Norwith Rd *DONS/BSCR* DN4.......... 66 B1
Norwood Av *CHNE* S41.................. 191 F5
  SHEFN S5 .... 109 F3
Norwood Cl *SHEFN* S5 .... 109 F3
Norwood Crs *ECK/KIL* S21............ 167 D1
Norwood Dr *BTLY* DN5 .... 16 B3
  SHEFN S5 .... 109 F3
Norwood Grange Dr *SHEFN* S5 .... 109 F2
Norwood Pl *ECK/KIL* S21............... 167 D1
Norwood Rd *CONI* DN12 .... 84 C1
  SHEFN S5 .... 109 F3
Norwood St *RHAM/THRY* S65........ 95 E5
Nostell Fold *DOD/DAR* S75 .... 20 A4 🔢
Nostell Pl *DONS/BSCR* DN4............ 66 B1
Nottingham Cliff *OWL* S3 .... 122 B1
Nottingham Cl *BSLYN/ROY* S71 .... 24 B3
  BTLY DN5 .... 28 B3 🔢
Nottingham St *OWL* S3 .... 109 F5
  RHAM/THRY S65............................. 7 A3
Nowill Ct *SHEFS* S8........................ 135 E4 🔢
Nowill Pl *SHEFS* S8........................ 135 E4 🔢
Nunnery Crs *RHAM* S60.................. 127 D1
Nunnery Dr *SHEFP/MNR* S2.......... 124 A3
Nunnery Ter *SHEFP/MNR* S2......... 123 E1
Nursery Dr *CHPT/GREN* S35.......... 98 C1
  RHAM S60 .... 127 D1
Nursery Gdns *BSLY* S70 .... 23 F3 🔢
Nursery Gv *CHPT/GREN* S35.......... 98 C1
Nursery La *OWL* S3.......................... 9 F2
Nursery Rd *AU/AST/KP* S26 .... 142 A2
Nursery St *BSLY* S70 .... 21 F2
  OWL S3 .... 9 E2
Nuttall Pl *SHEFP/MNR* S2.............. 123 E4
Nutwell Cl *DONS/BSCR* DN4........... 66 C1
Nutwell La *ARMTH* DN3.................. 33 F5

Oak Av *DEARNE* S63........................ 56 B3
Oak Bank Av *CHNE* S41 .... 178 C3
Oakbank Cl *MEX/SWTN* S64............ 81 E3
Oakbank Ct *TOT/DORE* S17 .... 156 C3 🔢
Oakbrook Rd *ECC* S11..................... 133 D2
Oak Cl *ECK/KIL* S21........................ 166 A3
  HOY S74.. 51 D3

MEX/SWTN S64................................ 57 F3
Oak Ct *BTLY* DN5............................. 42 B3
  MEX/SWTN S64............................. 57 F3
Oakcrest *DONS/BSCR* DN4.............. 67 F3
Oakdale *BSLY* S70 .... 22 C5
Oakdale Pl *KIMB* S61 .... 102 A3
Oak Dale Rd *DONS/BSCR* DN4......... 62 A3
Oakdale Rd *ECC* S11...................... 134 B4
  KIMB S61 .... 102 A4
Oakdell *DRON* S18.......................... 160 B5
Oaken Wood Cl *KIMB* S61 .... 90 B1
Oaken Wood Rd *KIMB* S61 .... 90 B1
Oakes Gn *DARN/MH* S9 .... 124 A1
Oakes Park Vw *SHEFS* S8 .... 148 B4 🔢
Oakes St *DARN/MH* S9 .... 100 C5 🔢
Oakfern Gv *CHPT/GREN* S35.......... 73 E3
Oakfield Av *CHSW* S40 .... 188 C3
Oakfield Wk *DOD/DAR* S75 .... 12 C5
Oak Gv *CONI* DN12........................... 84 C2
Oak Grove Gn *TOT/DORE* S17 .... 156 C4
Oakham Dr *OWL* S3........................ 122 A1
Oakham Pl *DOD/DAR* S75 .... 13 D4
Oakhill Rd *ABRD* S7........................ 134 B4
  DRON S18..................................... 160 A5
  WHHL DN2...................................... 31 F3
Oakholme Ms *ECC* S11 .... 134 A1 🔢
Oakholme Rd *ECC* S11................... 134 A1
Oaklands Av *BSLYN/ROY* S71......... 15 E3
Oaklands Dr *DONS/BSCR* DN4........ 46 B4
Oaklands Gdns *DONS/BSCR* DN4..... 46 B5
Oaklands Pl *DEARNE* S63................ 55 F3
Oak Lea *KIMB* S61 .... 92 C3
Oak Lea Av *DEARNE* S63................. 55 D1
Oaklea Gv *BSLY* S70 .... 37 D1 🔢
Oakley Av *CHSW* S40...................... 10 B4
Oakley Rd *HAN/WDH* S13............... 125 F5
Oak Lodge Rd *CHPT/GREN* S35...... 73 D4
Oak Pk *FUL* S10 .... 120 C5
Oak Rd *ARMTH* DN3........................ 33 E1
  DEARNE S63.................................... 27 D3
  DEARNE S63.................................... 56 B3
  HACK/IN S12.................................. 149 E3
  MEX/SWTN S64............................. 57 F3
  MOS S20.. 153 D1
Oaks Av *STKB/PEN* S36................... 68 B2
Oaks Cl *DEARNE* S63....................... 56 B4
Oaks Crs *BSLY* S70 .... 23 D2
Oaks Fold Av *SHEFN* S5.................. 99 F3
Oaks Fold Rd *SHEFN* S5.................. 99 F4
Oaks La *BSLY* S70............................ 23 D2
  BSLYN/ROY S71 .... 23 D1
  KIMB S61 .... 91 D5
  SHEFN S5 .... 99 F5
Oak St *BSLY* S70.............................. 2 A6
  MOS S20.. 152 A5
  SHEFS S8 .... 135 E3
  STV/CWN S43 .... 180 B5
Oak Ter *AU/AST/KP* S26 .... 141 F2
  DONS/BSCR DN4........................... 44 A3
Oak Well La *BSLY* S70 .... 22 B2
  BSLYN/ROY S71 .... 3 F6
Oakwell Ter *BSLYN/ROY* S71 .... 22 B2 🔢
Oakwell Vw *BSLYN/ROY* S71 .... 3 C6
Oakwood Av *SHEFN* S5 .... 98 A2
Oakwood Cl *BSLY* S70..................... 37 D1
Oakwood Crs *RAW* S62 .... 79 F4
Oakwood Dr *ARMTH* DN3................ 33 E4
  RHAM S60 .... 115 F1
Oakwood Gv *RHAM* S60................. 104 B5
Oakwood Rd *DONS/BSCR* DN4........ 43 D5
Oakwood Rd East *RHAM* S60......... 115 E1
Oakwood Rd West *RHAM* S60........ 115 D1
Oakworth Cl *DOD/DAR* S75 .... 12 C4 🔢
  MOS S20.. 164 C2 🔢
Oakworth Dr *MOS* S20................... 164 B2 🔢
Oakworth Gv *MOS* S20................... 164 B2
Oakworth Vw *MOS* S20.................. 164 B2
Oates Av *RAW* S62........................... 94 B1
Oates Cl *KIMB* S61.......................... 102 B2
Oates St *KIMB* S61.......................... 102 B2
Oats Orch *MOS* S20........................ 164 B2 🔢
Occupation La *HACK/IN* S12.......... 151 D2
Occupation Rd *CHNE* S41............. 184 A1
  RAW S62 .... 75 E2
  RAW S62 .... 93 F2
Ochre Dike La *MOS* S20................. 152 C3 🔢
Ochre Dike La *MOS* S20................. 152 B3
Octavia Cl *RHAM* S60.................... 114 A2 🔢
Odom Ct *SHEFS* S8......................... 135 F4
Ogden Rd *WHHL* DN2...................... 32 B1
Oil Mill Fold *RHAM* S60................... 6 D6
Oldale Cl *HAN/WDH* S13................ 140 A5
Oldale Ct *HAN/WDH* S13................ 140 A4
Oldale Gv *HAN/WDH* S13................ 140 A4
Old Bakery Cl *CHNE* S41................ 178 B4 🔢
Old Cross La *DEARNE* S63............... 56 A2
Old Farm Ct *MEX/SWTN* S64.......... 57 F2
Oldfield Av *CONI* DN12................... 84 A1
  ST/HB/BR S6................................. 119 E1
Oldfield Cl *HOY* S74....................... 51 F2
Oldfield Gv *ST/HB/BR* S6............... 119 E2
Oldfield Rd *RHAM/THRY* S65......... 105 E2

ST/HB/BR S6................................. 119 E2
Oldfield Ter *ST/HB/BR* S6.............. 119 E2
Old Fulwood Rd *ECC* S11.............. 132 B3
Old Garden Dr *RHAM/THRY* S65 ..... 7 H3
Oldgate La *RHAM/THRY* S65........... 95 F5
Old Hall Cl *BTLY* DN5....................... 42 A4
Old Hall Pl *BTLY* DN5...................... 29 F1
Old Hall Rd *BTLY* DN5..................... 29 F1
  CHSW S40..................................... 189 E2
Oldhay Cl *TOT/DORE* S17.............. 156 B2
Old Hay Gdns *TOT/DORE* S17 .... 156 A2
Old Hay La *TOT/DORE* S17 .... 156 A2
Old Hexthorpe *DONS/BSCR* DN4 ... 43 E3 🔢
Old House Cl *WMB/DAR* S73.......... 53 D1 🔢
Old House Rd *CHSW* S40............... 183 E3 🔢
Old La *MOS* S20.............................. 165 E1
Old Mill Dr *RCH* S42....................... 182 B2
Old Mill La *BSLY* S70......................... 2 C3
  BSLYN/ROY S71 .... 3 F2
Old Mill Rd *CONI* DN12.................... 85 D2
Old Park Av *SHEFS* S8.................... 158 B1
Old Park Rd *SHEFS* S8.................... 158 B1
Old Quarry Av *AU/AST/KP* S26 ..... 155 F2
The Old Railway Yd *SHEFS* S8........ 146 B2
Old Retford Rd *HAN/WDH* S13 ..... 140 A1
Oldridge Cl *CHSW* S40................... 182 B3
  CHSW S40..................................... 188 B1
  CONI DN12...................................... 84 A3
Old School Cl *HOY* S74................... 51 F1 🔢
Old School La *RHAM* S60............... 127 E1
Old Sheffield Rd *RHAM* S60........... 103 D4
Old St *SHEFP/MNR* S2.................... 123 D3
Old Warren V *RAW* S62................... 80 B4
Oldwell Cl *TOT/DORE* S17.............. 156 B4
Old Whittington La *DRON* S18 ...... 170 C5
Old Wortley Rd *KIMB* S61.............. 101 F1
Olive Cl *AU/AST/KP* S26................. 142 B3
Olive Crs *HACK/IN* S12................... 149 E3
Olive Grove Rd *SHEFP/MNR* S2..... 135 F2
Olive Rd *MOS* S20........................... 164 B1
  STKB/PEN S36................................ 68 C2 🔢
Oliver Rd *ABRD* S7.......................... 146 A1
  DONS/BSCR DN4........................... 43 E5
Olivers Dr *DARN/MH* S9................. 125 E3
Olivers Mt *DARN/MH* S9................. 125 F3
Oliver St *MEX/SWTN* S64................ 58 A3
Olivers Wy *RHAM* S60.................... 113 F5
Olivet Rd *SHEFS* S8......................... 147 D3
Onchan Rd *ST/HB/BR* S6............... 119 F2 🔢
Onslow Rd *ECC* S11........................ 133 F3
Orange St *SHEFS* S1.......................... 8 C5
Orchard Cl *ARMTH* DN3.................. 19 F2 🔢
  BSLYN/ROY S71 .... 15 D2
  CHPT/GREN S35............................ 98 C2
  RHAM S60 .... 127 E1
Orchard Crs *SHEFS* S5.................... 98 C2
Orchard Cft *AU/AST/KP* S26 .... 155 F2
  DOD/DAR S75 .... 20 B4
Orchard Flatts Crs *KIMB* S61........ 92 B4
Orchard La *AU/AST/KP* S26 .... 155 F3
  MOS S20.. 153 D3
  SHEF S1.. 9 E5
Orchard Lea Dr *AU/AST/KP* S26 ... 142 B3 🔢
Orchard Pl *DEARNE* S63................. 55 E2
  ECK/KIL S21................................. 166 B2
  RHAM S60 .... 6 A5
Orchard Rd *ST/HB/BR* S6............... 121 D1
Orchard Sq *DRON* S18................... 168 B1
Orchard St *DONS/BSCR* DN4.......... 43 F3
  SHEF S1.. 9 E5
  STKB/PEN S36................................ 70 A3 🔢
  WMB/DAR S73................................ 39 E2
Orchards Wy *CHSW* S40................ 189 D3
Orchard View Rd *CHSW* S40.......... 183 D5
Orchard Wy *DEARNE* S63................ 27 D3
  RHAM S60 .... 114 A5
Orgreave Dr *HAN/WDH* S13.......... 140 A1
Orgreave La *HAN/WDH* S13.......... 139 E1
Orgreave Pl *HAN/WDH* S13.......... 126 C5
Orgreave Rd *RHAM* S60................. 127 D2
Orgreave Wy *HAN/WDH* S13........ 140 A2
Oriel Rd *FUL* S10............................. 132 A3
Oriel Wy *BSLYN/ROY* S71............... 15 E4
Ormesby Cl *DRON* S18................... 168 A2 🔢
Ormesby Crs *BTLY* DN5................... 28 C4
Ormes Meadow *MOS* S20.............. 152 A3
Ormond Cl *CHSW* S40.................... 188 C5 🔢
  SHEFS S8 .... 159 F2
Ormond Dr *SHEFS* S8..................... 159 F2
Ormond Rd *SHEFS* S8..................... 159 F2
Ormond Wy *SHEFS* S8.................... 159 F1
Ormsby Cl *DONS/BSCR* DN4........... 63 E3
Ormsby Rd *CHNE* S41.................... 184 A2
Orpen Dr *SHEFS* S8........................ 148 C3
Orpen Wy *SHEFS* S8....................... 148 C3 🔢
Orwell Cl *WMB/DAR* S73................ 40 A4
Osberton Pl *ECC* S11...................... 134 A2
Osberton St *RAW* S62..................... 80 C5
  RHAM/THRY S65............................. 95 D5
Osbert Rd *RHAM* S60..................... 115 F1
Osborne Av *AU/AST/KP* S26.......... 142 C2
Osborne Cl *ECC* S11....................... 134 A3 🔢
Osborne Ms *BSLY* S70.................... 22 B2 🔢
Osborne Rd *ECC* S11...................... 134 A3

WHHL DN2 .... 31 D5
Osborne St *BSLY* S70 .... 22 B2
Osgathorpe Crs *ATT* S4 .... 110 A4
Osgathorpe Dr *ATT* S4 .... 110 B4
Osgathorpe Rd *ATT* S4 .... 110 A4
Osmaston Dr *SHEFS* S8 .... 147 D3
Osmond Dr *BSLY* S70 .... 22 B5
Osmond Rd *BSLY* S70 .... 22 B5
Osmond Wy *BSLY* S70 .... 22 B5
Osmund Rd *ECK/KIL* S21 .... 163 F5
Osprey Av *BSLY* S70 .... 36 A5
Osprey Gdns *SHEFP/MNR* S2 .... 123 F5
Osprey Rd *AU/AST/KP* S26 .... 142 C4
Oswestry Rd *SHEFN* S5 .... 99 D5
Oswin Av *DONS/BSCR* DN4 .... 43 D4
Otley Cl *CONI* DN12 .... 85 E1
Otter St *DARN/MH* S9 .... 124 A1
Oughton Wy *ATT* S4 .... 110 B5
Oulton Ri *MEX/SWTN* S64 .... 59 E2
Ouseburn Cft *DARN/MH* S9 .... 124 B2
Ouseburn Rd *DARN/MH* S9 .... 124 B2
Ouseburn St *DARN/MH* S9 .... 124 B2
Ouse Rd *DARN/MH* S9 .... 124 B2
Ouslethwaite Ct *BSLY* S70 .... 21 F4
Outram Rd *CHNE* S41 .... 184 A3
SHEFP/MNR S2 .... 123 F5
Oval Rd *RHAM/THRY* S65 .... 104 C2
The Oval *CONI* DN12 .... 61 D5
DONS/BSCR DN4 .... 46 A3
SHEFN S5 .... 110 A1
Overcroft Ri *TOT/DORE* S17 .... 156 A4
Overdale Av *BSLY* S70 .... 22 C4
Overdale Gdns *TOT/DORE* S17 .... 156 A4
Overdale Ri *TOT/DORE* S17 .... 156 A2
Overdale Rd *WMB/DAR* S73 .... 39 F4
Overend Cl *GLV* S14 .... 148 B1
Overend Dr *GLV* S14 .... 148 B1
Overend Rd *GLV* S14 .... 148 B1
Overend Wy *GLV* S14 .... 148 B1
Oversley Rd *WHHL* DN2 .... 31 D3
Oversley St *DARN/MH* S9 .... 112 C1
Overton Rd *ST/HB/BR* S6 .... 107 F2
Owen Cl *RHAM/THRY* S65 .... 7 F2
ST/HB/BR S6 .... 97 E3
Owen Pl *ST/HB/BR* S6 .... 97 E3
Owler La *ATT* S4 .... 110 B3
SHEFS S8 .... 160 C3
Owler La *DRON* S18 .... 160 C4
SHEFS S8 .... 160 C3
Owlings Pl *ST/HB/BR* S6 .... 107 E4
Owlings Rd *ST/HB/BR* S6 .... 107 E4
Owlthorpe Av *MOS* S20 .... 151 F5
Owlthorpe Cl *MOS* S20 .... 151 F5
Owlthorpe Dr *MOS* S20 .... 151 F5
Owlthorpe Greenway *MOS* S20 .... 152 C4
Owlthorpe Gv *MOS* S20 .... 151 F5
Owlthorpe La *MOS* S20 .... 151 F5
Owlthorpe Ri *MOS* S20 .... 151 F5
Ox Carr *ARMTH* DN3 .... 33 E3
Ox Close Av *KIMB* S61 .... 91 F5
TOT/DORE S17 .... 157 E3
Oxclose Dr *DRON* S18 .... 168 A2
Oxclose La *DRON* S18 .... 168 A2
Oxclose Park Rd *MOS* S20 .... 165 D2
Oxclose Park Rd North *MOS* S20 .... 165 D2
Oxford Cl *KIMB* S61 .... 93 D3
STV/CWN S43 .... 186 A1
Oxford Pl *BSLYN/ROY* S71 .... 23 F2
DON DN1 .... 4 D6
Oxford Rd *STV/CWN* S43 .... 186 A1
Oxford St *BSLY* S70 .... 22 B3
BSLYN/ROY S71 .... 23 F2
MEX/SWTN S64 .... 57 F5
RHAM/THRY S65 .... 104 B2
ST/HB/BR S6 .... 108 C3
Ox HI *MOS* S20 .... 165 E3
Oxley Cl *STKB/PEN* S36 .... 69 D1
Oxley Gv *RHAM* S60 .... 104 A5
Oxspring Bank *SHEFN* S5 .... 108 B2
Oxted Rd *DARN/MH* S9 .... 111 E2
Oxton Dr *DONS/BSCR* DN4 .... 62 B1

P

Packer's Rw *CHSW* S40 .... 11 F6
Pack Horse La *CHPT/GREN* S35 .... 73 F3
Packington Rd *DONS/BSCR* DN4 .... 47 E5
Packman Rd *DEARNE* S63 .... 54 C1
Packman Wy *DEARNE* S63 .... 54 C2
Paddock Cl *BTLY* DN5 .... 28 C4
Paddock Crs *SHEFP/MNR* S2 .... 136 C5
Paddock Cft *MEX/SWTN* S64 .... 56 C5
The Paddocks *AU/AST/KP* S26 .... 142 C3
BTLY DN5 .... 28 B4
BTLY DN5 .... 61 E2
The Paddock *KIMB* S61 .... 90 C2
WMB/DAR S73 .... 39 D5
Paddock Wy *DRON* S18 .... 169 F1
Padley Wy *SHEFN* S5 .... 99 D5
Page Hall Rd *SHEFN* S5 .... 110 B3
Pagenall Dr *AU/AST/KP* S26 .... 142 B2
Paget St *DARN/MH* S9 .... 111 D5
Pagnall Av *DEARNE* S63 .... 26 B4
Paisley Cl *STV/CWN* S43 .... 187 D1

Palgrave Crs *SHEFN* S5 .... 97 F5
Palgrave Rd *SHEFN* S5 .... 97 E5
Pall Ml *BSLY* S70 .... 2 C6
Palmer Crs *DRON* S18 .... 169 F2
Palmer Rd *DARN/MH* S9 .... 125 D1
Palmersgate *CHSW* S40 .... 11 F6
Palmerston Rd *FUL* S10 .... 121 E4
Palmer St *DARN/MH* S9 .... 124 A2
DONS/BSCR DN4 .... 44 C3
Palm Gv *CONI* DN12 .... 84 B3
Palm La *ST/HB/BR* S6 .... 121 D1
Palm St *DOD/DAR* S75 .... 13 D4
ST/HB/BR S6 .... 121 D1
Pamela Dr *DONS/BSCR* DN4 .... 62 A1
Pangbourne Rd *DEARNE* S63 .... 26 C2
Pantry Gn *BSLY* S70 .... 37 D1
Pantry Hl *BSLY* S70 .... 23 D5
Pantry Well *BSLY* S70 .... 37 D1
Paper Mill Rd *SHEFN* S5 .... 99 E2
The Parade *RAW* S62 .... 79 F4
Paradise La *SHEF* S1 .... 9 E4
Paradise Sq *SHEF* S1 .... 9 E4
Paradise St *SHEF* S1 .... 9 E4
Parish Wy *BSLYN/ROY* S71 .... 15 E4
Park Av *ARMTH* DN3 .... 2 B6
BSLY S70 .... 42 A3
BTLY DN5 .... 42 A3
CHPT/GREN S35 .... 85 D2
CONI DN12 .... 85 D2
DRON S18 .... 169 F1
ECC S11 .... 133 F1
MEX/SWTN S64 .... 58 B3
RHAM S60 .... 116 A2
Park Cl *BTLY* DN5 .... 42 A3
CHSW S40 .... 190 B5
MEX/SWTN S64 .... 57 D5
Park Ct *DEARNE* S63 .... 27 D3
Park Crs *CHPT/GREN* S35 .... 98 C1
DONS/BSCR DN4 .... 62 A1
FUL S10 .... 121 E5
Park Dr *AU/AST/KP* S26 .... 141 F3
BTLY DN5 .... 42 A3
CHNE S41 .... 190 C3
Parkdrive *DOD/DAR* S75 .... 34 C1
Park Dr *STKB/PEN* S36 .... 68 C2
Park Drive Wy *STKB/PEN* S36 .... 68 C1
Parker's La *FUL* S10 .... 121 D4
Parkers La *TOT/DORE* S17 .... 144 A5
Parker's Rd *FUL* S10 .... 121 D4
Parker St *BSLY* S70 .... 2 A6
Park Farm *DRON* S18 .... 168 A1
Parkfield Ct *RAW* S62 .... 94 A3
Parkfield Rd *RHAM/THRY* S65 .... 7 G6
Parkgate Av *CONI* DN12 .... 84 B1
Parkgate Cl *MOS* S20 .... 151 E5
Parkgate Cft *MOS* S20 .... 151 E5
Parkgate Dr *HACK/IN* S12 .... 151 E4
Parkgate La *ECK/KIL* S21 .... 179 F1
Park Grange Cl *SHEFP/MNR* S2 .... 136 A1
Park Grange Cft *SHEFP/MNR* S2 .... 136 A1
Park Grange Dr *SHEFP/MNR* S2 .... 136 A2
Park Grange Mt *SHEFP/MNR* S2 .... 136 A2
Park Grange Rd *SHEFP/MNR* S2 .... 135 F1
Park Grange Vw *SHEFP/MNR* S2 .... 136 B3
Park Gv *BSLY* S70 .... 21 F2
RAW S62 .... 80 A4
STKB/PEN S36 .... 68 C1
Park Hall Av *CHSW* S40 .... 188 B4
Park Hall Cl *CHSW* S40 .... 188 C4
Park Hall Gdns *CHSW* S40 .... 188 C4
Parkhead Cl *ECC* S11 .... 145 D1
Parkhead Crs *ECC* S11 .... 145 D1
Parkhead Rd *ECC* S11 .... 145 D2
Park Hl *AU/AST/KP* S26 .... 141 F3
ECK/KIL S21 .... 164 C5
Park Hill Rd *WMB/DAR* S73 .... 39 F2
Park Hollow *WMB/DAR* S73 .... 40 A3
Park House La *DARN/MH* S9 .... 113 D3
Park La *CHNE* S41 .... 184 A1
CHPT/GREN S35 .... 69 E1
DONS/BSCR DN4 .... 46 A2
FUL S10 .... 121 E5
Park Mt *RHAM/THRY* S65 .... 7 F6
Park Nook *RHAM/THRY* S65 .... 95 F4
Park Pl *RHAM/THRY* S65 .... 104 C2
Park Rd *BSLY* S70 .... 36 B1
BTLY DN5 .... 16 B4
BTLY DN5 .... 16 B5
CHSW S40 .... 11 E6
CONI DN12 .... 84 C2
DEARNE S63 .... 26 C3
DEARNE S63 .... 55 F3
DON DN1 .... 5 F3
MEX/SWTN S64 .... 80 C1
MEX/SWTN S64 .... 80 C1
RHAM/THRY S65 .... 104 B2
ST/HB/BR S6 .... 120 A1
Parkside La *ST/HB/BR* S6 .... 119 E2
Parkside Ms *BSLY* S70 .... 22 B5
Parkside Rd *HOY* S74 .... 50 C4
ST/HB/BR S6 .... 108 A3
Parkson Rd *RHAM* S60 .... 115 F2
Park Spring Dr *SHEFP/MNR* S2 .... 136 A2
Park Spring Gv *SHEFP/MNR* S2 .... 136 A2

Park Spring Pl *SHEFP/MNR* S2 .... 136 A2
Park Spring Wy *SHEFP/MNR* S2 .... 136 A2
Park Square Rbt *ATT* S4 .... 9 G5
Parkstone Delph *HACK/IN* S12 .... 149 E3
Parkstone Wy *WHHL* DN2 .... 32 A2
Park St *AU/AST/KP* S26 .... 142 A3
BSLY S70 .... 21 F2
CHSW S40 .... 190 B5
KIMB S61 .... 102 C2
RAW S62 .... 80 A5
WMB/DAR S73 .... 39 F3
Park Ter *CHPT/GREN* S35 .... 88 C2
DON DN1 .... 5 F3
Parkview *BSLY* S70 .... 22 C5
Park Vw *CHNE* S41 .... 191 E5
DOD/DAR S75 .... 20 A3
Park View Av *MOS* S20 .... 164 C1
Park View Rd *CHPT/GREN* S35 .... 88 B2
KIMB S61 .... 101 D4
ST/HB/BR S6 .... 108 A3
Parkway *ARMTH* DN3 .... 33 F4
Parkway Av *DARN/MH* S9 .... 124 A3
Parkway Cl *DARN/MH* S9 .... 124 A3
Parkway Dr *DARN/MH* S9 .... 124 B3
Parkway North *WHHL* DN2 .... 31 D3
Parkway South *WHHL* DN2 .... 31 E3
Parkwood Rd *OWL* S3 .... 108 C5
Parkwood Rd North *SHEFN* S5 .... 109 D3
ST/HB/BR S6 .... 109 D3
Parliament St *ECC* S11 .... 134 C1
Parma Ri *WMB/DAR* S73 .... 25 F1
Parsley Hay Cl *HAN/WDH* S13 .... 139 D1
Parsley Hay Dr *HAN/WDH* S13 .... 139 D1
Parsley Hay Gdns *HAN/WDH* S13 .... 139 D1
Parsley Hay Rd *HAN/WDH* S13 .... 139 D1
Parsonage Cl *MOS* S20 .... 164 B2
Parsonage Crs *ST/HB/BR* S6 .... 121 D1
Parsonage St *ST/HB/BR* S6 .... 121 D1
Parson Cross Rd *ST/HB/BR* S6 .... 97 D5
Partridge Cl *ECK/KIL* S21 .... 163 F5
Partridge Flatt Rd 67 D1
Partridge Pl *AU/AST/KP* S26 .... 142 C4
Partridge Ri *DONS/BSCR* DN4 .... 67 D1
Partridge Vw *SHEFP/MNR* S2 .... 123 F5
Parwich Cl *CHSW* S40 .... 182 B4
Pashley Cft *WMB/DAR* S73 .... 38 C3
Passhouses Rd *ATT* S4 .... 109 F4
Pasture Cl *ARMTH* DN3 .... 33 E4
Pasture Gv *ECK/KIL* S21 .... 164 A5
Pasture La *BTLY* DN5 .... 60 C2
DEARNE S63 .... 41 E1
Pastures Rd *MEX/SWTN* S64 .... 59 F3
Paternoster Rw *SHEF* S1 .... 122 C5
Paterson Cl *STKB/PEN* S36 .... 68 B1
Paterson Ct *STKB/PEN* S36 .... 68 B1
Paterson Cft *STKB/PEN* S36 .... 68 B1
Paterson Gdns *STKB/PEN* S36 .... 68 B1
Patmore Rd *SHEFN* S5 .... 99 E5
Paton Gv *STV/CWN* S43 .... 185 E1
Patrick Stirling Ct
DONS/BSCR DN4 .... 43 E3
Patterdale Cl *DRON* S18 .... 168 C2
Pavilion La *RHAM* S60 .... 113 F2
Pavillion Cl *CONI* DN12 .... 62 A4
Paxton Crs *ARMTH* DN3 .... 33 D2
Paxton La *FUL* S10 .... 121 E5
Paxton Rd *CHNE* S41 .... 185 D4
Payler Cl *SHEFP/MNR* S2 .... 137 D2
Payne Crs *RAW* S62 .... 79 F4
Peacock Cl *ECK/KIL* S21 .... 166 A2
KIMB S61 .... 76 A5
Pea Fields La *CHPT/GREN* S35 .... 72 A1
Peakdale Crs *HACK/IN* S12 .... 138 C5
Peake Av *CONI* DN12 .... 84 B1
Peak Pl *STV/CWN* S43 .... 187 E2
Peaks Mt *MOS* S20 .... 152 C2
Peak View Rd *CHSW* S40 .... 183 E5
Pearce Dr *DARN/MH* S9 .... 125 D4
Pearce Wk *DARN/MH* S9 .... 125 D4
Pearl St *ECC* S11 .... 134 C2
Pea Royd La *STKB/PEN* S36 .... 69 D1
Pearson Crs *WMB/DAR* S73 .... 38 C1
Pearson Pl *SHEFS* S8 .... 147 D1
Pearson's Cl *RHAM/THRY* S65 .... 105 D5
Pearson's Fld *WMB/DAR* S73 .... 39 E2
Pearson St *STKB/PEN* S36 .... 68 C1
Pear St *ECC* S11 .... 134 C1
Peartree Av *DEARNE* S63 .... 26 C3
Pear Tree Cl *ECK/KIL* S21 .... 166 A3
RHAM S60 .... 114 B4
STV/CWN S43 .... 186 B1
Pear Tree Rd *SHEFN* S5 .... 99 E3
Pearwood Crs *DONS/BSCR* DN4 .... 63 D2
Peasehill Cl *BSLY* S70 .... 21 F2
Peashill St *RAW* S62 .... 94 A1
Peatfield Rd *ECK/KIL* S21 .... 167 D1
Peckham Rd *CHPT/GREN* S35 .... 74 A5
Pedley Av *MOS* S20 .... 152 C4
Pedley Cl *MOS* S20 .... 152 C5
Pedley Dr *MOS* S20 .... 152 C5
Pedley Gv *MOS* S20 .... 152 C4
Peel Pde *BSLY* S70 .... 2 B5
Peel Pl *BSLYN/ROY* S71 .... 3 F1
Peel Sq *BSLY* S70 .... 2 C5

Peel St *BSLY* S70 .... 2 B5
FUL S10 .... 121 D5 ⁵
Pell's Cl *DON* DN1 .... 4 D4 ²
Pembrey Ct *MOS* S20 .... 153 E3
Pembroke Av *DONS/BSCR* DN4 .... 63 E1
Pembroke Cl *CHSW* S40 .... 189 D3 ²
Pembroke Crs *CHPT/GREN* S35 .... 75 E5
Pembroke Ri *BTLY* DN5 .... 28 B3
Pembroke Rd *DRON* S18 .... 169 E3
Pembroke St *ECC* S11 .... 134 C1 ⁹
KIMB S61 .... 102 A5
Pendeen Rd *ECC* S11 .... 133 D2 ⁶
Pendlebury Gv *HOY* S74 .... 51 D3 ⁸
Pendle Cft *MOS* S20 .... 153 F4 ⁴
Penistone Rd *CHPT/GREN* S35 .... 87 C3
OWL S3 .... 8 B1
Penistone St *DON* DN1........................... 5 F2
Penley St *ECC* S11 .... 135 D2 ⁷
Penmore Cl *CHNE* S41 .... 191 D3
Penmore Gdns *CHNE* S41 .... 191 D4
Penmore La *CHNE* S41 .... 191 D4
Penmore St *CHNE* S41 .... 191 D4
Pennine Vw *STKB/PEN* S36 .... 68 C4
Pennine Wy *CHSW* S40....................... 183 D4
DOD/DAR S75 .... 12 C5
Pen Nook Cl *STKB/PEN* S36 .... 69 E4
Pen Nook Ct *STKB/PEN* S36 .... 69 F4 ⁴
Pen Nook Dr *STKB/PEN* S36 .... 69 F4
Pen Nook Gdns *STKB/PEN* S36 .... 69 F4
Penns Rd *SHEFP/MNR* S2 .... 136 A4
Penny Engine La *ECK/KIL* S21 .... 164 C4
Penny La *TOT/DORE* S17 .... 156 A3
Penrhyn Rd *ECC* S11 .... 134 A3
Penrhyn Wk *BSLYN/ROY* S71 .... 24 B2
Penrith Cl *SHEFN* S5 .... 108 C2
Penrith Crs *SHEFN* S5 .... 108 C2
Penrith Gv *BSLYN/ROY* S71 .... 24 A2
Penrith Rd *SHEFN* S5 .... 108 C2
Penrose Pl *HAN/WDH* S13 .... 139 E4
Penthorpe Cl *HACK/IN* S12 .... 137 F4 ⁸
Pentland Cl *CHSW* S40 .... 183 D4 ⁸
Pentland Gdns *MOS* S20 .... 152 B3
Pentland Rd *DRON* S18 .... 168 B2
Penton St *SHEF* S1 .... 8 D5 ⁵
Penyghent Cl *CHPT/GREN* S35 .... 74 A5 ⁷
Pepper Cl *KIMB* S61 .... 91 E3 ⁷
Pepper St *HOY* S74 .... 37 F5
Percy St *OWL* S3 .... 8 C1
RHAM/THRY S65 .... 7 E5
Peregrine Dr *BSLY* S70 .... 36 A5
Perigree Rd *SHEFS* S8 .... 146 C2
Periwood Av *SHEFS* S8 .... 146 C2 ⁸
Periwood Cl *SHEFS* S8 .... 146 C2 ⁸
Periwood Dr *SHEFS* S8 .... 146 C2 ⁸
Periwood Gv *SHEFS* S8 .... 146 C2 ⁸
Perkyn Rd *SHEFN* S5 .... 99 D2
Perkyn Ter *SHEFN* S5 .... 99 D2
Perran Gv *BTLY* DN5 .... 29 D4
Perseverance St *BSLY* S70 .... 21 E1 ⁸
Perth Cl *MEX/SWTN* S64 .... 59 D2
Peterborough Cl *FUL* S10 .... 131 E2
Peterborough Dr *FUL* S10 .... 131 E1
Peterborough Rd *FUL* S10 .... 131 E1
Peterdale Cl *STV/CWN* S43 .... 185 F1
Peterdale Rd *STV/CWN* S43 .... 185 F1
Petersgate *BTLY* DN5 .... 29 D1
Peter St *KIMB* S61 .... 101 F2
Petre Dr *ATT* S4 .... 110 C4
Petre St *ATT* S4 .... 110 B5
Pettyclose La *CHNE* S41 .... 178 A5
Petworth Dr *ECC* S11 .... 145 D3
Pevensey Av *CHNE* S41 .... 183 F3
Peveril Rd *CHNE* S41 .... 184 A2 ¹
ECC S11 .... 133 F3
ECK/KIL S21.................................... 164 C4
Pexton Rd *ATT* S4 .... 110 A4
Philadelphia Dr *ST/HB/BR* S6 .... 8 A1
Philadelphia Gdns *ST/HB/BR* S6 .... 8 A1
Philadelphia Gv *ST/HB/BR* S6 .... 8 A1
Philip Rd *BSLY* S70 .... 23 E3
Phillimore Rd *DARN/MH* S9 .... 124 C1
Phillips Rd *ST/HB/BR* S6 .... 106 B3
Phoenix Ct *HACK/IN* S12 .... 150 C4
Phoenix Gv *RHAM* S60 .... 113 F3
Phoenix La *DEARNE* S63 .... 27 E4
Phoenix Rd *DARN/MH* S9 .... 112 C1
HACK/IN S12 .... 150 C4
Piccadilly *BTLY* DN5 .... 29 E1
Piccadilly Rd *CHNE* S41 .... 190 C2
MEX/SWTN S64.................................. 81 D2
Pickering Crs *AU/AST/KP* S26 .... 142 A4
Pickering Rd *BTLY* DN5 .... 16 B5
OWL S3 .... 109 D5
Pickering St *DARN/MH* S9 .... 111 F4 ⁸
Pickhill's Av *DEARNE* S63 .... 27 F5
Pickmere Rd *FUL* S10 .... 120 C3
Pickton Cl *CHSW* S40 .... 189 D2 ⁸
Pickup Crs *WMB/DAR* S73 .... 39 E4
Pickwick Dr *RHAM* S60 .... 126 C1
Piece End *CHPT/GREN* S35 .... 73 E3
Piece End Cl *CHPT/GREN* S35 .... 73 E3 ⁸
The Pieces North *RHAM* S60 .... 115 F4
The Pieces South *RHAM* S60 .... 115 F4
Pighills La *DRON* S18 .... 159 F4
Pike Cl *CHSW* S40 .... 182 C4 ⁸

Pike Rd *RHAM* S60 .... 114 A3
Pilgrim St *OWL* S3 .... 109 F5
Pilley Gn *DOD/DAR* S75 .... 49 E3
Pilley Hl *DOD/DAR* S75 .... 20 A4 ⁸
Pilley La *DOD/DAR* S75 .... 49 E2
Pinchfield Ct *MALT* S66 .... 117 F1
Pinchfield Holt *MALT* S66 .... 117 F1
Pinchfield La *MALT* S66 .... 117 F1
Pinchmill Hollow *MALT* S66................ 117 F2
Pinch Mill La *RHAM* S60 .... 116 C3
Pindale Av *STV/CWN* S43 .... 187 D2
Pindar Oaks Cottages *BSLY* S70 .... 22 C3 ⁸
Pindar Oaks St *BSLY* S70 .... 22 B2
Pindar St *BSLY* S70 .... 22 C2 ⁸
Pine Cl *BSLY* S70 .... 23 D4
ECK/KIL S21 .... 166 A5
HOY S74 .... 51 F3
Pine Cft *CHPT/GREN* S35 .... 88 B2
Pinecroft Wy *CHPT/GREN* S35 .... 88 B2
Pine Gv *CONI* DN12 .... 84 B3
Pinehall Dr *BSLYN/ROY* S71 .... 15 E3
Pinehurst Ri *MEX/SWTN* S64 .... 81 E1
Pine Rd *DONS/BSCR* DN4 .... 47 D4
The Pines *FUL* S10 .... 131 E2
Pine St *STV/CWN* S43 .... 186 B1
Pine Vw *CHSW* S40 .... 188 C1
Pine Wk *MEX/SWTN* S64 .... 81 E3
Pinewood Av *ARMTH* DN3 .... 33 F1
DONS/BSCR DN4 .... 62 C2 ⁸
Pinfold Cl *BSLYN/ROY* S71 .... 23 F2 ⁸
MEX/SWTN S64 .... 81 D1
Pinfold Hl *BSLY* S70 .... 22 B4
Pinfold Lands *MEX/SWTN* S64 .... 58 C4
Pinfold La *OWL* S3 .... 109 E5
RHAM/THRY S65 .... 7 F6 ⁸
RHAM/THRY S65 .... 103 F4 ⁸
Pinfold St *ECK/KIL* S21 .... 164 B5
Pingle Av *ABRD* S7 .... 146 A2
Pingle Gra *STV/CWN* S43 .... 185 F2
Pingle Rd *ABRD* S7 .... 146 A2
ECK/KIL S21................................... 166 C1
Pingles Crs *RHAM/THRY* S65 .... 95 F4
Pinner Rd *ECC* S11 .... 134 A5
Pipe House La *RAW* S62 .... 80 A4 ⁸
Piper Cl *SHEFN* S5 .... 109 F1
Piper Crs *SHEFN* S5 .... 109 E1 ⁸
Piper Crs *SHEFN* S5 .... 109 E1
Pipering La (East) *BTLY* DN5 .... 29 D2
Pipering La (West) *BTLY* DN5 .... 28 C2
Piper La *AU/AST/KP* S26 .... 143 D3
Piper Rd *SHEFN* S5 .... 109 F1
Pipeyard La *ECK/KIL* S21 .... 164 A5
Pipworth Gv *SHEFP/MNR* S2 .... 138 A1
Pipworth La *ECK/KIL* S21 .... 165 D4
Pisgah House Rd *FUL* S10 .... 121 D4 ⁸
Pitchford La *FUL* S10 .... 132 B1
Pithouse La *AU/AST/KP* S26 .... 154 A2
Pit La *HAN/WDH* S13 .... 137 E4
KIMB S61 .... 90 A3
RHAM S60 .... 128 A3
Pitman Rd *CONI* DN12 .... 59 F5
Pitsmoor Rd *ATT* S4 .... 109 F5
OWL S3 .... 122 B1
Pittam Cl *ARMTH* DN3 .... 33 F3
Pitt Cl *SHEF* S1 .... 8 B6
Pitt La *SHEF* S1 .... 8 B6 ⁸
Pitt St *BSLY* S70 .... 2 B6
ECK/KIL S21 .... 174 A1
KIMB S61 .... 102 A3
MEX/SWTN S64 .... 59 D3
SHEF S1 .... 8 B6
WMB/DAR S73 .... 25 F5
Pitt St West *BSLY* S70 .... 2 A6 ⁸
Plank Ga *STKB/PEN* S36 .... 70 B4
Plantation Av *DONS/BSCR* DN4 .... 67 F3
Plantation Rd *SHEFS* S8 .... 135 E4 ⁸
Plantin Ri *MOS* S20 .... 164 C1 ⁸
The Plantin *MOS* S20 .... 164 C1
Platts Dr *MOS* S20 .... 153 E1
Platt St *OWL* S3 .... 122 B1
Pleasant Cl *HACK/IN* S12 .... 137 F4 ⁸
Pleasant Rd *HACK/IN* S12 .... 137 F4
Pleasley Rd *RHAM* S60 .... 115 E3
Plover Cl *SHEFP/MNR* S2 .... 123 F5 ⁸
Plover Cft *KIMB* S61 .... 76 B5
Plover Dr *BSLY* S70 .... 36 A5
Plowright Dr *SHEFP/MNR* S2 .... 136 B5
Plowright Ms *SHEFP/MNR* S2 .... 136 B5
Plowright Wy *SHEFP/MNR* S2 .... 136 B5 ⁸
Plumber St *BSLY* S70 .... 2 A5
Plumbley Hall Ms *MOS* S20 .... 164 A2
Plumbley Hall Rd *MOS* S20 .... 164 A1 ⁸
Plumbley La *MOS* S20 .... 163 F2
Plum La *OWL* S3 .... 8 C1
Plumper's Rd *DARN/MH* S9 .... 112 B2 ⁸
Plumpton Av *MEX/SWTN* S64 .... 59 D2
Plumpton Gdns *DONS/BSCR* DN4 .... 67 E1
Plumpton Park Rd
DONS/BSCR DN4 .... 67 E2
Plum St *OWL* S3 .... 9 E3
Plunket Rd *WHNL* DN2 .... 31 D5
Plymouth Rd *ABRD* S7 .... 134 C5
Pogmoor La *DOD/DAR* S75 .... 12 B5
Pogmoor Rd *DOD/DAR* S75................. 20 C1
Pole Hl *SHEFS* S8 .... 147 E3

Polka Ct *OWL* S3 .... 122 B1
Pollard Av *SHEFN* S5 .... 108 C1
Pollard Crs *SHEFN* S5 .... 108 C1
Pollard Rd *SHEFN* S5 .... 108 C1
Pollard St *KIMB* S61 .... 101 F3
Pollitt St *DOD/DAR* S75 .... 2 A2
Pomona St *ECC* S11 .... 134 C1
Pond Cl *ST/HB/BR* S6 .... 119 E1
Pond Hl *SHEF* S1 .... 9 G5
Pond Rd *ST/HB/BR* S6 .... 119 E1
Pond St *BSLY* S70 .... 21 F2
CHSW S40 .... 190 B2
SHEF S1 .... 9 F5
Pondwell Dr *STV/CWN* S43 .... 186 A2
Pontefract Rd *BSLYN/ROY* S71 .... 3 F6
DEARNE S63 .... 54 C1
Pool Dr *DONS/BSCR* DN4 .... 67 F1
Poole Pl *DARN/MH* S9 .... 125 D3
Poole Rd *DARN/MH* S9 .... 125 D3
Pool's La *ECK/KIL* S21 .... 172 A4
Pool Sq *SHEF* S1 .... 9 E5
Pope Av *CONI* DN12 .... 84 A1
Poplar Av *CHSW* S40 .... 188 C3
MOS S20 .... 141 D5
RHAM/THRY S65 .... 95 F4
STKB/PEN S36................................. 68 C3
Poplar Cl *DRON* S18 .... 170 A4 ⁸
ECK/KIL S21 .... 166 A3
MEX/SWTN S64................................ 58 A2
Poplar Dr *DEARNE* S63 .... 56 A4
RHAM S60 .... 113 F4
Poplar Gv *BSLYN/ROY* S71 .... 15 F3
CONI DN12 .... 84 C2
DONS/BSCR DN4.............................. 62 A3
MEX/SWTN S64............................... 57 E5 ⁸
Poplar Pl *ARMTH* DN3 .... 33 F3
Poplar Rd *ECK/KIL* S21 .... 174 A1
WMB/DAR S73 .... 39 F4
Poplars Rd *BSLY* S70 .... 22 C3
The Poplars *CONI* DN12 .... 84 C2
Poplar Ter *BTLY* DN5 .... 29 F1 ⁸
Poplar Wy *RHAM* S60 .... 126 B2
Popple St *ATT* S4 .... 110 C3
Porter Brook Vw *ECC* S11 .... 134 B2
Porter St *STV/CWN* S43 .... 181 F4
Porter Ter *DOD/DAR* S75 .... 12 C5 ⁸
Portland Av *AU/AST/KP* S26 .... 142 C3
Portland Ct *ST/HB/BR* S6 .... 121 F1
Portland La *SHEF* S1 .... 8 B6
Portland Pl *DON* DN1 .... 4 D5
Portland Rd *MOS* S20 .... 153 E3
Portland St *BSLY* S70 .... 22 C2
MEX/SWTN S64............................... 57 E5
ST/HB/BR S6 .... 121 F2
Portobello *SHEF* S1 .... 8 B5
Portobello St *SHEF* S1 .... 8 C5
Portsea Rd *ST/HB/BR* S6 .... 107 F4
Pot House La *STKB/PEN* S36 .... 80 A3
Potterdyke Av *RAW* S62 .... 80 A3
Potter Hl *KIMB* S61 .... 93 D3
Potter Hill La *CHPT/GREN* S35 .... 73 D4
Potteric Carr Rd *DONS/BSCR* DN4 ...... 44 C3
Potters Cl *CHNE* S41 .... 178 C4
Potters Ga *CHPT/GREN* S35 .... 73 D4
Pottery Cl *RAW* S62 .... 94 A1
Pottery La East *CHNE* S41 .... 184 C1
Pottery La West *CHNE* S41 .... 184 B2
Poucher St *KIMB* S61 .... 101 D3
Poulton St *BSLYN/ROY* S71 .... 15 E1
Powder Mill La *BSLY* S70 .... 37 D2
Powell Dr *ECK/KIL* S21 .... 166 A2
Powell St *BSLY* S70 .... 36 C1
OWL S3 .... 121 F3
Power Station Rd *BTLY* DN5 .... 4 A1
Powley Rd *ST/HB/BR* S6 .... 97 D4
Poynton Av *AU/AST/KP* S26 .... 129 F4
Poynton Wy *AU/AST/KP* S26 .... 129 F4
Poynton Wood Crs
TOT/DORE S17 .... 157 E2 ⁸
Poynton Wood Gld
TOT/DORE S17 .... 157 E2
Prescott Rd *ST/HB/BR* S6 .... 107 E2
President Wy *ATT* S4 .... 123 D2
Preston Av *HOY* S74 .... 52 B1
Preston St *SHEFP/MNR* S2 .... 135 E3 ⁷
Preston Wy *BSLYN/ROY* S71 .... 15 E1
Prestwich St *DARN/MH* S9 .... 100 C5 ⁷
Priestfield Gdns *CHSW* S40 .... 182 C2 ⁸
Priestley Av *RAW* S62 .... 80 C4
Priestley Cl *DONS/BSCR* DN4 .... 63 D2
Priestley St *SHEFP/MNR* S2 .... 135 F1
Primrose Av *RHAM* S60 .... 114 B5 ⁸
SHEFS S8 .... 99 F5
Primrose Cl *ECK/KIL* S21 .... 166 C1
Primrose Crs *MOS* S20 .... 153 D2 ⁸
Primrose Dr *CHPT/GREN* S35 .... 98 C1
Primrose Hl *KIMB* S61 .... 6 B2
ST/HB/BR S6 .... 121 F1 ⁸
Primrose La *ECK/KIL* S21 .... 154 C5
Primrose Wy *HOY* S74 .... 51 F4 ⁸
Prince Arthur St *DOD/DAR* S75 .... 2 A3
Prince of Wales Rd *DARN/MH* S9 ..... 125 D4
SHEFP/MNR S2............................... 137 F2 ⁷
Prince's Rd *DONS/BSCR* DN4 .... 46 A3 ⁸

Princess Ct *SHEFF/MNR* S2 .... **137** F2 🔲
Princess Dr *DEARNE* S63 .... **27** E4
   STKB/PEN S36 .... **69** D4
Princess Gdns *WMB/DAR* S73 .... **39** E3
Princess Gv *DOD/DAR* S75 .... **49** D3
Princess Rd *DRON* S18 .... **169** E1
   MEX/SWTN S64 .... **58** C3
Princess St *ATT* S4 .... **123** E2
   BSLY S70 .... **2** B6
   CHNE S41 .... **10** D3
   DEARNE S63 .... **55** E1
   HOY S74 .... **50** C3
   STV/CWN S43 .... **180** A5
   WMB/DAR S73 .... **39** D2 🔲
Prince's St *DON* DN1 .... **5** F4
Princes St *RHAM* S60 .... **102** C3
Prince St *MEX/SWTN* S64 .... **57** E4
Pringle Rd *RHAM* S60 .... **113** F3
Printing Office St *DON* DN1 .... **4** D4
Prior Rd *CONI* DN12 .... **84** C2
Priory Av *ECC* S11 .... **135** D2
Priory Cl *BSLY* S70 .... **36** A3
   CHPT/GREN S35 .... **88** B5
   CONI DN12 .... **61** D5
Priory Crs *BSLYN/ROY* S71 .... **15** F4
Priory Pl *ABRD* S7 .... **135** D2
   BSLYN/ROY S71 .... **15** F3
   DON DN1 .... **4** D4
Priory Rd *ABRD* S7 .... **134** C3
   BSLYN/ROY S71 .... **15** F3
   CHPT/GREN S35 .... **88** B5
Priory Wy *AU/AST/KP* S26 .... **142** C3
Pritchard Cl *HACK/IN* S12 .... **151** F2
Private Dr *STV/CWN* S43 .... **186** B1
Proctor Pl *ST/HB/BR* S6 .... **108** A4
Prospect Dr *TOT/DORE* S17 .... **157** C3
Prospect Pl *TOT/DORE* S17 .... **157** E2
Prospect Rd *BTLY* DN5 .... **16** B2
   CHNE S41 .... **178** A4
   DRON S18 .... **160** A5
   SHEFP/MNR S2 .... **135** E3
   SHEFS S8 .... **135** E3
   TOT/DORE S17 .... **157** E3
Prospect St *BSLY* S70 .... **2** A5
Providence Ct *BSLY* S70 .... **22** A2 🔲
Providence Rd *ST/HB/BR* S6 .... **120** C1
Providence St *KIMB* S61 .... **93** D3
   RHAM S60 .... **6** A6
   WMB/DAR S73 .... **40** A1 🔲
Psalter La *ECC* S11 .... **133** D3
Psalters Ct *KIMB* S61 .... **102** A2
Purbeck Av *CHSW* S40 .... **185** E5
Purbeck Cl *MOS* S20 .... **152** B3 🔲
Purbeck Gv *MOS* S20 .... **152** B3
Purbeck Rd *MOS* S20 .... **152** B3
Pye Bank Cl *OWL* S3 .... **122** B1 🔲
Pye Bank Dr *OWL* S3 .... **122** B1
Pye Bank Rd *OWL* S3 .... **122** B1
Pym Rd *MEX/SWTN* S64 .... **58** B3
Pynot Rd *CHNE* S41 .... **178** C4 🔲

Q

The Quadrant *TOT/DORE* S17 .... **156** C3
Quail Ri *SHEFP/MNR* S2 .... **125** F5 🔲
Quaker Cl *DEARNE* S63 .... **55** E3
Quaker La *BSLYN/ROY* S71 .... **24** A2
   DONS/BSCR DN4 .... **62** B1
Quantock Wy *CHSW* S40 .... **182** C4
Quarry Bank *DEARNE* S63 .... **54** C2
Quarry Bank Rd *CHNE* S41 .... **191** D2 🔲
Quarry Cl *RHAM* S60 .... **113** E4
Quarry Field La *MALT* S66 .... **117** F2
Quarry Flds *MALT* S66 .... **117** F1
Quarry Hl *ECK/KIL* S21 .... **172** B1
   HACK/IN S12 .... **151** E5
   RHAM S60 .... **6** D6
Quarry Hill Rd *DEARNE* S63 .... **55** F4
Quarry La *CHSW* S40 .... **189** D2
   ECC S11 .... **134** A4
   KIMB S61 .... **6** A2
Quarry Rd *DRON* S18 .... **171** E2 🔲
   ECK/KIL S21 .... **166** A1
   HAN/WDH S13 .... **125** F4
   HOY S74 .... **37** E4 🔲
   TOT/DORE S17 .... **156** C3
Quarry St *BSLY* S70 .... **22** A2 🔲
   BSLYN/ROY S71 .... **14** B2 🔲
   MEX/SWTN S64 .... **58** C4
   RAW S62 .... **80** A5
Quarry Vale Gv *HACK/IN* S12 .... **150** A1
Quarry Vale Rd *HACK/IN* S12 .... **150** A1
Queen Gdns *WMB/DAR* S73 .... **39** E3
Queen Mary Cl *SHEFP/MNR* S2 .... **137** E3 🔲
Queen Mary Crs *SHEFP/MNR* S2 .... **137** E2
Queen Mary Gv *SHEFP/MNR* S2 .... **137** D3 🔲
Queen Mary Ms *SHEFP/MNR* S2 .... **137** E3 🔲
Queen Mary Rd *CHSW* S40 .... **188** C3
   SHEFP/MNR S2 .... **137** D2
Queen's Av *DOD/DAR* S75 .... **13** E5
   MEX/SWTN S64 .... **57** E4
Queensberry Rd *WHHL* DN2 .... **32** A5
Queen's Ct *BTLY* DN5 .... **29** E3 🔲

Queens Crs *HOY* S74 .... **50** B3 🔲
Queen's Dr *BTLY* DN5 .... **29** E3
   DOD/DAR S75 .... **13** D4
   DOD/DAR S75 .... **20** A3
Queens Gdns *DOD/DAR* S75 .... **13** D4
   HOY S74 .... **50** C3 🔲
Queensgate *CHPT/GREN* S35 .... **97** E1 🔲
Queens Rd *AU/AST/KP* S26 .... **142** A3
   BSLYN/ROY S71 .... **3** E5
   DON DN1 .... **5** G1
   MOS S20 .... **153** D1
   SHEFP/MNR S2 .... **135** E2
Queen's Rw *OWL* S3 .... **8** C2
Queen's Ter *MEX/SWTN* S64 .... **58** B3
Queen St *BSLY* S70 .... **2** C5
   CHPT/GREN S35 .... **74** B5
   CHSW S40 .... **10** D4
   DEARNE S63 .... **27** E4
   DONS/BSCR DN4 .... **43** F4 🔲
   ECK/KIL S21 .... **164** C5
   HOY S74 .... **50** B3
   MEX/SWTN S64 .... **57** E5
   MOS S20 .... **164** A5
   RAW S62 .... **80** B4
   RHAM/THRY S65 .... **104** B2
   SHEF S1 .... **9** E4
   STV/CWN S43 .... **180** A5
   STV/CWN S43 .... **187** E1
Queen St North *CHNE* S41 .... **184** B1
Queensway *BSLY* S70 .... **36** C1
   DOD/DAR S75 .... **13** D4 🔲
   HOY S74 .... **52** A2
   RHAM S60 .... **115** D2
Queen Victoria Rd *TOT/DORE* S17 .... **157** D3
Quest Av *WMB/DAR* S73 .... **38** C5
Quiet La *ECC* S11 .... **131** F4
Quintec Ct *RAW* S62 .... **93** F5
Quoit Gn *DRON* S18 .... **169** F2
Quorn Dr *CHSW* S40 .... **182** B4 🔟

R

Raby Rd *WHHL* DN2 .... **31** D4
Raby St *DARN/MH* S9 .... **112** C1
Racecommon La *BSLY* S70 .... **21** E3
Racecommon Rd *BSLY* S70 .... **21** E3
Racecourse Mt *CHNE* S41 .... **184** A1
Racecourse Rd *CHNE* S41 .... **178** A5 🔲
   CHNE S41 .... **184** A1
   MEX/SWTN S64 .... **56** B5
Racecourse Rd East *CHNE* S41 .... **184** C1
Race St *BSLY* S70 .... **2** B6 🔲
Racker Wy *ST/HB/BR* S6 .... **107** F5
Radcliffe Rd *BTLY* DN5 .... **16** B4
Radford St *OWL* S3 .... **8** B4
Radnor Cl *MOS* S20 .... **153** D3
Radnor Wy *WHHL* DN2 .... **32** A4
Raeburn Cl *GLV* S14 .... **148** C3
Raeburn Pl *GLV* S14 .... **148** C2
Raeburn Rd *GLV* S14 .... **148** C2
Raeburn Wy *SHEFS* S8 .... **148** C3
Rail Mill Wy *RAW* S62 .... **94** A4
Rails Rd *ST/HB/BR* S6 .... **118** B3
Railway Av *RHAM* S60 .... **127** D2
Railway Ter *RHAM* S60 .... **6** B5 🔲
Rainbow Av *HACK/IN* S12 .... **151** F1
Rainborough Ms *DEARNE* S63 .... **54** C1 🔲
Rainborough Rd *DEARNE* S63 .... **54** C2
Rainbow Av *HACK/IN* S12 .... **151** F1
Rainbow Crs *HACK/IN* S12 .... **152** A1
Rainbow Dr *HACK/IN* S12 .... **152** A1
Rainbow Gv *HACK/IN* S12 .... **152** A1
Rainbow Pl *HACK/IN* S12 .... **152** A1
Rainbow Rd *HACK/IN* S12 .... **152** A1
Rainbow Wy *HACK/IN* S12 .... **151** F1
Rainford Dr *BSLYN/ROY* S71 .... **15** E1
Rainton Gv *DOD/DAR* S75 .... **12** C4
Rainton Rd *DONS/BSCR* DN4 .... **5** G6
Raintree Ct *BTLY* DN5 .... **29** D4
Raisen Hall Pl *SHEFN* S5 .... **109** E3
Raisen Hall Rd *SHEFN* S5 .... **109** D1
Rake's La *NROS/TKH* DN11 .... **64** B5
Raleigh Ct *WHHL* DN2 .... **45** F1
Raleigh Dr *CHPT/GREN* S35 .... **74** A5
Raleigh Rd *SHEFS* S8 .... **135** F4
Raleigh Ter *DONS/BSCR* DN4 .... **62** C1
Raley St *BSLY* S70 .... **21** E2
Ralph Ellis Dr *STKB/PEN* S36 .... **68** C3
Ralston Ct *MOS* S20 .... **164** B3 🔲
Ralston Cft *MOS* S20 .... **164** C2 🔲
Ralston Gv *MOS* S20 .... **164** B3
Rampton Rd *ABRD* S7 .... **135** D3 🔟
Ramsden Rd *RHAM* S60 .... **103** F2
Ramsey Av *CHSW* S40 .... **189** E3
Ramsey Rd *FUL* S10 .... **121** D3
Ramshaw Cl *CHSW* S40 .... **183** D2 🔲
Ramshaw Rd *DRON* S18 .... **170** C5 🔲
Ramsker Dr *ARMTH* DN3 .... **33** F4
Ramsworth Cl *BTLY* DN5 .... **28** C4 🔲
Ranby Rd *ECC* S11 .... **133** F3
Randall Pl *SHEFP/MNR* S2 .... **135** D3
Randall St *ECK/KIL* S21 .... **173** F1 🔲
   SHEFP/MNR S2 .... **135** E1
Randerson Dr *MEX/SWTN* S64 .... **81** F2

Ranelagh Dr *ECC* S11 .... **133** F5
Raneld Mt *CHSW* S40 .... **189** D4
Rangeley Rd *ST/HB/BR* S6 .... **120** B2
Ranmoor Cl *CHNE* S41 .... **191** D4 🔟
Ranmoor Cliffe Rd *FUL* S10 .... **132** C1
Ranmoor Crs *FUL* S10 .... **133** D1
Ranmoor Park Rd *FUL* S10 .... **133** D1
Ranmoor Ri *FUL* S10 .... **133** D1 🔲
Ranmoor Rd *FUL* S10 .... **133** D1
Rankill Ct *DARN/MH* S9 .... **112** A5
Ranyard Rd *DONS/BSCR* DN4 .... **43** D5 🔲
Raseby Av *MOS* S20 .... **152** C3
Raseby Cl *MOS* S20 .... **152** C3
Raseby Pl *MOS* S20 .... **152** C3 🔲
Rasen Cl *MEX/SWTN* S64 .... **58** C2
Ratcliffe Rd *ECC* S11 .... **134** B2
Ravencar Rd *ECK/KIL* S21 .... **163** F5
Ravencarr Pl *SHEFP/MNR* S2 .... **137** E1
Ravencarr Rd *SHEFP/MNR* S2 .... **137** E1
Raven Dr *KIMB* S61 .... **76** B5
Ravenfield Cl *MOS* S20 .... **151** E3
Ravenfield Dr *BSLYN/ROY* S71 .... **14** B1
Ravenfield St *CONI* DN12 .... **60** A3
Ravenholt *BSLY* S70 .... **36** B1
Raven Mdw *MEX/SWTN* S64 .... **81** D3
Raven Rd *ABRD* S7 .... **134** B4
Ravenscar Cl *CONI* DN12 .... **60** A3
Ravenscourt *BSLY* S70 .... **36** C1
Ravenscroft Av *HAN/WDH* S13 .... **138** C2
Ravenscroft Cl *HAN/WDH* S13 .... **138** C2 🔲
Ravenscroft Ct *HAN/WDH* S13 .... **138** C2 🔲
Ravenscroft Crs *HAN/WDH* S13 .... **138** C2
Ravenscroft Dr *HAN/WDH* S13 .... **138** C2
Ravenscroft Ov *HAN/WDH* S13 .... **138** C2 🔲
Ravenscroft Pl *HAN/WDH* S13 .... **138** C2 🔲
Ravenscroft Rd *HAN/WDH* S13 .... **138** C3
Ravenscroft Wy *HAN/WDH* S13 .... **138** C3
Ravensdale Cl *STV/CWN* S43 .... **187** D3
Ravensdale Rd *DRON* S18 .... **168** A2
Ravenshaw Cl *DOD/DAR* S75 .... **12** C4 🔲
Ravens Wk *CONI* DN12 .... **85** F1
Ravenswood Rd *RCH* S42 .... **182** B4 🔟
Ravensworth Rd *DON* DN1 .... **5** G6
The Ravine *SHEFN* S5 .... **99** F2
Rawmarsh Hl *RAW* S62 .... **94** A2
Rawmarsh Rd *RHAM* S60 .... **6** D2
Rawson Cl *DONS/BSCR* DN4 .... **47** D3 🔲
Rawson Spring Rd *ST/HB/BR* S6 .... **108** B2
Rawson Spring Wy *SHEFN* S5 .... **108** B2
Raybould Rd *KIMB* S61 .... **92** A5 🔲
Rayleigh Av *STV/CWN* S43 .... **185** E1
Raymond Rd *BSLY* S70 .... **23** D3
   BTLY DN5 .... **29** D3
Raynald Rd *SHEFP/MNR* S2 .... **137** E1
Reader Crs *MEX/SWTN* S64 .... **57** E4
Reaper Crs *CHPT/GREN* S35 .... **73** F5
Reasbeck Ter *BSLYN/ROY* S71 .... **14** A2 🔲
Rebecca Ms *BSLY* S70 .... **22** A2 🔟
Rebecca Rw *BSLY* S70 .... **22** A2
Recreation Rd *DEARNE* S63 .... **56** A1
   STV/CWN S43 .... **186** A4
Rectory Cl *DEARNE* S63 .... **26** B3
   ECK/KIL S21 .... **164** C4
   STKB/PEN S36 .... **69** D2
   WMB/DAR S73 .... **39** E3
Rectory Gdns *DON* DN1 .... **5** H1
   ECK/KIL S21 .... **166** B2
Rectory La *DEARNE* S63 .... **26** B3
Rectory Rd *ECK/KIL* S21 .... **164** C4
   STV/CWN S43 .... **181** F4
Rectory St *RAW* S62 .... **94** A2
Rectory Wy *BSLYN/ROY* S71 .... **15** E4 🔲
Redbourne Rd *BTLY* DN5 .... **16** C5
Redbrook Av *CHNE* S41 .... **190** C4
Redbrook Cl *DOD/DAR* S75 .... **13** D3 🔲
Redbrook Cft *HACK/IN* S12 .... **151** E2 🔲
Redbrook Gv *MOS* S20 .... **151** E2 🔲
Redbrook Rd *DOD/DAR* S75 .... **12** B3
Redbrook Vw *DOD/DAR* S75 .... **13** D3
Redbrook Wk *DOD/DAR* S75 .... **13** D3
Redcar Cl *CONI* DN12 .... **83** F1
Redcar Rd *FUL* S10 .... **121** D4
Redcliffe Cl *DOD/DAR* S75 .... **12** C4
Redfearn St *BSLYN/ROY* S71 .... **3** E5 🔲
Redfern Av *MOS* S20 .... **152** B4
Redfern Ct *MOS* S20 .... **152** B4 🔲
Redfern Dr *MOS* S20 .... **152** B4
Redfern Gv *MOS* S20 .... **152** B4
Red Fern Gv *STKB/PEN* S36 .... **68** C2
Redgrove Wy *CHSW* S40 .... **189** D4
Red Hl *SHEF* S1 .... **8** C4
Redhill Av *BSLY* S70 .... **23** D5
Redhouse Cl *STV/CWN* S43 .... **179** E2 🔲
Red La *CHNE* S41 .... **179** D5
   ECC S11 .... **134** A1
Redmarsh Av *RAW* S62 .... **79** F4
Redmires La *FUL* S10 .... **130** B1
Redmires Rd *FUL* S10 .... **119** D5
Rednall Cl *CHSW* S40 .... **182** B4 🔟
Red Oak La *ST/HB/BR* S6 .... **106** A5 🔲
Redrock Rd *RHAM* S60 .... **115** E2
Redscope Crs *KIMB* S61 .... **91** E4
Redscope Rd *KIMB* S61 .... **91** E5
Redthorn Rd *HAN/WDH* S13 .... **139** D2

Redthorpe Crest *DOD/DAR* S75 .... 12 B3 🔢
Redvers Buller Rd *CHSW* S40 .... 190 B3
Redwood Av *ECK/KIL* S21 .... 166 A3
Redwood Cl *HOY* S74 .... 51 E3
  STV/CWN S43 .... 186 B1
Redwood Gln *CHPT/GREN* S35 ...... 88 A2
Regent Gdns *BSLY* S70 .... 2 B3
Regent Gv *BTLY* DN5 .... 29 D4
Regent Sq *DON* DN1 .... 5 F4
Regent St *BSLY* S70 .... 2 D4
  DONS/BSCR DN4 .... 43 E5
  HOY S74 .... 50 B3
  KIMB S61 .... 102 A3
  SHEF S1 .... 8 B5
Regents Wy *AU/AST/KP* S26 ...... 142 C3 🔢
Regent Ter *OWL* S3 .... 8 B3
Reginald Rd *BSLY* S70 .... 23 E3
  WMB/DAR S73 .... 40 A3 🔢
Rembrandt Dr *DRON* S18 .... 168 C2
Remington Av *SHEFN* S5 .... 98 A2
Remington Dr *SHEFN* S5 .... 98 A2 🔢
Remington Rd *SHEFN* S5 .... 98 A3
Remount Rd *KIMB* S61 .... 91 E4
Remount Wy *KIMB* S61 .... 91 E4 🔢
Renathorpe Rd *SHEFN* S5 .... 99 E3
Rencliffe Av *RHAM* S60 .... 115 D1
Reneville Cl *SHEFN* S5 .... 98 B1
Reneville Ct *SHEFN* S5 .... 98 B1
Reneville Crs *SHEFN* S5 .... 98 B1
Reneville Dr *SHEFN* S5 .... 98 B1 🔢
Reneville Rd *RHAM* S60 .... 103 E5
Reney Av *SHEFS* S8 .... 158 B2
Reney Dr *SHEFS* S8 .... 158 B2
Reney Rd *SHEFS* S8 .... 158 C1
Renishaw Av *RHAM* S60 .... 115 F2
Renshaw Cl *CHPT/GREN* S35 .... 73 D3
Renshaw Rd *ECC* S11 .... 133 E4
Renville Cl *RAW* S62 .... 79 F4
Renway Rd *RHAM* S60 .... 104 B5
Repton Cl *CHSW* S40 .... 182 B4
Repton Pl *DRON* S18 .... 168 A2 🔢
Reresby Crs *RHAM* S60 .... 116 A3
Reresby Dr *RHAM* S60 .... 116 A2
Reresby Rd *RHAM* S60 .... 115 F2
Reservoir Rd *AU/AST/KP* S26 ...... 129 D3
  FUL S10 .... 121 D4
Retford Rd *HAN/WDH* S13 .... 139 E1
Revell Cl *RHAM/THRY* S65 .... 105 E2
Revill La *HAN/WDH* S13 .... 140 A4
Rex Av *ABRD* S7 .... 145 F1
Reynard Crs *ECK/KIL* S21 .... 175 F3
Reynard La *ST/HB/BR* S6 .... 118 C2
Reynolds Cl *DRON* S18 .... 168 C3
Rhodes Av *CHNE* S41 .... 10 B1
  KIMB S61 .... 91 F4
Rhodes Dr *RHAM* S60 .... 116 A2
Rhodesia Rd *CHSW* S40 .... 188 C2
Rhodes St *SHEFP/MNR* S2 .... 9 H5
Ribble Cft *CHPT/GREN* S35 .... 74 A5
Ribblesdale Dr *HACK/IN* S12 .... 151 D4
Ribble Wy *SHEFN* S5 .... 110 A1
Riber Cl *ST/HB/BR* S6 .... 106 B5
  STV/CWN S43 .... 187 D4
Ribston Ct *RAW* S62 .... 80 A4
Ribston Ms *DARN/MH* S9 .... 124 C3
Ribston Pl *DARN/MH* S9 .... 124 C3
Ribston Rd *DARN/MH* S9 .... 124 B3
Richard Av *BSLYN/ROY* S71 .... 14 B1
Richard Rd *BSLYN/ROY* S71 .... 14 B1
  RHAM S60 .... 103 F4
Richards Ct *SHEFP/MNR* S2 .... 135 F4 🔢
Richards Rd *SHEFP/MNR* S2 .... 135 E3
Richard St *BSLY* S70 .... 2 A6 🔢
Richards Wy *RAW* S62 .... 80 B5
Rich Farm Cl *BTLY* DN5 .... 17 E3
Richmond Av *HAN/WDH* S13 ...... 138 C2
Richmond Cl *CHSW* S40 .... 189 F4 🔢
Richmond Farm Ms
  HAN/WDH S13 .... 138 B3 🔢
Richmond Gv *HAN/WDH* S13 ..... 138 C2 🔢
Richmond Hall Av *HAN/WDH* S13.... 138 B2
Richmond Hall Crs
  HAN/WDH S13 .... 138 B3 🔢
Richmond Hall Dr
  HAN/WDH S13 .... 138 B2 🔢
Richmond Hall Rd *HAN/WDH* S13 . 138 B2
Richmond Hall Wy
  HAN/WDH S13 .... 138 B3 🔢
Richmond Hill Rd *BTLY* DN5 ...... 42 C2 🔢
  HAN/WDH S13 .... 138 B3 🔢
Richmond Park Av *HAN/WDH* S13.. 125 F5
  KIMB S61 .... 101 E3
Richmond Park Cl
  HAN/WDH S13 .... 138 C1 🔢
Richmond Park Crs
  HAN/WDH S13 .... 125 F5
Richmond Park Cft
  HAN/WDH S13 .... 125 E5
Richmond Park Dr *HAN/WDH* S13.. 138 C1
Richmond Park Gv *HAN/WDH* S13.. 138 B1
Richmond Park Ri *HAN/WDH* S13 . 125 E5
Richmond Park Rd *HAN/WDH* S13.. 138 C1
Richmond Park Vw
  HAN/WDH S13 .... 138 C1

Richmond Park Wy
  HAN/WDH S13 .... 138 C1
Richmond Pl *HAN/WDH* S13 ..... 138 B3 🔢
Richmond Rd *BTLY* DN5 .... 28 B2
  DEARNE S63 .... 26 C3
  HAN/WDH S13 .... 138 A4
  KIMB S61 .... 101 F3
Richmond St *BSLY* S70 .... 21 E1 🔢
  OWL S3 .... 122 C1
Richworth Rd *HAN/WDH* S13 ..... 139 D2
Ricknald Cl *AU/AST/KP* S26 .... 129 E5
Ridal Av *STKB/PEN* S36 .... 68 B1
Ridal Cl *STKB/PEN* S36 .... 68 B1
Ridal Cft *STKB/PEN* S36 .... 68 B1 🔢
Riddings Cl *SHEFP/MNR* S2 .... 137 E3
Rider Rd *ST/HB/BR* S6 .... 108 A4
Ridgehill Av *HACK/IN* S12 .... 137 E5
Ridgehill Av *HACK/IN* S12 .... 137 F5
Ridge Rd *ECK/KIL* S21 .... 172 C1
  RHAM/THRY S65 .... 7 F4
The Ridge *FUL* S10 .... 132 A1
Ridge View Cl *DARN/MH* S9 .... 111 E1
Ridge View Dr *DARN/MH* S9 .... 111 E1
Ridgewalk Wy *BSLY* S70 .... 22 A4
Ridgeway *DRON* S18 .... 160 B5
  RHAM/THRY S65 .... 105 D2
Ridgeway Cescent *HACK/IN* S12 . 137 E5
Ridgeway Cl *RHAM/THRY* S65 ..... 105 E2
Ridgeway Crs *HACK/IN* S12 .... 137 E4
Ridgeway Dr *HACK/IN* S12 .... 137 E4
Ridgeway Moor *HACK/IN* S12 ..... 162 C2
Ridgeway Rd *HACK/IN* S12 .... 137 E5
  RHAM S60 .... 113 F4
  SHEFP/MNR S2 .... 137 E4 🔢
Riding Cl *DONS/BSCR* DN4 .... 67 F1
Ridings Av *BSLYN/ROY* S71 .... 14 C2
The Ridings *BSLYN/ROY* S71 ...... 15 D2 🔢
Rig Cl *KIMB* S61 .... 92 A5
Rig Dr *MEX/SWTN* S64 .... 56 B5
Riggs High Rd *ST/HB/BR* S6 .... 118 A2
Riggs Low Rd *ST/HB/BR* S6 .... 118 A2
Riley Av *DONS/BSCR* DN4 .... 63 D1
Riley Rd *DEARNE* S63 .... 56 A3
Rimington Rd *WMB/DAR* S73 .... 39 E2
Rimini Ri *WMB/DAR* S73 .... 25 F5
Ringinglow Rd *ECC* S11 .... 132 B5
Ringstead Av *FUL* S10 .... 119 F5
Ringstead Crs *FUL* S10 .... 120 A5
Ringwood Av *CHNE* S41 .... 183 F2
  STV/CWN S43 .... 187 D1
Ringwood Crs *MOS* S20 .... 153 E3
Ringwood Dr *MOS* S20 .... 153 E3
Ringwood Gv *MOS* S20 .... 153 E3
Ringwood Rd *MOS* S20 .... 155 E3 🔢
  STV/CWN S43 .... 186 A1
Ringwood Vw *STV/CWN* S43 .... 186 A2
Ripley Gv *DOD/DAR* S75 .... 12 C3
Ripley St *ST/HB/BR* S6 .... 108 A5
Ripon Av *WHHL* DN2 .... 31 D3
Ripon St *DARN/MH* S9 .... 124 A2
Ripon Wy *AU/AST/KP* S26 .... 142 A3
Rippon Ct *RAW* S62 .... 80 A4
Rippon St *ST/HB/BR* S6 .... 107 F4
Rippon Rd *ST/HB/BR* S6 .... 107 F4
The Rise *MEX/SWTN* S64 .... 80 C1
Rising St *OWL* S3 .... 122 C1
Rivelin Bank *ST/HB/BR* S6 .... 107 F5
Rivelin Mill Br *ST/HB/BR* S6 .... 118 B4
Rivelin Park Crs *ST/HB/BR* S6 ..... 120 A1
Rivelin Park Dr *ST/HB/BR* S6 .... 120 A1
Rivelin Park Rd *ST/HB/BR* S6 ...... 120 B2
Rivelin Rd *ST/HB/BR* S6 .... 120 B1
Rivelin St *ST/HB/BR* S6 .... 120 C1
Rivelin Ter *ST/HB/BR* S6 .... 120 B1
Rivelin Valley Rd *ST/HB/BR* S6 .... 118 B4
Riverdale Av *ECC* S11 .... 133 D2
Riverdale Dr *FUL* S10 .... 133 D1
Riverdale Rd *ST/HB/BR* S6 .... 120 C3
  ECC S11 .... 133 D1
Riverside Cl *ST/HB/BR* S6 .... 107 D4
Riverside Dr *BTLY* DN5 .... 42 A3
Riverside Wy *RHAM* S60 .... 103 D4
River Ter *ST/HB/BR* S6 .... 108 A4
Riviera Pde *BTLY* DN5 .... 29 F4
Rix Rd *MEX/SWTN* S64 .... 81 E3
Roach Rd *ECC* S11 .... 134 A1
Robert Av *BSLYN/ROY* S71 .... 15 E5
Robert Cl *DRON* S18 .... 177 F1
Robert Rd *SHEFS* S8 .... 159 D1
Roberts Av *CONI* DN12 .... 85 E2
Robertshaw Crs *STKB/PEN* S36 .... 69 E2 🔢
Robertson Dr *ST/HB/BR* S6 .... 120 B1
Robertson Rd *ST/HB/BR* S6 .... 120 B2
Roberts Rd *DONS/BSCR* DN4 .... 43 D4
Roberts St *WMB/DAR* S73 .... 39 D3 🔢
Robert St *BSLY* S70 .... 36 B1 🔢
  RHAM S60 .... 102 C3 🔢
Robey St *ATT* S4 .... 110 B3
Robincroft *CHSW* S40 .... 190 A5 🔢
Robinets Rd *KIMB* S61 .... 92 B5
Robin Hood Cha *ST/HB/BR* S6 ...... 106 A5
Robin Hood Rd *DARN/MH* S9 ..... 100 B5 🔢
Robin La *MOS* S20 .... 153 D4
Robin Pl *AU/AST/KP* S26 .... 142 C4
Robins Cl *AU/AST/KP* S26 .... 142 C3

Robinson Rd *SHEFP/MNR* S2 ..... 123 D5 🔢
Robinson St *RHAM* S60 .... 103 E5
Rob Royd *DOD/DAR* S75 .... 20 A4 🔢
Rob Royd La *BSLY* S70 .... 21 E4
Roche Cl *BSLYN/ROY* S71 .... 3 H2
Rocher Av *SHEFN* S5 .... 97 F2
Rocher Cl *SHEFN* S5 .... 97 F2
Rocher Gv *SHEFN* S5 .... 97 F2
Rochester Cl *FUL* S10 .... 131 E1 🔢
Rochester Dr *FUL* S10 .... 131 E1
Rochester Rd *BSLYN/ROY* S71 ...... 14 C3
  FUL S10 .... 131 E1
Rochester Rw *BTLY* DN5 .... 28 B4
Rockcliffe Rd *RAW* S62 .... 94 A3
Rockingham Cl *BSLY* S70 .... 49 F2
  CHSW S40 .... 189 D1
  DRON S18 .... 168 A2 🔢
  SHEF S1 .... 122 B5 🔢
Rockingham Ga *SHEF* S1 .... 122 B5 🔢
Rockingham La *SHEF* S1 .... 8 D5
Rockingham Rd *DOD/DAR* S75 ...... 20 B5
  MEX/SWTN S64 .... 80 B1
  RAW S62 .... 80 B5
Rockingham Rw *BSLY* S70 .... 50 A2
  BSLYN/ROY S71 .... 13 F3
  HOY S74 .... 50 B2
  SHEF S1 .... 8 C5
Rockingham Wy *SHEF* S1 .... 122 B5 🔢
Rocklea Cl *MEX/SWTN* S64 .... 81 D1 🔢
Rockley Av *BSLY* S70 .... 35 F4
  WMB/DAR S73 .... 38 C4
Rockley Cl *CHSW* S40 .... 190 A5
Rockley Crs *BSLY* S70 .... 49 F1
Rockley La *BSLY* S70 .... 35 E5
  DOD/DAR S75 .... 35 D2
Rockley Mdw *BSLY* S70 .... 21 D3
Rockley Nook *WHHL* DN2 .... 31 F2 🔢
Rockley Rd *ST/HB/BR* S6 .... 107 F2
Rockley Vw *DOD/DAR* S75 .... 49 E2
Rock Mt *HOY* S74 .... 52 A2 🔢
Rock Mount Rd *DARN/MH* S9 ..... 100 C5
Rock St *BSLY* S70 .... 2 A4
  OWL S3 .... 9 F1
Rockwood Cl *CHPT/GREN* S35 ..... 87 F1 🔢
Roden Wy *RAW* S62 .... 79 D3
Rodge Cft *CHNE* S41 .... 178 B3
Rodger Rd *HAN/WDH* S13 .... 140 B3
Rodger St *KIMB* S61 .... 102 C2
Rodman Dr *HAN/WDH* S13 .... 140 B2
Rodman St *HAN/WDH* S13 .... 140 B2
Rod Moor Rd *TOT/DORE* S17 ...... 157 F4
Rodney Hl *ST/HB/BR* S6 .... 106 B4
Rodsley Cl *CHSW* S40 .... 182 C4 🔢
Roebuck Hl *HOY* S74 .... 38 A5
Roebuck Rd *ST/HB/BR* S6 .... 121 E3
Roebuck St *WMB/DAR* S73 .... 39 F4
Roecar Cl *CHNE* S41 .... 178 C4
Roehampton Ri *BSLYN/ROY* S71 ... 24 A2
  BTLY DN5 .... 28 C4 🔢
  RHAM S60 .... 113 E3
Roe La *ATT* S4 .... 109 F4
Roger Rd *BSLYN/ROY* S71 .... 15 F5
Rojean Rd *CHPT/GREN* S35 .... 97 E1
Rokeby Dr *SHEFN* S5 .... 98 B3
Rokeby Rd *SHEFN* S5 .... 98 B3
Rolleston Rd *SHEFN* S5 .... 99 D5
Rollet Cl *SHEFP/MNR* S2 .... 137 E2
Rollin Dr *ST/HB/BR* S6 .... 107 F3
Rolls Crs *RAW* S62 .... 79 D3
Roman Ct *KIMB* S61 .... 101 F3 🔢
Roman Crs *RAW* S62 .... 79 F5
  RHAM S60 .... 114 A3
Romandale Gdns *SHEFP/MNR* S2 . 138 A1
Roman Ridge Rd *DARN/MH* S9 .... 111 F1
Roman Rd *DONS/BSCR* DN4 .... 5 H5
Roman St *DEARNE* S63 .... 27 E2
Romney Dr *DRON* S18 .... 168 C2
Romney Gdns *SHEFP/MNR* S2 .... 135 F4 🔢
Romsdal Rd *FUL* S10 .... 121 D3 🔢
Romwood Av *MEX/SWTN* S64 .... 56 B5
Ronald Rd *DARN/MH* S9 .... 125 D5 🔢
  DONS/BSCR DN4 .... 43 E5 🔢
Ronksley Crs *SHEFN* S5 .... 99 E3
Ronksley Rd *SHEFN* S5 .... 99 E3
Rookdale Cl *DOD/DAR* S75 .... 12 C3
Rookery Bank *STKB/PEN* S36 ..... 70 A3 🔢
Rookery Cha *STKB/PEN* S36 .... 70 A3 🔢
Rookery Cl *STKB/PEN* S36 .... 70 A3 🔢
Rookery Dell *STKB/PEN* S36 .... 70 A3 🔢
Rookery Ri *STKB/PEN* S36 .... 70 A4
Rookery Rd *MEX/SWTN* S64 .... 80 C1
The Rookery *STKB/PEN* S36 .... 70 A3 🔢
Rookery V *STKB/PEN* S36 .... 70 A3 🔢
Rook Hl *BSLY* S70 .... 23 D5
Roper Hl *FUL* S10 .... 130 B3
Rosamond Av *TOT/DORE* S17 ..... 157 E2
Rosamond Cl *TOT/DORE* S17 ...... 157 E2
Rosamond Dr *TOT/DORE* S17 ...... 157 E3
Rosamond Gld *TOT/DORE* S17 ... 157 E2 🔢
Rosamond Pl *TOT/DORE* S17 ..... 157 E2 🔢
Rosa Rd *FUL* S10 .... 121 D3
Roscoe Bank *ST/HB/BR* S6 .... 119 F2
Roscoe Dr *ST/HB/BR* S6 .... 120 A2
Roscoe Mt *ST/HB/BR* S6 .... 120 A2

Roscoe Rd OWL S3 .... 8 C2
Rose Av DONS/BSCR DN4 .... 43 F4
  MOS S20 .... 153 D2
Roseberry Cl HOY S74 .... 51 F4 🔢
Rosebery St KIMB S61 .... 102 B3
Rosebery Ter BSLY S70 .... 22 A2 🔢
Rose Cl RHAM S60 .... 114 B5
Rose Ct DONS/BSCR DN4 .... 43 E4 🔢
Rose Crs BTLY DN5 .... 28 C2
  RAW S62 .... 80 C5
Rosedale Av CHSW S40 .... 190 C4
  RAW S62 .... 80 A5
Rosedale Gdns BSLY S70 .... 21 D1
  ECC S11 .... 134 B2 🔢
Rosedale Rd AU/AST/KP S26 ... 142 C2
  BTLY DN5 .... 16 B4
  BTLY DN5 .... 28 B2
  ECC S11 .... 134 B2 🔢
Rosedale Vw CHSW S40 .... 188 C5 🔢
Rose Garth Av AU/AST/KP S26 .. 142 C2
Rosegarth Cl BTLY DN5 .... 28 C2 🔢
Rose HI CHSW S40 .... 10 D6
  DONS/BSCR DN4 .... 46 A3
  MOS S20 .... 151 F5
Rose Hill Av MOS S20 .... 151 F5
Rosehill Av RAW S62 .... 80 B4
Rose Hill Cl MOS S20 .... 151 F5
Rosehill Ct BSLY S70 .... 2 C3
Rose Hill Dr DOD/DAR S75 .... 20 A3 🔢
  MOS S20 .... 151 E5
Rose Hill East CHSW S40 .... 11 E6
Rose Hill Ri DONS/BSCR DN4 .... 46 A3
Rosehill Rd RAW S62 .... 80 A5
Rose HI West CHSW S40 .... 10 D6
Roselle St ST/HB/BR S6 .... 108 A4 🔢
Rosemary Gv BTLY DN5 .... 61 F3 🔢
Rosemary Rd MOS S20 .... 153 D1
Rose Pl WMB/DAR S73 .... 39 D1
Rose Wy ECK/KIL S21 .... 166 B3
Rose Wood Cl CHNE S41 .... 183 E1 🔢
Roslin Rd FUL S10 .... 121 D4
Rossendale Cl CHSW S40 .... 189 F4 🔢
Rosser Av HACK/IN S12 .... 149 D3
Rossington Dr DONS/BSCR DN4 ... 67 F5
Rossington Rd ECC S11 .... 134 A2
Rossington St CONI DN12 .... 60 A4
Rossiter Rd KIMB S61 .... 93 D2
Rosslyn Av AU/AST/KP S26 ...... 142 C2
Rosslyn Crs BTLY DN5 .... 16 C4
Ross St DARN/MH S9 .... 125 E3
Roston Cl DRON S18 .... 168 B2 🔢
Rothay Cl DRON S18 .... 168 C3
Rothay Rd ATT S4 .... 111 D3
Rothbury Cl MOS S20 .... 153 E3 🔢
Rothbury Ct MOS S20 .... 153 E3 🔢
Rothbury Wy RHAM S60 .... 114 A3 🔢
Rother Av STV/CWN S43 .... 185 E1
Rother Cl CHSW S40 .... 189 F4
Rother Crs RHAM S60 .... 127 F4
Rotherham Cl ECK/KIL S21 .... 155 D5
Rotherham Rd AU/AST/KP S26 ... 153 E3
  BSLYN/ROY S71 .... 14 B1
  DEARNE S63 .... 54 C2
  ECK/KIL S21 .... 155 D5
  HAN/WDH S13 .... 126 C5
  MOS S20 .... 165 D1
  RAW S62 .... 93 F5
  RHAM S60 .... 127 E1
  RHAM/THRY S65 .... 7 F2
Rotherham Rd North MOS S20 .. 165 D1 🔢
Rotherham Roundwalk KIMB S61.. 102 C1 🔢
  RAW S62 .... 77 E3
  RHAM S60 .... 128 A1
Rotherham St DARN/MH S9 ...... 111 E5 🔢
Rotherhill Cl RHAM/THRY S65 ...... 104 B2
Rother Rd RHAM S60 .... 114 B1
Rotherside Rd ECK/KIL S21 ...... 165 D4
Rotherstoke Cl RHAM S60 .... 103 F5
Rother St WMB/DAR S73 .... 40 B5
Rother Ter RHAM S60 .... 114 B1
Rothervale Cl MOS S20 .... 153 E1
Rothervale Rd CHSW S40 .... 190 B5
Rother Valley Wy MOS S20 .... 153 F5
Rother View Rd RHAM S60 .... 114 B1
Rother Wy CHNE S41 .... 184 C3
Rotherway RHAM S60 .... 114 C4
Rotherwood Av HAN/WDH S13 ... 140 B2
Rotherwood Cl BTLY DN5 .... 28 B3
Rotherwood Rd ECK/KIL S21 .... 166 C1
Rothesay Cl BTLY DN5 .... 29 D4 🔢
Rothey Gv RCH S42 .... 182 A4
Rough La CHPT/GREN S35 .... 71 D3
  CHPT/GREN S35 .... 86 C5
Roughwood Rd KIMB S61 .... 91 F4
Roundel St DARN/MH S9 .... 124 A2
Round Green La DOD/DAR S75 .... 34 C1
Roundwood Ct BSLY S70 .... 36 B1 🔢
Roundwood Gv RAW S62 .... 94 B1
Rowan Cl BSLY S70 .... 22 A3
  CHPT/GREN S35 .... 88 B2
Rowan Ct WHHL DN2 .... 32 A3
Rowan Dr DOD/DAR S75 .... 12 C4
Rowan Garth BTLY DN5 .... 29 E3 🔢
Rowan Mt WHHL DN2 .... 31 F3

Rowan Rd ECK/KIL S21 .... 174 A2
Rowan Tree Dell TOT/DORE S17 .. 156 C5
Rowan Tree Rd ECK/KIL S21 ..... 165 F2
Rowborn Dr CHPT/GREN S35 ...... 96 A5
Rowdale Crs HACK/IN S12 .... 138 B5 🔢
Rowel La ST/HB/BR S6 .... 106 A4
Rowena Dr BTLY DN5 .... 28 A3
Rowena Rd CONI DN12 .... 84 C1 🔢
Rowland Rd DOD/DAR S75 .... 13 D4
  SHEFP/MNR S2 .... 135 D2
Rowland St OWL S3 .... 8 D1
Rowms La MEX/SWTN S64 .... 58 A5
Rowsley Crs STV/CWN S43 .... 187 D1
Rowsley St SHEFP/MNR S2 ...... 135 F1
Roxby Cl DONS/BSCR DN4 .... 66 B2
Roxton Av SHEFS S8 .... 147 D5 🔢
Roxton Rd SHEFS S8 .... 146 C4
Royal Av DON DN1 .... 5 G2
Royal Ct HOY S74 .... 52 A2
Royale Cl ECK/KIL S21 .... 164 C5
Royal St BSLY S70 .... 2 C5
Royd Cl BSLY S70 .... 36 A1
Roydfield Cl MOS S20 .... 152 B3 🔢
Roydfield Dr MOS S20 .... 152 B3
Roydfield Gv MOS S20 .... 152 B3
Royd La STKB/PEN S36 .... 69 E4
Royds Av RHAM S60 .... 116 A3
Royds Close Crs RHAM/THRY S65 ... 95 F5
Royds La HOY S74 .... 53 D3
Royds Moor HI RHAM S60 .... 116 C3
The Royd STKB/PEN S36 .... 69 E4
Roy Kilner Rd WMB/DAR S73 ..... 38 C1 🔢
Royston Av BTLY DN5 .... 29 E2
  MOS S20 .... 151 E3
Royston Cl MOS S20 .... 151 E3 🔢
Royston Gv MOS S20 .... 151 E3 🔢
Royston HI HOY S74 .... 51 E2
Rubens Cl DRON S18 .... 169 D2
Rudyard Rd ST/HB/BR S6 .... 108 A4
Rufford Cl CHSW S40 .... 189 F3
Rufford Ct MOS S20 .... 153 E3 🔢
Rufford Ri MOS S20 .... 153 E5
Rufford Rd DONS/BSCR DN4 ...... 45 D3
Rugby St OWL S3 .... 122 B1
Rundle Dr ABRD S7 .... 134 C3
Rundle Rd ABRD S7 .... 134 C3
  STKB/PEN S36 .... 68 C2
Runnymede Rd WHHL DN2 .... 45 F1
Rupert Rd ABRD S7 .... 134 C5
Rural La ST/HB/BR S6 .... 107 D2
Rushby St ATT S4 .... 110 C3
Rushdale Av SHEFS S8 .... 135 E5
Rushdale Mt SHEFS S8 .... 135 E5 🔢
Rushdale Rd SHEFS S8 .... 135 E5
Rushdale Ter SHEFS S8 .... 135 E5 🔢
Rushey Cl RAW S62 .... 79 F3
Rushley Av TOT/DORE S17 .... 144 B5
Rushley Cl TOT/DORE S17 .... 144 B5
Rushley Dr TOT/DORE S17 .... 144 B5
Rushley Rd TOT/DORE S17 .... 156 B1
Ruskin Av MEX/SWTN S64 .... 58 C2
Ruskin Cl DEARNE S63 .... 55 D1
Ruskin Rd DONS/BSCR DN4 .... 63 E1 🔢
Ruskin Sq SHEFS S8 .... 135 E4
Russell Cl BSLYN/ROY S71 .... 14 C2
Russell Ct ECC S11 .... 145 E3
Russell Rd MEX/SWTN S64 .... 81 F4
Russell St OWL S3 .... 8 D2
  RHAM/THRY S65 .... 7 F2
Rustlings Rd ECC S11 .... 133 E2
Ruston Cl CHSW S40 .... 182 C3
Ruthin St ATT S4 .... 110 C4
Ruth Sq FUL S10 .... 121 F5 🔟
Ruthven Dr DONS/BSCR DN4 ...... 42 B3
Rutland Pk FUL S10 .... 121 D5
Rutland Pl WMB/DAR S73 .... 38 C5
Rutland Rd CHSW S40 .... 10 C6
  OWL S3 .... 122 B1
Rutland St CHNE S41 .... 178 B4 🔢
  DON DN1 .... 5 G2 🔢
  OWL S3 .... 122 B1
Rutland Wy DOD/DAR S75 .... 13 D4
  OWL S3 .... 8 B1
Ryan Dr HAN/WDH S13 .... 140 C3
Ryan Pl RAW S62 .... 94 A2
Rydal Cl DRON S18 .... 168 B2
Rydal Crs CHNE S41 .... 183 F1
Rydalhurst Av ST/HB/BR S6 ...... 107 D2
Rydall Pl BTLY DN5 .... 29 D1
Rydal Rd SHEFS S8 .... 134 C5
Rydal Wy MEX/SWTN S64 .... 59 D2
Rye Bank RHAM S60 .... 116 B3
Rye Cft BSLYN/ROY S71 .... 14 B1
  CONI DN12 .... 85 F1
Ryecroft Glen Rd TOT/DORE S17 .. 157 D1
Ryecroft Rd RAW S62 .... 81 D5
Ryecroft Vw TOT/DORE S17 ...... 144 B5
Ryefield Gdns ECC S11 .... 133 E5
Rye Flatt La CHSW S40 .... 188 C3
Ryegate Crs FUL S10 .... 120 C4
Ryegate Rd FUL S10 .... 120 C5
Ryehill Av CHSW S40 .... 188 B2
Ryeview Gdns KIMB S61 .... 92 C4
Ryhill Dr HACK/IN S12 .... 151 E3

Ryle Rd ABRD S7 .... 134 C4
Rylstone Ct HACK/IN S12 .... 151 F3 🔢
Rylstone Gv HACK/IN S12 .... 151 F3
Rylstone Wk BSLY S70 .... 23 E4 🔢
Ryton Av WMB/DAR S73 .... 40 A4
Ryton Wy DONS/BSCR DN4 .... 67 E1

S

Sackerville Ter ECK/KIL S21 ..... 165 F1
Sackville Cl CHSW S40 .... 188 C4 🔢
Sackville Rd FUL S10 .... 120 C3
Sackville St BSLY S70 .... 2 A4
Saddler Av MOS S20 .... 152 B4
Saddler Cl MOS S20 .... 152 B4
Saddler Gn MOS S20 .... 152 B4 🔢
Saddler Gv MOS S20 .... 152 B4
Sadler Ga BSLY S70 .... 2 C4
Sadler's Ga WMB/DAR S73 .... 39 D1 🔢
St Agnes' Rd DONS/BSCR DN4 .. 45 E2
St Aidan's Av SHEFP/MNR S2 ... 136 B2
St Aidan's Cl SHEFP/MNR S2 .. 136 C1 🔢
St Aidan's Dr SHEFP/MNR S2 .. 136 C1
St Aidan's Mt SHEFP/MNR S2 . 136 C2 🔢
St Aidan's Pl SHEFP/MNR S2 .. 136 C2
St Aidan's Rd SHEFP/MNR S2 . 136 C2 🔢
St Aidan's Wy SHEFP/MNR S2 . 136 C2
St Albans Cl FUL S10 .... 132 A1 🔢
St Albans Dr FUL S10 .... 131 F1
St Albans Rd FUL S10 .... 131 F1
St Andrew St STKB/PEN S36 ...... 69 F3 🔢
St Andrew's Cl ABRD S7 .... 134 B3 🔢
  MEX/SWTN S64 .... 81 E2
St Andrews Crs HOY S74 .... 51 F2 🔢
St Andrews Ri CHSW S40 .... 189 D4 🔢
St Andrew's Rd ABRD S7 .... 134 B3
  CONI DN12 .... 84 C2
  HOY S74 .... 51 F2
St Andrew's Ter DONS/BSCR DN4 ... 44 C3
St Andrews Wk RHAM S60 .... 113 E3
St Andrews Wy BSLYN/ROY S71 ... 24 B3
St Anne's Rd DONS/BSCR DN4 .. 45 E2
St Ann's Rd RHAM/THRY S65 ...... 7 E2
  STKB/PEN S36 .... 69 E2 🔢
St Anthony Rd FUL S10 .... 120 B3
St Augustines Av CHSW S40 .... 190 B3
St Augustines Dr CHSW S40 .... 190 B3
St Augustines Mt CHSW S40 ... 190 B3
St Augustines Ri CHSW S40 ..... 190 B4 🔢
St Augustines Rd CHSW S40 .... 190 A4
St Augustine's Rd DONS/BSCR DN4.. 46 A3
St Barnabas La SHEFP/MNR S2 .. 135 E2
St Barnabas Rd SHEFP/MNR S2 ... 135 E2
St Bartholomews Ri
  DONS/BSCR DN4 .... 46 B3 🔢
St Bedes Rd RHAM S60 .... 6 A5
St Catherine's Av DONS/BSCR DN4 .. 43 F4
St Catherines Wy DOD/DAR S75 ... 20 C1 🔢
St Cecilia's Rd DONS/BSCR DN4 .. 45 E3
St Chad's Wy BTLY DN5 .... 42 E1
St Charles St DARN/MH S9 ...... 123 F1
St Christophers Cl
  BSLYN/ROY S71 .... 24 B3 🔢
St Christopher's Crs BTLY DN5 .. 28 C3
St Clements Cl BSLYN/ROY S71 ... 24 B3 🔢
St Clement's Cl BTLY DN5 .... 28 B3 🔢
St David Rd STKB/PEN S36 .... 69 F3
St David's Dr BSLYN/ROY S71 ... 24 A2
  BTLY DN5 .... 28 B3
  RHAM S60 .... 113 E3
St David's Ri CHSW S40 .... 189 E4
St David's Rd CONI DN12 .... 84 C1
St Edwards Av BSLY S70 .... 21 E2
St Elizabeth Cl SHEFP/MNR S2 . 135 F2 🔢
St Eric's Rd DONS/BSCR DN4 .... 46 B4
St George Ga DON DN1 .... 4 D3
St George St STKB/PEN S36 .... 69 F3
St George's Av MEX/SWTN S64 .. 56 C5
St George's Cl OWL S3 .... 8 A4
St Georges Dr RHAM S60 .... 113 E3 🔢
St George's Rd BSLY S70 .... 2 B6
St George's Ter SHEF S1 .... 8 B5
St Giles Cl CHSW S40 .... 190 C4
St Giles Ga BTLY DN5 .... 28 B4
St Giles Sq CHPT/GREN S35 .... 88 A1
St Helen Rd STKB/PEN S36 .... 69 F4 🔢
St Helen's Av BSLYN/ROY S71 .... 14 C2
St Helen's Cl CHNE S41 .... 11 E4
Saint Helens Cl DEARNE S63 ...... 26 B3
St Helens Rd DONS/BSCR DN4 .. 45 E2 🔢
St Helen's St CHNE S41 .... 11 E3
  HOY S74 .... 52 B2
St Helens Wy BSLYN/ROY S71 ... 15 E2
St Helier Dr DOD/DAR S75 .... 12 C5
St Hilda Av BSLY S70 .... 21 D1
St Hilda Cl STKB/PEN S36 .... 69 F4
St Hildas Cl DEARNE S63 .... 27 E2
St Hilda's Rd DONS/BSCR DN4 .. 45 E2
St James Cl CHNE S41 .... 191 D3 🔢
  DEARNE S63 .... 56 B2
St James' Gdns DONS/BSCR DN4 .. 43 F3
St James's Br DONS/BSCR DN4 ... 4 C6

St James St *DON* DN1...... 4 C6
  SHEF S1 ...... 9 E5
St James Wk *HAN/WDH* S13...... 140 B2
St Joan Av *STKB/PEN* S36 ...... 69 F4
St John's Av *RHAM* S60 ...... 102 C3
St Johns Cl *CHSW* S40...... 188 C5
  RHAM/THRY S65...... 104 B1
St John's Mt *CHNE* S41 ...... 184 A1
St Johns Pl *STV/CWN* S43...... 181 E5
St John's Rd *BSLY* S70 ...... 21 F2
  CHNE S41...... 184 A1
  DONS/BSCR DN4...... 43 E4
  DRON S18 ...... 170 C3
  MEX/SWTN S64...... 57 D5
  RHAM/THRY S65...... 104 B1
  SHEF/MNR S2...... 123 E3
  STKB/PEN S36 ...... 70 A3
  STV/CWN S43 ...... 181 D5
St Joseph's Rd *HAN/WDH* S13...... 126 A5
St Lawrence Rd *DARN/MH* S9...... 112 C1
St Leonards Ct *SHEFN* S5 ...... 109 F1
St Leonard's La *RHAM/THRY* S65 ...... 7 H3
St Leonard's Lea *BTLY* DN5 ...... 28 C3
St Leonard's Rd *RHAM/THRY* S65 ...... 7 F4
St Leonards Wy *BSLYN/ROY* S71 ...... 24 B3
St Lukes Wy *BSLYN/ROY* S71 ...... 15 D4
St Margaret Av *STKB/PEN* S36 ...... 69 F3
St Margaret's Dr *CHSW* S40...... 10 D5
St Margaret's Rd *CHPT/GREN* S35 ...... 98 C1
  DONS/BSCR DN4 ...... 45 E3
St Mark Rd *STKB/PEN* S36 ...... 69 F3
St Mark's Crs *FUL* S10 ...... 121 E5
St Mark's Rd *CHSW* S40 ...... 10 A6
St Martin St *STKB/PEN* S36 ...... 69 F3
St Martin's Av *BTLY* DN5 ...... 29 D4
St Martins St *DOD/DAR* S75 ...... 12 C5
St Mary Crs *STKB/PEN* S36 ...... 69 F3
St Mary's Cl *CHPT/GREN* S35 ...... 88 B5
St Mary's Crs *DON* DN1 ...... 5 G1
  MEX/SWTN S64...... 57 D4
St Mary's Dr *RHAM* S60 ...... 127 D1
St Mary's Gdn *BSLY* S70 ...... 36 B3
St Mary's Ga *BSLY* S70 ...... 2 C4
  CHNE S41 ...... 11 G6
  SHEF/MNR S2 ...... 135 D1
St Mary's La *CHPT/GREN* S35 ...... 88 B5
St Mary's Pl *BSLY* S70 ...... 2 C4
St Mary's Rd *DEARNE* S63 ...... 27 F5
  DON DN1 ...... 30 C4
  RAW S62 ...... 94 B1
  SHEF S1 ...... 135 E1
  WMB/DAR S73 ...... 135 E1
St Mary's Sq *SHEF/MNR* S2 ...... 135 D1
St Mary's Vw *KIMB* S61 ...... 92 C3
St Matthews Wy *BSLYN/ROY* S71 ...... 15 D4
St Matthias Rd *STKB/PEN* S36 ...... 69 F4
St Michael's Av *BSLYN/ROY* S71 ...... 15 E1
  MEX/SWTN S64...... 57 E4
  NROS/TKH DN11...... 67 E5
St Michael's Cl *CHPT/GREN* S35 ...... 98 C1
St Michael's Crs *CHPT/GREN* S35 ...... 98 C1
St Michael's Rd *CHPT/GREN* S35...... 98 C1
  DONS/BSCR DN4 ...... 45 F3
St Nicholas Cl *ARMTH* DN3 ...... 19 F4
St Nicolas Rd *RAW* S62 ...... 80 B5
St Oswald's Dr *ARMTH* DN3...... 19 F4
St Owens Dr *DOD/DAR* S75 ...... 12 C5
St Patrick Rd *STKB/PEN* S36 ...... 69 F3
St Patrick's Rd *WHHL* DN2...... 31 E5
St Patrick's Wy *BTLY* DN5 ...... 28 B4
St Paul Cl *STKB/PEN* S36 ...... 69 F3
St Paul's Pde *BSLYN/ROY* S71 ...... 24 A2
  BTLY DN5 ...... 28 B4
St Peter Av *STKB/PEN* S36 ...... 70 A3
St Peter's Cl *RHAM* S60 ...... 113 E4
St Peter's Ga *DEARNE* S63 ...... 26 C2
St Peter's Rd *CONI* DN12 ...... 84 C2
  DONS/BSCR DN4 ...... 42 C5
St Peter's Ter *BSLY* S70 ...... 22 B3
St Philip's Dr *CHNE* S41 ...... 190 C4
St Philip's La *OWL* S3 ...... 8 B2
St Philip's Rd *OWL* S3 ...... 8 A3
St Quentin Cl *TOT/DORE* S17 ...... 157 E3
St Quentin Dr *TOT/DORE* S17 ...... 157 F3
St Quentin Mt *TOT/DORE* S17 ...... 157 F3
St Quentin Ri *TOT/DORE* S17 ...... 157 F3
St Quentin Vw *TOT/DORE* S17 ...... 157 F3
St Ronan's Rd *ABRD* S7 ...... 135 D3
St Sepulchre Ga *DON* DN1 ...... 4 D4
St Sepulchre Ga West *DON* DN1 ...... 4 C6
St Stephen's Dr *AU/AST/KP* S26 ...... 142 B2
St Stephen's Rd *RHAM/THRY* S65 ...... 7 F3
St Stephens Wk *BTLY* DN5...... 28 B4
St Stephen's Wk *OWL* S3 ...... 121 F3
St Thomas Rd *FUL* S10 ...... 120 C4
St Thomas's Cl *DONS/BSCR* DN4.. ...... 62 C1
St Thomas's Rd *DOD/DAR* S75 ...... 12 B3
St Thomas' St *CHSW* S40 ...... 189 D2
St Thomas St *SHEF* S1 ...... 8 C5
St Ursula's Rd *DONS/BSCR* DN4 ...... 45 E2
St Veronica Rd *STKB/PEN* S36 ...... 69 F4
St Vincent Av *DON* DN1...... 5 G2
St Vincent Rd *DON* DN1 ...... 5 G2

St Wandrilles Cl *CHPT/GREN* S35 ...... 88 C5
St Wilfrid's Rd *DONS/BSCR* DN4 ...... 46 A3
  SHEF/MNR S2...... 135 E2
Salcey Sq *CHSW* S40 ...... 189 E3
Sale Hl *FUL* S10 ...... 120 C5
Salerno Wy *WMB/DAR* S73 ...... 25 F4
Sale St *HOY* S74 ...... 50 B3
Salisbury Av *CHNE* S41 ...... 183 F2
  DRON S18...... 169 E3
Salisbury Crs *CHNE* S41 ...... 184 A2
Salisbury Rd *CHNE* S41 ...... 43 E3
  DRON S18...... 169 F4
Salisbury St *DOD/DAR* S75...... 2 A2
Salmon St *ECC* S11 ...... 135 D2
Salt Box Gv *CHPT/GREN* S35 ...... 97 D1
Salt Box La *CHPT/GREN* S35 ...... 97 D2
Saltergate *CHSW* S40 ...... 10 C5
Samson St *SHEF/MNR* S2 ...... 123 D5
Samuel Cl *SHEF/MNR* S2 ...... 136 B3
Samuel Dr *SHEF/MNR* S2 ...... 136 B3
Samuel Pl *SHEF/MNR* S2 ...... 136 B3
Samuel Rd *DOD/DAR* S75...... 12 C4
  SHEF/MNR S2 ...... 136 B3
Samuel Sq *DOD/DAR* S75 ...... 12 C4
Samuel St *DONS/BSCR* DN4...... 63 D1
Sandall Beat La *WHHL* DN2...... 32 B3
Sandall Beat Rd *DONS/BSCR* DN4 ...... 45 F1
Sandall Carr Rd *ARMTH* DN3 ...... 19 F3
Sandall La *ARMTH* DN3...... 19 E2
Sandall Park Dr *WHHL* DN2...... 32 A2
Sandall Ri *WHHL* DN2 ...... 31 F3
Sandall Stones Rd *ARMTH* DN3 ...... 19 E3
Sandall Rd *CONI* DN12 ...... 84 B2
Sandalwood Cl *WHHL* DN2 ...... 32 A1
Sandalwood Ri *MEX/SWTN* S64 ...... 81 E3
Sandbeck Cl *BSLYN/ROY* S71 ...... 2 D1
Sandbeck Pl *ECC* S11 ...... 134 B3
Sandbeck Rd *DONS/BSCR* DN4 ...... 45 D2
Sandbed Rd *OWL* S3 ...... 108 C5
Sandbergh Rd *KIMB* S61 ...... 91 F4
Sandby Ct *SHEFS* S8 ...... 148 C3
Sandby Cft *SHEFS* S8 ...... 148 C3
Sandby Dr *SHEFS* S8 ...... 148 C3
Sandcliffe Rd *WHHL* DN2...... 31 F3
Sandcroft Cl *HOY* S74 ...... 51 D3
Sanderson St *DARN/MH* S9 ...... 111 D5
Sandford Ct *BSLY* S70 ...... 21 E2
Sandford Grove Rd *ABRD* S7 ...... 134 C4
Sandford Rd *DONS/BSCR* DN4 ...... 63 E1
Sandhill Cl *RAW* S62 ...... 80 C4
Sandhill Rd *RAW* S62 ...... 80 C5
Sandhurst Rd *DONS/BSCR* DN4 ...... 29 E1
Sandiway *CHSW* S40...... 189 D4
Sandown Cl *ECK/KIL* S21 ...... 163 F5
Sandown Gdns *DONS/BSCR* DN4 ...... 46 B2
Sandown Rd *MEX/SWTN* S64 ...... 58 C2
Sandpiper Rd *KIMB* S61 ...... 76 A5
Sandringham Av *RHAM* S60 ...... 115 F3
Sandringham Cl *STV/CWN* S43 ...... 186 A5
Sandringham Rd *DARN/MH* S9 ...... 100 B5
  WHHL DN2...... 45 E1
Sandrock Dr *DONS/BSCR* DN4 ...... 46 C5
Sands Cl *GLV* S14 ...... 148 C1
Sandstone Av *CHSW* S40 ...... 188 C4
  DARN/MH S9...... 111 D2
Sandstone Dr *DARN/MH* S9 ...... 111 E1
Sandstone Dr *DARN/MH* S9 ...... 111 D2
Sandstone Rd *DARN/MH* S9 ...... 111 D2
Sandy Acres Cl *MOS* S20 ...... 153 D4
Sandy Acres Dr *MOS* S20 ...... 152 F4
Sandycroft Crs *DONS/BSCR* DN4 ...... 62 C1
Sandy Flat La *MALT* S66 ...... 117 F2
Sandygate *DEARNE* S63 ...... 56 A2
Sandygate Grange Dr *FUL* S10 ...... 119 F5
Sandygate Gv *FUL* S10 ...... 119 E5
Sandygate Pk *FUL* S10 ...... 119 D5
Sandygate Park Crs *FUL* S10 ...... 119 E5
Sandygate Park Rd *FUL* S10 ...... 119 E4
Sandygate Rd *FUL* S10 ...... 119 E5
Sandy La *DONS/BSCR* DN4 ...... 45 E3
  WMB/DAR S73...... 37 F3
Sandymount Rd *DEARNE* S63 ...... 56 B3
Sanforth St *CHNE* S41 ...... 184 B3
Sarah St *KIMB* S61 ...... 102 C3
  MEX/SWTN S64...... 58 B4
Sark Rd *SHEF/MNR* S2 ...... 135 E3
Saundby Ct *DONS/BSCR* DN4 ...... 46 A5
Saunders Pl *SHEF/MNR* S2 ...... 123 F4
Saunders Rd *SHEF/MNR* S2 ...... 123 F4
Saunders Rw *WMB/DAR* S73...... 39 D3
Savage La *TOT/DORE* S17 ...... 156 B1
Savile St East *ATT* S4 ...... 123 E1
Savile Hall La *DOD/DAR* S75 ...... 20 A4
Savile Rd *DEARNE* S63 ...... 55 F3
  DOD/DAR S75 ...... 20 B4
  RHAM S60...... 115 F3
Saville St *RHAM/THRY* S65 ...... 95 D5
Sawdon Rd *ECC* S11 ...... 134 C1
Sawston Cl *DONS/BSCR* DN4 ...... 63 E3
Saxon Crs *BSLY* S70 ...... 22 B5
Saxonlea Av *SHEF/MNR* S2 ...... 138 A1
Saxonlea Cl *SHEF/MNR* S2 ...... 138 A1
Saxonlea Ct *SHEF/MNR* S2 ...... 138 A1
Saxonlea Dr *SHEF/MNR* S2 ...... 137 F1

Saxon Rd *KIMB* S61 ...... 101 E3
  SHEFS S8...... 135 E4
Saxon Rw *CONI* DN12 ...... 85 F2
Saxon St *DEARNE* S63...... 27 E3
Saxton Av *DONS/BSCR* DN4...... 46 A4
Saxton Cl *HOY* S74 ...... 52 C1
Saxton Dr *RHAM* S60 ...... 115 D3
Scaftworth Cl *DONS/BSCR* DN4 ...... 66 A1
Scammadine Cl *RHAM* S60 ...... 114 A4
Scarborough Rd *DARN/MH* S9 ...... 125 D2
Scarfield Cl *BSLYN/ROY* S71 ...... 24 A2
Scargill Cft *SHEF* S1 ...... 9 E4
Scar La *BSLYN/ROY* S71 ...... 24 A2
Scarlett Oak Meadow
  ST/HB/BR S6 ...... 119 D1
Scarll Rd *DONS/BSCR* DN4 ...... 43 E3
Scarsdale Cl *DRON* S18...... 169 F3
Scarsdale Crs *STV/CWN* S43 ...... 185 E2
Scarsdale Cross *DRON* S18 ...... 169 F2
Scarsdale Rd *CHNE* S41 ...... 184 B1
  DRON S18...... 169 F2
  SHEFS S8...... 147 D2
Scarth Av *DONS/BSCR* DN4 ...... 43 F4
Schofield Rd *STKB/PEN* S36 ...... 69 D3
Schofield St *MEX/SWTN* S64 ...... 58 A3
Scholes Gn *KIMB* S61 ...... 91 D3
Scholes La *KIMB* S61 ...... 90 B3
Scholes Vw *CHPT/GREN* S35 ...... 88 C5
Scholey St *OWL* S3 ...... 9 G2
School Av *MOS* S20 ...... 164 C1
School Board La *CHSW* S40 ...... 10 A6
School Cl *AU/AST/KP* S26 ...... 155 F2
  MOS S20...... 164 C1
Schoolfield Dr *RAW* S62 ...... 80 A4
School Green La *FUL* S10 ...... 131 F3
School Gv *AU/AST/KP* S26 ...... 142 C3
School Hl *RHAM* S60 ...... 115 F3
School La *ARMTH* DN3 ...... 47 F4
  CHPT/GREN S35...... 87 D5
  DRON S18...... 169 E2
  ECK/KIL S21...... 162 C5
  RAW S62...... 93 F3
  SHEF/MNR S2...... 123 D4
  SHEFS S8...... 148 A4
  SHEFS S8...... 159 D1
  ST/HB/BR S6...... 119 D2
School Lane Cl *SHEFS* S8 ...... 148 A4
School Rd *AU/AST/KP* S26 ...... 155 E3
  CHNE S41...... 184 B2
  CHPT/GREN S35...... 73 F4
  FUL S10...... 120 C4
  MOS S20...... 153 F3
School St *AU/AST/KP* S26 ...... 142 A3
  BSLY S70...... 23 E2
  DEARNE S63...... 13 E4
  DOD/DAR S75...... 13 E4
  ECK/KIL S21...... 164 B5
  MOS S20...... 164 B1
  RHAM/THRY S65...... 95 F4
  WMB/DAR S73...... 39 E2
  WMB/DAR S73...... 53 D1
School Wk *CONI* DN12 ...... 60 A4
Scotia Cl *SHEF/MNR* S2 ...... 137 D2
Scotia Dr *SHEF/MNR* S2 ...... 137 D2
Scotland St *OWL* S3 ...... 8 C3
Scot La *DON* DN1 ...... 5 E3
Scott Av *CONI* DN12 ...... 84 B2
Scott Crs *ARMTH* DN3...... 19 F3
Scott Rd *ATT* S4 ...... 110 A4
Scott St Wy *CHPT/GREN* S35 ...... 88 A2
Scovell Av *RAW* S62 ...... 79 F4
Scowerdons Cl *HACK/IN* S12 ...... 139 D5
Scowerdons Dr *HACK/IN* S12 ...... 139 D5
Scraith Wood Dr *SHEFN* S5 ...... 108 B2
Scrooby Dr *RAW* S62 ...... 93 D3
Scrooby La *RAW* S62 ...... 93 E3
Scrooby Pl *RAW* S62 ...... 93 D3
Scrooby St *KIMB* S61 ...... 93 D3
Seabrook Rd *SHEF/MNR* S2 ...... 123 E5
Seagrave Av *HACK/IN* S12 ...... 149 F1
Seagrave Cr *HACK/IN* S12 ...... 149 E2
Seagrave Dr *HACK/IN* S12 ...... 149 E1
Seagrave Rd *HACK/IN* S12 ...... 149 E1
Seaton Cl *SHEF/MNR* S2 ...... 124 A5
Seaton Crs *SHEF/MNR* S2 ...... 124 A5
Seaton Pl *SHEF/MNR* S2 ...... 124 A5
Seaton Wy *SHEF/MNR* S2 ...... 124 A5
Sebastion Vw *RHAM* S60 ...... 114 A2
Sedan St *ATT* S4...... 110 A5
Sedbergh Cts *CHNE* S41 ...... 183 E2
Sedgefield Wy *MEX/SWTN* S64 ...... 58 C2
Sedgemoor Cl *CHSW* S40...... 188 C5
Sedgley Rd *ST/HB/BR* S6...... 108 B4
Sefton Rd *ECC* S11 ...... 132 C3
Selborne Rd *FUL* S10 ...... 120 B4
Selborne St *RHAM/THRY* S65 ...... 7 E2
Selby Cl *AU/AST/KP* S26 ...... 142 A3
  CHSW S40...... 189 D4
Selby Rd *SHEFN* S5 ...... 110 B3
  WHHL DN2...... 31 E4
Selhurst Crs *DONS/BSCR* DN4 ...... 46 C5
Selhurst Rd *CHNE* S41 ...... 10 D1
Selkirk Rd *WHHL* DN2 ...... 32 A3
Sellars Rd *KIMB* S61 ...... 91 F5

Sellers St *SHEFS* S8 .... **135** D3 🔢
Selly Oak Gv *SHEFS* S8 .... **160** A2
Selly Oak Rd *SHEFS* S8 .... **160** A2 🔢
Selmer Ct *STV/CWN* S43 .... **185** E1 🔢
Selwyn St *RHAM/THRY* S65 .... 7 F2
Senior Rd *DARN/MH* S9 .... **125** D3
  DONS/BSCR DN4 .... **43** E2
Sennen Cft *BSLYN/ROY* S71 .... 14 C4 🔢
Setcup La *ECK/KIL* S21 .... **174** A1
Seth Ter *BSLY* S70 .... 22 B2 🔢
Sevenairs Rd *MOS* S20 .... **152** C2
Sevenfields Ct *ST/HB/BR* S6 .... **107** E3
Sevenfields La *ST/HB/BR* S6 .... **107** E3
Severn Ct *FUL* S10 .... **121** E4 🔢
Severn Rd *FUL* S10 .... **121** E4 🔢
Severnside Dr *HAN/WDH* S13 ..... **139** E3
Severnside Gdns *HAN/WDH* S13 ... **139** E3
Severnside Pl *HAN/WDH* S13 ...... **139** E3
Sewell Rd *MOS* S20 .... **165** D2
Seymore Rd *AU/AST/KP* S26 .... **142** B4
Shackleton La *WHHL* DN2 .... 19 E5
Shady Side *DONS/BSCR* DN4 .... 43 E3
Shaftesbury Av *CHSW* S40 .... **189** E1
  WHHL DN2 .... 45 F1
Shaftesbury Dr *HOY* S74 .... 51 E3
Shaftesbury St *BSLY* S70 .... 23 E2
Shaftholme Rd *BTLY* DN5 .... 17 E1
Shafton Rd *RHAM* S60 .... **115** F3
Shaftsbury Sq *RHAM/THRY* S65 .... 7 E3
Shakespeare Av *BTLY* DN5 .... 29 D5
Shakespeare Crs *DRON* S18 .... **170** A3
Shakespeare Rd *BTLY* DN5 .... 16 C5 🔢
  DEARNE S63 .... 55 E1
  RHAM/THRY S65 .... 7 H1
Shaldon Gv *AU/AST/KP* S26 .... **142** B3
Shalesmoor *OWL* S3 .... 8 C2
Shambles St *BSLY* S70 .... 2 C5 🔢
Shap Cl *CHSW* S40 .... **183** D4
Shardlow Gdns *DONS/BSCR* DN4 ... 67 D3
Sharman Cl *DRON* S18 .... **171** E2
Sharpe Av *SHEFS* S8 .... **146** C5
Sharpfield Av *RAW* S62 .... 79 F3
Sharrard Cl *HACK/IN* S12 .... **137** F5
Sharrard Dr *HACK/IN* S12 .... **137** F5
Sharrard Gv *HACK/IN* S12 .... **137** F4
Sharrard Rd *HACK/IN* S12 .... **137** F5
Sharrow La *ECC* S11 .... **134** C2
Sharrow St *ECC* S11 .... **135** D2
Sharrow Vale Rd *ECC* S11 .... **134** A2
Sharrow Vw *ABRD* S7 .... **134** C2
Shawfield Rd *BSLYN/ROY* S71 .... 15 D1
Shaw La *BSLY* S70 .... 21 D1
  WHHL DN2 .... 32 B1
Shaw Rd *RHAM/THRY* S65 .... **104** B1
Shawsfield Rd *RHAM* S60 .... **104** A5
Shaw's Rw *CHSW* S40 .... **189** E2 🔢
Shaw St *BSLY* S70 .... 21 E2
  CHNE S41 .... **184** B1
Shaw Wood Wy *WHHL* DN2 .... 32 B2
Shay House La *STKB/PEN* S36 ...... 68 C3
Shay Rd *STKB/PEN* S36 .... 68 C2
The Shay *DONS/BSCR* DN4 .... 46 C5
Sheaf Bank *SHEFP/MNR* S2 .... **135** E3 🔢
  SHEFP/MNR S2 .... **123** E6
Sheaf Cl *CONI* DN12 .... 85 E2
Sheaf Ct *BSLY* S70 .... 23 E3
Sheaf Gdns *SHEFP/MNR* S2 .... **135** F1 🔢
Sheaf St *SHEF* S1 .... 9 G6
Sheards Cl *DRON* S18 .... **169** D2
Sheards Dr *DRON* S18 .... **168** C2 🔢
Sheards Wy *DRON* S18 .... **168** C2
Shearman Av *KIMB* S61 .... 91 F4
Shear Square Rbt *SHEF* S1 .... **122** C5
Shearwood Rd *FUL* S10 .... **121** E4 🔢
Sheep Bridge La *NROS/TKH* DN11 ... 64 F3
Sheepcote Rd *ECK/KIL* S21 .... **166** A2
Sheep Cote Rd *RHAM/THRY* S65 ... **116** B1
Sheffield La *RHAM* S60 .... **127** D3
Sheffield Pkwy *HAN/WDH* S13 .... **125** F4
  SHEFP/MNR S2 .... **123** E3
  SHEFP/MNR S2 .... **125** E5
Sheffield Rd *BSLY* S70 .... 22 A2
  BSLY S70 .... 50 A1
  CHNE S41 .... 11 F1
  CHNE S41 .... **178** B5 🔢
  CHNE S41 .... **184** B1 🔢
  CONI DN12 .... 84 A3
  DARN/MH S9 .... **112** A3
  DONS/BSCR DN4 .... 62 A2
  DRON S18 .... **159** D5
  DRON S18 .... **177** F2
  ECK/KIL S21 .... **166** A1
  HACK/IN S12 .... **151** D3
  HAN/WDH S13 .... **139** E4 🔢
  HAN/WDH S13 .... **141** E3
  MOS S20 .... **164** B3
  RHAM S60 .... **103** E4
Sheldon Av *CONI* DN12 .... 85 C2
Sheldon La *ST/HB/BR* S6 .... **119** D1 🔢
Sheldon Rd *ABRD* S7 .... **182** C4 🔢
  CHSW S40 .... **182** C4 🔢
  STKB/PEN S36 .... 68 C2
Sheldon Rw *ATT* S4 .... 9 G3
Sheldon St *SHEFP/MNR* S2 .... **135** E1 🔢
Sheldrake Cl *KIMB* S61 .... 90 A1
Shelley Av *DONS/BSCR* DN4 .... 63 F1

Shelley Dr *BSLYN/ROY* S71 .... 3 G1
  DRON S18 .... **170** A4
  RHAM/THRY S65 .... **104** C4
Shelley Gv *BTLY* DN5 .... 29 D5 🔢
Shelley Rd *RHAM/THRY* S65 ...... **104** C3
Shelley Wy *DEARNE* S63 .... 55 D1 🔢
Shenstone Dr *RHAM/THRY* S65 ... **104** C5
Shenstone Rd *RHAM/THRY* S65 .. **104** C5
  ST/HB/BR S6 .... **107** F2
Shepcote La *DARN/MH* S9 .... **112** A5
Shepcote Wy *DARN/MH* S9 .... **112** A5
Shephard's Cl *CONI* DN12 .... 60 A5
Shepherd Dr *CHPT/GREN* S35 ..... 73 F5 🔢
Shepherd La *DEARNE* S63 .... 27 D4
Shepherd St *OWL* S3 .... 8 C3
Shepley Cft *CHPT/GREN* S35 ...... 73 F5 🔢
Shepley St *SHEF* S2 .... **189** E2
Sheppard Rd *ST/HB/BR* S6 .... **107** F3
Shepperson Rd *ST/HB/BR* S6 .... **107** F3
Sherbourne Av *CHNE* S41 .... **183** F1
Sherburn Ga *CHPT/GREN* S35 ..... 74 A5
Sherde Rd *ST/HB/BR* S6 .... **121** E1
Sheridan Av *DONS/BSCR* DN4 ...... 64 A1
Sheridan Ct *BSLYN/ROY* S71 .... 3 H1
Sheridan Dr *RHAM/THRY* S65 .... **105** D3
Sheringham Cl *CHPT/GREN* S35 ... 73 E4
Sherwood Av *BTLY* DN5 .... 28 B3
  CONI DN12 .... 84 B2
Sherwood Crs *RHAM/THRY* S65 .... 7 E6
Sherwood Dr *DONS/BSCR* DN4 .... 62 C2
Sherwood Gln *SHEFS* S8 .... **145** F4
Sherwood Rd *DRON* S18 .... **168** B2
  ECK/KIL S21 .... **166** C1
Sherwood St *BSLYN/ROY* S71 .... 3 E5
  CHSW S40 .... **190** C3
Shetland Rd *DRON* S18 .... **169** F3
Shield Av *BSLY* S70 .... 22 A5
Shinwell Av *STV/CWN* S43 .... **186** C2
Ship HI *RHAM* S60 .... 6 D6
Shipman Ct *MOS* S20 .... **164** B1 🔢
Shipton St *ST/HB/BR* S6 .... **121** F2 🔢
Shirburn Gdns *DONS/BSCR* DN4 .. 46 C3
Shirebrook Rd *SHEFS* S8 .... **135** E4
Shirecliffe Cl *OWL* S3 .... **109** F5
Shirecliffe La *OWL* S3 .... **109** F5
Shirecliffe Rd *SHEFN* S5 .... **109** E5
Shiregreen La *SHEFN* S5 .... 99 F5
Shiregreen Ter *SHEFN* S5 .... 99 F4
Shirehall Crs *SHEFN* S5 .... 99 E2
Shirehall Rd *SHEFN* S5 .... 99 F5
Shireoaks Rd *DRON* S18 .... **170** A1
Shirland Av *BSLYN/ROY* S71 .... 14 B1
Shirland Ct *DARN/MH* S9 .... **124** C2 🔢
Shirland La *DARN/MH* S9 .... **124** A1
Shirland Ms *DARN/MH* S9 .... **124** C2 🔢
Shirland Pl *DARN/MH* S9 .... **124** C2 🔢
Shirland St *CHNE* S41 .... 11 F3
Shirley Cl *CHSW* S40 .... **182** C4
Shirley Rd *DONS/BSCR* DN4 .... 43 E3 🔢
Shoreham Av *RHAM* S60 .... **115** E3
Shoreham Dr *RHAM* S60 .... **115** D3
Shoreham St *SHEF* S1 .... **122** C5
Shore La *FUL* S10 .... **120** B5
Shortbrook Bank *MOS* S20 .... **152** C5 🔢
Shortbrook Cl *MOS* S20 .... **152** C5
Shortbrook Cft *MOS* S20 .... **153** D5 🔢
Shortbrook Dr *MOS* S20 .... **152** C5
Shortbrook Rd *MOS* S20 .... **152** C5
Shortbrook Wy *MOS* S20 .... **152** C5
Short La *DONS/BSCR* DN4 .... 45 F5
Shortridge St *DARN/MH* S9 .... **124** A1
Short Rd *WHHL* DN2 .... 32 A5
Short Wood Cl *BSLY* S70 .... 36 A4
Shrewsbury Cl *MEX/SWTN* S64 .... 58 A3 🔢
Shrewsbury Rd *SHEFP/MNR* S2 .. **122** C5
Shrewsbury Ter *KIMB* S61 .... **102** A3
Shrogswood Rd *RHAM/THRY* S65 .. **116** B1
Shubert Cl *HAN/WDH* S13 .... **139** F2
Shude HI *SHEF* S1 .... 9 G5
Sicey Av *SHEFN* S5 .... 99 E1
Sicey La *SHEFN* S5 .... 99 E3
Sicklebrook La *DRON* S18 .... **160** C4
Siddall St *OWL* S3 .... 8 B5
Sidings Ct *DONS/BSCR* DN4 .... 44 C4
Sidlaw Cl *CHSW* S40 .... **189** D4 🔢
Sidney Rd *WHHL* DN2 .... 31 F5
Sidney St *MEX/SWTN* S64 .... 57 E5
  SHEF S1 .... **122** B5
Sidons Cl *KIMB* S61 .... 91 F4 🔢
Siemens Cl *DARN/MH* S9 .... **112** C2 🔢
Siena Cl *WMB/DAR* S73 .... 25 F4
Silkstone Cl *DOD/DAR* S75 .... 49 E3
  HACK/IN S12 .... **150** C1
Silkstone Crs *HACK/IN* S12 .... **150** C1
Silkstone Dr *HACK/IN* S12 .... **150** B1
Silkstone Pl *HACK/IN* S12 .... **150** C1
Silkstone Rd *HACK/IN* S12 .... **150** C1
Silver Birch Av *FUL* S10 .... **132** A3 🔢
Silverdale Cl *CHNE* S41 .... **177** F5
  ECC S11 .... **133** E5
Silverdale Crs *ECC* S11 .... **133** E5
Silverdale Cft *ECC* S11 .... **145** E1
Silverdale Dr *BSLYN/ROY* S71 .... 15 E2

Silverdale Gdns *ECC* S11 .... **145** E1 🔢
Silverdale Gld *ECC* S11 .... **145** E1 🔢
Silverdale Rd *ECC* S11 .... **145** E1
Silver Hill Rd *ECC* S11 .... **133** F5
Silver Jubilee Cl *WHHL* DN2 .... 32 A3
Silver Mill Rd *SHEFP/MNR* S2 .... **135** E2 🔢
Silver St *BSLY* S70 .... 21 F2
  DOD/DAR S75 .... 20 A4
  DON DN1 .... 5 E3
  RHAM/THRY S65 .... 95 F4
  SHEF S1 .... 9 E4
Silver Street Head *SHEF* S1 .... 8 D4
Simcrest Av *ECK/KIL* S21 .... **166** B3
Simmonite Rd *KIMB* S61 .... 92 A5
Simons Wy *WMB/DAR* S73 .... 24 C5
Sims Cft *CHNE* S41 .... **179** D3 🔢
Sims St *SHEF* S1 .... 8 D4
Singleton Crs *ST/HB/BR* S6 .... **108** A5 🔢
Singleton Gv *ST/HB/BR* S6 .... **108** A5 🔢
Singleton Rd *ST/HB/BR* S6 .... **108** A5
Sitwell Av *CHSW* S40 .... **190** A3
  RHAM S60 .... 68 B2
Sitwell Dr *RHAM* S60 .... **115** F1
Sitwell Gv *MEX/SWTN* S64 .... 81 E1
  RHAM S60 .... **115** E2
Sitwell La *MALT* S66 .... **117** F1 🔢
Sitwell Park Rd *RHAM/THRY* S65 ... **116** B1
Sitwell Pl *SHEFP/MNR* S2 .... **135** D2 🔢
Sitwell Rd *ABRD* S7 .... **135** D2
Sitwell St *ECK/KIL* S21 .... **174** A1
Sitwell V *RHAM* S60 .... **115** D1
Sitwell Vw *RHAM* S60 .... **116** B3
Sivilla Rd *MEX/SWTN* S64 .... 81 E3
Skeldale Dr *CHSW* S40 .... **190** C4
Skelton Dr *HAN/WDH* S13 .... **140** A5
Skelton Gv *HAN/WDH* S13 .... **139** F4
Skelton La *HAN/WDH* S13 .... **139** F4
  MOS S20 .... **153** D2
Skelton Rd *SHEFS* S8 .... **135** E5
Skelwith Cl *ATT* S4 .... **111** D3
  CHNE S41 .... **183** E1 🔢
Skelwith Dr *ATT* S4 .... **111** D3
Skelwith Rd *ATT* S4 .... **111** D3
Skew Hill La *CHPT/GREN* S35 ...... 96 C1
Skiddaw Cl *CHSW* S40 .... **183** E3
Skiers View Rd *HOY* S74 .... 51 D3
Skiers Wy *HOY* S74 .... 51 D3
Skinnerthorpe Rd *ATT* S4 .... **110** B3
Skipton Cl *CONI* DN12 .... 59 F5
Skipton Rd *ATT* S4 .... **110** A4
  AU/AST/KP S26 .... **142** A3
Skipwith Cl *NROS/TKH* DN11 .... 64 A5
Skye Edge Av *SHEFP/MNR* S2 .... **123** E5
Skye Edge Rd *SHEFP/MNR* S2 .... **123** E5
Slack La *CHSW* S40 .... **188** C1
Slade Rd *MEX/SWTN* S64 .... 81 D1
Slag La *ECK/KIL* S21 .... **172** B5
Slaidburn Av *CHPT/GREN* S35 ...... 74 A5
Slate St *SHEFP/MNR* S2 .... **135** E3 🔢
Slayleigh Av *FUL* S10 .... **132** A2
Slayleigh Delph *FUL* S10 .... **132** A2
Slayleigh Dr *FUL* S10 .... **132** B2
Slayleigh La *FUL* S10 .... **132** A2
Sleaford St *DARN/MH* S9 .... **124** A1 🔢
Sledgate Dr *MALT* S66 .... **117** D1
Sledgate La *MALT* S66 .... **117** D1
Sledmere Rd *BTLY* DN5 .... 28 C3
Slinn St *FUL* S10 .... **121** D3
Slitting Mill La *DARN/MH* S9 ..... **124** A1 🔢
Sloade La *HACK/IN* S12 .... **162** B1
Smallage La *HAN/WDH* S13 ...... **141** E1
Smalldale Rd *HACK/IN* S12 .... **150** B1
Smeaton St *CONI* DN12 .... **135** D2 🔢
Smeckley Wood Cl *DRON* S18 ... **177** D3
Smelter Wood Av *HAN/WDH* S13 ... **138** C3
Smelter Wood Cl *HAN/WDH* S13 ... **138** C3 🔢
Smelter Wood Crs *HAN/WDH* S13 ... **139** D3
Smelter Wood Dr *HAN/WDH* S13 ... **138** C3
Smelter Wood La *HAN/WDH* S13 ... **138** C3
Smelter Wood Pl *HAN/WDH* S13 ... **139** D3
Smelter Wood Ri *HAN/WDH* S13 ... **139** D4
Smelter Wood Rd *HAN/WDH* S13 ... **138** C3
Smelter Wood Wy *HAN/WDH* S13 ... **138** C3
Smith Av *STV/CWN* S43 .... **186** C2
Smith Crs *CHNE* S41 .... **191** D5
Smithey Cl *CHPT/GREN* S35 ...... 73 E5
Smithfield *OWL* S3 .... 8 D3
Smithfield Av *CHNE* S41 .... **191** D5
Smithfield Rd *HACK/IN* S12 .... **149** E3
Smithies La *BSLYN/ROY* S71 .... 13 F3
Smithies Rd *MEX/SWTN* S64 ...... 57 D2
Smithies St *BSLYN/ROY* S71 .... 13 F3
Smithley La *WMB/DAR* S73 .... 38 B1
Smith Rd *STKB/PEN* S36 .... 68 B2
Smith Sq *DONS/BSCR* DN4 .... 43 D5
Smith St *CHPT/GREN* S35 .... 88 B1
  DONS/BSCR DN4 .... 43 D5
  WMB/DAR S73 .... 39 F2 🔢
Smithy Bridge La *WMB/DAR* S73 ... 53 E1
Smithy Carr Av *CHPT/GREN* S35 ... 88 A1
Smithy Carr Cl *CHPT/GREN* S35 ... 88 A1
Smithy Cl *KIMB* S61 .... 92 A5
Smithy Cft *DRON* S18 .... **168** A1
Smithy Fold La *CHPT/GREN* S35 ... 71 F2

Smithy Wood Crs *SHEFS* S8 .... **147** D1 ⁵
Smithy Wood La *DOD/DAR* S75 .... **20** A4
Smithy Wood Rd *CHPT/GREN* S35 .... **89** D2
   SHEFS S8 .... **146** C1
Snail Hl *RHAM* S60 .... 6 D6
Snaithing La *FUL* S10 .... **132** C1
Snaithing Park Cl *FUL* S10 .... **132** C1 ²
Snaithing Park Rd *FUL* S10 .... **132** C1
Snake La *CONI* DN12 .... **85** E2
Snape Hl *DRON* S18 .... **169** E1
Snapehill Cl *DRON* S18 .... **159** E5 ²
Snapehill Crs *DRON* S18 .... **159** E5
Snape Hill Dr *DRON* S18 .... **159** F5 ²
Snape Hill La *DRON* S18 .... **169** E1
Snelston Cl *DRON* S18 .... **168** A2 ¹⁴
Snig Hl *SHEF* S1 .... 9 F4
Snowberry Cl *MEX/SWTN* S64 .... **81** D3
Snowden Ter *WMB/DAR* S73 .... **39** E2
Snowdon La *ECK/KIL* S21 .... **161** F5
Snowdon Wy *RHAM* S60 .... **114** B5
Snow La *SHEF* S3 .... 8 D3
Soaper La *DRON* S18 .... **169** E1
Soap House La *HAN/WDH* S13 ...... **140** C3
Sokell Av *WMB/DAR* S73 .... **39** D3
Solly St *SHEF* S1 .... 8 B4
Solway Ri *DRON* S18 .... **168** D1
Somercotes Rd *HACK/IN* S12 .... **138** B5
Somersall Cl *CHSW* S40 .... **188** B3
Somersall La *CHSW* S40 .... **188** B3
Somersall Park Rd *CHSW* S40 ...... **188** C3 ²
Somersall Willows *CHSW* S40 .... **188** B3
Somersby Av *BTLY* DN5 .... **29** D5
   CHSW S40 .... **188** C3
Somerset Dr *STV/CWN* S43 .... **186** A1
Somerset Rd *DON* DN1 .... 5 F6
   OWL S3 .... **122** C1
Somerset St *BSLY* S70 .... 2 A4 ¹
   OWL S3 .... **122** C1 ⁵
Somerton Dr *DONS/BSCR* DN4 ...... **46** A2
Somerville Dr *ST/HB/BR* S6 .... **121** E1
Sorby Rd *AU/AST/KP* S26 .... **141** F3
Sorby St *ATT* S4 .... 9 H1
Sorby Wy *MALT* S66 .... **117** F1
Soresby St *CHSW* S40 .... **11** E6
Sorrelsykes Cl *RHAM* S60 .... **115** F4 ¹
Sothall Cl *MOS* S20 .... **153** D2
Sothall Ct *MOS* S20 .... **153** D2 ⁵
Sothall Gn *MOS* S20 .... **153** D2
Sothall Ms *MOS* S20 .... **153** D2 ²
Sough Hall Av *KIMB* S61 .... **90** A1
Sough Hall Cl *KIMB* S61 .... **90** A1
Sough Hall Crs *KIMB* S61 .... **90** A1
Sough Hall Rd *KIMB* S61 .... **90** A2
Soughley La *CHPT/GREN* S35 .... **70** B1
   FUL S10 .... **130** C2
Southall St *SHEFS* S8 .... **135** E4 ¹¹
South Av *MEX/SWTN* S64 .... **80** C1
Southbourne Rd *ECC* S11 .... **121** D5
South Cl *DRON* S18 .... **170** C5
Southcote Dr *DRON* S18 .... **168** B2
South Crs *DOD/DAR* S75 .... **20** A3
   ECK/KIL S21 .... **166** C1
   RHAM/THRY S65 .... **104** C2
Southcroft Gdns *SHEFS* S8 .... **135** D4 ⁵
Southdown Av *CHSW* S40 .... **188** D5
Southend Pl *SHEFP/MNR* S2 .... **123** F5
Southend Rd *SHEFP/MNR* S2 ...... **136** C1 ⁹
Southey Av *SHEFN* S5 .... **109** E1
Southey Cl *SHEFN* S5 .... **109** D1 ¹
Southey Crs *SHEFN* S5 .... **109** D1
Southey Dr *SHEFN* S5 .... **109** E1
Southey Green Cl *SHEFN* S5 .... **109** D1 ²
Southey Green Rd *SHEFN* S5 .... **97** D5
Southey Hall Dr *SHEFN* S5 .... **109** D1
Southey Hall Rd *SHEFN* S5 .... **97** D5
Southey Hl *SHEFN* S5 .... **109** D1
Southey Pl *SHEFN* S5 .... **109** D1
Southey Ri *SHEFN* S5 .... **109** D1
Southfield Crs *DEARNE* S63 .... **26** B4
Southfield Dr *DRON* S18 .... **170** A3
Southfield La *DEARNE* S63 .... **26** B4
Southfield Mt *DRON* S18 .... **170** A3 ²
Southfield Rd *ARMTH* DN3 .... **33** E4
Southgate *DOD/DAR* S75 .... **13** D4
   ECK/KIL S21 .... **164** C5
   HOY S74 .... **51** F3
Southgate Ct *ECK/KIL* S21 .... **164** C5
Southgate Wy *STV/CWN* S43 .... **180** C2
South Grimesthorpe Rd *ATT* S4 .. **123** D1 ⁵
Southgrove Rd *FUL* S10 .... **134** B1
Southlands Wy *AU/AST/KP* S26 .. **142** C3
South La *SHEF* S1 .... **135** E1
Southlea Av *HOY* S74 .... **52** A3
Southlea Cl *HOY* S74 .... **52** A3 ¹
Southlea Dr *HOY* S74 .... **51** F3
Southlea Rd *HOY* S74 .... **51** F2
South Lodge Ct *CHSW* S40 .... **188** C1
Southmoor Av *ARMTH* DN3 .... **33** E4
Southmoor Cl *STV/CWN* S43 .... **186** A5
Southmoor La *ARMTH* DN3 .... **33** E4
South Pde *DON* DN1 .... 5 G4
   OWL S3 .... 8 D2
South Pl *CHSW* S40 .... **190** B3 ²
   DOD/DAR S75 .... **12** C4
   WMB/DAR S73 .... **38** C2 ¹

South Rd *CHPT/GREN* S35 .... **73** E4
   DOD/DAR S75 .... **20** A2
   KIMB S61 .... **101** F2
Southsea Rd *HAN/WDH* S13 .... **139** E4
South St *BSLY* S70 .... **21** D1 ⁵
   DOD/DAR S75 .... **20** A2
   DONS/BSCR DN4 .... **44** B3
   KIMB S61 .... **93** D3
   KIMB S61 .... **101** F4
   MOS S20 .... **164** B2
   RAW S62 .... **80** B5
South St North *STV/CWN* S43 ...... **179** E2
South Street Pk *SHEFP/MNR* S2 .. 9 H5
South Vw *MOS* S20 .... **165** E1
South View Cl *ST/HB/BR* S6 .... **106** C3
South View Crs *ABRD* S7 .... **135** D3 ¹⁴
South View Ri *ST/HB/BR* S6 .... **106** C3
South View Rd *ECC* S11 .... **135** D2
   HOY S74 .... **51** E2
South View Ter *RHAM* S60 .... **127** D2 ²
Southview Ri *MEX/SWTN* S64 ...... **58** C2 ²
Southwell Rd *ATT* S4 .... **111** D3 ⁴
   RAW S62 .... **80** C5
   WHHL DN2 .... **31** D3
Southwell St *DOD/DAR* S75 .... **13** E5 ¹⁰
Southwood Av *DRON* S18 .... **169** E4
Sowters Rw *CHSW* S40 .... **11** E6
Spa Brook Cl *HACK/IN* S12 .... **151** D1
Spa Brooke Dr *HACK/IN* S12 .... **139** D5
Spa La *CHNE* S41 .... **11** G6
   HAN/WDH S13 .... **140** A5
Spa Lane Cft *HAN/WDH* S13 .... **140** A4
Spalton Rd *RAW* S62 .... **94** A2
Spansyke St *DONS/BSCR* DN4........ 4 B5
Spa View Av *HACK/IN* S12 .... **151** D2
Spa View Dr *HACK/IN* S12 .... **151** D2
Spa View Pl *HACK/IN* S12 .... **151** D2
Spa View Rd *HACK/IN* S12 .... **151** D2
Spa View Ter *HACK/IN* S12 .... **151** D2 ¹
Spa View Wy *HACK/IN* S12 .... **151** D2
Spa Well Crs *RHAM* S60 .... **127** F2
Speeton Rd *ST/HB/BR* S6 .... **108** A5 ⁶
Spencer Gn *RHAM* S60 .... **116** B3 ¹
Spencer Rd *SHEFP/MNR* S2 .... **135** E3
Spencer St *BSLY* S70 .... **21** F2
   CHSW S40 .... **11** E4
   MEX/SWTN S64 .... **57** F3
Spenser Rd *RHAM/THRY* S65 ...... **104** B4
Spilsby Cl *DONS/BSCR* DN4 .... **67** E1
Spink Hall Cl *STKB/PEN* S36 .... **69** D3 ¹
Spink Hall La *STKB/PEN* S36 .... **68** C3
Spinkhill Av *HAN/WDH* S13 .... **138** A2
Spinkhill Dr *HAN/WDH* S13 .... **138** B2
Spinkhill Rd *ECK/KIL* S21 .... **166** C4
   HAN/WDH S13 .... **138** B3
Spinney Cl *RHAM* S60 .... **115** E1
Spinneyfield *RHAM* S60 .... **115** E2
The Spinney *DONS/BSCR* DN4 ...... **63** D2 ²
Spital Brook Cl *CHNE* S41 .... **191** D3
Spitalfields *OWL* S3 .... 9 F2
Spital Gdns *CHNE* S41 .... **191** D3
Spital Hl *ATT* S4 .... 9 H2
Spital La *CHNE* S41 .... **190** C2
   OWL S3 .... 9 H1
Spital St *OWL* S3 .... 9 G1
Spofforth Rd *DARN/MH* S9 .... **124** B2 ⁶
Spooner Rd *ECK/KIL* S21 .... **166** A2
Spooner Rd *FUL* S10 .... **121** D4
Spoon Gld *ST/HB/BR* S6 .... **119** D1 ⁶
Spoonhill Rd *ST/HB/BR* S6 .... **120** A1
Spoon La *ST/HB/BR* S6 .... **118** B1
Spoon Ms *ST/HB/BR* S6 .... **119** D1
Spoon Wy *ST/HB/BR* S6 .... **119** D1
Spotswood Cl *GLV* S14 .... **148** C1 ⁵
Spotswood Dr *SHEFP/MNR* S2 .... **136** C5 ³
Spotswood Mt *GLV* S14 .... **136** C5 ⁵
Spotswood Pl *GLV* S14 .... **148** B1
Spotswood Rd *SHEFS* S8 .... **148** B1
Spout La *ST/HB/BR* S6 .... **118** C1
Spout Spinney *ST/HB/BR* S6........ **118** C1
Spring Bank Rd *CHSW* S40 .... **10** C5
   CONI DN12 .... **84** C3
Spring Close Dell *GLV* S14 .... **149** D1
Spring Close Mt *GLV* S14 .... **149** D1
Spring Close Vw *GLV* S14 .... **149** D1
   HACK/IN S12 .... **137** F5
   SHEFP/MNR S2 .... **135** E1
Spring Cft *KIMB* S61 .... **92** A5
Springcroft Dr *BTLY* DN5 .... **28** C1
Spring Dr *WMB/DAR* S73 .... **40** B5
Springfield Av *CHSW* S40 .... **189** D1
   ECC S11 .... **134** A5
Springfield Cl *ABRD* S7 .... **146** A1
   ECK/KIL S21 .... **164** A5
   KIMB S61 .... **93** D3
Springfield Ct *BTLY* DN5 .... **28** C4 ⁷
Springfield Crs *HOY* S74 .... **51** D3
Springfield Gln *ECC* S11 .... **145** F1
Springfield Pl *BSLY* S70 .... **21** E1 ¹⁰
Springfield Rd *ABRD* S7 .... **146** A1
   CONI DN12 .... **62** A5
   HOY S74 .... **50** C3
   MEX/SWTN S64 .... **81** F4
Springfield St *BSLY* S70 .... **21** D1

Spring Gdns *BSLYN/ROY* S71 .... **15** D3 ⁴
   DON DN1 .... 4 D4
   HOY S74 .... **51** F2
Spring Hl *FUL* S10 .... **121** D3
Springhill Av *WMB/DAR* S73 .... **40** B5
Spring Hill Rd *FUL* S10 .... **121** D3
Spring House Cl *RCH* S42 .... **182** A4
Spring House Rd *FUL* S10 .... **121** D3 ⁷
Spring La *SHEFP/MNR* S2 .... **136** C2
Spring St *BSLY* S70 .... **21** F2
   OWL S3 .... 9 E3
   RHAM/THRY S65 .... 7 F4
Spring Vale Rd *BSLY* S70 .... **36** A1 ³
Springvale Rd *ST/HB/BR* S6 .... **121** E3
Spring View Rd *STV/CWN* S43 .... **185** F1
Spring View Rd *FUL* S10 .... **121** D3 ⁸
Spring Water Av *HACK/IN* S12...... **151** D2
Spring Water Cl *HACK/IN* S12 .... **151** E2 ⁶
Spring Water Dr *HACK/IN* S12 .... **151** D1
Springwood Av *AU/AST/KP* S26 .. **142** A1
Spring Wood Cl *CHNE* S41 .... **183** D1
Springwood La *CHPT/GREN* S35 .. **73** D5
Springwood Rd *BTLY* DN5 .... **28** C1
   HOY S74 .... **51** D3
   SHEFS S8 .... **135** E4 ¹²
Sprotbrough Rd *BTLY* DN5 .... **43** D1
Spruce Ri *ECK/KIL* S21 .... **166** A3
Spurley Hey Gv *STKB/PEN* S36 .... **69** D3
Spurr St *SHEFP/MNR* S2 .... **135** F2
The Square *AU/AST/KP* S26 .... **155** F3 ⁵
   BSLY S70 .... **21** E2
   RAW S62 .... **75** E2
The Stables *MEX/SWTN* S64 .... **56** C4
Stacey Dr *RHAM/THRY* S65 .... **95** F3 ⁸
Stacye Av *HAN/WDH* S13 .... **140** B4
Stacye Ri *HAN/WDH* S13 .... **140** B4
Stadium Ct *RAW* S62 .... **93** F4
Stadium Wy *DARN/MH* S9 .... **98** A2
   RHAM/THRY S65 .... **94** A5
Stafford Cl *DRON* S18 .... **168** A1 ⁸
Stafford Crs *RHAM* S60 .... **115** D3
Stafford Dr *RHAM* S60 .... **115** D3
Stafford Gv *BSLY* S70 .... **50** A3
Stafford La *SHEFP/MNR* S2 .... **123** E3
Stafford Rd *SHEFP/MNR* S2 .... **123** E5
Stafford St *SHEFP/MNR* S2 .... 9 H6
Stafford Wy *CHPT/GREN* S35 .... **88** A1 ⁸
Stag Cl *RHAM* S60 .... **116** A1
Stag Crs *RHAM/THRY* S65 .... **116** A1
Stag La *RHAM* S60 .... **115** F1
Stainborough Cl *DOD/DAR* S75 .... **20** A4
Stainborough Rd *DOD/DAR* S75 .. **20** A4
Stainborough Vw *BSLY* S70 .... **22** A5 ⁸
   DOD/DAR S75 .... **49** E2 ⁸
Staindrop Vw *CHPT/GREN* S35 .... **74** B5
Stainley Cl *DOD/DAR* S75 .... **12** C3 ⁸
Stainmore Av *MOS* S20 .... **153** E3
Stainton Cl *BSLYN/ROY* S71 .... **15** D3
Stainton Rd *ECC* S11 .... **133** F2
Stainton St *CONI* DN12 .... **60** A5
Stair Rd *ATT* S4 .... **110** A4
Stalker Lees Rd *ECC* S11 .... **134** B2
Stamford St *DARN/MH* S9 .... **111** D5 ⁸
Stampers Hl *DOD/DAR* S75 .... **35** E3
Stanage Ri *HACK/IN* S12 .... **138** B5
Stanage Wy *RCH* S42 .... **182** A4 ⁸
Stanbury Cl *DOD/DAR* S75 .... **12** C4
Standish Av *SHEFN* S5 .... **109** E3
Standish Cl *SHEFN* S5 .... **109** E3
Standish Dr *SHEFN* S5 .... **109** E3
Standish Rd *SHEFN* S5 .... **109** E3
Standon Crs *DARN/MH* S9 .... **100** A4
Standon Dr *DARN/MH* S9 .... **100** A4
Standon Rd *DARN/MH* S9 .... **100** B4
Stand Rd *CHNE* S41 .... **184** A1
Staneford Ct *MOS* S20 .... **152** B4
Stanford Rd *DRON* S18 .... **168** A2 ⁸
Stanforth Wy *CHSW* S40 .... **188** C4
Stanhope Gdns *DOD/DAR* S75 ...... **13** D4
Stanhope Rd *DON* DN1 .... **30** C4
   HACK/IN S12 .... **138** A5
Staniforth Av *ECK/KIL* S21 .... **163** F5
Staniforth Rd *DARN/MH* S9 .... **124** B2
Stanley Av *STV/CWN* S43 .... **186** C3
Stanley Gdns *DONS/BSCR* DN4 .... **43** F3 ⁵
Stanley Gv *AU/AST/KP* S26 .... **143** D2 ¹
Stanley La *OWL* S3 .... 9 F2
Stanley Rd *BSLY* S70 .... **23** F2
   BTLY DN5 .... **28** B2
   CHPT/GREN S35 .... **73** F5
   SHEFS S8 .... **135** F5
   STKB/PEN S36 .... **69** D2 ⁴
Stanley St *BSLY* S70 .... 2 A5
   CHNE S41 .... **190** C2
   ECK/KIL S21 .... **166** B1
   OWL S3 .... 9 F2
Stannington Gln *ST/HB/BR* S6 .... **119** F1

Stannington Ri ST/HB/BR S6 ...... 107 E5 [1]
Stannington Rd ST/HB/BR S6..... 118 C1
Stannington View Rd FUL S10 .... 120 B3
Stanton Crs HACK/IN S12 .... 150 B1 [1]
Stanwell Av DARN/MH S9 .... 100 B5
Stanwell St DARN/MH S9........... 100 B5
Stanwood Av ST/HB/BR S6 .... 120 A1
Stanwood Crs ST/HB/BR S6 .... 120 A1
Stanwood Dr CHSW S40 .... 188 C4 [1]
ST/HB/BR S6 .... 120 A1
Stanwood Ms ST/HB/BR S6 .... 120 A1 [2]
Stanwood Rd ST/HB/BR S6......... 120 A1
Stapleton Rd DONS/BSCR DN4 ..... 62 B2
Star La BSLY S70 .... 2 B5
Starling Md SHEFP/MNR S2 .... 123 F5 [1]
Starnhill Cl CHPT/GREN S35....... 89 D5
Station La CHNE S41.................. 178 B4
DARN/MH S9............................ 111 E2
Station Rd BSLY S70 .... 13 E5
BSLY S70 .... 37 D1
BTLY DN5 .... 17 E4
CHNE S41 .... 11 G6
CHNE S41................................ 184 B1
CHPT/GREN S35 .... 74 C5
CHPT/GREN S35 .... 89 D5
CONI DN12................................ 61 D5
DARN/MH S9 .... 125 D3 [3]
DEARNE S63 .... 27 D3
DEARNE S63 .... 56 A2
ECK/KIL S21 .... 164 C5
ECK/KIL S21............................ 165 F2
ECK/KIL S21 .... 175 D1
HAN/WDH S13 .... 140 B3
MEX/SWTN S64........................ 58 B4
MOS S20 .... 164 B1 [6]
MOS S20 .... 165 D1
RHAM S60 .... 102 C3
RHAM S60 .... 127 D1
RHAM S60 .... 127 D1
STKB/PEN S36.......................... 70 B2
STV/CWN S43 .... 180 B5
STV/CWN S43 .... 180 C3
STV/CWN S43 .... 185 D1
WMB/DAR S73 .... 39 F2
Station St MEX/SWTN S64 .... 57 E5
Staton Av MOS S20 .... 153 E1
Staton La DRON S18 .... 171 E2
The Statutes RHAM S60.............. 6 B5
Staunton Rd DONS/BSCR DN4 ..... 47 E5
Staveley La ECK/KIL S21............ 173 E4
ECK/KIL S21............................ 174 C3
Staveley Rd BSVR S44 .... 187 F5
SHEFS S8 .... 135 E3 [10]
STV/CWN S43 .... 179 F3
Steade Rd ABRD S7.................... 135 D3
Steadfield Rd HOY S74............... 50 C4 [1]
The Steadlands RAW S62 .... 79 E4 [1]
Stead La HOY S74 .... 50 C3
Stead St ECK/KIL S21 .... 164 B5
Steele Av STV/CWN S43 .... 180 C3
Steele St HOY S74 .... 50 B3
Steel Hl CHPT/GREN S35 .... 97 D2
Steelhouse La OWL S3 .... 9 E3 [1]
Steel Rd ECC S11 .... 134 A2
Steel St RHAM S60 .... 102 B4
Steeping Cl STV/CWN S43 .... 185 F1
Steeton Rd HOY S74................... 52 B2
Stemp St ECC S11 .... 135 D2 [11]
Stenton Rd SHEFS S8................ 159 D1
Stephen Dr CHPT/GREN S35........ 96 C1
FUL S10 .... 120 A4
Stephen Hl FUL S10 .... 120 A4
Stephen Hill Rd FUL S10 .... 120 A4
Stephen La CHPT/GREN S35 .... 96 C1
Stephenson Pl CHNE S41 .... 11 F6 [1]
Stephenson Rd STV/CWN S43 ..... 181 F5
Stepney St SHEFP/MNR S2 .... 9 H4
Stepping La CHPT/GREN S35....... 86 C5
Sterland St CHSW S40................ 10 C6
Sterndale Rd ABRD S7 .... 146 A2
Steven Cl CHPT/GREN S35 .... 88 A2
Steven Crs CHPT/GREN S35 .... 88 A1
Steven Pl CHPT/GREN S35 .... 88 A2
Stevenson Dr RHAM/THRY S65.... 104 C4
Stevenson Rd DARN/MH S9 .... 123 F1
DONS/BSCR DN4 .... 63 F1
Stevenson Wy DARN/MH S9 .... 123 F1
Stevens Rd DONS/BSCR DN4 ...... 43 F3 [4]
Stewart Rd ECC S11 .... 134 B2
Stewarts Rd RAW S62 .... 80 B5
Stewart St DON DN1 .... 4 C5
Sticking La MEX/SWTN S64 .... 57 F1
Stillman Cl CHNE S41 .... 191 D4
Stirling Cl HOY S74................... 52 B2 [1]
Stirling St DON S74 .... 4 D6
Stockarth Cl CHPT/GREN S35 ...... 96 A5
Stockbridge Av BTLY DN5 .... 29 E2 [1]
Stockbridge La BTLY DN5 .... 17 D4
Stockil Rd DONS/BSCR DN4........ 5 H6
Stock Rd SHEFP/MNR S2 .... 136 C1
Stocks Green Ct TOT/DORE S17 .. 156 A4
Stocks Green Dr TOT/DORE S17 .. 156 B4 [1]
Stocks Hl CHPT/GREN S35 .... 88 B5
Stock's La DOD/DAR S75............ 13 E5
RAW S62 .... 94 A1

Stockwell La AU/AST/KP S26....... 155 F4
Stoke St DARN/MH S9 .... 123 F2
Stokewell Rd DEARNE S63.......... 55 D1
Stoneacre Av HACK/IN S12 .... 151 F1
Stoneacre Cl HACK/IN S12 .... 151 F2 [4]
Stoneacre Dr HACK/IN S12 .... 151 F1
Stoneacre Ri HACK/IN S12 .... 151 F2
Stonecliffe Cl SHEFP/MNR S2 .... 137 E1
Stonecliffe Dr STKB/PEN S36 ...... 68 C4
Stonecliffe Pl SHEFP/MNR S2 .... 137 E1
Stonecliffe Rd SHEFP/MNR S2 ... 137 E1
Stone Cl DRON S18 .... 160 A5
Stone Close Av DONS/BSCR DN4 ... 4 A6
Stonecroft Rd TOT/DORE S17..... 156 C5
Stonecross Gdns DONS/BSCR DN4... 47 E4
Stonedale Cl MOS S20 .... 164 B1 [3]
Stone Delf FUL S10 .... 132 A1
Stone Font Gv DONS/BSCR DN4... 47 D5
Stonegravels La CHNE S41 .... 11 F1
Stonegravels Wy MOS S20 .... 165 D2
Stone Gv FUL S10 .... 121 E5
Stone Hill Dr AU/AST/KP S26...... 142 A3
Stonehill Ri BTLY DN5 .... 28 C1 [1]
Stone La HAN/WDH S13 .... 139 E5
STV/CWN S43 .... 179 E2
Stoneleigh Cft BSLY S70 .... 22 A3 [11]
Stoneley Cl HACK/IN S12 .... 149 F4
Stoneley Crs HACK/IN S12 .... 149 F4
Stoneley Dell HACK/IN S12........ 149 F4
Stoneley Dr HACK/IN S12........... 149 F4
Stonelow Crs DRON S18 .... 170 B1
Stonelow Rd DRON S18 .... 169 F1
Stone Moor Rd STKB/PEN S36 .... 68 B4
Stone Rd DRON S18 .... 160 A4
Stone Rw CHSW S40.................. 189 E2
Stone st BSLYN/ROY S71 .... 13 F3
MOS S20 .... 164 B1
Stonewood Ct FUL S10 .... 119 E5 [3]
Stonewood Gv FUL S10 .... 119 E5
Stoney Ga CHPT/GREN S35 .... 73 E3
Stonyford Rd WMB/DAR S73 .... 40 A1
Stoops Cl CHSW S40 .... 183 E3 [5]
Stoops La DONS/BSCR DN4 .... 45 F5
Stoops Rd DONS/BSCR DN4 .... 46 B5
Stopes Rd ST/HB/BR S6 .... 118 B1
Store St SHEFP/MNR S2 .... 135 F1
Storey's Ga WMB/DAR S73 .... 38 C2
Storey St MEX/SWTN S64 .... 57 D5
Storforth La CHNE S41 .... 191 D5
CHSW S40 .... 190 B5
Storrs Hall Rd ST/HB/BR S6 ...... 120 C1
Storrs La CHPT/GREN S35 .... 72 C1
Storrs Rd CHSW S40 .... 188 C2
Storth Av FUL S10 .... 132 C2
Storth La FUL S10 .... 132 C1
Stortholme Ms FUL S10 .... 133 D1 [1]
Stotfold Dr DEARNE S63 .... 26 C3
Stothard Rd FUL S10 .... 120 C3
Stour Cl STV/CWN S43 .... 185 F1
Stour La ST/HB/BR S6 .... 107 D2
Stovin Cl DARN/MH S9 .... 124 C1
Stovin Dr DARN/MH S9 .... 124 C1
Stovin Gdns DARN/MH S9 .... 111 F5
Stow Bridge La RHAM S60 .... 129 F1
Stowe Av ABRD S7 .... 146 A1
Stradbroke Av HAN/WDH S13..... 138 B3
Stradbroke Cl HAN/WDH S13 ..... 138 C3
Stradbroke Crs HAN/WDH S13 ... 138 C3
Stradbroke Dr HAN/WDH S13 .... 138 C3
Stradbroke Pl HAN/WDH S13 ..... 138 C3
Stradbroke Ri CHSW S40 .... 189 D4
Stradbroke Rd HAN/WDH S13 .... 138 B3
Stradbroke Wy HAN/WDH S13 ... 138 C3
Strafford Av BSLY S70 .... 22 A4
HOY S74.................................. 52 B2
Strafford Cl KIMB S61 .... 89 F1
Strafford Rd KIMB S61 .... 91 F4
Strafford Wk DOD/DAR S75 .... 20 A4
Strafford Rd FUL S10 .... 132 B1
Strathmore Gv DEARNE S63 .... 56 A2
Strathtay Rd ECC S11................ 133 F3
Strawberry Av SHEFN S5 .... 98 C3
Streetfield Crs MOS S20 .... 164 B2 [5]
Streetfields MOS S20 .... 164 C3
Street La RAW S62 .... 77 F1
Strelley Av SHEFS S8 .... 146 C4
Strelley Rd SHEFS S8 .... 146 B4
Stretton Cl DONS/BSCR DN4 ...... 47 E4
Stretton Rd BSLYN/ROY S71 ...... 14 B2
ECC S11 .... 134 A3
Stringers Cft RHAM S60 .... 116 B3 [1]
Struan Rd ECC S11 .... 134 A5
Strutt Rd OWL S3 .... 109 E5
Stuart Cl CHNE S41 .... 184 C3
Stuart Gv CHPT/GREN S35 .... 88 B2
Stuart Rd CHPT/GREN S35 .... 88 C2
Stuart St DEARNE S63 .... 27 E3
Stubbin Cl RAW S62 .... 79 E4
Stubbing House La
CHPT/GREN S35 .... 96 B2
Stubbing La CHPT/GREN S35 ..... 106 A1
Stubbing Rd CHSW S40 .... 190 A5
Stubbin La RAW S62 .... 79 E3
SHEFN S5 .... 99 D5
Stubbin St RAW S62 .... 78 C4

Stubbs Crs KIMB S61 .... 92 A5
Stubbs Rd WMB/DAR S73 .... 39 D3
Stubley Cl DRON S18 .... 168 C1
Stubley Cft DRON S18 .... 168 B1
Stubley Dr DRON S18 .... 168 C1
Stubley Hollow DRON S18.......... 168 C1
Stubley La DRON S18 .... 168 B1
Stubley Pl DRON S18 .... 168 C1
Studfield Crs ST/HB/BR S6 .... 107 D4
Studfield Dr ST/HB/BR S6 .... 107 D4
Studfield Gv ST/HB/BR S6 .... 107 D4
Studfield Hl ST/HB/BR S6 .... 107 D3
Studfield Ri ST/HB/BR S6 .... 107 D3
Studfield Rd ST/HB/BR S6......... 107 D4
Studley Ct DARN/MH S9 .... 125 D3 [7]
Studmoor Rd KIMB S61 .... 91 E4
Stump Cross Rd DEARNE S63 ..... 55 F3
Stumperlowe Av FUL S10 .... 132 C2 [3]
Stumperlowe Cl FUL S10 .... 132 C2 [3]
Stumperlowe Crescent Rd
FUL S10 .... 132 B2
Stumperlowe Cft FUL S10 .... 132 B2
Stumperlowe Hall Cha FUL S10 .. 132 B1 [2]
Stumperlowe Hall Rd FUL S10 ... 132 B3
Stumperlowe La FUL S10 .... 132 B2
Stumperlowe Park Rd FUL S10 ... 132 B2
Stumperlowe Vw FUL S10 .... 132 B1
Stupton Rd DARN/MH S9 .... 111 E2
Sturge Cft SHEFP/MNR S2 .... 135 F4 [3]
Sturton Cl DONS/BSCR DN4........ 66 A1
Sturton Cft RHAM/THRY S65....... 95 F5
Sturton Rd ATT S4.................... 110 A4
Sudbury Cl CHSW S40............... 189 D4 [3]
Sudbury Dr AU/AST/KP S26........ 142 C3
Sudbury St OWL S3..................... 8 B2
Sudhall Cl CHNE S41 .... 183 E1
Suffolk Rd DONS/BSCR DN4 ...... 63 F1 [10]
SHEFP/MNR S2....................... 122 C5
Sulby Gv BSLY S70 .... 23 E4
Summerfield RHAM/THRY S65 ...... 7 F5
Summerfield Crs STV/CWN S43 .. 185 F1
Summerfield Rd CHSW S40 .... 190 A3
DRON S18 .... 159 F5
Summerfield St FUL S10 .... 134 C1
Summer La TOT/DORE S17 .... 156 A4
WMB/DAR S73 .... 38 B3
Summerley Lower Rd DRON S18 .. 170 C1
Summerley Rd DRON S18 .... 170 C1
Summerskill Gn STV/CWN S43 ... 187 D2
Summer St BSLY S70 .... 2 A4
OWL S3 .... 121 F3
Summerwood La DRON S18 .... 159 D5
Summerwood Pl DRON S18 .... 169 D1
Summer Rd RHAM/THRY S65 .... 7 G2
Sunderland St ECC S11 .... 134 C1 [4]
Sunderland Ter BSLY S70 .... 22 B2 [6]
Sundew Cft CHPT/GREN S35 ...... 73 E3 [7]
Sundew Gdns CHPT/GREN S35 ... 73 E2
Sundown Pl HAN/WDH S13 .... 139 D2
Sundown Rd HAN/WDH S13 ...... 139 D2
Sunningdale Cl ARMTH DN3 .... 67 F1 [3]
CHSW S40 .... 189 F4 [3]
MEX/SWTN S64........................ 81 E2
Sunningdale Mt ECC S11 .... 133 F5
Sunningdale Ri CHSW S40......... 189 D4 [8]
Sunningdale Rd WHHL DN2 .... 31 E4 [2]
Sunny Bank FUL S10................. 134 C1
HOY S74.................................. 52 A1
Sunnybank Crs RHAM S60 .... 114 A4 [1]
Sunny Bank Ri HOY S74 .... 52 B2 [2]
Sunny Bank Rd STKB/PEN S36 .... 69 D5
Sunny Bar DON DN1 .... 5 E3
Sunnybrook Cl HOY S74.............. 51 F4
Sunnyside ARMTH DN3 .... 19 F4
Sunny Springs CHNE S41 .... 11 F3
Sunnyvale Av TOT/DORE S17 ..... 156 B4
Sunnyvale Rd TOT/DORE S17 .... 156 B4
Surbiton St DARN/MH S9........... 111 F4
Surrey Cl BSLY S70 .... 22 A3
Surrey La SHEF S1 .... 122 C5
Surrey Pl SHEF S1 .... 9 F6 [2]
Surrey St DONS/BSCR DN4 .... 43 F5
SHEF S1 .... 9 E6
Sussex Rd ATT S4 .... 123 D2
CHPT/GREN S35 .... 88 B1
Sussex St ATT S4 .... 123 D3
Suthard Cross Rd FUL S10 .... 120 C3 [6]
Sutherland Rd ATT S4................ 123 D1
Sutherland St ATT S4 .... 123 E2 [1]
Sutton Crs STV/CWN S43 .... 187 D2
Sutton St OWL S3....................... 8 A5
Swaddale Av CHNE S41 .... 184 C3
Swaddale Cl CHNE S41 .... 184 C3 [1]
Swaith Av BTLY DN5.................. 29 D2
Swale Cl BTLY DN5 .... 29 D2
Swaledale Rd BSLY S70 .... 23 D5
Swaithe Vw BSLY S70 .... 23 E5
Swaledale Rd ABRD S7 .... 134 B5
Swale Dr CHPT/GREN S35 .... 87 F1
Swale Gdns DARN/MH S9 .... 125 D3 [8]
Swale Rd KIMB S61 .... 92 B3
Swallow Cl BSLY S70 .... 36 A5
Swallow La AU/AST/KP S26........ 142 C4
Swallow Wood Ct HAN/WDH S13.. 139 E4
Swamp Wk ST/HB/BR S6............ 108 B5
Swanbourne Pl SHEFN S5 .... 99 D5 [2]

Swanbourne Rd *SHEFN* S5 .... 99 D4
Swanee Rd *BSLY* S70 .... 22 C4
Swannington Cl *DONS/BSCR* DN4 .... 47 E5
Swan Rd *AU/AST/KP* S26 .... 142 C4
Swan St *BTLY* DN5 .... 16 C5 🔟
  RHAM S60 .... 103 E4
Swanwick St *CHNE* S41 .... 178 B4 🔟
Swarcliffe Rd *DARN/MH* S9 .... 124 B2
Sweyn Cft *BSLY* S70 .... 22 B5 🔢
Swifte Rd *RHAM* S60 .... 115 E1 🔟
Swift Ri *KIMB* S61 .... 76 B5
Swift Rd *CHPT/GREN* S35 .... 97 E1
Swift St *DOD/DAR* S75 .... 2 A3
Swift Wy *SHEFP/MNR* S2 .... 123 F5
Swinburne Av *DONS/BSCR* DN4 .. 63 F1 🔢
Swinburne Pl *RHAM/THRY* S65 .... 104 C4
Swinburne Rd *RHAM/THRY* S65 ..... 104 C4
Swinscoe Wy *RCH* S42 .... 182 A4
Swinton Rd *MEX/SWTN* S64 .... 58 A4
Swinton St *OWL* S3 .... 9 E1
Sycamore Av *AU/AST/KP* S26 .... 155 F3
  CHSW S40 .... 189 F3
  DRON S18 .... 159 E5
Sycamore Crs *DEARNE* S63 .... 56 A3 🔟
Sycamore Dr *CHNE* S41 .... 191 E1
  ECK/KIL S21 .... 166 A3
Sycamore Farm Cl *MALT* S66 .... 117 F1 🔟
Sycamore Gv *CONI* DN12 .... 84 B2 🔟
  DONS/BSCR DN4 .... 47 D4
Sycamore House Rd *SHEFN* S5 ..... 100 A3
Sycamore La *STV/CWN* S43 .... 180 B5
Sycamore Rd *CHPT/GREN* S35 .... 98 C1
  MEX/SWTN S64 .... 57 F3
  RHAM/THRY S65 .... 94 C5
  STKB/PEN S36 .... 68 B3
  STV/CWN S43 .... 180 A5
The Sycamores *BTLY* DN5 .... 28 A1
Sycamore St *DOD/DAR* S75 .... 13 D5 🔟
  MOS S20 .... 152 A5
  MOS S20 .... 153 D1 🔟
Sycamore Vw *BTLY* DN5 .... 42 B3
Sydney Rd *ST/HB/BR* S6 .... 121 E5
Sydney St *CHSW* S40 .... 10 A6
Sykes Av *DOD/DAR* S75 .... 2 A5
Sykes Ct *MEX/SWTN* S64 .... 81 E2
Sykes St *BSLY* S70 .... 21 E3
Sylvan Cl *CHNE* S41 .... 190 C3 🔟
Sylvester Av *DONS/BSCR* DN4 .... 44 A3
Sylvester Gdns *SHEF* S1 .... 122 B5
Sylvester St *SHEF* S1 .... 135 E1
Sylvia Cl *HAN/WDH* S13 .... 140 B3 🔟
Sylvia Rd *DRON* S18 .... 177 E1
Symes Gdns *DONS/BSCR* DN4 .... 47 D3
Symonds Av *RAW* S62 .... 79 D3
Symons Crs *SHEFN* S5 .... 98 A4

T

Tadcaster Cl *CONI* DN12 .... 83 F1
Tadcaster Crs *SHEFS* S8 .... 147 D1
Tadcaster Rd *SHEFS* S8 .... 147 D1
Tadcaster Wy *SHEFS* S8 .... 147 D1 🔟
Taddington Rd *CHSW* S40 .... 182 C4 🔟
Talbot Crs *CHNE* S41 .... 191 E5
  SHEFP/MNR S2 .... 123 D5 🔟
Talbot Gdns *SHEFP/MNR* S2 .... 123 D5 🔢
Talbot Pl *SHEFP/MNR* S2 .... 123 D5 🔢
Talbot Rd *MEX/SWTN* S64 .... 58 A5
  SHEFP/MNR S2 .... 123 D4 🔢
Talbot St *CHNE* S41 .... 191 E5
  SHEFP/MNR S2 .... 123 D5
Talmont Rd *ECC* S11 .... 133 F4
Tanfield Rd *ST/HB/BR* S6 .... 108 B3
Tankersley La *HOY* S74 .... 50 A4
Tank Rw *BSLY* S70 .... 23 E1
Tannery Cl *HAN/WDH* S13 .... 139 F4
Tannery St *HAN/WDH* S13 .... 139 F4
Tansley Dr *CHSW* S40 .... 182 B4
  DARN/MH S9 .... 100 C5
Tansley St *DARN/MH* S9 .... 100 C5
Tansley Wy *STV/CWN* S43 .... 187 D3
Tap La *CHSW* S40 .... 10 B6
Taplin Rd *ST/HB/BR* S6 .... 107 F4
Tapton Bank *FUL* S10 .... 120 B5 🔟
Tapton Crescent Rd *FUL* S10 .... 120 B4
Tapton Hill Rd *FUL* S10 .... 120 B4
Tapton House Rd *FUL* S10 .... 120 C5
Tapton La *CHNE* S41 .... 11 C5
Tapton Ms *FUL* S10 .... 120 C4
Tapton Park Rd *FUL* S10 .... 133 D1
Tapton V *CHNE* S41 .... 185 D4
Tapton View Rd *CHNE* S41 .... 10 B2
Taptonville Crs *FUL* S10 .... 121 D5 🔟
Taptonville Rd *FUL* S10 .... 121 D4
Tapton Wy *STV/CWN* S43 .... 186 A5
Tasker Rd *FUL* S10 .... 120 C4
Tatenhill Gdns *DONS/BSCR* DN4 ... 67 E1
Taunton Av *DARN/MH* S9 .... 111 F1
Taunton Gdns *MEX/SWTN* S64 .... 59 D2
Taunton Gv *DARN/MH* S9 .... 111 F1 🔟
Taverner Cl *CHPT/GREN* S35 .... 73 E2

Taverner Cft *CHPT/GREN* S35 .... 73 F3 🔟
Taverner Wy *CHPT/GREN* S35 .... 73 F3
Tavistock Rd *SHEFS* S8 .... 135 D4
Tay Cl *DRON* S18 .... 68 B1
Taylor Crs *CHNE* S41 .... 191 E5
Taylor Rw *BSLY* S70 .... 22 A2 🔢
Taylors Cl *RAW* S62 .... 93 F4
Taylors La *RAW* S62 .... 93 F3
Taylor St *CONI* DN12 .... 84 A3
T Benedict Ct *SHEFP/MNR* S2 .... 136 B2 🔟
Teesdale Rd *HACK/IN* S12 .... 151 D4
  KIMB S61 .... 92 A3
Teeside Cl *BTLY* DN5 .... 28 B4
Telford Rd *BTLY* DN5 .... 29 C4
Telson Cl *MEX/SWTN* S64 .... 56 B5
Temperance St *MEX/SWTN* S64 ... 57 E5 🔟
Temple Gdns *DONS/BSCR* DN4 .... 47 D5
Temple Rd *RHAM* S60 .... 113 D1
Templestowe Ga *CONI* DN12 .... 85 F1 🔢
Temple Wy *BSLYN/ROY* S71 .... 15 E4 🔢
Ten Acre Rd *KIMB* S61 .... 102 A1
Tenby Gdns *DONS/BSCR* DN4 .... 43 E5
Tennyson Av *ARMTH* DN3 .... 33 F3
  BTLY DN5 .... 29 D5
  CHSW S40 .... 10 D5
  MEX/SWTN S64 .... 58 C2
Tennyson Ri *DEARNE* S63 .... 55 D1
Tennyson Rd *BSLYN/ROY* S71 .... 3 H1
  BTLY DN5 .... 16 C5
  RHAM/THRY S65 .... 104 C3
  ST/HB/BR S6 .... 121 E1
Ten Pound Wk *DONS/BSCR* DN4 ... 44 B4
Tenterden Rd *SHEFN* S5 .... 111 D1 🔟
Tenter La *DONS/BSCR* DN4 .... 62 A1
Tenter Rd *DONS/BSCR* DN4 .... 62 A1
Tenters Gn *BSLY* S70 .... 36 A1
Tenter St *RHAM* S60 .... 6 A3
  SHEF S1 .... 8 D4
Terminus Rd *ABRD* S7 .... 146 A2 🔟
Terrace Rd *RAW* S62 .... 94 A2
Terrey Rd *TOT/DORE* S17 .... 156 C3
Terry St *DARN/MH* S9 .... 111 F5
Tetney Rd *FUL* S10 .... 133 D1
Tewitt Rd *BTLY* DN5 .... 16 B2 🔟
Teynham Dr *SHEFN* S5 .... 109 D2
Teynham Rd *SHEFN* S5 .... 108 C2
Thackeray Av *RAW* S62 .... 80 C4
Thames St *RHAM* S60 .... 6 B4
Thealby Gdns *DONS/BSCR* DN4 ..... 46 A5
Theatre La *CHNE* S41 .... 11 C5 🔟
Thellusson Av *BTLY* DN5 .... 28 A3
Theobald Av *DONS/BSCR* DN4 .... 45 D2
Theobald Cl *DONS/BSCR* DN4 .... 44 C3 🔟
Thirlmere Dr *DRON* S18 .... 169 E1
Thirlmere Rd *BSLYN/ROY* S71 .... 3 F5
  BSLYN/ROY S71 .... 3 F6
  CHNE S41 .... 183 D2 🔟
  CHNE S41 .... 183 E2
  SHEFS S8 .... 134 C5 🔟
Thirlwall Av *CONI* DN12 .... 84 B1
Thirlwell Rd *SHEFS* S8 .... 135 E4
Thirsk Cl *CONI* DN12 .... 83 F1
Thomas St *BSLY* S70 .... 21 F2
  BSLY S70 .... 36 B1 🔟
  MEX/SWTN S64 .... 57 E5
  MEX/SWTN S64 .... 81 F4
  SHEF S1 .... 122 A5
Thompson Cl *CHNE* S41 .... 184 B1 🔟
  RAW S62 .... 79 D3 🔟
Thompson Dr *MEX/SWTN* S64 .... 81 D2
Thompson Gdns
  CHPT/GREN S35 .... 73 D3 🔟
Thompson Hl *CHPT/GREN* S35 .... 73 D4
Thompson Rd *FUL* S10 .... 134 B1
  WMB/DAR S73 .... 39 E3
Thompson St *CHNE* S41 .... 184 B1
Thomson Av *DONS/BSCR* DN4 .... 43 D5
Thomson Cl *DEARNE* S63 .... 56 A2
Thoresby Av *BSLYN/ROY* S71 .... 14 C3
  DONS/BSCR DN4 .... 45 D3
Thoresby Cl *AU/AST/KP* S26 .... 143 D2
Thoresby Pl *STV/CWN* S43 .... 187 D3 🔟
Thoresby Rd *ST/HB/BR* S6 .... 108 A5
Thornborough Cl
  SHEFP/MNR S2 .... 136 A3 🔟
Thornborough Pl
  SHEFP/MNR S2 .... 136 A3 🔟
Thornborough Rd *SHEFP/MNR* S2 . 135 F3
Thornbridge Av *HACK/IN* S12 .... 150 B2
Thornbridge Cl *HACK/IN* S12 .... 150 C2
Thornbridge Crs *HACK/IN* S12 ...... 150 C2
Thornbridge Dr *HACK/IN* S12 .... 150 B2
Thornbridge Gv *HACK/IN* S12 .... 150 B2 🔟
Thornbridge La *HACK/IN* S12 .... 150 C2 🔟
Thornbridge Pl *HACK/IN* S12 .... 150 B2 🔟
Thornbridge Ri *HACK/IN* S12 .... 150 C2
Thornbridge Rd *HACK/IN* S12 .... 150 B2
Thornbridge Wy *HACK/IN* S12 ...... 150 C2
Thornbrook Cl *CHPT/GREN* S35 ..... 74 B5
Thornbrook Gdns *CHPT/GREN* S35 . 74 B5
Thornbrook Ms *CHPT/GREN* S35 .. 74 B5 🔟
Thorncliffe La *CHPT/GREN* S35 ...... 74 A4
Thorndale Ri *RHAM* S60 .... 114 B4 🔟
Thorndene Cl *CHNE* S41 .... 184 A3
Thorndon Wy *CHSW* S40 .... 189 D4

Thorne Cl *CHSW* S40 .... 182 A5 🔟
Thornely Av *DOD/DAR* S75 .... 20 A2
Thorne Rd *ABRD* S7 .... 134 C5 🔟
  ARMTH DN3 .... 19 F5
  DON DN1 .... 5 F3
Thornfield Av *CHSW* S40 .... 188 C3
Thorn Garth *BTLY* DN5 .... 29 E3
Thornham Cl *ARMTH* DN3 .... 33 F4 🔟
Thornhill Av *RHAM* S60 .... 113 F5
  WHHL DN2 .... 31 F3
Thornhill Edge *RHAM* S60 .... 6 A4
Thornhill Pl *DEARNE* S63 .... 55 F2 🔟
Thorn La *WHHL* DN2 .... 19 E4
Thornley Sq *DEARNE* S63 .... 26 B3 🔟
Thorn Rd *MEX/SWTN* S64 .... 81 E2
Thornsett Gdns *TOT/DORE* S17 ..... 157 D1
Thornsett Rd *ECC* S11 .... 134 C2
Thorntondale Rd *BTLY* DN5 .... 28 B3
Thornton Pl *DRON* S18 .... 168 A2 🔢
Thornton Rd *BSLY* S70 .... 22 C3
Thornton St *KIMB* S61 .... 101 F4
Thornton Ter *BSLY* S70 .... 23 D5 🔟
Thorntree Cl *KIMB* S61 .... 90 A2 🔟
Thorntree La *DOD/DAR* S75 .... 13 E4 🔟
Thorntree Rd *KIMB* S61 .... 90 A3
Thornwell La *KIMB* S61 .... 76 A5
Thorogate *RAW* S62 .... 80 A4
Thorpe Cl *SHEFP/MNR* S2 .... 135 E2
Thorpe Av *DRON* S18 .... 160 A4
Thorpe Cl *CHNE* S41 .... 184 A1 🔟
Thorpe Dr *MOS* S20 .... 152 C4
Thorpefield Cl *KIMB* S61 .... 90 A1
Thorpefield Dr *KIMB* S61 .... 90 A1
Thorpe Gn *MOS* S20 .... 152 B3 🔟
Thorpe House Av *SHEFS* S8 .... 147 F1
Thorpe House Ri *SHEFS* S8 .... 147 E1
Thorpe House Rd *SHEFS* S8 .... 147 E1
Thorpe St *KIMB* S61 .... 90 A1
Threshfield Wy *HACK/IN* S12 .... 151 F2 🔟
Thrush Av *RHAM* S60 .... 114 B4 🔢
Thrush St *ST/HB/BR* S6 .... 120 C1
Thrybergh Ct *CONI* DN12 .... 60 C5 🔟
Thrybergh Hall Rd *RAW* S62 .... 80 C5
Thundercliffe Rd *KIMB* S61 .... 100 C2
Thurnscoe Bridge La *DEARNE* S63 .. 27 D5
Thurstan Av *SHEFS* S8 .... 146 C5
Tiber Vw *RHAM* S60 .... 114 A2 🔟
Tickhill Rd *DONS/BSCR* DN4 .... 63 E1
Tickhill Sq *CONI* DN12 .... 60 A5
Tickhill St *CONI* DN12 .... 60 A4
Tideswell Cl *STV/CWN* S43 .... 186 C1
Tideswell Rd *SHEFN* S5 .... 99 E5
  SHEFN S5 .... 110 A1
Tilford Rd *HAN/WDH* S13 .... 140 A4
Tillotson Cl *SHEFS* S8 .... 135 E4 🔢
Tillotson Ri *SHEFS* S8 .... 135 E4 🔢
Timothy Wood Av *BSLY* S70 .... 36 A5
Tingle Bridge Av *WMB/DAR* S73 ..... 53 D1
Tingle Bridge Crs *WMB/DAR* S73 .. 53 D1 🔟
Tingle Bridge La *WMB/DAR* S73 ..... 53 D1
Tingle Cl *WMB/DAR* S73 .... 53 D1
Tinker La *HOY* S74 .... 50 B5
  ST/HB/BR S6 .... 120 C2
Tinker Rd *RAW* S62 .... 80 B5
Tinsley Park Cl *DARN/MH* S9 .... 112 A5
Tinsley Park Rd *DARN/MH* S9 .... 111 F5
Tinsley Rd *HOY* S74 .... 51 E1
Tipton St *DARN/MH* S9 .... 111 E2
Tissington Cl *CHSW* S40 .... 182 C4
Tithe Barn Av *HAN/WDH* S13 .... 139 F3
Tithe Barn Cl *HAN/WDH* S13 .... 140 A3
Tithe Barn La *HAN/WDH* S13 .... 140 A4
Tithe Barn Wy *HAN/WDH* S13 .... 139 F3
Tithe Laithe *HOY* S74 .... 51 F2 🔟
Titterton Cl *DARN/MH* S9 .... 124 B1
Titterton St *DARN/MH* S9 .... 124 B1 🔟
Tiverton Cl *MEX/SWTN* S64 .... 81 E1 🔟
Tockwith Rd *DARN/MH* S9 .... 124 C2 🔟
Todmorden Cl *CONI* DN12 .... 59 F5
Todwick Rd *SHEFS* S8 .... 146 C1
Tofts La *ST/HB/BR* S6 .... 119 D3
Toftstead *ARMTH* DN3 .... 33 F4
Toftwood Av *FUL* S10 .... 120 B3 🔟
Toftwood Rd *FUL* S10 .... 120 C3
Togo St *DEARNE* S63 .... 26 C4 🔟
Toll Bar Av *HACK/IN* S12 .... 136 C5 🔟
Toll Bar Cl *HACK/IN* S12 .... 136 C5
Toll Bar Dr *HACK/IN* S12 .... 136 C5
Toll Bar Rd *MEX/SWTN* S64 .... 56 C5
  RHAM/THRY S65 .... 105 F5
Toll House Md *MOS* S20 .... 164 A1
Tom La *FUL* S10 .... 132 B1
Tomlinson Rd *HOY* S74 .... 52 A2
Tompson Hl *CHPT/GREN* S35 .... 72 C4
Tontine Rd *CHSW* S40 .... 190 B2 🔟
Tooker Rd *RHAM* S60 .... 103 F4
Topcliffe Rd *BSLYN/ROY* S71 .... 14 B2
Top Field La *RHAM/THRY* S65 .... 105 E1
Top Hall Rd *DONS/BSCR* DN4 .... 67 D2
Toppham Dr *SHEFS* S8 .... 159 D2
Toppham Rd *SHEFS* S8 .... 159 D2
Toppham Wy *SHEFS* S8 .... 159 D2
Top Pingle Cl *STV/CWN* S43 .... 185 F2
Top Side *CHPT/GREN* S35 .... 86 C5
Torbay Rd *ATT* S4 .... 110 B5

Tor Cl *BSLYN/ROY* S71 .... **14** B2
Torksey Cl *DONS/BSCR* DN4 ...... **66** C2 ⓶
Torksey Rd *SHEFN* S5 .... **99** E5
Torne Cl *DONS/BSCR* DN4 .... **67** E1
Torry Ct *HAN/WDH* S13 .... **140** A4
Tor Wy *RHAM* S60 .... **114** B5
Torwood Dr *SHEFS* S8 .... **158** C1 ⓶
Totley Brook Cl *TOT/DORE* S17 .. **156** B3 ⓵
Totley Brook Cft *TOT/DORE* S17 .. **156** B3 ⓶
Totley Brook Gln
TOT/DORE S17 .... **156** B3 ⓵
Totley Brook Gv *TOT/DORE* S17 .. **156** B3
Totley Brook Rd *TOT/DORE* S17 .. **156** B2
Totley Brook Wy
TOT/DORE S17 .... **156** B3 ⓵
Totley Grange Cl *TOT/DORE* S17 .. **156** B4 ⓶
Totley Grange Rd *TOT/DORE* S17 .. **156** B4
Totley Hall La *TOT/DORE* S17 .... **156** B4
Totley La *TOT/DORE* S17 .... **157** F3
Totley Mt *STV/CWN* S43 .... **185** E1
Towcester Wy *MEX/SWTN* S64 .... **59** D2
Tower Cl *SHEFP/MNR* S2 .... **136** A2 ⓵
Tower Dr *SHEFP/MNR* S2 .... **136** A2
Tower St *BSLY* S70 .... **21** F3
Town End *DRON* S18 .... **171** D2
Town End Av *AU/AST/KP* S26 ...... **142** B2
Townend Av *RHAM/THRY* S65 ...... **95** F4
Townend La *STKB/PEN* S36 .... **69** F4
Town End Rd *CHPT/GREN* S35 .... **98** A1
Townend St *FUL* S10 .... **121** D3
Town Fields Av *CHPT/GREN* S35 .. **98** C1
Townhead Rd *TOT/DORE* S17 .... **156** A2
Townhead St *SHEF* S1 .... **8** D5
Town La *KIMB* S61 .... **91** E4
Town Moor Av *WHHL* DN2 .... **31** D5
Town St *DARN/MH* S9 .... **112** B1
RHAM S60 .... **103** E5
Toyne St *FUL* S10 .... **120** C3
Trafalgar St *ST/HB/BR* S6 .... **97** D5
Trafalgar St *SHEF* S1 .... **8** C6
Traffic Ter *STV/CWN* S43 .... **180** C2
Trafford Ct *DON* DN1 .... **4** C4 ⓵
Trafford Wy *DON* DN1 .... **4** C4
Tranmoor Av *DONS/BSCR* DN4 .... **46** C5
Tranmoor Ct *HOY* S74 .... **50** C3 ⓷
Tranmoor La *ARMTH* DN3 .... **33** F4
Trans Pennine Trail *CONI* DN12 .. **60** B4
DARN/MH S9 .... **111** D5
ECK/KIL S21 .... **175** F2
HAN/WDH S13 .... **138** C1
KIMB S61 .... **102** A4
RAW S62 .... **51** E5
Trap La *ECC* S11 .... **132** C4
Travey Rd *SHEFP/MNR* S2 .... **137** E3 ⓷
Travis Gdns *DONS/BSCR* DN4 .... **43** D3
Travis Pl *FUL* S10 .... **121** F5
Tredis Cl *BSLYN/ROY* S71 .... **3** H2
Treecrest Ri *DOD/DAR* S75 .... **13** F3
Treefield Cl *KIMB* S61 .... **92** B3
Treelands *DOD/DAR* S75 .... **12** C4
Treeneuk Cl *CHSW* S40 .... **188** C1 ⓵
Tree Root Wk *FUL* S10 .... **121** E4 ⓶
Treeton La *AU/AST/KP* S26 .... **128** C4
RHAM S60 .... **127** E2
Treetown Crs *RHAM* S60 .... **127** F2
Treherne Rd *RHAM/THRY* S65 .... **104** A4
Trelawney Wk *BSLY* S70 .... **22** A5 ⓶
Trent Cl *CONI* DN12 .... **60** B4
Trent Gv *DRON* S18 .... **159** F5
Trentham Cl *RHAM* S60 .... **114** B4 ⓵
Trenton Cl *HAN/WDH* S13 .... **140** B4
Trenton Ri *HAN/WDH* S13 .... **140** B4
Trent St *DARN/MH* S9 .... **123** F1
Treswell Crs *ST/HB/BR* S6 .... **108** A4 ⓶
Trewan Ct *BSLYN/ROY* S71 ...... **14** C4 ⓶
Tricket Rd *CHPT/GREN* S35 ...... **73** D3
Trickett Rd *ST/HB/BR* S6 .... **108** A5
Trinity Cl *CHNE* S41 .... **10** D3
Trinity St *OWL* S3 .... **8** D3
Trippet La *SHEF* S1 .... **8** D5
Tristford Cl *RHAM* S60 .... **127** E1
Troon Cl *CHSW* S40 .... **189** D4
Troughbrook Rd *STV/CWN* S43 .. **180** C5
Troutbeck Cl *DEARNE* S63 .... **26** C4
Troutbeck Rd *SHEFS* S8 .... **146** C4
Trueman Ter *BSLYN/ROY* S71 .... **15** F5 ⓷
Truman Gv *STKB/PEN* S36 .... **70** A2 ⓵
Truman St *BTLY* DN5 .... **16** B5
Truro Av *WHHL* DN2 .... **32** A1
Truro Ct *BSLYN/ROY* S71 .... **14** C4
Truswell Av *FUL* S10 .... **120** B3
Truswell Rd *FUL* S10 .... **120** B4
Tudor Rd *WHHL* DN2 .... **31** F5
Tudor St *DEARNE* S63 .... **27** E3
Tudor Wy *BSLY* S70 .... **22** B5
Tuffolds Cl *SHEFP/MNR* S2 ...... **137** E3
Tulip Tree Cl *MOS* S20 .... **141** E5
Tullibardine Rd *ECC* S11 .... **133** F4
Tummon Rd *SHEFP/MNR* S2 .... **125** F5
Tummon St *KIMB* S61 .... **102** C3 ⓷
Tune St *BSLY* S70 .... **22** B2
WMB/DAR S73 .... **39** D3
Tunstall Gn *CHSW* S40 .... **189** E3
Tunstall Wy *CHSW* S40 .... **189** E3

Tunwell Av *SHEFN* S5 .... **98** C2
Tunwell Dr *SHEFN* S5 .... **98** C2
Tunwell Greave *SHEFN* S5 .... **98** C2
Turie Av *SHEFN* S5 .... **98** B3
Turie Crs *SHEFN* S5 .... **98** B3
Turnberry Cl *CHSW* S40 .... **189** D4 ⓵
Turnberry Ct *BTLY* DN5 .... **29** E1 ⓷
Turner Av *WMB/DAR* S73 .... **38** C2
Turner Cl *DRON* S18 .... **169** D2 ⓷
RAW S62 .... **94** B2
Turner Dr *STV/CWN* S43 .... **186** C2
Turner La *RHAM* S60 .... **115** F3
Turner's Cl *HOY* S74 .... **52** A1
Turners La *FUL* S10 .... **121** D5 ⓾
Turner St *SHEFP/MNR* S2 .... **122** C5
Turnesc Gv *DEARNE* S63 .... **27** D4
Turnoaks La *CHSW* S40 .... **190** B5
Turnpike Cft *CHPT/GREN* S35 .... **87** D5 ⓵
Turnshaw Av *AU/AST/KP* S26 .... **142** A1
Tutbury Gdns *DONS/BSCR* DN4 .. **47** E5
Tuxford Crs *BSLYN/ROY* S71 .... **15** E5
The Twenty Lands *RHAM* S60 .. **127** F4
Twentywell Dr *TOT/DORE* S17 .. **157** F2 ⓵
Twentywell La *TOT/DORE* S17 .. **157** E1
Twentywell Ri *TOT/DORE* S17 .. **157** F1
Twentywell Rd *TOT/DORE* S17 .. **157** F3
Twentywell Vw *TOT/DORE* S17 .. **157** F3
Twibell St *BSLYN/ROY* S71 .... **3** F2
Twickenham Cl *MOS* S20 .... **164** C2 ⓷
Twickenham Ct *MOS* S20 .... **164** C2 ⓾
Twickenham Crs *MOS* S20 .... **164** C3
Twickenham Gld *MOS* S20 .... **164** C2 ⓵⓵
Twickenham Gln *MOS* S20 .... **165** D3 ⓷
Twickenham Gv *MOS* S20 .... **164** C2 ⓵⓶
Twitchill Dr *HAN/WDH* S13 .... **139** F4
Twyford Cl *MEX/SWTN* S64 .... **56** B5
Tyas Pl *MEX/SWTN* S64 .... **58** C3 ⓵
Tyas Rd *SHEFN* S5 .... **98** B2
Tye Rd *MOS* S20 .... **153** E2
Tyler St *DARN/MH* S9 .... **111** F1
Tyler Wy *DARN/MH* S9 .... **111** F1
Tylney Rd *CHSW* S40 .... **188** C5
SHEFP/MNR S2 .... **136** B1
Tynker Av *MOS* S20 .... **153** E2
Tyzack Rd *SHEFS* S8 .... **146** C3

U

Ulley Crs *HAN/WDH* S13 .... **137** F3
Ulley La *AU/AST/KP* S26 .... **129** F4
AU/AST/KP S26 .... **142** C2
Ulley Rd *HAN/WDH* S13 .... **137** F3
Ulley Vw *AU/AST/KP* S26 .... **129** E5
Ullswater Av *MOS* S20 .... **164** C2
Ullswater Cl *DRON* S18 .... **168** C1
MOS S20 .... **164** C2
Ullswater Pl *DRON* S18 .... **168** C2
Ullswater Rd *BSLYN/ROY* S71 .. **24** C2 ⓷
MEX/SWTN S64 .... **59** E2
Ulverston Rd *CHNE* S41 .... **183** E2
SHEFS S8 .... **146** C1
Undercliffe Rd *ST/HB/BR* S6 .... **120** A1 ⓷
Underhill *BSLY* S70 .... **36** C1
Underhill La *ST/HB/BR* S6 .... **96** C4
Underwood Av *BSLY* S70 .... **22** C4
Underwood Rd *SHEFS* S8 .... **147** D1
Union Cl *BSLY* S70 .... **22** A2
Union La *SHEF* S1 .... **122** B5 ⓵⓸
Union Rd *ECC* S11 .... **134** B4
Union St *BSLY* S70 .... **22** A2
DON DN1 .... **4** D5
KIMB S61 .... **102** C3
SHEF S1 .... **122** B5 ⓵⓶
Unity Pl *RHAM* S60 .... **6** D6
Unstone-Dronfield By-pass
DRON S18 .... **159** D5
Unstone Hl *DRON* S18 .... **170** B3
Unstone Rd *DRON* S18 .... **178** A1
Unstone St *SHEFP/MNR* S2 ...... **135** E1
Upland Ri *CHSW* S40 .... **189** E3
Uplands Wy *RAW* S62 .... **79** F5
Upper Albert Rd *SHEFS* S8 ...... **135** F5
Upper Allen St *OWL* S3 .... **8** B4
Upper Clara St *KIMB* S61 .... **102** A3
Upper Croft Cl *STV/CWN* S43 .... **185** F2
Upper Folderings *DOD/DAR* S75 .. **20** A3 ⓷
Upper Gate Rd *ST/HB/BR* S6 .... **118** C2
Upper Hanover St *OWL* S3 .... **8** A6
OWL S3 .... **121** F5 ⓵⓾
Upper Hoyland Rd *HOY* S74 ...... **51** D1
Upper Ley Ct *CHPT/GREN* S35 .. **88** B1 ⓷
Upper Ley Dell *CHPT/GREN* S35 .. **88** B1 ⓵
Upper Moor St *CHSW* S40 .... **188** C2 ⓶
Upper Newbold Cl *CHSW* S40 .. **182** C2 ⓷
Upper New St *BSLY* S70 .... **22** A3 ⓵⓷
Upper Rye Cl *RHAM* S60 .... **116** B3
Upper School La *DRON* S18 ...... **169** E3 ⓶
DRON S18 .... **169** E3 ⓷
Upper Sheffield Rd *BSLY* S70 .... **22** B4
Upperthorpe *ST/HB/BR* S6 .... **121** E2 ⓷
Upperthorpe Gln *ST/HB/BR* S6 .. **121** E2 ⓷
Upperthorpe Rd *ECK/KIL* S21 .. **166** B3

ST/HB/BR S6 .... **8** A2
Upper Valley Rd *SHEFS* S8 ...... **135** F5
Upper Whiston La *RHAM* S60 .. **116** A5
Upperwood Rd *WMB/DAR* S73 .. **25** F4
Upper Wortley Rd *KIMB* S61 .... **90** A3
Upton Cl *WMB/DAR* S73 .... **38** C1
Upwell Hl *ATT* S4 .... **110** C3
Upwell La *ATT* S4 .... **110** C3
Upwell St *ATT* S4 .... **110** C3
Upwood Cl *CHSW* S40 .... **182** B4 ⓵⓷
Upwood Rd *ST/HB/BR* S6 .... **107** F3
Urban Rd *DONS/BSCR* DN4 ...... **43** F3
Urch Cl *CONI* DN12 .... **85** D2
Uttley Cft *DARN/MH* S9 .... **124** C1
Uttley Cl *DARN/MH* S9 .... **124** C1
Uttley Dr *DARN/MH* S9 .... **124** C1
Uttoxeter Av *MEX/SWTN* S64 .... **59** D2

V

Vaal St *BSLY* S70 .... **22** C2
Vainor Rd *ST/HB/BR* S6 .... **107** E2
Vale Cl *DRON* S18 .... **169** F2 ⓷
Vale Gv *ST/HB/BR* S6 .... **106** C4
Valentine Cl *SHEFN* S5 .... **99** D4
Valentine Cr *SHEFN* S5 .... **99** D4
Valentine Rd *SHEFN* S5 .... **99** D4
Vale Rd *OWL* S3 .... **109** D5
Valiant Gdns *BTLY* DN5 .... **42** C1
Valley Dr *DEARNE* S63 .... **55** E2
ECK/KIL S21 .... **166** B1 ⓷
Valley Rd *CHNE* S41 .... **191** D2
CHPT/GREN S35 .... **73** F5
ECK/KIL S21 .... **166** B1
HACK/IN S12 .... **152** A3
MEX/SWTN S64 .... **80** C1
SHEFS S8 .... **135** E4
WMB/DAR S73 .... **39** F1
Valley View Cl *CHNE* S41 .... **191** F5
ECK/KIL S21 .... **174** A1 ⓵
Valley Wy *HOY* S74 .... **51** F2
Varney Rd *DEARNE* S63 .... **55** F3
Vaughan Av *DON* DN1 .... **5** F2
Vaughan Rd *DOD/DAR* S75 ...... **12** C4 ⓷
Vaughton Hl *STKB/PEN* S36 .... **70** B2
Vauxhall Cl *DARN/MH* S9 .... **100** C5
Vauxhall Rd *DARN/MH* S9 .... **100** C5
Velvet Wood Cl *DOD/DAR* S75 .. **12** B4
Ventnor Cl *DONS/BSCR* DN4 .... **43** D5 ⓶
Ventnor Pl *ABRD* S7 .... **135** D2 ⓵⓶
Venture Wy *CHNE* S41 .... **178** A5
Venus Ct *RHAM* S60 .... **114** A2
Verdant Wy *SHEFN* S5 .... **99** E4
Verelst Av *AU/AST/KP* S26 ...... **142** B1
Vere Rd *ST/HB/BR* S6 .... **108** A2
Vernon Cl *BSLY* S70 .... **22** A3
Vernon Crs *BSLY* S70 .... **22** A5
Vernon Delph *FUL* S10 .... **120** A4
Vernon Dr *CHPT/GREN* S35 ...... **74** A5
Vernon Rd *BSLY* S70 .... **22** A5
CHSW S40 .... **189** E1
RHAM/THRY S65 .... **115** F1
TOT/DORE S17 .... **156** C2
Vernon St *BSLY* S70 .... **50** A2
BSLYN/ROY S71 .... **3** E3
HOY S74 .... **51** D3
Vernon St North *BSLYN/ROY* S71 .. **3** E3
Vernon Ter *FUL* S10 .... **120** B5
Vernon Wy *DOD/DAR* S75 .... **12** C4
Vesey St *RAW* S62 .... **94** A2
Vicarage Cl *CHPT/GREN* S35 .... **97** D1
DONS/BSCR DN4 .... **47** E5
HOY S74 .... **51** F2 ⓷
MEX/SWTN S64 .... **59** D4
RHAM/THRY S65 .... **105** E1
Vicarage Crs *CHPT/GREN* S35 .. **97** D1
Vicarage La *TOT/DORE* S17 ...... **156** B1
Vicarage Rd *CHPT/GREN* S35 .... **97** D1
DARN/MH S9 .... **111** D3
Vicarage Wy *BTLY* DN5 .... **17** E4
Vicar La *CHSW* S40 .... **11** F6
HAN/WDH S13 .... **139** F3
SHEF S1 .... **9** E4
Vicar Rd *DEARNE* S63 .... **55** E1
Vickers Dr *SHEFN* S5 .... **110** B1
Vickers Rd *CHPT/GREN* S35 .... **73** E4
SHEFN S5 .... **110** B2
Victoria Av *RHAM/THRY* S65 .... **7** H6
Victoria Cl *STKB/PEN* S36 .... **68** C2
Victoria Ct *BTLY* DN5 .... **16** C3
Victoria Crs *BSLY* S70 .... **49** F1 ⓷
DOD/DAR S75 .... **2** A3
Victoria Crs West *DOD/DAR* S75 .. **2** A4
Victorian Crs *WHHL* DN2 .... **31** D5
Victoria Park Rd *STV/CWN* S43 .. **186** A4
Victoria Rd *BSLY* S70 .... **2** B3
BTLY DN5 .... **16** C4
DEARNE S63 .... **55** E1
DONS/BSCR DN4 .... **43** F4
FUL S10 .... **134** C1
MEX/SWTN S64 .... **58** B3
MOS S20 .... **153** D1

RAW S62 .... **94** A2
STKB/PEN S36 .... **69** D2
WMB/DAR S73 .... **39** D2
Victoria Station Rd ATT S4 .... **9** C3
Victoria St BSLY S70 .... **2** B4
BSLY S18 .... **23** E2
CHNE S41 .... **11** E4
DRON S18 .... **169** D1
HOY S74 .... **52** A2
MEX/SWTN S64 .... **57** F3
MEX/SWTN S64 .... **F4** F1
OWL S3 .... **8** B6
RHAM S60 .... **102** C3
RHAM S60 .... **127** E1
STKB/PEN S36 .... **68** C2
STV/CWN S43 .... **180** A5
Victoria St North CHNE S41 .... **178** A4
Victoria St West CHSW S40 .... **189** D2
Victoria Ter BSLY S70 .... **22** B2 10
Victor Rd TOT/DORE S17 .... **157** D1
Victor St ST/HB/BR S6 .... **108** B5
View Rd RHAM/THRY S65 .... **104** B3
SHEFS S8 .... **135** E3
Viewtree Cl RAW S62 .... **75** E2
Vikinglea Cl SHEFP/MNR S2 .... **137** F2 7
Vikinglea Dr SHEFP/MNR S2 .... **137** F2
Vikinglea Gld SHEFP/MNR S2 .... **137** F1 8
Vikinglea Rd SHEFP/MNR S2 .... **137** F1
Villa Gdns BTLY DN5 .... **16** B1
Villa Park Rd DONS/BSCR DN4 .... **46** C4
Villiers Cl SHEFP/MNR S2 .... **136** C5
Villiers Dr SHEFP/MNR S2 .... **136** C5
Vincent Crs CHSW S40 .... **188** C2
Vincent La CHSW S40 .... **188** C2
Vincent Rd ECC S11 .... **135** D2
Vine Cl BSLYN/ROY S71 .... **15** D3
RHAM S60 .... **6** A5
Viola Bank STKB/PEN S36 .... **68** C2
Violet Av MOS S20 .... **152** C2
Violet Bank Rd ABRD S7 .... **134** C4 8
Vivian Rd SHEFN S5 .... **110** B2
Vizard Rd HOY S74 .... **52** A2
Vulcan Rd DARN/MH S9 .... **111** F3

W

Wadbrough Rd FUL S10 .... **134** B1
Waddington Rd DOD/DAR S75 .... **12** C5
Wade Cl RHAM S60 .... **104** A5
Wade Meadow ST/HB/BR S6 .... **107** E3 1
Wade St ATT S4 .... **110** C3 1
DOD/DAR S75 .... **12** C5
Wadsley La ST/HB/BR S6 .... **107** E2 10
Wadsley Park Crs ST/HB/BR S6 .... **107** E3
Wadsworth Av HACK/IN S12 .... **138** A5
Wadsworth Cl HACK/IN S12 .... **138** B5 1
Wadsworth Dr HACK/IN S12 .... **138** B4
RAW S62 .... **79** D3
Wadsworth Rd HACK/IN S12 .... **138** A5 8
Wadsworth Ri RHAM/THRY S65 .... **95** F5
Wadworth St CONI DN12 .... **60** B5
Wagon Rd SHEFN S61 .... **92** C3
Waingate OWL S3 .... **9** F4
Wainwright Av HAN/WDH S13 .... **138** B2
WMB/DAR S73 .... **38** C2
Wainwright Crs HAN/WDH S13 .... **138** A2
Wainwright Pl WMB/DAR S73 .... **38** C2 2
Wainwright Rd DONS/BSCR DN4 .... **5** H6
KIMB S61 .... **92** A5 3
Wakefield Rd BSLYN/ROY S71 .... **14** A1
Wake Rd ABRD S7 .... **134** C3
Walbert Av DEARNE S63 .... **26** C4
Walbrook BSLY S70 .... **36** C1
Walden Rd SHEFP/MNR S2 .... **135** F3
Walders Av ST/HB/BR S6 .... **107** E2
Walders La STKB/PEN S36 .... **69** D5
Wales Pl ST/HB/BR S6 .... **121** E1
Wales Rd AU/AST/KP S26 .... **155** F3
Waleswood Rd AU/AST/KP S26 .... **154** A1
Waleswood Vw AU/AST/KP S26 .... **142** B4
Walford Rd ECK/KIL S21 .... **166** A2
Walgrove Av CHSW S40 .... **189** E3
Walgrove Rd CHSW S40 .... **189** E2 10
Walker Cl CHPT/GREN S35 .... **97** D1
Walker La RHAM/THRY S65 .... **7** F5
Walker Rd DOD/DAR S75 .... **50** A3 5
KIMB S61 .... **92** A5
Walkers La ECK/KIL S21 .... **166** B2
Walker St MEX/SWTN S64 .... **57** F5
OWL S3 .... **9** G2
RAW S62 .... **80** C5
Walker Vw RAW S62 .... **80** C5
Walkley Bank Cl ST/HB/BR S6 .... **121** D1
Walkley Bank Rd ST/HB/BR S6 .... **120** C1
Walkley Crescent Rd
ST/HB/BR S6 .... **120** C1
Walkley La ST/HB/BR S6 .... **108** A4
Walkley Rd ST/HB/BR S6 .... **121** D2
Walkley St ST/HB/BR S6 .... **121** E1
Walkley Ter ST/HB/BR S6 .... **120** B5
The Walk BSLY S70 .... **49** F2
Wallace Rd DONS/BSCR DN4 .... **62** C1

OWL S3 .... **122** A1
Waller Rd ST/HB/BR S6 .... **120** B2
Walling Cl DARN/MH S9 .... **111** F2
Walling Rd DARN/MH S9 .... **111** F2 8
Wall St BSLY S70 .... **21** F2
Walney Fold BSLYN/ROY S71 .... **15** E1 10
Walnut Dr ECK/KIL S21 .... **166** A3 2
Walnut Gv MEX/SWTN S64 .... **58** A2
Walnut Pl CHPT/GREN S35 .... **88** A2
Walpole Cl DONS/BSCR DN4 .... **63** D2
Walpole Gv AU/AST/KP S26 .... **142** B1
Walsham Dr BTLY DN5 .... **28** C4
Walter St RHAM S60 .... **6** A4
ST/HB/BR S6 .... **108** B5 9
Waltham Gdns MOS S20 .... **153** E3 10
Waltham St BSLY S70 .... **22** A2
Waltheof Rd SHEFP/MNR S2 .... **137** E2
Walton Back La RCH S42 .... **188** A4
Walton Cl CHPT/GREN S35 .... **73** D3 5
CHSW S40 .... **188** C4 6
DRON S18 .... **168** A1
Walton Crs CHSW S40 .... **189** E3
Walton Dr CHSW S40 .... **189** F5
Walton Fields Rd CHSW S40 .... **189** E2
Walton Rd CHSW S40 .... **189** E3
FUL S10 .... **134** B1
Walton St DOD/DAR S75 .... **13** D4
Walton St North DOD/DAR S75 .... **12** C4
Walton Wk CHSW S40 .... **189** F2
Wannop St RAW S62 .... **94** A3
Wansfell Rd ATT S4 .... **111** D3
The Wapping RHAM/THRY S65 .... **83** E4
Warburton Cl SHEFP/MNR S2 .... **136** A3 8
Warburton Gdns
SHEFP/MNR S2 .... **136** A3 4
Warburton Rd SHEFP/MNR S2 .... **136** A3
Warde Av DONS/BSCR DN4 .... **63** D1
Warden Cl DONS/BSCR DN4 .... **47** E4
Warden St RHAM S60 .... **114** B1
Wardgate Wy CHSW S40 .... **182** B4
Ward La STV/CWN S43 .... **167** F5
Wardlow Cl CHSW S40 .... **190** A4
Wardlow Rd HACK/IN S12 .... **138** B5
Ward Pl SHEFP/MNR S2 .... **135** D2 18
Wardsend Rd SHEFN S5 .... **108** B2
Wardsend Rd North ST/HB/BR S6 .. **108** A1
Ward St OWL S3 .... **8** D2
Ware Rd MOS S20 .... **153** E3 10
Wareham Gv DOD/DAR S75 .... **20** B2
Warehouse La DEARNE S63 .... **55** F2
Warminster Cl SHEFS S8 .... **147** E1
Warminster Crs SHEFS S8 .... **147** F1
Warminster Dr SHEFS S8 .... **147** F2 1
Warminster Pl SHEFS S8 .... **147** F3
Warminster Rd SHEFS S8 .... **147** E1
Warmsworth Rd DONS/BSCR DN4... **62** C1
Warner Av DOD/DAR S75 .... **12** C5
Warner Pl DOD/DAR S75 .... **13** D5
Warner Rd DOD/DAR S75 .... **12** C5
ST/HB/BR S6 .... **107** F3
Warner St CHNE S41 .... **190** C3 18
Warnington Dr ARMTH DN3 .... **67** F3
DONS/BSCR DN4 .... **67** E2
Warning Tongue La ARMTH DN3 .... **47** F5
Warren Av RAW S62 .... **79** F4
Warren Cl DONS/BSCR DN4 .... **62** A1
WHHL DN2 .... **31** E5
Warren Crs BSLY S70 .... **22** A3
ECK/KIL S21 .... **172** C1
Warren Dr KIMB S61 .... **102** A1
Warren Gdns CHPT/GREN S35 .... **74** B3
Warren Hl KIMB S61 .... **102** A1
Warren La CHPT/GREN S35 .... **74** C3
DONS/BSCR DN4 .... **67** D2
HOY S74 .... **74** A2
Warren Mt KIMB S61 .... **102** A1
Warren Pl BSLY S70 .... **22** A3 8 2
Warren Quarry La BSLY S70 .... **22** A2
Warren Ri DRON S18 .... **160** A5
Warren St ATT S4 .... **123** E2
Warren V MEX/SWTN S64 .... **80** B2
RAW S62 .... **80** B4
Warren Vale Rd MEX/SWTN S64 .... **56** B5
Warren Vw HOY S74 .... **51** D4
Warrington Rd FUL S10 .... **121** E3 8
Warris Cl SHEFP/MNR S2 .... **91** F5
Warris Pl SHEFP/MNR S2 .... **123** E4
Warwick Rd WHHL DN2 .... **31** H4
Warwick St CHSW S40 .... **190** C5
FUL S10 .... **121** D3 9
RHAM/THRY S65 .... **103** F4
Warwick Ter FUL S10 .... **121** D3 10
Wasdale Av MOS S20 .... **164** C2 13
Washdale Cl MOS S20 .... **164** C2
Washfield Crs RHAM S60 .... **127** F3
Washfield La RHAM S60 .... **127** F4
Washford Rd DARN/MH S9 .... **123** F1
Wash House La CHSW S40 .... **189** D2
Washington Av CONI DN12 .... **84** A1
WMB/DAR S73 .... **38** C3
Washington Gv BTLY DN5 .... **29** E2
Washington Rd CHPT/GREN S35 .... **88** C5
ECC S11 .... **135** D2
Washington St MEX/SWTN S64 .... **58** C3
Watch House La BTLY DN5 .... **29** D3

Watch St HAN/WDH S13 .... **140** B2
Waterdale DON DN1 .... **5** E5
Waterdale Cl BTLY DN5 .... **42** B4 1
Waterdale Rd BSLY S70 .... **36** A1
Waterfield Ms MOS S20 .... **152** C4 2
Waterfield Pl BSLYN/ROY S71 .... **23** F2 3
Waterford Rd OWL S3 .... **108** C5
Waterhouse Cl RHAM/THRY S65 .... **95** F5
Water La RAW S62 .... **52** B5
RHAM S60 .... **103** E4
TOT/DORE S17 .... **157** D1
Waterloo Rd BSLY S70 .... **2** A6
BSLY S70 .... **21** E1 18
Waterloo Wk OWL S3 .... **8** C1
Watermeade ECK/KIL S21 .... **173** F1
Water Meadow La CHSW S40 .... **182** C3
Water Royd Dr DOD/DAR S75 .... **20** A3
Water Slacks Cl HAN/WDH S13 .... **139** F4 8
Water Slacks Dr HAN/WDH S13 .... **139** F4
Water Slacks La HAN/WDH S13 .... **139** F4
Watersmeet Rd ST/HB/BR S6 .... **107** F5
Water St OWL S3 .... **9** E3
RHAM S60 .... **103** E4
Waterthorpe Cl MOS S20 .... **153** D5 4
Waterthorpe Crs MOS S20 .... **153** D5
Waterthorpe Gdns MOS S20 .... **152** C5
Waterthorpe Gld MOS S20 .... **152** C5
Waterthorpe Gln MOS S20 .... **153** D5 9
Waterthorpe Greenway MOS S20 .. **152** B2
Waterthorpe Ri MOS S20 .... **153** D5
Watery St OWL S3 .... **8** B2
Wath Rd ABRD S7 .... **134** C4
HOY S74 .... **52** B4
MEX/SWTN S64 .... **57** E3
WMB/DAR S73 .... **40** A4
Wath Wood Bottom DEARNE S63 ...... **55** F5
Wath Wood Dr DEARNE S63 .... **56** A4
Wath Wood Rd DEARNE S63 .... **56** A4
Watkinson Gdns MOS S20 .... **152** C3
Watson Cl KIMB S61 .... **102** A1
Watson Gln KIMB S61 .... **101** D3
Watson Rd FUL S10 .... **121** D5 11
KIMB S61 .... **102** A1
Watson St HOY S74 .... **50** C3 8
Watt La FUL S10 .... **120** A5
Waverley Av CONI DN12 .... **85** D1
DONS/BSCR DN4 .... **42** C5
Waverley Ct BTLY DN5 .... **16** B2
Waverley Rd DARN/MH S9 .... **125** D3 9
Waverley Vw RHAM S60 .... **127** D2
Waycliffe BSLYN/ROY S71 .... **15** D4
Wayford Av CHNE S41 .... **190** C3 3
Wayland Av BSLY S70 .... **22** A5
Wayland Rd ECC S11 .... **134** B2
Wayside Cl STV/CWN S43 .... **185** E1
Wayside Ct STV/CWN S43 .... **185** E1 8
Weakland Cl HACK/IN S12 .... **151** D3
Weakland Crs HACK/IN S12 .... **151** D2
Weakland Dr HACK/IN S12 .... **151** D2
Weakland Wy HACK/IN S12 .... **151** D2 2
Weavers Cl CHPT/GREN S35 .... **87** D5
Webb Av STKB/PEN S36 .... **69** E5
Webbs Av ST/HB/BR S6 .... **119** F1
Webster Cl KIMB S61 .... **101** E1 2
Webster Crs KIMB S61 .... **101** E1
Webster Cft CHNE S41 .... **178** C4 8
Webster St DARN/MH S9 .... **111** F3 1
Wedgewood Cl RAW S62 .... **94** A1
Weedon St DARN/MH S9 .... **111** F2
Weetwood Dr ECC S11 .... **133** F5 1
Weetwood Rd RHAM S60 .... **115** E2
Weigh La SHEFP/MNR S2 .... **123** D4 10
Weir Head DARN/MH S9 .... **111** F3
Welbeck Cl DRON S18 .... **168** A1
STV/CWN S43 .... **187** E3
Welbeck Dr AU/AST/KP S26 .... **143** D3
Welbeck Rd DONS/BSCR DN4 .... **45** D2
Welbeck St DOD/DAR S75 .... **13** E5
Welbury Gdns MOS S20 .... **164** C2
Welby Pl SHEFS S8 .... **147** D1
Welfare Av CHSW S40 .... **189** E1
CONI DN12 .... **84** B1
Welfare Rd DEARNE S63 .... **26** C3
Welham Dr RHAM S60 .... **103** F5
Welland Cl OWL S3 .... **122** A1
Welland Crs HOY S74 .... **52** B2
Wellbeck Rd ST/HB/BR S6 .... **120** C1
Wellbourne Cl CHPT/GREN S35 .... **89** D2
Wellcarr Rd SHEFS S8 .... **147** E3
Wellcroft Cl WHHL DN2 .... **32** A3
Wellesley Rd FUL S10 .... **121** E4
Wellfield Cl HACK/IN S12 .... **150** C4
ST/HB/BR S6 .... **121** E2
Wellfield Rd DOD/DAR S75 .... **13** E4
KIMB S61 .... **91** H4
ST/HB/BR S6 .... **121** E2
Wellgate CONI DN12 .... **85** D1
RHAM/THRY S65 .... **7** E5
Wellgate Mt RHAM/THRY S65 .... **7** E6
Well Green Rd ST/HB/BR S6 .... **118** C3
Wellhead Rd SHEFS S8 .... **135** E4 13
Wellington Cl BSLYN/ROY S71 .... **14** C3
Wellington Crs BSLY S70 .... **23** D5
Wellington Gv BTLY DN5 .... **29** E2
Wellington Rd ST/HB/BR S6 .... **119** F2

Wellington St *BSLY* S70 .... 2 D6 ②
  MEX/SWTN S64 .... 58 B3
  SHEF S1 .... 8 D6
  STV/CWN S43 .... 179 E2
Welling Wy *KIMB* S61 .... 101 F2
Well La *AU/AST/KP* S26 .... 129 D5
  BSLYN/ROY S71 .... 15 D2
  RHAM S60 .... 115 F3 ①
  RHAM S60 .... 116 B5
  RHAM S60 .... 127 F3
  ST/HB/BR S6 .... 107 D2
Well Meadow Dr *OWL* S3 .... 8 B4
Well Meadow St *OWL* S3 .... 8 B4
Well Pl *SHEFS* S8 .... 135 E4 ⑯
Well Rd *SHEFS* S8 .... 135 E4 ⑰
Well Spring Cl *STV/CWN* S43 ... 185 F2 ①
Wells Rd *WHHL* DN2 .... 31 D3
Well St *BSLY* S70 .... 2 A6
Well View Rd *KIMB* S61 .... 101 E1
Welney Pl *ST/HB/BR* S6 .... 97 D5
Welton Cl *DONS/BSCR* DN4 .... 66 A1
Welwyn Cl *CHSW* S40 .... 189 E1
  HACK/IN S12 .... 149 F1 ①
Welwyn Rd *HACK/IN* S12 .... 149 F1
Wembley Av *CONI* DN12 .... 84 B1
Wembley Cl *WHHL* DN2 .... 32 A4 ②
Wendel Gv *HOY* S74 .... 52 C2 ②
Wenlock Cl *CHSW* S40 .... 183 E5
Wenlock Crs *CHSW* S40 .... 183 D5
Wenlock St *HAN/WDH* S13 ...... 139 D1 ②
Wensley Cl *ATT* S4 .... 110 C3
Wensley Crs *DONS/BSCR* DN4 .... 47 D5
Wensley Cft *ATT* S4 .... 110 C2
Wensley Dale Dr *RHAM* S60 ..... 114 B5
Wensleydale Rd *BTLY* DN5 .... 28 B2
  KIMB S61 .... 92 A3
Wensley Gdns *ATT* S4 .... 110 C2
Wensley Gn *ATT* S4 .... 110 C2
Wensley St *ATT* S4 .... 110 C2
  DEARNE S63 .... 26 B3
Wensley Wy *STV/CWN* S43 ...... 187 D1
Wentworth Av *AU/AST/KP* S26 .. 143 D4
  CHSW S40 .... 189 F4
  ECC S11 .... 145 D3
  ECC S11 .... 145 E3 ③
Wentworth Cl *KIMB* S61 .... 89 F1
Wentworth Ct *RAW* S62 .... 92 C2
Wentworth Dr *RAW* S62 .... 94 A2
Wentworth Gdns *MEX/SWTN* S64 .. 81 D3
Wentworth Pl *KIMB* S61 .... 91 D4
Wentworth Rd *DRON* S18 .... 168 A2
  HOY S74 .... 37 E4
  HOY S74 .... 52 B1
  HOY S74 .... 52 B5
  KIMB S61 .... 90 A1
  RAW S62 .... 79 E3
  WHHL DN2 .... 30 C4
Wentworth St *BSLY* S70 .... 49 F1
  BSLYN/ROY S71 .... 2 C1
Wentworth Vw *HOY* S74 .... 52 A3 ③
  WMB/DAR S73 .... 39 E4
Wentworth Wy *DOD/DAR* S75 ... 20 A4
  DOD/DAR S75 .... 49 E4
Wesley Av *AU/AST/KP* S26 ...... 142 B2
Wesley Ct *KIMB* S61 .... 90 A1
Wesley La *FUL* S10 .... 120 C4 ⑤
Wesley Rd *CHPT/GREN* S35 .... 73 D4
Wesley St *BSLY* S70 .... 2 D6
Wessenden Cl *DOD/DAR* S75 .... 20 B1 ⑥
Wessex Gdns *TOT/DORE* S17 ... 156 B3
Wessington Dr *STV/CWN* S43 ... 187 D1
West Av *DONS/BSCR* DN4 .... 43 E5
  RAW S62 .... 80 A5
  WMB/DAR S73 .... 38 C2
Westbank Cl *DRON* S18 .... 159 F4
West Bar *SHEF* S1 .... 9 E4
West Bars *CHSW* S40 .... 10 D6
West Bawtry Rd *RHAM* S60 ..... 114 B3
Westbourne Gdns
  DONS/BSCR DN4 .... 63 D1 ④
Westbourne Gv *CHSW* S40 ..... 188 C3
  DOD/DAR S75 .... 13 E4 ④
Westbourne Rd *ECC* S11 .... 121 D5
Westbourne Ter *DOD/DAR* S75 ... 21 D1
Westbrook Bank *ECC* S11 .... 134 C5
Westbrook Cl *CHSW* S40 .... 188 A2
Westbrook Dr *CHSW* S40 .... 188 A2
Westbrook Rd *CHPT/GREN* S35 ... 88 B1
Westbury Av *CHPT/GREN* S35 .... 88 B3
Westbury Cl *DOD/DAR* S75 .... 12 C3
Westbury St *DARN/MH* S9 ...... 124 A2
Westby Crs *RHAM* S60 .... 115 F3
West Cl *KIMB* S61 .... 101 F1
West Crs *STKB/PEN* S36 .... 68 B2
West Croft Ct *STV/CWN* S43 ... 186 C4
Westcroft Crs *MOS* S20 .... 152 C5
Westcroft Dr *MOS* S20 .... 152 C5
West Croft Dr *STV/CWN* S43 ... 186 C4
Westcroft Gdns *MOS* S20 .... 152 C5
Westcroft Gln *MOS* S20 .... 164 C1 ⑤
Westcroft Gv *MOS* S20 .... 164 C1
West Don St *ST/HB/BR* S6 ...... 121 F1
West End Av *BTLY* DN5 .... 29 E2
West End La *NROS/TKH* DN11 ... 65 B5
West End Rd *DEARNE* S63 .... 54 C2

West End Vw *ECK/KIL* S21 ...... 174 A1
Westerdale Rd *BTLY* DN5.......... 28 B3
Western Bank *FUL* S10 .... 121 E4
  FUL S10 .... 121 F4 ⑤
Western Rd *FUL* S10 .... 120 C5
  RHAM/THRY S65............... 104 B2
Western St *BSLY* S70 .... 2 B3
Western Ter *WMB/DAR* S73 ...... 39 D2
Westfield Av *AU/AST/KP* S26 .... 142 A1
  CHSW S40 .... 188 C3 ⑧
  HACK/IN S12 .... 152 A2
Westfield Centre *MOS* S20 ...... 152 C5
Westfield Cl *CHSW* S40 .... 188 C2
Westfield Crs *DEARNE* S63 .... 26 B3
  MOS S20 .... 152 B5
Westfield Gdns *CHSW* S40 ...... 188 C3 ⑧
Westfield Gv *HACK/IN* S12 ..... 151 F2 ⑧
Westfield La *ECK/KIL* S21 .... 172 B3
Westfield Northway *MOS* S20 .. 152 C5
Westfield Rd *ARMTH* DN3 .... 33 E3 ①
  DEARNE S63 .... 54 B1 ②
  DONS/BSCR DN4 .... 43 F3
  DRON S18 .... 170 A3
  ECK/KIL S21 .... 166 A3
  RAW S62 .... 93 F2
Westfields *BSLY* S70 .... 36 B1
Westfield Southway *MOS* S20 .. 152 C5
Westfield St *BSLY* S70 .... 21 E1 ⑬
Westfield Ter *SHEF* S1 .... 8 C6
Westgate *BSLY* S70 .... 2 B5
  BSLYN/ROY S71 .... 14 C3
West Ga *MEX/SWTN* S64 .... 59 D3
Westgate *RHAM* S60 .... 6 D6
West Green Dr *ARMTH* DN3........ 19 F2
West Gv *WHHL* DN2 .... 31 E4
West Hill *KIMB* S61 .... 101 D3
Westhill La *SHEF* S1 .... 8 B6
Westholme Rd *DONS/BSCR* DN4 .. 43 F3 ③
West Laith Ga *DON* DN1 .... 4 D4
Westland Cl *MOS* S20 .... 152 C4
Westland Gdns *MOS* S20 .... 152 B4
Westland Gv *MOS* S20 .... 152 C5 ⑪
Westland Rd *MOS* S20 .... 152 C4
West La *AU/AST/KP* S26 .... 141 F1
West Lea *CHSW* S40 .... 188 C2 ③
Westleigh Ct *CHSW* S40 .... 10 B3
Westminster Cl *FUL* S10 .... 131 F1 ⑬
Westminster Crs *FUL* S10 ...... 131 F1
  WHHL DN2 .... 32 A4 ④
West Moor Crs *DOD/DAR* S75 ... 20 B1
Westmoor Rd *STV/CWN* S43 ... 186 A5
Westmoreland St *ST/HB/BR* S6 121 F2 ⑬
Westmorland St *DONS/BSCR* DN4 .. 63 D1
Westmount Av *DEARNE* S63 ..... 41 D5 ②
Westnall Rd *SHEFN* S5 .... 99 E2
Westnall Ter *SHEFN* S5 .... 99 E2
Weston Cl *CHSW* S40 .... 182 B3
Weston St *OWL* S3 .... 8 A4
Westover Rd *FUL* S10 .... 119 F5
West Park Dr *AU/AST/KP* S26 .. 141 F3
Westpit Hl *DEARNE* S63 .... 54 B1
West Pl *BTLY* DN5 .... 16 C5
West Qd *SHEFN* S5 .... 110 B1
West Rd *DOD/DAR* S75 .... 12 C5
  MEX/SWTN S64 .... 58 A3
Westside Gra *DONS/BSCR* DN4 43 E4 ②
West St *BSLY* S70 .... 36 C1
  CHSW S40 .... 10 C4
  CONI DN12........................ 85 D1
  DEARNE S63 .... 27 E5 ①
  DEARNE S63 .... 55 F2
  DON DN1 .... 4 C4
  DRON S18 .... 169 D1 ②
  ECK/KIL S21 .... 174 A1
  HOY S74 .... 51 D2
  MEX/SWTN S64 .... 58 A4
  MOS S20 .... 153 D2
  SHEF S1 .... 8 C6
  WMB/DAR S73 .... 39 D2
West Street La *SHEF* S1 .... 8 D5
Westthorpe Fields Rd
  ECK/KIL S21 .... 166 A4
Westthorpe Rd *ECK/KIL* S21 ... 166 B3
West Vw *STV/CWN* S43 .... 181 E5
West View Cl *TOT/DORE* S17 ... 157 D2 ①
West View Ri *TOT/DORE* S17 ... 157 D2 ①
West View Rd *CHSW* S40 .... 183 F3
  KIMB S61 .... 101 D3
  MEX/SWTN S64 .... 58 B4
Westville Rd *DOD/DAR* S75 ...... 13 E4
West Wy *BSLY* S70 .... 2 D6
Westwell Pl *MOS* S20 .... 164 B2
Westwick Crs *TOT/DORE* S17 .. 158 B1
Westwick Gv *SHEFS* S8 .... 158 B1
Westwick Rd *SHEFS* S8 .... 158 B1
Westwood Av *STV/CWN* S43 ... 187 D1
Westwood Cl *STV/CWN* S43.... 187 D4
Westwood Ct *BSLY* S70 .... 2 B3
  CHPT/GREN S35 .... 73 E3
Westwood Dr *STV/CWN* S43 ... 186 C4
Westwood La *CHPT/GREN* S35 ... 48 B2
  STV/CWN S43 .... 186 A5
Westwood New Rd *DOD/DAR* S75 .. 49 E5

Westwood Rd *ECC* S11 .... 133 D2
  STV/CWN S43 .... 186 B5
Wetherby Cl *BTLY* DN5............. 28 B4
Wetherby Ct *DARN/MH* S9 ...... 125 D3
Wetherby Dr *AU/AST/KP* S26 ... 142 A3
  MEX/SWTN S64 .... 58 C2
Wetlands La *CHNE* S41 .... 185 F5
Wet Moor La *DEARNE* S63 .... 56 A1
Whaley Rd *DOD/DAR* S75 .... 12 A2
Wharf Cl *MEX/SWTN* S64 .... 57 F5 ②
Wharfedale Dr *CHPT/GREN* S35 .. 87 F1
Wharfedale Rd *DOD/DAR* S75.... 12 B4
Wharf La *CHNE* S41 .... 11 F3
Wharf Rd *DARN/MH* S9 .... 112 B1
  DON DN1 .... 30 B4
  MEX/SWTN S64 .... 81 F3
Wharf St *ATT* S4 .... 9 G4
  BSLYN/ROY S71 .... 3 F7
  MEX/SWTN S64 .... 57 F5
Wharncliffe *DOD/DAR* S75 ...... 20 B4 ⑧
Wharncliffe Av *AU/AST/KP* S26 .. 142 C2 ⑧
  DEARNE S63 .... 56 A2
Wharncliffe Cl *HOY* S74 .... 51 E4
  RAW S62 .... 79 E3 ①
Wharncliffe Rd *CHPT/GREN* S35 .. 73 E4 ⑧
  FUL S10 .... 121 F5
Wharncliffe St *BSLY* S70 .... 2 A5
  DONS/BSCR DN4 .... 43 E2 ②
Wharton Av *AU/AST/KP* S26 ... 142 B1
Wheatacre Rd *STKB/PEN* S36 ... 69 D2
Wheata Dr *SHEFN* S5 .... 98 B2
Wheata Pl *SHEFN* S5 .... 98 B3
Wheata Rd *SHEFN* S5 .... 98 B3
Wheatbridge Rd *CHSW* S40 ...... 10 B6
Wheat Cft *CONI* DN12 .... 85 F1
Wheatcroft Rd *RAW* S62 .... 80 C5
Wheatfield Crs *SHEFN* S5 .... 99 E3
Wheatfield Dr *DEARNE* S63 ...... 27 D4 ②
Wheatfield Wy *RCH* S42 .... 182 A4 ④
Wheathill Cl *CHSW* S40 .... 182 B4 ④
  CHSW S40 .... 182 B4 ②
  STV/CWN S43 .... 186 A5
Wheathill La *CHNE* S41 .... 185 F5
Wheathill St *RHAM* S60 .... 103 E4 ②
Wheatley Cl *BSLYN/ROY* S71 ... 14 A3 ③
Wheatley Hall Rd *WHHL* DN2 .... 19 E5
  WHHL DN2 .... 31 D3
Wheatley La *DON* DN1 .... 5 F1 ②
Wheatley Pl *CONI* DN12 .... 60 A5 ①
Wheatley Rd *BSLY* S70 .... 23 F5 ②
  BTLY DN5......................... 16 B4
  KIMB S61 .... 91 F5
  MEX/SWTN S64 .... 81 F3
Wheatley St *CONI* DN12 .... 60 A5
Wheeldon Crs *STV/CWN* S43 ... 185 E2
Wheeldon St *SHEF* S1 .... 8 B5
Wheel La *CHPT/GREN* S35 .... 97 E1
The Wheel *CHPT/GREN* S35 ...... 97 F1
Wheldrake Rd *SHEFN* S5 .... 110 B2
Whernside Av *CHPT/GREN* S35 .. 74 A5 ⑤
Whinacre Cl *SHEFS* S8 .... 159 F2 ③
Whinacre Pl *SHEFS* S8 .... 159 F2 ①
Whinby Cft *DOD/DAR* S75 .... 20 A3 ④
Whinfell Ct *ECC* S11 .... 144 C3
Whin Gdns *DEARNE* S63 .... 27 D2
Whin Hill Rd *DONS/BSCR* DN4 ... 46 B4
Whinmoor Rd *CHPT/GREN* S35 ... 73 D4
  SHEFN S5 .... 111 D1 ③
Whinside Crs *DEARNE* S63 .... 26 C2
The Whins *RAW* S62 .... 93 D1
Whiphill Cl *DONS/BSCR* DN4 .... 46 C5 ③
Whirlow Court Rd *ECC* S11 ..... 145 D3
Whirlowdale Cl *ECC* S11 .... 145 D3 ②
Whirlowdale Crs *ECC* S11 .... 145 F2
Whirlowdale Ri *ECC* S11 .... 145 D3 ③
Whirlowdale Rd *ABRD* S7 .... 145 E3
  ECC S11 .... 145 D5
Whirlow Gv *ECC* S11 .... 145 D2 ③
Whirlow La *ECC* S11 .... 145 D2 ①
Whirlow Ms *ECC* S11 .... 145 D2 ⑤
Whirlow Park Rd *ABRD* S7 ...... 145 D4
Whisperwood Dr *DONS/BSCR* DN4 .. 63 F3
Whiston Brook Vw *RHAM* S60 .. 116 A3
Whiston Gra *RHAM* S60 .... 115 E3
Whiston Grn *RHAM* S60 .... 115 E4 ②
Whiston Gv *RHAM* S60 .... 104 A5
Whiston V *RHAM* S60 .... 115 F4
Whitbourne Cl *BSLYN/ROY* S71 .. 14 A2 ②
Whitburn Rd *DON* DN1 .... 5 F6
Whitby Rd *DARN/MH* S9 .... 124 C3 ③
  DARN/MH S9 .... 125 D2 ⑦
Whitebank Cl *CHNE* S41 .... 190 C3
Whitecoats Pk *CHSW* S40 ...... 190 A4
Whitecotes Cl *CHSW* S40 .... 189 F4
Whitecotes La *CHSW* S40 .... 189 F4
White Cft *SHEF* S1 .... 8 C4
Whitecroft Crs *RHAM* S60 ...... 114 A4
White Cross La *BSLY* S70 .... 23 E5
White Cross Ri *BSLY* S70 .... 23 E5
White Edge Cl *CHSW* S40 .... 183 E4
Whitehall Rd *KIMB* S61 .... 92 A2
Whitehead Av *STKB/PEN* S36 ... 69 E3
White Hill Av *BSLY* S70 .... 20 B1
Whitehill Av *RHAM* S60 .... 114 A4

Whitehill Dr *RHAM* S60.................... **114** A5
White Hill Gv *BSLY* S70..................... **20** C1 ⬛
Whitehill La *RHAM* S60..................... **114** A3
Whitehill Rd *RHAM* S60.................... **114** A4
White Hill Ter *BSLY* S70..................... **20** B1 ⬛
Whitehouse La *ST/HB/BR* S6............. **121** E1
Whitehouse Rd *ST/HB/BR* S6............ **121** E1
Whitehouses *CHNE* S41..................... **190** C3 ⬛
White La *CHPT/GREN* S35.................. **74** C4
  HACK/IN S12................................. **149** E2
Whitelea Gv *MEX/SWTN* S64............. **58** A4
White Leas *CHSW* S40....................... **182** C5
Whitelee Rd *MEX/SWTN* S64............. **57** F4
Whiteley La *ECC* S11......................... **132** A3
Whiteley Wood La *ECC* S11............... **132** C3
Whiteley Wood Rd *ECC* S11.............. **132** C4
White Rose Ct *BTLY* DN5.................... **17** D5
White Rose Wy *DONS/BSCR* DN4........ **44** C4
  DONS/BSCR DN4............................... **65** D1
White's La *SHEFP/MNR* S2................. **125** E4
White Thorns Cl *SHEFS* S8............... **159** F2 ⬛
White Thorns Dr *SHEFS* S8............... **159** F3
White Thorns Vw *SHEFS* S8.............. **159** F2
Whiteways Cl *ATT* S4........................ **110** B4
Whiteways Dr *ATT* S4....................... **110** B4 ⬛
Whiteways Gv *ATT* S4....................... **110** B4
Whiteways Rd *ATT* S4....................... **110** B4
Whitfield Rd *FUL* S10....................... **132** A3
  RAW S62.. **79** D3
Whiting St *SHEFS* S8........................ **135** E4 ⬛
Whitley Carr *CHPT/GREN* S35............ **87** F4
Whitley La *CHPT/GREN* S35............... **87** E5
Whitley Vw *CHPT/GREN* S35.............. **88** C4
Whitley View Rd *KIMB* S61............... **100** C4
Whitney Cl *DONS/BSCR* DN4.............. **62** C2 ⬛
Whittier Rd *DONS/BSCR* DN4............. **63** E1
Whittington Hl *CHNE* S41................. **178** B5
Whittington La *DRON* S18................. **178** B2
Whittington St *STV/CWN* S43............ **179** F2
Whittington St *DON* DN1.................... **30** B4
Whitting Valley Rd *CHNE* S41........... **178** B5
Whitton Cl *DONS/BSCR* DN4.............. **66** A1
Whitwell Crs *STKB/PEN* S36.............. **68** C2
Whitwell La *STKB/PEN* S36................ **68** B3
Whitwell St *DARN/MH* S9................. **125** E3
Whitworth La *DARN/MH* S9.............. **111** E5
Whitworth Rd *CHNE* S41................... **184** A3 ⬛
  FUL S10.. **132** C1
Whitworth Wy *DEARNE* S63............... **55** F1
Whyn Vw *DEARNE* S63...................... **26** C3 ⬛
Wicker *OWL* S3..................................... **9** G2
Wicker La *OWL* S3................................ **9** G3
Wickersley Rd *RHAM/THRY* S65......... **104** B5
Wicket Wy *CONI* DN12....................... **62** A4
Wickfield Cl *HACK/IN* S12................ **139** D5
Wickfield Dr *HACK/IN* S12................ **150** C1
Wickfield Gr *HACK/IN* S12................ **138** C5
Wickfield Pl *HACK/IN* S12................ **138** C5
Wickfield Rd *HACK/IN* S12............... **151** D1
Wicklow Rd *WHHL* DN2...................... **31** E4
Widdop Cl *HAN/WDH* S13................ **138** B2
Widdop Cft *HAN/WDH* S13............... **138** B2
Wigfield Dr *BSLY* S70....................... **22** A5
Wigfull Rd *ECC* S11......................... **134** A1
Wigley Rd *STV/CWN* S43................. **187** D3
Wikeley Wy *STV/CWN* S43................ **185** E2
Wike Rd *BSLYN/ROY* S71................... **15** F5
Wilberforce Rd *WHHL* DN2................ **19** E5
Wilbrook Ri *DOD/DAR* S75................. **12** B3
Wilby La *BSLY* S70............................ **22** B2 ⬛
Wilcox Cl *ST/HB/BR* S6..................... **97** E4
Wilcox Rd *ST/HB/BR* S6.................... **97** E4
Wild Av *RAW* S62............................... **79** D4
Widene Dr *MEX/SWTN* S64................ **58** B2
Wilding Cl *KIMB* S61...................... **101** F1
Wilding Wy *KIMB* S61..................... **101** F1
Wilfred Cl *DARN/MH* S9................. **124** B2 ⬛
Wilfred Dr *DARN/MH* S9.................. **124** B2
Wilfred St *RHAM* S60.......................... **6** D6
Wilfrid Rd *DARN/MH* S9................. **124** B2
Wilkinson La *FUL* S10......................... **8** A6
Wilkinson Rd *HOY* S74....................... **52** B3
Wilkinson St *BSLY* S70.................... **22** A2 ⬛
  FUL S10.. **121** F1
Willan Dr *RHAM* S60....................... **127** D2
Willbury Dr *HACK/IN* S12................ **137** E4
Willey St *OWL* S3................................. **9** J3
William Cl *MOS* S20......................... **164** B2 ⬛
William Crs *MOS* S20........................ **164** B1
Williamson Rd *ECC* S11................... **134** A3
Williams Rd *BTLY* DN5....................... **29** D3
William St *BSLY* S70.......................... **22** B3
  CHNE S41....................................... **184** B3 ⬛
  DEARNE S63...................................... **56** A2
  ECK/KIL S21.................................... **164** B5
  FUL S10... **121** F5
  MEX/SWTN S64................................. **57** F5
  RAW S62.. **94** B2
  RHAM/THRY S65................................ **7** F6
  WMB/DAR S73.................................. **39** D2 ⬛
William St North *CHNE* S41............. **178** A4
Willingham Cl *MOS* S20.................. **153** E4
Willingham Gdns *MOS* S20............. **153** E3 ⬛
Willington Rd *SHEFN* S5.................... **99** D5

Willis Rd *ST/HB/BR* S6..................... **107** F3
Willoughby St *ATT* S4...................... **110** B2
Willow Av *DONS/BSCR* DN4............... **47** D4
  RAW S62.. **94** B1
Willow Bank *BSLYN/ROY* S71............ **13** E5
Willow Cl *HOY* S74........................... **51** D3
  RHAM S60....................................... **114** B5
Willow Crs *CHPT/GREN* S35............... **88** B2
Willowdale Cl *BTLY* DN5.................... **42** B4
Willow Dr *CONI* DN12....................... **62** A4
  DARN/MH S9.................................. **125** F4
  MEX/SWTN S64................................. **58** A3
Willow Garth *RAW* S62...................... **80** B5
Willowgarth Av *RHAM* S60.............. **114** A5
Willow Garth Rd *CHNE* S41............. **183** D1
Willow Gv *AU/AST/KP* S26............... **143** D2 ⬛
Willowlees Ct *DONS/BSCR* DN4......... **46** C5 ⬛
Willow Rd *DEARNE* S63...................... **27** D3
  DEARNE S63...................................... **56** B4
  ECK/KIL S21................................... **166** A3
  STKB/PEN S36.................................. **68** C4
The Willows *KIMB* S61...................... **91** E4
Willow St *CONI* DN12....................... **85** F4
Willow Wk *BTLY* DN5......................... **16** B3 ⬛
Wilmington Dr *DONS/BSCR* DN4........ **45** D5
Wilsden Gv *DOD/DAR* S75.................. **12** C3 ⬛
Wilson Av *RAW* S62........................... **79** F5
Wilson Dr *RHAM/THRY* S65............... **95** F5
Wilson Gv *BSLYN/ROY* S71................ **15** F3
Wilson Pl *SHEFS* S8......................... **135** E4 ⬛
Wilson Rd *DRON* S18........................ **160** A4
  ECC S11.. **134** A2
  STKB/PEN S36................................... **70** A3
Wilson St *DRON* S18........................ **169** F3 ⬛
  OWL S3... **122** B1
  WMB/DAR S73.................................. **38** C2
Wilthorpe Av *DOD/DAR* S75.............. **13** D3
Wilthorpe Crs *DOD/DAR* S75............. **13** D3
Wilthorpe Farm Rd *DOD/DAR* S75... **13** D5
Wilthorpe Gdns *HACK/IN* S12........ **151** E2 ⬛
Wilthorpe Gn *DOD/DAR* S75............. **13** D3 ⬛
Wilthorpe La *DOD/DAR* S75............... **12** C5 ⬛
Wilthorpe Rd *DOD/DAR* S75.............. **12** B3
Wilton Cl *RAW* S62........................... **94** A1
Wilton Ct *KIMB* S61........................ **102** B3
Wilton Gdns *KIMB* S61.................... **102** B3
Wilton La *KIMB* S61........................ **102** B3
Wilton Pl *FUL* S10........................... **121** F5
Wiltshire Rd *WHHL* DN2.................... **32** A5
Wimborne Crs *CHNE* S41................. **183** F2
Wincanton Cl *MEX/SWTN* S64........... **58** C2
Winchester Av *FUL* S10................... **131** F2 ⬛
  WHHL DN2....................................... **31** E3
Winchester Crs *FUL* S10.................. **131** F2
Winchester Dr *FUL* S10................... **131** F2 ⬛
Winchester Rd *CHNE* S41................ **183** F2
  FUL S10... **131** F2
Winchester Wy *BSLYN/ROY* S71......... **24** B3 ⬛
  BTLY DN5.. **28** B3
  RHAM S60....................................... **113** E5
Wincobank Av *SHEFN* S5................. **110** C1
Wincobank Cl *SHEFN* S5................. **111** D1 ⬛
Wincobank La *ATT* S4...................... **111** D3
Wincobank Rd *SHEFN* S5................. **111** D1
Windermere Av *DRON* S18................ **168** C2
  WHHL DN2....................................... **32** A4 ⬛
Windermere Rd *BSLYN/ROY* S71......... **3** F5
  CHNE S41....................................... **183** D2
  SHEFS S8....................................... **134** C5 ⬛
Winders Pl *WMB/DAR* S73................. **39** E3 ⬛
Windgate Hl *CONI* DN12................... **61** E5
Windham Cl *BSLYN/ROY* S71............... **2** D2
Windhill Av *MEX/SWTN* S64.............. **59** D3
Windhill Crs *MEX/SWTN* S64............. **59** D2
Windhill Ter *MEX/SWTN* S64............. **59** D2
The Windings *DEARNE* S63................ **27** E4
Windle Rd *DONS/BSCR* DN4............... **43** E3
Windmill Av *CONI* DN12.................... **85** E2
Windmill Greenway *MOS* S20......... **164** C3
Windmill Hill La *CHPT/GREN* S35..... **87** F2
Windmill La *DRON* S18.................... **171** E5
  SHEFN S5.. **110** C1
Windmill Rd *WMB/DAR* S73.............. **38** C3
Windsor Av *MOS* S20....................... **189** D3
Windsor Crs *BSLYN/ROY* S71.............. **3** H1
Windsor Dr *DOD/DAR* S75................. **20** A3 ⬛
  DRON S18....................................... **168** A2
  MEX/SWTN S64................................. **59** D2
Windsor Ri *AU/AST/KP* S26.............. **142** C4
Windsor Rd *CONI* DN12.................... **60** C5 ⬛
  KIMB S61.. **90** A2
  SHEFS S8....................................... **135** D4
  WHHL DN2....................................... **31** D5
Windsor Sq *DEARNE* S63................... **27** E3
Windsor St *ATT* S4.......................... **123** E1 ⬛
  DEARNE S63...................................... **27** E3
  HOY S74.. **51** E1
Windsor Wk *BTLY* DN5....................... **28** C3
  CHNE S41....................................... **191** D3
Windy House La *SHEFP/MNR* S2...... **137** D3
Windy Rdg *AU/AST/KP* S26.............. **142** A1
Winfield Rd *DEARNE* S63................... **56** A3
Wingerworth Av *SHEFS* S8.............. **158** B1
Wingerworth Wy *CHSW* S40............ **190** A5
Wingfield Cl *DRON* S18................... **168** A3

  KIMB S61.. **92** B3
Wingfield Crs *HACK/IN* S12............ **138** A5
Wingfield Rd *BSLYN/ROY* S71........... **14** B1
  KIMB S61.. **91** F3
Winifred St *RHAM* S60........................ **6** A4
Winkley Ter *SHEFS* S8........................ **99** F4
Winlea Av *RHAM/THRY* S65.............. **105** F5
Winnat Pl *STV/CWN* S43................. **187** D2
Winnats Cl *CHSW* S40..................... **183** D4 ⬛
Winn Cl *ST/HB/BR* S6...................... **107** F1
Winn Dr *ST/HB/BR* S6...................... **107** F1
Winn Gdns *ST/HB/BR* S6................. **107** F1
Winn Gv *ST/HB/BR* S6..................... **107** E1
Winnipeg Rd *BTLY* DN5..................... **16** C5
Winsford Rd *ST/HB/BR* S6................. **97** D4
Winster Cl *BSLY* S70......................... **36** A5
Winster Rd *ST/HB/BR* S6................. **108** A3
  STV/CWN S43.................................. **187** D1
Winston Av *STKB/PEN* S36................ **68** A1
Winter Av *DOD/DAR* S75.................... **13** D5
Winter Hill La *KIMB* S61.................. **101** F2
Winterhill Rd *KIMB* S61................... **101** E3
Winter Rd *DOD/DAR* S75................... **13** D5
Winter St *OWL* S3............................ **121** F3
Winter Ter *DOD/DAR* S75.................. **13** D5
Winterton Cl *DONS/BSCR* DN4.......... **66** B1 ⬛
Winterton Gdns *HACK/IN* S12......... **152** A2
Winterwell Rd *DEARNE* S63............... **55** D1
Winton Cl *BSLY* S70......................... **22** B3 ⬛
Winton Rd *WHHL* DN2........................ **31** F5
Wisbech Cl *CHSW* S40..................... **189** F4
Wiseton Rd *ECC* S11....................... **134** A1
Wisewood Av *ST/HB/BR* S6............. **107** E4
Wisewood La *ST/HB/BR* S6.............. **107** E4
Wisewood Pl *ST/HB/BR* S6.............. **107** E4
Wisewood Rd *ST/HB/BR* S6............. **107** E4
Witham Cl *CHNE* S41...................... **185** D3 ⬛
Witham Rd *FUL* S10........................ **121** D5
Withens Av *ST/HB/BR* S6................. **107** F2
Witney St *SHEFP/MNR* S2................ **135** E2 ⬛
Wivelsfield Rd *DONS/BSCR* DN4........ **82** B5
Woburn Cl *DONS/BSCR* DN4.............. **62** C2
Woburn Pl *DOD/DAR* S75.................. **20** A4 ⬛
  ECC S11.. **145** D3
Wolfe Cl *CHSW* S40........................ **189** E3
Wolfe Dr *ST/HB/BR* S6...................... **97** E4 ⬛
Wolfe Rd *ST/HB/BR* S6...................... **97** E4
Wollaton Av *TOT/DORE* S17............. **157** E3 ⬛
Wollaton Dr *TOT/DORE* S17............. **157** E3 ⬛
Wollaton Rd *TOT/DORE* S17............. **157** D4
Wolseley Rd *SHEFS* S8.................... **135** D3
Wolsey Av *WHHL* DN2........................ **31** F5
Wolverley Rd *HAN/WDH* S13........... **139** E4
Wombwell Av *DEARNE* S63................ **55** E3 ⬛
Wombwell La *BSLY* S70.................... **24** A3
  WMB/DAR S73.................................. **37** E3
Wombwell Rd *HOY* S74...................... **51** F1
Wood Acres *DOD/DAR* S75................ **12** B3
Woodall Rd *ECK/KIL* S21................. **167** D3
  RHAM/THRY S65.............................. **105** D4
Woodall Rd South
  RHAM/THRY S65.............................. **105** D4
Woodbank Crs *SHEFS* S8................. **135** D5
Woodbank Rd *ST/HB/BR* S6............ **118** A3
Woodbine Rd *DARN/MH* S9............ **111** D5
Woodbourn Hl *DARN/MH* S9.......... **124** A3
Woodbourn Rd *DARN/MH* S9......... **124** A3
Woodburn Dr *CHPT/GREN* S35.......... **88** C1
Woodbury Cl *DARN/MH* S9............. **100** B4
Woodbury Rd *DARN/MH* S9............ **100** B4
Wood Cliffe *ECC* S11....................... **131** F4
Wood Cl *CHPT/GREN* S35.................. **89** D2
  RAW S62.. **79** F4
Wood Close Cobnar *DRON* S18....... **176** C3
Woodcock Cl *KIMB* S61..................... **92** A4
Woodcock Pl *SHEFP/MNR* S2........... **123** E4
Woodcock Rd *HOY* S74...................... **51** F3
Wood Cft *KIMB* S61........................... **92** A5
Woodcross Av *DONS/BSCR* DN4........ **47** E5
Woodend Cl *ST/HB/BR* S6............... **107** E5
Woodend Dr *ST/HB/BR* S6............... **107** E5
Woodfarm Av *ST/HB/BR* S6............. **120** A1
Woodfarm Cl *ST/HB/BR* S6............. **119** F1
Woodfarm Dr *ST/HB/BR* S6............ **119** F1
Woodfarm Pl *ST/HB/BR* S6............. **119** F1
Woodfield Av *MEX/SWTN* S64........... **58** C3
Woodfield Rd *DEARNE* S63................ **54** C2
  DONS/BSCR DN4............................... **63** F1
  DONS/BSCR DN4............................... **64** A1
  FUL S10... **120** C3
Wood Fold *OWL* S3.......................... **109** E5
Woodfoot Rd *RHAM* S60................. **115** D3
Woodgrove Rd *DARN/MH* S9.......... **100** C4
  RHAM/THRY S65.............................. **105** D2
Woodhall Ri *MEX/SWTN* S64............. **81** E1 ⬛
Woodhead Dr *HOY* S74...................... **37** E4
Woodhead La *HOY* S74...................... **37** F4
Woodhead Rd *CHPT/GREN* S35......... **71** E2
  SHEFP/MNR S2................................ **135** E2
Woodholm Pl *ECC* S11.................... **133** F5 ⬛
Woodholm Rd *ECC* S11.................... **133** F5
Woodhouse Cl *RAW* S62.................... **79** E3 ⬛
Woodhouse Ct *MOS* S20.................. **140** C5
Woodhouse Crs *MOS* S20................ **153** D1

Woodhouse La *MOS* S20 .... 140 C5
   MOS S20 .... 141 D5
Woodhouse Rd *HACK/IN* S12 .... 137 F4
   HOY S74 .... 51 E3
   WHHL DN2 .... 30 C3
Woodland Cl *MALT* S66 .... 117 F1
   RHAM S60 .... 126 C2
Woodland Dr *BSLY* S70 .... 20 C2
   HACK/IN S12 .... 149 F3 🖪
Woodland Gv *DEARNE* S63 .... 56 A4
Woodland Pl *TOT/DORE* S17 .... 157 D3
Woodland Rd *DEARNE* S63 .... 56 A4
   SHEFS S8 .... 147 F2
Woodlands *STV/CWN* S43 .... 185 E2
Woodlands Av *MOS* S20 .... 141 D5
Woodlands Cl *AU/AST/KP* S26 .... 142 B1 🖪
Woodlands Crs *MEX/SWTN* S64 .... 80 B1
Woodlands Rd *HOY* S74 .... 37 F5
Woodlands Vw *HOY* S74 .... 51 F1
   WMB/DAR S73 .... 38 B5
Woodland Vw *HACK/IN* S12 .... 149 F3
   MEX/SWTN S64 .... 59 D4 🖪
Woodland View Rd
   ST/HB/BR S6 .... 120 B1 🖪
Woodland Wk *RCH* S42 .... 182 A4
Woodland Wy *RHAM/THRY* S65 .... 105 D5
Wood La *NROS/TKH* DN11 .... 63 D5
   RHAM S60 .... 113 E5
   RHAM S60 .... 128 A4
   RHAM S60 .... 120 A1
Wood Lane Cl *ST/HB/BR* S6 .... 119 F1
Woodlea Gdns *DONS/BSCR* DN4 .... 47 D5
Woodlea Gv *ARMTH* DN3 .... 33 F3
Woodlea Wy *WHHL* DN2 .... 32 A3 🖪
Woodleigh Cl *RCH* S42 .... 182 A4 🖪
Woodleys Av *RAW* S62 .... 79 F3
Woodman Dr *MEX/SWTN* S64 .... 80 B1
Woodnook Cl *CHSW* S40 .... 182 A5
Woodnook Gv *ECK/KIL* S21 .... 172 C1
Woodnook Wy *CHSW* S40 .... 182 A5
Woodpecker Cl *AU/AST/KP* S26 .... 142 C4
Wood Rd *KIMB* S61 .... 92 A5
   ST/HB/BR S6 .... 107 F4
Woodrove Av *HAN/WDH* S13 .... 137 F3
Woodrove Cl *HAN/WDH* S13 .... 137 F3
Wood Royd Rd *STKB/PEN* S36 .... 69 E2
Wood Seats *CHPT/GREN* S35 .... 87 E3
Woodseats Cl *SHEFS* S8 .... 146 C1
Woodseats House Rd *SHEFS* S8 .... 147 D3
Woodseats Rd *SHEFS* S8 .... 146 C1
Wodseet Wk *CONI* DN12 .... 61 F5
Woodside Av *DEARNE* S63 .... 167 D1
   ECK/KIL S21 .... 167 D1
Woodside Cl *CHSW* S40 .... 182 C5 🖪
Woodside La *CHPT/GREN* S35 .... 87 D5
   OWL S3 .... 122 B1 🖪
Woodside Rd *BTLY* DN5 .... 28 C1
Woodside Wk *RHAM* S60 .... 92 B4
Wood Spring Ct *ATT* S4 .... 110 C4
Wood's Riding *DONS/BSCR* DN4 .... 32 B5
Woodstock Dr *CHNE* S41 .... 191 D4
Woodstock Rd *ABRD* S7 .... 134 C4
   DOD/DAR S75 .... 13 E3
   DONS/BSCR DN4 .... 62 C1
   ST/HB/BR S6 .... 106 C3
Wood St *BSLY* S70 .... 22 A2
   DON DN1 .... 5 E4
   MEX/SWTN S64 .... 57 F5
   MEX/SWTN S64 .... 58 A3
   RHAM/THRY S65 .... 95 F4
   ST/HB/BR S6 .... 121 F1
   WMB/DAR S73 .... 39 D3
Wood Syke *DOD/DAR* S75 .... 20 B3
Wood Ter *RHAM* S60 .... 114 B1
Woodthorpe Cl *SHEFP/MNR* S2 .... 137 E2

Woodthorpe Crs *HAN/WDH* S13 .. 138 A2 🖪
Woodthorpe Rd *HAN/WDH* S13 .... 138 A3
Woodvale Cl *CHSW* S40 .... 188 B4
Woodvale Rd *ECC* S11 .... 133 F1
Wood Vw *CONI* DN12 .... 62 A4
   CONI DN12 .... 85 F2
   HOY S74 .... 52 B3
Woodview La *DOD/DAR* S75 .... 12 C4 🖪
Wood View Pl *RHAM* S60 .... 114 B1
Woodview Rd *ST/HB/BR* S6 .... 108 A5
Woodview Ter *ECC* S11 .... 132 C2 🖪
Wood Wk *HOY* S74 .... 37 F5
   MEX/SWTN S64 .... 58 A2
   WMB/DAR S73 .... 38 B5
Woofindin Av *ECC* S11 .... 132 C3
Woofindin Rd *ECC* S11 .... 132 B3
Wooldale Cl *MOS* S20 .... 151 E3
Wooldale Cft *MOS* S20 .... 151 E3
Wooldale Dr *MOS* S20 .... 151 E3
Wooldale Gdns *MOS* S20 .... 151 E3
Wooley Av *WMB/DAR* S73 .... 39 D3
Woolley Rd *STKB/PEN* S36 .... 68 B2
Woolley Wood Rd *SHEFN* S5 .... 99 F2
Wootton Ct *RHAM/THRY* S65 .... 95 F4 🖪
Worcester Av *WHHL* DN2 .... 31 D2
Worcester Cl *FUL* S10 .... 131 F1 🖪
Worcester Dr *FUL* S10 .... 131 F1
Worcester Rd *FUL* S10 .... 131 E1
Wordsworth Av *DONS/BSCR* DN4 .... 63 F1
   SHEFN S5 .... 98 A3
   SHEFN S5 .... 108 C1
Wordsworth Cl *SHEFN* S5 .... 97 F3
Wordsworth Crs *SHEFN* S5 .... 97 F5
Wordsworth Dr *BTLY* DN5 .... 29 D5
   RHAM/THRY S65 .... 104 B3
   SHEFN S5 .... 97 F5
Wordsworth Pl *DRON* S18 .... 170 A4
Wordsworth Rd *BSLYN/ROY* S71 .... 14 C3
   CHNE S41 .... 184 A1
   DEARNE S63 .... 55 D1
Workhouse La *OWL* S3 .... 9 E3
Worksop Rd *AU/AST/KP* S26 .... 142 B3
   DARN/MH S9 .... 124 B1
Works Rd *STV/CWN* S43 .... 180 C3
Worral Av *RHAM* S60 .... 127 F3
Worral Cl *BSLY* S70 .... 22 A4
Worrall Rd *CHPT/GREN* S35 .... 73 F5
Worry Goose La *RHAM* S60 .... 116 A2
Worsborough Vw *DOD/DAR* S75 .... 49 E2
Worsbrough Rd *BSLY* S70 .... 36 A5
   HOY S74 .... 37 E4
Worsley Cl *BSLY* S70 .... 22 C4
Worthing Crs *CONI* DN12 .... 85 E1
Worthing Rd *DARN/MH* S9 .... 123 F3
Wortley Av *MEX/SWTN* S64 .... 81 E1
   WMB/DAR S73 .... 38 C1
Wortley Ms *KIMB* S61 .... 89 F2
Wortley Rd *CHPT/GREN* S35 .... 70 B1
   CHPT/GREN S35 .... 73 D3
   KIMB S61 .... 101 F1
   KIMB S61 .... 102 B2 🖪
   STKB/PEN S36 .... 70 A2
Wortley St *BSLY* S70 .... 2 C6
Wortley Vw *HOY* S74 .... 37 E4
Wostenholm Rd *ABRD* S7 .... 135 D5
Wragby La *AU/AST/KP* S26 .... 141 F5
Wragg Rd *SHEFP/MNR* S2 .... 123 F5
Wreakes La *DRON* S18 .... 169 D1
Wren Bank *SHEFP/MNR* S2 .... 123 F5 🖪
Wren Park Cl *CHSW* S40 .... 190 A5
   HACK/IN S12 .... 150 C5
Wrens Wy *BSLY* S70 .... 36 A5
Wright Crs *WMB/DAR* S73 .... 39 E3
Wright's Hl *SHEFP/MNR* S2 .... 135 D1
Wrightson Av *DONS/BSCR* DN4 .... 62 A2

Wrightson Ter *BTLY* DN5 .... 29 F3 🖪
Wroxham Wy *BTLY* DN5 .... 28 C4
Wulfric Cl *SHEFP/MNR* S2 .... 137 D2
Wulfric Pl *SHEFP/MNR* S2 .... 137 D2
Wulfric Rd *ECK/KIL* S21 .... 164 A5
   SHEFP/MNR S2 .... 137 D3
Wyatt Av *ECC* S11 .... 134 A4
Wybourn House Rd
   SHEFP/MNR S2 .... 123 F4 🖪
Wybourn Ter *SHEFP/MNR* S2 .... 123 F4 🖪
Wychwood Cl *DONS/BSCR* DN4 .... 63 D3
Wychwood Cft *MOS* S20 .... 153 E3 🖪
Wychwood Gln *MOS* S20 .... 153 E3 🖪
Wychwood Gv *MOS* S20 .... 153 E3 🖪
Wycombe St *BSLYN/ROY* S71 .... 15 F5 🖪
Wyedale Cft *MOS* S20 .... 153 D1
The Wynd *ECK/KIL* S21 .... 175 F4
Wyn Gv *WMB/DAR* S73 .... 54 B1
Wynmoor Crs *WMB/DAR* S73 .... 40 B5
Wynyard Rd *ST/HB/BR* S6 .... 107 F5
Wythburn Rd *CHNE* S41 .... 183 D2
Wyvern Gdns *TOT/DORE* S17 .... 156 C2

Y

Yarborough Ter *BTLY* DN5 .... 29 F4
Yardley Sq *OWL* S3 .... 121 F3 🖪
Yarmouth St *DARN/MH* S9 .... 111 F3 🖪
Yarncliff Cl *CHSW* S40 .... 183 E4
Yates Cl *MALT* S66 .... 117 E1
Yearling Cha *MEX/SWTN* S64 .... 56 C5
Yeldersley Cl *CHSW* S40 .... 182 C4
Yeomans Rd *ST/HB/BR* S6 .... 121 F2 🖪
Yewdale *BSLY* S70 .... 22 C5
Yew Greave Crs *SHEFN* S5 .... 98 A2
Yew La *CHPT/GREN* S35 .... 98 B1
   SHEFN S5 .... 98 A2
Yews Av *BSLY* S70 .... 22 C5
Yews La *BSLY* S70 .... 22 C5
Yews Pl *BSLY* S70 .... 22 C3
Yew Tree Crs *NROS/TKH* DN11 .... 67 E5
Yew Tree Dr *DARN/MH* S9 .... 113 D3
   ECK/KIL S21 .... 166 A3 🖪
   RCH S42 .... 188 B4
Yoredale Av *CHPT/GREN* S35 .... 74 A5
York Gdns *DONS/BSCR* DN4 .... 46 B5
York La *MALT* S66 .... 117 F5
York Ri *AU/AST/KP* S26 .... 142 A3
York Rd *BTLY* DN5 .... 28 B1
   DARN/MH S9 .... 125 D2
   RHAM/THRY S65 .... 7 F3
   STKB/PEN S36 .... 68 C2 🖪
York St *BSLY* S70 .... 2 B6
   CHNE S41 .... 191 D5
   DEARNE S63 .... 27 E4
   HOY S74 .... 51 F1
   MEX/SWTN S64 .... 58 A3
   NROS/TKH DN11 .... 66 C5
   SHEF S1 .... 9 E4
   WMB/DAR S73 .... 39 E2
Youlgreave Dr *HACK/IN* S12 .... 138 B5
Young St *DON* DN1 .... 5 E4
   SHEF S1 .... 122 A5
Yvonne Gv *WMB/DAR* S73 .... 38 C2

Z

Zetland Rd *HOY* S74 .... 52 C3
   WHHL DN2 .... 31 D5
Zion Pl *DARN/MH* S9 .... 124 A1

Abbeydale Grange School
  ABRD S7.................................. 146 B1
Abbeydale Park Sports Club
  TOT/DORE S17......................... 157 E1
Abbeydale Primary School
  ABRD S7.................................. 135 D4
Abbey Lane Primary School
  SHEFS S8................................ 146 C3
Abbey School
  KIMB S61................................ 101 E2
Abercrombie Primary School
  CHNE S41................................. 11 E3
A C E Business Centre
  ATT S4...................................... 9 G3
Acorn Business Park
  SHEFS S8................................ 146 C1
Acres Hill Primary School
  DARN/MH S9............................ 124 C4
Adwick Road Surgery
  MEX/SWTN S64.......................... 58 C3
Akwaaba Surgery
  CHPT/GREN S35........................ 88 C2
The Alhambra Shopping Centre
  BSLY S70.................................... 2 D6
All Saints RC School
  SHEFP/MNR S2........................ 136 A1
Amber Business Centre
  RHAM S60.................................. 6 D3
Ambergate Clinics
  KIMB S61................................ 102 C3
Ambler Junior School
  DONS/BSCR DN4........................ 63 D1
Anchorage School
  BTLY DN5.................................. 28 C3
Anns Grove Primary School
  SHEFS S8................................ 135 E3
Apperknowle County
    Primary School
  DRON S18............................... 171 D2
Arbourthorne Junior School
  SHEFP/MNR S2........................ 136 B4
Ardsley Oaks Junior
    & Infant School
  BSLY S70.................................. 24 A2
Arksey County Junior
    & Infant School
  BTLY DN5.................................. 17 E4
Armthorpe High School
  ARMTH DN3.............................. 33 E2
Armthorpe Southfield Infant
    & Junior School
  ARMTH DN3.............................. 33 F4
The Armthorpe Surgery
  ARMTH DN3.............................. 33 E3
Art Gallery & Museum
  RHAM/THRY S65.......................... 7 G5
Ashdell Preparatory School
  FUL S10................................. 120 C5
Ashley Industrial Estate
  RHAM S60.................................. 6 D2
Ash Lodge Medical Centre
  CHSW S40............................... 189 E2
Ashville Medical Centre
  BSLY S70.................................. 23 E2
Ashwood Road Junior
    & Infant School
  RAW S62.................................. 94 A3
Asian Mosque Centre
  SHEFP/MNR S2........................ 135 E3
Askern CP School
  BTLY DN5.................................. 16 B1
Aston Comprehensive School
  AU/AST/KP S26........................ 142 A1
Aston Fence Junior
    & Infant School
  HAN/WDH S13.......................... 141 E2
Aston Hall Cricket Club
  AU/AST/KP S26........................ 143 E3
Aston Lodge School
  AU/AST/KP S26........................ 142 C4
Aston Springwood
    Junior School
  AU/AST/KP S26........................ 142 C2
Aston Swallownest Junior
    & Infant School
  AU/AST/KP S26........................ 141 F2
Athron Industrial Estate
  DON DN1.................................... 5 F1
Atlas Business Park
  CHPT/GREN S35........................ 89 D5
Aughton Junior & Infant School
  AU/AST/KP S26........................ 142 B1
Avenue House Surgery
  CHSW S40................................ 10 D5

The Avenue Medical Practice
  SHEFS S8................................ 158 B1
Badsley Moor Lane Jmi School
  RHAM/THRY S65....................... 104 C3
Balby Carr School
  DONS/BSCR DN4......................... 64 A1
Balby Waverley First School
  DONS/BSCR DN4......................... 62 C1
Ballifield Primary School
  HAN/WDH S13.......................... 139 E2
Bank End Junior & Infant School
  BSLY S70.................................. 23 D4
Bankwood Lane Industrial Estate
  NROS/TKH DN11......................... 66 B5
Bankwood Primary School
  SHEFS S8................................ 136 B5
Barnsley Borough Council
  BSLY S70.................................... 2 D5
Barnsley Christian School
  BSLY S70.................................... 2 C6
Barnsley College
  BSLY S70.................................... 2 C3
Barnsley College
  DOD/DAR S75.............................. 2 C2
Barnsley County Court
  BSLY S70.................................... 2 C4
Barnsley District General Hospital
  DOD/DAR S75............................ 13 D4
Barnsley Football Club Ltd
  BSLYN/ROY S71............................ 3 G5
Barnsley Magistrates Court
  BSLY S70.................................... 2 B4
Barnsley Metropolitan
    Borough Council
  BSLY S70.................................... 2 C4
Barnsley Metropolitan
    Borough Council
  BSLY S70.................................... 2 B3
Barnsley Metropolitan
    Borough Council
  BSLY S70.................................... 2 D3
Barnsley Metropolitan
    Borough Council
  BSLY S70.................................. 21 E3
Barnsley Metropolitan
    Borough Council
  BSLY S70.................................. 36 B1
Barnsley Metropolitan
    Borough Council
  BSLYN/ROY S71............................ 3 E5
Barnsley Metropolitan
    Borough Council
  BSLYN/ROY S71............................ 3 F2
Barnsley Metropolitan
    Borough Council
  DOD/DAR S75............................ 49 D2
Barnsley Metropolitan
    Borough Council
  WMB/DAR S73............................ 39 F2
Barnsley Metropolitan
    Borough Council
  WMB/DAR S73............................ 40 A2
Barnsley Private Clinic
  DOD/DAR S75.............................. 2 B2
Barrow Hill Primary School
  STV/CWN S43........................... 180 C3
The Basement Gallery
  FUL S10................................. 132 A3
Baslow Road Surgery
  TOT/DORE S17.......................... 156 C3
Beauchief Golf Club House
  SHEFS S8................................ 145 F4
Beevor Industrial Estate
  BSLYN/ROY S71......................... 14 C5
Beighton Health Centre
  MOS S20................................. 153 D1
Belgrave Medical Centre
  SHEFP/MNR S2......................... 135 E2
Bentley Colliery Cricket Club
  BTLY DN5.................................. 16 C4
Bentley Health Centre
  BTLY DN5.................................. 16 B5
Bentley High Street
    Primary School
  BTLY DN5.................................. 29 F1
Bentley Sunnyfields
    Infant School
  BTLY DN5.................................. 28 C2
Bentley Sunnyfields
    Junior School
  BTLY DN5.................................. 29 D2
Bents Green Special School
  ECC S11................................. 132 C5

Birdwell Health Centre
  BSLY S70.................................. 50 A2
Birdwell Primary School
  BSLY S70.................................. 50 A1
Birkdale Preparatory School
  FUL S10................................. 134 B1
Birkdale School
  ECC/KIL S21............................ 134 A1
Birkhill Primary School
  ECK/KIL S21............................ 173 F1
Birley First School
  HACK/IN S12............................ 150 B2
Birley Health Centre
  HACK/IN S12............................ 150 B3
Birley Middle School
  HACK/IN S12............................ 150 B2
Birley Primary School
  HACK/IN S12............................ 150 B2
Birley Spa Primary School
  HACK/IN S12............................ 151 D1
Blackburn County
    Junior Mixed School
  KIMB S61................................ 100 C3
Bluebell Medical Centre
  SHEFN S5................................ 111 D1
Bluestone Middle School
  SHEFP/MNR S2......................... 136 B2
Bluestone Primary School
  SHEFP/MNR S2......................... 136 B2
Bond's Picture Gallery
  CHNE S41................................. 10 D4
Bracken Moor Sports Club
  STKB/PEN S36........................... 69 D3
Bradmarsh Business Park
  RHAM S60............................... 103 D4
Brampton Ellis Infant School
  DEARNE S63.............................. 55 D2
Brampton Health Centre
  WMB/DAR S73............................ 40 B5
Brampton Junior
    & Infant School
  CHSW S40................................ 10 A6
Brantwood Independent
    School for Girls
  ABRD S7................................. 134 B2
Brimington Clinic
  STV/CWN S43........................... 185 F1
Brimington Manor County
    Infant School
  STV/CWN S43........................... 186 A4
Brinsworth Clinic
  RHAM S60............................... 113 F3
Brinsworth Comprehensive
    School
  RHAM S60............................... 113 E4
Brinsworth Medical Centre
  RHAM S60............................... 113 E3
Brinsworth Whitehill Jm School
  RHAM S60............................... 114 A5
Broad Elms School
  ECC S11................................. 145 D1
Broadway School
  BSLY S70.................................. 20 C2
Brockwell Junior School
  CHSW S40............................... 183 E5
Brookfield Community School
  CHSW S40............................... 188 B2
Brook House Junior School
  MOS S20................................. 153 F2
Broomhill Clinic
  FUL S10................................. 121 D5
Broomhill Infant School
  FUL S10................................. 121 D5
Broomhill Medical Centre
  FUL S10................................. 121 E5
Broomhill Medical Surgery
  FUL S10................................. 120 C5
Broom Lane Medical Centre
  RHAM S60............................... 115 E1
Broom Valley Junior
    & Infant School
  RHAM S60............................... 103 F5
Brunswick Primary School
  HAN/WDH S13.......................... 140 B3
Burncross Surgery
  CHPT/GREN S35........................ 88 A1
Burns Medical Centre
  DONS/BSCR DN4......................... 46 C4
The Burns Practice
  WHHL DN2................................... 5 G4
Burton Road Junior
    & Infant School
  BSLYN/ROY S71............................ 3 G1

The Business Centre
RHAM S60 6   D5
The Business Centre
RHAM S60 103   D5
Byron Wood Primary School
ATT S4 109   F5
Camms Endowed C of E
Primary School
MOS S20 164   B4
Canklow Meadows
Industrial Estate
RHAM S60 114   B3
Canklow Woods Junior
& Infant School
RHAM S60 114   B2
Cantley Hawthorn First School
DONS/BSCR DN4 46   C3
Cantley Hawthorn Junior School
DONS/BSCR DN4 46   C3
Cantley Health Centre
DONS/BSCR DN4 47   D5
Carbrook Hall Industrial Estate
DARN/MH S9 111   F3
Carfield Primary School
SHEFS S8 135   E5
Caribbean Sports Club
CHPT/GREN S35 99   D1
Carrfield Medical Centre
SHEFP/MNR S2 135   F4
Carterknowle & Dore
Medical Practice
ABRD S7 134   C5
Carter Knowle Junior School
ABRD S7 134   B5
Castle Market
ATT S4 9   G4
Cathedral Church of
St Peter & St Paul
SHEF S1 9   E4
Cavendish Junior School
CHNE S41 184   A1
Cedar Special School
DONS/BSCR DN4 63   D1
Central Business Park
RHAM S60 6   B5
Central Sheffield
University Hospitals
FUL S10 121   E4
Chapeltown Surgery
CHPT/GREN S35 88   C2
Charnock Hall Primary School
HACK/IN S12 149   F3
Charter Gallery Museum
CONI DN12 84   C1
Chatsworth Surgery
CHSW S40 188   C2
Chaucer School
SHEFN S5 97   F4
Chesterfield Borough Council
CHNE S41 184   B3
Chesterfield Borough Council
CHSW S40 190   A3
Chesterfield Bowl
CHSW S40 190   C5
Chesterfield Caravan &
Leisure Centre
DRON S18 177   F3
Chesterfield College of
Technology & Arts
CHNE S41 11   F4
Chesterfield Football Club Ltd
CHSW S40 10   C5
Chesterfield Museum
CHNE S41 11   G6
Chesterfield Rugby Club
CHNE S41 11   F1
Chesterfield Small
Business Centre
CHNE S41 184   B2
Childrens Hospital N H S Trust
FUL S10 121   E4
Child Welfare & School Clinic
RHAM/THRY S65 7   H2
Christ Church School
CHNE S41 11   E1
Cifford C of E Grammar School
ECC S11 134   B2
City Museum & Mappin
Art Gallery
FUL S10 121   E4
Civic Building
RHAM/THRY S65 6   D4
Civic Theatre
BSLY S70 2   D5

Claremont Hospital
FUL S10 119   E5
Claycliffe Business Park
DOD/DAR S75 12   A2
Clayfield Industrial Estate
DONS/BSCR DN4 63   E1
Clocktower Business Centre
STV/CWN S43 180   B3
Clough House Medical Centre
SHEFP/MNR S2 135   F1
Coit Primary School
CHPT/GREN S35 88   B2
Coleridge Road Jmi School
RHAM/THRY S65 104   B1
College of Technology
RHAM/THRY S65 6   D5
Colonnades Centre
DON DN1 4   D4
Concord Middle School
SHEFN S5 99   F5
Conisbrough Castle
CONI DN12 61   F5
Contour Health Centre
RHAM S60 103   E4
Cooper Gallery
BSLY S70 2   C4
Cope Street Surgery
BSLY S70 22   B3
Coroners Court
DON DN1 4   D5
Cortonwood County
Primary School
WMB/DAR S73 40   B5
The Crookes Practice
FUL S10 121   D3
Crown Court
DON DN1 5   E5
Crown Court
OWL S3 9   E3
Crucible Theatre
SHEF S1 9   F6
The Culvert Gallery
ECC S11 134   B2
Cupola Gallery
ST/HB/BR S6 108   A2
Curlew Junior School
WHHL DN2 19   E5
The Curtain Gallery
ECC S11 134   B2
Cusworth Hall
BTLY DN5 28   B5
Dalton Foljambe Infant School
RHAM/THRY S65 95   F5
Dalton Health Centre
RHAM/THRY S65 95   E5
Danum Grammar School
WHHL DN2 32   B4
Darfield Valley Primary School
WMB/DAR S73 40   A1
Darnall Health Centre
DARN/MH S9 125   D2
Darnall Road Surgery
DARN/MH S9 124   C2
Dead Earnest Theatre
ST/HB/BR S6 121   D1
Deepcar Junior School
STKB/PEN S36 69   F3
Deerlands Special School
SHEFN S5 98   C4
Deer Park Surgery
ST/HB/BR S6 119   F1
Denaby Lane Industrial Estate
CONI DN12 59   F5
Derbyshire County Council
CHNE S41 11   F4
Derbyshire County Council
CHNE S41 184   A1
Derbyshire County Council
CHSW S40 10   C5
Derbyshire County Council
ECK/KIL S21 164   C5
Devonshire Green Medical Centre
SHEF S1 8   C6
Dobcroft Infant School
ECC S11 145   F1
Dobcroft Junior School
ECC S11 145   F2
Dodworth Health Centre
DOD/DAR S75 20   A3
Dodworth Junior School
DOD/DAR S75 20   A3
Doncaster Area Health Authority
CONI DN12 84   C1

Doncaster Area Health Authority
DON DN1 5   F4
Doncaster Area Health Authority
MEX/SWTN S64 58   C4
Doncaster Balby
Central First School
DONS/BSCR DN4 43   F3
Doncaster Civic Theatre
DON DN1 5   F4
Doncaster College
DON DN1 4   D2
Doncaster Golf Course
DONS/BSCR DN4 67   E3
Doncaster Health Authority
DONS/BSCR DN4 44   B4
Doncaster Health Authority
DONS/BSCR DN4 63   F2
Doncaster Magistrates Court
DON DN1 4   D5
Doncaster Metropolitan Borough
Council
ARMTH DN3 19   F4
Doncaster Metropolitan Borough
Council
BTLY DN5 4   B1
Doncaster Metropolitan Borough
Council
CONI DN12 85   D1
Doncaster Metropolitan Borough
Council
DON DN1 4   D6
Doncaster Metropolitan Borough
Council
DON DN1 4   D4
Doncaster Metropolitan Borough
Council
DON DN1 5   F3
Doncaster Metropolitan Borough
Council
DON DN1 5   G5
Doncaster Metropolitan Borough
Council
DONS/BSCR DN4 46   C4
Doncaster Metropolitan Borough
Council
MEX/SWTN S64 59   D3
Doncaster Museum & Art Gallery
DON DN1 5   F4
Doncaster Road Infant School
MEX/SWTN S64 59   D4
Doncaster Road Jmi School
RHAM/THRY S65 104   B1
Doncaster Road Junior School
MEX/SWTN S64 59   D4
Doncaster Road Primary School
BSLY S70 22   B2
Doncaster Rovers Football Club
DONS/BSCR DN4 45   E2
Doncaster Royal Infirmary
& Montagu Hospital N H S Trust
WHHL DN2 31   D4
Doncaster & South Humber
Healthcare Nhs Trust
DONS/BSCR DN4 63   F2
Doncaster Town Cricket Club
WHHL DN2 5   H4
Don Valley High School
BTLY DN5 28   B1
Dore Junior & Infant School
TOT/DORE S17 156   B2
Dovercourt Surgery
SHEFP/MNR S2 136   C1
Dr Chambers & Partners
CHPT/GREN S35 73   E3
Dr John Bingham Junior
& Infant School
SHEFS S8 159   E3
Dr John Worrall School
DARN/MH S9 111   E5
Dronfield County Junior School
DRON S18 169   E2
Dronfield Health Centre
DRON S18 169   E2
Dronfield Infant School
DRON S18 169   E2
The Dronfield School
DRON S18 168   C1
Dronfield Sports Centre
DRON S18 169   D2
Dunston Primary School
CHNE S41 183   E1
Dunston Trading Estate
CHNE S41 177   F4

Dykeshall Medical Centre
ST/HB/BR S6.................................. **107** F3
Eastwood Trading Estate
RHAM/THRY S65......................... **94** B5
Ecclesall Infant School
ECC S11....................................... **133** D4
Ecclesall Medical Centre
ECC S11....................................... **133** E5
Ecclesfield Comprehensive
School
CHPT/GREN S35........................ **88** B3
Ecclesfield Health Centre
CHPT/GREN S35........................ **88** C5
Ecclesfield Parish Council
CHPT/GREN S35........................ **73** F4
Eckington Health Centre
ECK/KIL S21............................... **164** C5
Eckington Junior School
ECK/KIL S21............................... **164** B5
Eckington School
ECK/KIL S21............................... **163** E5
Edward Sheerien School
BSLYN/ROY S71......................... **14** C1
Ellers Middle School
DONS/BSCR DN4......................... **45** F4
Ellesmere Teaching School
ATT S4... **123** D1
Emmett Carr Surgery
ECK/KIL S21............................... **175** F3
Eppic Theatre
CHPT/GREN S35........................ **87** D5
Fairfield School of Art
BSLY S70...................................... **2** B4
Falkland House Surgery
ECC S11....................................... **133** E4
Far Lane Medical Centre
ST/HB/BR S6.............................. **107** F3
Ferham House Clinic
KIMB S61..................................... **102** B3
Fernham Junior & Infant School
KIMB S61..................................... **102** B3
Fire Police Museum
OWL S3.. **8** D4
Firs Hill Junior School
ATT S4... **109** F4
Firth Park Medical Centre
SHEFN S5..................................... **110** B1
Firth Park School
SHEFN S5..................................... **110** A1
Foxhill Medical Centre
ST/HB/BR S6.............................. **97** E3
Fox Hill Primary School
ST/HB/BR S6.............................. **97** E3
Frame Gallery
RHAM S60.................................... **6** D4
Frenchgate Centre
DON DN1..................................... **4** D3
Fullerton House School
CONI DN12................................... **60** A5
The Gables School
WMB/DAR S73............................ **39** E3
The Gallery
DON DN1..................................... **5** E3
Gawber Junior & Infant School
DOD/DAR S75............................. **12** B4
Gilbert Heathcote Infant School
CHNE S41..................................... **184** A1
Gladys Buxton School
DRON S18.................................... **170** A1
Gleadless Clinic
HACK/IN S12............................... **149** F2
Gleadless Primary School
HACK/IN S12............................... **137** F5
Globe Business Centre
OWL S3.. **8** C1
Goldthorpe RC Jmi School
DEARNE S63................................ **27** E5
Gooseacre Primary School
DEARNE S63................................ **26** C2
Grange Gate Junior School
BSLYN/ROY S71......................... **15** F5
Grange Lane Industrial Estate
BSLYN/ROY S71......................... **23** F2
Graves Art Gallery
SHEF S1....................................... **9** F6
Greasbrough Health Centre
KIMB S61..................................... **92** C3
Greasbrough Junior & Infant School
KIMB S61..................................... **92** C3
Greengate Lane Primary School
CHPT/GREN S35........................ **73** F4
Greenhill Health Centre
SHEFS S8..................................... **158** C2

Greenhill Primary School
SHEFS S8..................................... **158** C1
Greenlands Junior School
DARN/MH S9................................ **125** D3
Greenside Surgery
KIMB S61..................................... **92** C3
Greenway Natural Health Centre
TOT/DORE S17............................ **156** B4
Grenoside Primary School
CHPT/GREN S35........................ **87** D5
Greystones First School
ECC S11....................................... **133** E3
Greystones Medical Centre
ECC S11....................................... **133** F3
Greystones Primary School
ECC S11....................................... **133** F3
Grove Street Junior & Infant
School
BSLYN/ROY S71......................... **3** F5
Guildhall Industrial Estate
ARMTH DN3................................. **19** F3
Hackenthorpe Medical Centre
HACK/IN S12............................... **151** E2
Hady School
CHNE S41..................................... **191** E2
Halfway Infant School
MOS S20...................................... **164** C1
Halfway Junior School
MOS S20...................................... **164** C1
Hallam Primary School
FUL S10....................................... **132** A1
Hallamshire Business Park
FUL S10....................................... **134** C1
The Hallamshire Gallery
ECC S11....................................... **133** F3
Hallamshire Natural
Health Centre
ECC S11....................................... **134** A2
Hall Cross Comprehensive
School
DON DN1..................................... **5** G3
Handsworth Branch Clinic
HAN/WDH S13............................. **139** D1
Handsworth Road
Medical Centre
HAN/WDH S13............................. **139** D1
Hanover Medical Centre
FUL S10....................................... **121** F5
Hartington Industrial Estate
STV/CWN S43.............................. **181** F2
Hasland Hall Community School
CHNE S41..................................... **191** E5
Hasland Primary Infant School
CHNE S41..................................... **191** D4
Hasland Primary Junior School
CHNE S41..................................... **191** D5
Hatfield Primary School
SHEFN S5..................................... **99** E4
Healthcare Surgery
SHEFN S5..................................... **97** E5
Heeley Business Centre
SHEFP/MNR S2........................... **135** E2
Heeley Green Surgery
SHEFP/MNR S2........................... **135** F4
Heeley Retail Park
SHEFS S8..................................... **147** D2
Hemingfield Ellis C of E
Junior & Infant School
WMB/DAR S73............................ **39** D5
Hemsworth Primary School
GLV S14....................................... **148** B3
Henry Bradley County
Infant School
STV/CWN S43.............................. **186** A1
Herdings Primary School
GLV S14....................................... **148** C3
Herries School
SHEFN S5..................................... **108** C2
Herringthorpe Junior
& Infant School
RHAM/THRY S65......................... **104** C5
Hexthorpe First School
DONS/BSCR DN4......................... **43** E2
Hexthorpe Primary School
DONS/BSCR DN4......................... **43** E3
Highfields Junior School
WMB/DAR S73............................ **39** D2
High Greave Jmi School
RHAM/THRY S65......................... **105** D1
High Green Health Centre
CHPT/GREN S35........................ **73** E3
High Green Primary School
CHPT/GREN S35........................ **73** E3

High Storrs School
ECC S11....................................... **133** D4
High Street Medical Centre
STV/CWN S43.............................. **181** F4
Highwoods Infant School
MEX/SWTN S64.......................... **57** F2
Hill House Preparatory School
DON DN1..................................... **5** H2
Hill Primary School
DEARNE S63................................ **27** F2
Hillsborough Health Centre
ST/HB/BR S6.............................. **108** A5
Hillsborough Primary School
ST/HB/BR S6.............................. **108** A3
Hinde House School
SHEFN S5..................................... **99** F5
Hm Prison
BTLY DN5..................................... **4** B3
Holgate School
BSLY S70...................................... **21** D1
Hollies Medical Centre
ECC S11....................................... **134** B3
Hollingwood Junior
& Infant School
STV/CWN S43.............................. **180** B5
Hollis Hospital
TOT/DORE S17............................ **144** C3
Holly House School
CHNE S41..................................... **178** B3
Hollywood Bowling
DARN/MH S9................................ **112** A4
Holme Hall Primary School
CHSW S40................................... **182** C4
Holt House Infant School
ABRD S7...................................... **146** B1
Holy Cross Deanery C of E Junior
& Infant School
BSLYN/ROY S71......................... **14** C1
Holyrood RC Junior
& Infant School
BSLY S70...................................... **21** E2
Howarth Junior & Infant School
RHAM S60.................................... **114** A5
Hoyland Common
Primary School
HOY S74....................................... **50** B3
Hoyland Elsecar C of E Junior
& Infant School
HOY S74....................................... **52** C3
Hoyland Greenfield Junior
& Infant School
HOY S74....................................... **52** A2
Hoyland St Helens RC Junior
& Infant School
HOY S74....................................... **51** E2
Hoyland Sports Centre
HOY S74....................................... **51** D2
H S B C Sports Club
TOT/DORE S17............................ **144** B4
Hucklow Primary School
SHEFN S5..................................... **110** A2
Hunloke Secondary School
CHSW S40................................... **190** B5
Hunningley Junior
& Infant School
BSLY S70...................................... **23** F3
Hunters Bar Junior
& Infant School
ECC S11....................................... **134** A2
Industrial Centre
MEX/SWTN S64.......................... **58** B4
Inkersall Primary School
STV/CWN S43.............................. **187** D2
Intake High School
WHHL DN2.................................... **32** B4
Intake Junior & Infant School
HACK/IN S12............................... **137** F4
Ironbridge Industrial Estate
HAN/WDH S13............................. **140** A2
Ivanhoe Junior & Infant School
CONI DN12................................... **84** B2
Jamiyat Tabliq Ul Islam Mosque
DARN/MH S9................................ **124** B1
Jaunty Springs Health Centre
HACK/IN S12............................... **149** F1
Jessop Hospital for Women
OWL S3.. **8** A5
Jordanthorpe Health Centre
SHEFS S8..................................... **159** F2
Junction 34 Industrial Estate
DARN/MH S9................................ **112** B3
Keir House Surgery
BSLY S70...................................... **2** A3

Kelham Island Museum
   OWL S3 .... 8 D2
Kelvin Grove Surgery
   WMB/DAR S73 .... 39 F3
Kendray Hospital
   BSLY S70 .... 23 D2
Kendray Infant School
   BSLY S70 .... 23 D3
Kendray Primary School
   BSLY S70 .... 22 C3
Keresforth Primary School
   DOD/DAR S75 .... 20 B4
Killamarsh County Junior
   & Infant School
   ECK/KIL S21 .... 166 C1
Killamarsh Leisure Centre
   ECK/KIL S21 .... 166 B1
Killamarsh Medical Centre
   ECK/KIL S21 .... 166 A1
Kilnhurst Business Park
   MEX/SWTN S64 .... 81 F5
Kilnhurst Junior & Infants School
   MEX/SWTN S64 .... 82 A4
Kimberworth
   Comprehensive School
   KIMB S61 .... 102 A3
Kimberworth Infants School
   KIMB S61 .... 102 A2
Kimberworth Park Clinic
   KIMB S61 .... 91 F5
Kimberworth Park Medical Centre
   KIMB S61 .... 101 F1
King Ecgbert Secondary School
   TOT/DORE S17 .... 156 B2
King Edward Vii School
   FUL S10 .... 121 E5
Kingfisher First School
   WHHL DN2 .... 31 E2
Kingthorne Group Practice
   DON DN1 .... 5 G2
Kirk Balk School
   HOY S74 .... 51 D2
Kirkby Avenue Primary School
   BTLY DN5 .... 29 E3
Kitchen Gallery
   RHAM S60 .... 6 D6
Lakeside First School
   DONS/BSCR DN4 .... 45 D3
Lantern Theatre
   ABRD S7 .... 134 C2
Lecture Theatre
   SHEF S1 .... 8 B5
Lenthall School
   DRON S18 .... 159 F5
Limpsfield Junior School
   DARN/MH S9 .... 111 E2
Listerdale Shopping Centre
   RHAM/THRY S65 .... 105 F5
The Little Gallery
   RAW S62 .... 76 C2
Little Theatre
   DEARNE S63 .... 26 C4
Littleworth Lane Infant School
   BSLYN/ROY S71 .... 15 E4
Lobwood Junior & Infant School
   BSLY S70 .... 22 B5
Lodge Moor Medical Centre
   FUL S10 .... 131 E1
Longcar Junior & Infant School
   BSLY S70 .... 21 E2
Lound Infant School
   CHPT/GREN S35 .... 74 A5
Lound Junior School
   CHPT/GREN S35 .... 74 B5
Lowedges Primary School
   SHEFS S8 .... 159 D2
Loxley Primary School
   ST/HB/BR S6 .... 106 B3
Lundwood Medical Centre
   BSLYN/ROY S71 .... 15 E5
The Lyceum Theatre
   SHEF S1 .... 9 F6
Lydgate Infant School
   FUL S10 .... 120 B4
Lydgate Junior School
   FUL S10 .... 120 B5
Makki Mosque
   SHEFS S8 .... 135 E4
Malin Bridge Primary School
   ST/HB/BR S6 .... 107 F4
Manor Clinic
   SHEFP/MNR S2 .... 137 D4
Manor Lodge Middle School
   SHEFP/MNR S2 .... 136 C1

Manor Lodge Primary School
   SHEFP/MNR S2 .... 136 C1
Manor Park Medical Centre
   SHEFP/MNR S2 .... 124 B5
Manor Top Medical Centre
   HACK/IN S12 .... 137 E4
Market Hall
   DON DN1 .... 5 E2
Market Junior School
   HOY S74 .... 51 F1
Maricliffe Primary School
   ST/HB/BR S6 .... 107 F2
Marshgate Industrial Estate
   BTLY DN5 .... 4 B2
Marsh Lane Primary School
   ECK/KIL S21 .... 162 C5
Mary Swanick Primary School
   CHNE S41 .... 178 B3
The Mcauley School
   DONS/BSCR DN4 .... 47 E4
Meadow Bank Industrial Estate
   KIMB S61 .... 102 A3
Meadowhall Centre
   DARN/MH S9 .... 112 A1
Meadowhall Junior School
   KIMB S61 .... 101 F3
Meadowhall Retail Park
   DARN/MH S9 .... 112 A4
Meadowhead School
   SHEFS S8 .... 159 E1
Meadows Community School
   CHNE S41 .... 178 C3
Meersbrook Bank
   Primary School
   SHEFS S8 .... 135 D5
Melrose Surgery
   OWL S3 .... 122 C1
Merlin Gallery
   ABRD S7 .... 134 B3
Merlin Theatre
   ST/HB/BR S6 .... 106 C3
Metrodome sports
   & Leisure complex
   BSLYN/ROY S71 .... 3 F4
Mexborough Business Centre
   MEX/SWTN S64 .... 58 C3
Mexborough Comprehensive
   School
   MEX/SWTN S64 .... 58 A2
Mexborough Windhill
   Junior & Infant School
   MEX/SWTN S64 .... 59 D2
Middlecroft Leisure Centre
   STV/CWN S43 .... 187 E2
Mill Road Surgery
   CHPT/GREN S35 .... 88 C5
Mill Trading Estate
   BSLYN/ROY S71 .... 22 C1
Monk Bretton Health Centre
   BSLYN/ROY S71 .... 15 D3
Monkwood Health Centre
   RAW S62 .... 79 F4
Montagu Hospital
   MEX/SWTN S64 .... 58 B2
Monteney Middle
   & Primary School
   SHEFN S5 .... 98 B2
Montgomery House
   Medical Centre
   ST/HB/BR S6 .... 8 B1
Montgomery Theatre
   SHEF S1 .... 9 E5
Monument
   DON DN1 .... 5 G4
Moorgate Business Centre
   RHAM S60 .... 7 E6
Moorgate Mosque &
   Community Centre
   RHAM S60 .... 6 D6
Morley Place Junior School
   CONI DN12 .... 84 B1
Mosborough Medical Centre
   MOS S20 .... 164 A1
Mosborough Primary School
   MOS S20 .... 164 B1
Mosque
   OWL S3 .... 122 C1
Mosque
   RHAM S60 .... 6 A5
Mossbrook Special School
   SHEFS S8 .... 148 A5
The Mount Group Practice
   DON DN1 .... 5 H2

Mount Osborne Industrial Park
   BSLYN/ROY S71 .... 3 H6
Mount Vernon Hospital
   BSLY S70 .... 22 A4
Museum
   ECC S11 .... 134 A2
Myers Grove School
   ST/HB/BR S6 .... 107 E5
National Music Centre
   SHEF S1 .... 122 C5
The Nelson Practice
   BTLY DN5 .... 28 C2
Nether Edge Hospital
   ECC S11 .... 134 B4
Nether Green Infant School
   FUL S10 .... 132 B2
Nether Green Junior School
   FUL S10 .... 132 C2
Netherthorpe Primary School
   OWL S3 .... 8 B3
Newbold C of E School
   CHNE S41 .... 183 F2
Newbold Community School
   CHNE S41 .... 183 F3
Newbold Community School
   CHSW S40 .... 183 E3
Newfield School
   SHEFS S8 .... 148 A2
Newman Special School
   RHAM S60 .... 115 E3
New Street Health Centre
   BSLY S70 .... 21 F2
New Surgery
   MEX/SWTN S64 .... 58 C4
Newton Business Centre
   BTLY DN5 .... 43 D1
New Village Primary School
   BTLY DN5 .... 16 C4
New Whittington Infant School
   STV/CWN S43 .... 179 E2
New Whittington Primary
   Junior School
   CHNE S41 .... 179 E3
Nightingale Primary School
   DONS/BSCR DN4 .... 62 C1
Nook Lane Junior School
   ST/HB/BR S6 .... 106 A5
Norfolk Middle School
   SHEFP/MNR S2 .... 136 C2
Norfolk Park Health Centre
   SHEFP/MNR S2 .... 136 A2
Northcliffe School
   CONI DN12 .... 60 B5
North Derbyshire
   Health Authority
   CHSW S40 .... 11 E4
North East Derbyshire
   District Council
   CHSW S40 .... 10 D5
North East Derbyshire
   District Council
   DRON S18 .... 169 E2
North East Derbyshire
   District Council
   DRON S18 .... 169 F2
Northfield Junior School
   DRON S18 .... 160 A5
Northlands Community
   Health Centre
   SHEFN S5 .... 98 A5
Norton Free Primary School
   SHEFS S8 .... 148 A4
Norton Oakes Cricket Club
   SHEFS S8 .... 148 B4
Notre Dame School
   FUL S10 .... 133 E1
Oakes Park Special School
   SHEFS S8 .... 148 A3
Oakfield Junior School
   WMB/DAR S73 .... 39 E3
Oakwell Business Centre
   BSLYN/ROY S71 .... 3 H6
Oakwood Surgery
   DONS/BSCR DN4 .... 46 C5
Oakwood Swimming Baths
   RHAM S60 .... 115 D1
Odeon Cinema
   BSLY S70 .... 2 D4
Odeon Cinema
   DON DN1 .... 5 F4
Odeon Cinema
   SHEF S1 .... 9 F5
Old College of Technology
   BSLY S70 .... 2 C4

Old Forge Business Park
SHEFP/MNR S2 .... **135** E3

Old Hall Comprehensive School
KIMB S61 .... **101** F2

Ora Gallery
ECC S11 .... **134** B2

Our Lady of Sorrows RC School
ARMTH DN3 .... **33** E2

Our Lady RC Primary School
BTLY DN5 .... **16** C5

Our Ladys & St Josephs
RC JMI School
DEARNE S63 .... **56** A2

Owlthorpe Surgery
MOS S20 .... **151** E3

Parkgate Business Park
RAW S62 .... **94** A4

Parkgate Medical Centre
RAW S62 .... **94** A2

Park Health Centre
SHEFP/MNR S2 .... **9** H6

Park Hill Primary School
SHEFP/MNR S2 .... **9** H6

Park Infant School
WHHL DN2 .... **31** D3

Park Primary School
WHHL DN2 .... **31** D3

Park Road Infant School
MEX/SWTN S64 .... **58** B2

Parkside Community School
CHSW S40 .... **190** A2

Park Street Junior
& Infant School
WMB/DAR S73 .... **39** F3

Parson Cross C of E
Primary School
ST/HB/BR S6 .... **97** E5

Peacock Trading Estate
ST/HB/BR S6 .... **108** C4

Pearsons Trading Estate
CHNE S41 .... **178** C5

The Petersgate Medical Centre
BTLY DN5 .... **28** C1

Peveril School of Art
ECC S11 .... **133** F2

Phillimore Park Primary School
DARN/MH S9 .... **124** C1

Phoenix Surgery
DON DN1 .... **5** F4

Pipworth Junior School
SHEFP/MNR S2 .... **137** F1

Pitsmoor Dental Health Centre
ATT S4 .... **109** F5

Pitsmoor Surgery
OWL S3 .... **109** E5

Platts Common Industrial Estate
HOY S74 .... **51** E1

Plumb Estates
ARMTH DN3 .... **19** E4

Pomegranate Theatre
CHNE S41 .... **11** G6

Ponds Forge International
Sports Centre
SHEF S1 .... **9** G5

Porter Croft School
ECC S11 .... **134** C1

Portland Business Park
HAN/WDH S13 .... **138** C1

Prince Edward Middle School
SHEFP/MNR S2 .... **137** E3

Prince Edward Primary School
SHEFP/MNR S2 .... **137** E3

Prince of Wales Road
Medical Centre
DARN/MH S9 .... **125** D4

Priory School
DONS/BSCR DN4 .... **46** C5

Public Baths
DEARNE S63 .... **56** A2

Public Baths
ST/HB/BR S6 .... **121** F2

Public Swimming Baths
ECK/KIL S21 .... **164** C5

Pye Bank Trinity C of E
Junior School
OWL S3 .... **122** C1

Queens Road Clinic
BSLYN/ROY S71 .... **3** E5

Queen Street Junior
& Infant School
MEX/SWTN S64 .... **57** E5

Ragged School
CHSW S40 .... **190** B2

Railway Staff Social
& Sports Club
STV/CWN S43 .... **180** A5

Rawmarsh Leisure Centre
RAW S62 .... **94** B2

Rawmarsh Monkwood
Jmi School
RAW S62 .... **79** F4

Rawmarsh Thorogate
Junior & Infant School
RAW S62 .... **80** A4

Redbrook Business Park
DOD/DAR S75 .... **12** C2

Redscope Junior & Infant School
KIMB S61 .... **91** F5

Reflex Theatre
SHEFS S8 .... **135** E4

Regent Square Group Practice
DON DN1 .... **5** G3

Register Office
DON DN1 .... **5** G5

Reignhead Primary School
MOS S20 .... **153** D2

Renishaw Primary School
ECK/KIL S21 .... **175** F3

Revolution House
CHNE S41 .... **178** B3

The Richmond Fellowship
MEX/SWTN S64 .... **57** E5

Richmond Hill Junior
& Infant School
BTLY DN5 .... **42** C1

Richmond Medical Centre
HAN/WDH S13 .... **138** B3

Ridgeway Medical Centre
RHAM/THRY S65 .... **105** D2

Ridgeway Primary School
HACK/IN S12 .... **150** C5

Ridgewood Comprehensive
School
BTLY DN5 .... **28** A3

Rivelin Primary School
ST/HB/BR S6 .... **107** F5

Rockingham Business Park
BSLY S70 .... **50** A2

Rockingham College of Further
Education
DEARNE S63 .... **55** F2

Rockingham Junior
& Infant School
KIMB S61 .... **92** A3

Rockley Mount School
BSLY S70 .... **21** D3

Rosedale Middle School
BTLY DN5 .... **28** B2

Rosedale Road Infant School
BTLY DN5 .... **28** B2

Rossington Swimming Pool
NROS/TKH DN11 .... **67** D5

Rother County Junior School
CHSW S40 .... **190** B4

Rotherham Civic Theatre
RHAM/THRY S65 .... **7** E5

Rotherham College of Arts
& Technology
RHAM/THRY S65 .... **7** E4

Rotherham County Court
RHAM S60 .... **7** E6

Rotherham District
General Hospital
RHAM S60 .... **115** D2

Rotherham Health Authority
RHAM S60 .... **114** C2

Rotherham Health Authority
RHAM/THRY S65 .... **104** B3

Rotherham Magistrates Court
RHAM S60 .... **6** C5

Rotherham Metropolitan
Borough Council
RAW S62 .... **93** F1

Rotherham Metropolitan
Borough Council
RHAM S60 .... **6** D6

Rotherham Metropolitan
Borough Council
RHAM S60 .... **6** C3

Rotherham Metropolitan
Borough Council
RHAM/THRY S65 .... **7** E5

Rotherham Metropolitan
Borough Council
RHAM/THRY S65 .... **7** E3

Rotherham Priority Health Trust
RHAM/THRY S65 .... **7** E5

Rotherham Road Medical Centre
BSLYN/ROY S71 .... **14** B1

Rotherham Rugby Club
RHAM/THRY S65 .... **104** A4

Rotherham Town Cricket Club
RHAM/THRY S65 .... **104** A4

Rotherham Town Hall
RHAM S60 .... **6** D6

Rotherham United Football Club
RHAM S60 .... **102** C4

Rotunda Business Centre
CHPT/GREN S35 .... **74** A4

Roughwood Junior School
KIMB S61 .... **91** F4

Rowan School
TOT/DORE S17 .... **156** C2

Rowena Infant School
CONI DN12 .... **84** C1

Royal Hallamshire Hospital
FUL S10 .... **121** E5

Rudston Preparatory School
RHAM/THRY S65 .... **104** A4

Ruskin Gallery
SHEF S1 .... **9** E6

Rustlings Road Medical Centre
ECC S11 .... **133** E2

Rutland Business Park
OWL S3 .... **122** A1

Ryecroft Infant School
RAW S62 .... **80** B5

Sacred Heart R C Primary School
ST/HB/BR S6 .... **108** A5

St Albans RC School
CONI DN12 .... **60** B5

St Andrews C of E
Methodist Aided School
DRON S18 .... **168** B2

St Anns Medical Centre
RHAM/THRY S65 .... **6** D3

St Anns Surgery
KIMB S61 .... **91** F5

St Bedes Primary School
KIMB S61 .... **101** F1

St Bernards RC School
RHAM/THRY S65 .... **105** D1

St Catherines RC
Primary School
OWL S3 .... **109** E4

St Francis Xavier RC School
DONS/BSCR DN4 .... **44** A3

St Georges Church
SHEF S1 .... **8** B5

St Georges Hospital
ST/HB/BR S6 .... **121** E3

St Giles C of E (aided)
Primary School
ECK/KIL S21 .... **166** A2

St Helens Junior & Infant School
BSLYN/ROY S71 .... **15** E2

St James Swimming Pool
DON DN1 .... **5** E5

St John Fisher RC Junior
& Infants School
HACK/IN S12 .... **151** E2

St Johns Business Centre
CHNE S41 .... **184** A1

St Johns C of E (Park)
Primary School
SHEFP/MNR S2 .... **123** E4

St Johns C of E School
MEX/SWTN S64 .... **58** C2

St Josephs Convent School
CHSW S40 .... **10** D4

St Josephs Junior
& Infants School
RAW S62 .... **94** A1

St Josephs RC Primary School
STV/CWN S43 .... **181** E5

St Maries R C Primary School
FUL S10 .... **133** E1

St Mary School
FUL S10 .... **121** D2

St Marys C of E Junior
& Infant School
DOD/DAR S75 .... **13** D5

St Marys C of E Junior
& Infant School
RAW S62 .... **94** A1

St Marys C of E Primary School
ST/HB/BR S6 .... **121** E1

St Marys High Green
RC Primary School
CHPT/GREN S35 .... **73** F3

St Marys RC High School
  CHSW S40 .... 183 D2
St Marys RC Primary School
  CHSW S40 .... 10 D4
St Marys RC School
  RHAM/THRY S65 .... 105 D3
St Marys School
  DONS/BSCR DN4 .... 46 B4
St Marys School
  DRON S18 .... 171 D3
St Matthews Infant School
  DOD/DAR S75 .... 13 D5
St Michaels RC Junior
  & Infant School
  WMB/DAR S73 .... 40 A1
St Oswalds RC Primary School
  SHEFP/MNR S2 .... 123 F5
St Patricks RC School
  SHEFN S5 .... 99 D5
St Peter & St Paul School
  CHNE S41 .... 191 D2
St Peters RC Primary School
  DONS/BSCR DN4 .... 45 E3
St Peters & St Pauls School
  CHNE S41 .... 191 D4
St Theresas School
  SHEFP/MNR S2 .... 137 F3
St Thomas More R C
  Primary School
  CHPT/GREN S35 .... 97 E2
St Thomas of Canterbury R C
  Primary School
  SHEFS S8 .... 147 D5
Saint Vincent Medical Centre
  DON DN1 .... 5 G2
St Wilfrids RC Primary School
  ABRD S7 .... 146 A1
Saltergate Health Centre
  CHSW S40 .... 11 E5
Sandall Wood School
  WHHL DN2 .... 32 B4
Sandhill J M I School
  RAW S62 .... 81 D5
The Sandringham Practice
  WHHL DN2 .... 31 F4
Scawsby College
  BTLY DN5 .... 28 A3
Scawsby Health Centre
  BTLY DN5 .... 28 C3
Scawthorpe Clinic
  BTLY DN5 .... 28 C2
Shardlows Sports Club
  CHPT/GREN S35 .... 88 C4
Sharrow Junior School
  ECC S11 .... 135 D2
Shaw Lane Industrial Estate
  WHHL DN2 .... 32 C1
Shaw Wood Junior
  & Infant School
  ARMTH DN3 .... 33 E1
Sheaf Heaf Gardens
  Industrial Estate
  SHEFP/MNR S2 .... 135 F1
Sheaf Market
  SHEF S1 .... 9 G4
Sheepbridge Business Centre
  CHNE S41 .... 177 F4
Sheffield Area Health
  Authority Sports & Social Club
  ECC S11 .... 132 B3
Sheffield Area Health Authority
  (Teaching)
  FUL S10 .... 121 F4
Sheffield City Council
  ATT S4 .... 9 H1
Sheffield City Council
  ATT S4 .... 109 F5
Sheffield City Council
  ATT S4 .... 110 A4
Sheffield City Council
  CHPT/GREN S35 .... 97 E2
Sheffield City Council
  DARN/MH S9 .... 112 A3
Sheffield City Council
  DARN/MH S9 .... 125 D3
Sheffield City Council
  HACK/IN S12 .... 150 C2
Sheffield City Council
  HAN/WDH S13 .... 139 F4
Sheffield City Council
  MOS S20 .... 152 C3
Sheffield City Council
  OWL S3 .... 8 B5

Sheffield City Council
  OWL S3 .... 122 B1
Sheffield City Council
  SHEF S1 .... 9 F4
Sheffield City Council
  SHEF S1 .... 9 E5
Sheffield City Council
  SHEFN S5 .... 99 F2
Sheffield City Council
  SHEFP/MNR S2 .... 9 H5
Sheffield City Council
  SHEFP/MNR S2 .... 123 F4
Sheffield City Council
  SHEFP/MNR S2 .... 135 F2
Sheffield City Council
  SHEFP/MNR S2 .... 136 B5
Sheffield City Council
  SHEFP/MNR S2 .... 137 E3
Sheffield City Council
  SHEFS S8 .... 135 E5
Sheffield City Council
  SHEFS S8 .... 158 C2
Sheffield City Council
  ST/HB/BR S6 .... 8 A2
Sheffield City Council
  ST/HB/BR S6 .... 108 A4
The Sheffield College
  MOS S20 .... 153 D5
The Sheffield College
  SHEFN S5 .... 98 A2
The Sheffield College
  SHEFP/MNR S2 .... 135 F1
The Sheffield College
  SHEFS S8 .... 159 F1
Sheffield Eagles R L F C Ltd
  DARN/MH S9 .... 124 B1
Sheffield Hallam University
  FUL S10 .... 121 E5
Sheffield Hallam University
  SHEF S1 .... 9 F6
Sheffield Health Authority
  FUL S10 .... 121 F4
Sheffield Health Authority
  SHEFN S5 .... 99 E5
Sheffield High School
  ECC S11 .... 121 D5
Sheffield Magistrates Court
  SHEF S1 .... 9 F4
Sheffield Medical Centre
  OWL S3 .... 9 G1
Sheffield Natural Health Centre
  SHEFS S8 .... 135 D3
Sheffield Sports Stadium Ltd
  ST/HB/BR S6 .... 108 B3
Sheffield Technology Park
  DARN/MH S9 .... 124 A1
Sheffield United AFC
  SHEFP/MNR S2 .... 135 E1
Sheffield United Cricket Club
  DARN/MH S9 .... 113 D3
Sheffield Wednesday
  Football Club Plc
  ST/HB/BR S6 .... 108 A2
Shirecliffe Junior School
  SHEFN S5 .... 108 C2
Shire Green Medical Centre
  SHEFN S5 .... 99 F3
Shooters Grove Primary School
  ST/HB/BR S6 .... 107 D5
Shopping Centre
  BSLY S70 .... 2 D5
Shopping Centre
  CHSW S40 .... 183 D4
Shopping Centre
  RAW S62 .... 93 F1
Shortbrook Primary School
  MOS S20 .... 153 D5
Shrewsbury Hospital
  SHEFP/MNR S2 .... 123 D5
Sikh Temple
  ATT S4 .... 110 A5
Sikh Temple
  DON DN1 .... 5 E5
Silverdale School
  ECC S11 .... 132 C5
Sir Harold Jackson
  Primary School
  TOT/DORE S17 .... 157 F3
Sitwell Junior & Infants School
  RHAM S60 .... 115 F1
The Sloan Practice
  SHEFS S8 .... 148 B3
Sothall Medical Centre
  MOS S20 .... 153 D3

Sothall Snooker & Leisure Centre
  MOS S20 .... 153 D2
South Cantley Middle School
  DONS/BSCR DN4 .... 67 D1
Southey Green Medical Centre
  SHEFN S5 .... 109 D1
Southey Hill Surgery
  SHEFN S5 .... 98 A5
South Yorkshire
  Business Centre
  RAW S62 .... 93 F4
Speedwell County
  Infants School
  STV/CWN S43 .... 181 F5
Springfield Primary School
  OWL S3 .... 122 A5
Springwell Community School
  STV/CWN S43 .... 187 E2
Springwood Junior
  & Infant School
  HOY S74 .... 51 E3
Sprotbrough Health Centre
  BTLY DN5 .... 42 C2
Stag Medical Centre
  RHAM/THRY S65 .... 116 A1
Stairfoot Health Centre
  BSLY S70 .... 23 E3
Stannington Health Centre
  ST/HB/BR S6 .... 119 D1
Stannington Infant School
  ST/HB/BR S6 .... 119 D1
Station Lane Industrial Estate
  CHNE S41 .... 178 C4
Station Road Industrial Estate
  WMB/DAR S73 .... 39 F2
Station Road Junior
  & Infant School
  CONI DN12 .... 61 D5
Staveley Council Office
  STV/CWN S43 .... 181 F4
Staveley Health Clinic
  STV/CWN S43 .... 181 F5
Staveley Junior School
  STV/CWN S43 .... 181 E5
Staveley Urban District Council
  STV/CWN S43 .... 181 F5
Stirling First School
  DON DN1 .... 4 D6
Stirling Junior School
  DON DN1 .... 5 E6
Stocksbridge Golf Club
  STKB/PEN S36 .... 69 E4
Stocksbridge High School
  STKB/PEN S36 .... 68 C2
Stocksbridge Junior School
  STKB/PEN S36 .... 68 C3
Stocksbridge Leisure Centre
  STKB/PEN S36 .... 68 B2
Stocksbridge Rugby Club
  STKB/PEN S36 .... 68 C1
Stonelow Junior School
  DRON S18 .... 169 F1
Storm House School
  DEARNE S63 .... 57 D1
Stradbroke Primary School
  HAN/WDH S13 .... 138 B3
Sunday School
  DEARNE S63 .... 26 B3
Superbowl Two Thousand
  KIMB S61 .... 101 F1
Superintendent Swimming Baths
  CHPT/GREN S35 .... 88 B1
Swallownest Health Centre
  AU/AST/KP S26 .... 142 B3
Swinton Brookfield
  Primary School
  MEX/SWTN S64 .... 81 E1
Swinton Comprehensive School
  MEX/SWTN S64 .... 81 D1
Swinton Fitzwilliam
  Infants School
  MEX/SWTN S64 .... 80 C1
Swinton Meadows Business Park
  MEX/SWTN S64 .... 58 A5
Swinton Meadows
  Industrial Estate
  MEX/SWTN S64 .... 58 A5
Swinton Milton Special School
  MEX/SWTN S64 .... 57 D5
Swinton Swimming Pool
  MEX/SWTN S64 .... 57 F5
Sycamore Hall Preparatory
  School
  DONS/BSCR DN4 .... 43 E5

Tapton Golf Course
CHNE S41 .... **185** D4

Tapton Secondary School
FUL S10 .... **120** B5

Tates Gallery
DARN/MH S9 .... **125** D3

Tates Gallery
ST/HB/BR S6 .... **108** A4

Templeborough Business Centre
RHAM S60 .... **103** D5

Tertiary College
ECK/KIL S21 .... **164** B5

Thomas Rotherham College
RHAM S60 .... **103** F5

Thornbridge School
HACK/IN S12 .... **150** B3

Thornhill Industrial Estate
KIMB S61 .... **6** B2

Thornhill Jmi School
RHAM S60 .... **6** A4

Thorpe Hesley Clinic
KIMB S61 .... **90** A2

Thorpe Hesley Infant School
KIMB S61 .... **89** F2

Thorpe Hesley Junior School
KIMB S61 .... **90** A2

Thrybergh St Gerards RC M
& I School
RHAM/THRY S65 .... **95** E4

Thurnscoe Business Centre
DEARNE S63 .... **27** E4

Thurnscoe Business Park
DEARNE S63 .... **27** E4

Thurnscoe Gooseacre J M School
DEARNE S63 .... **26** C2

Tinsley Junior School
DARN/MH S9 .... **112** C2

Totley All Saints C of E
Primary School
TOT/DORE S17 .... **156** A4

Totley Primary School
TOT/DORE S17 .... **156** B4

Town Fields Primary School
WHHL DN2 .... **5** H2

Trafalgar House Medical Centre
ST/HB/BR S6 .... **97** E5

Tramways Medical Centre
ST/HB/BR S6 .... **108** A4

Treeton C of E Junior
& Infant School
RHAM S60 .... **127** F3

U C I Cinema
MOS S20 .... **152** C2

University of Sheffield
ECC S11 .... **133** F1

University of Sheffield
FUL S10 .... **121** D4

University of Sheffield
OWL S3 .... **121** F4

University of Sheffield
SHEF S1 .... **8** C5

Unstone Junior School
DRON S18 .... **170** C4

Untitled Gallery
SHEF S1 .... **122** C5

Valley Medical Centre
STKB/PEN S36 .... **68** C1

Vanguard Trading Estate
CHSW S40 .... **190** B5

Verdon Recreation Centre
OWL S3 .... **9** F1

Victoria Primary School
DEARNE S63 .... **56** B2

Wales Junior & Infant School
AU/AST/KP S26 .... **155** F3

Walkley Medical Centre
FUL S10 .... **121** D1

Walk Talk Galleries
ECC S11 .... **133** F2

Waltheof School
SHEFP/MNR S2 .... **124** C5

Walton Hospital
CHSW S40 .... **189** F5

Ward Green Junior School
BSLY S70 .... **22** A5

Warmsworth Primary School
DONS/BSCR DN4 .... **62** A1

Warren House Surgery
BSLY S70 .... **22** A2

Warwick Street Industrial Estate
CHSW S40 .... **190** C5

Watergate Centre
DON DN1 .... **5** E4

Wath C of E JMI School
DEARNE S63 .... **55** F1

Wath Park Infant School
DEARNE S63 .... **55** F3

Wath Pope Pius R C
Secondary School
DEARNE S63 .... **56** B4

Wath R U F C
DEARNE S63 .... **56** A1

Wath Upon Dearne
Comprehensive School
DEARNE S63 .... **56** A3

Wath West Industrial Estate
DEARNE S63 .... **41** D5

Waverley Junior School
DONS/BSCR DN4 .... **62** C1

Welfare Clinic
ECK/KIL S21 .... **164** B5

Wentworth Castle College
of Education
DOD/DAR S75 .... **34** A2

Wentworth C of E School
RAW S62 .... **76** B2

Westfield Health Centre
MOS S20 .... **152** C5

Westfield Infant School
CHSW S40 .... **188** C2

West Melton J & I School
DEARNE S63 .... **55** D1

Weston Park Hospital
N H S Trust
FUL S10 .... **121** E4

Westside Gallery
FUL S10 .... **134** B1

Westways Middle
Primary School
FUL S10 .... **121** D3

Wheatley Hall Business Centre
WHHL DN2 .... **31** E2

Whiston Grange School
RHAM S60 .... **115** E3

Whiston Junior & Infant School
RHAM S60 .... **115** F3

Whiston Worry Goose
Jmi School
RHAM S60 .... **116** B3

Whitecotes Primary School
CHSW S40 .... **190** A4

White House Surgery
SHEFP/MNR S2 .... **137** F2

Whitelea Grove Trading Estate
MEX/SWTN S64 .... **57** F4

Whiteley Wood Clinic
ECC S11 .... **132** C3

Whiteways Junior School
ATT S4 .... **110** B4

Whitley Hall Cricket Club
CHPT/GREN S35 .... **87** F5

Whittington Medical Centre
CHNE S41 .... **178** B3

Whittington Moor Surgery
CHNE S41 .... **184** B1

Whittington Moor Surgery
CHNE S41 .... **184** C2

William Levick Infant School
DRON S18 .... **168** A1

William Levick Primary School
DRON S18 .... **168** A1

William Rhodes Primary School
CHSW S40 .... **189** F2

Wilthorpe Junior School
DOD/DAR S75 .... **13** D3

Wincobank Surgery
DARN/MH S9 .... **100** C5

Windermere Surgery
CHNE S41 .... **183** E2

Windmill Hill Primary School
CHPT/GREN S35 .... **88** A2

Wingfield Comprehensive School
KIMB S61 .... **92** B4

Wisewood Secondary School
ST/HB/BR S6 .... **107** D3

Wombwell Aldham Junior
& Infant School
WMB/DAR S73 .... **38** B2

Wombwell Clinic
WMB/DAR S73 .... **39** D2

Wombwell Cricket Club
WMB/DAR S73 .... **38** C3

Wombwell High School
WMB/DAR S73 .... **39** F4

Wombwell Jump Junior
& Infant School
HOY S74 .... **52** A1

Wombwell Public Baths
WMB/DAR S73 .... **39** E3

Woodfield First School
DONS/BSCR DN4 .... **63** F1

Woodgrove Surgery
DEARNE S63 .... **56** A2

Woodhouse Clinic
HAN/WDH S13 .... **139** F4

Woodhouse Medical Centre
HAN/WDH S13 .... **139** F4

Woodseats Medical Centre
SHEFS S8 .... **147** D3

Woodseats Primary School
SHEFS S8 .... **147** D2

Woodstock Bower Group Practice
KIMB S61 .... **102** B3

Woodthorpe Community
Primary School
HAN/WDH S13 .... **138** A3

Works
ARMTH DN3 .... **19** E2

Works
CHSW S40 .... **190** C2

Works
RHAM/THRY S65 .... **95** D3

Worsbrough Bridge RC School
BSLY S70 .... **22** C5

Worsbrough C of E Junior
& Infant School
BSLY S70 .... **36** A4

Worsbrough Common County
Primary School
BSLY S70 .... **22** A4

Worsbrough Health Centre
BSLY S70 .... **22** C5

Worsbrough High School
BSLY S70 .... **37** E1

Worsbrough Mill Museum
BSLY S70 .... **36** B2

Wybourn Primary School
SHEFP/MNR S2 .... **123** E4

Yewlands School
CHPT/GREN S35 .... **97** F2

York House Medical Centre
SHEFP/MNR S2 .... **137** D2

Page 13

F5
1 Aireton Rd
2 Churchfield
3 Church La
4 Church St
5 Eastgate
6 Lancaster Ga
7 Rosehill Ct
8 Sadler Ga
9 St Mary's Ga
10 St Mary's Pl
11 Victoria St
12 Westwood Ct

Page 22

A1
1 Burleigh Ct
2 Burlington Ar
3 Cheapside
4 Freemans Yd
5 Hayes Cft
6 Malthouse Rd
7 May Day Gn
8 Midland St
9 Pall Mall
10 Sherwood St
11 Wesley St

A2
1 Britannia Cl
2 Buckley Ct
3 Copper Cl
4 Denison Ct
5 Duke Crs
6 Duke St
7 Freeman St
8 Providence Ct
9 Quarry St
10 Rebecca Ms
11 Rosebery Ter
12 Taylor Rw
13 Upper New St
14 Wilkinson St

A3
1 California Crs
2 Chestnut Ct
3 Dickinson Pl
4 Dickinson Rd
5 Essex Rd
6 Frederic Pl
7 Hornby St
8 Howard St
9 Kelsey Ter
10 Kenworthy Rd
11 Stoneleigh Cft
12 Warren Pl

B2
1 Clifton St
2 Gold Cft
3 Henshall St
4 Milnes St
5 Oakwell Ter
6 Osborne Ms
7 St Peter's Ter
8 Seth Ter
9 Sunderland Ter
10 Victoria Ter
11 Wilby La

B5
1 Blackburn St
2 Brockfield Cl
3 Croft St
4 Henry St
5 John St
6 Kingwell Cft
7 Kingwell Ms
8 Mill Ct
9 Norman Cl
10 Osmond Pl
11 Osmond Wy
12 Parkside Ms
13 Sweyn Cft

Page 103

E3
1 College St
2 The Crofts
3 Domine La
4 Down's Rw
5 Quarry Hl
6 Snail Hl
7 Stanley St
8 The Statutes
9 Unity Pl

F3
1 Catherine St
2 Chatham St
3 Doncaster Ga
4 Douglas St
5 Morpeth St
6 Percy St
7 Summerfield
8 Whybourne Gv

Page 121

D3
1 Ainsley Rd
2 Clementson Rd
3 Cobden Pl
4 Conduit La
5 Leamington St
6 Romsdal Rd
7 Spring House Rd
8 Spring View Rd
9 Warwick St
10 Warwick Ter

D5
1 Ashdell
2 Ashdell La
3 Ashgate La
4 Caxton Rd
5 Chandos St
6 Hoole La
7 Nile St
8 Peel St
9 Taptonville Crs
10 Turners La
11 Watson Rd

E3
1 Barber Crs
2 Barber Pl
3 The Coach Houses
4 Crookesmoor Dr
5 Elliot Rd
6 Ivy Dr
7 Ivy Gv
8 Moorgate Av
9 Warrington Rd

E4
1 Claremont Crs
2 Damer St
3 Harcourt La
4 Palmerston Rd
5 Severn Ct
6 Severn Rd
7 Shearwood Rd
8 Tree Root Wk

F2
1 Blake Grove Rd
2 Brandeth Rd
3 Brandreth Cl
4 Burlington Ct
5 Carnarvon St
6 Daniel Hill Ter
7 Gilpin La
8 Philadelphia Dr
9 Philadelphia Gv
10 Portland St
11 Shipton St
12 Straw La
13 Westmoreland St
14 Yeomans Rd

F3
1 St Stephen's Wk
2 Yardley Sq

F4
1 Brightmore Dr
2 Conway St
3 Durham Rd
4 Favell Rd
5 Hounsfield La
6 Hounsfield Rd
7 Leavygreave Rd
8 Western Bank
9 Wilkinson La
10 Wilkinson St

F5
1 Broomspring Cl
2 Broomspring La
3 Exeter Wy
4 Gloucester Crs
5 Hanover St
6 Holberry Cl
7 Holberry Gdns
8 Mackenzie Crs
9 Monmouth St
10 Ruth Sq
11 Upper Hanover St

Page 122

A2
1 Bedford St
2 Dixon St
3 Downing La
4 Dun Flds
5 Dun La
6 Henry St
7 Infirmary Rd
8 Lancaster St
9 Lister La
10 Matthew St
11 Montgomery Terrace Rd
12 Percy St
13 St Philip's Rd
14 Sudbury St
15 Waterloo Wk

A3
1 Blue Boy St
2 Brocco St
3 Brownell St
4 Burnt Tree La
5 Craven St
6 Ellison St
7 Morpeth St
8 Nethertorpe St
9 Queen's Rw
10 Well Meadow Dr
11 Well Meadow St

A4
1 Abney St
2 Boden La
3 Broad Lane Ct
4 Canning St
5 Charlotte La
6 Chester St
7 Congress St
8 Convent Pl
9 Devonshire La
10 Devonshire St
11 Orange St
12 Pitt Cl
13 Pitt La
14 Portland La
15 Red Hl
16 Regent St
17 St George's Ter
18 St Thomas St
19 Siddall St
20 Westhill La
21 Wheeldon St

B3
1 Bower Spring
2 Cupola
3 Lee Cft
4 North Church St
5 Paradise La
6 Paradise Sq
7 Paradise St
8 Plum La
9 St Peter's Cl
10 Silver Street Head
11 Water St
12 Workhouse La

B4
1 Barker's Pool
2 Bells Sq
3 Cambridge St
4 Chapel Wk
5 Charles La
6 Cross Burgess St
7 East Pde
8 Fargate
9 Holly La
10 Norfolk La
11 Orchard La
12 Orchard St
13 Penton St
14 Pool Sq
15 St James' St
16 Wellington St
17 West Street La

B5
1 Cambridge St
2 Clay La
3 Cumberland Wy
4 Duke La
5 Froggatt La
6 Hallam La
7 Jessop St
8 Matilda Wy
9 Moor Head
10 Newton La
11 Rockingham Cl
12 Rockingham Ga
13 Rockingham Wy
14 Union La
15 Union St

C3
1 Castle Gn
2 Harts Head
3 Haymarket
4 Johnson La
5 Joiner St
6 Lady's Br
7 Meetinghouse La
8 Shude Hl
9 Waingate
10 Wharf St
11 Willey St

C5
1 Brittain St
2 Cross Turner St
3 Fornham St
4 Granville St
5 Leadmill Rd

Page 123

D4
1 Anson St
2 Blackwell Cl
3 Blackwell Ct
4 Crown Pl
5 High Street La
6 Manor Oaks Rd
7 Manor Oaks Gdns
8 Rhodes St
9 Talbot Rd
10 Weigh La

D5
1 Coates St
2 Glencoe Dr
3 Glencoe Pl
4 Robinson Rd
5 Samson St
6 Talbot Crs
7 Talbot Gdns
8 Talbot Pl

F5
1 Kestrel Gn
2 Magpie Gv
3 Maltravers Cl
4 Osprey Gdns
5 Partridge Vw
6 Plover Ct
7 Quail Ri
8 Starling Mead
9 Wren Bank

Page 124

B2
1 Bray St
2 Cattal St
3 Chinley St
4 Faranden Rd
5 Fearnehough St
6 Garth Cl
7 Harry Firth Cl
8 Ouseburn St
9 Spofforth Rd
10 Wilfred Cl

Page 134

B2
1 Ashford Rd
2 Berresford Rd
3 Bruce Rd
4 Dyson Pl
5 Eastwood Rd
6 Gordon Rd
7 Harefield Rd
8 Hickmott Rd
9 Jarrow Rd
10 Lynton Rd
11 Rosedale Gdns
12 Rosedale Rd

C4
1 Archibald Rd
2 Catefield Rd
3 Herbert Rd
4 Marden Rd
5 Violet Bank Rd

Page 135

D2
1 Asher Rd
2 Bennett St
3 Crowther Pl
4 Croydon St
5 Grosvenor Sq
6 Mount Pleasant Rd
7 Penley St
8 Salmon St
9 Sitwell Pl
10 Smeaton St
11 Stemp St
12 Ventnor Pl
13 Ward Pl

D3
1 Ainsty Rd
2 Aizlewood Rd
3 Alcester Rd
4 Brookfield Rd
5 Cutts Ter
6 Dalton Ct
7 Farrar Rd
8 Herschell Rd
9 Marples Cl
10 Marples Dr
11 Miller Rd
12 Rampton Rd
13 Sellers St
14 South View Crs

E2
1 Alderson Rd North
2 Atkin Pl
3 Batt St
4 Belgrave Sq
5 Harrington Rd
6 Holland Pl
7 St Barnabas La
8 Silver Mill Rd
9 Witney St

E3
1 Alderney Rd
2 Fieldhead Rd
3 Gifford Rd
4 Glover Rd
5 Guernsey Rd
6 Jersey Rd
7 Preston St
8 Sark Rd
9 Sheaf Bank
10 Staveley Rd

E4
1 Arthington St
2 Bradbury St
3 Gleadless Rd
4 Goodwin Rd
5 Gregory Rd
6 Maxey Pl
7 Molloy St
8 Nowill Ct
9 Nowill Pl
10 Plantation Rd
11 Southall St
12 Springwood Rd
13 Tillotson Cl
14 Tillotson Rd
15 Wellhead Rd
16 Well Pl
17 Well Rd
18 Whiting St
19 Wilson Pl

F4
1 Farish Pl
2 Gerard Cl
3 Gleadless Ct
4 Jeffery St
5 Nicholson Pl
6 Richards Ct
7 Romney Gdns
8 Sturge Cft

Page 136

B4
1 East Bank Cl
2 East Bank Vw
3 East Bank Wy
4 Gleadless Rd
5 Hartopp Dr

Page 137

F4
1 Applegarth Cl
2 Bagshaw's Rd
3 Holbrook Gv
4 Penthorpe Cl
5 Pleasant Cl

Page 152

C5
1 Birchwood Cl
2 Birchwood Gdns
3 Birchwood Ri
4 Birchwood Wy
5 Challoner Gn
6 Garland Mt
7 Meadowcroft Gld
8 Meadowcroft Ri
9 Pedley Dr
10 Shortbrook Bank
11 Westland Gv

Page 153

E3
1 Byron Rd
2 Charnwood Ct
3 Grizedale Cl
4 Hartland Av
5 Hartland Ct
6 Ringwood Rd
7 Rothbury Cl
8 Rothbury Ct
9 Rufford Cl
10 Waltham Gdns
11 Wareham Ct
12 Willingham Gdns
13 Wychwood Cft
14 Wychwood Gln
15 Wychwood Gv

Page 164

C2
1 Ambleside Cl
2 Borrowdale Av
3 Borrowdale Cl
4 Ennerdale Av
5 Ennerdale Dr
6 Murrayfield Dr
7 Oakworth Cl
8 Ralston Cft
9 Twickenham Cl
10 Twickenham Ct
11 Twickenham Gld
12 Twickenham Gv
13 Wasdale Av

Page 182

A4
1 Briardene Cl
2 Easedale Cl
3 Foxbrook Cl
4 Hollens Wy
5 Langdale Cl
6 Stanage Wy
7 Wheatfield Wy
8 Wheathill Cl
9 Woodleigh Cl

B4
1 Ashbourne Cl
2 Bretton Cl
3 Butterton Dr
4 Cauldon Dr
5 Cornfield Cl
6 Harvest Wy
7 Langley Cl
8 Mercaston Cl
9 Parwich Cl
10 Quorn Dr
11 Ravenswood Rd
12 Rednall Cl
13 Upwood Cl
14 Wheathill Cl

Notes

Notes

Notes

Notes

Notes